$35.00

Retta S. Osteen
216 Cook Rd
Yorktown, Va
23690

Osteen @ pinn.net

D1174124

COLONIAL BERTIE COUNTY
NORTH CAROLINA
DEED BOOKS A-H
1720-1757

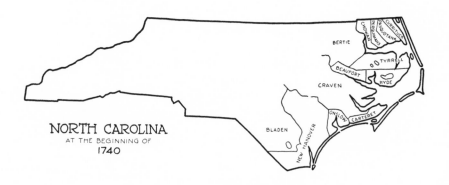

ABSTRACTED BY: MARY BEST BELL
2ND. EDITION PUBLISHED BY: SOUTHERN HISTORICAL PRESS

Please Direct all Correspondence & Orders to:

Southern Historical Press, Inc.
P.O. Box 1267
375 West Broad Street
Greenville, S.C. 29602-1267

TABLE OF CONTENTS

i

FOREWORD

A brief history of the formation of Bertie Precinct is necessary background for an understanding of the importance of these early Bertie County records to North Carolina history

While Bertie Precinct was not formed until 1722, the area had long been settled. The earliest known settler in North Carolina, NATHANIEL BATTS, lived here as early as 1657. Documentary evidence of this is the map prepared in 1657 by NICHOLAS COMBERFORD, London map maker. This map shows a house, labeled "BATTS House", on the neck of land between the mouth of the Roanoke River and Salmon Creek.[1] In 1707 ROBERT LAWRENCE of Isle of Wight County, Virginia testified that in 1660/61 he "seated" and occupied for seven years a plantation on the southwest side of the Chowan River "three or four miles from the mouth of the Moratuck.[2] Certainly in the 1660's there were other settlers in what is now Bertie County.

By 1722 the area was so densely populated that an act was passed to establish a separate precinct: "...that part of Albemarle County lying on the west side of Chowan River to be a precinct, bounded to the Northward by the line dividing this Government from Virginia, and the Southward by Albemarle Sound and Morattuck (Roanoke) River as far up as Welch's Creek, and then including both sides of said River, and the Branches thereof, as far as the limits of this Government...."[3]

An explanation of the formation of the counties in North Carolina is not within the scope of such a sketch as this, but brief enumeration will illustrate that many northern and central counties now in North Carolina were, in 1722-25, a part of Bertie Precinct. Tyrell County was formed in part from Bertie in 1729. Edgecombe and Northampton counties were formed from Bertie in 1741. Later Granville (1746), Halifax (1758), Nash (1777), and Wilson (1855) counties were formed in part or in whole from Edgecombe. Hertford County was formed in part from Bertie in 1759. Martin County was formed from Halifax and Tyrell in 1774. Washington County was formed from Tyrell in 1799. Orange (1752), Vance (1881) were formed in part or in whole from Granville. Franklin (1779) and Warren (1779) counties were formed from Bute.[4]

Deed Book A is the earliest deed book in the county. An excerpt, quoted below, indicates that the first three books were combined into this one book in 1796:
   A 99. "February Court 1796. It was ordred that STEPHEN OUTERBRIDGE, FRANCIS PUGH, and JONATHAN JACOCKS go to (the) Register's office & examine the state of the records kept therein...(signed GEORGE GRAY, Clerk of Court)...Agreeable to the (amendment) ordered we called at the Register's Office and Examined the books in the same, and it appeared to us that the whole of the first three books, A,B,C, ought to be new copied in a New Book of Books....our direction is that the said Register proceed in the above manner given - under our hands and seal this sixth day of April Anno 1796." (signed)

SPELLING: There has been no attempt to edit these deeds. All proper names throughout have been copied exactly from the original deed book. Only the word patent has been given consistent spelling. See EXPLANATION on page ii for codes covering spelling.

DATES: Prior to 1752 England used the Julian Calendar, which began the first of each year on March 25th. Other European countries used the Gregorian Calendar, which begins each year on January 1st.[5] Therefore, between January 1st and March 25th, double dates are often given. Sometimes a deed appears to have been recorded a year before its execution. This is merely a reflection of the difference in dates acceptable at the time. All dates have been copied exactly from the original deed book [except those that have been abbreviated in the interest of space]. Many deeds throughout were recorded prior to the 1722 formation of Bertie Precinct. These were recorded in what was then Chowan Precinct of Albemarle County.

REFERENCES:
(1) Powell, William S. Ye Countie of Albemarle in Carolina, p.xxiii.

(2) Saunders, William L. The Colonial Records of North Carolina. Vol. I,p.677.

(3) Clark, Walter. <u>The State Records of North Carolina</u>. Vol. XXIII, p.100.

(4) Corbitt, David L. <u>The Formation of the North Carolina Counties 1663 - 1943</u>. p.295 (chart). See under index the name of each county.

(5) "Calendar", <u>Encyclopedia Britannica</u>. Vol. LV, p. 572.

EXPLANATION

A.	acres
ack.	acknowledges
adj.	adjoins
appt.	appoint(S)
atty.	attorney
C/C	Clerk of Court
C.J.	Chief Justice
Coll. (Col.)	Colonel
cont.	contains
D.C/C.	Deputy Clerk of Court
dec'd.	deceased
ES	East Side
Jun.	Junior
NS, NES, SWS.	North Side, North East Side, North West Side
pds.	pounds, money
Sen.	Senior
sh.	shilling(s)
SS, SES, SWS	South Side, South East Side, South West Side
WS	West Side
wit.	witnesses
( )	more than one spelling
(?).	spelling unclear
*	date or other data omitted

<u>DATES</u>: All dates are copied exactly from the original deed book. [Some dates have been abbreviated by the editor in the interest of space.]

<u>SPELLING</u>: All spelling except the word <u>patent</u> is copied exactly from the original.

<u>PLACE DESIGNATIONS</u>: Unless otherwise indicated, the persons in the deeds are residents of Bertie Precinct.* In the original deeds the terms "Chowan Precinct of Albemarle County" and "Bertie Precinct of Albemarle County" are used almost interchangeably to indicate Bertie Precinct (now Bertie County). *Or the place of residence was not mentioned.

<u>MONEY</u>: The abbreviation <u>pds</u> is used for pounds. Sometimes the purchase is expressed "pounds Sterling of Great Britain"; sometimes it is "pounds of the colony of Virginia"; sometimes "pounds of this province".

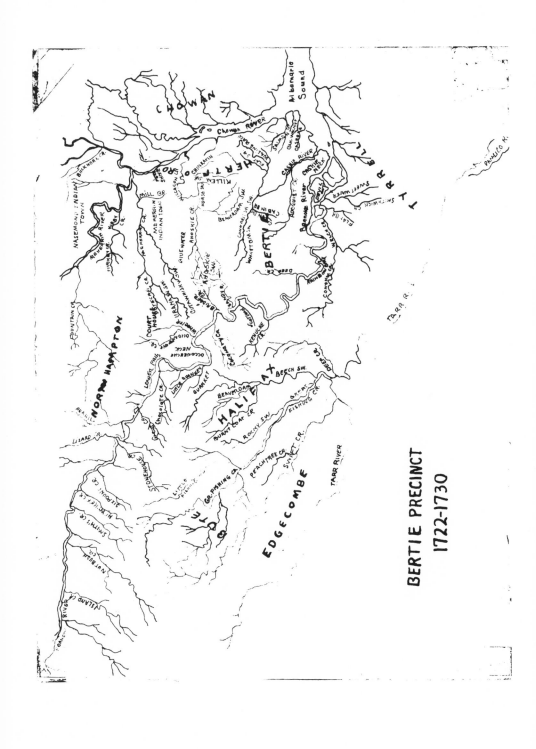

BERTIE PRECINCT
1722-1730

BERTIE COUNTY DEED BOOK A

1720 - 1725

A 1   JAMES BLOUNT (BLUNT) & WIFE CATHERINE TO WILLIAM MAULE (MAUL)
      July 15, 1721. For 40 pds. 600 A. on SW Chowan River adj. "MAULE'S
Haven". Wit: WILLIAM GRAY, JOHN WILLIAMS. Oct. 31, 1722. C. Gale C.J.+

A 2   HENRY SIMMS TO WILLIAM THOMAS of Isle of Wight, Virginia
      Aug. 20, 1722. 7 pds. for 180 A. Part of a patent dated March 1,1719
on NS Morattock River adj. WILLIAM CARRE (CARR) on Yourah Swamp. Wit:
WILLIAM GRAY, PATRICK MAULE, JOHN GRAY. Oct. 31, 1722. C. GALE, C.J. +

A 3   THOMAS WHITMELL & WIFE ELIZABETH TO RICHARD CUERTON of Prince George
      Co., Va. Aug. 20, 1722. 15 pds. for 200 A. on NS Morratuck River
granted to ARTHUR CAVENAUGH. On Double Bottom Branch adj. RICHARD TUBER-
VILLE. WIT: JOHN GRAY, WILLIAM GRAY. Oct. 31, 1722. C. GALE C.J. +

A 5   JAMES BOON & WIFE ELIZABETH TO JOHN GRAY
      March 11, 1721. 24 pds. for 200 A. on WS Chowan River. Wit: THOMAS
STONEHANE(?), WILLIAM MAULE, WILLIAM GRAY. Dec. 30, 1721. C. GALE C.J.+

A 7   MARTIN FREDERICK RAZOR (RASOR) & WIFE FRANCES TO PETER OZBORN
      Nov. 19, 1722. 100 pds. for 640 A. in SW Parish of Bertie Prec't.
near Salmon Creek Adj. land formerly LAURANCE's, WILLIAM GRILL'S dec'd.,
Hon. President THOMAS POLLOCK. Wit: ROBERT FORSTER, CATHERINE LINCH.
Nov. 19, 1722. C. GALE C.J.+

A 8   PETER OZBORN TO MARTIN FREDERICK RASOR & WIFE FRANCES
      Nov. 19, 1722. 640 A. on ES Salmon Creek adj. LAURANCE's, WILLIAM
GRILL's dec'd., THOMAS POLLOCK dec'd. To "...the longest liver of them..."
At their deaths one half to EDWARD, son of M.F. & FRANCES RASOR the other
one half to CHRISTINA RASOR, daughter of M.F. & FRANCES RASOR. If these
children die without heirs of their bodies...to the eldest two daughters
of FRANCES RASOR: ELIZABETH PERROT & SUSANNAH PERROT. Part land adj. Widow
HILL. Wit: ROBERT FOSTER, CATHERINE LINCH. Nov. 19, 1722. C. GALE C.J.+

A 10 JAMES PEEKE (JAMES PEEK) & WIFE MARGARET & RICHARD WASHINGTON & WIFE
      HANAH TO JAMES HUTCHINSON (HUTCHENSON). July 2, 1722. 12 pds. for
600 A. in Chowan at HARDY COUNCIL's. Wit: signers, ELIZABETH HUNTRIDGE(?).
Feb. Court 1722. ROBERT FORSTER, Public Register.

A 12 ROBERT LANIER & WIFE SARAH TO MATTHER SWANNER (SWANER)
      Feb. 13, 1722. 41 pds for 250 A. on Beaver Dam adj. GEORGE WINN's
Mill to Horsing Branch. Wit: WILLIAM CRANFORD (CRAWFORD), JOHN FANIM.
Feb. Court 1722. ROBERT FORSTER, D.C/C.

A 14 ROBERT SHERWOOD (SHERRWOOD) TO ROBERT MACRARY
      Feb. 13, 1722. 5 pds. for 100 A. whereon ROBERT MACRARY now lives adj.
Sandy Run. Wit: ISAAC HILL, ROBERT FORSTER. Feb. Court 1722. ROBERT
FORSTER, C/C.

A 15 WILLIAM BUSH TO JOHN BUSH
      Feb. 8, 1723. 30 pds. for 300 A. at Pole Cat Branch adj. THOMAS
MACLENDON, WILLIAM HOOKER. Wit: JAMES BATE, JOHN SMITH. Feb. Court 1722.
ROBERT FORSTER C/C. (dates as written)

A 17 JOHN BUSH TO WILLIAM BUSH
      Feb. 8, 1723. 25 pds. for 156 A. adj. GEORGE WINN. Wit: JAMES BATE,
JOHN SMITH. Feb. Court 1722. ROBERT FORSTER C/C.

A 19 JAMES ANDERSON of Bath County to JOHN GRAY (CAPT.)
      March 3, 1721/22. 400 A. NS Morattock River in Occoneeche Neck.
Part of 640 A. surveyed by Coll. WILLIAM MAULE for WILLIAM BRASWELL then
sold to MATTHEW CAPPS, and by CAPPS sold to JAMES ANDERSON. Adj. WILLIAM
BOON, JOHN NELLSON. Wit: PATRICK MAULE, MAU. MOORE. April 20, 1722.
C. GALE, C/C.

+ C.J. by name C. GALE probably means Chief Justice. Also written C/C.

A 20 TREDALL (TREDDAL, TRADELL) KEEFE TO ROBERT EVANS
    Jan. 9, 1723. 160 A. adj. Col. WILLIAM MAULE, THOMAS MANN on Kellum
Swamp. Wit: WILLIAM MEARS, ARON DRAB. Feb. Court 1722. ROBERT FORSTER C/C.

A 22 PETER PARKER & WIFE GRACE TO GEORGE POWELL
    Feb. 7, 1723. 290 A. in Holsky Woods by patent dated Aug. 10, 1720.
Adj. CHRISTOPHE FIRYBENT(?). Wit: JOHN SPEIR, JOHN BRYAN, JOHN MAINER. Feb.
Court 1722. JOHN SUTTON Dep. C/C.

A 24 JOHN KEELE TO JACOB LEWIS
    Feb. 12, 1722. 20 pds. for 50 A. on Dawses Road "beginning at a tree
of Rasberries" adj. JACOB LEWIS. Wit: THOMAS BIRD, DEBORAH KEELE. Feb.
Court 1722. JOHN SUTTON Dep. C/C.

A 26 CHARLES JONES & WIFE SARAH TO THOMAS BONNER
    * 60 pds. for 640 A. Ahotsky Swamp by patent dated Dec. 3, 1720. Wit:
WILLIAM WHITFIELD, JAMES HOWARD. Feb. Court 1722. JOHN SUTTON Dep. C/C.

A 28 JOHN BUSH & WIFE MARY TO JOHN HOLLY
    * 1722. 3 pds for 70 A. adj. WILLIAM HOOKER on Neetops Branch. Wit:
JAMES BATE, THOMAS BLAKE. Feb. Court 1722. JOHN SUTTON Dep. C/C.

A 30 GEORGE POWELL & WIFE ANN TO DENNIS MACKLENDON
    40 pds. for 140 A. adj. WILLIAM CRAFORD, GEORGE WINN, ABRAHAM BLEW-
LITTS, WILLIAM BUSH, JAMES WILKINSON on Neetops Branch. Formerly surveyed
for WILLIAM HOOKER, SEN. Wit: JOHN EARLY, *. Feb. Court 1722. WILLIAM
CRAFORD was atty. for ANN POWELL to ack. her right of dower in above sale.
JOHN SUTTON D. C/C.

A 32 ANN POWELL TO WILLIAM CRANFORD
    Feb 13, 1722. Power of Atty. given (CRAWFORD) to "acknowledge her
right fo thirds & dower" in 440 A. sold by her husband, GEORGE POWELL, to
DENNIS MACKLENDON. Wit: JOHN BRYAN, WILLIAM HINTON. JOHN SUTTON D. C/C.

A 32 JOHN MOLTON, SEN. TO JOHN JERNIGAN
    5 pds. for 100 A. on SS Ahotsky Swamp adj. JOHN MOLTON JUN., JOHN
BARFIELD. Part of 400 A. patent date 1717. Wit: JOHN BARFIELD, THOMAS
JENKINS. Feb. Court 1722. JOHN SUTTON D. C/C.

A 34 AARON DRAKE TO SAMUEL ELSON of Salem New England.
    Feb. 12, 1722/23. 220 A. Part of 640 A. patent dated Nov. 11, 1719.
On SS Meherrin River. Wit: WILLIAM RICKS, ESTER RICKS, CHARLES KIRBY. Feb.
Court 1722. JOHN SUTTON D. C/C.

A 36 THOMAS ROODS & WIFE MARY TO JEFFRY BUTLAR
    Feb. 9, 1722. 6 pds. for 100 A. on Jumping Run. Wit: WILLIAM JONES,
THOMAS JONES. Feb. Court 1722. JOHN SUTTON D. C/C.

A 37 ARTHUR DAVIS & WIFE TO WILLIAM KINCHEN
    Feb 12, 1722. 25 pds. for 112 A. on Meherrin River patented Aug. 2,
1720. "...my wife relinquishes her dower...". Wit: SIMON JEFFREYS, STEWART
WILLIAM WILSON. Feb. Court 1722. JOHN SUTTON D. C/C.

A 38 JOHN MOULTON TO JOHN BARFIELD
    Oct. 8, 1722 10 pds. for 50 A. on SS Ahotsky Swamp adj. JOHN JERNI-
GAN. Part of a 400 A. patent to MOULTON dated 1717. Wit: THOMAS JENKINS,
RICHARD BARFIELD, HENRY BAKER. Feb. Court 1722. JOHN SUTTON D. C/C.

A 41 JOHN MAINARD TO JAMES FAIRCHILD
    Oct. 16, 1722. 6 pds. for 200 A. part of 540 A. patent surveyed by
MAINARD. Adj. WILLIAM AIRLES, COLL. POLLOCK, WILLIAM BAKER. Wit: JOHN
MANEAR(?), WILLIAM BARENCE, TRADDELL KEEF. Feb. Court 1722. JOHN SUTTON
D. C/C.

A 42 JOHN MOLTON TO STEPHEN HOWARD
    Feb. 1, 1723. 50 pds. for 250 A. on SS Ahotsky Swamp adj. JOHN DAVI-
SON. Wit: JOSEPH JONES, CHARLES JONES, JOHN NAIRNE. Feb. Court 1722. JOHN
SUTTON D. C/C.

A 44 JOHN ELA of Boston in New England to THOMAS SPIRES (SPIERS)
    Power of atty. to collect all account book debts, bond bills, and

other debts owed him in N.C. Wit: ROBERT HICKS, DAVID ATKINS. Feb. Court
1722. JOHN SUTTON D. C/C.

A 44 JOHN BYRD (BIRD) TO JAMES CURRY (CURRIE)
     May 1, 1723. 5 pds. for 250 A. Part of 500 A. adj. Coll. ROBERT WEST
on Will's Quarter Swamp. Wit: JAMES CASTELLAW, EDWARD BYRD. May Court 1723.
JOHN SUTTON D C/C.

A 46 CHRISTOPHER VANLUVEN TO MICHAEL KING
     Feb. 9, 1721/22. 15 pds for 100 A. on Cashoke Creek Swamp adj.
THOMAS BALL, VANLUVEN's dwelling house. Wit: JOHN CROMBIE, JOHN BATTS,
RICHARD ABEE, JAMES BLACK. May Court 1723. JOHN SUTTON D. C/C.

A 47 CHRISTOPHER VANLUVEN & WIFE ELIZABETH TO JAMES CURRIE
     May 13, 1723. Power of atty. to ack. sale to Michael King. Wit:
JAMES CURRIE, JOHN BYRD, JOSEPH HUDSON. May Court 1723. JOHN SUTTON D. C/C.

A 48 JAMES BRYANT & WIFE SARAH TO JOHN DICKINSON
     May 14, 1723. 10 pds. for land on Yowarrah Swamp. Part of 640 A.
patent bearing date Mar. 9, 1717/18. Wit: NICHOLAS BAGGET, JOHN SMITH.
May Court 1723. JOHN SUTTON D. C/C.

A 49 SARAH BRYANT TO THOMAS BRYANT
     May 14, 1723. SARAH, wife of JAMES BRYANT, gives power of atty. to
THOMAS BRYANT to adk. sale of 640 A. to JOHN DICKINSON. Wit: NICHOLAS
BAGGETT, JOHN SMITH. May Court 1723. JOHN SUTTON D. C/C.

A 50 JOHN LANE & WIFE MARY TO JOHN DICKINSON
     May 11, 1723. 10 pds. for 225 A. on (Urha) Swamp at mouth of Cabin
Creek, Pottecasi Creek. Patent date Nov. 11, 1719. Wit: JOHN SUTTON, MARY
SUTTON, JAMES BRYANT. May Court 1723. JOHN SUTTON D. C/C.

A 52 MARY LANE TO THOMAS BRYANT
     May 11, 1723. MARY LANE gives power of atty. to THOMAS BRYANT to sell
225 A. to JOHN DICKINSON. Wit: JAMES BRYANT, NICHOLAS BAGGETT. Mary Court
1723. JOHN SUTTON D. C/C.

A 52 JOHN COTTON & WIFE MARTHA TO JOHN SPIER (SPEIR)
     April 26, 1723. 221 pds. 10 sh. for 300 A. NW Horskey (Ahorskey)
surveyed by THOMAS DIALL. Patent dated June 8, 1719. Adj. JOHN COTTON JUN,
Col. MAULE. Wit: WILLIAM MARTIN, THOMAS JORDAN, THOMAS JENKINS. May Court
1723. JOHN SUTTON D. C/C.

A 55 ISAAC LEWIS TO JAMES WILKINSON
     May 15, 1723 50 pds. for 160 A. NS Horse Swamp. Wit: ROBERT FORSTER,
BARNABE MACKINNE. May Court 1723. JOHN SUTTON D. C/C.

A 56 JAMES BLUNT & WIFE KATHERINE TO WILLIAM HINTON of Upper Parish Nansi-
     mond County. Feb. 12, 1722. 31 pds. for 640 A. between Moratuck and
Cashay on "ye Village Pond". Part of 640 A. patent date March 30, 1721. Wit:
STEPHEN HOWARD, JOHN NAIRN. May Court 1723. *

A 59 BARNABE MACKINNE, SEN. TO BARNABE MACKINNE, JUN.
     May 11, 1723. "For love I bear my son"...100 A. on SS Moratuck River
adj. NATHANIEL HOLLEY, PHILLIP RAYFORD. Wit: ROBERT UMPHREY, JOHN BROWN.
May Court 1723. JOHN SUTTON D. C/C.

A 59 BARNABE MACKINNE, JUN. TO JOSEPH LANE, JUN.
     May 14, 1723. 12 pds. for 250 A. on SS Moratuck on Conocannar Swamp
and Beaver Dam Swamp. Part of 500 A. patented to William Murphey April 5,
1720 and bought by MACKINNE. Wit: BARNABE MACKINNE, JOHN PAGE. May Court
1723. JOHN SUTTON D. C/C.

A 61 VALINTINE BRASSWELL & WIFE JEAN TO JOHN BLACKMAN
     Dec. 3, 1722. 50 pds. for 440 A. adj. JOHN POPE, WILLIAM BRYANT
(BRIANT). Pagent bearing date March 9, 1717/18. Wit: SAMUEL WILLIAMS,
NATHANIEL PIGOTT. May Court 1723. Ack. by JOHN COTTON, Esq. atty of VALEN-
TINE & JANE BRASSWELL. JOHN SUTTON D. C/C.

A 63 VALENTINE BRASSWELL & WIFE JENE TO JOHN BLACKMAN
     Sept. 3, 1721. 30 pds. for 150 A. purchased of JEAMES BRIANT patent

date April 1, 1719...now in possession of JOHN BLACKMAN. On WS (Quonk's) Branch. Wit: JEAMES BRYANT, SARAH BRYANT. Mary Court 1721. JOHN SUTTON D.CC.

A 64   VALENTINE BRASSWELL & WIFE JEANE TO JOHN COTTON, ESQ.
       Apr. 15, 1721. Power of Atty to sell land on Urharra Swamp, "the manor plantation of VALENTINE BRASSWELL" to JOHN BLACKMON. Wit: JOSIAH BRIDGES, ROBERT PATTERSON.

A 65   DANIEL O'QUIN TO BRIAN O'QUIN & PATRICK O'QUIN
       May 11, 1723. 12 pds. for 200 A. granted to DANIEL O'QUIN by patent dated Oct. 10, 1722. On Catawhiskey Swamp. FRANCES PRIDGON (PRIDGSON), JACOB (HORN). May Court 1723. JOHN SUTTON D. C/C.

A 67   THOMAS VINCENT & WIFE ISABELL TO WILLIAM VINCENT
       May 10, 1723. 10 pds. for 100 A. Part of 300 A. patent dated Mar. 9 1717/18 on WS Meherrin Creek adj. WILLIAM HARRELL, JOHN JERNAGIN (JORNAKEN). Wit: THOMAS JENKINS, JEAMES BRYANT, JOHN DICKINSON. May Court 1723. JOHN SUTTON D. C/C.

A 69   JOHN LANE TO JOHN COOK
       May 14, 1723. 10 pds for 225 A. by patent dated Nov. 11, 1719. On SW Urah Swamp adj. JOHN DICKINSON down Cabin Branch..along Pottecasie Creek. Wit: THOMAS FEWTRELL, MOORE CARTER, JOHN SUTTON. May Court 1723. J.S.+

A 70   WILLIAM BRYANT TO WILLIAM BRIDGERS
       May 13, 1723. WILLIAM BRYANT and wife MARY, 320 A. for 50 sh. on Urharra Swamp. Patent dated March 9, 1717/18. (no witnesses). May Court 1723. J.S.+

A 72   NOVEMBER COURT 1723
       JOHN STEPHENS brought in on complaint of MARY GRAY, wife of PETER GRAY, that he slandered her by false reports. He denied the reports in court, and owned himself a "lyer". Wit: WILLIAM LATTIMORE, PHILLIP WALSTON.+

A 73   BENJAMIN FOREMAN & VERRILY (VERRELY) HIS WIFE TO ROBERT SHERWOOD
       May 13, 1723. 30 pds. for 360 A. on Kirby's Creek. Wit: CORNELIUS (CORNELIONS) PIERCE, JOHN BRYANT. May Court 1723. +

A 74   JACOB LEWIS TO DEBORAH KEEL
       May 14, 1723. "For love I bear my sister-in-law" 200 A. on Petty Shore adj. THOMAS WIGGAN's, WILLIAM KEEL, ABRAHAM BLEWLETT, THOMAS BIRD. Wit: THOMAS BIRD, JOHN NAIRNE. May Court 1723. +

A 75   JOHN HOLLY & WIFE SARAH TO CHRISTIAN CHURCH
       Dec. 22, 1721. To her & her heirs...50 A. for 6 pds. On Wiccacon Creek adj. DENNIS MACKLENDON. Wit: WILLIAM CRANFORD(CRAWFORD), GEORGE POWELL, JAMES BATE, SARAH DAVIS. May Court 1723. +

A 77   OWEN MCDANIEL TO JAMES BLOUNT
       May 15, 1723. 160 A. on Sandy Run. Patent Date March 1, 1719. Wit: EDWARD HOWARD, JOHN NAIRNE. May Court 1723. +

A 78   STEPHEN HOWARD & WIFE SARAH TO GEORGE MARTIN, CAPT. of Maryland
       March 5, 1723. 20 pds. land SS Chowan River adj. RICHARD BARFIELD. Wit: EDWARD HOWARD, SAMUEL WILLIAMS, JEAMES HOWARD. May Court 1723. +

A 80   JEAMES BOON & WIFE ELIZABETH TO GEORGE MARTIN of Maryland.
       March 7, 1722/23. 45 pds for 900 A. SS Chowan adj. JOHN GRAY, JOHN BEVERLY, JOHN HOLMES, Elm Swamp, RICHARD BARFIELD. Wit: WILLIAM MAULE, FRANCIS BROWN, RICHARD BROWN. May Court 1723. +

A 81   GEORGE MARTIN TO WILLIAM MAULE
       March 20, 1723. 50 pds. for 320 A. NS Meherrin River adj. Chowan River, Indian Creek. Wit: JOHN (VIJAN), FRAN. HATTON, WILLIAM GRAY. * + *

A 83   LAZARUS WHITEHEAD & WIFE MARY of Isle of Wight, Va. to BARNABY THOMAS
       May 10, 1723. 15 pds. for 150 A. on Holly Creek by patent March 1, 1719. Wit: WILLIAM WHITEHEAD, BENJAMIN THOMAS, WILLIAM MURPHEY. May Ct.1723.

+ JOHN SUTTON, Dep. C/C. As he is listed in every deed, his name will be omitted from here on.

A 86   THOMAS BONNER & WIFE ELIZABETH TO MARGARET MOORE
        May 13, 1723. 80 pds. for 670 A. in three tracts. One: land BONNER
bought of THOMAS BROWN by deed dated July 16, 1717. Another: land BONNER
holds by patent dated March 9, 1717/18. Another: BONNER holds by patent
dated April 7, 1722. Wit: WILLIAM WHITFIELD, JOHN DUFFIELD. May Court 1723.

A 88   EDWARD CHITTY of Isle of Wight, Va. to FRANCIS PRIDGEON
        May 14, 1723. 12 pds. for 90 A. Urah Swamp. Wit: JAMES BRYANT, JOHN
DICKENSON, JOHN SUTTON. May Court 1723.

A 90   PHILLIP RAYFORD & WIFE MARTHA TO ROBERT WARREN
        Oct. 9, 1722. 7 pds. for 200 A. on SS Morractucky River on Conacon-
aro Swamp adj. NATHANIEL HOLLY. Wit: JOHN GRAY, DAVID BUN. May Court 1723.

A 92   MARTIN GARDINER & WIFE ANNE TO JOHN EDWARDS, JUN.
        May 14, 1723. 5 pds. for 100 A. WS Cushy Swamp between GARDINER and
EDWARDS. Wit: OWEN(?) DANILL, WILLIAM JONES. May Court 1723. MATTHEW
EDWARDS by power of atty. from MARTIN GARDINER & wife ack. sale to JOHN
EDWARDS.

A 93   MARTIN GARDINER & WIFE ANNE TO MATTHEW (MARTHA) EDWARDS
        May 14, 1723. Power of atty to MATTHEW EDWARDS to sell land to JOHN
EDWARDS, JUN. Wit: OWEN DANIEL, WILLIAM JONES. (no court date here).

A 94   RICHARD TURBERVILLE TO JOHN GRAY
        May 10, 1723. 12 pds. for 450 A. on Marrattack River adj. WALTER
TURBERVILLE, JOHN PACE. Wit: ROBERT FOSTER, *. May Court 1723.

A 96   WILLIAM GREEN & WIFE ELIZABETH TO JOHN GRAY
        May 10, 1723. 10 pds for 100 A. in Society Parish on SS Merratack
River adj. THOMAS WHITMELL. Wit: LEWIS BRYAN, JEAMES BROGDEN, THOMAS BECK-
MAN. May Court 1723.

A 97   JOHN PACE & WIFE ELIZABETH TO JOHN GRAY
        May 13, 1723. 30 pds. for 320 A. NS Morrattuck River adj.RICHARD
TURBERVILLE. Wit: HENRY JONES, FRANCES JONES. May Court 1723.

A 100 JOHN BRYAN TO NICHOLAS SMITH
        Feb. 19, 1723 35 pds. for 450 A. SS Morattock River adj. JOHN HAM-
ELTON. Wit: JOHN GRAY, LEWIS BRYAN, HENRY THIGPEN. May Court 1723.

A 102 JOHN BRYAN, JUN. TO THOMAS BOYKEN
        May 23, 1722. 11 pds. for 420 A. SS Meherrin River adj. REBECCA
BRASSWELL, MOYE's Branch, THOMAS MOYE. Wit: HENRY ROADES, JOHN GRAY. May
Court 1723.

A 104 RICHARD BRASSWELL & WIFE ELEANOR TO WILLIAM KINCHEN
        Feb. 12, 1722/23. 30 pds. for 145 A. SS Meherrin River now in poss-
ession of WILLIAM KINCHEN. Wit: JAMES BRYANT, WILLIAM BRYANT, HARDY
COUNCILL. May Court 1723.

A 105 RICHARD BRASSWELL & WIFE ELEANOR TO WILLIAM KINCHEN
        Feb. 12, 1722/23. 30 pds. for 145 A. part of a patent for 245 A.
dated April 6, 1722 on SS Meherrin River. Now in possession of WILLIAM
KINCHEN. Adj. "the Islands of the River". Wit: JAMES BRYANT, WILLIAM
BRYANT, HARDY COUNCILL. May Court 1723.

A 105 WILLIAM BENNETT & WIFE GRACE TO JOHN BASS, JUN. of Perquimmons Pre-
        cinct. July 16, 1722. 37 pds. for 200 A. between Urharra Swamp &
Yeorhaugh(?) adj. RICHARD WASHINGTON, Esq. POLLOCK, VALENTINE BRASSWELL,
Part of a patent of 400 A. dated March 9, 1717/18. Wit: WILLIAM WHITE,
WILLIAM BRYANT, BENJAMIN THOMAS. May Court 1723.

A 108 WILLIAM BENNETT & WIFE GRACE TO JOHN BASS
        April 10, 1722. 15 pds. for 200 A. between Urharra & Yeorhaugh(?)
adj. WILLIAM BRYANT, THOMAS KIRBY, RICHARD WASHINGTON. Part of a 400 A.
patent dated March 9, 1717/18. Wit: WILLIAM WHITEHEAD, WILLIAM BRYANT,
BENJAMIN THOMAS. May Court 1723.

A 110 GRACE BENNETT TO THOMAS BRYANT
        May 13, 1723. Power of atty. at court held at JAMES HOWARD's to ack.

to JOHN BASS, SEN. & JOHN BASS, JUN. "my right of Dowrie and power of thirds" to all lands sold by my husband, WILLIAM BENNETT, to aforesaid BASSES. Wit: HENRY SIMS, CHARLES MERRITT. (No court date here).

A 111   FRANCIS McKLENDON & WIFE ELEANOR TO RICHARD WILLYFORD
        May 10, 1723   20 pds. for 200 A. on Quakeson Swamp. Wit: SARAH SCOTT, FRANCIS McKLENDON. May Court 1723.

A 113   RICHARD BRASSWELL & WIFE ELEANOR TO WILLIAM BENNETT
        May 14, 1723. 30 pds for 100 A. Part of patent for 245 A. dated April 6, 1722 on SS Meherrin River Adj. WILLIAM KINCHEN. Wit: HARDY COUN-CILL, JEAMES BRYANT, WILLIAM BRYANT. May Court 1723.

A 115   TIMOTHY HINDS TO ROBERT EDWARDS of Isle of Wight Va.
        December 21, 1722. 14 pds. for 320 A. SS Meherrin River being half of 640 A. patent dated March 1, 1719. Wit: RICHARD WASHINGTON, JOHN COLSON, JOHN BACLOR(?). May Court 1723.

A 117   JOHN COTTON & WIFE JUDITH TO BARREBE MILTON (MELTON)
        May 13, 1723. 10 pds. for 130 A. SS Morratacky River adj. WILLIAM GREEN, Island Creek. Wit: JAMES BROKEDON, JOHN MELTON. May Court 1723.

A 118   WILLIAM GREEN & WIFE ELIZABETH TO BARRABE MELTON
        May 13, 1723. 6 pds. for 40 A. on SS Morratacky River on Reedy Branch. Wit: JAMES BROKDON, JOHN MELTON. May Court 1723.

A 120   WILLIAM GREEN & WIFE ELIZABETH TO JOHN MELTON
        May 13, 1723. 10 pds for 100 A. on SS Morattacky River on Island Creek. Wit: JAMES BROKDON, BARRABEE MELTON. May Court 1723.

A 122   WILLIAM GREEN & WIFE ELIZABETH TO JAMES SMITH
        May 13, 1723. 10 pds. for 100 A. on SS Marrattacky River. Wit: JANES BROKDON, JOHN MELTON. May Court 1723.

A 124   BARRABE MELTON TO WILLIAM HOLLINGSWORTH (HILLINGSWORTH)
        May 13, 1723. 10 pds. for 140 A. on SS Morratacky River on Island Swamp, Reedy Branch. Adj. JOHN RIVERS. Wit: JOHN LENARD, GEORGE SMITH. May Court 1723.

A 126   BARRYBE MELTON TO JOHN RIVERS
        May 13, 1723. 3 pds. for 100 A. on SS Morattacky River adj. WILLIAM HILLINGSWORTH. (No witnesses). May Court 1723.

A 127   THOMAS BROWN (BROWNE) & WIFE JANE TO JAMES DENTON
        May 11, 1723. 12 pds. for 240 A. on NS Pottacasie Branch of Moher-rin Creek by patent dated Aug. 30, 1714. Wit: ROBERT BRASSWELL, JOHN BROWN. May Court 1723.

A 124   WILLIAM WHITEHEAD & WIFE RACHEL TO JOHN BASS, SEN.
        Feb. 12, 1722. 15 pds. for 300 A. on SS Swamp Urah adj. JAMES FIELD. Part of patent surveyed by RICHARD WASHINGTON and lapsed. Then seated by WILLIAM WHITEHEAD. Patent of 600 A. dated March 30, 1721. Wit: R. FOSTER clerk of court. May Court 1723. Ack. in court by WILLIAM WHITEHEAD and THOMAS BRYANT, Esq., atty for RACHEL WHITEHEAD.

A 132   RACHILL WHITEHEAD TO THOMAS BRYANT
        May 13, 1723. Appts. THOMAS BRYANT power of atty at court held at JAMES HOWARD's to ack. to JOHN BASS, SEN. and EDWARD BASS all rights in lands sold by husband, WILLIAM WHITEHEAD, to aforesaid BASSES. Wit: HENRY SIMS, CHARLES MERRIT.

A 133   ROBERT BRASSWELL & WIFE SARAH TO JOHN GARLAND of Isle of Wight, Va.
        May 15, 1723. 15 pds. for 290 A. now in possession of JOHN GARLAND. By patent dated March 1, 1719 for 500 A. on NS Moherrin River adj. Mill Meadow, JONATHAN SANDERSON, JOHN WIGGAINS. Wit: MARY BRASSWELL, ELIZABETH MOLTON. May Court 1723.

A 135   JOHN MACKMIEL TO CHARLES STEPHENS
        May 15, 1723. 12 pds. for 160 A. on NES Uraka Meadow. Part of a patent granted to JOHN McMIEL, and dated Aug. 10, 1720. Wit: JAMES BRYANT, JOHN HOMES, ROBERT ORANGE(?). May Court 1723.

A 136 CHARLES SOWELL & WIFE ELIZABETH TO JOHN HICKS
        Aug. 12, 1723. 18 pds. for 100 A. on WS Chowan River at mouth of
Horse Creek Swamp. Wit: JOHN BAYLY, JOHN HAIRNE(?). Aug. Court 1723.

A 138 JENNETT PATTERSON TO HER CHILDREN
        Aug. 12, 1723. "For love and good will"...all household goods and
breeding horses and stock. (named) Daughters: ELIZABETH PATTERSON, JENNETT
(JINNETTE) PATTERSON. Son: JOHN PATTERSON. Wit: WILLIAM HOWETT, JOHN
NAIRNE. August Court 1723.

A 140 ROBERT BRASSWELL TO JONATHAN SANDERSON
        Aug. 15, 1723. 10 pds. for 200 A. on Buckhorn Swamp. Part of 580 A.
Wit: ROBERT HICKS, JUN., JOHN WIGGINS. August Court 1723.

A 141 ROBERT BRASSWELL TO JOHN WIGGANS
        Aug. 15, 1723. 10 pds. for 100 A. Part of 580 A. patent. Wit:
ROBERT HICKS, JONATHAN SANDERSON. August Court 1723.

A 141 JOHN BLACKMAN & WIFE ELIZABETH TO THOMAS SEALEY
        Aug. 12, 1723 22 pds. for 320 A. Part of 640 A. patent dated Mar. 9, 1717/18 on
SS Yowaruh Swamp. Wit: NATHL. PIGOTT, NICHOLAS BAGGATT. Aug. Court 1723.

A 143 JOHN SMITHSON of ye Sloop James & Mary of New England to ROBERT
        EVANS. Jan. 25, 1722/23. The Sloop now on the Petty (Pette) Shore
(Shoar) in North Carolina "wishes to return home". ROBERT EVANS appt.
power of atty. to "call for and receave" my debts in N.C. Wit: JOHN MEANER,
ELIZABETH MEANER. Aug. Court 1723.

A 145 EDWARD MOORE & WIFE MARGRATT TO GARRETT KELLEY
        April 27, 1723. 161 pds. for 100 A. adj. JOHN WILLIAMS on Roquiess
Swamp. Wit: JAMES CASTELLOW, ELIZABETH GRIFFET. Aug. Court 1723. (Note:
The name MARGRATT is used in the body of deed. It is signed ELIZABETH
MOORE.)

A 147 NICHOLAS SESSOME & WIFE ELIZABETH TO JAMES PAGE
        Aug. 13, 1723. 12 pds. for 80 A. on Wickacorne Creek adj. JOHN
WILLIAMS. Wit: NEEDHAM BRYANT, JOHN NAIRNE. Aug. Court 1723.

A 149 RALPH MASON, JUN. TO FOSTER MASON
        Aug. 12, 1723. 10 pds. for 160 A. on SS Morrattacky River. Wit:
RALPH MASON, SEN., THOMAS BROWNE. Aug. Court 1723.

A 151 JOHN BAYLEY TO LAWRENCE HOBBY
        May 6, 1723. 14 pds. for 300 A. purchased of RICHARD WASHINGTON in
1717. On SS Moherrin River adj. ARTHUR WILLIAMS. Wit: HICKS(?), HENRY
WHEELER, ARON DRAKE. August Court 1723.

A 152 JOHN BLACKMAN & WIFE ELIZABETH TO NICHOLAS BAGGETT
        Aug. 12, 1723. 25 pds. for 150 A. Part of tract granted WILLIAM
BRASSWELL on April 1, 1714. On WS Quonke Branch. Wit: NEEDHAM BRYANT,
JAMES PARKER. August Court 1723.

A 155 JOHN BLACKMAN & WIFE ELIZABETH TO JAMES PARKER
        Feb. 12, 1722. 20 pds. for 320 A. on Yauerah Swamp "betwixt" THOMAS
KIRBY & DANIEL McDANIEL. Wit: NEEDHAM BRYAN, THOMAS SEALEY. Aug. Court 1723.

A 156 THOMAS BONNER & WIFE ELIZABETH TO WILLIAM REED
        Aug. 13, 1723. 7 pds for 100 A. Part of two tracts: one, granted
March 9, 1717; the other, " a elaps patten" dated April 17, 1722. Adj.
THOMAS BONNER & WILLIAM REED on Reedy Branch and THOMAS BROWNE. Wit: JOHN
SUTTON, BARNABE MACKINNE. August Court 1723.

A 150 JOHN BRYAN, SON OF EDWARD BRYAN TO LEWIS BRYAN
        Aug. 13, 1723. 37 pds. for 640 A. on St. John's Neck on Chinkopin
Creek adj. THOMAS BRAY, WILLIAM WEST. Wit: EDWARD HOWARD, JAMES REEK(?).
August Court 1723.

A 160 RALPH MASON, JUN. TO RALPH MASON, SEN.
        Aug. 12, 1723. 10 pds for 150 A. on SS Morrattacky River adj.
FOSTER MASON. Wit: FOSTER MASON, THOMAS BROWN. Aug. Court 1723.

A 162 WILLIAM POPE of Isle of Wight, Va. to HENRY POPE
        Aug. 15, 1722. 60 pds. or 1/2 money paid by my father, HENRY POPE,
to GEORGE SMITH. 290 A. or 1/2 patent cont. 500 A. dated Dec. 3, 1720.
Sold by GEORGE SMITH to HENRY POPE. On SS Morattacky River adj. THOMAS
GOODWIN, AFTER(?) CRAFORD, JOHN POPE. Wit: JOHN BRYAN, JOHN GRIFFITH,
THOMAS BOONE. August Court 1723.

A 164 ABELL JOHNSON alias JOHN BUTLER & WIFE RACHILL JOHNSON alias RACHILL
        BUTLER TO JOHN BIRD. Oct. 30, 1723. 25 pds. for 70 A. WS Cushie
River where JOHNSON now lives. Wit: JOHN ARMSTRONG, JOSEPH HUDSON, ROGER
SNELL. November Court 1723. C. Gale C/C.

A 166 RACHILL BUTLER TO JOHN BIRD
        Nov. 9, 1723. "I, RACHILL BUTLER or RACHILL JOHNSON, wife to ABELL
JOHNSON or JOHN BUTLER, planter.." appt. JAMES CORRIE power of atty. to ack.
sale by husband to JOHN BIRD. Wit: JOHN HENRE, JAMES CORRIE. Nov. 2, 1723.

A 166 HON. JOHN LORD CARTERRETT, PALLATINE & rest of Lords to EDWARD
        STANDEN. Oct. 19, 1716. "...according to our grant..May 1, 1668.."
229 A. on Kesiah River adj. M. RIVERS, J. RIVERS, LUKE MEZLES. Recorded in
Sec'y. Office Oct. 19, 1716. J. KNIGHT.

A 167 WILLIAM STANDING, SON OF EDWARD STANDING TO MARTIN CROWMAN
        Oct. 22, 1723. 30 pds: 20 lbs. pitch delivered to EDWARD SMITHWICK's
landing before May 31, 1724; remaining 10 lbs. corn and barrelled pork delivered same place before Dec. 31, 1724...any part can be paid in current
bills double the amount according to rated currency...land belonging to
MARTIN CROWMAN. Wit: S. WARNER, JOHN PALIN, THOMAS HENMAN. Nov. 1, 1723.

A 168 JOHN BROWN & WIFE MARY TO JOSEPH JOYNER
        October 25, 1723. 10 pds for 80 A. SS Morrattacky River adj.WILLIAM
BROWN dec'd. Part of patent to WILLIAM BROWN for 640 A. and resurveyed by
JOHN BROWN. Wit: BAR. MACKINNE, NATHANIEL HOLLEY. Nov. 23, 1723.

A 170 TARLE (TARLO) O"QUIN TO WILLIAM EASON
        Nov. 11, 1723.*. 200 A. on Meadow adj. WILLIAM EASON. Wit: JOHN
SUTTON, JOHN STEWARD. Nov. Court. JOHN SUTTON D. C/C.

A 171 JOHN SMITH & WIFE JUDITH TO BENJAMIN WARREN
        Nov. 9, 1723. 19 pds. for 200 A. Obrey's (?) Branch on Chinkopin
Swamp. Wit: JAMES BATE, JAMES PEEKE. Nov. Court 1723.

A 172 RICHARD WILLIAMS & WIFE MARTHA TO JAMES HOWARD
        Nov. 13, 1723. 6 pds for 200 A. "betwaxt Ahotsky & Catawhitskey
Swamps" adj. JOSEPH JONES, EDWARD HOWARD. Patent dated April 6, 1722. Wit:
JOHN SUTTON, JAMES SAUDERS, JOSEPH HOWARD. November Court 1723.

A 175 JAMES HOWARD & WIFE SARAH TO ALEXANDER BRAYSON of North Brittain
        November 12, 1723. 7 pds. for 440 A. on Timber Branch adj. ROBERT
LENISR's (?), EDWARD HOWARD, JOSEPH JONES, JOHN JONES, JUN., JOHN JONES
SEN. Wit: WILLIAM CRANFORD, JAMES MOORE, JAMES SANDERS. Nov. Court 1723.

A 176 HENRY TURNER TO THOMAS HART
        June 13, 1723. *. 376 A. SS Meherren River on Sypress Swamp in
Upper part of patent granted to HENRY TURNER for 476 A. by CHARLES EDEN,
Esq. dated March 1, 1719. Wit: JOSEPH PLATTS, HOPKINS HOWELL, JOSHUA
SIKES. November Court 1723.

A 182 JAMES WOOD TO DANIEL PUGH of Nansimond Co., Va.
        Dec. 17, 1723. 40 pds. for 500 A. on Catawhitskey Meadow. ROBERT
HICKS patent dated Nov. 1, 1719 and by him "elapsed". Came to JAMES WOOD
by order of Councill April 1, 1723. Wit: JOHN DICKINSON, JOHN STONE,
MOORE CARTER. Feb. Court 1723.

A 180 JOHN YELVERTON & WIFE ELIZABETH TO JOHN STEWARD
        Nov. 12, 1723. 10 pds. for 100 A. on SS Morrattacky River on Flaggy
Run. By patent dated March 13, 1724. Adj. ROBERT WEST. Wit: NEEDHAM BRYAN,
JOHN PAGE. November Court 1723.

A 184 JOHN DICKINSON TO EDWARD MASHBORNE of Upper Parish Nansimond Co, Va.
        June 30, 1719. 11 pds. for 300 A. on NS Catawitskey Meadow formerly

seated by JOHN BAYLEY. Part of 640 A. patent to JOHN BRYANT, JUN. dated
Aug. 28, 1714...with additional part of Catashitskey Meadow surveyed by
JOHN GRAY, deputy surveyor, on Indian Springs. Adj. EDWARD MASHBORNE & JOHN
DICKINSON. Wit: JAMES BRYANT, JAMES WOOD, MICHAEL DORMAN. Feb. Court 1723.

A 186 CHARLES SOWELL & WIFE ELIZABETH TO THOMAS JENKINS
        Feb. 12, 1723. 15 pds. for 100 A. adj. ANDREW BARROW and DANIEL
O'QUIN. Wit: JOHN SUTTON, JACOB BRASSWELL, SIMON JEFFREYS. Feb. Court 1723.

A 188 NATHANIEL MERIOT TO JOSEPH BALLARD of Nansimond Co., Va.
        Nov. 10, 1723. 10 pds for 50 A. on SS Roanoaky River on Plumtree
Island. Adj. ROBERT LONG, JOSEPH SEWARDS, FRANCIS VARNUMS(?), WILLIAM
REEVES. Wit: JOHN GRAY, WILLIAM GRAY, THOMAS WHITTMELL. Feb. Court 1723.

A 190 GEORGE STEPHENS TO CLEMENT STRADFORD
        Feb. 12, 1723. 3 pds. for 60 A. Part of 620 A. patent dated April
1, 1723. On Bridger's Creek. Wit: JOHN SUTTON, ISAAC HILL. Feb. Court 1723.

A 191 WILLIAM WHITFIELD & WIFE ELIZABETH TO THOMAS WILSON
        Feb. 10, 1723/24. 25 pds. for 600 A. part of grant to JOHN HOMES
now "relapsed" and seated by WILLIAM WHITFIELD. On Hot House Branch called
Reed's Clearing. Wit: R. FOSTER, JOHN SUTTON. Feb. Court 1723.

A 193 ROBERT LANEER (LANIER) & WIFE SARAH TO JAMES SPEIR of Nansemond Co.
        Va. Jan. 24, 1723. 25 pds. for 420 A. "lately taken up & pattened"
by ROBERT LANEER dated April 1, 1723. On Spring Branch adj. ANTHONY
WILLIAMS, JAMES SUMNER on Ahotskey. Wit: CHARLES JONES, WILLIAM MEARS.
Feb. Court 1723.

A 197 ROBERT LANEER (LANIER) & WIFE SARAH TO JAMES SPIER of Nansimond Co.
        Va. Jan. 24, 1723. 25 pds. for 300 A. on Ahotskey Ridge. Patent
date April 1, 1723. Wit: CHARLES JONES, WILLIAM MEARS. Feb. Court 1723.

A 200 WILLIAM WHITFIELD & WIFE ELIZABETH TO THOMAS JOHNSON
        Jan. 29, 1723. 30 pds. for 300 A. "called Red Ridge". Patent dated
April 6, 1722. Wit: MARY DURDINO, WILLIAM MOOR, JANE GILBERT. Feb. Ct.1723.

A 202 GEORGE STEPHENS TO CLEMENT STANFORD.
        May 12, 1724. 40 sh. for 60 A. on NS Morratacky River on Bridger's
Creek. Part of 620 A. patent dated April 1, 1723. Wit: THOMAS HART, JOHN
HART. Feb. Court 1723.

A 203 DANIEL O'QUIN TO THOMAS JENKINS
        Feb. 12, 1723. 5 pds. for 100 A. adj. ANDREW BARROW, LEWIS WILLIAMS,
JAMES WOOD. Wit: WILLIAM RICKS, JAMES SPEIR, JUN. Feb. Court 1723.

A 205 WILLIAM WHITFIELD & WIFE ELIZABETH TO JOHN GILBERT
        Feb. 12, 1723. 20 pds. for 150 A. on Pottacasie Branch adj. Coll.
JONES, McTHOMAS Path, JOHN BEVERLEY. Wit: R. FORSTER, JOHN SUTTON. Feb.
Court 1723.

A 207 EDMUND SMITHWICK TO JOHN GRIFFIN
        Feb. 12, 1723. "..for love...I do bare JOHN GRIFFIN, son of MARTIN
and ELIZABETH GRIFFIN..." 124 A. on SS Casia River. Part of patent of 420 A.
surveyed by EDMUND SMITHWICK, SEN. and 300 A. of which he disposed of to
DANILL SMITH. Wit: R. FORSTER, JAMES CASTELLOW. Feb. Court 1723.

A 208 WILLIAM WHITFIELD & WIFE ELIZABETH TO THOMAS WILSON
        Feb. 10, 1724. 20 pds. for 580 A. on Watt Tom Swamp being in "two
patents in his name the other in his wife's name". Wit: THOMAS BANKS, ROB.
FORSTER. Feb. Court 1723.

A 210 SAMUEL CANADY & WIFE MARY TO ELIAS FORT
        Nov. 6, 1723. 15 pds. for 100 A. on SS Meherrin River purchased of
WILLIAM BOON on July 15, 1721. Now in actual possession of ELIAS FORT.
Wit: THOMAS BOON, ISAAC STERLING, ROBERT SCOTT. Feb. Court 1723.

A 212 LAURENCE HOBBY & WIFE SARAH TO ROBERT SCOTT
        Feb 10, 1723 30 pds for 50 A. on SS Meherrin River at mouth of
"Pudle Duck". Wit: RICHARD HORN, WILLIAM RICKS, ARON DICKENSON. Feb. Court
1723.

A 214   WILLIAM HOWELL of Isle of Wight Co., Va. TO HOPKINS HOWELL
        Dec. 5, 1720. *. 150 A. on SS Meherrin River of Cypress Swamp adj.
THOMAS HART. Part of 260 A. patent dated March 1, 1719. Wit: WILLIAM
WHITEHEAD, RICHARD WASHINGTON, ELIAS FORT. Feb. Court 1723.

A 217   WILLIAM HOWELL of Isle of Wight Co. Va. TO THOMAS HART
        Dec. 5, 1720. *. 110 A. on SS Meherrin River on Sypress Swamp and
Beaver Dam Branch. Part of 260 A. patent dated March 1, 1719. Wit: WILLIAM
WHITEHEAD, JOHN HART, RICHARD WASHINGTON. Feb. Court 1723.

A 220   JOHN GRIFFIN & WIFE JOYCE TO WILLIAM GRIFFIN
        June 1, 1720 "for love...I do bare my son WILLIAM GRIFFIN..." 200 A.
on SWS Kesai Swamp adj. WILLIAM WILSON. Wit: EDWARD MOORE, MARTIN GARDINER,
JAMES CASTELLOW. June 4, 1724. C. Gale C/C.

A 222   ELINOR KEEFE TO GEORGE WINN
        May 13, 1724. 20 pds. for * commonly called "Elexander's Neck" adj.
ANTHONY WILLIAMS on Wickorcan Creek. Wit: WILLIAM MAUL, ROBT. FORSTER.
May Court 1724.

A 224   DIANAH BALLENTINE (BALENTINE) TO JOSEPH WATFORD
        Jan. 24, 1723/4. "...Whereas GEORGE BALLENTINE dyed the twenty-first
day this Instant January...leaving me...by will January 14, 1723...execu-
trix..." I do appoint JOSEPH WATFORD to make proof of said will, and have
power of atty. to manage estate. Wit: WILLIAM CRANFORD, FRANCIS BROWN.
May Court 1724.

A 225   PHILLIP RAYFORD & WIFE MARTHA TO EDWARD SIMMONS
        May 9, 1724. 10 pds. for 125 A. on SS Marrattacky River NS Conconary
adj. NATHANIEL HOLLY, ROBERT WARREN. Part of 450 A. patent dated Aug. 10,
1720. Wit: BAR. MACKINNE, WILLIAM MURPHEY. May Court 1724.

A 227   MICHAEL MACKINNE TO JOHN FORT
        Nov. 12, 1723. 10 pds for 122 A. on SS Morattacky River on Looking
Glass Swamp. Wit: BAR. MACKINNE, GEORGE PACE. May Court 1724.

A 229   HENRY WHEELER (WHELER) TO PETER JONES
        Jan. 31, 1723. 6 pds. for 100 A. Part of 640 A. granted WILLIAM
BRASSWELL in 1711 and sold to HENRY WHEELER. On NS Morrattacky River on
Cypress Swamp called "Aukaneachey". Wit: ROBERT SIMMS, MARTHEW JONES.
May Court 1724.

A 231   THOMAS WHITMELL TO JOHN HOY of James Citty Co., Va.
        May 12, 1724. 15 pds. for 630 A. adj. Capt. YEDES (?), WILLIAM
GREE(N). Wit: JOHN GREEN, JOHN GRIFFETH. May Court 1724.

A 232   NEEDHAM BRYAN & WIFE ANNE TO JOHN HART
        Nov. 12, 1723. 16 pds. for 640 A. NES Morrattacky River adj. HENRY
JONES, SAMUEL MERIET. Patent dated April 3, 1721. Wit: WILLIAM COLLINS,
JONATHAN CHRISTMAS. May Court 1724. Deed of Sale ack. and proved by power
of atty. given TARLOW O'QUIN.

A 235   ANN BRYAN TO JAMES TURNER & TARLOW O'QUIN
        Nov. 14, 1723. Either or both JAMES TURNER of Isle of Wight, Va.
or TARLOW O'QUIN of County Albemarle in Bertie to appear in court in Bertie
to ack. right of dowrie in sale of land. Wit: JAMES TURNER, TARLOW O'QUIN.

A 235   JAMES BOON & WIFE ELIZABETH TO JOSEPH WATFORD
        March 21, 1723. 6 pds. for 100 A. on Killem Swamp adj. ANDREW STE-
VENSON, GOFERRY HOOKER, THOMAS MAIR. Wit: WILLIAM CRANFORD, JAMES NORVILL.
May Court 1724.

A 237   JAMES BOON & WIFE ELIZABETH TO JAMES NORVILL
        March 21, 1723. 8 pds. for 100 A. on Killem Swamp adj. THOMAS MANN,
ANDREW STEPHENSEN, JAMES BOON. Wit: WILLIAM CRANFORD, JOSEPH WATFORD. May
Court 1724.

A 239   JOHN STEWARD & WIFE SARAH TO ROBERT BRASSWELL
        Feb. 8, 1723. 25 pds. for 200 A. on Yourah Swamp Part of a 600 A.
tract. Wit: THOMAS BONNER, MOORE CARTER. May Court 1724.

A 242   JAMES NORVILL TO JOHN BROWN, JUN.
        May 12, 1724. 8 pds. for 100 A. adj. JOHN THOMAS on Horse Swamp adj.
LAZARUS THOMAS. Wit: HENRY BAKER, JOSEPH MAINOR. May Court 1724.

A 244   RICHARD BAREFIELD, SEN. TO EDWARD OUTLAW
        Feb. 10, 1723. 64 pds. for 250 A. on Chowan River adj. PETER EVANS
on Gum Branch. Wit: GEORGE MARSHHAM, JOHN POWER. May Court 1724.

A 246   WILLIAM CURLEE & WIFE MARTHA TO THOMAS BIRD
        May 2, 1724. 26 pds. for 400 A. on SS Ahotskey Swamp. Wit: WILLIAM
MEARS, CHARLES CAVENAH. May Court 1724.

(The following two transactions are not clear. They appear to be recipro-
cating leases between FRANCIS PARKER of Bertie and JOHN PARKER of Nansemond
County, VA.)

A 248   FRANCIS PARKER TO JOHN PARKER of Nansemond, Va.
        Feb. 10, 1723. 5 sh.(see above note) 640 A. in Bertie adj. JAMES
BLOUNT. 300 A. in Nansimond by lease signed May 20, 1721. "Interchangeably
sealed" FRANCIS PARKER AND JOHN PARKER. Wit: WILLIAM HORTON, ELIZABETH
PARKER, FRANCIS PARKER, JUN. May Court 1724.

A 251   FRANCIS PARKER TO JOHN PARKER OF NANSEMOND, VA.
        Feb. 10, 1720. 5 sh. (see note above) for one year lease on 640 A.
in Bertie adj. JAMES BLOUNT, THOMAS BEESLEY. Also land on Southern Branch
Nansimond "Indenture of Lease dated May 20, 1721 and another release dated
May 20, 1721" of 300 A. "Interchangeably signed and sealed" by FRANCIS
PARKER AND JOHN PARKER. Wit: WILLIAM HORTON, ELIZABETH PARKER, FRANCIS
PARKER, JUN. May Court 1724.

A 255   JACOB LEWIS & WIFE MARY TO JOHN MAINER
        May 12, 1724. 35 pds. for 170 A. *. Wit: JOSEPH WATFORD, NICHOLAS
SESSUMS, JOHN SUTTON. May Court 1724.

A 257   RICHARD BRASSWELL TO JOHN HILLIARD
        May 12, 1724. 9 pds. for 200 A. on NS Moratucky River adj. "Miry
Meadow alias Bridge Meadow" on Usara Meadow. Part of 300 A. patent dated
March 1, 1721. Wit: THOMAS BRYANT, JOHN HART. May Court 1724.

A 250   JOHN DICKENSON TO MOORE CARTER
        Oct. 10, 1720. 10 pds. for 210 A. on NS Catawhiskey Meadow on
Crakelast Branch adj. BROWN. Wit: JONATHAN WOODALL, JOHN CROPLY. August
Court 1724.

A 259   JACOB LEWIS TO CHARLES JONES
        Aug. 11, 1724. 4 pds. for 200 A. on Horse Swamp and Cowhall adj.
JAMES HOWARD, PETER WEST. Wit: JOHN SUTTON, JAMES PEEKE, JOHN RASBERRY.
Aug. Court 1724.

A 261   PETER STANSELL TO ARTHUR DUGALL
        Aug. 11, 1724. 10 pds. for 150 A. on SS Morattucky River and ES
Smithwick Creek. Part of 300 A. patent to STANSELL dated April 1, 1723.
Wit: JAMES CASTELLOW, OWEN O'DANIEL, JONATHAN RIDINGS. Aug. 1724.

A 262   JOHN BLOUNT & WIFE ELIZABETH TO JAMES BLOUNT
        *. 10 pds. paid by our brother JAMES BLOUNT for 200 A. on Cashiah
Swamp. Wit: THOMAS ROADS, WILLIAM JONES. August Court 1724.

A 264   EDWARD HOWCUTT TO WILLIAM WILLIAMSON
        Aug. 19, 1723. 50 pds. for 80 A. on Vickens (Vickis) Branch and
Stancell Neck adj. JOHN SMITH. Wit: ROBERT FORSTER, WILLIAM LITTLE. August
Court 1724.

A 266   JAMES BRYANT & WIFE SARAH TO THOMAS FEWTRELL
        Aug. 11, 1724. 10 pds. for 100 A. on Yourah Swamp. Part of 640 A.
patent surveyed by WILLIAM BRASSWELL. Wit: MOORE CARTER, MARTHEW MASHBORN.
Aug. Court 1724.

A 267   BARRABE (BARNABE, BARNEBE) MACKINNE, JUN. TO JOHN LANE
        Aug. 12, 1724. 5 pds. for 150 A. at mouth of Reedy Branch on SS
Conocanaro Swamp. Part of a patent formerly granted to WILLIAM MURPHREY

dated April 5, 1724. Wit: JOHN SUTTON, JAMES CASTELLOW. Aug. Court 1724.

A 269 WILLIAM PADGETT & WIFE JANE TO MICHAEL RISHAW
     March 31, 1724. 20 pds. for 230 A. adj. THOMAS WANS(?). Wit: WILL-
IAM KELLEY, JOHN YOUNG. Aug. Court 1724.

A 271 ARTHUR DUGALL & WIFE SARAH TO PETER STANSELL
     July 20, 1724. 30 pds. for 100 A. on SS Casia River. Part of tract
"whereon I now live". Near "Old Plantation Spring" adj. PETER GRAY. Wit:
JAMES CASTELLOW, SARAH CASTELLOW, JONATHAN RIDINGS. Aug. Court 1724.

A 273 ANDREW STEVENSON & WIFE ELIZABETH TO JOSEPH WATFORD
     March 13, 1724. 34 pds. for 130 A. on Killem Swamp adj. STEVENSON.
Wit: ANDREW MURRY, ANDREW STEVENSON. Aug. Court 1724.

A 275 WILLIAM JONES TO THOMAS JONES
     Aug. 10, 1724. "for good will I do bare" my kinsman and the heirs
of his body...200 A. in Casiah Swamp. Wit: PHILL WALSTON, FRANCIS HOBSON.
Aug. Court 1724.

A 277 GEORGE STEVENS TO CHARLES STEVENS
     Aug. 1, 1724. 10 pds. for 500 A. on Bridger's Creek adj. CLEMENT
STANDFORD, CHARLES STEVENS. Wit: JOHN SUTTON, THOMAS SPIVES (SPIRES).
Aug. Court 1724.

A 278 JOHN EDWARDS, JUN. & WIFE ELIZABETH TO OWEN O'DANIEL
     Aug. 8, 1724. 5 pds. for 100 A. Casiah Swamp. Wit: HENRY OVERSHEET,
WILLIAM JONES. Aug. Court 1724. Ack. in open court by JOHN EDWARDS, JUN.
OWEN O'DANIEL & PETER STANCELL BY Power of Atty. ELIZABETH EDWARDS ack. her
right of dower in sale above as proved by oath of PHILLIP WALSTON.

A 280 OWEN O'DANIEL TO JOHN BLOUNT
     Nov. 8, 1723. 15 pds. for 480 A. SWS Cusiah Swamp. Wit: ROBT.
FORSTER, WILLIAM LITTLE. Aug. Court 1724.

A 282 ARTHUR DUGALL TO JOHN (STANSILL) STANSELL
     Oct. 12, 1724. 17 pds. for 150 A. SS Morrattucky River on ES Smith-
wick Creek. Part of tract bought of PETER STANCILL. Wit: JOHN SMITHWICK,
PETER STANSELL. Nov. Court 1724. Ack. by JAMES CASTELLOW by power of atty
from ARTHUR DUGALL.

A 284 ARTHUR DUGALL TO JAMES CASTELLOW
     Oct. 25, 1724. Appt. JAMES CASTELLOW power of atty. to ack. in open
court sale of 150 A. to JOHN STANSELL. Wit: JOHN MAICAKEY (?), PETER
STANSELL.

A 284 WILLIAM CRANFORD TO EDWARD WILLIAMS
     *, 1720. For "love and natural affection" for EDWARD, son of JOHN &
MARY WILLIAMS, 143 A. adj. JAMES BOON, WILLIAM BUSH, GEORGE WINN, EDWARD
shall build a house and seat plantation by 30 March next. Wit: THOMAS
SPIRES, ROBT. FORSTER. Nov. Court 1724.

A 286 JOHN BUTLER & WIFE SARAH TO GEORGE STEVENS
     Sept. 7, 1724. 7 pds. for 240 A. between Ahotsky Swamp and Sandy
Run. Adj. OWEN MACK DANIEL. Patent 1722. Wit: NEDHAM BRYAN, THOMAS BUNTON.
Nov. Court 1724. NEDHAM BRYAN by power of atty. of SARAH BUTLER duly ack.
her right of dower.

A 288 SARAH BUTLAR TO NEDHAM BRYAN & THOMAS BUNTON
     Sept. 7, 1724. Power of atty. to either or both to ack. sale unto
GEORGE STEVENS. (No witnesses; no court date).

A 289 JOHN GILBERT & WIFE JANETT TO WILLIAM WHITFIELD
     May 16, 1724. 30 pds. for 150 A. on Pottacasia adj. Coll. JONES,
McTHOMAS' Path. Wit: JAMES COLE, JOHN GILBERT, JUN. Nov. Court 1724.

A 291 MARTIN CROMEN TO JOHN VANPELT of New York
     June 13, 1724. 35 pds. for 200 A. on Casiah Neck on NS Herrin Creek.
Wit: WILLIAM LATTIMER, EDWARD WINGATE. By power of atty. from MARTIN CRO-
MEN to WILLIAM CHARLTON proved by oath of WILLIAM (LATTEMER). July 23, 1724.
C. GALE C.C.

A 292   WILLIAM BENNETT & WIFE GRACE TO THOMAS WEST
        Nov. 11, 1724. 20 pds for 150 A. Part of patent dated April 1,
1724. On NS Morrattacky River adj. Coll. POLLOCK. Wit: WILLIAM WHITEHEAD,
_____PARKER, THOMAS BOAN(?). November Court 1724.

A 294   THOMAS MACKLENDON & WIFE ELIZABETH TO WILLIAM MACKHENRY
        Nov. 10, 1724. 30 pds. for 438 A. on Cannan Swamp adj. WILLIAM BUSH,
JOHN HILL. Wit: WILLIAM CRANFORD, WILLIAM BUSH. Nov. Court 1724.

A 296   JOHN HOLBROOK & WIFE DOROTHY TO JOHN CAKE
        Jan 22 1723. 22 pds. for 140 A. WS Squareena(?) Swamp adj. WM. HEN-
DERSON, _____WEST, & COLL. POLLOCK. Wit: WILLIAM GRIMES, JOHN DAVIS. Nov.
Court 1724.

A 298   JOHN JONES, JUN. TO THE JUSTICES OF THE COURT
        Nov. 12, 1724. 5 sh. for 1 A. of land whereon a Court House and
prison is to be built. Justices: WILLIAM MAULE, GEORGE POLLOCK, BAR.
MACKINNE, WILLIAM LATTIMORE, GEORGE WINN, JAMES CASTELLOW, JAMES BOON, JOHN
HOLLBROOK, NATHANIEL HILL, JOHN DEW(DUN), EDWARD HOWARD. Wit: WILLIAM
LITTLE, ROBERT HICKS, SIMON JEFFREYS, THOMAS BOYILN(?), ROBERT FOSTER,
THOMAS JONES. Nov. Court 1724.

A 299   LORD CARTERET & OTHER LORDS TO HENRY OVERSTREET
        HENRY OVERSTREET & WIFE ANN TO JOHN EDWARDS, JUN.
        Aug. 4, 1723. "LORD JOHN CARTERET PALATINE & rest of ye true &
absolute Lords Proprietors..." by grant of May 1, 1668...150 A. NS Casay
Swamp adj. JAMES PARKER. Signed WILLIAM REED.
        HENRY OVERSTREET & WIFE ANN..."We the Subscribers do assigne all
right...of within...patent to JOHN EDWARDS, JUN. Nov. 10, 1724." OWNE
O'DANIEL power of atty. to ack. aforementioned deed.

A 300   HENRY OVERSTREET & WIFE ANN TO OWEN O"DANIEL
        Nov. 9, 1724. Power of atty. to ack. sale of land to JOHN EDWARDS,
JUN. Wit: MARTIN GARDNER, EDWARD MOORE. (No court date here.)

A 301   WILLIAM CARLEE TO RICHARD WILLYFORD
        Nov. 11, 1724. 7 pds. for 100 A. on Ahotskey Swamp adj. "whereon
I now live". Wit: WILLIAM CRANFORD, JOHN BUSH. Nov. Court 1724.

A 303   JOHN WOOD & WIFE JANE TO BENJAMIN WOOD
        April 6, 1724. 40 sh. for 320 A. on SS Morrattucky River on Clay-
hill. "To my loving brother, BENJAMIN WOOD." Wit: RICHARD MYRICK, WILLIAM
MERRITT, JOHN SPEIR. Nov. Court 1724.

A 305   JAMES WOOD TO JOHN WOOD
        April 19, 1720. 5 pds. for 100 A. on SS Catawhiskey Meadow surveyed
CESI(?) WILLIAMS. *,*,*.*.*.

A 307   JOHN WOOD TO JAMES WOOD
        Nov. 10, 1724. 20 pds. *. "plantation". Wit: ROBERT HICKS, ANTHONY
PRANCE. Nov. Court 1724.

A 307   JAMES SWAIN TO JOHN STANCELL
        May 22, 1723. 5 pds. for 100 A. on SS Marattucky River known as
"Abihonntah" on Devil's Gutt. Wit: HENRY SPELLER, PETER STANCELL. Nov.
Court 1724. WILLIAM LATTEMORE by virtue of power of atty. ack. sale from
JAMES SWAIN to JOHN STANCELL.

A 309   JAMES SWAIN TO WILLIAM LATTEMORE
        Nov. 9, 1724. Appt. power of atty. to ack. deed to EDWARD SMITHWICK
for use of JOHN STANCELL. *,*.*.*.

A 309   EDMUND SMITHWICK TO JOHN SMITHWICK
        Nov. 7, 1724. 50 pds. for 250 A. on Smithwick Creek. Wit: NATHANIEL
MING, WILLIAM LATTEMORE. Nov. Court 1724.

A 311   JAMES WILKENSON & WIFE SARAH TO WILLIAM SCOTT
        Nov. 11, 1724 14 pds. for 300 A. on Chinkapen Creek adj. "WILLIAM
WILSON's former corner tree", WILLIAM BUSH, JAMES BOON. Wit: JAMES
WILLIAMSON, ROBERT FORSTER. Nov. Court 1724.

A 315   JOHN SMITHWICK TO JOHN JOHNSON
        Feb. 23, 1723/24. 50 pds. for 365 A. on Shojottack(?) adj. JAMES
WILLIAMSON. Patent date June 25, 1723. Wit: JAMES WILLIAMSON, EDMUND
SMITHWICK. Nov. Court 1724. HENRY SPELLER by virtue of power of atty.
from JOHN SMITHWICK ack. deed in open court.

A 313   PETER STANCILL (STANSILL) TO JOHN STANSILL
        Oct. 14, 1724. 17 pds. for 150 A. on SS Morattucky River. Wit:
JOHN MACARKEY, JONATHAN RIDINGS. Nov. Court 1724

A 317   ARTHUR DAVIS & WIFE ELIZABETH TO RICHARD KILLINGSWORTH
        Aug. 3, 1724. 7 pds. for 200 A. on SS Morrattucky River adj. JOHN
HAMILTON. Wit: JOHN BRYAN, WILLIAM BINUM. Nov. Court 1724.

A 319   LAWRENCE HOBBY & WIFE SARAH TO ROBERT SCOTT
        Nov. 10, 1724. 30 pds. for 320 A. adj. ROBERT SCOTT, _____ GANEY.
Part of patent granted HENRY WHEELER Nov. 5, 1714. Wit: W. RICKS, ESTHER
RICKS, WILLIAM WILSON. Nov. Court 1724.

A 321   THOMAS JOHNSTON & WIFE ANN TO JOHN GILBERT
        July 19, 1724. 40 pds. for 270 A. on Deep Creek where JOHNSTON
formerly lived. Adj. JOHN BEASES, JOHN WILLIAMS. Wit: WILLIAM WHITFIELD,
CHARLES CAVENAH. Nov. Court 1724.

A 323   JOHN JOHNSON TO JAMES WILLIAMSON, "DOCTER"
        March 27, 1723. 20 pds. for 150 A. on Roquies Swamp. Wit: SARAH
HERRICK, MARY JOHNSON. Nov. Court 1724. HENRY SPELLER by virtue of power
of atty. with WILLIAM LATTIMORE ack. sale in open court.

A 325   BENJAMIN FOREMAN TO JOHN HALL
        Nov. 9, 1724. *. for 150 A. on SS Morattucky River on a Meadow.
(witnesses omitted). November Court 1724.

A 326   WILLIAM RICKS & WIFE ESTHER TO ISAAC RICKS
        Nov. 10, 1724. 30 pds. for 240 A. on SS Kirby's Creek and Reedy
Branch. Patent date April 6, 1722. Wit: JAMES BRYANT, WILLIAM WILSON,
MATHEW SELLERS. Nov. Court 1724.

A 328   ARTHUR DAVIS & WIFE ELIZABETH TO WILLIAM KILLINGSWORTH
        Aug. 4, 1724. 7 pds. for 150 A. on SS Morrattuck River adj. RICHARD
KILLINGSWORTH. Wit: JOHN BRYAN, RICHARD KILLINGSWORTH, WILLIAM BINUM.
Nov. Court 1724.

A 330   CHARLES JONES TO STEPHEN WILLIAMS
        Nov. 9, 1724. 30 pds. for 550 A. adj. GEORGE SMITH, JOHN WILLIAMS.
Wit: WILLIAM CRANFORD, SAMUEL (?) WILLIAMS. Nov. Court 1724.

A 332   BENJAMIN FOREMAN TO CORNELIUS PIERCE
        Nov. 10, 1724. 5 pds. for 540 A. "CORNELIUS PIERCE son in law to ye
said BENJAMIN". Patent dated March 1, 1719 excepting 100 A. on Indian Swamp.
*. Nov. Court 1724.

A 333   JAMES WILLIAMS TO JOSEPH MOORE
        May 11, 1724. 20 sh. for 35 A. on Little Roquess Swamp adj. SAMUEL
HERRING. Wit: JOHN HART, NEEDHAM BRYAN. Nov. Court 1724.

A 334   JAMES BLOUNT TO JOHN YELVERTON
        Nov. 7, 1724. 20 sh. for 211 A. "Deed of gift...to my brother-in-
law" on Marrattuck River, adj. THOMAS BEESLEY. Wit: FRANCIS PARKER,
BENJAMIN FOREMAN. Nov. Court 1724.

A 336   JAMES BLOUNT TO WILLIAM MELTON
        Nov. 7, 1724. 20 sh. for 213 A. adj. JOHN YELVERTON on Morrattuck
River. Wit: FRANCIS PARKER, BENJAMIN FOREMAN. Nov. Court 1724.

A 337   WILLIAM BENNETT & WIFE GRACE TO THOMAS THORNTON
        2000 lbs. pork for 230 A. Patent dated March 1, 1719 on NS Meherrin
River. Wit: THOMAS THORNTON(?), WILLIAM ELDRIGE(?), THOMAS BOON. Nov. Court
1724. * .

A 339   WILLIAM BENNETT & WIFE GRACE TO THOMAS BOON

Nov. 9, 1724. 20 pds. for 300 A. Part of 600 A. patent dated April 1, 1723. On SS Meherrin River adj. WILLIAM BOON. Wit: WILLIAM ELDRIGE, THOMAS THORNTON. Nov. Court 1724.

A 341 WILLIAM BENNETT & WIFE GRACE TO WILLIAM ELDRIGE
Nov. 10, 1724. 10 pds. for 300 A. Part of 600 A. patent dated April 1, 1723 on SS Meherrin River. Now in possession of ELDRIGE on Meadow Branch. Wit: THOMAS BOON, ROBERT SCOTT, FRANCIS PARKER. Nov. Court 1724.

A 342 TAYLOR O'QUIN TO WILLIAM EASON
August 6, 1724. 12 pds. for 150 A. adj. WILLIAM MAUL. Part of two patents: (1) dated March 1, 1721; (2) part of 300 A. patent dated August 4, 1723. Wit: NEEDHAM BRYAN, THOMAS BUNTON, JAMES SMITH. Nov. Court 1724.

A 345 THOMAS WILLIAMSON TO JONATHAN RIDINGS
Nov. 6, 1724. 10 pds. for 100 A. on Sims Branch adj. ARTHUR DUGALL. (see note below) Wit: PETER STANCELL, EDWARD MOORE. Nov. Court 1724.
Note: In one place in the above deed it read "...that JAMES CASTELLOW shall peacefully occupy..." A margin note in the 1796 copy said: "Same as in ye old book."

A 346 JAMES CASTELLOW (CASTELLAW) & WIFE SARAH TO THOMAS WILLIAMSON
Feb. 21, 1723. *. 550 A. on Kesiah River adj. ARTHUR DUGALL, TERENCE BOURN, JOHN SMITHWICK. Wit: JONATHAN RIDINGS, PETER STANCELL. EDWARD MOOR by virtue of power of atty. from "ye above SARAH, wife of JAMES.." ack. in open court the sale.

A 340 SARAH CASTELLAW TO EDWARD MOORE
Nov. 8, 1724. Ordains EDWARD MOORE lawful atty. to ack. sale of land on Kesiah Neck. Wit: PETER STANCELL, JURAT. No court date.

A 341 WILLIAM WILSON & WIFE REBECCA TO THOMAS CLERK
Nov. 10, 1724. 7 pds. for 265 A. on SS Meherrin River. Land formerly granted to REBECCA BRASSWELL for 530 A. March 1, 1719. REBECCA "now ye wife of WILLIAM WILSON". Wit: SAMUEL WILLIAMS, JOHN HART. Nov. Court 1724.

A 350 RICHARD ABBE & WIFE ANN TO EDWARD MOORE (MOOR)
Sept. 12, 1724. 20 pds. for 320 A. "whereon he now does live" on SS Roquis Swamp. Wit: JOHN BRYAN, ALICE BRYAN, MARTIN GARDNER. Nov. Court 1724. By virtue of power of atty. RICHARD ABBE & ANN RICHARD ROBERTS proved above deed in open court.

NOTE HERE SAYS: "N.B. SO FAR DONE BEFORE AUGUST COURT 1796".

A 352 RICHARD ABBE & WIFE ANN TO JAMES ROBERTS
*. JAMES ROBERTS appt. true and lawful atty. to ack. sale of 320 A. between lines of FRANCIS HOBSON, GEORGE COCKBOURN, WILLIAM SMITH on Roquis Swamp to EDWARD MOORE. Sale bearing date Sept. 12, 1724. Wit: JAMES CASTELLAW.

A 352 RICHARD HORN & WIFE SARAH TO ARTHUR WILLIAMS
Nov. 9, 1724. 10 pds. for 120 A. Same purcharsed of THOMAS KIRBY May 14, 1716. Part of tract granted said KIRBY of 1200 A. dated Jan. 9, 1712 on SS Meherrin River and Turkey Creek. Adj. HENRY WHEELER, and Mill Path. Wit: FRANCIS MORECOCK, WILLIAM ARING. Nov. Court 1724.

NOTE HERE: (354): "N.B. The last sheet or two of the old book badly...defaced...which was cause of blanks."

A 354 ARTHUR DAVIS & WIFE ELIZABETH (ELIZA) TO WILLIAM BYNUM
Aug. 4, 1724. 10 pds. for 200 A. on Morrattack River. Wit: JOHN B____, _____LLINGSWORTH, WILLIAM KILLINGSWORTH. ____Court 1724. No clerk signing. PLEASE SEE ABOVE NOTE.

A 356 JOHN EDWARDS & WIFE ELIZABETH TO PETER STANCELL
Aug. 10, 1724. Power of atty. to sell land to OWEN O'DANIEL. Wit: PHILLIP WALSTON. Court date omitted.

A 356 LAWRANCE HOBBY & WIFE SARAH TO AARON DRAKE
May 14, 1723. 12 pds. for 100 A. Part of parcel purchased from

JOHN (BAYLEY) on SS Meherrin River adj. "place called Crag's", ARTHUR WILLIAMS. Wit: JOHN PROCTOR, J. RICKS, JOHN BAYLY. Feb. Court 1724.

A 350 THOMAS AVENT of Surry Co., Va. TO JOHN JONES of Surry Co, Va.
        Feb. 5, 1724/25. 10 pds. for 640 A. at Mount Ryall(?) on River low ground. Surveyed and patented for THOMAS AVENT by JOHN GRAY on March 30, 1721. Adj. JACOB COLSON. Wit: JOHN GRAY, jurat, RALPH MASON. Feb. Ct. 1724.

A 359 FRANCIS McKLENDON & WIFE ELINOR TO RICHARD WILLYFORD
        May 10, 1723. 20 pds. for 200 A. on Quakeson Swamp. Wit: SARAH SCOTT, FRANCIS McKLENDON. May Court 1723.

A 360 RICHARD WILLYFORD TO ALEXANDER KENNEDY
        Feb. 9, 1724. 12 pds. for "all land I do hold by virtue of within deed.." Wit: WILLIAM GRAY, THOMAS KEARNY. Feb. Court 1724.

A 361 JOHN BARNS & WIFE CATHERINE TO EDWARD WOOD, JUN.
        Feb. 4, 1724. 10 pds. for 200 A. by patent dated August 4, 1723. Wit: NATHANIEL WILLIAMS, EDWARD MARK. Feb. Court 1724.

A 363 RICHARD BRASSWELL & WIFE ELINOR TO WILLIAM WILLSON
        Feb. 8, 1724/25. 10 pds. for 180 A. in Urah Meadow and Fish Meadow. Adj. ARTHUR WHITEHEAD, RICHARD BRASSWELL, JOHN COTTON. Part of 365 A. patent. Wit: JOHN DUFFIELD, HENRY WHEELER, JOHN PAGE. Feb. Court 1724.

A 364 JOSEPH CALVERT TO JOHN GRAY
        June 24, 1724. 12 pds. for 250 A. on NS Morattuck River and Plum-tree Island adj. WILLIAM GREEN. "Near Foltera Fort". Wit: WILLIAM GRAY, THOMAS WHITMELL. Feb. Court 1724.

A 365 THOMAS HOWELL, JUN. & WIFE ELIZABETH TO GEORGE WILLIAMS
        Nov. 9, 1724. *. 225 A. Part of patent for 450 A. dated Aug. 4, 1723. Granted to THOMAS HOWELL by WILLIAM REED, Esq. President and Commander-in-chief of Province. Adj. Beaverdam Branch & GREAL (?) JOYNER. Wit: JAMES TURNER, JOSEPH WALL, JUN. Feb. Court 1724.

A 367 RICHARD FLEWALLEN of Surrey in Virginia TO RICHARD BUTLER
        Oct. 28, 1724. 12 pds. for 250 A. Land granted PHILLIP JONES by patent dated Feb. 20, 1721/22, and transferred to RICHARD FLEWELLEN. On NS Morttuck adj. _____JONES. Wit: JOHN GRAY, JOHN LEONARD. Feb. Court 1724.

A 368 JAMES RUTLAND & WIFE ELIZABETH TO WILLIAM DANIEL
        Feb. 9, 1724. 50 pds. for 100 A. at Deep Creek Bridge. Adj. "FIERY-BENT's former line". Wit: JOHN SUTTON, JOHNSON NAIRNE, THOMAS WHIPPLE. Feb. Court 1724.

A 369 BARNABE MACKINNE & WIFE MARY TO HENRY WHEELER
        Feb. 9, 1724/25. 40 pds. for 90 A. patent date August 20, 1720. On NS Morattack River and Mill Swamp. Wit: ANDREW GRIFFES, THOMAS JENKINS. Feb. Court 1724.

A 371 WILLIAM JONES & WIFE ELIZABETH TO JOSEPH LANE, JUN.
        May 14, 1723. 20 pds. for 640 A. on NS Morattack River at Spring Branch. Wit: ROBERT JONES, JUN., MATTHEW JONES. Feb. Court 1724. JOSEPH SIMMS by virtue of power of atty. from WILLIAM JONES ack. sale in open court.

A 372 WILLIAM JONES of Surry Co., Va. to JOSEPH SIMMS
        Oct. 12, 1720. Power of atty. to ack. sale of 640 A. on Morrttack River by patent dated Feb. 26, 1711/12 to JOSEPH LANE, JUN. Wit: BAR. MAKINNE, WILLIAM WHITEHEAD. Feb. Court 1724. *.

A 373 CHARLES KIMBLE of Surry Co., Va. to THOMAS EVANT
        Feb. 5, 1724/25. 20 pds. for 330 A. on NS Morattuck River adj. EVANT, JONATHAN CAVES. Wit: JOHN GRAY, RALPH MASON. Feb. Court 1724.

A 374 DANIEL O'QUIN TO JAMES CASTEN of Nansimond, Va.
        Feb. 9, 1724. 9 pds. for 150 A. on Catawhistskey Road. Wit: JOHN SUTTON, JACOB LEWIS. Feb. Court 1724.

A 375 PROPRIETORS TO JOSEPH HOWARD

August 4, 1723. His Excel. JOHN LORD CARTERET, PALATINE and other Lords by virtue of "our great deed of grant" dated May 1, 1668 do grant to JOS. HOWARD 310 A. to be seated and planted within three years. This patent to be dated August 4, 1723. Signed WILLIAM REED, Esq. Wit: THOMAS POLLOCK, LOVICK RICHSANDSON. * .

A 376   JOSEPH HOWARD TO JOHN BARNES
     Feb. 9, 1724. I assign my right and title to above patent to JOHN BARNES. Ack. by JOSEPH HOWARD & JOHN BARNES. *.*.

A 376   ANTHONY LEWIS & WIFE ELIZABETH TO LAZARUS THOMAS
     Feb. 9, 1724. 40 pds. for 300 A. on Deep Creek. Adj. FIERYBENT.
Wit: WILLIAM LITTLE, JOHN SUTTON. Feb. Court 1724.

A 378   DANIEL MACKGEE & WIFE MARY TO CHARLES SOWELL
     Feb. 8, 1724. 50 pds. for 100 A. on WS Chowan on Horse Swamp adj. RICHARD MALPASS, CHARLES GAVIN. Wit: BARNABE MACKINNE. Feb. Court 1724.

A 379   DANIEL MACKDANIEL & WIFE SARAH TO LAWRANCE HOBBY
     Nov. 10, 1724. 14 pds. for 600 A. adj. WILLIAM BRASSWELL on Yorworhah Swamp. Patent date March 9,1717. Wit: JAMES BRYANT, THOMAS WILSON, W. MAUL. Feb. Court 1724.

A 381   ROBERT RADFORD & WIFE SUSANNA TO JAMES RUTLAND
     Jan. 11, 1724. 5 pds. for 200 A. adj. JAMES RUTLAND, ROBERT SHERRWOOD. Wit: ANN FURGARRELL, THOMAS WATSON. Feb. Court 1724.

A 382   JOHN MITCHEL(MITCHELL) & WIFE HANNAH TO DENIS(DENNIS) McLENDON
     Sept. 7, 1724. 5 pds. for 600 A. adj. "former corner tree of GEORGE WINN". Wit: WILLIAM CRANFORD, JOHN WILLIAMS. Feb. Court 1724.

A 384   CHARLES KIMBLE of Surry Co., Va. to JOHN DAVIS
     Feb. 5, 1724. 20 pds. for 200 A. on NS Morattack River. Wit: JOHN GRAY, jurat, RALPH MASON, THOMAS AVENT. Feb. Court 1724.

A 385   CHARLES MERRITT & WIFE ELEANOR & PETER EVANS TO RICHARD BARFIELD of Va. April 16, 1715. 30 pds. for 280 A. on SS Chowan on Deep Creek. By patent of PETER EVANS. Adj. JAMES PEEK, JOHN FIERYBENT. Wit: WILLIAM WILSON, PETER EVANS.

A 386   ELINOR MERRITT TO WILLIAM MIXON
     April 16, 1715. Power of atty. to WILLIAM MIXON to ack. sale of 280 A. to RICHARD BARFIELD (BAREFIELD). Wit: PETER EVANS, RICHARD BARFIELD. April Court 1715. ROBERT HICKS C/C. Registered June 19, 1715 in Chowan.

A 387   RICHARD BARFIELD TO WILLIAM REED of Papstank Precinct
     Jan. 1, 1724. 80 pds. for "aforementioned deed"..."unto Collonell WILLIAM REED, Esq. Wit: JOHN POWER, WILLIAM MOORE, DAVID LINSEY. Feb. Court 1724.

A 387   JACOB LEWIS TO JEREMIAH BARNES
     Feb. 10, 1724. 6 pds. for 260 A. at EDWARD HOWARD's corner tree on NW side Horse Swamp. Wit: JOHN SUTTON, WILLIAM WILLIFORD. Feb. Court 1724.

A 389   HENRY BAKER TO RICHARD BARFIELD
     Feb. 9, 1724. 10 pds. for 200 A. on WS Ahoskey Marsh. Part of patent granted BAKER for 840 A. dated April 1, 1723. Wit: JOHN MOLTON, JOHN HENARD(?). Feb. Court 1724.

A 390   JOHN BEVERLY & WIFE MARGRETT of Ahorsky to ELIZABETH LOKER of Nansimond. Dec. 4, 1724. Two negro women, Betty and Nann, for 500 A. on Horsky Swamp as defined by patent. Wit: JAMES PEEKE, THOMAS JONES. Feb. Court 1724.

A 391   JOSEPH SIMMS & WIFE SARAH TO JOSEPH LANE, JUN.
     Feb. 6, 1724/25. 50 pds. for 330 A. on SS Morrattack adj. GEORGE GOODWIN on String Meadow. Wit: ROBERT WARREN, PETER JONES. Feb. Court 1724. ROBERT JONES by virtue of Power of atty. from SARAH SIMMS ack. sale in open court. Proved by oath of BARNABE MACKINNE.

A 393   SARAH SIMMS TO ROBERT JONES

Feb. 6, 1724 SARAH SIMMS, wife of JOSEPH SIMMS, appts. ROBERT JONES power of atty. to ack. sale to JOSEPH LANE, JUN. Wit: BARNABE MACKINNE, ROBERT WARREN. Feb. Court 1724.

A 393 WILLIAM HOWETT TO SAMUEL ELSON
Feb. 9, 1724. 18 pds. for 230 A. on Meherin River adj. THOMAS KIRBY, JOHN BAYLY, ARTHUR WILLIAMS. On Spring Branch. Wit: JOHN SUTTON, JOHN HART. Feb. Court 1724.

A 394 LAZARUS THOMAS TO THOMAS SNOWDEN of Perquimmons Precinct
Feb. 9, 1724. 50 pds. for 515 A. on Flat Swamp. adj. ISAAC LEWIS. On Horse Swamp. Wit: JOHN ALSTON, JOHN SUTTON. Feb. Court 1724.

A 395 HENRY JONES of Surry Co., Va. to SIMON JEFFREYS
Feb. 8, 1724. 25 pds. for 140 A. "where JEFFREYS now lives" Patent date July 8, 1713. On Morrattuck River. *. Feb. Court 1724. Ack. in open court by HENRY JONES.

A 397 JACOB COLSON & WIFE MARY of Isle of Wight, Va. to JOHN SPANN
May 12, 1724. 30 pds. for 270 A. on NS Morrattuck River. Called Mount Royall. Wit: JOHN GRAY, JOHN THACKER, WILLIAM LIONS. Feb. Court 1724.

A 398 JOHN HICKS, executor of JOHN HAWTHORN, TO ROBERT JONES
Dec. 7, 1724. JOHN HICKS of Surry County, Va. "JOHN HAWTHORN by last will and testament did...give me full power to make sale of tract... granted him Feb. 26, 1711/12 for 470 A." On NS Morattuck River at Cypress Swamp. Sold for 20 pds. (Signed JOHN HICKS) Wit: ROBERT JONES, JUN., MATHEW JONES, WILLIAM ATKINSON. JOSEPH SIMMS by power of atty. from JOHN HICKS ack. above deed in open court.

A 399 JOHN HICKS of Surry County, Va. to JOSEPH SIMMS
Dec. 7, 1724. JOHN HICKS, executor of last will and testament of JOHN HAWTHORNE, appts. JOSEPH SIMMS power of atty. to convey 420 A. Wit: ROBERT JONES, JUN., MATHEW JONES, WILLIAM ATKINSON.

A 400 BARNABE MACKINNE TO JOHN MACKINNE
Feb. 6, 1724/25. "For love I do bare my son, JOHN MACKINNE...and the heirs of his body" 100 A. known as Walnut Fork. Part of tract granted WILLIAM BROWN "which elapsed". Also by Capt. JOHN GRAY "for want of seating elapsed". On SS Morrattack River dividing land of JOSEPH JOYNER on Walnut Fork Gutt. If JOHN MACKINNE shall die without heirs...to his next of kin. Wit: ISAAC RICH, THOMAS FOXHALL. Feb. Court 1724.

A 400 JAMES BLOUNT & WIFE CATHERINE TO GEORGE STEVENS
Feb. 3, 1724. 20 pds. for 160 A. on Sandy Run granted to OWEN MCDANIEL for 160 A. March 1, 1719. Wit: JAMES WOOD, JOHN HART. Feb.Ct.1724.

A 401 JOHN SHORT & HIS MOTHER ELIZABETH ROSE TO JONATHAN STANDLEY
Feb. 3, 1719/20. "For my suply of corn, cloathes and other diet and in consideration of 10 pds." 100 A. on Cashia River adj. where STANDLEY now lives. Wit: B. STEWARD, JOHN COMES. Feb. Court 1724.

A 402 JOHN COTTON & WIFE JUDETH TO JAMES BROCKDON
May 10, 1725. 5 pds. for 50 A. on SS Morrattuck River adj. JOHN GREEN, WILLIAM GREEN. Wit: JOHN KELLY. May Court 1725.

A 404 JOHN KELLEY TO JOHN COTTON
May 10, 1725 6 pds. for 50 A. on NS Morrattuck River adj. HENRY JONES. Wit: JAMES BROCKDON, (*omitted). May Court 1725.

A 405 THOMAS ROADS & WIFE MARY TO JAMES MARROW(MURROW) of Nansimond Co.Va.
May 10, 1725. 10 pds. for 250 A. at fork of Casiah Swamp on Bever Dam adj. Major WEST. Wit: PHILLIP EDENS, EDWARD POWERS. May Court 1725

A 406 JOSEPH LANE, SEN. & WIFE JELIAN (JUELIAN) TO ROBERT HOUSE
*. for *. Part of patent granted for 640 A. on March 1, 1719. On ES Hunting Quarter Swamp in actual possession of ROBERT HOUSE between ROBERT NEWSOME, JOSEPH LANE, JUN. Wit: THOMAS BRYANT, HEN. BAKER, THOMAS JONES. Feb. Court 1725.

A 408 RICHARD BARFIELD THE ELDER TO THOMAS BARFIELD

Feb. 13, 1724/25. 10 pds. for 100 A. on SS Ahotskey Marsh "out of FIREBENT's patent". Part of 470 A. Wit: RICHARD BARFIELD, SEN., RICHARD BARFIELD, JUN, HENRY BAKER. May Court 1725.

A 409 JAMES WOOD & WIFE SARAH TO RICHARD SUMNER
     May 10, 1725. 25 pds. for 600 A. on NS Catawhitskey Meadow adj. JAMES BRYANT. Patent dated Nov. 11, 1719 to ROBERT HICKS lapsed "for want of seating and planting". Land came to JAMES WOOD by order of Councill April 1, 1723. Wit: THOMAS JENKINS, DANIEL O'QUIN. May Court 1725.

A 411 BENJAMIN WOOD TO JAMES WOOD
     May 11, 1725. 12 pds. for 100 A. adj. JAMES WOOD, PATRICK O'QUIN. Wit: _____CLAYTON, JOHN PARK, JOHN SUTTON. May Court 1725.

A 412 JOHN NAIRNE TO OWEN McDANIELL
     April 20, 1725. 8 pds. for 300 A. on NS Morrattack River adj. JOHN WILLIAMS on Flaggy Run. Wit: JOHN BUTLAR, JAMES CANNADAY. May Court 1725.

A 413 JOHN BRYAN TO WILLIAM CURLEE
     May 12, 1725. "JOHN BRYAN, son of EDWARD BRYAN". 35 pds. for 634 A. on ES Canaan Swamp. Wit: JOHN SMITH, LEWIS BRYAN. May Court 1725.+

A 414 THOMAS BANKS TO WIFE JENNETT(JENNET) BANKS of Edenton
     Nov. 17, 1725. JENNET BANKS formerly JENNET BLEWLET. "I constitute my wife to be my absolute attorney.." To have "to her own use...all lands (etc.)..that were hers at the time of our intermarriage..." To recover all debts belonging to the estate of BLEWLETT. Wit: ROBERT FORSTER, WILLIAM LITTLE. Nov. 17, 1725. Registered by C. GALE, C/C.

A 415 WILLIAM MAULE TO ARTHUR GOFF, ESQ.
     Oct. 28, 1724. 30 pds. for 130 A. adj. JOHN JONES, JUN., JOSEPH JONES, RICHARD WILLIAMS, JOHN BEAVERLY, PHILLIP CORSLEY, ABRAHAM BLEWLETT on Catawhitskey Swamp. Wit: ISAAC HILL, WILLIAM GRAY. Oct. 28, 1724. T. POLLOCK, Chief Justice.

A 416 THOMAS JOHNSTON & WIFE ANN TO THOMAS STEPHENSON
     May 10, 1725. 10 pds. for 300 A. on both sides of Elm Swamp. Part of patent granted THOMAS JOHNS Dec. 3, 1720. Wit: WILLIAM WHITFIELD, ELIZABETH WHITFIELD. May Court 1725. JOHN WINNS D.C/C.

A 418 JOHN HARLOE TO WILLIAM COWARD
     Dec. 4, (1725). 60 pds. for 600 A. on NS Moratork River "formerly granted to me ye said JOHN HARLOE and more lately unto EDWARD MOSELY by patent April 1, 1723." Adj. _____COGSWILL, _____DOWNING, MARTIN GRIFFIN. On Roquish Creek. Wit: THOMAS JONES, W. BADHAM (Mem d)(?) Oct. 9, 1725. C. GALE, C/C.

A 419 THOMAS HOSKINS TO ARTHUR GOFF of Edenton
     Aug. 6, 1725. 60 pds. for one half of tract of 640 A. granted THOMAS HOSKINS. Adj. COLL. EDWARD MOSELY, CAPT. NIE S(?) CRISP. 320 A. Wit: R. HICKS, CHRISTIAN HIDELLBURGH(HEDELBREY). Sept. 6, 1725. C. GALE.

A 421 HENRY SPELLER TO JOHN DUGGAN
     Aug. 9, 1725. 60 pds. for 250 A. on SMITHWICK's Creek adj. RICHARD SWAIN, EDMOND SMITHWICK. Wit: WILLIAM CHARLTON, WILLIAM CHARLTON, JUN. Aug. 18, 1725. C. Gale ch.J. (chief justice?)

A 422 JAMES BLOUNT & WIFE CATHERINE TO SAMUEL WOODARD
     July 30, 1716. 15 pds. for 200 A. on SS Chowan River adj. "WILLIAM MAUL's corner tree", BLUNT's Spring Branch. By patent dated JAN. 19, 1715/16. Granted by Hon. CHARLES EDEN, ESQ. Wit: JA. THRNER, DAVID ATKINS, JOHN ROBERSON, JOHN THACKRARY. Registered in Chowan Precinct Aug. 1716. C. GALE, R. HICKS, Clk.

A 424 SAMUEL WOODARD TO THOMAS BRAY
     Jan. 3, 1718. "I do make over to THOMAS BRAY the lands mentioned in within deed." Wit: WM. SHORPE, THOS. CRANK. Chowan July Court 1719. R. HICKS C/C. Registered in Chowan Precinct August 24, 1719.

+This is the last deed in Book A that JOHN SUTTON signs as Deputy C/C.

NOTE HERE: "N.B. so far new registered before November Court 1796."

A 424 THOMAS BRAY TO ROBERT FORSTER
        "N.B. This following assignment and the above assignment this same
page page 406, seems to be assignments of the Deed of Sale & conveyance No.
56, page 404."

A 424 THOMAS BRAY of Virginia TO ROBERT FORSTER
        Apr. 1, 1725. 20 pds. for "all my right title...to within mentioned
tract unto ROBERT FORSTER..." Wit: J. CLAYTON, THOMAS PARVIS. April 1, 1725.
THOMAS POLLOCK, JOHN WINNS D.C/C.

A 425 SARAH SMITH, WIDOW, TO THOMAS BRAY
        July 15, 1719. 50 pds. for 150 A. "now occupied by me & whereon
TREDDLE KEEFE lately dwelt" on Wicacon Creek adj. THOMAS MAN, JAMES BOON.
Wit: ABRAHAM BLEWLETT, JOHN RAMSEY (?), JOHN SAWYER. N.C. General Court
July 20, 1719. ROBERT HICKS by virtue of power of atty. to him directed by
SARAH SMITH, ack. within deed. ROBERT HICKS Cl. General Court. Registered
in Chowan Precinct. Oct. 3, 1719. ROBERT HICKS, C/C.

A 427 THOMAS BRAY of Virginia to ROBERT FORSTER
        April 1, 1725. 50 pds. for 150 A. Wit: J. CLAYTON, THOMAS PAIRIS.
April 1, 1725. THOMAS POLLOCK C.J.(Chief Justice) JOHN WINNS D.C/C.

A 428 SARAH SMITH TO HENRY BARFIELD
        Nov. 10, 1723. 20 pds. for 640 A. granted to SARAH SMITH by patent
dated March 1, 1712. On "head of Ahotskey". Wit: THOMAS POLLOCK, JOHN
RASBURY. May 2, 1725. THOMAS POLLOCK Chief Justice.

A 430 CHARLES JONES & WIFE SARAH TO JOHN RASBERY
        April 25, 1725. 70 pds. for 610 A. adj. LANSLET JONES, WILLIAM BUSH.
Wit: THOMAS BIRD, STEPHEN WILLIAMS. Ack. by CHARLES CAVENER of atty. to
CHARLES & SARAH JONES. May 2, 1725. THOMAS POLLOCK, Chief Justice.

A 431 CHARLES JONES & WIFE SARAH TO THOMAS BIRD
        April 23, 1725. 20 pds. for "extent of patent" on SS Ahotskey Swamp
at BIRD's corner tree to Loosing Swamp. Wit: STEPHEN WILLIAMS, JOHN RAS-
BEARY. Ack. by CHARLES CAVENER as atty. to CHARLES & SARAH JONES. May 2,
1725. THOMAS POLLOCK, Chief Justice.

A 432 NOTE HERE "N.B. The following No.8 (CHAS. JONES to BRIGET RASBEARY)
was in order before this last No.7 (CHAS. JONES to THOS. BIRD) in the old
book, but by mistake, was tooked over and ought to have bin No.7 & No.7
here ought to have bin No.8, It makes no other difference."

A 433 CHARLES JONES TO BRIGET RASBEARY
        April 23, 1725. For "love I do bare BRIGET RASBEARY the daughter of
JOHN RASBEARY and BRIGET his wife..."100 A. at Hors(Horse) Swamp adj. JAMES
HOWARD, PETER WEST to Cow Hall (Haule). Wit: THOMAS BIRD, STEPHEN WILLIAMS.
May 1725. THOMAS POLLOCK, C. Justice.

A 433 CHARLES JONES & WIFE SARAH TO STEPHEN WILLIAMS
        April 23, 1725. 20 pds. for 640 A. on NS Wicacon Swamp at CHARLES
JONES, AARON OLIVER, JACOB LEWIS. Wit: THOMAS BIRD, JOHN RASBEARY. Ack. in
open court by CHARLES CAVENER as atty. to CHARLES & SARAH JONES. May 2,1725.
THOMAS POLLOCK, C. Justice

A 434 CHARLES JONES & WIFE SARAH TO CHARLES CAVEANER
        April 22, 1725. Power of atty. to CHARLES CAVEANER to ack. to JOHN
RASBEARY one tract of land unto STEPHEN WILLIAMS and one tract unto THOMAS
BIRD. Wit: JOHN RASBAY (RASBURY), STEPHEN WILLIAMS. May 2, 1725. THOMAS
POLLOCK, C.Justice.

A 435 SARAH WILKINSON TO ROBERT HICKS
        May 10, 1724 April 6, 1725 (both given). For 55 pds. "plantation
whereon I now dwell and all stocks of of Cattle Hoggs..". SARAH WILKINSON
"wife and (atty.) of JAMES WILKINSON...by instruement by date May 12,1724..
doth empower SARAH to sell or dispose of lands..." Wit: JOHN RASBERRY,
CHRISTIAN LANE.*. THOMAS POLLOCK C. Justice.

A 436 GEORGE POLLOCK TO HENRY KING

March 25, 1725. 130 pds. for * A. on NES Mouth of Caseay River belonging to Coll. THOMAS POLLOCK, ESQ. Wit: CATHERINE LINCH, ROBERT FORSTER.
March 25, 1724/25. THOMAS POLLOCK, C. Justice.

A 437 JOHN JOHNSON & WIFE MARY of PERQUECEMONS (?) PRECINCT to MARTIN
       CROMAN. Oct. 8, 1724. 15 pds. for 100 A. adj. JAMES FROST. Former
dwelling of WILLIAM FROST. MARY JOHNSON, daughter of WILLIAM FROST "formerly of Casia but now deceased...before his death (willed) to MARY JOHNSON
..." within named land. Land also adj. AFFRICA SMITH. Wit: ARTHUR DUGLASS,
THOMAS (THOMS) COPLIN, JONATHAN RIDINGS. Ack. in court by JAMES SANDERLIN
by power of atty. March 10, 1724/25. THOMAS POLLOCK, C. Justice. (Note:
MARTIN CROMEN also spelled CORMEN, CROMAN.)

A 439 JOHN JOHNSON & WIFE MARY (MARRY) TO JAMES SANDERLY
       *. Appt. JAMES SANDERLY lawful atty. to ack. sale to MARTIN CROMEN.
Wit: JONATHAN RIDINGS, ARTHUR DUGALL, THOMAS COOLEN (COPLIN). March 10,
1724/25. THOMAS POLLOCK, C Justice.

A 440 RICHARD BARFIELD & WIFE MARY TO WILLIAM MOORE (MOOR)
       May 11, 1725. for love to our son-in-law WILLIAM MOORE 150 A. on ES
Blew Water. Wit: WILLIAM HOWETT, JOHN SUTTON. Mary Court 1725. JOHN WINNS
D.C/C.

A 440 RICHARD BARFIELD & WIFE MARY TO JOHN GRADY
       May 11, 1725. "for love unto our loveing Grandson, JOHN GRADY..."
150 A. adj. WILLIAM MOOR (MOORE), PETER WEST. Wit: WILLIAM HOWETT, JOHN
SUTTON. May Court 1725. JOHN WINNS D.C/C.

A 441 MARTIN GARDNER (GARDNIER) & WIFE ANNA TO THOMAS WHITMELL
       Jan. 13, 1724/25. 27 pds. for 310 A. on WS Casia River adj. EDWARD
MORE's plantation. Wit: GEORGE EUBANCK (ENBANCK), JA. CASTELLAW. May
Court 1725. Ack. in open court by virtue of power of atty.

A 443 MARTIN GARDNER TO THOMAS WHITMELL
       Feb. 8, 1724/25. 27 pds. for 50 A. "along old dividing line". Wit:
JAMES CASTELLAW, GARRET KELLY. May Court 1725. The within deed of sale
ack. by JAMES CASTELLAW by power of atty. from MARTIN GARDNER & ANNA his
wife. * . JOHN WINNS D.C/C.

A 444 MARTIN GARDNER & WIFE TO JAMES CASTELLAW
       May 10, 1725. Appt. JAMES CASTELLAW lawful atty. to ack. in open
court two parcels of land lying on Kesia River. 310 A. by our deed Jan. 13
last and 50 A. a deed of sale given bearing date Feb. 8 last. Wit: JONATHAN
STANDLEY, jurat, JOHN EDWARDS. May Court 1725. JOHN WINNS D.C/C.

A 445 JAMES HOWARD & WIFE SARAH TO JAMES SANDERS
       May 11, 1725. 12 pds. for 300 A. on Horse Swamp at _____ LEWIS's
corner, adj. EDWARD HOWARD, ROBERT LANIER. Wit: RICHARD OLDNER(?), THOMAS
BETTERLY. May Court 1725. JOHN WINNS D.C/C.

A 447 HENRY SIMS & WIFE GRACE TO HENRY IRBY
       May 10, 1725. 30 pds. for 200 A. Part of 600 A. patent to WILLIAM
BOON dated Nov. 11, 1711/12 on NS Moratock River on Beaverdam at WILLIAM
POWELL's corner tree. Adj. WILLIAM BRASSWELL, JOHN PACE. Wit: ROGER CASSE,
HUBORD GIBSON, ANN EVENS. May Court 1725. JOHN WINNS D.C/C.

A 449 WILLIAM EASON TO JAMES SMITH
       August 6, 1724. 18 pds. for 150 A. on NS Moratock River. Part of
328 A. granted WILLIAM EASON by patent August 4, 1723. Adj. JAMES PARKER,
OEN (OWEN) DANIEL. Wit: NEEDHAM BRYAN, THOMAS BUNTON, TARLON OGWIN. May
Court 1725. JOHN WINNS D.C/C.

A 451 JAMES TURNER & WIFE ANN of Isle of White, Va. to THOMAS HOWELL, SEN.
       Nov. 7, 1724. 4 pds. 10 sh. for 100 A. Part of 640 A. granted
JAMES TURNER March 1, 1719 on SS Meherrin River at mouth of Branch adj.
JOSEPH WALL, THOMAS HOWELL. Wit: THOMAS HOWELL, JUN., GEORGE WILLIAMS.
May Court 1725. JOHN WINNS D.C/C.

A 452 THOMAS TURNER TO RICHARD WALL
       Feb. 13, 1724/25. 20 pds. for 290 A. on SS Maherrin River. Land
being granted THOMAS TURNER Dec. 3, 1720 on Cypress Swamp. Wit: JAMES

TURNER, JOSEPH WALL, SEN.   May Court 1725.   JOHN WINNS D. C/C.

A 452   ROBERT HAMILTON TO JOHN GRAY (SE)
        "Mr. JOHN GRAY SE...If you deale so by others as you have done by me
you will get but few commissions from London.   I am sure you have not acted
the fair part by me Neither was it ever my (wishing) that you should hade
ye disposel of my 1/4 of Lueas Cargo the trifeling (excuses) you have mead
about delaying to Sending Effects because of a deference betwixt McCOCKBURN
& me is as (inexcusable) as your declining to (warn) me about my affaires &
nott to tel me my Effects is turned to pitch & you have (Skyred) ye Pitch
this 6 or 7 years in ye possession, hade you assigned my advantage your
hade sent me returns 5 years agoe I expect you will (alone) me interest for
the time you heave kepd me out of my effects & if McSTENTON hes not gote
them alredey I disayer you may give Mr. JOHN MAUL ye rest deer skins or
money yt.   All may be sent me per first opertunity & send me some snake
(_____?) for the books I give you, I am Sr. your humble sert.   R. HAMILTON
Lond. ye 23 (dim) 1723. (Endorsed)."
To JOHN GRAY I JOHN MAUL grant 89 barrels pitch on acct. of ROBERT HAMILTON,
MERCHANT IN Capt. WALL Court London...in full account between ROBERT HAMIL-
TON & JOHN GRAY...all debts prodeeding date of within letter.   February 9,
1724/25.   JO. MAULE.

A 455   EDWARD OUTLAW TO THOMAS JONES
        Dec. 9, 1724.   5 sh. for 100 A. on SES of tract of EDWARD HOWARD.
Adj. _____BARNELL. Wit: WIL DANIEL, jurat, WILLIAM MEARS. August Court
1725. JOHN WINNS D.C/C.

A 456   JOHN CHESHERE & WIFE ELIZABETH TO JAMES SANDER(S)
        Aug. 10, 1725. 43 pds. 15 sh. for 300 A. on Ahotskey Swamp. Wit:
JOHN SUTTON, WILLIAM MARSHILL. *. JOHN WINNS D.C/C.

A 457   ROBERT SHERWOOD (SHEROD) TO JAMES RUTLAND
        May 12, 1725. 15 pds. for 540 A. bounded by Patent granted me April
5, 1720 "100 A. out of patent to ROBERT McCREARY only excepted where he now
dwells..." Wit: WILLIAM WHITEHEAD, THOMAS BOON. August Court 1725.   JOHN
WINNS D.C/C.

A 458   JAMES PEEKE (PEAKE) & WIFE MARGARET (MARGRETT) TO JOHN EARLY, SEN.
        Aug. 10, 1725. 4 pds. for 500 A. adj. FRANCIS MACKLENDON on Myrey
Branch. Adj. JOHN BUSH at Head of Holly Swamp. Wit: JOHN ROBERTS, JOHN
EARLY, JUN. August Court 1725.   JOHN WINNS D.C/C.

A 460   JAMES SUMNER TO JAMES HOWARD
        August 11, 1725. 20 pds for 400 A. on Ahotskey Swamp at JAMES
HOWARD's corner. Adj. CHARLES JONES, ROBERT LENIER. Wit: WILLIAM CRANFORD,
JOHN HOWARD. August Court 1725.   JOHN WINNS, D. C/C.

                         End of Deed Book A

DEED BOOK B
1725 - 1727

B 1   RICHARD BARNES & WIFE MARY of Nansemond Co., Va. to JENNET VINCINT
      1725. 30 barrells Tar for 100 A. On Meherrin Creek near a "small
Savannah". Wit: JNO. SUTTON, JOHN ROGERS. August Court 1725. JOHN WINNS
D. C/C.

B 2   WILLIAM BENNET (BENNETT) & WIFE GRACE TO NICHOLAS BOON
      Aug. 10, 1725. 8 pds. for 100 A. "which I purchased of RICHARD
BRASSWELL, dec'd. on May 14, 1723. On SS Meherrin River. Adj. WILLIAM
KINCHIN on Middle Branch. Wit: THOS. JENKINS, (FR.?) PARKER, JOSEPH COL-
PEPER. Aug. Court 1725. Capt. JOHN WINNS D. C/C.

B 3   THOMAS WHITMEL (WHITMELL) TO EDWARD YOUNG
      * 1725 40 pds. for 570 A. "my plantation...on Stonehouse Creek" on
the river bank to HUBBARD's Creek. Wit: JOHN NAIRN, JOHN BROWN. August
Court 1725.

B 5   JOHN DICKINSON TO JOSEPH CARTER
      Aug. 11, 1725. 9 pds. for 320 A. on Meherrin Creek. Land I pur-
chased of JAMES BRYANT, JUN. Wit: JNO. SUTTON, MATHEW MARSHBURN. August
Court 1725.

B 6   JOHN GRAY TO NICHOLLAS SMITH
      Aug. 11, 1725. 60 pds. for 500 A. "...on the river side..." at Reedy
Branch. Adj. ARTHUR DAVIS. Wit: ROBERT FORSTER, THOMAS BOYD. Aug. Court 1725.

B 7   WILLIAM BRIDGERS TO JOSEPH & SAMUEL(SAMUELL) BRIDGERS
      Feb. 23, 1724/25. "...for tender love and good will I bear unto my
loving sons...land that I purchased of JAMES GEE(?)..." on NS Meherrin. (1)
To Joseph : part on which he now dweleth, lowest part. 200 A. on eastimost
side of survey, by Island Side "to the headline of the government (2) Residue of above parcel to son SAMUEL...should SAMUEL die without "isher" then
his part to return to BENJAMIN. Wit: RICHARD WASHINGTON, JOHN BAYLEY,
THOMAS HORN. August Court 1725.

B 8   BARNABE MACKENNE (MACKINE) & WIFE MARY TO JOSEPH JOYNER
      Aug. 5, 1723. *. 150 A. "deed of gift made by WILLIAM BROWN late de-
ceased...by his last will did give to his daughter MARTHA...which is to say
MARTHA BROWN which land was laps before the aforesaid BROWN's death and is
now come due to me by virtue of relapsed patent bearing date Nov. 22, 1723..
and now being exchanged by WILLIAM STRICKLAND(?) the husband of said MARTHA
(MARTHAN) BROWN with JOSEPH JOYNER wee doe for this reason...bargain and
confirm to JOSEPH JOYNER..." On SS Moratuck River. Part of a survey called
"Walnutt fork Gutt". Wit: ISAAC RICKS, WILLIAM MURPHREY. Aug. Court 1725.

B 10 THOMAS BRIT (BRITT) (BRETT) TO JOHN BARDEN
      March 11, 1724. 15 pds. for 320 A. on NS Meherin River. Adj. WILLIAM
WORRILL and Mill Creek. Wit: JOHN DEW, ABRAHAM DEW. Aug. Court 1725.

B 11 THOMAS WHITMELL TO JOSEPH TURNER of Isle of Wight Co., Va.
      Aug. 10, 1725. 40 pds. for 460 A. on SS Moratok River Adj. JOHN
NAIRNE in "Cheastfield" at Cypress Swamp. Adj. DANIEL McDANIEL, JOHN
HAMILTON. Wit: JOHN NAIRNE, JOHN BROWN. Aug. Court 1725

B 13 ARTHUR WILLIAMS TO WILLIAM JONES
      Aug. 10, 1725. 10 pds. for 100 A. "...land I purchased of RICHARD
WASHINGTON by deed April 21, 1717..." On SS Moharing River on run of Cray(?)
Branch. Wit: RICHARD HORNE, NICHOLAS SIKES (LIKER?). Aug. Court 1725.

B 14 WILLIAM WHITEHEAD & WIFE RACHILL TO FRANCIS PARKER & WIFE MARY
      Aug. 10, 1725. 50 pds for 140 A. on SS Patterkersey Creek. Part of
tract granted ROBERT PATESON and elapsed...By WILLIAM WHITEHEAD patented
Aug. 10, 1720. On the "Island Side". Adj. PETER DANIELS..."Furthermore, I,
FRANCIS PARKER, do bind and oblige myself not...to sell this land...without
free consent of my wife, MARY...otherwise this deed will be null and void.."
Wit: THOS. JENKINS, JOSEPH CULPEPER, JOHN TAYLOR. Aug. Court 1725.

B 16 THOMAS WHITMELL & WIFE ELIZABETH TO THOMAS BARROT (BARRAT) of Colony
      of Va. Aug. 7, 1725. 25 pds. for 200 A. on NS Roanoke River adj.

JOHN GRAY, RICHARD CUERLEN, ISAAC PRICE. Wit: JA. CASTELLAW, EDWARD MOOR (MOORE). Aug. Court 1725. Ack. by EDWARD MOOR, lawful atty. of ELIZABETH WHITMELL.

B 18   ELIZABETH WHITMELL TO EDWARD MOORE
      Aug. 9, 1725. ELIZABETH, wife of THOS. WHITMELL, do make and ordain EDWARD MOORE my lawful atty. to ack. sale of 200 A. on NS Moratuck River to THOMAS BARRAT. Wit: GEO. EUBANCK (ENBANCK), JAS. CASTELLAW, jurat. August Court 1725.

B 18   WILLIAM GREEN TO JOHN ROTTENBERRY
      May 8, 1725. 10 pds for 100 A. on SS Moratuck River in Plumtree Island. Adj. JOHN GRAY, ROBERT LANGE. Wit: JOHN GRAY, jurat, SETH HATCHER, RICHARD CUERTON. Aug. Court 1725.

B 20   JOHN GRAY TO THOMAS ELEBY
      * 1725. 40 pds. for 640 A. on Stonehouse Creek. Adj. THOMAS WHITMELL. Wit: BENJAMIN HILL, ROBT. FORSTER. Aug. Court 1725.

B 22   JAMES TURNER & WIFE ANN of Isle of Wight TO THOMAS JARRELL (JERRELL) SEN. of Isle of Wight, Va. Dec. 11, 1722. 15 pds. for 250 A. on SS Moratock River in the Low Ground at the Great Marsh. Adj. JOHN BRYANT (BRYAN). Wit: JOHN BRYAN, JOHN BROWN, W. SIMMONS. Aug. Court 1725.

B 24   ARTHUR GOFFE of Chowan Prac't. TO HON. GEORGE BURRINGTON, ESQ.
      Aug. 12, 1725. 30 pds. for 130 A. On Catawitsky Swamp. Adj. JOHN JONES, JUN., JOSEPH JONES, RICHARD WILLIAMS, JOHN BEAVERLY, PHILLIP CORSLEY, ABRAHAM BLEWLETT. Wit: ISAAC HILL, JOHN NAIRNE. Aug. Court 1725.

B 25   WILLIAM WHITEHEAD & WIFE RACHEL TO PETER (PEATH, PEATER) DANIEL
      Oct. 10, 1725. 8 pds. for 200 A. on SS Pottycasy Creek adj. PARKER's line. Wit: JOSEPH CARTER, ROBERT SCOTT. Nov. Court 1725.

B 26   JOHN CHESHIRE TO NICHOLLAS TYNER
      Nov. 9, 1725. 48 Bar. Tar for 460 A. on SWS Little Swamp. Wit: JOHN SUTTON, JOHN SMITH. Nov. Court 1725.

B 28   OWEN O'DANIEL TO JOHN EDWARDS, JUN.
      Oct. 25, 1725. 20 pds. for 640 A. on NS Roquis, a branch of Casia. Adj. MARTAIN (MARTIN) GARDNER, JOHN EDWARDS, THEO. WILLIAMS. Wit: GEORGE SMITH, THOMAS BUSBIE. Nov. Court 1725.

B 29   WILLIAM MACKHENRY TO JOHN MITCHELL
      April 7, 1725. 100 pds. for 431 A. on Canaan Swamp. Adj. WM. BUSH, JOHN HILL. Wit: WM. CRANFORD, JOHN WILLIAMS. Nov. Court 1725.

B 31   JOHN MITCHELL & WIFE HANNAH TO WILLIAM MACKHENRY
      April 7, 1725. 50 pds. for 295 A. on Wiccacon Creek and Bear Swamp. Adj. WM. HOOKER, GEORGE WINN, THOMAS SESSOMS. Wit: WM. CRANFORD, JOHN WILLIAMS. Nov. Court 1725.

B 32   JOHN CHESHIRE (CHESHER) & WIFE ELIZABETH of Chowan to JOHN HOMES of Chowan. Oct. 14, 1721. 15 pds. for 300 A. on SS Ahotsky Swamp at upper side Cabin Branch. Adj. _____ McTHOMAS. By patent bearing date Dec. 3, 1720 for 606 A. Wit: WILLIAM MOORE, JOHN CHESHER. Edenton, N.C. 1722. C. GALE, C.J. (Note: The deeds recorded by C. GALE are stated to be North Carolina Court.)

B 34   ROBERT RADFORD & WIFE SUSANNA TO JAMES RUTLAND
      Nov. 9, 1725. 10 pds. for 450 A. adj. LAWRANCE BAKER, WILLIAM WHIT-FIELD. Wit: JOHN SUTTON JAMES DUASSLESS (DUAFLESS?). Nov. Court 1725.

B 36   HENRY ROADS & WIFE ELIZABETH TO JAMES BLUNT (BLOUNT)
      Aug. 6, 1725. 3 pds. *. NWS Casay Swamp. Adj. THOMAS BUSBY, JAMES PARKER. Wit: JOHN DUFFIELD, THOMAS BUNTIN. Nov. Court 1725.

B 37   HENRY RODES (RODS, ROODS) TO THOMAS BUSBY
      *. 10 pds. for 170 A. on ES Cashie Swamp. Wit: OWEN O'DANIEL, JAMES MURRAY. Nov. Court 1725.

B 38   THOMAS ROADS & WIFE MARY TO JAMES MURRY (MURRAY)

Nov. 9, 1725. 7 pds. for 200 A. At fork of Cashia Swamp on Beaverdam and Wattom Swamp. Adj. JOHN BARFIELD, ELIZABETH BARFIELD. Nov. Court 1725.

B 40 HENRY ROADS TO PETER PARKER
Nov. 9, 1725. 7 pds. for 150 A. on Casiah Swamp on line between HENRY ROADS & THOMAS BUSBY. Wit: JAMES MURRAY, THOMAS BUFE(?). Nov. Court 1725.

B 41 JOHN BRYAN (BRYANT) & WIFE ELIZABETH TO JOHN SPEIR
Sept. 14, 1725. 20 "barrills of Merchantable Pork". for 200 A. on SS Maratock River. Adj. JOHN NAIRN on NS meadow "where JOHN BRYAN did live.." Wit: WM. DEW, EDW. MACKGIER. Nov. Court 1725.

B 43 GEORGE WINNS & WIFE ROSE TO JOHN FANNEY
Nov. 8, 1725. 6 pds. for 100 A. on Beaverdam branch. Adj. MATHEW TOBIAS SWANNER. Wit: WM. MARSHALL, JENNET BANKS. Nov. Court 1725.

B 45 JOHN LEONARD & WIFE ELIZABETH TO BARRABEE MELTON (MILTON)
Nov. 8, 1725. 3 pds. for 20 A. on NS Moratock River. Wit: JOHN BOBBETT, HEZEKIAH MESSEE. Nov. Court 1725.

B 46 JOHN BOBBITT & WIFE SARAH TO ZEKIAH (HEZEKIAH) MESSEE(?)
Nov. 8, 1725. 10 pds. for 300 A. on WS Occonecheh Swamp. Adj. ROBERT LANG (LONG), PHILLIP JONES. JOHN LEONARD, BARAB. MILTON. Nov. Court 1725.

B 48 JOHN BEVERLY (BEAVERLY) & WIFE MARGARETT TO JAMES DUGLASS
Nov. * 1725. 20 pds. for 200 A. On Poplar Swamp. Adj. LEWIS WILLIAMS, RICHARD WILLIAMS, ABRAHAM BLEWLET. Wit: JOHN BEVERLY, JUN., THOS. JONES. Nov. Court 1725.

B 49 RICHARD KILLINGSWORTH & WIFE MARY TO WILLIAM WHITEHEAD
Oct. 10, 1725. 15 pds. for 640 A. on SS Moratuck River called "Spring Medis" (Meadows?). Wit: JOHN HART, THOS. FUHILL(?). Nov. Court 1725.

B 50 WILLIAM MARTIN TO FRANCIS PUGH of Chowan
Nov. 10, 1725. 30 pds. for 520 A. on Pottecasey Creek. Adj. ROBERT PATERSON, JOHN DICKINSON, JAMES BRYANT. Wit: JOHN SUTTON, THOMAS WHIPPLE. Nov. Court 1725.

B 52 JOHN HOMES & WIFE DOROTHY TO FRANCIS PUGH of Nansemond Co, Va.
Nov. 10, 1725. 10 pds. for 80 A. on Elm Swamp and Tuscarora Path. Adj. JOHN BAREFIELD. Wit: JOHN SUTTON, RICH. OLDNER. Nov. Court 1725.

B 53 ROBERT JONES TO MATTHEW JONES
Nov. 9, 1725. *. 140 A. "For love and affection I do bear to my son MATTHEW JONES. On NS Moratock River Pocoson. Part of tract granted JOHN HATHHORN by patent Feb. 26, 1711/12. Wit: THOMAS BRYANT, JOSEPH SIMES. Nov. Court 1725.

B 54 ROBERT JONES TO ROBERT JONES, JUN.
Nov. 9, 1725. *. 230 A. "For love and affection...to my son ROBERT JONES, JUN. On Moratock River Pocoson at mouth of Cypress Swamp. Land formerly granted to JOHN HAWTHORN by patent dated Feb. 2, 1711/12. Wit: THOS. BRYANT, JOSEPH SIMES. Nov. Court 1725.

B 55 EDWARD HOWCUTT of Chowan to JOHN PERRY of Nansemond, Va.
Nov. 10, 1725. 50 pds. for 640 A. "...my plantation in Bertie..." Wit: THOS. SPIRES, JOHN SUTTON. Nov. Court 1725.

B 57 JOHN NELSON TO JOSEPH BOON
Nov. 9, 1725. 3 pds. for 40 A. on SS Meherring. Adj. WILL BOON. Part of 500 A. patent dated April 1, 1723. Wit: MATHEW SELLERS, CATHA.(?) SELLERS

B 58 JOHN PAGE (PAIDGE) & WIFE HANNER TO SAMUEL GARLAND (SAMMEWELL GARLEN)
Nov. 9, 1725. "a valuable consideration already reserved" for 320 A. On Horse Pasture Creek and Dogwood Neck. By patent. Wit: NEDHAM BRYAN, JOHN PROTIS, THOS. BUSBY. Nov. Court 1725.

B 59 WILLIAM WHITE & WIFE RACHEL (RACHELL) TO SAMUELL CANADY
July 10, 1725. 10 pds. for 195 A. on NS Moratock River. Adj. WILLIAM WHITEHEAD, RICHARD BRASSWELL. Wit: JOSEPH CARTER, PETER DANIEL.Nov.Ct.1725.

26

B 60   WILLIAM DOWNING TO THOMAS JOHNSTON
      Nov. 6, 1725 15 pds. for 150 A. Between "BLEWLETT's line & BIRD's..."
at Petty Shore. Was bought by DOWNING of STEPHEN WILLIAMS. At Deep Creek.
Wit: WILLIAM COOK, EDWARDS TIDMON. Nov. Court 1725.

B 62   SAMUEL GARLEN & WIFE ABIGALL(ABIGALE) TO ARTHUR BENN of New Port of
      Isle of Whit, Va. Aug. 11, 1725. For "consideration already reserv-
ed" 80 A. "Part of JOHN PAIDGES patron" Side of "Medo Pown" (Meadow Pond).
Wit: JOHN PORTIS, JOHN JORNOR. Nov. Court 1725.

B 63   SAMUEL GARLAND & WIFE ABIGAIL TO JOHN PORTIS
      * Nov. 1725. 10 pds. for 100 A. Part of patent for 250 A. dated Nov.
7, 1723. On NS Meherring River at Hogpen Branch. Adj. JOHN PAGE, ARTHUR
BENN. Wit: ROBT SCOTT, ARTHUR BENN. Nov. Court 1725.

B 64   DANIEL MACK DANIEL & WIFE SARAH TO JOHN WILLS, JUN. of Norwick Parish
      Va. Nov. 8, 1725. 20 pds. for 240 A. on SS Moratock River. Adj.
JOHN NARON, JAMES TURNER, HENRY TURNER. Wit: JOHN BRYAN, JOHN SPEIR, WM.
BROWN. Nov. Court 1725.

B 66   SARAH MACK DANIEL TO JOHN BRYAN
      Nov. 8, 1725. Power of atty. to ack. sale of land to JOHN WILLS, JUN.
(240A). Wit: JOHN SPEIR, jurat, WM. BROWN. Nov. Court 1725.

B 66   WILLIAM GRAY TO JOHN GRAY
      May 1726. Power of atty to "friend and brother" to collect debts,
rents and other demands...to lett and sell tenements. Wit: THOMAS WHITMELL,
GEO. EUBANCK. *.*.

B 68   JAMES RUTLAND TO HENRY BAKER of Virginia
      Feb. 7, 1725. 10 pds. for 100 A. on WS Katherine Creek which was
sold by MARY WILLIAMS to JAMES RUTLAND on March 18, 1717/18. Wit: JOSEPH
HORTON, THOMAS BARFIELD, JOHN HENORD(?). Feb. Court 1725.*.

B 70   THOMAS BARFIELD & WIFE MARY TO HENRY BAKER of Virginia
      Feb. 7, 1725/26. 13 pds. for 100 A. on NES Katherine Creek sold by
LEWIS WILLIAMS unto JAMES & ELIZA RUTLAND by deed dated April 6, 1708 & by
them sold to THOS. & MARY BARFIELD on Feb. 4, 1725/26. Wit: JOSEPH HORTON,
JOHN HENARD, HENRY BARFIELD. Feb. Court 1725.*.

B 72   RICHARD OLDNER & WIFE ELENOR (ELINOR) KEEFE, WIDOW TO ROBERT EVANS
      Feb. 10, 1725. 5 sh. together with what has already been paid. For
640 A. Land on Flatt Swamp. Adj. Coll. MAUL, ROBERT EVANS, THOS. MANOR.
ELENER KEEFE, widow of TRADDLE KEEFE and executrix of his last will and
testament. During his life TRADDLE KEEFE bargained with ROBERT EVANS to
sell parcill of land...Wit: WILLIAM LITTLE, WILLIAM DANIEL. Feb. Court 1725.*.

B 72   JAMES RUTLAND & WIFE ELIZA (ELIZABETH) TO THOMAS & MARY BARFIELD
      Feb. 4, 1725/26. For love and affection to our son-in-law & daughter.
100 A. NES Katherine Creek which was given by LEWIS WILLIAMS dec'd. unto
JAMES & ELIZABETH RUTLAND on April 6, 1708. Wit: JOSEPH HORTON, JOHN HENARD,
HENRY BAKER. Feb. Court 1725. *.

B 74   RICHARD MILTON TO FRANCIS PARKER
      Jan. 3, 1725. 15 pds. for 640 A. by patent dated 1720. Adj. JOHN
BLOUNT, THOMAS BUSBY. Wit: WILLIAM EASON, TARLER OQUIN. Feb. Court 1725.*.

B 76   WILLIAM MOORE (MOOR) late of Nansemond Co., Va. to HENRY BARFIELD.
      Nov. 20, 1725. 10 pds. for 220 A. WILLIAM, son and heir of RICHARD
MOORE late of Nansemond County, dec'd...Land at Ahorsky Marsh. Adj. LEONARD
LANGSTON. Granted by patent to THOMAS DYALLS and by DYALLS transferred to
"my hon'd Father by deed" in 1715. Wit: PETER WEST, MARY JONES. February
Court 1725. *.

B 77   JOHN SUTTON TO SAMUEL PARKER of Nansemond, Va.
      Feb. 8, 1725. 10 pds. 10 sh. for 400 A. on NS Cattawiskee Meadow.
Adj. JOHN DICKINSON, JAMES WOOD, NICH. DORMAN, WILLIAM MARTIN. Wit: PATRICK
O'QUIN, JOSEPH CARTER. Feb. Court 1725. *.

B 79   JOHN SPEIR & WIFE PATIENCE TO GEORGE POWELL
      Feb. 9, 1725. 30 sh. "being ye 1/2 charges of 400 A." for 200 A. On

SS Ahorskey Marsh. Adj. JOHN KING. Patent dated April 1, 1723. Adj. JAMES
RUTLAND. Wit: NEEDHAM BRYAN, HENRY BARFIELD, THOS. BARFIELD. Feb.Court1725.*.

B 80   WILLIAM MAUL (MAULE) TO ALEXANDER STEEL, labourer
       Aug. 12, 1725. 30 pds. for 640 A. on WS Chinkpin Swamp. Adj. JAMES
TURNER, JOHN BRYAN. Wit: WILLIAM GRAY, GEORGE HENDERSON. Feb. Court 1725.
JOHN SUTTON, P.Reg.

B 81   RICHARD MELTON TO JOHN HART
       May 12, 1724. 20 pds. for 320 A. on NS Moratock River. Part of
patent formerly granted to MELTON for 640 A. dated April 1, 1723. Wit:
THOS. FUTRELL, FRANCIS PARKER, jurat. Feb. Court 1725. *.

B 82   JOHN NAIRN, atty. for RICHARD MELTON, TO JOHN HART.
       Feb. 8, 1725. "5 sh. as well as within considerations" 320 A. Wit:
ROBERT FORSTER, JOHN WINNS. *.*.

B 83   JOHN DICKINSON & WIFE REBEKAH TO JOHN SUTTON
       Aug. 14, 1725. 5 pds. for 100 A. Adj. FRANCIS PRIGEON, EDWARD MARSH-
BORNE (MASHBORN). Wit: MARY MASHBORNE, JETHRO MASHBORNE. Feb. Court 1725.*.

B 84   JOHN TINEY & WIFE MARY TO JOHN DRAKE
       Oct. 8, 1725. 20 pds. for 340 A. In Hunting Quarter Swamp. Adj.
RICHARD WASHINGTON on NS Pottecarsie Creek. Wit: JOHN SUTTON, MARY SUTTON.
Feb. Court 1725.*.

Note here: "So far copyed to Feb'y Court 1797."

B 85   JOHN DICKINSON TO JOSEPH CARTER
       Feb. 8, 1725. 20 A. "...for love good will and affection which I bare
unto my well beloved kinsman JOSEPH CARTER..." Land Adj. CARTER on the
creek. Wit: MORE CARTER, JOHN SUTTON. Feb. Court 1725.

B 86   RICHARD MILTON (MELTON) TO SAMUEL WILLIAMS
       May 12, 1724. 8 pds. for 320 A. on NS Morattock River "upon ye Long
Meadow". Part of patent formerly granted MILTON for 640 A. dated April 1,
1723. FRANCIS PARKER, jurat. THOS. FUTRILL. Feb. Court 1725. *.

B 87   JOHN NAIRN, atty. to RICH'D. MILTON, TO SAMUEL WILLIAMS
       Feb. 8, 1725. "5 sh. as well as within consideration" for 320 A. Wit:
ROBERT FORSTER, JOHN WINNS. Feb. Court. * .

B 87   JOHN SPEIR TO RICHARD BARFIELD
       Feb. 1, 1726. 20 pds. for 300 A. NWS "of the uper Horskey Meadow".
Land formerly surveyed by THOMAS DYAL and for want of planting was "lapsed".
To JOHN COTTON by patent dated June 8, 1719. Land Adj. SPEIR, JOHN SUTTON,
JUN., COLL. MAUL. Land conveyed to SPEIR by deed dated April 26, 1723.
Wit: HENRY BAKER, JAMES RUTLAND, HENRY BARFIELD. Feb. Court 1725. *.

B 89   MULFORD LANGSTON & WIFE MARY TO SAMUEL WHEATLEY
       Oct. 16, 1725. 20 pds. for 200 A. on NS Pottacassey Creek. At Spring
Branch, Reedy Branch. Adj. LEONARD LANGSTON. Part of tract patented by
THOMAS BONNER. Wit: JOHN BROWN, SEN., THOMAS HOMES. Feb. Court 1725. *.

B 91   MULFORD LANGSTON & WIFE MARY TO THOMAS BONNER
       Oct. 16, 1725. Power of atty. to make over land to SAMUEL WHEATLEY.
Wit: JOHN BROWNE, SEN., jurat, THOMAS HOMES. Feb. Court 1725. *.

B 92   RICHARD WASHINGTON & WIFE HANNAH TO ROBERT SCOTT
       Feb. 5, 1725. 20 pds. for 100 A. on SS Meherrin River at Cragg
Bottom. Part of patent granted HENRY WHEELER on Nov. 5, 1714. Wit:
WILLIAM POPE, ISAAC RICKS, BARNABEE MACKINNE, JUN. Feb. Court 1725. *.

B 93   SAMUEL ELLSON (ELSON), marriner, of New England TO PHILLIP EDEN
       Feb. 8, 1725. 25 pds. For "within mentioned land". Wit: ROBERT
FORSTER, JOHN BONDE. Feb. Court 1725. *.

B 93   THOMAS JENKINS TO WILLIAM LITTLE
       Feb. 9, 1725. 20 pds. for 100 A. On "uper side" Deep Creek. Formerly
belonging to FREDERICK JONES, and purchased by JOHN WILLIAMS. Bounded by
Creek. Wit: ROBT. FORSTER, JOHN WINNS. Feb. Court 1725. *.

28

B 94 WILLIAM LITTLE TO WILLIAM DANIELL (DANIEL)
     Feb. 10, 1725. 30 pds. For "within mentioned lands". Wit: RICHARD
OLDNER, THOMAS JONES. Feb. Court 1725. *.

B 94 RICHARD WEBB of Nansemond Co. Va. to JAMES WOOD
     Feb. 5, 1725. 500 pds. For "cartain Negro wench". RICHARD WEBB
"firmly bound and Justly Indebted...the consideration of this obligation is
such...that (he and his heirs)...shall forever hereafter defend the sale...
already sold and bill of sale delivered to JAMES WOOD..." Wit: JOHN MOORE,
JAMES MOORE, JOHN SUTTON. *.*.

B 95 RICHARD WEBB of Nanssemond Co. Va. to JAMES WOOD
     Feb. 5, 1725. 32 pds. 15 sh. For "wench named Rose...and her in-
crease..." Wit: JOHN MOORE, JAMES MOORE, JOHN SUTTON. Feb. Court 1725. *.

B 95 LAZARUS THOMAS TO WILLIAM GARRET
     May 11, 1726. 9 pds. for 100 A. On Holley Branch and Long Pocoson.
Wit: JOHN SUTTON, ROBT. GARRET. May Court 1726.*.

B 97 JOHN COOK (COOKE) & WIFE SARAH TO MATTHEW MASHBORNE of Nansemond Co.
     Va. Sept. 7, 1725. 7 pds. for 225 A. On Urah Swampt. Adj. JOHN
DICKINSON on Cabin Branch and Pottakersey Creek. By patent dated Nov. 11,
1719. Wit: MOORE CARTER, jurat, JETHRO MASHBORNE, JOHN SUTTON, jurat.
May Court 1726. *.

B 99 JOHN BROWN & WIFE MARY TO BARNABE MACKINNE
     Aug. 8, 1725. 5 pds. for 80 A. on SS Morrattock River and Cypress
Gutt. Formerly surveyed for WILLIAM BROWN. Resurveyed for his son, JOHN
BROWN, by patent dated March 30, 1721. Patent Cont. 525 A. Wit: WILLIAM
MURPHEY(?), ISAAC RICKS. May Court 1726. *.

B 101 WILLIAM MAUL (MAULE) TO BARNABEE MACKINNE
     Feb. 10, 1725. 60 pds. for 200 A. on SS Morattock River Adj.
WILLIAM JONES. Survey made for JOHN LEWIS and by him "lapsed", and ye same
patent since granted to WILLIAM MAUL. Wit: EDWARD MOORE, GEORGE BURRINGTON,
THOS. BRYANT, jurat. May Court 1726. *.

B 102 JOHN BOWIN(?) of Isle of Whight, Va. TO BARNABEE MACKINNE
     April 25, 1726. 80 pds. for 610 A. On SS Morattock and NS Conacon-
aro Swamp Adj. GEORGE SMITH. Patent granted March 1, 1719 to WILLIAM LED-
BETTER of Surry County and sold by him to JOHN BOWIN. Wit: WILLIAM RICKS,
ISAAC RICKS, jurat. May Court 1726. *.

B 103 GEORGE STEVENS TO CHARLES STEVENS
     Aug. 12, 1724. 5 pds. for 100 A. On NS Morattock River "dividend
of woodland" Adj. JOHN COTTON, RICHARD MELTON to "ye Village Swamp". Patent
dated April 1, 1723. Wit: ROBT. FORSTER, *. May Court 1726. *.

B 103 JOHN BROWN & WIFE MARY TO RICHARD JACKSON
     Aug. 9, 1725. 30 pds for 100 A. On SS Morattock River. Adj. JOSEPH
JOYNER, WILLIAM STRICKLAND. "Being plantation whereon WILLIAM BROWN did
live and given by him to his son JOHN BROWN..." Wit: ISAAC RICKS, WILLIAM
MURPHRY. May Court 1726. *.

B 105 JOHN RASBERRY & WIFE BRIGET TO WILLIAM LEE
     May 9, 1726. 50 pds. for 200 A. On Deep Branch Adj. FRANCIS(?) DUNN
(DUN). Wit: CHARLES CAVENAH, WILLIAM BORFIELD (BARFIELD) May Court 1726.*.

B 106 BARNABEE MACKINNE JUN. TO ROBERT LANG
     May 9, 1726. 20 pds. for 520 (525) A. On SS Morattock River and NS
Elk Marsh. Patent dated Feb. 1, 1725. Wit: _____RAPIER(?), THOMAS BRYANT.*.

B 107 HENRY POPE of Virginia TO JOHN POPE
     *1726. 20 pds. for 90 A. To "JOHN POPE my son". Patent granted to
GEORGE SMITH for 580 A. and sold to WILLIAM POPE, and by him sold to HENRY
POPE, his father (290 A.) Land on SS Morrattock River and Beaverdam Swamp.
Wit: JOSEPH LANE, jurat. WM. BIRKHEAD. May Court 1726. *.8.

B 108 RICHARD JACKSON & WIFE SARAH TO BARNABE MCKINNE (MACKINNE)
     May 10, 1725. 30 pds. for 220 A. On SS Morrattock River Adj.WILLIAM
BROWN and BENJAMIN MACKINNE. Part of tract formerly granted to WILLIAM

BROWN for 640 A. dated April 1, 1713. Known by name "BROWN's lower Survey".
By BROWN sold to WILLIAM JONES & NATHANIEL HOLLEY, and by them sold to
RICHARD JACKSON. Wit: ISAAC RICKS, WILLIAM MURPHRY. May Court 1726. *.

B 110 JACOB BRASSWELL (BRACEWELL) TO JOHN SMITH, blacksmith
       * 1726. 10 pds. for 250 A. NS Morrattock River and Urssarah Meadow.
"...Where John now lives..." being "pt. and p'cill of a patent of 528 A."
granted to BRACEWELL April 1, 1723. On Holly Bush Meadow. Wit: *.*. May
Court 1726. *.

B 111 CHARLES MERRIT (MERRET) & WIFE ELINER TO JAMES PEEK (PEEKE) of
       Boston in New England. April 16, 1715. 50 pds. for 130 A. On SS
Chowan River in Chowan Precinct in ye County Albemarle at Deep Creek "on ye
hill side". Adj. JOHN FERREBENT. Wit: PETER EVENS, RICHARD BAREFIELD.*.*.

B 112 ELINOR MERRET (MERIET) TO WILLIAM MIXON (MELTON)
       April 16, 1715. Power of atty. to ack. in open court 130 A. for ye
said WILLIAM MERRET unto JAMES PEEKE. Wit: PETER EVENS, RICHARD BAREFIELD.*.

B 112 JAMES PEEKE TO WILLIAM DANIEL
       May 11, 1726. 20 pds. "Land within mentioned". Wit: ROBERT FORSTER,
THOS. JONES. May Court 1726. ROBERT FORSTER C/C. NOTE HERE: "The word Feb'r
being rassed and ye word May being Interlined and the figures 1726 being
added in presence of us, ROBERT FORSTER...THOS. JONES..."

B 112 BEALE (BAEL) BROWN TO JOHN POWER.
       Oct. 6, 1725. 50 pds. for 150 A. On Horse Pasture Creek. Adj. JOHN
CHESHER, JOHN PAGE. Wit: SAMUEL ELSON, ANNA DRAKE. May Court 1726. ED
MASHBORNE D.C/C.

B 114 HENRY WEST & WIFE SUSANAH TO JAMES SMITH
       Dec. 3, 1725. 20 pds. for 340 A. On NS Morrattock River between
ROBERT WEST & JOHN NAIRN. On Reedy Branch and Flagg Run. Wit: NEEDHAM BRYAN,
CHARLES CAVENAH. May Court 1726. *.

B 115 JAMES SMITH & WIFE MARY TO HENRY WEST
       Dec. 3, 1725. 20 pds. for 150 A. on NS Morrattock River. Adj. OWEN
(OWIN) DANIELS, JAMES PARKER on Flagg Run. Wit: NEEDHAM BRYAN, CHARLES
CAVENAH. May Court 1726. *.

B 117 ROBERT EVANS & WIFE ANN TO ALEXANDER BALLENTINE
       May 10, 1726 5 pds. for 150 A. At Royall Oak at fork of Killem
Swamp Adj. THOMAS MANS (MARS?). Formerly Coll. WILL'M MAWLES. Wit: WILLIAM
CRAWFORD, CORNELIONS PERCES. May Court 1726. *.

B 118 JAMES WILLIAMS TO ROBERT HOG (HOGH)
       * 1726. 10 pds. for 380 A. On Roquis and Flagg Branch. Adj. HENRY
OVERSTREET. Wit: THEOPH. WILLIAMS, RICHARD WASHINGTON. May Court 1726.*.

B 120 ANN TUBERVILLE, WILLIAM & MARGARETT TUBERVILLE TO RICHARD ALLEN of
       Hannover County, Virginia. May 7, 1726. *. 300 A. on NS Morrattock
River and SS Tuberville Branch. Adj. RICH. CURTON, WILLIAM GRAY, RALPH
MASON on NWS Reedy Run. Being in two patents: one granted to RICHARD TUBER-
VILLE in 1712; the other granted WILLIAM TUBERVILLE in 1720. "...ANN, wife
to RICH, dec'd. and WILLIAM our son with MARGARETT his wife..." Wit:
RICHARD CUERTON, SACKFIELD(?) BREWER. *.*.

B 121 ANN TUBERVILLE & MARGARETT TUBERVILLE TO SACKFIELD BREWER
       May 7, 1726. Power of atty. to ack. sale to RICHARD ALLEN. Wit:
RICHARD CUERTON, WALTER TUBERVILLE. May 1726. *.

B 121 SARAH ROSE TO ROBERT BELL
       May 7, 1726. 10 pds. for 640 A. Adj. Major GEO. POLLOCK, JOHN HOLE-
BROOK, JOHN COCK, LAURENCE LARSON. Patent granted THOMAS ROSE in ye Island
of Great Britain. Wit: THEO. WILLIAMS, JAMES WILLIAMS. *.*.

B 122 SARAH ROSE TO STEPHEN WILLIAMS
       May 7, 1726.*.*. Power of atty. to ack. sale of 640 A. to ROBERT
BELL. Wit: THEO. WILLIAMS, jurat, JAMES WILLIAMS, jurat. May Court 1726.*.

B 123 THOMAS KIRBY TO RICHARD VICK of Isle of Weight, Va.

May 9, 1726. 5 pds. for 100 A. In Potacarsie Woods. Adj. RICHARD WASHINGTON on Tinnes Branch. Patent granted Nov. 7, 1723. Wit: RICHARD WASHINGTON, THEOPHILUS WILLIAMS. May Court 1726.*.

B 124 JAMES MURRAY & WIFE ELIZABETH TO MOSES GRANDBURY of Nansemond Co.,Va.
. 10 pds. for 200 A. On Casiah Swamp. Adj. THOMAS RHODES. Wit: THOMAS COWLING, THOMAS ROADES. May Court 1726..

B 125 WILLIAM WILSON & WIFE REBEKAH TO SAMUEL ELDRIDGE (ELDREDGE)
May 9, 1726. 20 pds. for 265 A. "...being half tract granted said REBEKAH whose name was then BRACEWELL and now ye said WILLIAM WILSONS wife." 530 A. patent dated March 1, 1719. Wit: WILLIAM DRAKE, WILLIAM RICKS. May Court 1726.*.

B 126 HENRY SIMS TO THOMAS DYALL (DYAN)
Jan. 11, 1725. 12 pds. for 100 A. On NS Morattock River between HENRY SIMS & WILLIAM KELLY. land SIMS sold unto EDWARD GIBSON. Wit: HENRY IRBY, JACOB BROWN, WILLIAM KELLEY. May Court 1726. CG(?)

B 128 JOHN GREEN & WIFE AMMY (ELIMY) TO JOHN BROOKS (BROOCKS)
May 10, 1725. 2 pds. 10 sh. for 50 A. On SS Morrottock River Adj. JOHN GREEN. Wit: THOMAS SMITH, WILLIAM SPILLER. May Court 1726.*.

B 129 JOHN WILLIAMS & WIFE ANN TO JOHN MOORE
May 7, 1726. 24 pds. for 150 A. Adj. JONATHAN STANDLEY. Wit: THEO. WILLIAMS, SAMUEL WILLIAMS.*.*.

B 130 JOHN WILLIAMS & WIFE ANN TO STEPHEN WILLIAMS
May 7, 1726. Power of atty. to ack. sale of 150 A. to JOHN MOORE. Wit: THEOPH. WILLIAMS, jurat, JAMES WILLIAMS, jurat. May Court 1726. *.

B 131 WILLIAM GRAY TO NEEDHAM BRYAN
May 7, 1726. 30 pds. for 210 A. Plantation known as "Snowfield" in woods "betwixt" Cashay & Morrattock in Flint Pocoson. On Falling Run. Wit: JOHN SWAIN, J. WM. FON(?). May Court 1726. *.

B 132 RICHARD VICK of Isle of Whight, Va. TO THOMAS KIRBY
Feb. 1725. 2000 lbs. of Pork for 290 A. On NS Pottekerse Creek Adj. THOMAS DRAKE. Patent dated April 5, 1723. Wit: RICHARD WASHINGTON, THEOPH. WILLIAMS. May Court 1726.*.

NOTE HERE: "N.B. This following Deed WHITMELL to WILLIAMSON was in order before that above last one NO. 25 it makes no difference only not being in same order the mistake has no other Effect."

B 133 THOMAS WHITMELL TO JAMES WILLIAMSON
May 10, 1726. 12 pds. for 450 A. JAMES WILLIAMSON, Precinct Surgeon. Land on SS Canahoe Creek Adj. RICHARD MILTON. Wit: WILLIAM GRAY, GEORGE EUBANCKS. May Court 1726. *.

B 135 ANNE BIRD & HUSBAND BARNABEE BIRD TO BENJAMIN FOREMAN
March 10, 1725/26. 20 pds. for 625 A. On SS Kahukee (Kehukee) Swamp Adj. RICHARD MELTON, ANN MILTON. BENJAMIN to clear and plant an acre of land, and build a house by "ye last of March next coming". Wit: JOHN WILLIAMS, JACOB LEWIS. May Court 1726. *.

B 136 RICHARD JACKSON TO RICHARD PACE & RICHARD PACE, JUN.
May 1726. 20 pds. for 100 A. Being part of patent granted to BARTHO-LOMME CHAVEN for 300 A. dated March 1, 1719. Sold by CHAVEN to RICHARD JACKSON. On Youahaw Swamp. Wit: BARNABE MACKINNE, JUN. JOHN MACKINNE. May Court 1726. *.

B 137 JACOB LEWIS TO ISAAC LEWIS
May 1726. 5 pds. for "small pcill of land" On WS Brooks Creek. Wit: THOMAS JONES, JOHN WINNS. May Court 1726.*.

B 138 JOSEPH SIMS TO WILLIAM FROST
Nov. 9, 1725. 5 pds. for 150 A. On NS Morattock River and Mill Swamp. Patent dated March 1, 1719. Wit: THOMAS BRYANT, ROBERT JONES, JUN. May Court 1726. *.

B 139   HENRY WHEELER & WIFE ANN TO THOMAS LANE
        May 7, 1726. 15 pds. for 90 A. On NS Morottock River and ES Mill
Swamp. Formerly granted to BARNABEE MACKINNE. Patent dated Aug. 10, 1720.
Wit: ROBERT JONES, JUN., EMPOROR WHEELER. May Court 1726. *.

B 140   ROBERT LANIER (LENIER) & WIFE SARAH TO CHARLES ROYALL
        *. 30 pds. for 640 A. on Flat Swamp. Wit: *,*. May Court 1726. *.

B 141   ROBERT LONG (LANG) & WIFE ELINOR TO WILLIAM TUBERVILLE & WALTER
        TUBERVILLE. May 3, 1726. 10 pds. for 380 A. On SS Morattock River
in Plumtree Swamp at "Goose Pen". Adj. WILLIAM GREEN. Wit: JOHN ROTTEN-
BERRY, RICHARD ARDHILL. May Court 1726. *.

B 143   GEORGE SMITH TO BARNABEE MACKINNE, JUN.
        May 7, 1726. 20 pds. for 210 A. On SS Morattock River. Part of
patent 510 A. granted GEO. SMITH March 1, 1719. Adj. PHILLIP RAYFORD. Wit:
JOHN MACKINNE, jurat, WILLIAM LAW. May Court 1726. *.

B 144   JOHN BROWN & WIFE MARY TO WILLIAM STRICKLAND (STRICKLIN, STRICKLING)
        May 9, 1726. 20 pds. for 100 A. On SS Morrattock River at BROWN's
Spring Gutt. Wit: BARN. MACKINNE, JOHN ANDERSON. May Court 1726. ROBERT
FORSTER C/C

B 145   JOSEPH LANE, JUN. & WIFE PATIENCE TO ROBERT HOWSE
        May 9, 1725. 2 pds. for 50 A. On ES Hunting Quarter Swamp. Adj.
JOSEPH LANE, SEN. & JOSEPH LANE, JUN. Part of patent dated Aug. 10, 1720.
Wit: BARNABEE MACKINNY, ROBERT JONES, JUN. May Court *. ROBT. FORSTER.

B 146   LORDS PROPRIETORS TO ROBERT FORSTER
        March 30 1727. 1870 A. on SS Morrattock River on IRWIN's Island.
Due 50 A. for importation of each person. Rent 1 sh/A to be paid every
Sept. 29th. To be seated within three years. Signed SIR RICHARD EVERARD,
BARON. THOS. HARVEY, E. MOSELEY, J. LOVICK, R. FORSTER, R. EVERARD, C.
GALE, J. WORLEY, EDMD. GALE, FRAN. FOSTER.

B 148   JONATHAN SANDERSON TO JOHN WIGGANS
        Aug. 5, 1726. 2 pds. 10 sh. for 50 A. on NS Meherring River and
Buck Horne. Adj. ROBERT BRASSWELL. Part of patent belonging to JOHN HOBBS
dated Nov. 7, 1723. Wit: JOHN GARDNER, *. Aug. Court 1726. *.

B 149   CLEMENT STRADFORD TO GEORGE BLACKWELL
        Aug. 9, 1726. *. 60 A. "...for good will and affection I beare to my
son-in-law..." Land on Bridger's Creek. Wit: JOHN DUFFIELD, GEORGE STEVENS.
Aug. Court 1726. *.

B 150   BARNABE THOMAS TO JOHN DAWSON of Isle of Whight, Va.
        Aug. 1726. 15 pds. for 250 A. On NS Morattock called "Roanoke". Land
I bought of LAZARUS WHITEHEAD. Adj. SKIPPER's Land and THOMAS LANE. Wit:
THOMAS GALE, jurat, WM. CANE. Aug. Court 1726. *.

B 151   JOSEPH HOWARD & WIFE SARAH TO WILLIAM SHOLAR
        Aug. 8, 1726. 2 pds. 10 sh. for 182 A. On Cashiah Swamp. Wit: JOHN
BAREFIELD, ELIJA BAREFIELD. *.*.

B 152   LORDS PROPRIETORS TO ANTHONY LEWIS, JUN.
        March 1, 1721. 640 A. On SS Meherron River adj. ROBERT PATERSON,
ANTHONY LEWIS, SEN. Due for importation of persons. 50 A/person. To be
seated within three years or grant void. Rent of 1 sh/50A due yearly on
Sept. 29th. Reserved 1/2 of all gold and silver mined. Signed: CHARLES EDEN,
Esq., J. LOVICK, sec't'y., FRAN. FORSTER, RICHARD SANDERSON, WM. REED.

B 153   ANTHONY LEWIS, JUN. TO BENJAMIN HILL
        Aug. 9, 1726. 30 barrels of pitch for 640 A. On SS Meherin River,
"Butted and bounded as by within original patent dated March 1, 1719. Wit:
WILLIAM LITTLE, R. FOSTER. Aug. Court 1726. *.

B 154   JOSEPH SIMS (SIMMS) TO MARGARETT FOWLER
        1726. 5 pds. for 150 A. Part of patent dated March 1, 1719 on NS
Merottock River at Meadow Branch. Adj. WILLIAM BRACEWELL on Mill Swamp.
Wit: BARNA. MACKINNE, jurat, ROBERT JONES. Aug. Court 1726.*.

B 155   JOHN HOOKES (HOOKS), JUN. of Nansemond Co., Va. TO JONATHAN SANDER-
SON
        * 1725. 5 pds. for 320 A. Part of patent for 640 A. dated Nov. 7,
1723. On NS Meherin River. Adj. ROBERT BRACEWELL, BEAL BROWN, JOHN
MINSHEW. Wit: PETER GARLAND, EDW. JOHNSON, JOHN MACKELONE. August Court
1726. *.

B 156   JOHN STEWARD & WIFE SARAH TO JAMES WOOD
        * 1726. 30 pds. for 140 A. On NS Merattock River commonly called
"ye Peach Blossom". Adj. EDWARD HOWARD. Part of tract granted March 1,
1721. Wit: ROBERT BRASSWELL, ORLENDO CHAMPION, JOHN SUTTON. August Court
1726. *.

B 158   LEWIS BRYAN, "cooper", TO JOHN WRIGHT
        March 1725. 25 pds. for 200 A. On WS Chinkapine Swamp. Adj. JOHN
PETTEFORD. Wit: BENJ. SANDERS, HENRY BRADLEY. August Court 1726. *.

B 159   SIMON BRYAN TO WILLIAM WILLIAMS
        May 20, 1720. 32 pds. for 290 A. In Meherin Woods on Cypress
Swamp. Adj. HENRY TURNER. Wit: WILLIAM GRAY, A. COWLEY,
1726. *.

B 160   TIMOTHY HINDS & WIFE ANN TO ROBERT EDWARDS
        May 9, 1726. 7 pds. 10 sh. for 320 A. On SS Meherring River. Part
of grant for 640 A. dated March 1, 1719. Previously sold to EDWARDS by
deed dated November 21, 1722. Wit: JOHN DEW, THOS. HORNE, August Court
1726. *.

B 161   LORDS PROPRIETORS TO THOMAS SUTTON
        April 14, 1722. Grant. 262 A. In Chowan Precinct on SS Black
Walnut Swamp at mouth of Piping Branch. Formerly granted to ELIZABETH
JONES. Dated April 1, 1714. Now due to THOS. SUTTON April 3, 1721 by
order of council. Signed: J. LOVICK, Sec't'y., THOS. POLLOCK, JOHN BLOUNT,
RICH. SANDERSON, THOS. POLLOCK, JUN.

B 162   THOMAS SUTTON & WIFE ELIZABETH TO MARY JONES
        Sept. 7, 1723. *. 262 A. Land in fork of Black Walnut Swamp
bounded by Rocky Branch. Adj. _____ HILL. "...By patent and deed of gift
to my sister-in-law, MARY JONES ... 262 A. was in danger of having lapsed
... which was the true reason to gett the lapsed pattent in my name without
any intent to wrong my said sister-in-law, MARY JONES ... I ack. she has
right & good title to all that part of land lying below Black Walnut Swamp
..." Wit: JOHN LAERTON, JAMES FELLHAM. April Court 1726. *.

B 163   JOHN HOOKS, JUN. & WIFE MARTHA of Nansemond Co., Va. to FRANCIS
                                        CORBETT of Isle of Wight, Va.
        Aug. 9, 1726. 7 pds. for 145 A. On NS Meherren River and WS Chowan
River. Granted to HOOKS Nov. 7, 1723. Adj. Indian Creek Swamp, GODFREE
LEE, EDW. BARNES. Wit: EDW. BARNES, JOHN GARDNER, JONATHAN SANDERSON.
August Court 1726. *.

B 165   RICHARD JACKSON TO BARNABE MACKINNE, JUN.
        Aug. 6, 1726. 160 pds. for 100 A. Part of tract formerly granted
JOHN BROWN for 525 A. on March 3, 1721. Transferred to JACKSON by BROWN
and wife MARY. On SS Merattuck River. Adj. JOSEPH JOYNER, WILLIAM STRICK-
LAND, Spring Branch. Wit: BARN. MACKINNE, jurat, JOHN MACKINNE. August
Court 1726. *.

B 166   BEAL (BEALE) BROWN & WIFE SARAH TO JAMES HOWARD
        May 13, 1726. 100 pds. for 450 A. Known by name "Little Ahoskey."
Adj. JOHN PERRY on Ahosky Marsh. By patent dated Oct. 18, 1721 to WILLIAM
BROWN; now held by his son, BEAL BROWN. Wit: JOHN DICKINSON, JAMES HOL-
LAND, RD. HORSLEY. August Court 1726. *.

B 169   BEALE BROWN & WIFE SARAH TO JAMES HOWARD
        May 12, 1726. 5 sh. for 450 A. Lease for land known as "Little
Ahoskey." Adj. JOHN PERRY on Ahosky Marsh. (By patent as stated above in
B 166). "...and paying there of the rent of one pepper corn on the last
day of the said term..." Wit: JOHN DICKINSON, JAMES HOLLAND. August Court
1726. *.

B 171 WILLIAM RICKS & WIFE ESTHER TO THOMAS KIRBY, SEN.
     May 2, 1726. 10 pds. for 200 A. "...which land I obtained a patent
for the first day of Feb. anno Dom. 1725 for 640 A..." 200 A. Adj. THOMAS
BUSBY, ROBERT SCOTT. Wit: ROBERT SCOTT, ISAAC RICKS, THOMAS KIRBY. August
Court 1726. *.

B 172 LORDS PROPRIETORS TO AMBROSE ARRISS
     June 4, 1725. Grant. 150 A. On Fork of Gray Hall Swamp, which
land was granted by patent to DAVID STEWARD and by him "elapsed for want of
seating..." Signed: GEORGE BURRINGTON, Esq., Gov. Recorded J. LOVICK,
Sec'y. THOMAS HARVEY, FRAN. FORSTER, GOFFE, C. GALE, T. POLLOCK, E. MOSE-
LEY, WM. REED.

B 173 AMBROSE ARRISS (ARRIS) TO COLL. ROBERT WEST
     Apr. 25, 1726. *. *. "...my Right title to within mentioned deed
..." Wit: EDW. MOORE, JAMES CASTELLAW, jurat. August Court 1726. *.

B 173 LORDS PROPRIETORS TO GEORGE POWELL
     Apr. 1, 1725. Grant. 124A. ES Ahoskey Swamp adj. PETER PARKER,
LEONARD LANGSTON. "...being due for importation..." 50A/person. Signed:
WILLIAM REED, Esq., President of Council and Commander in Chief of Our
Province. RICH. SANDERSON, FRAN. FORSTER, M. MOORE, J. LOVICK. Recorded
in Sec'ty. Office. J. LOVICK, Sec'ty.

B 174 GEORGE POWEL TO JOHN ALSTON
     Aug. 11. 1726. 25 pds. "...within mentioned patent..." Wit: JOHN
NAIRN, JOHN POWER. August Court 1726. R. HICKS. *.

B 175 INVENTORY OF ESTATE OF NATHANIEL HOLLEY
     May 9, 1726. "An inventory of all the goods chattels and credits of
the estate of Nathaniel Holley, dec'd. Taken by me the Subscriber(?)...."

2 feather beds & furniture	16 pieces Earthenware
3 iron pots & pot hooks	1 bose(?) Iron & heater
2 frying pans	1 candlestick
7 puter dishes	1 pr. Fire Tongs
5 puter plates	2 small chests
puter basons	4 guns
5̄ puter poringers	1 pr. hand millstones
16 puter spoons	4 chairs slagg(?) bottom
1 grind stone	1 stone Jugg
1 puter Tankard	4 glass bottles
5 puter basons	a p'cill carpenters tools
1 Lattin(?) pan	1 saddle & bridle
1 Lattin sauce pan	1 mare & colt (1 yr)
1 pr. small stilliards	9 cows & calves= 30 MURPHEG

Eight pds the currency of Virginia due from WILLIAM MURPHEY alias /
Due from Estate known 20 sh. cash to (next) kin
40 sh. cost to (?) SOWARD
6 pds 15 sh currant to BARNABE MACKINNE
A small parcill of Hoggs of small acct. of widow RAISING
Being all at present yt is come to my hand to my knowledge Except some
     old washing Tubbs and water pails of little value.

This given by me....ISAAC RICKS.
August Court 1726. Proved by oath of ISAAC RICKS adm. to Dec'd. in open
court.

B 175 RICHARD WASHINGTON TO JOHN GANEY
     Nov. 17, 1726. 16 pds. for 400 A. Patent dated November 17, 1723.
In Pottakasey Woods..." ...at a Black Gum in Patties Delight..." Adj.
RICHARD VICK. Wit: THOS. SPIRES, JACOB POPE. November Court 1726. *.

B 177 JOHN BRYAN & WIFE ELIZABETH TO THOMAS JERREL, SEN.
     Dec. 10, 1725. 10 pds. for 150 A. On SS Morrattock River "in the
low ground" Adj. JOHN NEARNE, JAMES TURNER. Wit: JAMES IRELAND, WILLIAM
SIMMONS, DA. MACDANIEL, JOHN NAIRNE. November Court 1726. Ack. in open
Court by DAN'L MACDANIEL by Power of atty. from ELIZABETH BRYAN.

B 179 CHARLES JONES TO WILLIAM ASHLEY
     Nov. 7, 1726. 10 pds. for 100 A. On Beach Swamp and Bladoe (?)

Branch. Adj. JOHN JONES. Wit: JOHN WILLIAMS, JOHN ROBERTS. November Court 1726. *.

B 180   SAMUEL WILLIAMS & WIFE JANE TO WILLIAM RUFFIN of Surry Co., Va.
        Feb. 5, 1726. 21 pds. for 160 A. On NS Morrattock River and "the long meadow" at The Old Trading Path. Adj. CLEMMON STRADFORD. Tract formerly granted to RICHARD MILTON for 640 A. by patent dated April 1, 1723. Wit: THOMAS DEW, JUN., JOHN HART. November Court 1726. *.

B 181   SIMMON(SIMON) JEFFREYS TO EMANUEL ROGERS, "carpenter"
        Aug. 8, 1726. 30 sh. for 1 A. Adj. Bridger's Creek above the Mill Dam. Part of tract on Morrattock River. Wit: *. *. November Court 1726. *.

B 182   THOMAS BROWN & WIFE TO JOHN ROGERS, JUN.
        *. 1000 lbs. tobacco for 110 A. On NS Maeherrin River Adj. River Islands and JOSEPH DARDEN. Part of patent for 640 A. Wit: JACOB BRACE-WELL, MARY BRACEWELL. November Court 1726. *.

B 183   RICHARD MELTON TO WILLIAM MELTON
        Jan. 15, 1725. *. *. Power of atty. to "...ask demand sue....Recover and Receive all...debts due..." Wit: WILLIAM EASON, jurat, TARLOE O'QUIN, jurat. November Court 1726. ROBERT FORSTER C/C.

B 184   RICHARD MELTON TO WILLIAM MELTON
        Jan. 15, 1725. *. 26 head of cattle marked with Swallow Fork in right ear and half moon under same ear. Also 3 mares and 1 horse. Wit: WILLIAM EASON, jurat, TARLOE O'QUIN, jurat. November Court 1726. RT. FORSTER C/C.

B 184   JAMES SKEPER & WIFE MARY TO GEORGE SKEPER, SEN.
        Aug. 6, 1725. 10 pds. for 120 A. In Yeour Woods and NS Holly Bush or Quarter Swamp. Part of tract granted me for 160 A. dated Aug. 10, 1720. Wit: THOMAS BRYANT, JOHN SKEPER. November Court 1726. *.

B 186   WILLIAM BOUSH (BUSH) to BENJAMIN WARREN
        Nov. 7, 1726. 20 pds. for 130 A. On Bear Swamp Adj. BENJAMIN WARREN, HENRY BRADLEY, JUN. Wit: EDWARD TIDMAN, NICHOLAS FAIRLESS. November Court 1726. *.

B 187   MOSES GINN & WIFE MARY TO JOHN POWER
        Nov. 4, 1726. 20 pds. for 190 A. On NS Meherrin River. Wit: JOHN BOULE (BOUCLE), JOHN DEW. Ack. in court by JOHN DEW, Esq. by virtue of power of atty. from MARY GINN.

B 188   MOSES GINN & WIFE MARY TO JOHN POWER
        Nov. 4, 1726. 50 pds. for 300 A. On NS Meherring River. Adj. WILLIAM BRACEWELL. Wit: JOHN BONDE, JOHN DEW. Ack. by JOHN DEW, Esq. by power of atty. from MARY GINN. *. *.

B 189   MARY GINN TO JOHN DEW
        Nov. 7, 1726. Power of atty. to ack. sale to JOHN POWER. Wit: JOHN BONDE, SARAH BRASWELL. *. *.

B 190   JOHN DAVIS TO PHILLIP BROWN
        Nov. 8, 1726. 10 pds. for 213 A. On Cypress Swamp Adj. JOHN DAVIS and HENRY RHODES. *. *. November Court 1726. *.

B 191   SAMUEL WHEATLEY & WIFE SARAH TO JOSEPH SCOTT
        Nov. 10, 1726. 30 pds. for 200 A. On NS Pottakersy Creek at Spring Branch and Reedy Branch. Adj. LEONARD LANGSTON. Wit: JOHN WINNS, EDWARD CARTER. November Court 1726. (NOTE: In the body of the deed it also says, "...thirty pds. to me in hand by EDW. CARTER..." Probably copy error.)

B 193   JOHN COTTON TO RICHARD HOLLAND
        Aug. 8, 1723. 12 pds. for *. On SS Roanoke River and Broad Meadow. Adj. JOHN GREEN. Part of patent granted COTTON. Wit: WILLIAM WHITFIELD, JOHN SCOTT. November Court 1726. *.

B 194   JOHN COTTON & WIFE JUDITH TO BARABEE MILTON

Nov. 1726. 10 pds. for 200 A. On SS Meratock River & Quanhee Creek. Adj. JOHN COTTON. Wit: ELIZABETH MILTON, ROBERT DELJUM(?). November Court 1726.

B 196 JAMES WILLIAMSON, "doctor", TO ABRAHAM SHEEPHERD, "carpenter"
Nov. 5, 1726. 50 pds. for 100 A. Adj. "Windgate". Wit: JAMES MILLIKIN, THOMAS BUNTING. November Court 1726. *.

B 197 ELIZABETH MILTON TO BARABEE MILTON (MELTON)
Nov. 12, 1726. 10 pds. for 150 A. On NS Morattock River. Adj. PHILLIP JONES. Wit: JOHN COTTON, JUDITH COTTON. November Court 1726. *.

B 198 WILLIAM WHITEHEAD & WIFE RACHEL TO WILLIAM CAIN (CAN)
Nov. 6, 1726. 15 pds. for 290 A. Part of patent for 490 A. dated Aug. 10, 1720. Adj. THOMAS BRYANT, "said WHITEHEAD", WILLIAM BENET (BENNETS). Wit: JOHN SPEIR, GEORGE POWELL. November Court 1726. *.

B 200 JOHN KEEL TO NATHANIEL KEEL (KELLE)
Nov. 6, 1726. 100 A. For "...love and affection which I have and bear unto my Brother NATHANIEL KEELE..." On Cattawiskey Swamp. Wit: JOHN SPEIR, GEORGE POWELL. November Court 1726. *.

B 200 JOHN KEEL TO NATHANIEL KEEL
Nov. 9, 1726. 100 A. On WS Cattawiskey Swamp. For "...love and affection ...unto my Brother..." Wit: JOHN WINNS, LAZARUS THOMAS. November Court 1726. *.

B 201 Inventory of JOHN ROGERS
"A true inventory of all and singular the goods and chattels Rights and credits of John Rogers, Sen. dec'd. taken this 7th day of November 1726."

"4 coats | 1 pair Fire Tongs
1 jacket | 1 grid iron
4 shirts | 1 smothing Iron
2 hats | 1 pair still yards
2 pair shoes | 1 gun
2 pair stockings | 3 Iron wedges
6 pair drawers | 1 hoe
2 beds & furniture | 4 axes
2 chests | 1 carpenter adds
2 trunks | 1 cooper adds
1 table | hand saw & drawing knife
8 puter dishes | 1 pair compasses
3 basons | 2 hamers
8 plates | 1 chizel
2 porringers | 5 chears
2 Tankards | some niles
2 candlesticks | 2 door locks
29 spoons of Lighthorne | 1 Iron Ladle & flesh fork
1 Tunill (?) | 1 linen (linin) wheel
2 cups | 2 augars
1 mugg | 2 gimblets
3 stone Juggs | 17 cattle old & young
1 chamber pot | 6 sheep
4 glass bottles | 2 bridles
1 looking glass | 1 saddle
2 Iron Kettles | 1 pair sheep sheers
2 pots | 1 pair sisors
1 frying pan | 3 yds and 1/4 of Kersey (Jersey)
1 Iron pot Rack | 3 yds home spun cloth
1 pair pot hooks | some small smatter linene cloth
1 brass skillet | Some Trifeling lumber
1 Iron spit
Proved by the oath of JOHN ROGERS, Esq."

B 201 INVENTORY OF THE ESTATE OF ROBERT SMITH DECEASED
"Legies (?) to ye widow the best feather bed & furniture; a horse colt named Jockey. To his eldest Daughter ELIZABETH SMITH one feather bed & furniture. One colt a year old named Coney. To the youngest daug. MARY SMITH, one Bay Mare. To His son ROBT. SMITH a Bridle Saddle & new gun.

Debts Due from the sd. ROBT. SMITH estate to be paid in specie:

```
1 pd 10 sh
0     6
0     2    6 p.
1     9    0
0     1    0
3    08   06
```

By Bill money to Secretary & clk. fees 2=10

"5 cows
5 yearlings
1 3 yr. old steer
5 puter dishes (3 old 2 new)
2 wooden Trays
2 old puter plates
1 pr. cotton cards
1 Earthen plate
1 old wool wheel
1 Tankard
1 old hand saw
old candlestick
1 old coopers ax
1 Earthen Jugg
1 froo & drawing knife (?)
1 grubing hoe
4 d's cups
2 old broad hoes
2 old Iron pots & hooks
2 old hilling hoes
1 new (do) (ditto)
1 augar & guage
flat old smothing Iron
1 two edged (To war?)
1 old birding piece
2 wooden trays

1 pr cotton cards
1 powdering Tub
1 meal barrel
2 old water pails
1 beer cask
3 old slays
1 pair hand mill stones
1 old chamber pot
1 doz. spoons
2 or 3 meal sives
1 old pair bellows
6 glass bottles
1 Table
6 Joyner old hold fast
1 Joyner Rabbit
1 old age (adz)
1 old saddle Tree
1 small Earthen Jugg
1 old Looking Glass
1 334 #8 nails
540 single tens
1 old Earthen platter
1 old carpenters adds
2 Ews
1 ram

Proved in Court by oath of BARRABY MILTON, Ex."

B 202   ISAAC RICKS, administrator, OF NATHANIEL HOLLEY, Dec'd.
        "The whole Estate which is yet come to my hands of NATHANIEL HOLLEY
Dec'd. is 185 pds. 5 sh. After his debts paid and law charges 164 pds.
1 sh. His wodo. thirds taken out being 54 pds. 13 sh. 4 p. The remainder
being 110 pds. 12 sh. 4 p. There being five children and each part is
22:02:6. This being what I can find, but if there shall come any more to
my hands or a Remainder after I have paid all debts and Law charges, left
in my hands, I shall render a just (dect?) there of. This being given
under my hand. ISAAC RICKS, Administrator. Nov. 8, 1726. November Court
1726."

B 202   Aug. 17, 1726.   INVENTORY OF RICHARD TURBERVILLE, DEC'D.
        "1 bed sheet
1 rugg
1 blanket
1 Iron Pot & kittle
1 Frying pan
5 puter dishes
1 doz. spoons
1 qt. Tankard
4 plates
1 chest
1 Box Iron
2 wooling wheels
1 pr. cotton cards
1 hand saw
3 chissels
2 augers
3 gauges
1 set wedges
2 axes
3 hoes

1 froe (?)
1 sive
2 fleshing knives
1 pr. Carolina Mill Stones
2 Bread Trays
1 Sword
1 pad lock
1 prayer book & Bible
1 horse bridle & saddle
2 mares
1 horse colt
19 head of hoggs
6 cows & 5 yearlings
1 calf
2 steers 2 yr old
1 2 yr old heifer
200 A. land on SS Moratock River
1 2 gal Rundlet
1 pair sheep sheers
1 Barrel of gum

5 barrels	1 pair flesh forks
1 powdering tubb	2 pair sisers
1 beer cask	1 cowhide
1 pill	1 bull hide
1 pigm (?)	1 smothing Iron
1 washing Tubb	1 cart & wheels
2 slays	1 plough
1 loom	4 old hoes
2 stone Juggs	1 tennant Saw
3 bottles	

November Court 1726. Proved by WILLIAM TURBERVILLE, Esq.

B 203   ABEL (ABELL) CURTISS TO JAMES RUTLAND
        Feb. 15, 1726. 14 pds. for 200 A. On Cassiah Branch. Adj. JAMES
RUTLAND, ROBERT SHERRWOOD. Wit: JOHN SUTTON, JAMES_____. February Court
1726. *.

B 204   ROBERT EVANS & WIFE ANN TO JOHN MORRISE
        Feb. 14, 1726. 60 pds. for 100 A. On River Pocoson at Mile Branch.
Adj. Widow EARLEY, ROBERT EVANS. Wit: WILLIAM MARSHHURST, JOHN SUTTON.
February Court 1726. *.

B 205   JACOB LEWIS TO JEREMIAH BARNES (BARNS) of Perquimmons Precinct
        Feb. 10, 1726. 20 pds. for 200 A. "...beginning at JEREM BARNS
corner..." Adj. CHARLES JONES, GEORGE SMITH, JOHN EARLY. Wit: RICHARD
CHOASTEN, ROGER KENYON. February Court 1726. *.

B 206   WILLIAM STRICKLAND & WIFE MARTHA TO BARNABE MACKINNE, JUN.
        February 1726. 100 pds. for 100 A. At mouth of Spring Bottom &
Spring Gutt. On ye Great Ditch. Part of survey formerly surveyed for
WILLIAM BROWN and by him given to aforesaid MARTHA, but for want of patent
is now granted to his son JOHN BROWN...." Dated March 30, 1721. "...By
the said JOHN BROWN confirmed to us...." "...According to the said WILLIAM
BROWN's will it being a part of a patent of five hundr. and twenty five
(525 A.)". Wit: JOHN MACKINNE, RICHARD JACKSON. February Court 1726. *.

B 207   ARTHUR CRAWFORD TO JOHN POPE
        * 1726. 50 pds. 220 A. On SS Morattock River. "...it being one
patent for 220 A...." Adj. GEORGE SMITH, JOHN POPE, JACOB PATE. Wit:
BARN. MACKINNE, MATH. RAYFORD. February Court 1726. *.

B 208   GODFRY HOOKER & WIFE ELIZABETH TO WILLIAM HOOKER
        Jan. 16, 1726. 11 pds. 5 sh. for 100 A. On "ye Flatty Gut" at
mouth Deep Branch. Adj. COL. POLLOCK. Wit: JAMES BOON, WILLIAM CRAWFORD.
February Court 1726. *.

B 210   JACOB LEWIS & WIFE MARY TO SAMUEL KEEL
        Feb. 13, 1726. *. 200 A. On Chickapine Ridge at Clark Oak. Adj.
STEPHEN WILLIAMS, JAMES HOWARD, JOHN JONES. Wit:LAZARUS THOMAS, JOHN
WILLIAMS. February Court 1726. *.

B 211   JOHN DAVIS TO FRANCIS BROWN
        Jan. 11, 1726. 20 pds. for 440 A. On Mulberry Branch and WS
Cypress Swamp. Adj. FRANCIS BROWN, PHILLIP BROWN. Wit: JAMES PAGE, NICH-
OLAS FAIRLESS. February Court 1726. *.

B 213   JOHN DAVIS TO JAMES PAGE
        Jan. 14, 1726/27. Power of atty. to ack. sale of land on WS Cypress
Swamp. Wit: JOHN EARLY, SEN., JOHN EARLY, JUN. *. *.

B 213   TIMOTHY SPELLING of Isle of Wight, Va. TO ARTHUR CRAWFORD
        Feb. 2, 1726. 50 pds. for 300 A. On SS Merattock River. Adj.
WILLIAM GRAY. Patent dated Feb. 1, 1725. Wit: JOHN POPE, jurat, HENRY
CRAWFORD, JOSEPH LANE. February Court 1726. *.

B 214   MATTHEW SELLER TO TIMOTHY HIND
        Nov. 8, 1726. 5 pds. for 100 A. On SS Meherrin River at Redy
Swamp. Adj. OWIN CRAVIES (?). Part of patent cont. 170 A. granted Apr. 1,
1724. Wit: RICHARD WASHINGTON, JOHN COLSON (COLSSON). Feb. Court 1726. *.

38

38

B 215 PETER WEST & WIFE PRISSILLA (PRISCILLA) TO HENRY BAKER of Virginia
        Dec. 15, 1726. 400 A. "...for and in consideration of the rents
and covenants hereinafter to be paid done and performed...land at Little
Town whereon LEWIS WILLIAMS father of the above PRISCILLA lately lived and
dwelt and by his last will and testament devised to ...PRISCILLA..." BAKER
to have "...for and during the natural lives of HENRY BAKER, JUN. son of
said HENRY BAKER, JOHN BAKER another of the sons of said HENRY BAKER, and
JOHN PUGH, son of FRANCIS PUGH...and during the life of the longest liver
of them...paying yearly and every year...unto PETER and PRISCILLA ...on the
Feast of the Nativity...the rent of one eare of Indian Corn...." Wit: JOHN
_____, ROBERT RADFORD, RICHARD BARFIELD. February Court 1726. *.

B 217 WILLIAM POPE of Virginia to BARNABEE MACKINNE, JUN.
        *. 20 pds. for 100 A. On SS Merrattock River at Tuckahoe Marsh.
Land formerly granted to WILLIAM JONES by patent dated Apr. 5, 1720, and by
him elapsed for want of seating. Coming to said JONES by patent dated
Apr. 1, 1723. Wit: BARNABEE MACKINNE, JOHN MACKINNE. February Court
1726. *.

B 218 JOHN BROWN & JACOB BROWN TO BARNABEE MACKINNE, JUN.
        *. 40 pds. For 525 A. On SS Merattock River. Land formerly taken
up by WILLIAM BROWN and by him devised in his last will and testament to his
son JACOB BROWN. Lost and due to his son JOHN BROWN by patent dated
March 30, 1721. Adj. WILLIAM BROWN dec'd., JOHN BROWN, Cypress Gut. Wit:
JOHN MACKINNE, ISAAC RICKS. February Court 1726. *.

B 219 NICHOLAS BAGGET & WIFE MARY TO JOHN DICKINSON
        Feb. 4, 1726/27. 35 pds. for 150 A. On SS Yourah Swamp. Part of
tract granted to WILLIAM BRASSWELL by patent dated April 1, 1714. On WS
Quonkey Branch above "Oldfield." Wit: JOHN SUTTON, JAMES WOOD. February
Court 1726. *.

B 221 MARY BAGGET TO JOHN SUTTON
        Feb. 4, 1726/27. Power of atty. to ack. sale of land. Wit: JETHRO
MASHBORN, MARY SUTTON. February Court 1726. *.

B 221 LORDS PROPRIETORS TO AMBROSE AIRES
        Sept. 25, 1726. Grant. 178 A. Adj. MAJOR WEST. Land formerly
granted to Coll. THOMAS POLLOCK by patent granted April 5, 1720 "...and by
him elapsed for not seating and planting...." Signed: SIR RICHARD EVERARD,
Bar't., Gov. Recorded in Sec't'y. Office ROBERT FORSTER, Sec't'y. RICHARD
SANDERSON, THOMAS HARVEY, FRANCIS FORSTER, EDWARD MOSELEY, C. GALE, EDMOND
GALE, WILLIAM REED.

B 222 AMBROSE AIRES TO THOMAS POWELL
        Dec. 4, 1726. 15 pds. for 178 A. At Fork of Cashy River "in ye
other side the body of the Pattent...." Wit: THOMAS RYAN, JOHN PEAT.
May Court 1727. EDWARD MASHBORNE D. C/C.

B 223 AMBROSE AIRES (ARRISS) & WIFE MARY WHITE TO THOMAS POWELL
        Apr. 8, 1727. 15 barrels of pitch for 178 A. Adj. land formerly
COLL. ROBERT WEST's called "New Market" on Cashay Swamp. Wit: SAMUEL
HERRING, ANN HERRING. May Court 1727. COLL. ROBERT WEST by virtue power
of atty. ack. in open court. *.

B 225 WILLIAM RICKS TO JOHN COLSON (COLSSON)
        May 4, 1727. 10 pds. for 640 A. Adj. ESTHER RICKS. Being full
patent granted WILLIAM RICKS Feb. 1, 1725. Wit: ROBERT SCOTT, RICHARD
WASHINGTON. May Court 1727. *.

B 226 WILLIAM CURLEE & WIFE MARTHA TO EDWARD BRYAN, SEN.
        Feb. 9, 1727. 25 pds. for 317 A. On WS Canaan Swamp up "ye Great
Branch" between said BRYAN and JAMES MCGLOHON. Wit: LEWIS BRYAN, SIMON
BRYAN. May Court 1727. *.

B 227 LORDS PROPRIETORS TO WILLIAM JONES
        Dec. 6, 1720. Grant. 609 A. On WS Cashay Swamp (Casia). Which
land was granted July 20, 1717 to ROBERT HICKSON "...and by him elapsed..."
Due JONES by order of "councill" Aug. 10, 1720. Signed: CHARLES EDEN, Esq.,
Gov. Recorded in Sec't'y. Office J. LOVICK, Sec't'y. RICHARD SANDERSON,

THOMAS POLLOCK, FRED. JONES.

B 228 WILLIAM JONES, SEN. TO WILLIAM JONES, JUN.
        May 10, 1727. "...to my son WILLIAM JONES, JUN. all Right title to
within mentioned patent...." Wit: JOHN DEW, FRANCIS HOBSON. May Court
1727. *.

B 229 WILLIAM RICKS & WIFE ESTHER TO RICHARD WASHINGTON
        May 11, 1727. 20 pds. for 180 A. At Mill Swamp and Turkey Swamp.
"...according to courses of patent...." Wit: ROBERT SCOTT, JOHN COLSON.
May Court 1727. *.

B 230 PHILLIP EDEN TO JOHN BOND (BONDE) of Bath County
        Feb. 16, 1726. 35 pds. for 230 A. Part of patent of 950 A (?)
granted HENRY WHEELER in 1717. On SS Meherring River. Adj. THOMAS KIRBY.
Also adj. "land sold by JOHN BAYLEY and land I sold ARTHUR WILLIAMS." At
head Spring Branch. Wit: JOSEPH DARDEN, jurat, WILLIAM FOLK, May Court
1727. *.

B 231 WILLIAM CURLEE & WIFE MARTHA TO JAMES MACGLOHON
        Feb. 9, 1726/27. 25 pds. for 317 A. On WS Canaan Swamp. Adj.
EDWARD BRYAN, SEN. on "ye Great Branch." Wit: THOMAS SPIERS, CONF. (?)
LUTEN. May Court 1727. *.

B 233 THOMAS KIRBEY & WIFE ELIZABETH TO JOHN MCDANIEL
        April 21, 1727. 12 pds. for 95 A. NWS Yourah Swamp. Wit: ESTHER
RICKS, ROBERT SLAUTER (SLANTER?). May Court 1727. *.

B 234 WILLIAM RICKS & WIFE ESTHER TO THOMAS KIRBEY
        May 9, 1727. 5 pds. for 640 A. On SS Meherring River. Adj. HENRY
WHEELER. Patent granted ESTHER RICKS Feb. 1, 1725. Wit: ROBERT SCOTT,
JOHN COLSON. May Court 1727. *.

B 235 DAVID JONES & WIFE ANN TO JAMES NORWELL
        Feb. 25, 1726. 12 pds. 5 sh. for 30 A. On Wickacorne Creek at
mouth Little Creek. Wit: AARON OLIVER, SUSAN OLIVER. May Court 1727. *.

B 236 JOHN NAIRNE TO HENRY BONNER
        March 7, 1726/27. 20 pds. for 300 A. On SS Morattock River. Adj.
JAMES DENTON. Wit: DANIEL MCDANIEL, JOHN SURGINER. May Court 1727. *.

B 237 JOHN STEWARD & WIFE SARAH TO EDWARD HOWARD
        May 10, 1727. 25 pds. for 300 A. On NS Roanoke River "within 150
yds. of Peach Blossom oldfield." Adj. JAMES WOODS. Wit: TINAKER TAGNE,
THOMAS JONES. May Court 1727. *.

B 239 JOHN BRYAN (BRYANT) TO FRAN (CIS) BROWN
        Jan . 10, 1726. 16 pds. for 200 A. In St. John's Neck on ye
Cypress Swamp. Adj. HENRY RHODES. Wit: LAWRANCE MAGUE, *. ISAAC KIF
(KEEFE?) by power of Atty. from JOHN BRYAN ack. within deed of sale. *. *.

B 240 JOHN BRYAN TO ISAAC KIF (KIFF)
        May 8, 1727. Power of atty. to ack. sale of land adj. HENRY RHODES
and "where JOHN DAVIS lived" cont. 200 A. unto FRANCIS BROWN. Wit: LEWIS
BRYAN, JUN., SIMON BRYAN. *. *.

B 241 JOHN EARLY (EARLEY), JUN. TO THOMAS RYAN
        April 19, 1727. 40 pds. for 350 A. On Holly Swamp adj. JAMES
WILKSON. Land surveyed to JOHN EARLEY, SEN. JOHN EARLY, JUN. bound to
THOMAS RYAN for 40 pds. Assigns land to void obligation. Wit: CHARLES
PEAL, BEERSHABE EARLEY. May Court 1727. *.

B 242 INVENTORY OF ESTATE OF ROBERT EVANS, DEC'D.
        March 7 Court. Proved by oath of ANN EVANS.
        4 cows   3 hoes
        3 calves   4 axes
       35 head other cattle   14-1/2 lbs. old iron
        1 horse   1 earthen porringer
        8 puter dishes   1 half hour glass
        4 basons   3 chests

12 plates	1 table & form
1 tankard	2 water pails
1 qt. pot	2 piggons
2 puter porringers	2 cans
1 salt salter	1 tub
3 doz. spoons	2 chears
3 graters	2 feather beds and furniture
1 looking glass	1 bed steed
3 pocket bottles	1 gun
15 glass bottles	1 dutill knife
2 vinegar bottles	12 Turn.d. Trenchers
2 drinking glasses	3 wooden bowls
2 cups	3 iron hooks
23 earthen vessels	1 Iron chain
1 stone jugg	1 spinning wheel
4 Iron pots	2 pair cards
3 pair pot hooks	12 old barrels
1 frying pan	6 old hogs heads
1 pair fire tongs	1 saddle
1 pair flesh forks	1 bridle
1 Iron Ladle	1 bridle bit
1 Brass skinner	1 stock lock
1 candle stick	1 spring lock
1 grid iron	1 swivel stirup Iron
1 smoothing Iron	1 rasor
2 heaters	1 chisil
1 pair stilliards	1 pair sisers
3 iron wedges	2 meal senis
1 hammer	1 Bible
1 cross cut saw	1 pair Mill Stones

B 242   BEALE BROWN TO JOHN POWER
        Dec. 5, 1726. 60 pds. for 235 A. By patent bearing date Nov. 7,
1723. Wit: JOSEPH DARDEN, JOHN PORTIS. March Court 1727. *.

B 243   JOB MEADOR of Chowan Precinct TO SAMUEL WOODARD
        Oct. 25, 1726. 40 pds. for 640 A. On SS Chinkapeen at mouth of
Reedy Branch. Wit: JOHN JORDAN, JUN., WILLIAM BADHAM. Oct. 25, 1726.
N. C. Court. C. GALE C.J. "Is recorded for ED. MASHBORNE, D. C/C."

B 245   WILLIAM GRAY TO ROBERT HODGES
        March 7, 1726/27. 80 pds. for 180 A. On NES little Roquis Swamp.
Adj. JAMES WILLIAMS, RICHARD MILTON. Wit: JOHN GRAY, JOSEPH MOOR. March
Court. *. *.

B 246   JAMES PEEKE & WIFE MARGARET TO ROBERT WARREN
        March 7, 1726. 30 pds. for 340 A. On Horse Swamp Adj. JOHN BAR-
FIELD, THOMAS STURGES. Wit: RICHARD HORSLEY, SAMUEL WILLIAMS. March
Court. *. *.

B 247   LORDS PROPRIETORS TO JOHN DEW
        Feb. 1, 1725. Grant. 640 A. On SS Meherron River. Adj. "BUSBY's
line," JOHN BOND. Signed: RICHARD EVERARD, Baronet, Governor. Recorded
in Sec't'y. Office by ROBERT FOSTER, Sec't'y. C. GALE, THOS. HARVEY,
_____WORLEY, EDM. GALE, FRAN. FOSTER, J. LOVICK.

B 248   JOHN DEW TO JOHN BOND
        Feb. 14, 1726. 20 pds for *. "within mentioned tract." Wit: THOMAS
SPIRES, JOHN DARDEN, ROBERT FORSTER. March 7th Court. *. *.

B 249   THOMAS MANDEW & WIFE HANNAH of Ise of Wite, Va. to TINAKER HAYNE
                                        (HAYNES), (merchant)
        Feb. 14, 1726. 126 pds. for 370 A. Adj. SAMUEL WILLIAMS, JOHN
BROWN. Wit: EDW. HOWARD, STEPHEN HOWARD, RICHARD HORSLEY. March 7, 1727.
*.

B 250   BEALE BROWN TO JOHN POWER
        Nov. 10, 1726. 150 pds. for 320 A. According to patent dated
Nov. 6, 1706. Assigned to SARAH BROWN wife of WILLIAM BROWN. Wit: JAMES
JENKINS, FRAN. BENTON. March Court 1727. HENRY WEST by power of atty.

from BROWN ack. within deed of sale to JOHN POWER in open court. *. *.

B 251   BEALE BROWN TO HENRY WEST
        Feb. 24, 1726. *. *. Power of atty. to ack. sale to JOHN POWER of
235 A. Wit: WILLIAM WALL, JOHN RIAL. *. *.

B 251   ABEL CURTIS, (blacksmith), TO JOHN HENARD
        Feb. 15, 1726/27. 20 pds. For 440 A. "betwixt western & middle
Branch of Cushey." Part of patent of 640 A. dated Aug. 1, 1726. Wit:
WILLIAM WHITFIELD, JOHN DICKINSON, JAMES COSTON. March Court 1727. *.

B 253   PETER PARKER & HENRY RHODES & WIVES GRACE PARKER & ELIZABETH RHODES
        TO DANIEL HEISMITH
        *. 7 pds. for 150 A. on Cashay Swamp at Broad Branch. Wit: RICHARD
OLDNER, LAZARUS THOMAS. March Court 1727. *.

B 252   TARLOW O'QUIN (TARLOUGH) TO FRANCIS PUGH of Nancemond Co., Va.
        Feb. 15, 1726. 160 pds. for 300 A. plus * A. Place where TARLOW
O'QUIN now dwelleth called "Runaway Meadows" which was given him by WILLIAM
EASON by deed dated July 12, 1722. Recorded in Chowan Precinct Sept. 12,
1722 by ROBERT HICKS. One other piece of land cont. 300 A. which was
granted Aug. 4, 1723. Recorded in secretary's office. On NS Morratuck.
Wit: WILLIAM LITTLE, THOMAS SPIER. Bertie Court March 1727.

B 254   JOSEPH FROWELL & WIFE TIBITHA, (shoemaker), to EDWARD SMITHWICK
        Jan. 14, 1724/25. *. 273 A. in Kisianeck. Adj. PEANS LEGET, JOHN
LEGET, LUKE MEESSELL. Wit: WILLIAM MEESEL (?), JAMES LEGETT, ROBERT
FORSTER. March Court 1727. *.

B 255   EDMUND SMITHWICK TO WILLIAM SMITH
        June 27, 1723. *. "as the patent mentions." Adj. JOHN SEPHON,
ROBERT ANDERSON on Roquist Swamp. Wit: FRANCIS HOBSON, ANN HOBSON, ROBERT
FORSTER, jurat. March Court 1727. *.

B 255   WILLIAM JONES & WIFE MARY of Chowan Precinct TO JAMES CASTELAW
        April 12, 1721. 23 pds. for 150 A. On SS Kesai River Pocoson.
Adj. COLL. POLLOCK, RICHARD (FRYARS?), MARTEN GARDNER. Wit: J. PLOWMAN,
MARY WHITE. Chowan Court in Queen Ann's Town Tuesday April 3, 1721. JOHN
EDWARDS by power of atty. from CASTELAW accepted deed. THOMAS HENMAN C/C.

B 256   JAMES CASTELAW & WIFE SARAH TO GEORGE POLLOCK
        Jan. 1723/24. For "valuable consideration in hand" Assignment of
within mentioned deed to GEORGE POLLOCK, Esq. *. *. *. *.

B 257   JAMES CASTELAW & WIFE SARAH TO HENRY GUSTON & JAMES MILIKIN
        May 10, 1726. *. *. "...we...do assign all our right title and
interest in the within mentioned deed of sale...." Wit: THOMAS SMITH,
JAMES BLACK. N. C. Court Oct. 28, 1726. C. GALE C. J. Test. EDW. MASH-
BORNE D. C/C.

B 257   HENRY SPELLER TO RICHARD SWAIN
        Aug. 5, 1726. 25 pds. for 172 A. On "southmost branch of Roquist
butting and bounding on his own line...." Wit: WILLIAM CHARLTON, JOHN
DAVIS. N. C. Court Dec. 29, 1726. C. GALE C.J. Test. EDW. MASHBORNE
D. C/C.
                                                              BROMELEY
B 259   THOMAS BITTERLY, feltmaker, of Edenton in Chowan Prec't. TO GEORGE /
        June 15, 1726. 100 pds. for 1420 A. NS Merattuck River Adj. HENRY
SPELLER. Lands formerly granted COGSWELL & DOWNING. Wit: WILLIAM LITTLE,
JOHN JONES. N. C. Court March 20, 1726/27. C. GALE C.J. Test. EDW. MASH-
BORNE D.C/C.

B 260   MARTIN CROMEN of Cashia TO THOMAS ANDREWS
        Oct. 8, 1726. For "a sum of money agreed upon" 200 A. On SS Bear
(Bare) Swamp. Plantation formerly belonging to RICHARD PIERON. Adj. JOHN
HARDIN, COLL. POLLOCK. Wit: JOHN ARMSTRONG, THOMAS COPLIN. N. C. Court
Nov. 2, 1727. C. GALE C.J. Test. EDW. MASHBORNE D.C/C.

B 261   THOMAS MACCLENDON TO SAMUEL WOODARD of Chowan Prec't.
        Oct. 24, 1727. 25 pds. for 130 A. On Chinkapine Creek. Adj.

PHILLIP BROWN, COLL. MAULE. Wit: W. BADHAM, JOHN OVERTON. N. C. Court
Oct. 25, 1727. C. GALE C. J. Test. EDW. MASHBORNE D. C/C.

B 262 WILLIAM CHARLTON TO RICHARD SWAIN & WIFE ANN
    *. *. 600 A. "...for natural love and affection I have and do bear
unto RICHARD SWAIN & ANNA his wife...and heirs of said RICHARD begotten of
the body of aforesaid ANN..." Land on Sothhaca Creek and Roquist. Known
as "Meadow Tract." Wit: LUKE MIZELL, ALEXANDER RAY. N. C. Court June 6,
1726. C. GALE C. J. Test. EDW. MASHBORNE D. C/C.

B 264 MICHAEL KING TO MARY KING
    Nov. 9, 1726. 35 pds. for 100 A. "square." On Cushock(?) "betwixt"
CHRISTOPHER VON LUVEN's dwelling house, THOMAS BARBO (?)...All rights "ex-
cept all the aple trees and the planks of the upper floor in the house..."
Wit: MART. FRED. RASOR, ANN BALL. N. C. Court Jan.27, 1726. C. GALE C. J.
Test. EDW. MASHBORNE D. C/C.

B 265 JOHN LOVICK, Esq. Secretary of North Carolina & WIFE PENELOPE TO
    JOHN GALLANT
    5 sh. & "love & affection they do bear unto their brother JOHN GAL-
LANT, Esq." "...PENELOPE widow late relick of COLL. WILLIAM MAULE, dec'd.
...whereas WILLIAM MAULE by his last will and testament...did devise unto
PENELOPE his then wife...land on Chowan River att the ferrying place...
called Mount Gallant..." Wit: WILLIAM LITTLE, THOMAS LOVICK. N. C. Court
May 19, 1727. C. GALE C. J. Test. EDW. MASHBORNE D. C/C. "...PENELOPE
privately examined pursuant to an act of assembly for fem coverts to pass
land..."

B 266 WILLIAM LITTLE TO JOHN GALLANT
    "5 sh and love and affection too"....The boat at ye sd. Ferry with
her tackle and appurtenances rent bargained and acquit all my fees and
charges there on this 19th May 1727..." *. *. *.

B 266 EDMOND SMITHWICK TO JOHN STANCILL
    Nov. 29, 1726. *. 320 A. On SS Morattock River Adj. JOHN GARDNER
"down the Savannah...." Wit: THOMAS BRYANT, JOHN GARDNER, N. C. Court.
Oct. 31, 1727. C. GALE C. J. Test. EDMUND. MASBORNE D. C/C.

B 267 JOHN STANCILL & WIFE SARAH TO EDMOND SMITHWICK
    Jan. 12, 1726. 30 pds. for 100 A. On Kisah Neck adj. NATHAN MOORE,
known as "Deer Hall". "...she being first privately examined as by an act
of assembly of this province..." Wit: JOHN GARDNER, THOMAS BRYANT. N. C.
Court Oct. 3, 1727. C. GALE C. J. Test. ED. MASHBORNE D. C/C. Witnesses
to the private examination being: ELIZABETH CLAYTON and JOHN GARDNER.

B 268 SAMUEL SMITHWICK TO EDMOND SMITHWICK
    Jan. 12, 1726. 30 pds. for 520 A. On SS Morattock River called "The
Long Ridge" Butting and binding as the patent mentions. Wit: JOHN GARDNER,
THOMAS BRYANT, JOHN STANCILL. N. C. Court Oct. 31, 1727. C. GALE C. J.
Test. EDW. MASHBORNE D. C/C.

B 269 EDMOND SMITHWICK TO MICHAEL KING
    Oct. 7, 1726. 110 pds. for 200 A. In Kesia Neck called "Old House"
Adj. Kesia & Merattock River. "...excepting twenty foot square being a
burying place...." Wit: MART. FRED. RASOR, ROBERT BILL (BELL?). N. C.
Court Jan. 27, 1726. C. GALE C. J. EDW. MASHBORNE D. C/C.

B 270 JAMES SANDERS TO DAVID OSHEAL of Nansimond Co., Va.
    Oct. 10, 1726. 75 pds. for *. "...bound...in penal sum of 300 pds.
...the obligation is such that JAMES SANDERS...assigns a certain parcill of
land...on western branch of Nansemond River in Virginia which was devised
to him by will of RICHARD SANDERS his dec'd father...." DAVID OSHEAL does
settle on JAMES SANDERS lands, stock, etc. in Bertie. Wit: WILLIAM LITTLE,
JOHN BONDE. Nov. Court 1726. *.

B 272 JOHN JOHNSON & WIFE MARY of Perquimmons Precinct to MARTIN CROMEN
    Oct. 30, 1727. 30 pds. for 100 A. on Kesia River . Adj. JAMES
FROST, DANIEL HENDRICKS. Wit: JOSEPH GILBERT, JOHN GILBERT. N. C. Court
Nov. 16, 1727. C. GALE C. J. Test. EDW. MASHBORNE D. C/C.

B 273 EDWARD POWERS TO JOHN BONDE

May 15, 1727. 30 pds. for 410 A. On NS Meherrin River in the fork of Horse Pasture Creek. Adj. JOHN CHESHERS, BEAL BROWN. Wit: JOHN POWER, jurat, JAMES JENKINS. August Court 1727. *.

B 274   JOHN COTTON (COLTON) TO WILLIAM LITTLE
Aug. 9, 1727. 50 pds. for 450 A. "...the remaining part not sold out to ROGER CASE being 50 acres...out of 500 A. patent dated Feb. 1, 1726 ..." On Occanechee Swamp. Adj. JAMES ANDERSON. Wit: ROBERT FORSTER, EDWARD MASHBORNE. August Court 1727. *.

B 275   JOHN BONDE TO WILLIAM LITTLE
*. 30 pds. for 410 A. On Meherren Neck. Adj. JOHN CHESHER, BEAL BROWN. Land purchased by JOHN BONDE of EDWARD POWERS by deed dated May 15, 1727. Patent dated Nov. 7, 1723 to POWERS. Wit: ROBERT FORSTER, EDWARD MASHBORNE. August Court 1727. *.

B 275   JOHN POWERS TO WILLIAM LITTLE
May 15, 1727. 50 pds. for 190 A. On NS Meherren River. Wit: JOSEPH DARDEN, JOHN BONDE. August Court 1727. *.

B 276   FORTUNE HOLDBEE TO WILLIAM LITTLE
July 5, 1727. 15 pds. For *. "...plantation where I now live...formerly PAUL BUNCHes..." Wit: ROBERT FORSTER, JAMES MILLIKIN. "I FORTUNE HOLDEBEE do appoint WILLIAM LITTLE, Esq. my (atty.) in all causes and matters whatsoever July 5, 1727..." Test: JAMES MILLIKIN. Aug. Court 1727.*.

B 277   JOSEPH LANE, JUN. TO WILLIAM HOGGATT (HOGGATE)
Aug. 8, 1727. 50 pds. for 250 A. On NS Moratock River at mouth of Spring Branch. Part of patent of 640 A. formerly granted WILLIAM JONES and by him made over to JOSEPH LANE. Wit: BAR. MACKINNE, SIMON JEFFRYS. Aug. Court 1727. ROBERT FORSTER C/C.

B 278   THOMAS TAPLEY (TAPLIN) TO PHILLIP MULCEY
Feb. 26, 1726/27. 30 pds. for 240A. Part of patent granted for 340 A. dated Feb. 1, 1725. On SS Moratock River. Adj. ARTHUR DAVIS on Connocare Swamp. Wit: BAR. MACKINNE, MARY MACKINNE. August Court 1727. *.

Note: Page 278 followed immediately by page 289.

B 289   DANIEL CRAWLEY TO GIDEON GIBSON
Aug. 7, 1727. 20 pds. for 100 A. On NS Morattock River. Part of patent granted ROBERT LAND for 380 A. between JOHN PACE and EDWARD CLARK on mouth of Quincy Gutt. Wit: BARN. MACKINNE, jurat, BARN. MACKINNE, JUN. August Court 1727. ROBERT FORSTER C/C.

B 289   BARTHOLOMEW CHAVIS (CHAVERS) TO WILLIAM CHAVIS (CHAVERS)
*. *. 200 A. "...for love and natural affection I bear to my son WILLIAM CHAVERS. "Land on SS Morattock River. Part of tract granted to me for 630 A. dated July 30, 1726. Wit: BARN. MACKINNE, jurat, GEORGE PACE. August Court 1727. ROBERT FORSTER C/C.

B 290   JAMES TURNER & WIFE ANN of Isle of Wight Co., Va. TO JOHN SPEIR
July 24, 1727. 50 pds. for 400 A. On SS Morutuck River. Called "Cheslfield." Part of two tract. One by patent dated March 1, 1721. The other part of 640 A. granted WILLIAM GRAY dated April 5, 1720. Adj. JOHN NAIRN on Cattail Marsh on the "footway to JOHN JACKSON's," JOHN SPEIR, JOHN LOVICK, JAMES TURNER, JOHN BRYAN. In "Goose Meadow." Wit: WILLIAM HART, JOHN BRYAN, jurat. August Court 1727. ROBERT FORSTER C/C.

B 292   JOHN DICKINSON & WIFE REBEKAH TO RICHARD SUMNER
Apr. 15, 1727. 8 pds. for 150 A. Above "Oldfield" on WS Quonkey Branch. Wit: JOHN SUTTON, JETHRO MASHBORNE. August Court 1727. ROBERT FORSTER C/C.

B 293   JOSEPH SIMMS TO GIDEON GIBSON
Aug. 8, 1727. 30 pds. for 300 A. On SS Merottuck River by patent dated Feb. 1, 1725. On the "brow of a hill of Streite Marsh." Wit: BARN. MACKINNE, jurat, WILLIAM RICKS. August Court 1727. ROBERT FORSTER C/C.

B 294   WILLIAM LOWE TO GEORGE PACE
Aug. 7, 1727. 40 pds. for 125 A. On ES Elk Marsh and SS Morrattock River. Part of patent for 250 A. dated Aug. 4, 1723. Wit: BARN. MCKINNE,

44

jurat, BARN. MCKINNE, JUN. August Court 1727. ROBERT FORSTER C/C.

B 295 BENJAMIN JOYNER TO JOHN FARROW
      Aug. 7, 1727. 3 pds. 7 sh. for 50 A. On SS Meherrin River and Kir-
bey Creek. Part of patent for 200 A. dated April 1, 1723. Wit: FRANCIS
boikine(?), NICHOLAS (J)OYNER (TOYNER?). August Court 1727. ROBERT FORS-
TER C/C.

B 296 WILLIAMS SIMMS TO NICHOLAS TYNER
      Aug. 1, 1726. 15 pds. for 300 A. On SS Meherrin River on Little
Swamp. Wit: ROBERT SIMMS, WILLIAM BOON. August Court 1727. *.

B 297 THOMAS KIRBY TO JOHN GODLEY
      Aug. 8, 1727. 13 pds. for 240 A. In Pottakarsie Woods. Wit: WILL-
IAM RICKS, JAMES BRYAN, W. KINCHEN. August Court 1727. *.

B 298 LORDS PROPRIETORS TO ROBERT FORSTER
      Oct. 29, 1725. Grant for 300 A. On WS Ahorskey Marsh to side of
Catawitsky Pecoson. Land formerly granted JAMES BOON March 6, 1721 and "by
him elapsed." Signed: SIR RICH. EVERARD, Barrt. & Gov. ROBERT FORSTER
Sec't'y., C. GALE, RICH. SANDERSON, THOS. HARVEY, JOHN ALLEN, WM. REED, ED.
MOSELEY, FRAN. FORSTER, F(?) CLAYTON.

B 299 ROBERT FORSTER TO CAPT. JAMES BOON
      *. 5 pds. for "within mentioned tract." Wit: WILLIAM DANIEL, THOMAS
JONES. August Court 1727. *.

B 299 WILLIAM POPE TO WILLIAM EVANS
      Aug. 8, 1727. "considerable sum" for 350 A. On NS Merattuck River
on Mill Creek. Land was patented March 1, 1719 by DANIEL HAGAN and by him
"elapsed." Now due WILLIAM POPE by order of "Councill" dated April 1,
1723. Wit: ROBERT SHERED, WILLIAM ELDRIDGE. August Court 1727. *.

B 300 MARY COLSON & HER SON JOHN COLSON TO ROBERT GREEN of Surry Co., Va.
      Aug. 3, 1727. 10 pds. for 370 A. MARY COLSON, widow and relict of
JACOB COLSON. JOHN, son of said JACOB and MARY. Land on Morattock River
Adj. JOHN SPAN, HENRY JONES. Part of 640 A. granted JACOB COLSON. Wit:
ABRAHAM BURTON, JOHN GREEN, jurat, JOHN MASSEY, jurat. August Court 1727.*

B 302 JOHN SPEIR TO HENRY WALKER formerly of Virginia
      Aug. 7, 1727. 30 pds. for 200 A. On SS Meratuck River. Adj. JOHN
NAIRN on NS Meadow Marsh where JOHN BRYAN did live. Wit: JOHN SURGINOR,
WILLIAM DANIEL, CORNELIUS PERCE. August Court 1727. *.

B 304 JOHN GRAY TO THEOPHILUS WILLIAMS
      Aug. 8, 1727. 80 pds. 7 sh. for 640 A. WS Falling Run. Adj. WILLIAM
GRAY, JOHN WILLIAMS. Wit: JAMES CASTELAW, SAMUEL WILLIAMS. August Court
1727. *.

B 305 JAMES TURNER & WIFE ANN of Isie of Wight, Va. TO JOSEPH WALL, SEN.
      Nov. 7, 1724. 5 pds. for 100 A. On SS Morattock River at dividing
line between THOMAS HOWEL, SEN. and JOSEPH WALL. Part of 640 A. tract
dated March 1, 1719. Wit: THOMAS HOWEL, GEORGE WILLIAMS. Aug. Court 1727.*

B 306 JAMES TURNER of Isle of Wight, Va. TO FRANCIS BOYKIN
      Aug. 3, 1727. "...a valuable sum" for 240 A. On SS Meherrin River
in Chowan Precinct. Said land granted to JAMES TURNER by Hon. CHARLES
EDEN, Esq. by patent dated March 1, 1719. Part of 540 A. At mouth of Great
Branch. Wit: JOSEPH WALL, ROBERT HART. August Court 1727. *.

B 307 HENRY BRADLEY TO JOHN HOWELL (HOWEL) of Isle of Wight, Va.
      Aug. 3, 1727. Two Negro men called Cuffe & Frank for 340 A. On WS
Chowan River Adj. RICHARD BOOTH. "as mentioned in the patent." Wit: WILL-
IAM BRYAN, LEWIS BRYAN. August Court 1727. *.

B 309 DANIEL MACKDANIEL & WIFE SARAH TO HENRY TURNER
      Aug. 7, 1727. 10 pds. for 200 A. On SS Morattock River Adj. JOHN
NAIRN. JOHN WILL (JUNIERS). Patent dated Aug. 4, 1723. Wit: JOHN BENBO,
NATHANIEL PIGOTT. August Court 1727. *.

B 310 DANIEL MACDANIEL & WIFE SARAH TO THOMAS TURNER

May 8, 1727. 10 pds. for 200 A. On SS Morattock River Adj. JOHN NAIRN, "WHITMELL's corner." Patent date Aug. 4, 1723. Wit: JAMES TURNER, JOSEPH TURNER. August Court 1727. *.

B 312 BARTHO(LOMEW) CHAVERS TO EDWARD SIMMONS
Nov. 4, 1726. 40 pds. for 430 A. On SS Morattock River. Adj. WILL-IAM CHAVERS and Turkee(?) Pocoson. Part of patent to CHAVERS for 630 A. dated July 30, 1726. Wit: BARTHO. (?) MACKINNE, MARGARETT MURFREE. August Court 1727.

B 313 ANTHONY LEWIS & WIFE ELIZABETH TO JOHN SMITH
Aug. 7, 1727. 150 pds. for 640 A. Bounded according to patent obtained by ANTHONY LEWIS, SEN. Wit: BENJAMIN HILL, JAMES JENKINS. August Court 1727. *.

B 314 MATHEW SCELLER(S) TO JOHN SCELLER
Aug. 7, 1727. 10 pds. for 100 A. On SS Meherrin River at Patty's Delight. Part of patent for 192 A. dated Feb. 1, 1725. Wit: HENRY TURNER, DANIEL O'QUIN. August Court 1727. *.

B 315 CHARLES JONES & WIFE SARAH TO MOSES PRICE
Aug. 7, 1727. 12 pds. for 150 A. On western fork of White Oak Swamp Adj. JACOB LEWIS, CHARLES JONES, JUN. Wit: WILLIAM CRANFORD, ANTHONY WILLIAMS. August Court 1727. *.

B 317 HENRY EMERSON & WIFE MARY TO JAMES PEEKE
Feb. 14, 1726. *. 300A. Near Roanoke River on Flaggy Run. Adj. JOHN _____. Wit: BENJAMIN HILL, JAMES JENKINS, jurat. August Court 1727. *.

B 318 ROBERT CARLISLE & WIFE ELIZABETH of Surry Co., Va. to SAMUEL CHAPPEL and JAMES GEE of Surry Co., Va.
Nov. 13, 1727. 5 sh. for 500 A. On Ocoeneechee Plains at Cypress Meadow. Patent dated March 29, 1727. "...uper moiety or one half...to JAMES GEE...and other moiety or one half...to SAMUEL CHAPPELL..." Wit: WILLIAM WASHINGTON, RICHARD WASHINGTON. November Court 1727. *. (Land leased for one year.)

B 319 ROBERT CARLISLE & WIFE ELIZABETH of Surry Co., Va. to JAMES GEE & SAMUEL CHAPPELL
Nov. 14, 1727. 15 pds. for 500 A. On Ocoeneechee Plains. Land previously leased for one year; now sold "forever." Wit: WILLIAM WASHINGTON, RICHARD WASHINGTON. November Court 1727. *.

B 320 WILLIAM FROST TO RICHARD PACE, JUN.
*. 10 pds. for 50 A. Part of patent to DAVID CUMMINS for 340 A. dated March 1, 1726. Adj. ALEXANDER BANE (which land sold out of same patent), WILLIAM FROST. Wit: HENRY WHELLER (WHEELER), EMPEROR WHELLER, jurat. November Court 1727. *.

B 321 JAMES DENTON & WIFE CHRISTIAN TO CAPT. JOHN SPEIR
Dec. 7, *. 180 pds. for 580 A. on SS Morattock River according to patent dated April 6, 1722. Wit: THOMAS BRYAN, PETER WEST. November Court 1727. *.

B 322 LAZARUS THOMAS TO ROBERT ROGERS of Nansemond Co., Va.
Nov. 13, 1727. 20 pds. for 400 A. Between Deep Creek and Katherine Creek. Wit: JAMES HOLLAND, JAMES RUTLAND. November Court 1727. *.

B 324 WILLIAM BOON & WIFE ELIZABETH TO HUBBARD GIBSON, SEN. & DAUGHTER MARY
Nov. 13, 1727. 6 pds. 10 sh. for 100 A. On NS Morattock River, Cypress Swamp, Beaverdam Swamp. Adj. WILLIAM STRICKLAND, SEN., ROBERT SIMMS. Part of patent for 340 A. granted WILLIAM BOON March 8, 1711/12. Wit: NATHAN COOPER, THOMAS BOON, jurat. November Court 1727. *.

B 325 JOHN POPE TO RICHARD WASHINGTON
Nov. 14, 1727. 30 pds. for 216 A. On Looking Glass Swamp. Patent granted JOHN POPE November 7, 1723. Wit: SOLOMON JONES, SAMUEL CHAPPELL. November Court 1727. *.

B 326 WILLIAM BUSH (BOUSH) TO HENRY BRADLEY, JUN.

Dec. 5, 1727. 20 pds. for 130 A. On Bear Swamp. Adj. ROBERT EVANS, BENJAMIN WARREN. Wit: *. *. November Court 1727. *.

B 328 JOHN LEONARD TO HENRY JONES
Nov. 14, 1727. 10 pds. for 230 A. On NS Morattock River at Deep Bottom. Adj. WILLIAM REAVES, BARRY MELTON. Wit: JAMES GEE, SAMUEL CHAP-PELL. November Court 1727. *.

B 329 SAMUEL WILLIAMS TO CLEMON STRADFORD
Oct. 24, 1727. 8 pds. for 160 A. On NS Morattock River. Adj. RICHARD MELTON "above ye sd WILLIAMS dwelling house..." Part of 640 A. patent dated April 1, 1723. Wit: JOHN DUFFIELD, SAMUEL O CANNADAY. November Court 1727. *.

B 330 WILLIAM JONES, SEN. & WIFE MARY TO HENRY ROWELL
Nov. 7, 1727. 40 pds. for 440 A. On SS Kesai Swamp. Part of 640 A. tract 200 A. of which "...being by me already sold to John Steward wch. is hereby excepted...." Wit: THOMAS JONES, WILLIAM JONES. November Court 1727. *.

B 331 JOHN STEWARD TO SAMUEL GARLAND
Aug. 1, 1727. 4 pds. for 160 A. In Uriah Woods at head of Patenous Branch on Catawiskey Pocoson. Wit: WILLIAM COTTON, FRANCIS PARKER, jurat, CHRISTIAN HEIDELLBURG, jurat. November Court 1727. *.

B 331 RICHARD SOWELL, SEN. & WIFE MARGARET TO RICHARD SOWELL, JUN.
Sept. 16, 1727. *. 200 A. "...for love and natural affection they do owe and bear to their son..." Land on Horse Swamp. Wit: WILLIAM CRAW-FORD, RICHARD BROWNE. November Court 1727. *.

B 333 RICHARD SOWELL, SEN. & WIFE MARGARET TO WILLIAM CRAWFORD
Nov. 13, 1727. Power of atty. to ack. deed of gift of 200 A. to son RICHARD SOWELL, JUN. Wit: JOHN HIX, ANDREW STEVENSON, jurat. November Court 1727. *.

B 333 PETER JONES of Surry Co., Va. to ROBERT SIMMS
Nov. 13, 1727. 30 pds. for 100 A.(150 A.?) On NS Morattuck River on Cypress Swamp. Called Ocoeneechee. Part of patent 640 A. to WILLIAM BRACEWELL in 1711/12. Wit: EMPEROR WHEELER, ANN WHEELER. November Court 1727. *.

B 335 PETER JONES of Surry Co., Va. to ANDREW IRELAND
Nov. 13, 1727. Power of atty. to ack. deed of sale dated Nov. 13, 1727 to ROBERT SIMMS. Wit: EMPEROR WHEELER, ANN WHEELER. *. *.

B 335 JOHN BARNES & WIFE CATHERINE of Chowan Precinct TO THOMAS WALLIS
Jan. 25, 1726/27. 20 pds. for 310 A. On Fork Branch and Meadow Grounds. Surveyed and patented for JOSEPH HOWARD, and by HOWARD sold to BARNES. Patent date Aug. 4, 1727. Wit: THOMAS ROUNTREE, CHARLES ROUNTREE, EDWARD WOOD, SEN. November Court 1727. *.

B 337 RICHARD SUMNER & WIFE MARY TO JOHN COOK
Aug. 19, 1727. 20 pds. for 150 A. (250A.?) On SS Yourah Swamp "above Oldfield" and WS Geionkey(?) Branch. Wit: MATTHEW MASHBORNE, JOHN DICKINSON, JOHN SUTTON. November Court 1727. *.

B 338 THOMAS JERNAGAN & WIFE SARAH of Nansimond Co., Va. to THOMAS COWLING
         (CROWLING) of Nansemond Co., Va.
Feb. 8, 1727/28. 5 sh. for 300 A. (year lease). At Mouth of Pas-ture Branch on Elm Swmp on the Old Field Path. Adj. JOHN BEAVERLY, JOHN HOMES. Part of tract of 530 A. granted by patent dated March 9, 1717. THOMAS CROWLING is son of JAMES CROWLING. Wit: FRANCIS SPEIGHT, JAMES HOL-LAND, FRANCIS CLERK. February Court 1727. Deed ack. in open court by THOMAS JERNAGAN and by JOHN JONES, atty. for SARAH JERNAGAN. Duly proved by oath of JAMES HOLLAND. ED MASHBORNE D. C/C.

B 340 THOMAS JERNAGAN, SEN. & WIFE SARAH of Nansemond Co., Va. TO THOMAS
         COWLING
Feb. 9, 1727/28. 26 pds. and "3000 lbs. merch'able Tobacco" for 300 A. THOMAS COWLING, son of JAMES COWLING. Land formerly leased for a year. Patent date March 9, 1717 at Pasture Branch adj. JOHN BEAVERLY, JOHN

HOMES. Near Meherrin Creek. Wit: FRANCIS SPEIGHT, FRANCIS CLARK, JAMES
HOLLAND. February Court 1727. *.
JOHN JONES atty. for SARAH JERNAGAN ack. sale with JAMES JERNAGAN. Proved
by oath of JAMES HOLLAND.

B 342   SARAH JERNEGAN TO JOHN JONES
        Feb. 10, 1727/28. Pwer of atty. to ack. "according to law one paire
of Indentures of lease and release..." 300 A. unto THOMAS COWLING. Wit:
FRANCIS SPEIGHT, JAMES HOLLAND. February Court 1727. *.

B 343   WILLIAM HOWET TO BENJAMIN HILL of Nansemond Co., Va.
        Feb. 13, 1727. 200 pds. for 800 A. According to two patents: (1)
obtained by JOHN CROSBY for 400 A. and purchased by HOWET (2) One belonging
to JOHN SMITH and by him assigned to HOWET. Wit: WILLIAM LITTLE, ROBERT
FORSTER. February Court 1727. EDW. MASHBORNE D. C/C.

B 343   JONATHAN CLIFT TO FRANCIS PUGH of Nansemond Co., Va.
        Dec. 6, 1727. 30 pds. for 157 A. WS Chowan River where CLIFT now
lives. Wit: SIMON JEFFREYS, THOMAS BRYANT, WILLIAM DANIEL, CHRIS. HEIDEL-
BURG. February Court 1727. EDW. MASHBORNE D. C/C.

B 344   WILLIAM BYNAM TO RICHARD KILLINGSWORTH
        Feb. 14, 1727/28. 10 pds. for 300 A. On SS Morattock River. Wit:
WILLIAM SIMMS, WILLIAM KILLINGSWORTH, JOHN SUTTON. February Court 1727.
EDW. MASHBORNE D. C/C.

B 345   JOHN SMITH TO BENJAMIN HILL, merchant
        Jan. 23, 1727. 200 pds.

8 cows with calves	6 porringers
2 4 yr. old steers	1 pair Querin Stones
4 heifers 1 yr. old	1 Tenent Saw
2 steers 2 yr. old	1 cross cut saw
1 1 yr. old steer	1 carpenter adz
1 3 yr. old bull	2 Augars
3 heifers with calves	1 grind stone
2 2 yr. old steers	3 weading hoes
4 sows & 21 pigs	1 iron pestel
"the neat cattle"	3 hilling hoes
4 sows ANTHONY LEWIS mark	1 broad ax
the pigs not marked	3 narrow axes
2 feather beds & furniture	3 chests
6 iron pots	1 gilt trunk
6 puter Basons	1 chisil & gouge
8 puter dishes	2 drawing knives

"as also all goods and chattels not here particularly Inserted and belonging to JOHN SMITH." Wit: HENRY AMERSON, SAMUEL WHEATLEY. February Court
1727. EDW MASHBORNE D C/C.

B 346   JOHN SMITH TO BENJAMIN HILL, merchant
        Jan. 23, 1727. 200 pds. for 1110 A. Two patents. (1) obtained by
ANTHONY LEWIS for 640 A. and purchased by JOHN SMITH. (2) obtained by
SMITH. Wit: HENRY AMERSON, SAMUEL WHEATLEY, jurat, JOHN POWERS, jurat.
February Court 1727. EDW. MASHBORNE D. C/C.

B 347   DAVID VINCINT (VINCENT) TO BENJAMIN HILL
        Jan. 3, 1727. 90 pds. All cows, calves, horses, household goods,
tobacco. Wit: THOMAS JONES, jurat, WILLIAM LAND, jurat, THOMAS VINSON.
February Court 1727. EDW. MASHBORNE D. C/C.

B 348   DAVID VINCENT TO CAPT. BENJAMIN HILL
        Jan. 9, 1727. Power of atty. to act in all matters "as he sees
fitt." Wit: WILLIAM WHITFIELD, WILLIAM LAND, jurat, JAMES DENTON, jurat.
February Court 1727. ED. MASHBORNE D. C/C.

B 348   JAMES HUTCHENSON TO JOHN BASS, JUN.
        Jan. 17, 1727. 5 pds. for 100 A. At mouth of Plaquet Branch on An-
tonkey Marsh. Adj. HARDY COUNCIL. Part of greater tract of 600 A. Wit:
*. *. E. MASHBORNE D. C/C. Ack. in court by JAMES HUTCHINSON.

        NOTE HERE: "This Far New Registered to November Court 1797."

48

B 350   JOHN POWER TO PETER POWER
        Feb. 14, 1727/28. 50 pds. for 235 A. Land surveyed for BEALL BROWN
and by him sold to JOHN POWER. Wit: JOHN HOMES, THOMAS JONES. February
Court 1727. EDW. MASHBORNE D. C/C.

B 351   WILLIAM KILLINGSWORTH TO WILLIAM SIMMS
        Feb. 14, 1727/28. 10 pds. for 640 A. In Ahookey (Ahoskey) Woods.
Wit: RICHARD KILLINGSWORTH, JOHN SUTTON, WILLIAM BINUM. February Court
1727. EDW. MASHBORNE D. C/C.

B 353   JOHN ANDERSON of Henrico Co., Va. TO THOMAS BRYANT
        Jan. 6, 1727/28. Power of atty. to collect debts, wages etc. "...to
act as I myself might act...." Wit: ROBERT WARRIN, jurat, RICHARD PACE.
* Court 1727. EDW. MASHBORNE D. C/C.

B 353   WILLIAM DOWNING TO WILLIAM SHARP
        Feb. 9, 1727. 150 pds. for 380 A. On SS Wicacone Creek. Patent
granted August 27, 1716. Adj. COLL. POLLUCK. Wit: JOHN BOON, jurat, RICH-
ARD OLDNER. February Court 1727. EDW. MASHBORNE D. C/C.

B 354   JOHN SPEIR TO WILLIAM SPEIR
        Feb. 11, 1727/28. 5,500 lbs. "mer'table pork meat" For *. SS Mora-
ttuck River on "GEEs Meadow." Adj. HENRY WALKER, WILLIAM GRAY, JOHN LOVICK
(LOUCK), JOHN JACKSON. To Crop Marsh and Cattail Marsh. Wit: WILLIAM RUF-
FIN, THOMAS JENKINS, JOHN WORSLING. February Court 1727. EDW. MASHBORNE,
D. C/C.

B 355   JOHN HILLIARD, late of Virginia TO JOHN BEVERLEY, SEN.
        Dec. 14, 1727. 130 Pds. For Negro man called Tom about 24 years.
Wit: ANN THOMAS, ROBERT FORSTER. February Court 1727. EDW. MASHBORNE D.
C/C.

B 356   JOHN COLSTON TO JOHN HAYES
        Feb. 1727. 20 pds. for *. At fork of Roquist. Patent to LUKE MEA-
SLES and conveyed to GEORGE CLARK dec'd. and by CLARK's executors conveyed
to COLSTON. Wit: WILLIAM LITTLE, ROBERT FORSTER. February Court 1727.
EDW. MASHBORNE D. C/C.

B 357   JOHN SMITH TO BENJAMIN HILL, merchant
        Jan. 27, 1727/28. 50 pds. for 400 A. Land whereon Smith formerly
lived. Patent obtained Mar. 9, 1717/18. Wit: SPIAN(?) HEIDELBERG, jurat,
HENRY EMERSON, ANN SATOR. February Court 1727. EDW. MASHBORNE D. C/C.

B 358   JOHN SIMPSON & WIFE MARY of Isle of Wight Co., Va. TO WILLIAM WALL
        Feb. 10, 1727/28. 4 pds. for 180 A. On SS Meherrin River. Land
granted SIMPSON by WILLIAM REED, Esq. President of the Province of North
Carolina. Grant dated Nov. 7, 1723. Adj. JAMES TURNER, HOPKINS HOWEL.
Wit: JOSEPH WALL, SEN., JOSEPH WALL, JUN. February Court 1727. EDW. MASH-
BORNE D. C/C.

B 360   JAMES HUTCHENSON (HUTCHINSON) TO JOHN BASS, JUN.
        Jan. 17, 1727/28. 150 pds. for *A. Wit: JOHN SUTTON, ANDROS. JAN-
SEY(?). February Court 1727. EDW. MASHBORNE D. C/C.

B 361   JOHN CHERRY-HOLME, taylor, TO JOHN SWINNEY (SWINNER)
        Feb. 12, *. 50 pds. for 100 A. On ES Deep Branch at Neetops survey.
Wit: LEWIS BRYANT, RICHARD WILLIFORD. Feb. Court 1727. EDW. MASHBORNE D.C/C

B 362   JONATHAN TAYLOR TO JOHN COLSON
        Feb. 1727/28. 40 pds. for 600 A. On SS Rocquis Creek. Part of
patent by LUKE MEZELL and by him conveyed to TIMOTHY TRUELOVE. By TRUELOVE
conveyed to GOERGE CLARK. JONATHAN TAYLOR is legatee of last will and
testament of GEORGE CLARK. JAMES WILLIAMSON administrator of this will.
Land near JOHN STEVENS. Wit: EDMOND SMITHWICK, EDWARD WINGATE. February
Court 1727. EDW MASHBORNE D. C/C.

B 363   JAMES WILLIAMSON TO JOHN LEGGET
        Feb. 4, 1727/28. 45 pds. For 300 A. Adj. dividing line of SANDLEY
and LEGGET. Part of 1100 A. patented in name of LUKE MEZLE, and purchased
by GOERGE CLARK dec'd. Wit: JOHN COLLSON, THOMAS STREETER. February Court
1727/28. EDW. MASHBORNE D. C/C.

B 365   ROBERT SCOTT TO JOHN POWELL
        Nov. 14, 1727. 30 pds. for 640 A. On Cabbin Branch. Adj. ROBERT
EDWARDS. Patent granted SCOTT on Feb. 1, 1725. Wit: Capt. THOMAS BRYANT,
jurat, EDWARD POWERS. February Court 1727. EDW. MASHBORNE D. C/C.

B 366   CAPT. THOMAS BRYANT & WIFE ALICE TO JOHN POWERS
        Apr. 18, 1727. "Whereas several differences controversies and quar-
rels hath bin entertained between Capt. THOMAS BRYANT, ALICE his wife and
Mr. JNO. POWERS concerning several Negros (viz) Tom, Buck, Betty, Nanny,
Patty, Sara and an infant boy her son formerly in the possession of sd.
POWERS in right of his late deceased wife SARAH Mother to the sd. ALICE.
Now for quieting and avoiding all further strife debates law suits claims
controversies and demands whatsoever...Capt. THOMAS BRYANT and ALICE my
wife have...for...four of the sd Negros...quietly and peaceably made over
to me by said JOHN POWERS...by deed of sale...I do make over to JOHN POWERS
forever three of the Negros...." Wit: BENJAMIN HILL, SIMON JEFFREYS, WIL-
LIAM WHITEHEAD. February Court 1727. EDW. MASHBORNE D. C/C.

B 366   ROBERT JONES & SON WILLIAM of Surry Co., Va. TO BARNABE MCKINNE
        Nov. 13, 1727. 30 pds. for 470 A. On NS Morattuck. Patent formerly
granted to JOHN HATHHORN of Surry Co., Va. on Feb. 26, 1721/22. By last
will and testament of JOHN HATHHORN to be sold bv JOHN HIX for use of
ROBERT JONES and children. By deed Sept. 7, 1724, ROBERT JONES did make
over part of land to sons MATTHEW and ROBERT. Both these sons now deceased.
ROBERT JONES, SEN. "hole" executor, and WILLIAM JONES "heir at large" to
his brothers. Wit: ANDREW IRELAND, jurat, JOHN MCKINNE, JUN., ISAAC RICKS.
February Court 1727. EDW. MASHBORNE D. C/C.

B 368   ROBERT HUMPHRY (HUMPHREY) TO JOHN STEVENS
        Feb. 10, 1727/28. 40 pds. for 100 A. On SS Morattock River. Part
of 200 A. patent dated Feb. 1, 1727. On NS Conoconaro Swamp. Wit: BARNABE
MCKINNE, jurat, JOHN HENDRY. Feb. Court 1727. EDW. MASHBORNE D. C/C.

B 369   JOHN CHERRYHOLM (CHERRYHOLME) TO RICHARD WILLIFORD
        Oct. 17, 1726. 120 pds. for 150 A. At "Netops Messe" on Wicocorn
Creek. Adj. DENNIS MCCLANDONS, CHRISTIAN   . Wit: JOHN SWINNEE, WIL-
LIAM WILLIFORD. February Court 1727. EDW. MASHBORNE D. C/C. (JOHN CHERRY-
HOLM a "tailer").

B 370   CHARLES STEVENS (STEPHENS) TO HENRY OVERSTREET
        Nov. 7, 1727. 8 pds. 18 sh. for 240 A. On NS Morattock River on
Deep Creek. Adj. THEOPHILUS WILLIAMS, WILLIAMS GRAY. Wit: ABR(AHAM) SHEP-
PARD, DANIEL MCDANIEL. February Court 1727. EDW. MASHBORNE D. C/C.

B 371   JOHN EDWARDS, JUN. & WIFE ELIZABETH TO ABRAHAM SHEPPARD
        *. 20 pds. for 200 A. On Roquist. Adj. MARTIN GARDNER, JUN., MARTIN
GARDNER, SEN., HENRY OVERSTREET. Wit: HENRY OVERSTREET, WILLIAM GRIFFIN.
February Court 1727. EDW. MASHBORNE D. C/C.

B 372   JAMES MCGLOHON (MACGLAHAN) TO JAMES MCGLOHON
        Dec. 5, 1727. "for love and affection I bear JAMES MCGLOHON son of
JEREMIAH MCGLOHON." Land on Wiccacone Swamp and Round Pocoson. Wit: WIL-
LIAM WILLIFORD, EDW. MASHBORNE, JOHN EARLY. February Court 1727. EDW.
MASHBORNE D. C/C.

B 373   JOHN RASBERRY TO RICHARD WILSON of Chowan Precinct
        Jan. 4, 1727. 10 pds. for 317 A. On Loosing Swamp. Wit: R. ROUTE
(RONTE?), ROBERT FORSTER. February Court 1727. EDW. MASHBORNE D. C/C.

B 374   CHARLES KIRBEE TO ARTHUR WILLIAMS
        Feb. 12, 1727/28. *. 100 A. On SS Meherrin River Adj. plantation
whereon ARTHUR WILLIAMS lives on Mill Swamp. Part of patent of 1200 A.
granted THOMAS KIRBEE. Devised to me CHARLES KIRBEE by last will and testament of my father THOMAS KIRBEE. Wit: JOHN SIMPSON, JOHN BRYANT. February Court 1727. EDW. MASHBORNED. C/C.

B 375   SAMUEL KEEL TO FINCHER HAYNE
        Feb. 13, 1727. 11 barrels of pitch for 200 A. On Chinkapin Ridge.
Adj. STEPHENS WILLIAMS, JACOB LEWIS, JAMES HOWARD, JOHN JONES, Wading
Branch. Wit: THOMAS BRYANT, WILLIAM ASKEW. February Court 1727. EDW.
MASHBORNE D. C/C.

B 376   JOHN COLSON & WIFE SUSAN (SUSANNAH) TO THOMAS ARRINGTON
        Feb. 10, 1727. 20 pds. for 160 A. On NS Moratoc River. Adj. JOHN
TURBAVEL, RALPH MASON, FOSTER MASON. Wit: JOHN GRAY, WILLIAM BRYAN. February Court 1727. EDW. MASHBORNE D. C/C.

B 378   WILLIAM GRIFFIN TO SAMUEL BASS
        Nov. 10, 1727. 30 pds. for 200 A. On SS Kesia Swamp. Adj. WILLIAM
WILSON. Wit: WILLIAM GRIFFIN, JOHN GRAY, RICHARD FRYER. February Court
1727. EDW. MASHBORNE D. C/C.

B 379   SAMUEL CANNEDAY (CANNADAY) TO JOHN WOSLAND
        Feb. 10, 1727. 10 pds. for 100 A. Part of patent to WILLIAM WHITE-
HEAD dated April 1, 1723. Adj. RICHARD BRACEWELL. Wit: JOHN DUFFIELD,
CHARLES STEPHENS. JOHN DUFFIELD by power of atty. from SAMUEL CANNADAY
ack. in open court. * Court. EDW. MASHBORNE D. C/C.

B 380   HENRY BONNER TO FRANCIS WOOD
        Feb. 12, 1727/28. 8 pds. for 300 A. On SS Morattuck River Adj. JOHN
NAIRN, JAMES DENTON. Wit: JOHN JONES, PATRICK O'QUIN, WILLIAM SPEIR.
February Court 1727. EDW. MASHBORNE D. C/C.

B 381   ROBERT SCOTT & AARON DRAKE TO SAMUEL ELSON
        Dec. 16, 1727. 40 pds. for 300 A. On Crag Bottom Adj. GANEY
(GAINEY). Part of tract granted to HENRY WHEELER on Nov. 5, 1714. Wit:
RICHARD WASHINGTON, jurat, HENRY RODES. February Court 1727. EDW. MASH-
BORNE D. C/C.

B 382   DOCTOR JAMES WILLIAMSON TO EDWARD WINGATE
        Feb. 2, 1727. 95 pds. for 530 A. On NS Morattuck River at "COGSWELL
& DOMINEYs corner." Adj. SMITHWICK & WILLIAMSON, JONATHAN TAYLOR, ABRAHAM
SHEPERD. Wit: JOHN LEGGET, JOHN NAIRNER. February Court 1727. EDW. MASH-
BORNE D. C/C.

B 383   THOMAS JERNEGAN of Chowan Precinct TO FRANCIS PUGH of Nansemond Co.,
        Va.
        * 1727. 32 Barrels of Lawful Tar for 100 A. On Meherrin Creek and
Elm Swamp. Adj. JOHN BEVERLEY, JAMES BOON. Wit: JOSEPH NORFLEET, THOMAS
JONES, DAVID OSHEAL. February Court 1727. EDW. MASHBORNE D. C/C.

B 384   WILLIAM GRAY TO CHARLES STEVENSON
        May 13, 1727. 20 pds. for 640 A. On NS Morrattock River and WS
Falling Run. Adj. JOHN GRAY, JAMES CASTELLAW, JOHN WILLIAMS, COLL. MAULE,
COLL. JONES on Village Swamp. Wit: JOHN GRAY, HENRY GUSTON, GEORGE STEVEN-
SON. February Court 1727. EDW. MASHBORNE D. C/C.

B 385   RICHARD BRACEWELL & WIFE ELINOR TO OWIN KELLY
        *. 30 pds. for 150 A. On NS Morattock River within Arsaro Meadow at
Village Swamp and mouth of Holly Bush Meadow. Adj. JOHN COTTON, Green Pond
Meadow. Patent by BRACEWELL. Wit: WILLIAM RUFFIN, JOHN HART. February
Court 1727. EDW. MASHBORNE D. C/C.

B 386   ROBERT FORSTER of Edenton TO JOHN LOVICK of Edenton
        Aug. 8, 1728. 100 pds. for 3200 A. Near head of Fishing Creek. Adj.
SAMUEL SWANN. North Carolina Court Aug. 8, 1728. "ROBERT FORSTER, Gent.
personally appeared before (me) and ack. the within deed of sale." C. GALE
C. J. Test. EDW. MASHBORNE D. C/C.

        NOTE HERE: "So Far Done to Feb'y. Court 1798."

B 387   WILLIAM WHITEHEAD TO CAPT. THOMAS BRYANT
        May 11, 1728. 10 pds. for 100 A. On NS Moratock River and Yawreha
Swamp. Part of patent of 600 A. granted WHITEHEAD on March 9, 1717. Wit:
J. WILLIAMSON, J. BADHAM, JO. STAVART. May Court 1728. EDW. MASHBORNE
D. C/C.

B 388   JOHN WILLIAMS & WIFE ANN TO HENRY OVERSTREET
        Aug. 2, 1727. 12 pds. for 135 A. On Casiah Swamp and Roquist. "ly-
ing back of a survey of MARTIN GARDNER." Wit: ISAAC WILLIAMS, WILLIAM
JONES, ANNE HERRING. May Court 1728. EDW. MASHBORNE D. C/C.

B 389   JOHN WILLIAMS & WIFE ANNE TO ISAAC WILLIAMS

Nov. 13, 1727. Power of atty. to ack. sale to HENRY OVERSTREET. Wit: ISAAC WILLIAMS, jurat, WILLIAM JONES. May Court 1728. EDW. MASH-BORNE D. C/C.

B 390 WILLIAM REED & WIFE MARY TO SAMUEL GOODMAN
May 14, 1728. 5 pds. for 50 A. Part of tract bought of THOMAS BON-NER on Aug. 13, 1723. Wit: WILLIAM WHITFIELD, SAMUEL WHEATLY. May Court 1728. EDW. MASHBORNE D. C/C.

B 391 JONATHAN SANDERSON TO DANIEL CAMERRIN of Nansemond Co., Va.
May 13, 1728. 7 pds. for 120 A. On NS Meherrin River, SS Buckhorn Swamp, and Meadow Branch. Adj. "BEALL BOUND line." Part of patent to JOHN HOOKE dated Nov. 7, 1723. Wit: EDW. BARNES, BENJAMIN (JOHNSON?), JOHN WIGGANS. May Court 1728. EDW. MASHBORNE D. C/C.

B 392 JOHN SUTTON TO JAMES WYATE
May 15, 1728. 10 pds. for 370 A. On WS Yawreah Swamp. Adj. JOHN MACMIALS. Wit: CONF. LUTEN, JAHN MAINER, WILLIAM WHITEHEAD. May Court 1728. EDW. MASHBORNE D. C/C.

B 392 THOMAS BROWN TO JOHN CHESHIRE
May 14, 1728. 5 pds. for 100 A. On NS Meherrin River. Part of tract granted Thomas Brown for 540 A. Adj. JOHN ROGERS. JOSEPH DARDEN. Wit: JOHN SUTTON, WILLIAM FAULKE. May Court 1728. EDW. MASHBORNE D.C/C.

B 393 MATTHEW TOBIAS SWANNER TO GEORGE WINNS
May 13, 1728. 22 pds. for 100 A. On NS Wiccacon at mouth of "Beav-erdam or Mill Swamp." Adj. GEORGE WINNS to ES Round Pocoson, Horsehung Branch. Adj. GEO. WINNS Mill Dam. Wit: WILLIAM MARSHALL, JOHN WINNS. May Court 1728. EDW. MASHBORNE D.C/C.

B 394 JOHN SMITH, JOHN CROSBY & JOHN CROSBY, JUN. TO ROBERT FORSTER,
           blacksmith
May 16, 1727. 400 pds. for 640 A. "...the consideration of the above obligation is such...that JOHN SMITH in consideration of 100 pd. paid by ROBERT FORSTER for 640 A...On Catawitsky Swamp now occupied by JOHN SMITH...which doth in right belong to WILLIAM CROSBY son of JOHN CROSBY by patent...JOHN SMITH will procure a deed of sale from said WILLIAM CROSBY as soon as said CROSBY shall arrive at age 21...to confirm to ROBERT FORSTER ...." Wit: ROBERT FORSTER, BENJAMIN HILL. May Court 1728. EDW. MASHBORNE D. C/C.

B 395 DAVID CUMMINGS of Virginia TO RICHARD PACE
May 6, 1726. 20 pds. for 100 A. On NS Morrattock River. "bounded on the one hundred and ninety acres of patent sold to ALEX. BANE and fifty acres sold to WILLIAM FROST...." Patent dated March 1, 1719. Wit: LEWIS HOWEL, JOHN BRADFORD, jurat. May Court 1728. EDW. MASHBORNE D.C/C.

B 396 CHARLES CAVENAUGH TO WILLIAM FAULK
June 24, 1727. *.*. 3 heifers; one "pide" cow; 3 pide cows; one pide bull; one brown pide cow; one pide heifer; one bay mare and colt; one bed and furniture; 2 iron pots & pot hooks; one frying pan; 6 Flagg chairs; three pails; one tray; one spinning wheel and movables. Wit: ROBERT RAD-FORD, CHARLES CAVENAUGH. May Court 1728. EDW. MASHBORNE D.C/C.

B 396 JOHN SPEIR TO JAMES SPEIR
May 13, 1728. 30 pds. for 200 A. On SS Morattuck River. Adj. JOHN NAIRN, WILLIAM GRAY, WILLIAM SPEIR, HENRY WALKER. On Cattale Marsh and High Hills. Wit: DAVID OSHEAL(?), THOMAS BRYANT. May Court 1728. EDW. MASHBORNE D. C/C.

B 397 RICHARD KILLINGSWORTH TO THOMAS DREW
May 14, 1728. 36 pds. for 500 A. On SS Morattuck River and Cypress Swamp. Adj. JOHN WOODS. Wit: J. EDWARD, JOHN NAIRNER. May Court 1728. EDW. MASHBORNE D.C/C.

B 398 WILLIAM PERRY, carpenter, TO EMANUEL ROGERS, carpenter
May Last 1727. 10 pds. for 150 A. On SS Morattuck River on (Quel-que?) Creek. Granted to PERRY February 25, 1725. "...as also one hundred acres" On SS Morattuck River granted JOHN NAIRN and to PERRY by deed March 21, 1726. Wit: SIMON JEFFRYS, jurat, ELIZABETH JEFFREYS, THOMAS TURNER,

WILLIAM BAREFOOT. May Court 1728. EDW. MASHBORNE D.C/C.

B 399 JOSEPH LANE, JUN. & WIFE PATIENCE TO SAMUEL SWEARINGTON (SWEARINGEN)
     May 11, 1728. 40 pds. for 338 A. "all ye tract...said LANE formerly
bought of JOSEPH SIMMS." On SS Morattuck River and SS Connoconnare Swamp
at side of String Meadow at Reedy Pocoson and "GOODENs Corner." Wit: MAT-
THEW (RAEFORD), HENRY CRAFORD, JOSEPH WALL. May Court 1728. EDW. MASH-
BORNE D.C/C.

B 400 PATIENCE LANE TO MATTHEW RAIFORD
     May 11, 1728. PATIENCE, wife of JOSEPH LANE, JUN. Power of atty.
to ack. sale of land unto SAMUEL SWEARINGEN. Wit: MATTHEW RAIFORD, jurat,
HENRY CRAFFORD. May Court 1728. EDW. MASHBORNE D.C/C.

B 400 EDWARD BARNES TO GODFREY LEE
     May 7, 1728. 40 pds. for 550 A. On WS Chowan River and SS Indian
Creek. Adj. RICHARD HOLLAND. "...the whole paten of 550 (A) granted said
BARNES by relaps dated October 1726...." Wit: JAMES HOLLAND, THOMAS BIRD,
ROBERT LANIER. May Court 1728. EDW. MASHBORNE D.C/C.

B 402 JACOB OADHAM of Nansemond Co., Va. TO RICHARD MEADLING
     May 14, 1728. 20 pds. for 640 A. Adj. FRANCIS PARKER, THOMAS BUSBY
at BRANCH OF Casiey River. Wit: JOHN DUFFIELD, JOSEPH BALLARD. May Court
1728. EDW. MASHBORNE D.C/C.

B 403 CHARLES STEVENSON TO JAMES MOOR
     May 14, 1728. 20 pds. for 100 A. On NS Morattock River Adj. SAMUEL
MERRIT, SAMUEL WILLIAMSON. Wit: ANDREW IRELAND, THOMAS JENKINS, JOHN WILL-
IARD. May Court 1728. EDW. MASHBORNE D.C/C.

B 403 BENJAMIN WARREN (WARRAN) & WIFE HESTER TO BENJAMIN BAKER
     Nov. 11, 1727. 10 pds. for 50 A. "At a branch above BENJ. WARRENs
new dwelling house" to the Main Swamp. Wit: THOMAS BIRD, JOHN MITCHEL.
May Court 1728. EDW. MASHBORNE D.C/C.

B 405 WILLIAM JONES & WIFE MARY TO JONATHAN STANDLEY, JUN.
     Feb. 10, 1727/28. 10 pds. for 200 A. On Casiah Swamp. Adj. HENRY
ROWEL, _____ BRACEWELL. At Reedy Branch. Wit: WILLIAM JONES, JUN., ANN
JONES.

B 406 WILLIAM JONES TO EDWARD MOOR
     May 13, 1728. *.*. Power of atty. to ack. sale to JONATHAN STAND-
LEY, JUN. Wit: FRANCIS HOBSON, jurat, WILLIAM KENNEDAY. May Court 1728.
EDW. MASHBORNE D.C/C.

B 406 WILLIAM BOON TO CAROLUS ANDERSON
     May 13, 1728. For "valuable consideration in hand" 200 A. Part of
423 A. tract granted to BOON on December 3, 1720. On Heherrin River at the
Great Gutt. Wit: RICHARD BAYLY, NATHA. COOPER. May Court 1728. EDW.
MASHBORNE D.C/C.

B 407 HENRY CRAWFORD TO ELIAS FORD
     May 11, 1728. 10 pds. for 100 A. On SS Morattock River at Looking
Glass Swamp. Wit: JOHN POPE, jurat, SAMUEL SWEARINGEN. May Court 1728.
EDW. MASHBORNE D.C/C.

B 408 JOSEPH LANE, JUN. TO WILLIAM BALDWIN
     May 6, 1728. 18 pds. for 250 A. On Morattock River at dividing line
between JOSEPH LANE, JUN. and WILLIAM HOGGET. Half of a certain tract
granted WILLIAM JONES for 640 A. by patent dated Feb. 26, 1711/12. Wit:
JOHN (ONAILS?) (ONEAL?), ROBERT SIMS. May Court 1728. EDW. MASHBORNE DC/C

B 410 HENRY BRADLEY, JUN. TO JAMES PAGE
     Apr. 6, 1728. 50 pds. for 130 A. On Loosing Swamp. Adj. ROBERT
EVANS, WILLIAM BUSH, EDMOND TIDMAN. Wit: WILLIAM BUSH, jurat, EDW. TIDMAN.
May Court 1728. EDW. MASHBORNE D. C/C.

B 411 STEPHEN HOWARD & WIFE SARAH TO EDWARD MOORE (MOOR)
     April 5, 1728 (February 19, 1728). 115 pds. for 250 A. On SS Ahor-
skey Swamp at Turkey Swamp. Adj. JOHN DAVIDSON, STEPHEN HOWARD, JOHN BARE-
FOOT. Part of 485 A. patent. Wit: JONATHAN STANDLEY, jurat. *. May

Court 1728. EDW. MASHBORNE D.C/C.

B 412 JOHN POWERS TO BENJAMIN HILL
        July 3, 1727. "I JOHN POWERS (ack.) myself bound unto BENJ. HILL
for 100 pds.... I bind myself (my adm. & exec.)...the conditions are such
that BENJ. HILL shall have the first two children born of the body of the
Negro slave Sarah...they shall live with JOHN POWERS one year after they
are born (unless) Hill shall desire them sooner...." Wit: WILLIAM LITTLE,
ROBERT FORSTER. May Court 1728. EDW. MASHBORNE D.C/C.

B 413 ROBERT SHERWOOD TO JOHN MAHHA
        April 1, 1728. 6 pds. for 100 A. On Mill Path. Wit: JOHN BONDE,
jurat, MATTHEW SELLERS, NICHOLAS PERU(?). May Court 1728. EDW. MASHBORNE
D.C/C.

B 414 RICHARD MOLTON (MELTON), carpenter, to ANN YELVERTON
        Jan. 10, 1725. 200 A. "for love and affection I do owe and bear
unto ANN YELVERTON daughter of JOHN and ELIABETH YELVERTON...." Land on SS
Conaro Creek at mouth of Cabin branch adj. JOHN YELVERTON at Oldfield. "...
to her and her heirs forever...if she should die without heirs of her body
to return to her eldest sister Elizabeth and her heirs...." Wit: JOHN
YELVERTON, JOHN NAIRNE, jurat, ANDREW FRASHER. May Court 1728. EDW. MASH-
BORNE D.C/C.

B 415 EDWARD SIMMONS TO WILLIAM HOLLIDAY of Virginia
        May 10, 1728. 28 pds. for 430 A. On SS Marattuck River adj. ES
Quaque Pecoson, WILLIAM CHAVERS. Part of 630 A. patent granted to BARTHOL-
OMEW CHAVERS July 30, 1726. 200 A. of patent given by CHAVERS to his son,
WILLIAM CHAVERS. Wit: JOHN BEASSENT(?), GEORGE ROLLISSON, BAR. MACKINNE,
jurat. May Court 1728. EDW. MASHBORNE D.C/C.

B 416 JAMES WILLIAMSON & WIFE CONSTANCE TO WILLIAM BATTLE of Nansemond
        Co., Va.
        April 27, 1728. 120 pds. for 300 A. On Roquist Swamp. At dividing
line between WILLIAMSON and JONATHAN TAYLOR. Being part of grant to WILL-
IAMSON on April 5, 1720. Wit: JOHN HAYS, JOHN BATTLE, WILLIAM WALSTON.
PHILLIP WALSTON power of atty. May Court 1728. EDW. MASHBORNE D.C/C.

B 416 CONSTANCE WILLIAMSON TO PHILLIP WALSTONE
        April 7, 1728. Power of atty. to ack. right of dower in 300 A. sold
to WILLIAM BATTLE. Wit: WILLIAM WALSTON, JOHN HAYS. May Court 1728. EDW.
MASHBORNE D.C/C.

B 417 THEOPHILUS WILLIAMS TO JOSEPH BALLORD (BALLOR), SEN. of Nansemond
        Co., Va.
        March 4, 1727/28. 12 pds. for 200 A. *. Wit: NEEDHAM BRYAN, ELIAS
HOGHES, JAMES _____. May Court 1728. EDW. MASHBORNE D.C/C.

B 419 JOHN POPE TO JOHN DUFFIELD
        Feb. 10, 1727. 20 pds. for 200 A. On Horron Swamp. Land whereon
JOHN POPE formerly lived by patent. Wit: THOMAS JONES, JOHN DICKINSON.
May Court 1728. EDW. MASHBORNE D.C/C.

B 420 WILLIAM TURBERVILLE & WALTER TURBERVILLE TO PHILLIP MULKEY, carpen-
        ter
        Feb. 3, 1727. 20 pds. for 380 A. On SS Morattuck River at Plum Tree
Swamp. Adj. WILLIAM GREEN and Swan Pond. Part of patent granted to ROBERT
LONG on March 1, 1721. Wit: JOHN TURBERVILLE, FRAN(?) TURBERVILLE, ANN
COLSON, JOSEPH LANE, jurat. May Court 1728. EDW. MASHBORNE D.C/C.

B 422 JOHN NAIRNE TO ARTHUR DAVIS
        May 8, 1728. 20 pds. for 200 A. On SS Morattuck River at "Pappaw
Gum" on Deep Bottom. "...Tract of land ye I the said NAIRNE elapsed from
JOHN BAPTIST..." On the river pocoson. Wit: JOHN BUTLAR, SARAH BUTLAR.
May Court 1728. EDW. MASHBORNE D.C/C.

B 422 CHARLES STEPHENSON TO THOMAS JENKINS
        Nov. 13, 1728. 10 pds. for 140 A. Adj. RICHARD BRACEWELL. Wit:
ANDREW IRELAND, JAMES MOORE, JOHN HILLIARD. May Court 1728. EDW. MASH-
BORNE D.C/C.

B 423   BARTHOLOMME CHAVERS TO BARNABE MACKINNE
        May 10, 1728. 20 pds. for 100 A. On NS Morattock River and Yeorah
Swamp Adj. WILLIAM JONES. Part of patent of 640 A. granted to JOHN GREEN.
This 100 A. sold by GREEN to CHAVERS. Wit: EDW. SIMMONS, GEO. ROLLISON.
May Court 1728. EDW. MASHBORNE D.C/C.

B 424   JOHN GREEN TO RICHARD PACE, JUN.
        May 14, 1728. 20 pds. for 200 A. On NS Morattock River. Adj. 100 A.
sold to BARTHOLOMEW CHAVERS and 200 A. sold to RALPH MASON. Part of 640 A.
patent dated March 1, 1719. Wit: BENJAMIN THOMAS, JOHN BRADFORD. May
Court 1728. EDW. MASHBORNE D.C/C.

B 425   JOHN BIRD & WIFE MARY TO ROBERT BIRD
        February 1727/28. "divers good causes" For 200 A. Unto my son
ROBERT BIRD and his heirs lawfully begotten...and in default to my Daughter
REBEKAH BIRD and her heirs lawfully begotten...if both should die without
heirs unto my brother EDWARD BIRD..." ...and so successively to my other
Brother and Sisters in the same manner as NATHANIEL SUTTON late of Perquimmons Precinct did by his last will and testament bequeath a piece of land
containing (130 A.)...which I JOHN BIRD by a late act of assembly am empow-
ered to sell...." Wit: ROBERT BROWN, JAMES CORICE(?), THOMAS COPLIN.

B 426   MARY BIRD TO JAMES CURRIE (listed JOHN BIRD TO ROBERT BIRD)
        May 13, 1728. Power of atty. to ack. land unto ROBERT BIRD. Wit:
*, *. May Court 1728. EDW. MASHBORNE D.C/C.

B 426   JOSEPH BOON & WIFE ELIZABETH of Chowan Precinct TO RICHARD BAYLEY
        Jan. 27, 1727/28. "...value received" 200 A. At Kirbey's Creek and
Spring Branch on SS Meherrin River. Part of patent of 400 A. dated March 1,
1719. Wit: WILLIAM GREEN, NATHAN COOPER. May Court 1728. EDW. MASHBORNE
D.C/C.

B 427   WILLIAM GOODMAN & WIFE MARY TO BENJAMIN GRIFFIN
        May 15, 1728. 25 pds. for 400 A. "...two tracts of land hereafter
described is to say one certain plantation...." One 50 A. and one 350 A.
The 350 A. tract by patent dated Aug. 1, 1727. The 50 A. seated by GOOD-
MAN. Wit: WILLIAM WHITFIELD. May Court 1728. EDW. MASHBORNE D.C/C.

B 428   CHARLES STEVENS (STEVENSON) TO SAMUEL WILLIAMS
        Nov. 14, 1727. 10 pds. for 100 A. Patent granted July 13, 1726.
Adj. SAMUEL MERRIT, RICHARD BRACEWELL. Wit: THOMAS JENKINS, RICHARD SUM-
NER, JAMES MOORE. May Court 1728. EDW. MASHBORNE D.C/C.

B 429   WILLIAM MOOR, SEN. TO WILLIAM HOWET
        July 3, 1725. Power of atty. to recover and receive all debts "as
shall be found owing...." Wit: JOHN HUNT, jurat, THOMAS GANEY, jurat. May
Court 1728. EDW. MASHBORNE D.C/C.

B 430   WILLIAM KINCHIN (KINCHEN) TO JOHN FARROR (FARROUR)
        May 12, 1728. 5 pds. for 100 A. On Meherrin River and Kirbey's
Creek Adj. THOMAS MANDEW "...thence along windings of Coyray & Kirbey's
Creek...." Wit: NEDHAM BRYAN, ANDREW IRELAND. May Court 1728. EDW. MASH-
BORNE D.C/C.

B 431   LORDS PROPRIETORS TO JOHN MELTON
        March 9, 1717/18. Grant. 400 A. On SS Ahotske Swamp. Adj. JOHN
DAVISON. For transportation of persons @ 50 A./person. Recorded in
Sec't'y. Office, JOHN LOVICK, sec't'y. Signed: FRAN. FORSTER, WM. REED,
CHAS. EDEN, RICHARD SANDERSON, THOS. POLLOCK. *. *.

B 432   JOHN MOLTON, SEN. TO STEPHEN HOWARD
        Feb. 5, 1722. *. *. "I...do make over and assign unto STEPHEN HOW-
ARD all my right title and Interest to me belonging in the within mentioned
patent...." Wit: ROBERT LANIER, JAMES HOWARD, WILLIAM HOWETT. *. *.

B 432   STEPHEN HOWARD & WIFE SARAH TO EDWARD MOORE
        April 1, 1728. *. *. "I...do make over and assign to EDWARD MOORE
all my rite and Interest...of (250A.)...of within patent...." Wit: JOHN
HATCHER, JONATHAN STANDLEY. May Court 1728. EDW. MASHBORNE D.C/C.

B 432   LORDS PROPRIETORS TO STEPHEN HOWARD

Aug. 4, 1723. Grant. 235 A. On SS Ahotskey Swamp and SS Turkey Swamp. Adj. JOHN MOLTON, JOHN BARFIELD. Recorded in Sec't'y. Office JOHN LOVICK, sec't'y. Signed: RICH'D. SANDERSON, WILLIAM REED, C. GALE, THOMAS POLLOCK.

B 433 STEPHEN HOWARD & WIFE SARAH TO EDWARD MOORE (MOOR)
April 1, 1728. *. *. "...all my rite and title...of within patent ...." Wit: JOHN HATCHER, JONATHAN STANDLEY. May Court 1728. EDW. MASHBORNE D.C/C.

B 433 JOHN SESSIONS, yeoman, TO MOSES HARE, yeoman, of Nansemond Co., Va.
Feb. 23, 1727/28. 60 pds. for 490 A. On Rockquist Swamp. By patent dated April 16, 1722 for 490 A. Wit: EDWARD HARE, MOSES OADHAM, THOMAS SPEIGHT. N. C. Court April 2, 1728. C. GALE, C.J. Test. E. MASHBORNE D.C/C.

B 435 ALEX. VANGALL TO WILLIAM CHARLETON, SEN.
July 29, 1728. 10 pds. for 350 A. On SS Morattock River "bounded as the patent mentions..." Wit: WILLIAM LATTIMER, LUKE MIZELL. N.C. Court July 31, 1728. C. GALE, C.J.; Test. EDW. MASHBORNE D.C/C.

B 436 JOSEPH HUDSON, JUN. of Chowan Precinct TO DANIEL FRAZIER
April 18, 1728. 30 pds. for 100 A. On Cashoke Creek adj. WILLIAM BURT and CAPT. HUDSON. Land sold by JOHN CROMBEE to JACOB HARDY and by JACOB HARDY ack. to JAMES CASTELAW and by JAMES CASTELAW assigned to JOSEPH HUDSON, JUN. in October 16, 1722. North Carolina Court April 18, 1728. C. GALE, C.J., Test. EDW. MASHBORNE D.C/C. Wit: GEORGE ALLEN, RICHARD SWINSON.

B 437 MOSES HARE of Nansemond Co., Va. TO THOMAS SPEIGHT of Nansemond Co., Va.
Feb. 2, 1727/28. 30 pds. for 245 A. On Rockquist Swamp. Sold by JOHN SESSIONS to HARE on Feb. 23, 1727/28(?). Wit: CHARLES KING, MARY KING, HENRY KING. N. C. Court April 2, 1728. EDW. MASHBORNE D.C/C.

B 438 EDMOND SMITHWICK TO NATHANIEL MING
July 30, 1728. 28 pds. 5 sh. for 350 A. On SS Morattock River "... as patent mentions...." Wit: JOHN STANSEL, RICHARD SWAIN. N. C. Court July 31, 1728. C. GALE, C.J., ED. MASHBORNE D.C/C.

B 439 WILLIAM CHARLETON TO EDMOND SMITHWICK
July 24, 1728. 12 pds. for 350 A. On SS Morattock River "binding as the patent makes mention...." Wit: JOHN STANSELL, JOHN STACEY. N. C. Court July 31, 1728. C. GALE., C. J. Test: EDW. MASHBORNE D.C/C.

B 440 LORDS PROPRIETORS TO SAMUEL SWANN
May 9, 1728. Grant. 3,200 A. At head of Fishing Creek Adj. ROBERT FORSTER. Land which was formerly granted to HENRY IRWIN and "by him lapsed for want of seating." Recorded in Sec't'y. Office JOHN LOVICK, sec't'y. Signed: EDW. MOSELEY, RICHD. SANDERSON, EDM. GALE, RICHARD EVERARD, THOMAS POLLOCK, JOHN LOVICK, J. WORLEY.

B 441 SAMUEL SWANN of Perquimmons Precinct TO EDWARD MOSELEY of Chowan Prec't.
June 1, 1728. 45 pds. for 3200 A. Land at head of Fishing Creek. Granted to SWANN by patent dated May 29, 1728. Adj. ROBERT FORSTER. Wit: RICHD. SANDERSON, J. BADHAM. N. C. Court Sept. 10, 1728. C. GALE, C. J., R. FORESTER, Deputy Sec't'y. EDW. MASHBORNE D.C/C. (Book D, Fol. 479)

B 442 JEREMIAH BARNES of Perquimmons Precinct to JOSEPH, JAMES & JACOB BARNES
Aug. 13, 1728. 150 A. "love, good will and affection which I have ...unto my brothers...." Land Adj. JOSEPH BARNES, JACOB BARNES, CHARLES JONES, _____ WILLIAMS, EDW. HOWARD, JAMES BARNES. On Horse Swamp and "Chin-o-pine Ridge" Adj. JACOB LEWIS. Wit: ROBERT FORSTER, JOHN BARNES. August Court 1728. EDW. MASHBORNE D. C/C.

B 443 WILLIAM GRAY TO GEORGE STEVENSON
May 13, 1727. 35 pds. for 640 A. On NS Morattock River on Village Swamp. Adj. JOHN WILLIAMS. Land granted by patent to JAMES CASTELAW on April 1, 1727 and "by him elapsed for want of seating." Wit: JOHN GRAY,

HENRY GARTON. August Court 1728. EDW. MASHBORNE D.C/C. (Wit: CHAS. STEVENSON.)

B 444 THOMAS BRYAN (BRYANT) TO WILLIAM COWAN (COWIN)
Aug. 13, 1728. 12 pds. for 320 A. On SS Morattock River on Fishing Creek. Part of 640 A. grant to THOS. BRYANT dated April 14, 1727. Wit: SIMON JEFFREY, JOHN SUTTON. August Court 1728. EDW. MASHBORNE D. C/C.

B 444 STEPHEN HOWARD TO JACOB OADHAM
Aug. 14, 1728. 15 pds. for 320 A. On Casia Swamp Adj. JAMES HOWARD and JACOB OADHAM. Part of patent dated February 1725. Wit: JOHN SUTTON, ROBT. RADFORD. August Court 1728. EDW. MASHBORNE D.C/C.

B 445 SAMUEL ELSON, mariner, TO JOHN BONDE
Aug. 14, 1728. 20 pds. for 540 A. On NS Meherrin River bounded as appears by patent dated March 26, 1723. Adj. MARY BRACEWELL, _____ CHESHIRE. Wit: ELIAS FORD, PEACE ELSON. August Court 1728. EDW. MASHBORNE D.C/C.

B 446 STEPHEN HOWARD TO JAMES HOWARD
Aug. 14, 1728. 15 pds. for 320 A. On Cashia Swamp. Half patent granted Feb. 1, 1725. Wit: JOHN SUTTON, ROBERT RADFORD. August Court 1728. EDW. MASHBORNE D.C/C.

B 447 JOHN WILLIAMS TO WILLIAM WILLIFORD
Jan. 1, 1727. 50 pds. for 200 A. At mouth of Pit Bladder Branch òn Ahotskey Swamp. Adj. STEPHEN WILLIAMS. Wit: JOHN SWINNEY, WILLIAM ASKEW. August Court 1728. EDW. MASHBORNE D.C/C.

B 448 CHARLES STEVENSON TO JOHN CHESHIRE
July 6, 1728. 12 pds. for 400 A. Part of 640 A. patent granted WILLIAM GRAY on April 1, 1725. Adj. HENRY OVERSTREET, JAMES CASTELAW, JOHN WILLIAMS at Village Swamp and Falling Run Adj. COLL. MAULE, COLL. JONES. Wit: JOSEPH DARDEN, ANN THOMAS, JAMES ACKLAS(?). August Court 1728. EDW. MASHBORNE D.C/C.

B 449 WILLIAM FAULK TO HENRY BAKER
Aug. 12, 1728. 15 pds. for 110 A. On upper end of Hotskey Pecoson. Wit: ED. MASHBORNE, JOHN DICKINSON. August Court 1728. EDW. MASHBORNE D.C/C.

NOTE HERE: "N.B. This deed BEN. WARREN to GEO. WHITE; by an over-sight was not done in its place, it ought to have been in page 386 of this book it is done here and is as follows (Old Book p 367)."

B 450 BENJAMIN WARREN TO GEORGE WHITE
Feb. 13, 1728. 50 pds. for 150 A. On Oberrys Branch. Adj. HENRY BRADLEY, JOHN SMITH, BENJAMIN WARREN. Wit: LEWIS BRYANT, jurat, HENRY BRADLEY. February Court 1727. EDW. MASHBORNE D.C/C.

(End Book B)

NOTE HERE: "Page 7 KENNADAY to LEGATT Page 8 HOBSON to KENNEDY are both with the whole sheet one-- N.B. the original Deed KENNEDY to LEGGETT is in the office, but the other not....The sheet page 7 & 8 gone...mised Jan.12, 1796 & not before--LUKE(?) COLLINS, Esq."

C 1 JOHN WILLIAMS TO LAZARUS THOMAS
Aug. 14, 1728. 27 pds. for 560 A. Land on Holly Swamp Adj. MATTHEW TOBIAS SWANER, JAMES CURLEE. Wit: THOMAS BIRD, ED. HOWARD. August Court 1728. EDW. MASHBORNE D.C/C.

C 2 WILLIAM BRACEWELL TO JAMES WOOD
July 31, 1728. 25 pds. for 250 A. At mouth of Patterson Branch on Yourah Swamp. Wit: BRYAN O'QUIN, JOHN SUTTON. August Court 1728. EDW. MASHBORNE D.C/C.

C 2 WILLIAM GRIFFIN TO HENRY BAKER
Aug. 12, 1728. 20 pds. for 640 A. On NS Morattock River. Patent granted to WILLIAM GRAY on April 1, 1725 and by him conveyed to W. GRIFFIN by deed Feb. ?1, 1727/28. Wit: THOMAS HOLLAND, JAMES HOLLAND. August Court 1728. EDW. MASHBORNE D.C/C.

C 3   WILLIAM BRACEWELL TO ROBERT BRACEWELL
       July 31, 1728. 7 pds. for 100 A. On SS Yourah Swamp at Mirey Branch
and Poplar Branch. Wit: EDW. GREEN, JOHN SUTTON. August Court 1728. EDW.
MASHBORNE D.C/C.

C 4   DANIEL MACDANIEL (MCDANIEL) TO ANTHONY LEWIS of Isle of Wight Co.,
       Va.
       Aug. 13, 1728. 24 pds. for 410 A. On Beaverdam Swamp at Spring
Branch. Adj. JOHN CROSBEY (CROSBY), THOMAS ____INSON. Tract granted by
patent on March 9, 1717. Wit: LEONARD LANGSTON, JOHN NAIRRUR. August
Court 1728. EDW. MASHBORNE D.C/C.

C 5   WILLIAM BRACEWELL & WIFE MARGARETT TO THOMAS DAUGHTRY of Nansimond
       Co., Va.
       Aug. 13, 1728. 8 pds. for 200 A. On Yohohoh Swamp at Patterson
Branch. "WILLIAM BRACEWELL son and heir of WILLIAM BRACEWELL Dec'd...8
pds. paid to my father...bond dated Feb. 10, 1718...." Wit: JOHN DICKIN-
SON, PETER HASE, JAMES HOLLAND. August Court 1728. EDW. MASHBORNE D.C/C.

C 6   BENJAMIN FOREMAN & WIFE VERILAH TO GEORGE WILLIAMS
       Aug. 13, 1728. 30 pds. for 600 A. On NS Roanoke River. Adj. GEORGE
WILLIAMS known by name "Canoquinat." Wit: ROBERT FORSTER, HENRY TURNER,
JOHN NAIRN. JOHN MCDANIEL. *. *.

C 7   VERILAH FOREMAN TO JOHN NAIRNR
       Aug. 12, 1728. *. *. Power of atty. to ack. sale of "Canoquinal"
to GEORGE WILLIAMS, SEN. Wit: HENRY TURNER, jurat, JOHN MCDANIEL, jurat.
August Court 1728. EDW. MASHBORNE D.C/C.

C 8   JOHN STEWART TO THEOPHILUS PUGH, merchant, of Nansemond Co., Va.
       Feb. 12, 1727. 120 pds. for 750 A. On NS "Roanoke or Morattock
River." Adj. EDWARD HOWARD, OWEN MACDANIEL, ROBERT WEST. "...being two
surveys of land formerly taken up by JOHN ELVERTON...." Wit: JAMES EVERARD,
DANIEL PUGH, MARY GRUMSELL. August Court 1728. EDW. MASHBORNE D.C/C.

C 10   JOHN MORRIS TO GODFRY HOOKER
       Aug. 13, 1728. *. *. "...the within mentioned Deed of Sale...."
Wit: WILLIAM CRANFORD, JOHN WILLIAMS. August Court 1728. EDW. MASHBORNE
D.C/C.

C 10   JOHN BLOUNT & WIFE ELIZABETH TO HENRY OVERSTREET
       July 30, 1728. 30 pds. for 280 A. On Cashia Swamp. Adj. JAMES
BLOUNT. Wit: WILLIAM JONES, JOHN YELVERTON. August Court 1728. EDW.
MASHBORNE D.C/C.

C 11   EMPOROUR (EMPOROR) WHEELER TO BARNABE MCKINNE
       Aug. 10, 1728. 10 pds. for 100 A. On NS Morrattuck River at Occon-
nechee Swamp. Adj. JOHN HAWTHORNE. Part of tract of 640 A. formerly pat-
ented by WILLIAM BRASSWELL on March 4, 1711/12. By BRASSWELL sold to HENRY
WHEELER. By HENRY WHEELER's last will and testament left to his son EMPO-
ROR WHEELER. Wit: THOMAS CRAGHILL, BARNABE MCKINNE, JUN., JOHN POPE, jurat.
August Court 1728. EDW. MASHBORNE D.C/C.

C 12   BARNABE MCKINNE, JUN. TO WILLIAM STRICKLAND
       Aug. 10, 1728. 40 pds. for 100 A. On SS Morrattock River. Part of a
patent formerly granted to WILLIAM BROWN for 140 A. dated April 1, 1713.
"...and by him sold to ARTHUR DAVIS and by DAVIS sold to my father, BARNABE
MCKINNE, SEN. and by my father sold to me...." Wit: BARNABE MACKINNE,
jurat, JOHN POPE, THOMAS CRAGHILL. August Court 1728. EDW. MASHBORNE
D.C/C. Land at "caseway of the Cypress Gut nigh the Great Ditch...near
Warren's Old Path...."

C 13   THOMAS HART & WIFE ANN TO GEORGE WILLIAMS
       Aug. 3, 1728. 16 pds. 5 sh. for 110 A. On SS Meherrin River at Cy-
press Swamp and Beaverdam Run. Land granted HART in 1723 "and at this
present in the actual possession of GEORGE WILLIAMS...." Wit: JOHN SIMPSON,
WILLIAM WALL, ROBERT SAVIDGE. August Court 1728. EDW. MASHBORNE D.C/C.

C 15   HOPKINS HOWELL & WIFE ELIZABETH TO THOMAS HART
       Aug. 3, 1728. "a valuable sum" for 185 A. On Cypress Swamp branch
called Meherrin Cypress. Patent dated Feb. 1, 1725. Wit: JOHN SIMPSON,

WILLIAM WALL, ROBERT SAVIDGE. August Court 1728. EDW. MASHBORNE D.C/C.

C 16 JOHN HOLLEY TO BARNABE MCKINNE
     Aug. 1, 1728. 7 pds. 10 sh. for 50 A. "JOHN HOLLEY of uper parish
Bertie precinct, son and heir of NATHANIEL HOLLEY dec'd...." Land on SS
Morattock River. Part of patent for 640 A. formerly granted to WILLIAM
BROWN and sold to NATHANIEL HOLLEY. Patent date April 1, 1712. The remain-
der of the 640 A. sold by NATHANIEL HOLLEY to BARNABE MCKINNE and RICHARD
JACKSON "by several deeds." Wit: SAMUEL SWEARINGEN, ISAAC RICKS, THOMAS
CRAGHILL. August Court 1728. EDW. MASHBORNE D.C/C.

C 17 JOSEPH LANE & WIFE JULIAN TO WILLIAM BALDWIN
     July 29, 1727. 18 pds. for 213 A. On Little Swamp Adj. BENJAMIN
THOMAS. Patent dated Feb. 1, 1725. Wit: DANIEL REGAN, JOHN GLOVER. August Court 1728. EDW. MASHBORNE D.C/C.

C 17 JAMES SMITH TO JOSEPH HARRELL of Nansemond Co., Va.
     Aug. 12, 1725. 17 pds. for 200 A. On NS Morattock River Adj. WILL-
IAM EVANS, WILIAM EASON, JOHN ELVERTON. "nigh a place called Redy Branch"
at Flaggy Run. Wit: CHRISTOPHER GOWAN, jurat, JOSEPH WOOD. *. EDW. MASH-
BORNE. D.C/C.

C 18 BENJAMIN LANE TO ROBERT SIMS
     August 1728. 10 pds. for 640 A. On SS Morattock River at Conaconore
Swamp. Patent dated Feb. 1, 1725. Wit: JACOB POPE, WILLIAM CAIN. August
Court 1728. EDW. MASHBORNE D.C/C.

C 19 RICHARD BRACEWELL, JUN. TO RICHARD BRACEWELL, SEN.
     Aug. 13, 1728. 5 pds. for 640 A. On SS Cashy Swamp. Wit: THOMAS
BRYANT, THOMAS JENKINS. August Court 1728. EDW. MASHBORNE D.C/C.

C 20 JOHN HOBBSON (HOBSON) of Cashi TO FRANCIS HOBSON
     July 24, 1728. 100 pds. for 111 A. On NS Morattock River at Meadow
Branch and Spring Marsh. Part of patent for 222 A. Wit: JOHN HOBSON,
WILLIAM CRISP, JAMES RUTLAND, jurat. August Court 1728. EDW. MASHBORNE
D.C/C.

C 21 JOHN HOBSON TO JAMES RUTLAND
     Aug. 2, 1728. Power of atty. to ack. sale. Wit: THOMAS BAREFIELD,
THOMAS WALSON (WATSON?), jurat. August Court 1728. EDW. MASHBORNE D.C/C.

C 21 JOHN HALE TO HENRY BUNCH of Chowan Precinct
     Dec. 18, 1727. 60 pds. for 200 A. At mouth of Reedy Branch Adj.
JOHN HALE. Wit: ROBERT ROUTE, JOHN STEWARD. N.C. Court December 17, 1727.
C. GALE, C.J. Test. EDW. MASHBORNE D.C/C.

C 22 HENRY BAKER TO JOHN HARRELL, JUN.
     Aug. 12, 1728. 25 pds. for 630 A. (637 A.) On NS Morattock River at
Flaggy Run. Patent date April 6, 1722. Adj. JOHN NAIRN, JAMES PARKER.
Wit: CHRISTOPHER GEWIN, JOSEPH HARRELL. August Court 1728. EDW. MASH-
BORNE D.C/C.

C 23 JOHN SURGINER TO NICHOLAS SMITH
     Aug. 6, 1728. 20 pds. for 325 A. On SS Morattock River at Cahukee
Swamp. Adj. WILLIAM DREW (DEW). Wit: WILLIAM FAULK, JOHN NAIRNE. August
Court 1728. EDW. MASHBORNE D.C/C.

C 23 HENRY WEST TO CHRISTOPHER GEWIN
     March 25, 1728. 100 pds. for 150 A. On NS Morattock River. Adj.
JAMES PARKER, OWIN O'DANIEL, WILLIAM EASON. Wit: WILLIAM HUTCHINSON, JOHN
NAIRNR. August Court 1728. EDW. MASHBORNE D.C/C.

C 24 JOHN LOVICK & WIFE PENELOPE of Edenton TO JAMES LOCKHART, merchant
     Dec. 29, 1727. 280 pds. for 250 A. "...PENELOPE late widow and
relict of Coll. WILLIAM MAULE...MAULE did bequeath to PENELOPE...the plantation whereon he did live...called Scott's Hall...." Wit: WILLIAM LITTLE,
JOHN LOVICK. N. C. Court Dec. 29, 1727. "...PENELOPE privately Examined
pursuant to an act of Assembly of this province...did (ack.) sale...." C.
GALE, C.J. EDW. MASHBORNE D.C/C.

C 25 JOHN GARDNER TO WILLIAM GARDNER

Aug. 9, 1728. On Swift Creek and SS Morattock River. Wit: EDMOND
SMITHWICK, EDW. GRIFFIN, JOHN GRIFFIN. August Court 1728. EDW. MASHBORNE
D.C/C. (10 pds. for 175 A.)

NOTE HERE: "So Far done to Aug Court 1798"

C 26   THOMAS BUSBY TO JOHN PAGE, JUN.
        Aug. 6, 1728. *. 170 A. "...love good will and affection I have
and do bare toward my loving son in law JOHN PAGE, JUN...." Land on ES
Cashie Swamp. Wit: JOHN DUFFIELD, JOHN PAGE, SEN. August Court 1728. EDW.
MASHBORNE D.C/C.

C 27   JACOB POPE TO BENJAMIN LANE
        Aug. 10, 1728. 40 pds. for 120 A. On SS Morattock River. Part of
patent dated Nov. 7, 1723. At mouth of "Small Branch which makes into
Looking Glass pecoson...." Wit: WILLIAM CAIN, ROBERT SIMS. August Court
1728. EDW. MASHBORNE D.C/C.

C 28   JONATHAN DAVICE (DAVISE) (DAVIS) TO RICHARD MURICK
        Aug. 13, 1728. 20 pds. for 200 A. On NS Morattock. Wit: JOHN
NAIRNR, JOHN ALSTON. August Court 1728. EDW. MASHBORNE D.C/C.

C 29   JOHN NAIRNR TO JONATHAN DAVIS (DAVICE)
        March 20, 1727/28. 10 pds. for 200 A. On SS Morattock River at Cy-
press. Adj. JOHN WOODS. Wit: JAMES SPEIR, JOHN ALSTON. August Court 1728.
EDW. MASHBORNE D.C/C.

C 30   ROBERT WEST & WIFE MARY TO JOSEPH CLEPEHAM
        Jan. 29, 1727. 15 pds. for 150 A. In Runoroy Marshes at Flaggy Run.
Adj. HENRY RHODES. Wit: TIMOTHY RIALL, ANN YELVERTON, PETER KEIGHLEY.
August Court 1728. EDW. MASHBORNE D.C/C.

C 31   ROBERT WEST & WIFE MARY TO JOSEPH CLAPHAM
        Feb. 1727/28. "for divers causes" 20 A. At east corner of ROBERT
WEST's tract. Wit: TIMOTHY RIALL, ANN YELVERTON, PETER KEIGHTLEY. August
Court 1728. EDW. MASHBORNE D.C/C.

C 31   ROBERT WEST & WIFE MARY TO JOHN YELVERTON
        Feb. 2, 1727. 5 pds. for 125 A. Adj. OWIN DANIELS, WILLIAM EASON,
JAMES PARKER, HENRY BOOKES (BOOKERS) on Flaggy Run. Wit: TIMOTHY RIALL,
PETER KEIGHTLEY, ANN YELVERTON. August Court 1728. EDW. MASHBORNE D.C/C.

C 32   RICHARD BRACEWELL, SEN. & WIFE _____ TO JONATHAN STANDLEY, JUN.
        April 20, 1728. "a valuable consideration" for 640 A. On SS Kesiah
Swamp. Adj. patent of 451 A. of RICHARD BRACEWELL. Wit: THOMAS JENKINS,
JOHN ROWS. EDW. MASHBORNE D.C/C.

C 33   THOMAS MERREDETH of Hanover Co., Va. TO (CHRISTIAN) HEIDLEBERG(?),
        deputy marshall
        Sept. 17, 1728. Power of atty. to recover debts and to pay sums of
money and to contract as "he shall think fit." Wit: ED. MASHBORNE, JOHN
DICKINSON, jurat. August Court 1728. EDW. MASHBORNE D.C/C.

C 33   GEORGE CLEMENTS TO THOMAS MERREDETH of Hanover Co., Va.
        Sept. 12, 1728. 120 pds. *. "one Negro man named Tom of middleing
stature supposed to be aged about 25 years...." Wit: SPIAN (CHRIASTIAN)
HEIDELBERG, JOHN SUTTON. August Court 1728. *.

C 34   LORDS PROPRIETORS TO GEORGE WYNE
        Dec. 3, 1720. Grant. 150 A. At PETER WEST's corner adj. ROBERT
LANIER. For importation of persons 50/person. Signed: JOHN LOVICK, sec'-
t'y., C. EDEN, RD. SANDERSON, THOS. POLLOCK. *.*.

C 34   GEORGE WINNS TO JOHN WINNS
        Nov. 12, 1728. *. *. "for love and affection I have and bear unto
my son JOHN...." (Probably above patent.) Wit: JOHN WILLIAMS, JOSEPH
WILLIAMS. November Court 1728. EDW. MASHBORNE D.C/C.

C 35   THOMAS BOON, JUN. TO JOHN BRYAN, JUN.
        *. 13 barrels of tar for 150 A. Part of tract by Deed sold by
WILLIAM BENNETT unto THOMAS BOON (600 A.). Granted to BENNETT in 1723. On

On SS Meherrin River Adj. JOHN NELSON, WILLIAM BOON. Wit: THOMAS BOON, HENRY CRAMPTON. November Court 1728. EDW. MASHBORNE D.C/C.

C 36   GIDEON GIBSON & WIFE MARY TO JAMES MILLICAN & HENRY AUGUSTIN (GUSTIN)
        Oct. 22, 1728. 15 pds. for 150 A. On SS Merattuck River "bounded according to the will of WILLIAM BROWN, Gentleman, dec'd..." Wit: DANS RICH. HAINSWORTH, MICHEL MCKINSEY, RICH. JACKSON. November Court 1728. E. MASHBORNE D.C/C.

C 37   HUBBARD GIBSON, EDWARD GIBSON, HUBBARD GIBSON, JUN. TO SAMUEL CHAM-
        BERLIN of Hanover Co., Va.
        July 11, 1728. 5 sh. For one year lease on 370 A. On NS Morattock River Adj. ARTHUR HAVENNUGHS(?), RALPH MASON, JOHN HANTHORUS(?) on Falling Run. Land formerly granted to JOHN GIBSON dec'd. son of said HUBBARD, SEN. Patent dated Aug. 10, 1720. EDWARD and HUBBARD GIBSON, JUN. sons of HUB-BARD GIBSON, SEN. Wit: DAVIE HOPPER (KOPPER?), ROBERT SIMMS, JOHN EVANS. November Court 1728. E. MASHBORNE D.C/C.

C 38   HUBBARD GIBSON, EDWARD GIBSON, HUBBARD GIBSON, JUN. TO SAMUEL CHAM-
        BERLIN of Hanover Co., Va.
        July 12, 1728. 15 pds. for 370 A. Adj. ARTHUR KAVENAUGH, RALPH MASON, JOHN HANTHORN. Land granted by patent dated April 10, 1720 to JOHN GIBSON, dec'd. son of HUBBARD GIBSON, SEN. Wit: DAVIE HOPPER, ROBERT SIMES, _____ EVANS. November Court 1728. EDW. MASHBORNE D.C/C.

C 39   FOSTER MASON TO SAMUEL CHAMBERLAIN of Hanover Co., Va.
        Nov. 11, 1728. 5 pds. for 100 A. On NS Merattuck River Adj. RALPH MASON, JUN., RALPH MASON, SEN. Land formerly ack. by RALPH MASON "the elder" unto his son FOSTER MASON by deed of gift dated July 16, 1720. Wit: JOHN GRAY, WILLIAM GRAY. November Court 1728. EDW. MASHBORNE D.C/C.

C 40   FOSTER MASON TO SAMUEL CHAMBERLIN of Hanover Co., Va.
        Nov. 12, 1720. "for consideration therein mentioned." 100A. On NS Morattock River. Adj. RALPH MASON, JUN., RALPH MASON, JOHN HANTHORN. Land by Deed of gift July 16, 1720 by RALPH MASON to his son FOSTER MASON. Wit: JOHN GRAY, WILLIAM GRAY. November Court 1728. EDW. MASHBORNE D.C/C.

C 41   JOHN BRYAN TO JOHN GRAY
        Feb. 1727/28. 20 pds. for 640 A. On SS Morattick River on Cypress Swamp. Adj. JOHN BRYAN, JOHN HAMILTON, ARTHUR DAVIS. Wit: LEWIS BRYAN, SIMON BRYAN, jurat. November Court 1728. EDW. MASHBORNE D.C/C.

C 42   JOHN EDWARDS, SEN. & JOHN EDWARDS, JUN. TO JOHN GRAY
        Oct. 29, 1728. 40 pds. for 300 A. On NS Cashay River known as "Turkey Neck." Adj. THOMAS JONES on Licking Branch. Wit: EDW. MOORE, GEO. EUBANCK, jurat. November Court 1728. EDW. MASHBORNE D.C/C.

C 43   JOHN HART TO SIMON JEFFREYS
        Jan. 22, 1727. 60 pds. for 640 A. On NES Morattuck River. Land granted to NEEDHAM BRYAN by patent April 3, 1721 and deeded to HART November 12, 1723. Wit: THOMAS BRYANT, ROBERT HILLIARD, JOHN HILLIARD, SAMUEL WILLIAMS. November Court 1728. EDW. MASHBORNE D.C/C.

C 45   JOHN HART & WIFE MARY TO THOMAS HART
        Aug. 8, 1727. 6 pds. for 100 A. On NS Morattuck River and NS Vil-lage Swamp. Part of tract formerly granted to RICHARD MILTON for 640 A. by patent dated April 1, 1721. Wit: WILLIAM RUFFIN, JUN., JOHN BRYAN. Novem-ber Court 1728. EDW. MASHBORNE D.C/C.

C 46   SAMUEL GARLAND TO EDWARD POWERS
        May 14, 1727. 30 pds. for 220 A. On NS Meherin River and ES Horse Pasture Creek Adj. ARTHUR BENN. Part of 320 A. grant to GARLAND dated March 20, 1723. Wit: JOHN ROGERS, jurat, JOHN ROGERS, JUN. November Court 1728. EDW. MASHBORNE D.C/C.

C 47   GEORGE WILLIAMS, SEN. TO JOAN (JANE) BROWN (BROWNE)
        Nov. 14, 1728. 215 A. "for good will and affection I bear to JOAN the wife of THOMAS BROWN...." Land on Conaquinat Swamp. Adj. BENJAMIN FOREMAN. Wit: JOHN NAIRNR, *. November Court 1728. EDW. MASHBORNE D.C/C.

        NOTE HERE: "N.B. The blanks in the above last written Deed, with this I mark are parts in the old Book B that were Intirely defaced, and not Readable, being the last sheet of said Old Book-page 461-Test. DAVID TUR-NER, Public Register. September 28, 1798."

NOTE HERE: "N.B. Here begins the new copying the Old Book C-"

C 48   JOHN MENSHEW of Chowan Precinct to BRYANT MACLAINE
        Feb. 16, 1728. 15 pds. for 200 A. At "Old County Line." Adj. JOHN HOOKS, JUN. on Meadow Branch, and JOHN HOOKS, SEN. Part of patent granted MINSHEW for 640 A. on April 1, 1723. Wit: JOHN SMITH, JAMES HOLLAND. November Court 1728. EDW. MASHBORNE D.C/C.

C 49   JAMES WILLIAMSON, precinct surgeon, & JOHN TAYLOR TO DANSY STANDLEY
        Nov. 11, 1728. 39 pds. for 170 A. On Roquis Creek Adj. LUKE MEZEL. Wit: JAMES CASTELAW. *. EDW. MASHBORNE D.C/C. GEORGE EUBANCK by virtue of power of atty. ack. deed in open court.

C 50   DOCTOR JAMES WILLIAMSON & JONATHAN TAYLOR TO GEORGE EUBANCK
        Nov. 11, 1728. *. *. Power of atty. to ack. sale to DAVID STANDLEY. Wit: JAMES CASTELAW, MARY GRAY. *. EDW. MASHBORNE D.C/C.

C 50   WILLIAM WHITEHEAD TO EDWARD BASS
        Aug. 12, 1728. 10 pds. for 140 A. *. Wit: JAMES CASTELAW, JOHN GLISSON. November Court 1728. EDW. MASHBORNE D.C/C.

C 51   LORDS PROPRIETORS TO JOHN MOORE (MOOR) & BENTON MOOR
        Oct. 1, 1726. Grant. 640 A. On SES Meherrin at mouth of Elm Swamp. Adj. ED. COBB. Land surveyed for RICHARD MOORE, Father to the said JOHN and BENTON, and was by RICHARD devised to JOHN & BENTON. Signed: FRAN. FOSTER, C. GALE, EDM. GALE, THOS. HARVEY, RICHARD EVERARD, WILLIAM REED, ED MOSELEY, ROBERT FORSTER, Deputy Sec't'y.

C 51   JOHN MOORE TO WILLIAM HOWETT
        Nov. 13, 1728. 50 pds. for "aforementioned tract." Wit: THOMAS JONES, *. November Court 1728. ED. MASHBORNE D.C/C.

C 52   THOMAS TAPLEY TO JOSHUA GOODING of Nancymond Co., Va.
        Nov. 11, 1728. 20 pds. for 150 A. On SS Morattuck River & SS Connocanaro Swamp. Adj. BENJ. LANE. Wit: WILLIAM TURBERVILLE, WALTER TURBERVILLE. November Court 1728. ED. MASHBORNE D.C/C.

C 52   THOMAS BRIGMAN & WIFE ELIZABETH TO JOHN GIBSON
        Oct. 28, 1728 (Nov. 12, 1728). 15 pds. for 335 A. On NS Casay Swamp and NES Wattom Swamp. Wit: JAMES MURRY, THOMAS RODES, THOMAS BRIGMAN. November Court 1728. ED. MASHBORNE D.C/C.

C 53   ARTHUR WHITEHEAD & WIFE ISABELL (ISOBELL) of Isle of Wight C., Va.
        TO JOHN PERRIT
        April 10, 1728. 20 pds. for 640 A. On lower side of Bridgers Creek. Land granted by patent dated March 9, 1717/18. Adj. HENRY JONES. Wit: JOSEPH COTTON, THOMAS BOON. November Court 1728. ED. MASHBORNE D.C/C.

C 55   ED(WARD) YOUNG & WIFE SARAH TO FRANCIS YOUNG
        November 1728. 5 pds. for 150 A. On SS Morattuck River Adj. ROBERT HILL on Beaverdam. Part of 570 A. granted THOMAS WHITMELL April 6, 1722 and by him conveyed to ED. YOUNG. Wit: WILLIAM GRAY, JAMES JONES. November Court 1728. EDW. MASHBORNE D.C/C.

C 55   HENRY JONES, SEN., yeoman, TO HENRY JONES, JUN.
        Nov. 9, 1728. 200 A. for "love and affection I do bear unto my son ...." Part of 640 A. patented February 26, 1711. Wit: *, *. November Court 1728. ED. MASHBORNE D.C/C.

C 56   THOMAS TAPLEY & PHILLIP MULKEY TO VALTER(?) TUBELFIELD (TROUBLEFIELD)
        Feb. 5, 1727/28. 20 pds. for 240 A. On Con-a-conara Swamp Adj. WILLIAM TRUBELFIELD, ARTHUR DAVIS. Wit: JOHN TRUBELFIELD, FRANCIS TRUBELFIELD, WILLIAM TRUBELFIELD, jurat, JOSEPH LANE. November Court 1728. ED. MASHBORNE D.C/C.

C 57   PHILLIP MULKEY TO WILLIAM TRUBELFIELD
        Feb. 5, 1727/28. 10 pds. for 100 A. on SS Morattuck River and SS

Conacanora Swamp adj. ARTHUR DAVIS. Wit: JOSEPH LANE, VALTER TROULEFIELD, FRANCIS TROUBLEFIELD, JOHN TROUBLEFIELD. November Court 1728. ED. MASH-BORNE. D.C/C.

C 58   JONATHAN SANDERSON TO BARNARD BANGER, precinct school master
         July 26, 1728. 15 pds. for 100 A. On NS Meherring River Adj. ROBERT
BRACEWELL and Buckhorn Swamp, JOHN HOOKS, JONATHAN SANDERSON, County line,
JOHN MENSES, RICHARD KEMP. Part of patent granted to JOHN HICKS on Novem-
ber 7, 1723. Wit: RICHARD KEMP, JOHN GARDNER, THOMAS GRANGER. November
Court 1728. ED. MASHBORNE D.C/C.

C 58   WILLIAM ARINGTON TO THOMAS GOODSON
         Nov. 9, 1728. 5 pds. for 100 A. Part of patent dated Aug. 11, 1728.
Adj. JOSEPH RICHARDSON on Mill Swamp. Wit: WILLIAM BALDWIN, WALTER TROUB-
ELFIELD. November Court 1728. EDW. MASHBORNE D.C/C.

C 59   EDWARD YOUNG TO ROBERT HILL
         Nov. 8, 1728. 5 pds. for 100 A. On SS Morattuck River and Great
Meadow. Part of 625 A. patent dated Feb. 1, 1725. Wit: WILLIAM PERSON,
WILLIAM GRAY. November Court 1728. ED. MASHBORNE D.C/C.

C 60   WILLIAM HOGGET (HOGGATT) & WIFE JUDITH TO WILLIAM BALDWIN
         Nov. 2, 1728. 15 pds. for 215 A. On NS Morattuck River. Part of
640 A. survey granted to WILLIAM JONES Feb. 26, 1711, and by him conveyed
to JOSEPH LANE, JUN. Adj. HOGGAT and BALDWIN on Spring Branch. Wit: RICH-
ARD PACE, jurat, ANDREW IRELAND, jurat, THOMAS REYAN. November Court 1728.
EDW. MASHBORNE D.C/C.

C 60   JOHN GRIFFIN TO WILLIAM GRIFFIN
         Aug. 6, 1728. *. *. for "...love and affection I bear my son...all
my land Tenements and hereditants(?) which I now possess...also two Negroes
bought of OWIN O'DANIEL in Virginia...and one from Mr. FRANCIS...another
from Capt. HENRY POWERS upon York River...and a white servant named PETER
TEANGER bought of ALEXANDER GUSTON and MILLIKAN, merchants...with all my
Cattle Horses Hoggs and Household furniture...." Wit: HENRY GUSTON, GEORGE
EUBANCK, WILLIAM DAVIS. November Court 1728. ED. MASHBORNE D.C/C.

C 61   JOHN GRIFFIN TO JAMES MILLIKAN
         Aug. 6, 1728. *. *. Power of atty. to ack. Deed of Gift to WILLIAM
GRIFFIN. Wit: HENRY GUSTIN, GEORGE EUBANCK, WILLIAM DAVIS. November Court
1728. EDW. MASHBORNE D.C/C.

C 61   HENRY JONES TO FRANCIS JONES
         Nov. 9, 1728. 200 A. for "...love and affection I bear unto my son
..." Land adj. his brother HENRY. Part of 640 A. granted Feb. 26, 1711.
Wit: ROBERT JONES, C. EVANS. November Court 1728. EDW. MASHBORNE D.C/C.

C 62   THOMAS RHODES & WIFE MARY TO NATHANIEL ROWLAND of Chowan Precinct
         Nov. 11, 1728. 20 pds. for 390 A. On NES Casyah Swamp to Beaverdam.
Wit: JAMES MURRAY, JOHN EDWARDS, WILLIAM JONES. November Court 1728. EDW.
MASHBORNE D.C/C.

C 63   WILLIAM HARDING JONES of Chowan precinct TO WILLIAM DANIEL, ordinary
         keeper
         March 10, 1728/29. "one pistole and half...and 50 pds...." for 300
A. On Deep Creek at mouth of Mirey Branch adj. JAMES RUTLAND. Wit: ROBERT
PEARCE, CONST.(?) LUTON, W. BADHAM. N. C. Court March 10, 1728. C. GALE,
C. J. Test: EDW. MASHBORNE D.C/C.

C 63   JOHN BAREFIELD late of Nansemond Co., Va. but now of Strafford Co.,
         Va. TO THOMAS HOLLAND of Essex Co., Va.
         Sept 11, 1728. 8,000 lbs. of tobacco for 640 A. On SS Meherring
River. Adj. JOHN BEAVERLY, THOMAS ISMAY. Land formerly leased for one
year by HOLLAND. Taken up by JOHN BAREFIELD and lately in possession of
THOMAS JERNAGAN. Wit: CHRISTOPHER HOLLAND, MARY GRAY. N. C. Court Nov. 6,
1728. C. GALE, C. J. Test: *.

C 64   JOHN BAREFIELD of Stafford Co., Va. TO HENRY BAKER, FRANCIS PUGH,
         LEWIS JENKINS
         Sept. 11, 1728. *. *. Power of atty. to all or each to ack. "deeds

of lease and release" to THOMAS HOLLAND. Wit: CHRISTOPHER HOLLAND, MARY GRAY. *. *.

C 65   MARTHA BUSH TO MARY BUSH
        Sept. 13, 1728. "...for love and affection I bear unto MARY BUSH my Daughter in law late wife of my son JOHN BUSH dec'd. and my five grandchildren...ELIZABETH, JOHN, MARY, HARDY and ISAAC BUSH...the one half of all my goods and chattles and personal estate whatsoever ...to be equally divided among the mother and children...." Wit: NICH. FAIRLESS, JOHN BRYAN. N. C. Court Sept. 14, 1728. C. GALE, C.J. Test: EDW. MASHBORNE D.C/C.

C 65   LORDS PROPRIETORS TO JOHN HILL
        Apr. 1, 1710. Grant. 150 A. In Chowan Precinct on Loosing Swamp. For importation of persons @ 50 A./person. Wit: J. LOVICK, sec't'y., RD. SANDERSON, FRAN. FOSTER, THOS. POLLOCK, C. EDEN, WM. REED.

C 66   JOHN HILL TO ROBERT EVANS
        Dec. 14, 1724. *. *. "within mentioned patent." Signed: JOHN HILL, ISAAC HILL. N. C. Court *. C. GALE, C.J. Test: EDW. MASHBORNE D.C/C.

C 66   MARTHA BUSH TO WILLIAM BUSH
        Sept. 13, 1728. *. *. "for love and affection to...my son WILLIAM ...one half of my goods chattles and personal estate...." Wit: NICH. FAIRLESS, JOHN BRYAN. N. C. Court Sept. 14, 1728. C. GALE, C.J. Test: EDW. MASHBORNE D.C/C.

C 67   THOMAS HOWELL, SEN. TO THOMAS PHILLIPS, JUN.
        Aug. 27, 1724. "valuable sum" for 225 A. On SS Meherring River Adj. JAMES TURNER. Part of patent to THOMAS HOWELL for 450 A. dated April 1, 1723. Wit: THOMAS HOWELL, JUN., ROBERT HART, JOSEPH PLATTS. February Court 1728. EDW. MASHBORNE D.C/C.

C 68   MICHAEL RISHER TO JOHN AVERET
        Feb. 10, 1728. 21 pds. for 230 A. Adj. THOMAS WARR. Wit: WILLIAM CRANFORD, CONST. LUTON. February Court 1728. EDW. MASHBORNE D.C/C.

C 69   EDMOND WIGGINS (WICKINS) & JOHN WIGGANS TO FINCHER HAYNS, merchant
        Feb. 12, 1728. 35 pds. for 240 A. Adj. JOHN MAYNOR, JACOB LEWIS at Brooks Creek. (Signed: EDMOND WICKINS, JOHN WICKINS.) Wit: JOHN GRAY, JAMES MILLIKIN. February Court 1728/29. ED. MASHBORNE D.C/C.

C 69   THOMAS BOON, JUN. TO ELIAS FORT, SEN.
        Nov. 9, 1728. "13 barrells of tar" for 150 A. On SS Meherring River Adj. WILLIAM BOON, JOHN BRYAN. Being "part and parcel" of a deed from WILLIAM BENNET dated 1724. Part of 600 A. granted BENNET on April 1, 1723. Wit: THOMAS BOON, SEN., HENRY CRAMPTON. February Court 1728/29. ED MASHBORNE D.C/C.

C 70   JOHN EARLY, SEN. TO JAMES FOYLE
        Feb. 12, 1728/29. 10 pds. for 95 A. In Quarter Branch Adj. GEORGE SMITH. At Wiccacon Creek Swamp. Wit: JOHN WILLIAMS, jurat, CHRISTOPHER HOLLIMAN, jurat. February Court 1728/29. EDW. MASHBORNE D.C/C.

C 71   JOHN WILLIAMS TO JAMES FOYLE
        Feb. 12, 1728. "a negro man" for 200 A. On Wiccacon Creek Adj. WILLIAM WILLIFORD, STEPHEN WILLIAMS, CHRISTOPHER HOLLIMON. Wit: CHRISTOPHER HOLLIMON, CHARLES ROYALS. February Court 1728/29. EDW. MASHBORNE *.

C 72   JOHN GRAY TO EDWARD YOUNG
        Feb. 12, 1728/29. *. 600 A. On SS Roanoke River and ES Hobb. Quarter Creek. Adj. THOMAS WHITMELL. By patent dated Oct. 19, 1727. Wit: WILLIAM GRAY, GEORGE OTWAY. February Court 1728/29. ED. MASHBORNE D. C/C.

C 72   JOHN EARLY TO CHRISTOPHER HOLLIMON (HOLLIMAN)
        Feb. 12, 1728/29. 15 pds. for 400 A. On Wiccacon Creek Swamp Adj. JAMES FOYLE. Wit: JAMES FOYLE, jurat, CHARLES RYALS. February Court 1728/29. ED. MASHBORNE D.C/C.

C 73   WILLIAM ASKEY TO RICHARD WILLIFORD
        Feb. 6, 1728/29. 30 pds. for 100 A. In Beach Swamp at Pit Blade

64

Branch. Wit: JAMES FOYLE, jurat, WILLIAM WILLIFORD, jurat. February Court
1728/29. ED. MASHBORNE D.C/C.

C 74   JOHN NAIRN (NAIRNE) TO ROBERT SURGINER, cordwinder
        Feb. 12, 1728/29. 5 pds. for 50 A. On SS Morattuck River Adj.
DANIEL MCDANIEL, JOHN NAIRN, WILLIAM SURGINER. Wit: GEORGE WILLIAMSON,
EDWARD BROWN. February Court 1728/29. ED. MASHBORNE D.C/C.

C 75   JOHN NAIRNE TO WILLIAM SURGINER
        Feb. 12, 1728/29. 5 pds. for 50 A. On SS Morattuck River. Adj.
WILLIAM and ROBERT SURGINER, JOHN NAIRNE, JAMES ALLIN. Wit: GEORGE WILL-
IAMSON, EDWARD BROWN. February Court 1728. ED. MASHBORNE D.C/C.

C 75   THOMAS JARRELL of Isle of Wight Co., Va. TO GEORGE WILLIAMSON
        Feb. 12, 1728. 40 pds. for 250 A. On SS Morattuck River at Great
Marsh. Land formerly belonged to JAMES TURNER. Adj. JOHN NAIRNE. Wit:
BARNABE MACKINNE, ROBERT FORSTER. February Court 1728. ED. MASHBORNE *.

C 76   THOMAS JARRELL of Isle of Wight Co., Va. TO GEORGE WILLIAMSON
        Feb. 12, 1728. 20 pds. for 150 A. On SS Morattuck River. Part of
tract formerly granted to JOHN GRAY, and by GRAY sold to JARRELL. Adj.
TURNER and BRYAN, JOHN NAIRNE. Wit: BARNABE MACKINNE, ROBERT FORSTER. February Court 1728. ED. MASHBORNE D.C/C.

C 77   WILLIAM GRAY, merchant, TO WILLIAM LITTLE
        Feb. 22, 1727. 60 pds. for 640 A. On NS Maherrin River "at cypress
in Chowan and Maherrin Pocoson" at Indian Creek. Wit: J. LOVICK, ROBERT
FORSTER. N. C. Court February 22, 1727. C. GALE, C.J. Test: ED. MASH-
BORNE DCC.

C 77   THOMAS CHARLES MATTHEWS & WIFE MARGARET TO JOHN HARDY (HADY), weaver
        Feb. 8, 1728. 21 pds. 15 sh. for 150 A. On SS Morattuck River Adj.
JAMES BROGDON, JOHN GREEN. Wit: ELIAS BOOTH, JOHN WILLIAMS, SARAH WILLIAMS.
February Court 1728/29. ED. MASHBORNE D.C/C.

C 78   CHARLES KIRBY TO ARTHUR WILLIAMS
        Dec. 23, 1728. 24 pds. for 150 A. On SS Meherrin River on Mill
Swamp at Forkfield "including the Old Mill Pond." Part of Pai nt granted
"my Father" THOMAS KIRBY dec'd. for 1200 A. dated June 9, 171:...devised to
CHARLES KIRBEY by last will and testament of THOMAS KIRBY. Wit: JOHN
BAYLY, THOMAS KIRBY, ARTHUR WILLIAMS, JUN. February Court 1728/29. ED.
MASHBORNE D.C/C.

C 79   WILLIAM BRACEWELL TO MOSES GINN
        Aug. 7, 1728. 10 pds. for 240 A. On Youraha Swamp "betwixt" land of
THOMAS DAUGHTRY and HARDY COUCIL. Part of patent for 640 A. granted March
1717. Wit: JOSEPH DARDEN, WILLIAM CARTER. February Court 1728. ED. MASH-
BORNE D.C/C.

C 79   HENRY OVERSTREET TO THOMAS BUNTEN
        Feb. 11, 1728/29. 5 pds. for 100 A. On WS Deep Creek Adj. THEOPHI-
LUS WILLIAMS at Apple Tree Swamp. Wit: NEEDHAM BRYAN, EDMOND WICKING, ED.
OUTLAW. February Court 1728/29. ED. MASHBORNE D.C/C.

C 80   JAMES NORVILLE (NORVILL) & WIFE ELIZABETH TO BENJAMIN BAKER
        Jan. 29, 1728. 12 pds. for 100 A. At Killem Swamp adj. THOMAS MAN,
JAMES BOON, ANDREW STEVENSON at Mirey Branch. Wit: ELINOR OLDNER, RICHARD
OLDNER. February Court 1728. ED. MASHBORNE D.C/C.

C 81   LORDS PROPRIETORS TO JOHN HOBSON
        April 1, 1723. Grant. 190 A. On NS Rocquiss Swamp Adj. WILLIAM
SMITH, FRANCIS HOBSON, JAMES CASTELLAW. Due for importation of persons @
50A/person. Signed: J. LOVICK, sec't'y., M. MOORE, WM. REED, RICH. SANDER-
SON, FRAN. FOSTER.

C 81   JOHN HOBSON TO FRANCIS SINGLETON
        Dec. 3, 1728. *. *. "within mentioned patent" together with stock
of cattle, Hoggs. Wit: *. *. February Court 1728. ED. MASHBORNE D.C/C.

C 82   JAMES TURNER & WIFE ANN of Isle of Wight Co., Va. TO NICHOLAS
        MOUNGER

February 1728. "a valuable sum" for 100 A. On SS Meherrin River
Adj. WILLIAM HART at Deep Bottom Creek. Part of patent for 640 A. granted
March 1, 1719. Wit: JOHN SIMPSON, ROBERT HART. February Court 1728. ED.
MASHBORNE D.C/C.

C 82   FRANCIS HOBSON TO WILLIAM CRISP
       January 1728/29. *. 200 A. "for love good will and affection...for
my loving friend WILLIAM CRISP...." Land on Rocquiss Pocoson and Cheeska
Swamp Adj. WILLIAM PATE. Wit: SAMUEL HERRING, FRANCIS SINGLETON. February
Court 1728. ED. MASHBORNE D.C/C.

C 83   THOMAS JOHNSON & WIFE ANN TO THOMAS STEVENSON
       Aug. 14, 1728. 10 pds. for 100 A. Adj. PETER WEST. Being part of
tract granted WILLIAM WHITFIELD for 300 A. called "The Red Ridge." Wit:
WILLIAM WHITFIELD, JOHN(?) JONES, JOHN SUTTON. February Court 1728. ED.
MASHBORNE.

C 84   JAMES WOOD, yeoman, TO BRYANT DAUGHTRY, yeoman, of Nansemond Co., Va.
       Feb. 10, 1729. 27 pds. for 250 A. On Yourah Swamp at Patterson
Branch. Land formerly owned by WILLIAM BRACEWELL and sold to WOOD by sale
dated July 31, 1728. Wit: RICHARD SUMNER, THOMAS DAUGHTRY, JAMES HOLLAND.
February Court 1728. ED. MASHBORNE D.C/C.

C 85   THOMAS HOWELL, SEN. TO JOSEPH PLATTS
       Aug. 22, 1724. "a valuable sum" for 250 A. On SS Meherring River
Adj. JAMES TURNER, THOMAS PHILLIPS. Patent dated April 1, 1723. Wit:
THOMAS HOWELL, JUN., ROBERT HART, THOMAS PHILLIPS. February Court 1728.
ED. MASHBORNE D.C/C.

C 86   JAMES TURNER & WIFE ANN of Isle of Wight Co., Va. TO ROBERT HART
       February 1729. "a valuable sum" for 240 A. On SS Meherrin River
Adj. NICOLAS MOUNGER, THOMAS HOWELL, SEN. On the Low Grounds of the River.
Patent granted March 1, 1719. Wit: JOHN SIMPSON, NICH. MOUNGER. February
Court 1728. ED. MASHBORNE D.C/C.

C 87   THOMAS LANE TO JOHN WHEELER
       Oct. 20, 1728. 15 pds. for 90 A. On Mill Swamp. Land formerly
granted to BARNABE MACKINNE and by him sold to JOHN WHEELER and by WHEELER
sold to THOMAS LANE. Wit: ROBERT JONES, JUN., EMPOROR WHEELER. February
Court 1728. ED. MASHBORNE D.C/C.

C 87   HENRY RHODES & WIFE _____ of Chowan Precinct TO JOHN PAGE
       *. 5 sh. for 160 A. Part of 640 A. at Cochi(?) Swamp on BUSBEs
line Adj. DANIEL HIGHSMITH. Wit: PETER CONE, RICHARD MADLING. February
Court 1728. ED. MASHBORNE D.C/C.

C 88   JOHN WILLIAMS TO JAMES WOOD
       Dec. 16, 1728. 25 pds. for 640 A. On SS Morattuck River at River
Pocosin "below the Fort." Patent dated 1723. Wit: JOHN SUTTON, JOHN DICK-
INSON. February Court 1728. ED. MASHBORNE D.C/C.

C 88   GEORGE STEPHENSON TO TIMOTHY RIAL (RIALL)
       Aug. 2, 1728. 10 pds. for 200 A. On NS Flaggy Run Adj. HENRY BAKER,
JOHN BUTLAR, SAMUEL HERRING. Wit: WILLIAM DANIEL, JOHN BLACKMAN. February
Court 1728. ED. MASHBORNE D.C/C.

C 89   THOMAS JARRELL of Isle of Wight Co., Va. TO GEORGE WILLIAMSON
       (WILLIAMS)
       Feb. 12, 1728. 20 pds. for 640 A. On SS Morattock River adj. WIL-
LIAM GRAY. Land granted to _____ and by him sold to JARRELL. Patent date
Dec. 3, 1720. Wit: ROBERT FORSTER, BARNABE MCKINNE. February Court 1728.
ED. MASHBORNE D.C/C.

C 90   JOHN LOVICK of Edenton TO JOHN SPEIR
       Aug. 1, 1729. 120 pds. for 640 A. On SS Morattuck River at Goose
Meadow. Adj. JAMES TURNER at Gum Swamp "to the Governors corner tree."
Wit: THOMAS JONES, DAVID O'SHEAL. N. C. Court 1729. C. GALE, C.J. Test:
ED. MASHBORNE D.C/C.

C 91   JAMES MILLIKIN & HENRY GUSTIN TO BARNABE MACKINNE
       March 3, 1728/29. 15 pds. for 150 A. Part of 640 A. patented by

WILLIAM BROWN April 1, 1713. This 150 A. sold by GIDEON GIBSON and wife, MARY, to MILLIKIN & GUSTIN. Commonly called "Walnut Forte Survey" adj. JOSEPH JOYNER, WILLIAM BROWN. Wit: THOMAS CRAGHILL, WILLIAM DEWTT(?). May Court 1729. ROBERT FORSTER C/C.

C 91   JAMES MILLIKIN & HENRY GUSTIN TO JOHN MCKINNE
        March 5, 1728. Power of atty. to ack. deed of sale for 150 A. on SS Morrattuck River to BARNABE MACKINNE. Wit: THOMAS CRAGHILL, jurat, WILLIAM DUETT. May 13, 1729. ROBERT FORSTER C/C.

C 92   JOHN HOY of James City Co., Va. TO SAMUEL COBBS of York Co., Va.
        May 7, 1729. 5 sh. for 630 A. One year lease. Land at on Plum Tree Gut and Mill Path Adj. WILLIAM GREEN, JOHN GODDES (GODLIES). Wit: ANTHONY COLLINS, WILLIAM KENNEY. May Court 1729. ED. MASHBORNE D.C/C.

C 92   JOHN HOY of James City Co., Va. TO SAMUEL COBBS of York Co., Va.
        May 8, 1729. 60 pds. for 630 A. Land at Plum Tree Island and Mill Path Adj. WILLIAM GREEN, JOHN GODDES. Wit: ANTHONY COLLINS, WILLIAM KENNEY. May Court 1729. ED. MASHBORNE D.C/C.

C 93   ANTHONY WILLIAMS & WIFE MARY TO JAMES SPEIR
        April 6, 1729. 35 pds. for 640 A. on SS Cutawosky Meadow at mouth of Poplar Run. "ANTHONY WILLIAMS heir at law to LEWIS WILLIAMS, JUN. dec'd. late of the County of Albemarle...." Patent to LEWIS WILLIAMS dated August 14, 1714. Now due ANTHONY WILLIAMS by order Oct. 3, 1717. Patent to ANTHONY LEWIS dated April 5, 1720. Wit: HENRY BAKER, JOHN BAREFIELD, JAMES HOWARD, COST. SUTTON, WILLIAM CORLEE. May Court 1729. ED. MASHBORNE D.C/C.

C 95   GODFREY HOOKER TO JOHN MORRIS
        April 29, 1729. 80 pds. for 300 A. Adj. CAPT. BOON, WILLIAM HOOKER at the head of Tar Road and Tar Kiln Branch at Flatted Gut. Wit: JACOB :EWIS, NICHOLAS FAIRLESS. May 13, 1729. ROBERT FORSTER C/C.

C 95   JOHN GREEN & RALPH MASON TO RICHARD PACE, SEN.
        May 13, 1729. 20 pds. for 290 A. On Yaweehoke Swamp adj. BRTHOLOMEW CHAVIS, RALPH MASON, JOHN GREEN. Part of patent granted JOHN GREEN for 640 A. dated July 29, 1712. Wit: ABRA. BURTON, SETH HATCHER. May Court 1729. ED. MASHBORNE D.C/C.

C 96   SETH HATCHER & WIFE ELIZABETH TO THOMAS MASON
        Feb. 11, 1728/29. 15 pds. for 300 A. On SS Morrattock River and WS Little Run. Wit: JOHN ROTTENBERY, LEAH HATCHER. May Court 1729. ED. MASHBORNE D.C/C.

C 97   RICHARD BRACEWELL TO WILLIAM HARRIS
        May 13, 1729. 15 pds. for 320 A. On Kesiah Swamp at Steward's Branch. Part of patent to BRACEWELL for 675 A. dated Feb. 1, 1725. Wit: JOHN HERRING, JOHN HART. May 13, 1729. ROBERT FORSTER C/C.

C 97   ARTHUR CAVENAUGH of Surry Co., Va. TO EDWARD CHAMBERS, Hanover Co., Va.
        May 12, 1729. 28 pds. for 300 A. On NS Roneoke River adj. ARTHUR BEIGENESES. Adj. a tract calle "Mount Jeoye." Includes 200 A. patent dated Feb. 25, 1725. A 100 A. parcel part of 640 A. patent dated July 29, 1712. Wit: THOMAS BRYANT, JOHN BONDE. May 13, 1729. ROBERT FORSTER C/C.

C 98   GEORGE STEVENS TO JAMES RUTLAND
        * 1729. 120 pds. for 400 A. Between Ahoskey and Sandy Run. 160 A. patent by OWEN MCDANIEL on March 1, 1719. 240 A. granted GEORGE STEVENS July 30, 1729. Wit: ROBERT WILLKINS, HENRY RHODES, WILLIAM CRANFORD. May 13, 1729. ROBERT FORSTER C/C.

C 98   JAMES SWAIN TO WILLIAM CHARLTON, JUN.
        April 28, 1729. 7 pds. for 320 A. Part of survey by JAMES SWAIN on WS Smithwick's Creek adj. JOHN SWAIN. Wit: WILLIAM CHARLTON, JOHN DAVIS. N. C. Court September 13, 1729. C. GALE, C.J. *.

C 99   MOSES GINN TO JOHN BONDE, merchant
        Sept. 17, 1728. 40 pds. for 240 A. On Yourahaw Swamp "betwixt" THOMAS DAUGHTRY, HARDY COUNCIL. Granted to WILLIAM BRACEWELL dec'd. by

patent dated March 1717. Wit: SOLOMON SMITH, THOMAS IVE. May 14, 1729.
ROBERT FORSTER C/C.

C 100   JOHN GRAY TO RICHARD LEWIS (LEWES) of Isle of Wight, Va.
        May 13, 1729. 12 pds. for 250 A. On SS Morattuck River and NS
Arthur's Swamp (or Looking Glass Swamp). Being a survey made for WILLIAM
GRAY and by him "lapsed for not seating." Then granted to JOHN GRAY on
April 1, 1727. Wit: WILLIAM GRAY, THOMAS CRAGHILL. May 13, 1729.   ED.
MASHBORNE D.C/C.

C 100   RICHARD HOLLAND, yeoman, TO DAVIS JERNAGAN (JERNIGAN) of Nansemond
            Co., Va.
        Nov. 20, 1728. 60 pds. for 575 A. On Chowan River known by name
Indian Town on SS Indian Creek. Patent date April 1, 1723. Wit: STEPHEN
CATTER, JAMES HOLLAND. May 13, 1729. ROBERT FORSTER C/C.

C 102   JAMES SPEIR TO WILLIAM BOYKIN of Isle of Wight Co., Va.
        May 8, 1729. 21 pds. for 220 A. On SS Morettock River adj. JOHN
NAIRNE, WILLIAM GRAY, HENRY WALKER. On Cattale Marsh at Hill Marsh. Wit:
JOHN SPEIR, JOHN JONES. May 13, 1729. ROBERT FORSTER C/C.

C 102   SAMUEL SMITHWICK & WIFE MARY TO JAMES CASTELAW
        Feb. 8, 1728/29. 135 pds. for 400 A. Land in Kesai Neck "betwixt"
MICHAEL KING, SAMUEL SMITHWICK. On Herrin Creek. Wit: EDMOND SMITHWICK,
jurat, JOHN DAVIS. May Court 1729. ED. MASHBORNE D.C/C.

C 103   JAMES RUTLAND TO THOMAS BARFIELD
        May 12, 1729. 20 pds. for 100 A. On NS Sandy Run at mouth of Lick-
ing Root Run adj. ROBERT SHERWOOD. Part of grant to ROBERT SHERWOOD for
640 A. dated April 5, 1720. Wit: H. HORNE, JOSEPH LEWIS, MICHAEL HORNE.
May 13, 1729. ROBERT FORSTER C/C.

C 104   JOHN HENARD TO THOMAS BARFIELD
        May 8, 1729. 15 pds. for 150 A. At head of Cashy on WS Middle
Branch Adj. JAMES RUTLAND, HENRY HORNE. Part of patent of 640 A. to Abel
CURTIS. Wit: H. HORNE, JOSEPH LEWIS, MICHAEL LEWIS. May 13, 1729. ROBERT
FORSTER C/C.

C 104   JAMES SWAINE TO ALEXANDER RAY
        Jan. 6, 1728/29. *. 100 A. "for Love goodwill and affection...unto
my Loving friend ALEXANDER RAY...." Land on SS Morattock River Adj. JOHN
SMITHWICK. Wit: JOHN DAVIS, RICHARD SWAIN, WILLIAM SLOSS(?), WILLIAM
CHARLTON. N. C. Court Sept. 13, 1729. C. GALE, C.J. Test: ED. MASHBORNE.

C 105   ELIZABETH LOCKHART of Virginia TO JOHN BEVERLY of Ahoskey
        November 1727. Two negro women for 500 A. One woman named Betty;
one named Nann. Land on Ahoskey Swamp "as by patent." Wit: HENRY BAKER,
BENJAMIN HILL, DAVID O'SHEAL. N. C. Court April 1, 1729. C. GALE, C.J.
Test: ED. MASHBORNE D.C/C.

C 105   ELIZABETH LOCKHART TO JOHN BEVERLY
        Nov. 14, 1727. *. "two cows and calves and their increase...the
same I received from BEVERLY on a former bargain...." Wit: BENJAMIN HILL,
MAJOR DAVID O'SHEAL. N. C. Court April 1, 1729. C. GALE, C.J.

C 105   THOMAS LOVICK TO SAMUEL RATCLIFF
        * 1728. 120 pds. for 120 A. On Salmon Creek called "Myrtle Bluff"
Adj. EPHR(AIM) LEWERTON at Riscoris Branch. Wit: E. MOSELEY, EDMOND GALE.
N. C. Court 1728. C. GALE, C.J. Test: ED. MASHBORNE D.C/C.

C 106   THOMAS BARFIELD TO JAMES RUTLAND
        May 12, 1729. 15 pds. for 100 A. On SS Ahotskey Marsh. "being all
the land which was left out of FIREBENT's patent...." Part of 470 A.
granted to BARFIELD April 1, 1722. Wit: H. HORNE, JOSEPH LEWIS, MICHAEL
HORNE. May 13, 1729. ROBERT FORSTER C/C.

C 107   ANTHONY WILLIAMS TO HENRY BAKER of Chowan
        May 10, 1729. 50 pds. for 250 A. "land whereon WILLIAM CURLEE late-
ly did live...." Part of patent for 1175 A. granted to LEWIS WILLIAMS
dated April 1, 1713. Wit: PETER WEST, WILLIAM MOOR, JOHN HENARD. May
Court 1729. ROBERT FORSTER C/C.

NOTE HERE: "So far New Copyed before Nov. Court...."

C 108   ANTHONY WILLIAMS TO PETER WEST
        May 13, 1729. 10 sh. "...my right to that tract...left me by my
Grandfather LEWIS WILLIAMS to PRISCILLA WEST and her heirs...." Wit: BENJ-
AMIN HILL, ROBERT FORSTER, THOMAS JONES. May 13, 1729. ROBERT FORSTER C/C

C 108   WILLIAM CURLEE & WIFE MARTHA TO HENRY BAKER of Chowan
        May 8, 1729. 10 pds. for "...all right MARTHA now have or ought to
have...of land which LEWIS WILLIAMS by his last will and testament dated
Oct. 1, 1716...did devise unto his son ANTHONY WILLIAMS and MARTHA his wife
...dureing natural life of MARTHA and no longer...." Wit: ANTHONY WILLIAMS,
JOHN HENARD. May 13, 1719. ROBERT FORSTER C/C. "... MARTHA being first
privately examined...."

C 109   WILLIAM BRACEWELL TO JOHN BONDE, merchant
        Feb. 26, 1728/29. 50 pds. for 630 A. On NS Meherrin River. "...
land whereon my father live...." Patent granted Aug. 10, 1720. Wit: JAMES
BRYANT, SARAH DRAKE. May 14, 1729. ROBERT FORSTER C/C.

C 110   JOHN EARLY TO CHARLES JONES
        February 1728/29. 20 pds. for 145 A. On Wickacorne Creek Adj.
CHRISTOPHER WILLIAMS, SPIAN HOLLIMON. Wit: JOHN SWENNY, WILLIAM WILSON.
May 14, 1729. ROBERT FORSTER C/C.

C 111   CHARLES ROYAL (ROYALL) & WIFE ANN TO JOHN CHRISTOPHER TISWELL
        April 1729. *.   640 A. At Flat Swamp. Wit: ED. HOWARD, JOHN WILL-
IAMS, WILLIAM WILLIFORD. May 13, 1729. ROBERT FORSTER C/C.

C 111   EDMOND SMITHWICK TO WILLIAM ROBINSON & WIFE MARY
        April 25, 1729 (May 5, 1729). *. 100 A. "...for love and affection
...unto WILLIAM ROBINSON and wife MARY during their lives...(then) to WILL-
IAM ROBINSON, JUN.....my godson...." That plantation where the ROBINSONs
now live on SS Morrattuck River and Devil's Gut Swamp. Wit: JOHN MARDEN,
JOHN DUGGAN. May Court 1729. E. MASHBORNE D.C/C.

C 112   JAMES SPEIR & WIFE ANN TO WILLIAM CURLLEE (CORLEE, CURLEE)
        Feb. 25, 1726. 40 pds. for 300 A. At Ahotskey Ridge. Formerly
granted to ROBERT LANIER by patent dated April 1, 1723. Wit: HENRY BONNER,
JOHN SPEIRS, JOHN SUTTON, TERRENCE CONNER. May Court 1729. ED. MASHBORNE
D.C/C.

C 113   JOHN PERRITT & WIFE MARY TO JOHN DAWSON of Virginia
        Feb. 10, 1728. 50 pds. for 640 A. On NS Morrattock River at Brid-
ger's Creek. Adj. HENRY JONES..."being by patent 640 A." Wit: JOHN HART,
JAMES WILLIAMS. May Court 1729. ED. MASHBORNE D.C/C.

C 114   ANN WHEELER & EMPEROR WHEELER TO BARNABE MACKINNE (MCKINNE)
        March 22, 1728/29. 30 pds. for 350 A. Land on NS Morrattock River.
"...the plantation whereon both do now live...." ANN WHEELER, widow, and
son EMPEROR. "...the remainder of a tract formerly granted to WILLIAM
BRACEWELL by patent March 4, 1711/12 for (640 A.) and resurveyed to contain
seven hundred acres...and by BRACEWELL sold to HENRY WHEELER...by WHEELER
devised to EMPEROR WHEELER...." Except 160 A. formerly sold to MATTHEW
RUSKINS; 160 A. sold to PETER JONES: 100 A. sold to BARNABE MACKINNE. Wit:
THOMAS CRAGHILL, BARNABE MCKINNE, JUN., WILLIAM OPIE. *. E. MASHBORNE.

C 115   JOHN HENARD (HINARD) TO HENRY HORNE
        May 7, 1729. 20 pds. for 290 A. On western and middle branch of
Cashey Adj. JAMES RUTLAND. Part of tract granted ABEL CURTIS for 640 A.
dated August 1, 1726. Wit: JOSEPH LEWIS, MICHAEL HORNE, THOMAS BARFIELD.
May 13, 1729. ROBERT FORSTER C/C.

C 116   JOHN ONAILES TO JOSEPH BRIDGER
        *. 10 pds. for 327 A. On SS Morattock River. By patent dated Feb-
ruary 1, 1725. Wit: WILLIAM WHITEHEAD, JAMES HOLLAND. May 14, 1729. ROB-
ERT FORSTER C/C.

C 117   RALPH MASON & WIFE SARAH (+) TO WILLIAM REVES (REAVES)
        Feb. 8, 1728/29. 6 pds. for 30 A. On NS Morattock River. Wit:

RICHARD WHITINTUM, WILLIAM REVES, JUN. May Court 1729. ED. MASHBORNE DCC.
(+ also called JOHN MACON in body of deed--probably copiest error.)

C 117   RICHARD KEMP TO JOHN GARDNER
        May 12, 1729. 7 pds. for 150 A. Adj. GEORGE BEN, JOHN GARDNER. Part
of tract of 315 A. bearing date 1727. Wit: JONATHAN SANDERSON, JOHN BONDE.
May 13, 1729. ROBERT FORSTER C/C.

C 118   GEORGE SKIPPER, SEN. & WIFE MARY TO WILLIAM HALL
        Jan. 11, 1728. 45 pds. 5 sh. for 120 A. On NS Holly Bush or Quarter
Swamp. Adj. BARNABE THOMPSON. Wit: WILLIAM JOHNSON, DAVID HERRIN. May
Court 1729. ED. MASHBORNE D.C/C.

C 119   MOSES GINN & WIFE MARY TO WILLIAM BRACEWELL, JUN.
        May 12, 1729. 10 pds. for *. MARY GINN, late wife of WILLIAM
BRACEWELL, dec'd. to "...WILLIAM BRACEWELL son of WILLIAM BRACEWELL and
MARY MARY BRACEWELL alias GINN...all rights of dower of any kind in the
property of WILLIAM BRACEWELL dec'd...." Wit: JOHN BONDE, JOHN HOWARD.
May 13, 1729. ROBERT FORSTER C/C. "...MARY being first privately examined
as by act of assembly...."

C 119   JAMES SMITH TO JOHN HARRELL of Nansemond Co., Va.
        May 11, 1729. 32 sh. for 8 A. On NS Morattuck River and SS Flagg
Run. Adj. HENRY BAKER, JOHN HARRELL. Wit: JOSEPH HARRELL, ABRAHAM HURRELL
(HARRELL). May 13, 1729. ROBERT FORSTER C/C.

C 120   ROBERT GREEN of Surry Co., Va. TO GEORGE NORWOOD
        Aug. 11, 1729. 12 pds. for 370 A. On Morrattuck River Adj. JOHN
SPAR(?), HENRY JONES. Land called "Mount Royall." Part of 640 A. grant to
JACOB COLSON. Wit: JOHN GREEN, RICHARD MOORE. August Court 1729. THOMAS
CREW D.C/C.

C 121   THOMAS JENKINS TO THOMAS WIMBERLY
        July 19, 1729. 50 pds. for 140 A. Adj. RICHARD BRACEWELL. Wit:
WARREN ANDREWS, JAMES MOORE, ROBERT BUFFIN. August Court 1729. THOMAS
CREW D.C/C.

C 122   WILLIAM MOORE of Surry Co., Va. TO THOMAS AVENT of Surry Co., Va.
        Aug. 9, 1729. 20 pds. for 250 A. On NS Moraticoe River below "Mount
Royall." Surveyed for THOMAS AVENT by Capt. WILLIAM MAULE, Deputy Surveyor,
on May 18, 1713. Sold by AVENT to my father RICHARD MOORE. Wit: E. WING-
FIELD, JONES STOKES. August Court 1729. THOMAS CREW D.C/C.

C 122   JOHN GREEN TO RICHARD PACE, JUN.
        Aug. 11, 1729. 20 pds. for 440 A. On NS Moratuck River at WHEEL-
ER's Mill Swamp. To "include the bounds of patent dated March 1, 1719...."
Wit: THOMAS AVENT, RICHARD MOORE. August Court 1729. THOMAS CREW D.C/C.

        NOTE HERE: "So far done to Feb'y Court 1799."

C 123   JOHN MCDANIEL (MCDONALD) TO DANIEL MCDANIEL (MCDONALD)
        Aug. 12, 1729. 30 pds. for 640 A. On SS Morattuck River and SS
Connahoe Creek at NAIRNE's Branch. Adj. DONALD MCDONALD. By patent
granted JOHN MCDONALD. Wit: WILLIAM EVERITT, THOMAS BEUM, JOHN SUTTON.
August Court 1729. THOMAS CREW D.C/C.

C 124   JAMES WYAT TO JAMES LASSITER
        August 6, 1729. 10 pds. for 185 A. On NWS Yourah Swamp. Adj. JOHN
MCMIEL. Part of land formerly granted JOHN PIECTER(?) dated April 6, 1722
"and from him elapsed by JOHN SUTTON...March 31, 1726...." Wit: JOHN HART,
THOMAS FENTRILL. August Court 1729. THOMAS CREW D.C/C.

C 124   WILLIAM GREEN TO GEORGE NORWOOD of Surry Co., Va.
        Aug. 7, 1727. 12 pds. for 320 A. On NS Morrattuck River at "Mount
Royall" being uppermost half or moeity...of a tract...patented by HENRY
JONES July 3, 1713 cont. 640 A...." Wit: BARRYBY MILTON, THOMAS SHEPPARD,
C. EVANS, RICHARD MOORE, ROBERT GREEN. August Court 1729. THOMAS CREW *.

C 125   JOSEPH SIMS(SIMMS) & WIFE SARAH TO MARTHA MAPLES of James City Co.,
        Va.

May 13, 1729. *. 100 A. On NS Morrattock River adj. ROBERT SIMS. Part of a full survey to WILLIAM BRACEWELL on Cypress Swamp dated March 4, 1711/12. Wit: JOHN GROOM, ANDREW IRELAND. August Court 1729. THOMAS CREW.

C 126   THOMAS BRYANT TO JOHN BASS (ROBERT BASS)
August 12, 1729. 10 pds. for 100 A. On SS Yourah Swamp and NS Roanoke River. Adj. WILLIAM WHITEHEAD. Part of 640 A. patented to WILLIAM WHITEHEAD March 9, 1711. Granted to said BRYANT by deed. Wit: JAMES BRYANT, EDWARD OUTLAW. August Court 1729. THOMAS CREW D.C/C.

C 127   TIMOTHY HINDS TO JAMES WELSON (WILSON)
Aug. 11, 1729. 20 pds. for 200 A. On NS Hunting Quarter Swamp. By patent April 1, 1723. Wit: RICHARD HORN, ARTHUR WILLIAMS. August Court 1729. THOMAS CREW D.C/C.

C 127   GEORGE WILLIAMSON of Isle of Wight Co., Va. TO WILLIAM DREW of Surry
            Co., Va.
August 12, 1729. 40 pds. for 640 A. on SS Morattuck River. Adj. WILLIAM GRAY. Granted to THOMAS JERRELL and by him sold to WILLIAMSON. Patent dated Dec. 3, 1720. Wit: WILLIAM GRAY, JAMES CANY(?). August Court 1729. THOMAS CREW D.C/C.

C 128   JACOB LEWIS & WIFE MARY TO ISAAC LEWIS
Aug. 12, 1729. 75 pds. for 400 A. On WS Great Branch on Brooks Creek. Adj. WILLIAM DREW, JOHN RASBERRY, JACOB LEWIS, JOHN MAYNOR, WILLIAM KEEL. "...excepting always fifteen foot square about the Grave or burial place...." Wit: ED. MASHBORNE, JAMES BRYANT. August Court 1729. THOMAS CREW D.C/C.

NOTE HERE: "The following began January 22nd 1800...."

C 129   NICHOLAS SMITH TO RICHARD SESSOMS
Feb. 8, 1729. *. 100 A. "...good will and affection I bear unto my Nephew RICHARD SESSOMS...." Tract whereon RICHARD now lives adj. RICHARD KILLINGSWORTH, JOHN GRAY. Wit: JOHN SHELLY, SAMUEL SESSOMS. August Court 1729. THOMAS CREW D.C/C.

C 130   GEORGE WILLIAMSON of Isle of Wight Co., Va. TO WILLIAM DREW of Surry
            Co., Va.
Aug. 12, 1729. 20 pds. for 150 A. On SS Morattuck River. Adj. TURNER's and BRYANT's line, THOMAS JERRELL, JOHN NAIRN. At Great Marsh. Part of tract granted JOHN GRAY, and by GRAY sold to THOMAS JERRELL, and by JERRELL sold to WILLIAMSON. Wit: WILLIAM GRAY, JAMES MANY. August Court 1729. THOMAS CREW D.C/C.

C 131   GEORGE WILLIAMSON of Isle of Wight Co., Va. TO WILLIAM DREW of Surry
            Co., Va.
Aug. 12, 1729. 40 pds. for 250 A. On SS Morattuck River Adj. JOHN NARON at Great Marsh. Part of tract belonging to JAMES TURNER and JOHN BRYAN, and by them sold to THOMAS JERRELL, and by JERRELL sold to WILLIAMSON. Wit: WILLIAM GRAY, JAMES MANY. August Court 1729. THOMAS CREW D.C/C

C 132   JOHN GAVIN TO CHARLES GAVIN
Aug. 12, 1729. *. 90 A. For "...love and natural affection I do owe and bear unto my brother...." Land on Long Branch at Woodward's Creek. Wit: WILLIAM CRANFORD, JOHN WELSON. August Court 1729. THOMAS CREW D.C/C.

C 133   SIMON JEFFREYS TO WILLIAM WILLIARD (HILLIARD?)
May 13, 1729. 14 pds. for 182 A. On NS Morattuck River "within Ursara Meadows." Patent date August 10, 1720. Adj. JOHN HILLIARD. Wit: RICHARD HILLIARD, THOMAS JENKINS, JOHN HILLIARD. August Court 1729. THOMAS CREW D. C/C.

C 133   JAMES BOON TO ALEXANDER VALENTINE
May 14, 1729. 40 pds. for 100 A. On Kellum Swamp. Adj. GEORGE VALENTINE. Wit: JOHN ASKUE, JOSEPH WOODFORD. August Court 1729. THOMAS CREW D.C/C.

C 134   GEORGE STEVENSON TO HENRY OVERSTREET
June 26, 1729. 40 pds. for 490 A. On NS Morattuck River in Village

Swamp. Adj. JOHN WILLIAMS and Gray Marsh, JOHN BLACKMAN. Part of 640 A.
granted STEVENSON Aug. 8, 1728. Wit: JOHN HART, MARY WEST. August Court
1729. THOMAS CREW D.C/C.

C 135 WILLIAM WHITEHEAD TO JOHN BASS
       Aug. 13, 1729. 10 pds. for 100 A. At Headline adj. EDWARD BASS.
Part of tract granted RICHARD WASHINGTON March 9, 1717/18. Wit: JAMES HOW-
ARD, EDWARD OUTLAW. August Court 1729. THOMAS CREW D.C/C.

C 136 JOHN POPE & WIFE MARY (MURINING) TO WILLIAM BENNET
       Aug. 5, 1729. 3 pds(?). For 240 A. On SS Morrattuck and NS Elk
Swamp. Adj. JOHN POPE, THOMAS WEST, WILLIAM BENNET, "JOHN POPE's Old Wolf
Pit." Part of tract patented by JOHN POPE July 24, 1728. Wit: DAVID
HOPPER, BENJAMIN LANE, JOSEPH WATH. August Court 1729. THOMAS CREW D.C/C.

C 137 JOHN LEWERTON TO STEPHEN DROWERS
       Aug. 13, 1729. 4 pds. for 72 A. On WS Bear Swamp at head of JOHN
TOMSON's (THOMPSON) line adj. JOHN LEWERTON. Wit: JOHN ADDERLY. *. August
Court 1729. THOMAS CREW D.C/C.

C 137 JAMES SANDERS TO DAVID O'SHEAL of Nansemond Co., Va.
       Aug. 13, 1729. "several covenants and conditions in bond...." For
300 A. plus one Negro man called Coffee; 20 head meat cattle. On condition
DAVID O'SHEAL will allow JAMES SANDER's heirs to occupy said land within
six months after such heir shall come of age...also JAMES SANDERS makes
good title to land on west Branch Nansemond River in Virginia "pussuant to
condition of bond..." Wit: THOMAS CREW, THOMAS JONES. August Court 1729.
THOMAS CREW D.C/C.

C 138 JAMES WELSON (WILSON) TO TIMOTHY HINDS
       Aug. 11, 1729. 20 pds. for 450 A. "...the greatest part of patent
granted to my father JOHN WILSON dec'd. for (500A) dated April 1, 1723...."
On NS Little Swamp adj. WILLIAM BOON, JOSEPH BOON. Wit: RICHARD HORNE,
ARTHUR WILLIAMS. August Court 1729. THOMAS CREW D.C/C.

C 139 ARTHUR CRAFORD (CRAFFORD) & WIFE JANE TO JOSEPH WATTS
       Aug. 11, 1729. 20 pds. for 150 A. On SS Morattuck River and SS
Conoconero Swamp. Adj. CRAFORD. Part of tract formerly granted TIMOTHY
SPELLING in 1725. Wit: SAMUEL SWEARINGEN, HENRY CRAFFORD, WILLIAM MURPHREY,
JOHN POPE. *. THOMAS CREW D.C/C.

C 140 DANIEL MCDANIEL TO WILLIAM BROWN
       March 29, 1729. 30 pds. for 200 A. On SS Morattuck River at Beaver
Damm adj. DANIEL MCDANIEL. Wit: THOMAS HOLLAND, EDWARD MASHBORNE. August
Court 1729. THOMAS CREW D.C/C.

C 141 JOHN EDWARDS & WIFE ELIZABETH TO JAMES MURRY
       Aug. 11, 1729. 15 pds. for 240 A. At Little Rocquis "joining to
meadow between Casay and Roanoke." Adj.____OVERSTREET, JOHN EDWARDS.
Wit: THOMAS RODES, JAMES PARKER. August Court 1729. THOMAS CREW D.C/C.

C 142 BARNABE MCKINNE, JUN. TO JOHN BUNCH
       May 12, 1729. 20 pds. for 100 A. On SS Morattuck River adj. Tucka-
hoe Marsh. Land formerly patented April 3, 1720 by WILLIAM JONES and by
him "elapsed." Then granted to WILLIAM POPE April 1, 1723, and by him sold
to BARNABE MCKINNE, JUN. Wit: JOHN MACKINNE, THOMAS CRAGHILL, BARN. MC-
KINNE, SEN. August Court 1729. THOMAS CREW D.C/C.

C 143 DONALD MACKDANIEL (MACKDONALD) (MACK DONEIL) TO WILLIAM RICHARDSON
       of Isle of Wight Co., Va.
       April 5, 1729. 100 pds. for 100 A. On SS Morattuck River. Adj.
JOHN NAIRN and Canaan Marsh. Wit: JOHN SERGINER, JOHN NAIRN. August 13,
1729. THOMAS CREW D.C/C.

C 144 THOMAS AVENT of Surry Co., Va. TO RICHARD MERRICK
       Aug. 11, 1729. 5 pds. for 100 A. On NS Morattuck River. Wit: RICH-
ARD MOORE, JOHN GREEN. August Court 1729. THOMAS CREW D.C/C.

C 145 JOHN WILLIAMS & WIFE ANN TO THOMAS CASTELAW, SON OF JAMES CASTELAW
       *. 10 pds. for 250 A. On NS Roanoke River "being the plantation

whereon JOHN GLISSON now lives...." By Indian Village Pond. Adj. JAMES
BLUNT, ANTHONY HERRING, Indian Village Meadow and Great Swamp. Wit: EDM.
DAVIS, JOHN MATHEWS. August Court 1729. THOMAS CREW D.C/C.

C 146 WILLIAM STEVENS, SEN. TO JOHN BUNCH
    Feb. 8, 1728/29. 30 pds. for 270 A. On SS Morattuck River. Bounded
by patent dated Feb. 1, 1725. Wit: JAMES MILLIKIN, HENRY GUSTON, JOSEPH
JOYNER, BAR. MACKINNE, jurat. August Court 1729. THOMAS CREW D.C/C.

C 147 JACOB LEWIS & WIFE MARY TO PETER WEST
    August 1729. 10 pds. for 200 A. At Horse Swamp. Adj. _____ HOWARD,
JOHN JONES, Cowhall, "ye Round Pocoson," Wading Branch. Wit: *. *. August
Court 1729. THOMAS CREW D.C/C.

C 148 JOHN GALLAND TO CLEMENT HAMMOND(HEMMEND)
    May 29, 1728. 60 pds. for 190 A. Commonly called "Mount Galland."
Wit: MARTHA DUNSTAN, JOHN GALLAND, THOMAS BETTERLY. N. C. Court November
20, 1729. C. GALE, C.J. Test: THOMAS CREW D.C/C.

C 149 JOSEPH BALLARD of Chowan TO HENRY COPELAND of Virginia
    Aug. 12, 1729. 30 pds. for 182-1/2 A. One half patent granted
JAMES MANNY and JOSEPH BALLORD. Dated November 12, 1726. On Miery Meadow.
Adj. MANNY, BALLORD, RICHARD HOLLAND, EDWARD BARNES. Wit: JAMES HOLLAND,
JOHN THOMAS. August Court 1729. THOMAS CREW D.C/C.

C 150 JOHN GUILLIAM of Surry Co., Va. TO GEORGE JORDAN
    March 13, 1728. 5 sh. for 290 A. On NS Morattuck River. Adj. WILLIAM
WYCHE. Part of patent for 580 A. granted JOHN GUILLAM. Leased now for six
months. Wit: MARY SOUTHERLAND, ROBERT SOUTHERLAND, ALEXANDER SOUTHERLAND.
August Court 1729. THOMAS CREW D.C/C.

C 151 JOHN GUILLAM of Surry Co., Va. TO GEORGE JORDAN
    March 14, 1728/29. 1 pd. for 290 A. on NS Moratuck River adj.
WILLIAM WYCHE. Wit: MARY SOUTHERLAND, ROBERT SOUTHERLAND, ALEXANDER SOUTH-
ERLAND. August Court 1729. THOMAS CREW D.C/C.

C 153 MAJOR GEORGE POLLOCK TO JOHN LOVICK
    April 5, 1729. 510 pds. for 408 A. Two tracts. One: for 208 A.
bounded by Chowan River on east, CHARLES KING on north, and POLLOCK on the
west, LOVICK on the south. Two: for 200 A. bounded easterly by Chowan
River, northerly by LOVICK, westerly by POLLOCK, southerly by land which
formerly belonged to FRANCIS PARROTE. Wit: MARTIN FRED. RASOR, THOMAS
POLLOCK, JOSEPH BLAKE. N. C. Court November 7, 1729. C. GALE, C.J. Test:
THOMAS CREW D.C/C.

C 154 JAMES ROBERTS & WIFE CURDILLA TO JAMES PARKER
    May 12, 1729. 60 pds. for 270 A. On Buck Swamp. Adj. JOHN GRIFFET
and Rocquis Swamp. Wit: *. *. November Court 1729. THOMAS CREW D.C/C.

C 155 JOHN COUNCIL (COUNCEL) of Isle of Wight Co., Va. to SOLOMON ALSTON
    Nov. 11, 1729. 10 pds. for 100 A. On Wicken (Wiccacon?) Creek. Adj.
ISAAC LEWIS, JOHN EARLEY. Wit: CHRISTIAN HUDELBOYS(?), JAS. JOHN ALSTON.
November Court 1729. THOMAS CREW D.C/C.

C 156 JAMES MURRAY & WIFE ELISABETH TO JOHN WARD
    Nov. 10, 1729. 6 pds. for 100 A. Fork of Casay Swamp at Whattom
Swamp. Adj. SAMUEL PRESTON. Wit: THOMAS BRIGMAN, THOMAS QUICK. November
Court 1729. THOMAS CREW D.C/C.

C 156 JOHN BRYANT TO WILLIAM GAUSE
    May 29, 1729. 20 pds. for 300 A. On SS Morattuck River in the River
Pecoson. Adj. DANIEL MACK DANIEL. Wit: CHARLES CAVENAH, JOHN MACKMIALL.
November Court 1729. THOMAS CREW D. C/C.

C 157 JAMES MURRAY & WIFE ELISABETH TO THOMAS BRIGMAN
    Nov. 10, 1729. 10 pds. for 125 A. At Fork of Casay Swamp and What-
tom Swamp. Adj. JOHN WOOD and Poplar Branch. Wit: THOMAS QUICK, JOHN WARD
(WOOD?). November Court 1729. THOMAS CREW D.C/C.

C 158 HENRY OVERSTREET & WIFE ANN TO SILVANNA STOKES

Nov. 11, 1729. 14 pds. for 280 A. On Cashy Swamp at Great Marsh.
Adj. JAMES BLOUNT. Wit: OWEN MACK DANIEL, ROBERT IVEY. November Court
1729. THOMAS CREW D.C/C.

C 158   GEORGE POLLOCK TO PETER KEIGHLEY
Nov. 17, 1729. 15 pds. for 250 A. (200A.) On SS Morattuck River.
Adj. _____ YELVERTON. Wit: EDWARD WINGATE, JOHN BOYLE. N. C. Court November 18, 1729. C. GALE, C.J. Test: THOMAS CREW D.C/C.

C 159   CULLEN POLLOCK of Tyrell TO JESPER (JASPER) HARDISON
Nov. 22, 1729. 120 pds. for 1000 A. On SS Morattuck River called
"Rose's Plantation." Adj. JAMES BLOUNT. Wit: W. DOWNING, WM. MACKEY. N.C.
Court Nov, 22, 1729. THOMAS CREW D.C/C.

C 160   JAMES FAIRCHILD TO THOMAS JOHNSTON
Nov. 10, 1729. 7 pds. for 150 A. On Hare(?) Branch Adj. GODFREY
HACKER (HATCHER), ROBERT EVANDS, _____ POLLOCK, WILLIAM BAKER. Part of 250
A. which FAIRCHILD bought of JOHN MAINER, SEN. Wit: SAMUEL WILLIAMS, ELIZ-
ABETH WILLIAMS. November Court 1729. THOMAS CREW D.C/C.

C 160   MARTHA BUSH TO MARY BUSH +
Sept. 13, 1728. "...love and affection...unto Daughter in law late
wife of my son JOHN BUSH dec'd...and my five grandchildren...MARY, ELIZA-
BETH, JOHN HARDY, and ISAAC BUSH...." One half all chattels and personal
estate. Wit: NICHOLAS FAIRLESS, JOHN BRYAN. November Court 1729. *.
   +(this same deed appears on C 55.)

C 161   WILLIAM POWELL of Isle of Wight Co., Va. TO JAMES MILLIKIN
Nov. 7, 1729. 20 pds. for 200 A. On NS Roanock Ricer "bounded by
Deed given from WILLIAM BOON...." On Beaverdam Branch. Part of patent of
600 A. granted WM. BOON on March 5, 1712. Wit: JOSEPH JOYNER, WM. STRICK-
LAND, JOHN STRICKLAND, JOS. STRICKLAND. November Court 1729. *.

C 162   JOHN BEVERLEY, SEN. TO JOHN BEVERLEY, JUN.
Nov. 14, 1729. for "good causes" ..."a third part of a tract of
land...containing (110 A.)." On Cheskee Swamp in the Flatt Pocoson. Wit:
FRANCIS PUGH, EDWARD HOWARD, WILLIAM WHITFIELD. November Court 1729. *.

C 163   LORDS PROPRIETORS TO JAMES PARKER
Nov. 7, 1723. Grant. 540 A. On NES Casay Swamp. Adj. THOMAS
RODES, HENRY RODES. For importation of persons @ 50 A./person. Signed:
WILLIAM REED, J. LOVICK, sec't'y., RICH. SANDERSON, T. POLLOCK, C. GALE.

C 163   JAMES PARKER TO JOHN BEVERLEY
Nov. 11, 1729. 15 pds. for "right title and interest to within
mentioned patent...." Wit: *.*. Court *. THOMAS CREW D.C/C.

C 163   JOHN GRAY & WIFE ANN TO JOHN BRYANT
April 6, 1729. 10 pds. for 200 A. On SS Morrattuck River at Round
Pond and Broad Meadow. Adj. NICHOLAS SMITH. Wit: JOHN PERRITT, JOHN
HACHER. November Court 1729. THOMAS CREW D.C/C.

C 160?   WILLIAM GRAY (GREY) TO WILLIAM LITTLE
Feb. 22, 1729. 60 pds. for 640 A. On NS Meherrin River "at forked
cypress in Chowan and Meherrin River Pocoson" at Indian Creek. Wit: J.
LOVICK, ROBERT FOSTER. N. C. Court February 22, 1727? C. GALE, C.J. E.
MASHBORNE D.C/C.

C 165   JAMES FOYLE & WIFE ANN TO GEORGE NICHOLSON of Norfolk Co., Va.
Nov. 13, 1729. A Negro girl and 10 pds. for 295 A. On Wickacorne
Creek. Adj. WILLIAM WILLIFORD, STEPHEN WILLIAMS, CHRISTOPHER HOLLIMAN.
Wit: JOHN JONES, WILLIAM MEWRS(?), Nov. 14, 1729. THOMAS CREW D. C/C.

C 166   WILLIAM CURLEE & WIFE MARTHA TO JAMES JENKINS
Nov. 12, 1729. 7000 lbs. "Lawfull tobacco." Land on SWS Ahoskey
Swamp. Adj. CHARLES JONES. Wit: THOMAS BANKS, R. OLDNER. November Court
1729. THOMAS CREW D. C/C.

C 166   PETER PARKER & WIFE GRACE TO EPAPHRATES(?) MOORE of Nansemond Co.,Va.
Nov. 11, 1729. 160 pds. for 640 A. At Ford Branch on Ahoskey Swamp.

"the plantation that PETER PARKER now lives." Land devised unto PETER PARKER by PETER EVANS. Wit: THOMAS BRYANT, WILLIAM COTTON, JAMES HOLLAND. Court *. THOMAS CREW D.C/C.

C 167 JAMES MURRAY & WIFE ELIZABETH TO SAMUEL PRESTON
        Nov. 10, 1729. 25 pds. for 75 A. On Wattom Swamp. Adj. THOMAS BRIGMON, _____ WARD. Wit: THOMAS BRIGMAN, JOHN WARD. November Court 1729. THOMAS CREW D.C/C.

C 167(160) SUSANAH BROWN, JOHN WARREN & WIFE GRACE, SYLVESTER BROWN AND_____
            TO ELISABETH JOYNER
        Feb. 12, 1727/28. *. 256 A. "...love...for our sister ELISABETH JOYNER..." Land formerly belonging to our father, JOHN BROWN de'c'd. Patent July 28, 1713. On WS Chowan adj. J. CURLEE, J. SMITH. Wit: FINCHER HAYNE, CHARLES BROWN. Court *. THOMAS CREW D.C/C.

C 168 (163) EDWARD HOWARD of Chowan TO WILLIAM BARNES
        July 22, 1719. 12 pds. for 175 A. In Chowan Prec't. on Little Town path. Bounded as by patent dated Aug. 27, 1714 to RICHARD WILLIAMSON, and by him sold to HOWARD. Wit: JOHN GREEN, R. HICKS. Chowan Court July 1729. R. HICKS C/C. Registered in Chowan Aug. 25, 1719.

C 169 WILLIAM BARNS (BARNES) & WIFE LYDIA to WILLIAM ASKENE (ASKEWE?)
        Nov. 12, 1729. 60 pds. for "within mentioned plantation." Wit: WILLIAM LEE, JOHN ASKENE (ASKEWE?). November Court 1729. THOMAS CREW DCC

C 170 EDWARD HOWARD TO THEOPHILUS PUGH, merchant
        Nov. 13, 1729. 25 pds. for 300 A. Adj. JOHN STEWARD's (HOWARD's) cornfield on NS Roanoke River. Adj. JAMES WOOD. "...as by patent...." Wit: JAMES EVERARD, THOMAS JONES, FINCHER HAYNE. November Court 1729. THOMAS CREW D.C/C.

C 170 LAZARUS THOMAS TO JOHN BROWN
        February 7, 1729. 15 pds. for 250 A. On Holly Swamp and Catherine Creek Road. Adj. MATHEW TOBIAS SWANNER, JAMES CURLEE. Wit: JAMES PAGE, JOS.(?) JOHN ALSTON. February Court 1729. THOMAS CREW D.C/C.

C 171 SUSANNA BROWN & SILVESTER BROWN TO WILLIAM EVANS
        Nov. 22, 1729. 5 pds. for 100 A. On Horse Swamp. Adj. JOHN THOMAS, LAZARUS THOMAS. Wit: RICHARD WILLIFORD, MARY LUDEN (LADEN?). February Court 1729. THOMAS CREW D.C/C.

C 172 EDWARD YOUNG TO JOHN PARSONS of Isle of Wight Co., Va.
        February 1729/30. 7 pds. TO sh. for 300 A. On SS Morrattuck River and Stonehouse Creek. Part of 400 A. patent dated Dec. 1, 1727. Wit: MARTIN LYONS, THOMAS COVERLEY. February Court 1729. THOMAS CREW D.C/C.

C 173 WILLIAM HARDING JONES of Chowan Precinct TO LAZARUS THOMAS
        Nov. 1, 1729. 27 pds. for 50 A. On Holly Branch or Spring Branch at Main County Road. Wit: THOMAS HANSFORD, BENJAMIN HILL, CLEMENT HAMMAOND. February Court 1729. THOMAS CREW D.C/C.

C 173 DAVID BUN of Isle of Wight Co., Va. TO NATHAN JOINER
        Nov. 18, 1729. 20 pds. for 170 A. On SS Roanoke River. Adj. WILL-IAM ROBERTS, LEDBART's line(?), WILLIAM BROWN. Bounded by patent dated February 1, 1725. Wit: JAMES MILLIKIN, JOSEPH JOYNER. February Court 1729. THOMAS CREW D.C/C.

C 174 JOHN SMALEY of Isle of Wight Co., Va. to JOHN RACHEL of Isle of
            Wight Co., Va.
        Feb. 10, 1729. 50 sh. for 100 A. Part of patent for 300 A. granted Feb. 1, 1725. Wit: JAMES DENTON, PETER DANIEL. February Court 1729. THOMAS CREW D.C/C.

C 175 JOHN COWARD TO JOSEPH WHITE, cordwinder
        Feb. 9, 1729/30. 50 pds. for 100 A. Adj. MARTIN GRIFFIN. Patented by JOHN HARLOE, and by him sold to WILLIAM COWARD, dec'd. Wit: JAMES WILL-IAMSON, J. JONSON. February Court 1729. THOMAS CREW D.C/C.

C 175 JOHN COOK & WIFE ELISABETH TO FRANCIS SUMNER

Sept. 5, 1729. 20 pds. for 150 A. On SS Yourah Swamp and WS Quankey Branch. Wit: E. MASHBORNE, JOHN DICKINSON, JETHRO MASHBORNE. February Court 1729. THOMAS CREW D.C/C.

C 176 JEREMIAH BARNES of Perquimmons Precinct TO WILLIAM HALL
Feb. 12, 1729/30. 30 pds. for 250 A. On Horse Swamp. Adj. HENRY WISE, STEPHEN WILLIAMS. Wit: JOHN NAIRNE, WILLIAM EVANS. February Court 1729. THOMAS CREW D.C/C.

C 177 WILLIAM EASON TO EDWARD HARRELL of Nansemond Co., Va.
Dec. 20, 1729. 25 pds. for 350 A. On SES Unerry(?) Swamp. Adj. OWEN DANIELS, JAMES SMITH, WILLIAM EASON, JOSEPH HARRELL, _____ PARKER. Part of patent granted WILLIAM EASON Aug. 4, 1723, and of another patent granted EASON May 1, 1721, and part of a deed of sale of JAMES PARKER dated July 12, 1722. Wit: JOHN HARRELL, JOHN HARRELL (+), GRACE HARRELL. February Court 1729. THOMAS CREW D.C/C. (+Probably JOHN, SEN. and JUN.)

C 178 THOMAS MANN & WIFE BRIDGET TO FRANCIS BROWN
Nov. 15, 1729. 30 pds. for 250 A. On Flatt Swamp and Killem Swamp at Chinkapen Creek and "the Mill." Adj. _____ DAVIS. Wit: JOHN MANN, HENRY CROMBON (CRANTON). February Court 1729. THOMAS CREW D.C/C.

C 179 WILLIAM MOORE TO WILLIAM MEARS
February 1729. 7 pds. for 80 A. Adj. THOMAS STEPHENS. "...Mine by deed from PETER WEST dated Oct. 26, 1722...." Wit: WILLIAM LOVICE (LOVICK), JOHN GRADE (GRADY). February Court 1729. THOMAS CREW D.C/C.

C 180 JOHN EVANS of Chowan Precinct TO JOB MEADER
Jan. 17, 1725. 30 pds. for 640 A. On SWS Chinkapen Swamp at mouth of Ready Branch. Wit: JOHN JORDAN, JANE JORDAN. N.C. Court April 23, 1726. C. GALE, C.J.

C 181 JAMES PEEK TO JOHN WARREN
Aug. 9, 1727. 10 pds. for 100 A. On SS Chowan River. Adj. LAURANCE MARTIN, LAZARUS THOMAS. At Horse Swamp. Wit: JOHN BEVERLEY, JOHN SUTTON. November Court 1729. THOMAS CREW D.C/C.

C 182 JAMES SANDERS TO ROBERT WARREN
Feb. 13, 1728. 25 pds. for 300 A. On Horse Swamp. Adj. JACOB LEWIS at Howard's Swamp. Wit: GEORGE POWELL, WILLIAM CURLEE. February Court 1729. THOMAS CREW D.C/C.

C 184 JOHN HERRING (+) & WIFE REBECA TO GEORGE CLEMENTS
Feb. 9, 1729. 40 pds. for 100 A. On Rocquis Swamp adj. RICHARD FRYAR. Wit: HENRY GUTTON, JOHN EDWARDS, HENRY EDMONDS. February Court 1729. THOMAS CREW D.C/C. (+ Also spelled JOHN HERREN, JUN.)

C 183 THOMAS WEST & WIFE SARAH TO WILLIAM BENNETT (BENNET)
Sept. 29, 1729. 25 pds. for 150 A. On NS Morrattuck River Adj. CULLEN POLLOCK. Part of a survey patented by WILLIAM BENNET on April 1, 1724. The same "...as WILLIAM & GRACE BENNETT ack. to THOS. WEST by deed dated Nov. 11, 1724...." Wit: DAVICE HOPPER, GEORGE FORT, THOMAS BRYANT. February 1729. THOMAS CREW D.C/C.

C 185 JOSEPH HARRELL TO ABRAHAM HARRELL
Aug. 7, 1729. 8 pds. 10 sh. for 100 A. On an Island adj. WILLIAM EASON at Reedy Branch. Also adj. JOHN YELVERTON and Flag Run. Wit: PETER CANE, WILLIAM CANE. February Court 1729. THOMAS CREW D.C/C.

C 185 WILLIAM SHOLDRES & WIFE MARY TO HERBIRD PRITCHETT
Feb. 10, 1729. 20 pds. for 182 A. On Cashy Swamp. Wit: JOHN BAR-FIELD, THOMAS CREW. February Court 1729. THOMAS CREW D.C/C.

C 186 WILLIAM HARDEN JONES of Chowan TO THOMAS HANSFORD
Nov. 3, 1729. 13 pds. for 150 A. On SS Deep Creek at mouth of Miery Branch. Adj. LAZARUS THOMAS, Main County Road, Spring Branch and Holly Branch. Wit: BENJAMIN HILL, WILLIAM WHITFIELD, CLEMENT HAMAND. February Court 1729. THOMAS CREW D.C/C.

C 187 JOHN PACE TO JOHN COTTON

Feb. 10, 1729/30. 10 pds. for 200 A. At Miery Meadow. Adj. CHARLES EVANS,_____GRAY, COLL. LITTLE, JOHN GREEN, JOHN BOBBITT, WILLIAM BOON. Part of tract on Occanechy Neck and NS Morrattock River. Wit: C. EVANS, T. EVANS. February Court 1729. THOMAS CREW D.C/C.

C 189   JAMES PAGE, joiner, TO WILLIAM MCKENNEY
Feb. 10, 1729/30. 40 pds. for 100 A. On Loosing Swamp. Adj. ROBERT EVANS. "...along a concluded made between WILLIAM BUSH and said EVANS...." Adj. HENRY BRADLEY, EDWARD TIDMON. By deed of sale from HENRY BRADLEY dated April 6, 1728. Wit: JOHN WYNNS, JAMES SANDERS. February Court 1729.

C 190   JOHN BARFIELD TO JONATHAN STANDLEY, SEN.
*. 10 pds. for 260 A. On SS Ahosky Swamp. Part of patent formerly granted to JOHN MOLTON in 1717. Adj. JOHN MOLTON and Turkey Swamp. Wit: THOMAS CREW, ALEXANDER SOUTHERLAND, WILLIAM SHOLAR. February Court 1729. *.

NOTE HERE: "An act for the establishing of a ferry on Chowan River near the mouth of Meherrin River commonly called Mount Galland--and also one other act to Empower PETER WEST of Bertie precinct to make sale of a tract or parcill of Land in Said precinct is in this and several of the pages of the Old Book. Omitted to be Registered in this Book."

C 191   PETER WEST TO PRISCILLA WEST, JOHN WILLIAMS, SON OF ANTHONY WILLIAMS
Plantation where I now live including two tracts on Ahosky Ridge Adj. Cow Hall, JOHN WYNNS, WILLIAM MEARS, TERENCE COMES(?), WILLIAM MOORE, WILLIAM GRAY. Wit: THOMAS JONES, THOMAS KEARNEY. Justices Court Edenton: JOHN BONDE, BENJ. HILL, JOHN DEW, THOS. BRYANT. Thomas Crew D.C/C.

C 191   PETER WEST & WIFE PRICILLA
Feb. 11, 1729. *. 1000 A. "...At a General Assembly begun and held at Edenton the 3rd day of November 1729 one act was passed and ratified... to empower PETER WEST to sell land...Whereas LEWIS WILLIAMS late of Bertie dec'd. died seized...of (400A on SW side Chowan River)...and by his last will and testament...bequeathed (400 A.) to his daughter PRICILLA WEST wife of PETER WEST...further enacted that PETER WEST hath power to sell lands...provided...(that) 18 months after Ratification...(he) do make over Lands to as great or Greater value to aforesaid precinct..."

C 192   PETER WEST & WIFE PRICILLA TO HENRY BAKER
Feb. 11, 1729. 60 pds. for 400 A. Land near Little Town plantation whereon LEWIS WILLIAMS did live. Left PRICILLA by her father's will. Wit: JAMES EVERARD, THOMAS JONES. February Court 1729. Thomas Crew D.C/C.

C 193   JETHRO BUTLAR TO CHRISTIAN HEIDELBURG
Feb. 6, 1729. 10 pds. for 100 A. On Roanoke River at Jumping Run. Wit: PETER WEST, THOMAS CREW. Feb. 7, 1730. ROBERT FORSTER C/C.

C 194   RICHARD BRASWELL & WIFE ELENOR TO JAMES NORFLEET of Perquimmons Pre-
Cinct. Feb. 10, 1729. 100 pds. for 230 A. On NS Roanoke River in Ursara Meadow. Part of two tracts surveyed by BRASWELL. Adj. ELIZABETH JEFFREYS, JOHN HILLIARD, OWEN KELLEY, JOHN COTTON. At Holly Bush Meadow. Wit: THOMAS BRYANT, WILLIAM WILSON, JAMES MOORE. *. *.

C 195   GEORGE CLEMENT (CLEMONT) TO JOHN HERRIN, JUN.
Nov. 20, 1729. *. For one Negro man called Dick. Wit: WILLIAM JONES, JOHN HATCHER. *. *.

C 195   JOSEPH HOWARD TO EDMOND HOWARD
Aug. 23, 1729. To my well beloved brother...power of atty. to ack. sale of any land I have conveyed in Bertie Precinct. Wit: JOHN BARFIELD, JOSEPH SWAINNER. *. *.

C 196   JOHN ROUSE TO WILL HARRIS
Feb. 6, 1729. 5 sh. for 180 A. On Kersey up Conneritsat. Wit: HENRY GUSTAN, WILLIAM GRIFFIN, JOHN HERRING. *.*.

C 196   ROBERT HUMPHREYS & WIFE ELISABETH TO NATHAN JOINER
Feb. 2, 1729/30. 25 pds. for 150 A. On SS Roanoke River and NS Connocanero Swamp. Part of patent to HUMPHREY dated 1725. Wit: JAMES MILLIKIN, JOSEPH JOINER, JOHN JOINER. *. *.

C 197 JAMES WILLIAMSON, surgeon, TO ROBERT ANDERSON
        Feb. 9, 1729/30. 80 pds. for 450 A. On Connehow Creek adj. RICHARD
MELTON (MOLTON). Wit: JOHN SESSOMS, WILLIAM PACE. *. *.

C 198 THOMAS JOHNSTON & WIFE ANN TO WILLIAM WHITFIELD
        Oct. 24, 1729. 150 pds. for 200 A. Commonly called "Red Ridge."
Deed dated Jan. 9, 1723. Wit: JOHN GADDY, BENTON MOORE. *. *.

C 199 PETER KEIGHLEY TO JOHN SPEIR
        Nov. 11, 1729. 15 pds. for 250 A. On SS Morrattuck River Adj._____
YELVERTON. Wit: WILLIAM SPEIR, WILLIAM GAUSS(?), MARTHA PARNELL. *. *.

C 200 WILLIAM MOORE TO ROBERT GILBERT
        Feb. 10, 1729. 20 pds. for 538 A. Patent dated Feb. 1, 1725. Wit:
WILLIAM DEVECE(?), WILLIAM MEARS. *. *.

C 200 THOMAS JOHNSTON TO WILLIAM MOORE
        Oct. 25, 1729. Power of atty. to "...take in his charge and care
all my estate...." Wit: WILLIAM WHITFIELD, JOHN GADDY, BENTON MOORE. *. *.

C 201 WILLIAM BALDWIN TO EDWARD GOODSON, JUN.
        Oct. 13, 1729. 5 pds. for 100 A. On upper side of Little Swamp in
Northwest parish. Adj. BENJAMIN THOMAS. Wit: ABRAHAM DEW(?), JOSEPH
RICHARDSON, THOMAS GOODSON. *.*.

C 202 JACOB LEWIS & WIFE MARY TO HENRY VIZE
        Jan. 14, 1729/30. 14 pds. for 250 A. On Horse Swamp "...below the
house...." Wit: MOSES PRICE, NICHOLAS FAIRLESS. Feb. 12, 1729. ROBERT
FORSTER C/C.

C 203 JACOB LEWIS & WIFE MARY TO HENRY VIZE
        Jan. 14, 1730. 2 pds. for 100 A. On White Oak Pocoson. Adj. JERE-
MIAH BARNES. Wit: MOSES PRICE, NICHOLAS FAIRLESS. Feb. 12, 1729. ROBERT
FOSTER C/C.

C 204 JACOB LEWIS & WIFE MARY TO HENRY VIZE
        Jan. 14, 1730. 4 pds. for 50 A. At Mouth of Wading Branch at Horse
Swamp. Wit: MOSES PRICE, NICHOLAS FAIRLESS. Feb. 12, 1729. ROBERT FOSTER
C/C.

C 205 JOHN GAVIN (GAVEN) TO ISAAC WILLIAMS of Norfolk Co., Va.
        Oct. 25, 1729. 20 pds. for 500 A. "parallel to Head Line" Adj. ARON
OLLIVER. Wit: ARON OLLIVER, DAVID ATKINS. *. *.

C 206 JOHN SMEALEY of Isle of Wight Co., Va. TO WILLIAM SMEALEY
        Feb. 10, 1729/30. 5 pds. for 200 A. Part of patent granted to me
Feb. 1, 1725. On SS Moherine River "across the upper end of the patent..."
Wit: JAMES DENTON, PETER DANIEL. *. *.

C 207 EDWARD YOUNG TO THOMAS ELABE
        Feb. 10, 1729/30. 7 pds. for 100 A. Part of patent dated Dec. 1,
1727 on SS Morattuck River at Fork of Stonehouse Marsh. Adj. JOHN PARSON.
Wit: MARTIN LYONS, THOMAS COVERLY. *. *.

C 207 DANIEL MAGEE & WIFE MARY TO CHARLES SOWELL
        Feb. 8, 1724. 50 pds. for 100 A. on WS Chowan River at mouth of
Horse Swamp. Adj. RICHARD MALPASS, CHARLES GAVEN. Wit: BARNABE MACKINNE,
PETER WEST. Bertie Court 1729. ROBERT FOSTER C/C.

C 208 CHARLES SOWELL & WIFE ELIZABETH TO JOHN GRAVES
        Feb. 10, 1729. *. *. "...within mentioned sale...." Wit: JOHN YOUNG,
PHILLIP MCQUIRE. *. *.

C 208 RICHARD WILLIFORD TO JOHN MORRISS (MORRISH)
        Jan. 10, 1728. 50 pds. for 150 A. At Netops Marsh and Deep Branch.
Adj. DENNIS MCCLENDEN, CHRISTIAN CHURCH at Wiccacon Creek. Wit: JOHN
SWENNEY, MARY SWENNY. *. *.

C 209 JOHN BONDE TO THOMAS DAUGHTRY of Nansemond Co., Va.
        *. 8 pds. for 140 A. Part of tract formerly taken up by WILLIAM

78

BRASSWELL by patent dated March 8, 1717/18. "betwixt land of HARDY COUNCIL and THOMAS DAUGHTRY on Yowarha Swamp." Wit: BRYAN DAUGHTRY, JONATHAN FAULK. *.*.

C 210   THOMAS SOMERELL of Isle of Wight Co., Va. to SAMUEL THOMAS
        Dec. 22, 1729. Power of atty. to collect debts "and other dis-
charges in my name." Wit: WILLIAM ARRINGTON, JOHN WILLIAMS. *. *.

C 210   LORDS PROPRIETORS TO AMBROS AYERS
        June 4, 1725. Grant. 150 A. Land granted to DAVID STEWARD and by
him "elapsed." at Fork of Guize (?) Hall Swamp on Rocquis. Signed: J.
LOVICK, sec't'y., THOMAS HARVEY, GEORGE BURRINGTON, THOMAS POLLOCK, C. GALE,
E. MOSELEY, C. GOFFEE.

C 210   AMBROS AYERS TO COLL. ROBERT WEST
        Apr. 25, 1726. *.*. "all my right title to within mentioned patent."
Wit: EDWARD MORE, JAMES CASTELLAW. May 1726. ROBERT FOSTER C/C.

C 211   ROBERT WEST TO DAVID STEWARD, Precinct surgeon
        Sept. 27, 1729. *. *. "within mentioned patent." Wit: WILLIAM
FLEETWOOD, HENRY KING. *. *.

C 211   GEORGE STEPHENSON TO JOSEPH BLACKMON
        March 10, 1728. 10 pds. for 150 A. On NS Morattuck River Adj. JOHN
WILLIAMS, THEOPHILUS WILLIAMS, Gray's Marsh. Part of patent dated Aug. 8,
1728. Wit: NEEDHAM BRYAN, *. *. *.

C 212   JOHN BUTLAR (BUTLER) TO OWEN MCDANIEL
        Aug. 11, 1729. 5 sh. *. Land adj. JOHN NAIRN at Flaggy Run on
BUSBY's line. Wit: WILLIAM WHITEHEAD, JOHN ADERLEY. *. *.

C 212   SAMUEL BASS of Chowan Precinct TO JOSEPH THOMAS
        March 23, 1729. 36 pds. for 200 A. ON SS Kesai Swamp. Adj. WILLIAM
WILLIAMS. Wit: ANDERSON SUGG(?), JOHN PERRY. N. C. Court March 23, 1729.
C. GALE, C.J.

C 213   CULLEN POLLOCK of Terrell Precinct TO JOHN GRAY
        Dec. 5, 1729. 140 pds. for 1000 A. On WS Cashy called "Barfield."
Adj. WILLIAM JONES, mouth of Broad Branch. Granted to Hon. THOMAS POLLOCK.
Said POLLOCK excepts 100 A. on back part of WALSTON's line for himsel "to
be laid off square." Wit: JAS. CASTELLAW, JNO. BONDE, WM. MACKEY, JAS.
HOLLIS, THOS. BRYANT. N.C. Court April 10, 1730. C. GALE, C.J.

C 214   LORDS PROPRIETORS TO THOMAS POLLOCK
        June 27, 1717. 56 pds. 3 sh. 4 p. for 2,810 A. Called "Basefield"
(Barfield?) On WS Cashy Adj. WILLIAM JONES, WILLIAM WALSTON, PHILLIP WALS-
TON. Recorded in Secretary's Office June 24, 1717. Signed: W. KNIGHT,
sec't'y., N. CHEVIN, WM. REED, FRED. JONES, CHARLES EDEN, THOS. POLLOCK.
Recorded DANIEL RICHARDSON, Recorder General.

C 215   CULLEN POLLOCK TO GEORGE HENDERSON
        May 1, 1730. 100 pds. for 1710 A. "...all my right title to within
deed excepting 1000 acres already sold to Mr. JOHN GRAY...." Wit: THOMAS
BELL, JAMES CASTELLAW, jurat. *. *.

C 215   ANTHONY DEAN TO ABRAHAM SHEPHERD, carpenter
        May 11, 1730. 20 pds. for 100 A. In Roquis Pocoson at Deep Run.
Adj. JOHN EDWARDS, JUN., JAMES ROBERTS. Wit: JOHN EDWARDS, JAMES CASTELLAW.

C 216   MATHIAS TOBIAS SWANOR TO ISAAC BRAWLEY
        April 22, 1730. 20 pds. for 150 A. At Capt. GEORGE WINN's Mill.
Adj. JOHN COWARDE, JOSEPH MAINERS. Wit: JOHN SWANNER, MATHIAS TOBIAS
SWANNER. *. *.

C 217   STEPHEN WILLIAMS & WIFE ELIZABETH TO WILLIAM EVANS of Chowan Pre-
        cinct. May 12, 1729. 20 pds. for 400 A. On NS Wiccacon Creek
Adj. CHARLES JONES, ARON OLLIVER, JACOB LEWIS. Part of 640 A. tract. Wit:
ANTHONY WILLIAMS, HENRY VIZE. *. *.

C 218   RICHARD HOLLAND, cooper, TO JAMES BROGDEN

May 9, 1730. 2 mares and colts for 250 A. On SS Morrattuck River. Adj. JOHN GREEN on Broad Meadow. Part of patent granted to JOHN COTTON. Wit: JOHN HARDY, ELIZABETH HARDY. *. *.

C 219 ANTHONY DEAN (DEEN) TO JOHN EDWARDS, JUN.
May 11, 1720. 55 pds. for 80 A. On Roquis. Adj. JAMES PARKER, RICHARD FRYER at Buck Swamp. Wit: JAMES CASTELLAW, JOHN WARDS. *. *.

C 219 PHILLIS SYMES TO PETER JONES
*. 13 pds. for 100 A. On NS Morattuck River and Occaneche Swamp. Part of patent granted to WILLIAM BRASSWELL in 1711/12. Wit: WILL PAUL, JOSEPH SIMS. *. *.

C 220 JOSEPH MAINER (MAYNER) TO THOMAS JOHNSON
*. 20 pds. for 30 A. On NS Wiccacon Creek along Holly Bridge Branch. Wit: JOHN SWINE, ISAAC BRAWLER. May 12, 1730. THOMAS HANSFORD D.C/C.

C 221 GEORGE SMITH TO RICHARD MOORE
May 12, 1730. 40 pds. for 600 A. On NS Roquis Creek. Adj. JOHN GOREHAM. Wit: JOHN SUTTON, JOHN EDWARDS. May 12, 1730. THOMAS HANSFORD D. C/C.

C 222 JOHN BARNS (BARNES) & WIFE CATHERINE TO EDWARD WOOD, JUN.
Feb. 4, 1724/25. 10 pds. for 200 A. Part of grant to BARNES dated Aug. 4, 1723. Wit: NATHANIEL WILLIAMS. *. February Court 1724. ROBERT FORSTER C/C.

C 223 EDWARD WOOD TO EDWARD OUTLAW
Sept. 4, 1729. 40 pds. ("bills of credit") for 200 A. "within mentioned deed." Wit: GEORGE OTWAY, SARAH WILKINSON, RACHEL OTWAY, jurat. *.*.

C 223 JACOB POPE TO JOHN GODLEY, blacksmith
May 12, 1730. 80 pds. for 120 A. On SS Morattuck River on Looking Glass Pocoson. Wit: JAMES MILLIKIN, WILLIAM CUTTS, EDWARD OVERSTREET. *.*.

C 224 FRANCIS HOBSON & WIFE ANN TO JOHN HOBSON
May 9, 1730. 100 pds. for 111 A. On NS Morattock River on Meadow Branch. Part of patent for 222 A. Wit: SOLOMON MANNING, JEREMIAH MAGLAHON.

C 225 JAMES SMITH TO GEORGE HOUSE of Nansemond Co., Va.
May 11, 1730. 28 pds. for 140 A. On NS Morattock River and Flagg Run. Adj. JOSEPH HARRELL, JOHN NAIRN. Wit: JOHN HARRELL, JOSEPH HARRELL.*.

C 226 JAMES BROGDEN TO JOHN HARDY
May 9, 1730. 20 sh. for 8 A. On Morattuck River. Adj. Holland's Gut and HARDY's line. Wit: RICHARD HOLLAND, ANN DRINKWATER. *. *.

C 227 JAMES MOORE TO EMANUEL DEES
May 12, 1730. 20 pds. for 290 A. On SS Fishing Creek and NS Maple Swamp. Wit: JOHN GRAY, JOHN HARDY. *.*.

C 228 JOHN PRICE TO ANTHONY DEAN
Jan. 13, 1729. 25 pds. for 200 A. At Islands of Rocquis. Adj. JAMES ROBERTS. Wit: SAMUEL HERRING, WILLIAM JONES, SAMUEL WESTEN(?). *.*.

C 229 LAZARUS THOMAS TO THOMAS HANSFORD
Apr. 16, 1730. 60 pds. for 150 A. On Holly Branch at mouth of Spring Branch. Wit: BENJAMIN HILL, EDWARD OUTLAW, JOHN THOMAS. May 1730. ROBERT FORSTER C/C.

C 229 RICHARD WILLIFORD TO JAMES JENKINS
May 12, 1730. 30 pds. for 100 A. On Ahoskey Swamp. Wit: JOHN SWENNY. *. May Court 1730. THOMAS HANSFORD D.C/C.

C 230 GEORGE SKIPPER, JUN. TO JEAN HERRIN
March 17, 1729. 20 pds. for 615 A. On SS Potakasey Swamp. Patent dated January 1725. Wit: WILLIAM JOHNSON, jurat, JAMES STREET, WILLIAM WICKSIN. *. *.

C 231 JOHN SPEIR TO JOHN SURGINER
May 4, 1730. 100 pds. (Providince Bills) for 400 A. On Gum Swamp.

Adj. DONALD MACKDONALD, BENJAMIN FOREMAN, GOV. EDEN. On Beaverdam Swamp, Goose Meadow, SS Morattock River, and "on head of Scotland Neck." Part of 640 A. grant to JOHN LOVICK dated July 20, 1721, and by him conveyed to SPEIR. Wit: HENRY WALKER, WILLIAM SURGINER, JOHN NAIRN. *. *.

C 232 HENRY BAKER of Chowan Precinct TO HENRY (WILLIAM) HORN (HORNE)
       May 12, 1730. 30 pds. for 110 A. On Ahoskey Pocoson. Adj. JOHN
GRAY. Land bought of WILLIAM FAULK. Patent date Feb. 1, 1725. Wit: JOHN
BEVERLY, HENRY BEVERLY. *. *.

C 233 JOHN DEW, SEN. TO WILLIAM PAUL
       March 2, 1729. 20 pds. for 260 A. On ES Great Cypress Swamp to
Little Cypress Swamp. Adj. WILLIAM BRASSWELL. Wit: JAMES MUMFORD, JOHN
DARLING.

C 234 JOHN FANNING (FANNIN) TO JOSEPH MAINER (MANOR)
       May 13, 1730. 35 pds. for 100 A. On Beaverdam Branch. Wit: JOHN
WYNNS, THOMAS JOHNSON. May Court 1730. THOMAS HANSFORD D.C/C.

C 235 WILLIAM BUSH TO ISAAC BUSH
       May 8, 1730. 200 A. "...unto my loving kinsman ISAAC BUSH, Orphan
Son of JOHN BUSH lately deceased...." Land on Chincopen Neck, Wiccacon
Creek at Holly Branch. Adj. THOMAS MCCLENDON, THOMAS BAKER(?). "only
reserving liberty to MARY BUSH...until ISAAC BUSH be of age...." Wit:
WILLIAM CRAWFORD, JOHN WYNNS. May Court 1730. THOMAS HANSFORD D.C/C.

C 236 WILLIAM HOWET (HANET) of Tyrell Precinct to JOSEPH COTTON
       Jan. 9, 1729. 40 pds. for 640 A. On Elm Swamp and Moherrin Creek.
By patent taken out by JOHN MOORE and BENTON MOORE. Wit: GEORGE OTWAY,
ALEXANDER COTTON, THOMAS JONES, jurat. *. *.

C 236 WILLIAM BUSH TO HARDY BUSH AND MARY BUSH
       May 8, 1730. Deed of gift. "...my loving kinsman HARDY BUSH Orphan
Son of JOHN BUSH...lately deceased....MARY BUSH now possessing until HARDY
BUSH be of full age...." Land on Chincopen Neck at mouth of Pole Cat
Branch. Adj. THOMAS MCCLENDON on Wiccacon Creek. Wit: WILLIAM CRAWFORD,
JOHN WYNNS. May Court 1730. THOMAS HANSFORD D.C/C.

C 237 ROBERT DIXEN TO TIMOTHY PICKOD
       Aug. 27, 1729. 7 pds. for 80 A. Land on Musheets Island and Morat-
tock River. By patent dated Oct. 19, 1727. Wit: ROBERT SIMMS, WILLIAM
WILLIAMS, WILLIAM SIMMS. *. *.

C 238 ROBERT DIXEN (DIXON) TO THOMAS SHEPPARD
       Aug. 22, 1729. Power of atty. to ack. 80 A. to TIMOTHY PICKARD.
Wit: ROBERT SIMMS, WILLIAM SIMMS, WILLIAM WILLIAMS. *. *.

C 238 THOMAS MCCLENDON TO JOHN BUSH, JUN.
       May 1, 1730. 176 A. "...for love and affection...unto JOHN BUSH son
of JOHN BUSH lately deceased...." Land on Chincopen Creek. Wit: WILLIAM
CRAWFORD, WILLIAM BUSH. *. *.

C 239 ARTHUR DAVIS of Tyrell Precinct TO WILLIAM DREW
       May 1730. 15 pds. for 300 A. On SS Morattock River and Flat Swamp.
Two plantations. One: 200 A. adj. LEWIS DAVIS and CULLEN POLLOCK. Two:
100 A. Wit: JAMES MOORE, _____JENKINS(?). *. *.

C 240 LEWIS DAVIS TO THOMAS JENKINS
       May 11, 1730. 30 pds. for 200 A. On SS Roanoke River. Adj. CULLEN
POLLOCK. Wit: JAMES MOORE, JOHN HARDY, JOHN GRAY. May Court 1730. THOMAS
HANSFORD D.C/C.

C 241 THOMAS BONNER & WIFE ELISABETH TO JAMES JENKINS
       May 11, 1730. 35 pds. for 100 A. On Snake Branch adj. WILLIAM CAR-
LEE. Part of 350 A. tract. Wit: BENJAMIN HILL, THOMAS KEARNEY. May Court
1730. THOMAS HANSFORD D.C/C.

C 241 LEWIS DAVIS of Tyrell Precinct TO WILLIAM DREW of Surry Co., Va.
       May 12, 1730. 15 pds. for 350 A. On SS Morattock River and Flat
Swamp. Adj. CULLEN POLLOCK. Wit: JAMES MOORE, JOHN GRAY, THOMAS JENKINS.*.

C 242 THOMAS POLLOCK TO JOSEPH NEWBY, millwright, of Perquimmons Precinct
       Nov. 14, 1729. 70 pds. for 100 A. On Mill Creek. "...where THOMAS
POLLOCK late dec'd had a mill...." Where JOHN SMITH formerly lived. Wit:
JOHN PALIN, EDWARD HOWCUTT. *. *.

C 243 WILLIAM BAKER of Nansemond Co., Va. TO JAMES BARFIELD
       May 13, 1730. 15 pds. for 350 A. On Reedy Pocoson. Adj. HENRY
BAKER, JAMES RUTLAND. Wit: FRANCIS BROWN, JOHN WYNNS, HENRY BONNER. *. *.

C 244 JOHN LOVICK TO FRANCIS CLAXTON
       March 6, 1729. 150 pds. for 1250 A. (250 A.) On Quarter Swamp. adj.
MR. DUCKINFIELD on Ducking Run. Wit: ROBERT FOSTER, BENJAMIN CLAYHORN.
N.C. Court. *. C. GALE, C.J.

C 245 JOSEPH JOYNER, JUN. TO JAMES MILLIKIN, merchant
       June 19, 1730. 300 pds. for 230 A. On SS Roanoke River where JOSEPH
JOYNER did live. By two deeds of grant (1) Aug. 5, 1723. Signed by MAJ.
BARNABE MCKINNE for 150 A. land. (2) Dated Oct. 25, 1723. Signed by JOHN
BROWN & MARY BROWN for 80 A. of land. Wit: JOHN GREEN, EDMOND SIMMONS,
JAMES WILKESON, MARY SIMMONS. Aug. 11, 1730. THOMAS HANSFORD D.C/C.

C 247 JOHN BRANCH & WIFE ANN TO JAMES MILLIKIN, merchant
       Aug. 8, 1730. 26 pds. for 160 A. On SS Morrattock River "bounded
according to the _____ of WILLIAM BROWN dec'd...." Wit: JOHN BROOKS, JOHN
JOYNER, THOMAS JONES. August Court 1730. THOMAS HANSFORD D.C/C.

C 248 JOHN BOBBIT TO JAMES MILLIKIN
       July 23, 1730. *. 590 A. "in the Low Grounds near Clerk's Meadow
...." Adj. WILLIAM BOON. Wit: THOMAS BRYANT, SIMON JEFFREYS, HENRY GUSTON.

C 249 WILLIAM BENNET & WIFE GRACE TO DAVIE HOPPER
       Aug. 11, 1730. 430 A. On SS Morattock River and Eastimost side of
Deep Creek. Being patent granted WILLIAM BENNET on Aug. 1, 1726. Wit:
WILLIAM WHITEHEAD, WILLIAM CAIN. *. *. (Sale price 16 pds.)

C 250 WILLIAM WHITEHEAD & WIFE RACHEL TO DAVID (DAVIE)HOPPER
       Aug. 10, 1730. 80 pds. for 150 A. Adj. ARTHUR DAVIS, FRANCIS
POSE(?). Wit: THOMAS JOBEY(?), JOHN BRIGGS. August Court 1730. THOMAS
HANSFORD D.C/C.

C 251 JOHN FORT TO DAVIE HOPPER
       July 14, 1730. 50 pds. for 122 A. On SS Morattock River on Looking
Glass Swamp. Wit: WILLIAM FORT, ALEC FORT. *.*.

C 252 MARY FORT
       July 14, 1730. "MARY FORT wife of above mentioned JOHN FORT...free-
ly discharges right of Dower in land sold to DAVIE HOPPER...." Wit:
WILLIAM WHITEHEAD, WILLIAM BINUM. *. *.

C 252 WILLIAM WHITEHEAD TO DAVIE HOPPER
       Aug. 10, 1730. 17 pds. for 320 A. On SS Morattock River and Hood's
Creek. By patent dated Aug. 2, 1730. Wit: JOHN BRIGGS, THOMAS HOBY.
August Court 1730. THOMAS HANSFORD D.C/C.

C 253 JOHN POPE & WIFE MURINING TO THOMAS WEST
       Aug. 11, 1730. 10 pds. for 240 A. (200 A.) On SS Morattock River
and NS Elkmash Swamp. Part of patent of 480 A. dated July 9, 1728. Wit:
DAVIE HOPPER, jurat, BENJAMIN LANE, JOSEPH WATS. *. *.

C 254 EDWARD SIMMONS & WIFE MARY TO BENJAMIN LANE
       Feb. 18, 1729. "40 pds Virginia money amounting to 160 pds. Pro-
vince Bills...." For 124 A. On SS Morattock River and NS Conocano Swamp.
Adj. NATHANIEL HOLLEY (HOLLIS), RICHARD WARREN. Part of 450 A. patent
granted PHILLIP RAYFORD dated Aug. 13, 1720. Wit: DAVIE HOPPER, JANE
SIMONS, GRACE SIMONS. *. *.

C 255 JOSEPH LANE TO EZEKIEL FULLER
       May 11, 1730. *. For 250 A. On NS Morattock River bounded by Holly
Bush Swamp in Yourah Woods. Adj. BENJAMIN LANE änd THOMAS LANE. Part of
a tract granted to JOSEPH LANE March 1, 1729. Wit: BARNABEE THOMAS, THOMAS

LANE. August Court 1730. THOMAS HANSFORD D.C/C.

C 256   THOMAS MITCHELL & WIFE MARGARETT TO JOHN BYRD (BIRD)
        1729/30. 15 pds. for 60 A. On NS Cashy River "...being that land
which I bought from ABEL JOHNSON alias JOHN BUTLAR...." Wit: PATIENCE
WEST, WILLIAM WEST, MATTHEW RAYSONS. *.*.

C 257 THEOPHILUS WILLIAMS TO ARTHUR WILLIAMS
        Aug. 10, 1730. 100 pds. for 200 A. On ES Horse Swamp and Turkey
Swamp to Horse Spring Branch. Adj. SAMUEL HERRING. Wit: ISAAC WILLIAMS,
WILLIAM DANIEL, WILLIAM EASON. *.*.

C 258 LAZARUS THOMAS TO THOMAS STURGES
        Aug. 10, 1730. 3 pds. for 100 A. On Holly Swamp. Adj. MATTHEW
TOBIAS SWANNER, JOHN BROWN, JAMES CURLEE. Wit: WILLIAM CRAWFORD, WILLIAM
BUSH. *.*.

C 259 JOHN GRAY TO WILLIAM LITTLE
        Aug. 28, 1728. 80 pds. for 400 A. In Occaneachy Neck. Adj. JOHN
COTTON of Meherrin. Part of tract patented by WILLIAM BRACEWELL (BRASS-
WELL) and by him sold to JAMES ANDERSON and by him conveyed to JOHN GRAY.
Full tract except what was sold by GRAY to JOSEPH SYMS. Now adj. WILLIAM
LITTLE. Wit: ROBERT FOSTER, JOHN PATTERSON. *.*.

C 260 BENJAMIN LANE TO THOMAS TAYLOR
        Aug. 12, 1730. 20 pds. for 120 A. On SS Morattock River and Looking
Glass Pocoson. Part of patent granted JACOB POPE dated Nov. 17, 1723.
Wit:THOMAS CREW, DAVIE HOPPER. *.*.

C 260 JOSEPH JOHN ALSTON of Chowan TO WILLIAM WRIGHT, JUN. of Nansemond
        Co. Va. Aug. 10, 1730. 12 pds. for 480 A. On NS Elk Swamp be-
tween the marsh and Little Swamp...runs to Beaverdam Swamp. Part of patent
to ALSTON dated Jan. 22, 1729. Wit: EDWARD POORE(?), ELIZABETH POORE(?),
THOMAS MOYE. *.*.

C 262 GEORGE BLACKWELL & WIFE ANNE TO SAMUEL WIGGANS
        May 15, 1730. 7 pds. for 75 A. On SS Rocquiess Creek. Adj. GEORGE
STEVENS, CLEMENT STRADFORD. Part of patent granted GEORGE STEVENS. Wit:
WILLIAM BRYANT, THOMAS DAUGHTON. *.*.

C 263 FINCHER HAYNE TO ROBERT FORSTER
        Nov. 14, 1730. 400 pds. for 800 A. On Chowan River. Called Petty
Shore. Adj. SAMUEL WILLIAMSON. "...together with all the Stock of Cattle,
Horses and Hoggs...and also one Negro man slave called Captain...." Wit:
THOMAS BRYANT, J. PRATT, WILLIAM LITTLE. N.C. Court Dec. 5, 1730. C.GALE *.

C 264 JOSEPH LANE, SEN. TO WILLIAM WARR (WAR)
        May 16, 1730. 3 pds. for 100 A. On Quarter Swamp. Part of patent
for 640 A. Wit: JOHN DAWSON, BARNABE THOMAS. August Court 1730. THOMAS
HANSFORD D.C/C.

C 265 LORDS PROPRIETORS TO JOHN BIRD
        March 1, 1720. Grant. 500 A. On WS Will's Quarter Swamp. Adj.
MAJOR WEST. Due for importation of persons @50 A/person. Recorded in Sec-
retar's Office. J. LOVICK, sec't'y., Signed: C. EDEN, RICHARD SANDERSON,
FRANCIS FORSTER, WILLIAM REED, *.*.

C 265 JOHN BIRD & WIFE MARY TO JAMES CURRIE
        May 16, 1730. "a valuable consideration already in hand." For 500
A. "within mentioned lands." Wit: JOHN RAY, JOSEPH SKILELSHOOP. *.*.

C 266 JOHN BIRD (BYRD) TO COLL. ROBERT WEST
        .. Power of atty. to ack. sale of land on Will's Quarter Swamp to
JAMES CURRIE. Wit: JOHN COOK, jurat, MATTHEW RAYSON. *.*.

C 266 THOMAS POLLOCK TO HENRY BUNCH
        May 30, 1729. "...a valuable consideration...." Three tracts of
land. (1) On ED Conaritsa Swamp and Mulberry Branch cont. 315 A. (2) On
ES Conaritsa Swamp adj. JOHN RASBERRY and Mulberry Branch cont. 640 A. (3)
Bounded by HENRY BUNCH, Lazarus Pocoson, Reedy Branch. Wit: JOHN CRICKETT,

ROBER PERKS. *.*.

C 267   ROBERT FORSTER TO WILLIAM LITTLE
        Sept. 5, 1728. 50 pds. for 640 A. In Meherrin Neck adj. Horse Pas-
ture Creek adj. BEAL BROWN, JOHN GARDNER. By patent granted ROBERT FORSTER
May 25, 1728. Wit: J. LOVICK, _____BADHAM. N.C. Court Sep. 5, 1728. C.
GALE, C.J.

C 267   CULLEN POLLOCK TO THOMAS JENKINS
        May 27, 1730. 12 pds. 10 sh. for 125 A. On SS Roanoke River at
mouth of Cypress Swamp at dividing line between LEWIS DAVIS and CULLEN
POLLOCK. "...to come within ten feet of bank of creek...and no nigher...
and to keep that said distance from creek...onely giving THOS.JENKINS the
liberty to take any sypress...betwixt that line and the creek...if he
thinks proper...." Wit: J. EDWARDS, JAMES WALLIS. August Court 1730. *.

C 269   BARNABE MACKINNE TO WILLIAM RUSHIN
        1730. 16 pds. for 150 A. in NW Parrish of Bertie on NS Marattock
River Whereon MATTHEW RUSHIN, father of said WILLIAM, formerly lived. Sur-
vey granted to BARNABE MCKINNE by patent dated 1700. Adj. JOHN HAWTHORNE?,
HENRY WHEALER. On Mill Pond. Wit: JOHN GILL, jurat, JAMES CAIN. *.*.

C 270   JOSEPH RICHARDSON TO ELISABETH GOODSON
        Aug. 10, 1730. Gift. 100 A. "...unto my daughter Elisabeth the
wife of THOMAS GOODSON...." Land on lower side of Mill Swamp. Adj. JOSEPH
RICHARDSON, WILLIAM ARINGTON. Wit: EDWARD GOODSON, THOMAS MANDEN. August
1730. THOMAS HANSFORD D.C/C.

C 270   HENRY SIMES (SIMS) TO RICHARD KICKER (KECKER), "tayler"
        July 13, 1730. 20 pds. for 100 A. On SS Morattock River at
Kecker's Branch. Part of a larger tract granted HENRY SIMS by patent dated
Feb. 1, 1725. Wit: JAMES MILLIKIN, jurat, SYLVESTER DIGNAM, JOHN BROOKS.
Aug. 1730. THOMAS HANSFORD D.C/C.

C 272   THOMAS DYALL TO RICHARD KICKER, "tayler"
        Aug. 5, 1730. 10 pds. for 100 A. On SS Morattock River "the same
that lyeth between the land that HENRY SIMES sold to WILLIAM KELLY and
(that he) sold EDWARD GISS(?)...." Wit: JAMES MILLIKIN, ELIZABETH MILLI-
KIN, WILLIAM HOGGETT. *. THOMAS HANSFORD D.C/C.

C 273   THOMAS YEATS TO THOMAS MEWBURN (MEWBOURN)
        Aug. 16, 1730. 20 pds. for 500 A. On ES Eastmost Branch of Salmon
Creek. Adj. JOHN CAKE, _____GALLSON. Part of patent for 640 A. dated
Oct. 19, 1716. Wit: WILLIAM CRANFORD, RICHARD WILLSON. August Court 1730.
THOMAS HANSFORD D.C/C.

C 274   JOHN COOK (COCK) & WIFE ANN TO THOMAS SUTTON & WIFE ELIZABETH
        March 29, 1729. 50 pds. for 640 A. In Chowan Precinct at Cypress
Swamp Meadow adj. "DUCKINFIELD's Corner Tree." Wit: MARTIN FRED. RASOR,
ROGER SNALE. *. *.

C 275   ANN COOK TO JAMES CRIER
        Ann, "spous of JOHN COOK" gives Power of atty. to CRIER to ack. sale
of 640 A. to THOMAS SUTTON. Wit: THOMAS MITCHELL, MATTHEW RAYSON. August
Court 1730. THOMAS HANSEFORD D.C/C.

C 275   JOHN SCOT, SEN. TO ROBERT HEMPHRIES
        Aug. 8, 1730. 10 pds. for 100 A. on SS Morattock River and SS Conn-
canry Swamp at Reedy Branch. Wit: JAMES MILLIKIN, jurat, BARNABE MACKINNE,
EDWARD SIMMONS. AugustCourt 1730. THOMAS HANSFORD D.C/C.

C 276   GIDEON GIBSON (GUPSON) TO JAMES MOORE
        1729/30. 10 pds. for 108 A. In NW Parrish of Bertie on SS Morattock
River and NS Concacanry Swamp. Part of tract formerly granted to JOSEPH
SIMES for 300 A. by patent dated Feb. 1, 1725, and by SIMES sold to GIBSON.
Wit: JAMES MILLIKIN, WILLIAM WHITFIELD, ELIZABETH JOYNER. August Court
1730. THOMAS HANSFORD D.C/C.

C 277   THOMAS SUTTON & WIFE ELIZABETH TO JOHN COOK & WIFE ANN (ANNE)
        *. 50 pds. for 62 A. At fork of Black Walnut Swamp. Adj. MARY JONES,

Lawrance Pocoson, NATHANIEL HILL, JOHN HOLLBROOK. Wit: MART. FRED. RASOR, ROGER SNELL. *. *.

C 279   ELIZABETH SUTTON TO THOMAS MITCHELL
        Aug. 10, 1730. Power of atty. to ack. sale of 60 A. in Black Walnut
Swamp to JOHN COOK. Wit: JAMES CARRE, ROGER SNELL. *.*.

C 279   JOHN RASBERRY & WIFE BRIDGETT TO JOHN CRICKET
        1730. 30 pds. for 220 A. On Cashy Swamp. Adj. CHARLES JONES. Wit:
CHARLES BARBER, HENRY BRUCK (? BROOKS). August Court 1730. THOMAS HANS-
FORD D.C/C.

C 280   SARAH BRIDGERS TO ABRAHAM BAGGET
        Aug. 11, 1730. 10 pds. for 150 A. On NS Meherrin River. Part of
tract surveyed for WILLIAM BROWN. Wit: WILLIAM BRYANT, FRANCIS BROWN.
August Court 1730. THOMAS HANSFORD D.C/C.

C 281   WILLIAM LEWIS TO JOHN HOBBS of Nansemond Co., Va.
        Oct. 31, 1728. "10 Barrells of Everyway good merchantable Tar" for
30 A. Adj. WILLIAM LEWIS. Wit: WILLIAM SMITH, WILLIAM PARKER, JOHN DRURY.
August 1730. THOMAS HANSFORD D.C/C.

C 283   JOHN DAVISON TO WILLIAM LEWIS
        Aug. 12, 1730. 14 pds. for 364 A. Part of patent granted Aug. 1,
1723. Adj. RICHARD HOLLAND, _____ BARNES. Wit: JOHN HOBBS, HENRY SOUTHER-
LAND, JOHN CALLERD (?). August 1730. THOS. HANSFORD D.C/C.

C 284   JOHN RASBERRY TO RICHARD WILLSON of Chowan
        Jan. 4, 1737 (?27). 10 pds. for 317 A. On Loosing Swamp. Wit: R.
ROUTE, ROBERT FORSTER. *.*.

C 285   RICHARD WELLSON (WILSON) TO THOMAS YEATES
        Aug. 11, 1730. *.*. "I...make over all my right title...(to) within
mentioned deed...to THOMAS YEATES...." Wit: WILLIAM CRANFORD, THOMAS HANS-
FORD (HANNTH?). *.*.

C 285   SAMUEL PEACOCK TO WILLIAM BARDEN
        July 10, 1730. 16 pds. for 150 A. Part of 320 A. patent granted
Apr. 17, 1730. On SS Meherrin River and Craine Pond Swamp. Wit: JACOB
POPE, ELIAS FORT. *.*.

C 286   JOSEPH SIMES TO THOMAS MATTHEWS
        Aug. 17, 1730. *. 200 A. JOSEPH SIMES atty. for WILLIAM WILLIAMS and
wife MARY WILLIAMS. The WILLIAMS "late of this North West Parrish." Power
of atty. granted March 27, 1730. Land on SS Morattock River and SS Quanhee
Creek. Part of 340 A. granted WILLIAMS by patent May 17, 1730. Adj. _____
JONES, ROBERT WOOD. Wit: THOMAS CRAGHILL, JOHN MACKINNE, EDWARD RDISH(?),
JOHN HARDY. *.*.

C 287   THOMAS MATTHEWS TO JOSEPH SIMES
        Aug. 17, 1730. *. 200 A. THOMAS MATTHEWS atty. of WILLIAM WILLIAMS.
Power of atty. granted March 27, 1730. On SS Morattock and NS Quanhee
Creek. Patented May 17, 1730, which WILLIAMS sold to JOSEPH SIMES for 3
pds. Wit: THOMAS CRAGHILL, JOHN MACKINNE, E. REDISH(?), JOHN HARDY. *.*.

C 288   JOHN BUNCH TO WILLIAM LITTLE
        Aug. 28, 1728. 20 pds. for *. Land that my father PAUL BUNCH
bought of JAMES KELLY on Oceaneche. "...only I am to have the corn growing
...and fodder for my creatures...." Wit: R. FORSTER, jurat, JAMES WILLKIN-
SON. August Court 1730. THOMAS HANSFORD D.C/C.

C 288   JAMES FAIRCHILD TO SOLOMON ALSTON
        Aug. 8, 1730. 20 pds. for 240 A. Part of 450 A. Adj. COLL. POLLOCK,
JOHN BROWN, JAMES CURLEE, THOMAS WIGGINS, JOHN MAINER, WILLIAM BAKER. Wit:
FRANCIS BROWN, SAMUEL WILLIAMS, NICHOLAS FAIRLESS. August Court 1730. *.

C 289   WILLIAM FROST TO NICHOLAS BUSH (BOOSH) of Surry Co., Va.
        Aug. 20, 1730. 15 pds. for 150 A. On NS Roanoke River and WS
Whealer's Mill Swamp. Part and parcell of patent granted JAMES SIMES for
300 A. dated March 1, 1719. Wit: JAMES MILLIKAN, THOMAS BRYANT, EDWARD

PRICE. August Court 1730. THOMAS HANSFORD D.C/C.

C 290 JOHN GRADDY TO ELMER EARLEY
       August 1730. 10 pds. for 150 A. Adj. WILLIAM MOORE, PETER WEST.
Wit: WILLIAM WHITFIELD, THOMAS WHIPPLE. August Court 1730. *.

C 291 JOHN BEVERLY (BEAVERLY) TO EDWARD CARTER
       August 1730. 80 pds. for 300 A. On Potty Casy Branch and the Indian
Path. Adj. WILLIAM WHITFIELD, CAPT. FRED JONES. Wit: FRANCIS PUGH, EDWARD
OUTLAW. August Court 1730. THOMAS HANSFORD D.C/C.

C 292 LAZARUS THOMAS TO WILLIAM DANIEL
       Nov. 10, 1730. 10 pds. for 100 A. On SES Deep Creek. Adj. STEPHEN
WILLIAMS, ROBERT ROGERS. Wit: JOHN LEAKY, JAMES EVERARD, C. HEILDING(?).
November Court 1730. THOMAS HANSFORD D.C/C.

C 293 BARTHOLOMEW SHAVERS TO BENJAMIN DUKE & THOMAS WOOTEN
       Nov. 1, 1730. 5 pds. for 200 A. On NS Morattock River. Part of
640 A. granted SHAVERS. Adj. GEORGE POPE(?). Wit: BARNABE THOMAS, WILLIAM
HENDRICK (HENDRECK). November Court 1730. THOMAS HANSFORD D.C/C.

C 294 WILLIAM CRAWFORD TO CHARLES RICKETTS
       Nov. 9, 1730. 120 pds. (current money of N.C.) for 700 A. On Reed
Branch and Cypress Swamp. Wit: JOHN BRADDY, HENRY BRADDY, SEN. *.*.

C 295 FRANCIS BROWN & WIFE JANE TO RICHARD BROWN
       Nov. 10, 1730. 6 pds. for 100 A. On Chicopen Creek. Adj. FRANCIS
and RICHARD BROWN. Wit: THOMAS MACLANDON, NICHOLAS FAIRLESS. *.*.

C 296 CHARLES SOWELL & WIFE ELISABETH of Chowan Precinct TO JOHN HIX of
       Chowan. Aug. 12, 1720. 18 pds. (sterling) for 100 A. On WS
Chowan River at Horse Swamp. Wit: JOHN BAYLY, JOHN NANN. *.*.

C 297 JOHN HIX & WIFE JANE TO CHARLES SOWELL
       Nov. 5, 1730. *.*. "I...assign all my right title...of within men-
tioned deed of sale to CHARLES SOWELL...." Wit: JOHN EVERETT, *.*.*.

C 297 WILLIAM MAINER of New River TO HENRY MAINER
       Nov. 8, 1730. 30 pds. for 170 A. WILLIAM MAINER late of Bertie Pre-
cinct, but now of New River. Wit: WILLIAM LEE, THOMAS LEE. *.*.

C 298 JOHN GODLEY TO JOHN TULLY
       Nov. 10, 1730. 10 pds. for 240 A. In Potacasie Woods. Wit: JOHN
WILLIAMS, CHEIDELBERY(?), JOHN BRYAN. *.*.

C 299 JOHN WILLIAMS TO ROBERT WARREN
       April 6, 1728. 31 pds. 1 cr. for 640 A. Formerly granted by patent
to AARON OLLIVER on March 11, 1719. Wit: THOMAS JOHNSTON, EDWARD HOWARD,
jurat, OLLIF.(?) MELTON. *.*.

C 300 JOHN RASBERRY TO JOHN JERNIGAN of Nansemond Co., Va.
       Nov. 10, 1730. 10 pds. for 630 A. On WS Loosing Swamp. Adj. GEORGE
POLLOCK at Seqeah Swamp and Beaverdam Swamp. Wit: WILLIAM CRAWFORD, THOMAS
BIRD. *.*.

C 303 WILLIAM CRAWFORD TO JOHN WILLIAMS
       Nov. 9, 1730. 10 pds. for 240 A. In Chincopen Neck. Adj. JAMES
BOON. Wit: *. *. *. *.

C 301 THOMAS TAPLEY TO ROBERT HUMPHRIES
       Oct. 20, 1730. 30 pds. for 150 A. On SS Morattock River and SS
Conocanarie Swamp. Part of patent for 220 A. dated Feb. 1, 1725. Remain-
der of patent sold to JOSIAH GOODING. Wit: JAMES MILLIKIN, GEORGE RAWLISON,
EDWARD GIBSON. *.*.

C 304 JOHN BROWN TO BARNABE MACKINNE
       Sep. 27, 1730. 50 pds. for "...my whole right title and interest in
one patent of Land formerly patented to my father WILLIAM BROWN dec'd.
being for 640 A....dated April 1, 1713...." On SS Morattock River adj.
JOHN LEWIS, COLL. WILLIAM MAUL. "...I, the eldest son of WILLIAM BROWN..."

Wit: ROBERT HUMPHRIES, THOMAS HUMPHRIES, BARNABE MACKINNE, JUN. *.*.

C 304 WILLIAM LEWIS TO JOHN DRURY
     Oct. 8, 1730. 30 pds. for 100 A. On Eastermost branch of Miery
Meadow. Adj. JOHN HOBBS. Being greater part of tract purchased of JOHN
DAVISON. Wit: SARY(?) DRURY, JOHN HOBBS. *.*.

C 305 JAMES BOON TO CULMER SESSOMS (SESSIONS)
     Nov. 10, 1730. 40 pds. for 220 A. Part of larger tract granted to
JAMES BOON. Wit: J. LEAKY, JOHN WYNNS. *.*.

C 306 FRANCIS MECLENDEN TO JOHN WILLIAMS
     Nov. 10, 1730. 8 pds. for 100 A. On Quiokison Swamp adj. ALEXANDER
CANADY, JOHN WILLIAMS. "JOHN WILLIAMS of Chincopen Neck." Wit: JOHN WYNNS,
JOSEPH VARDEN. *.*.

C 307 BARNABE MACKINNE TO HENRY BOSEMAN (BOOSMAN)
     Nov. 18, 1730. 11 pds. for 296 A. In NW Parish of Bertie. On SS
Morattock River and Great Quanka Creek. Land formerly surveyed to STEVEN
DUNMADEN, and upon his death recovered by Lords Proprietors and granted to
BARNABE MACKINNE by patent May 15, 1730. Wit: J. PRATT, JAMES MILLIKIN,
ROBERT FORSTER. *.*.

C 308 JOHN MACKINNE TO MARY BROWN & WILLIAM BROWN
     Nov. 9, 1730. Gift. 200 A. to WILLIAM 150 A. to MARY. "for love
and affection to my cousins...son and daughter of JOHN & MARY BROWN dec'd.
...." (1) Land on SS Morattock River in NW Parish of Bertie adj. PHILIP
RAYFORD, ROBERT FORSTER, WILLIAM STEVENS. (2) On SS Morattock adj. her
brother WILLIAM and ROBERT FORSTER. Wit: BARNABE MACKINNE, JUN., SYLVESTER
DRYNTERN. *.*.

C 309 JOHN BONDE TO JOHN VICK
     *. 10 pds. for 300 A. One half of tract formerly BEAL BROWN's by
patent dated Nov. 27, 1729. Wit: JONATHAN SANDERSON, JOHN WIGGANS, BENJA-
MIN JOHNSTON. *.*.

C 309 ROGER CASE TO WILLIAM LITTLE
     Aug. 25, 1730. 5 pds. for 50 A. Sold to me by JOHN COTTON. Adj.
survey of"...old ROBERT LANG on Occaneachee...." Wit: J. PRATT, *.*.*.

C 309 JOHN CHRISTOPHER DEUALL TO EDWARD OUTLAW
     Nov. 11, 1730. 50 pds. for 640 A. That land "...which I had
CHARLES RYAL situate...." On SS Flat Swamp. Wit: WILLIAM WHITEHEAD, PETER
WEST. *.*.

C 310 JOHN MACKINNE TO SARAH GRIMES
     Nov. 9, 1730. 10 pds. for 50 A. "...whereon said SARAH now lives..."
Part of patent for 550 A. On SS Morattock River in NW Parish of Bertie.
Patent date May 1, 1730. Adj. PHILIP RAYFORD on Cattail Branch. Wit:
BARRIBE MACKINNE, JUN., SYLVESTER DIGNAM. *.*.

C 311 ABRAHAM BRAWLER (BRATER) TO MARY BRAWLER
     May 21, 1730. Gift. Household goods. "(for),,,good pure affection
... to my loving and dutiful daughter MARY BRAWLER....":
     2 beds & furniture   12 puter plates
     3 pots "last choice"   2 tankards
     8 puter basons   1 brass candlestick
     2 puter candlesticks   1 brass scimer
     3 puter salt sellers   1 great chest & trunk
     6 puter dishes   all stock cattle
    18 glass bottles   all hogs & other creatures marked with
     linnin wheel   crop & hole in left ear & 1/2
     whooling wheel   square on right ear
     young mare   3 porringers
     4 year old bridle & saddle all wearing gear
Wit: JOHN LOVICK, JOSEPH MAINER. *.*.

C 312 LORDS PROPRIETORS TO WILLIAM LITTLE
     July 4, 1726. Grant. 400 A. On SS Morattock River. For importa-
tion of persons @50 A/person. Signed: RICHARD EVERARD, Baronet, JOHN
BLOUNT, JOHN LOVICK, sec't'y., EDW. MOSELY, C. GALE, ROBT. WEST.

C 312 WILLIAM LITTLE TO JOHN ELLEBY
       April 29, 1730. 30 pds. for "within mentioned patent." Wit: THOMAS
JONES, JOHN GRAY. *.*.

C 313 JOHN MOHERA (MOHERE) TO MATTHEW SELLERS
       Dec. 19, 1729. 20 barrels of tar for 100 A. On SS Morattock River
at a branch of Kerby Creek. Part of a patent for 640 A. granted to ROBERT
SHERWOOD in 1719. Wit: JOHN DREW, jurat, JAMES MUMFORD. *.*.

       NOTE HERE: "So far done before May Term 1801"

C 314 BARNABE MACKINNE, JUN. TO EDWARD SIMONS (SIMMONS)
       Sep. 5, 1729. 30 pds. for 400 A. On SS Morattock River and SES
Conaconare Swamp. 350 A of which was granted to ARTHUR DAVIS by patent
Aug. 5, 1720 and by DAVIS sold to MACKINNE Aug. 5, 1722. The other 50 A.
part of a tract granted WILLIAM MURPHENE for 500 A. dated April 5, 1715 (?
at mouth of Barnes branch. By MURPHEW sold to MACKINNE on March 27, 1722.
Wit: BARNABE MACKINNE, THOMAS CRAGHILL, MICHAEL MACKINNE. *.*.

C 315 LORDS PROPRIETORS TO ROBERT FORSTER
       *. 400 A. On SS Morattock. For importation of persons @50 A/person.
Signed: Sir RICHARD EVERARD, Baronet, JOHN BLOUNT, C. GALE, ROBT. WEST,
J. LOVICK, sec't'y.

C 316 ROBERT FORSTER TO JOHN ELLEBY
       April 29, 1730. 30 pds. for *. "within mentioned lands...." Wit:
JAMES JENEURE(?), JOHN GRAY. *.*.

C 316 BARNABEE MACKINNE TO ABRAHAM MACKLEMARR (MACKELMARR)
       Nov. 9, 1730. 40 pds. for 625 A. On NS Morattock in NW Parish. By
patent dated Feb. 1, 1720. Wit: BARNABE MACKINNE, JUN., JOHN MACKINNE. *.*.

C 318 RICHARD PACE, JUN. TO RICHARD PACE, SEN.
Nov. 1, 1730. 30 pds. for 300 A. On NS Morattock River and Yowwehaugh
Swamp. Part of tract granted to RICHARD PACE, JUN. for 640 A. dated
March 1, 1719. Wit: WILLIAM CAIN, THOMAS PACE. *.*.

C 319 JACOB BROWN TO BARNABE MACKINNE, JUN.
       March 28, 1730. 40 pds. for 100 A. "...land...to me by last will
and testament of my father WILLIAM BROWN which Land since my father's
decease for want of patent hath been surveyed for my Eldest brother JOHN
BROWN...by date March 13, 1721...." Cont. 525 A. On SS Morattock River
"whereon my father did live and then dye...." Adj. RICHARD JACKSON, BARN-
ABE MACKINNE, _____ STRICKLAND. Wit: BARNABE MACKINNE, jurat, MARY MACKINNE.

C 320 HENRY OVERSTREET & WIFE ANN TO ABRAHAM SHEPPARD (SEPHERD)
       Nov. 10, 1730. 130 pds. for 235 A. "lying back of a survey of MAR-
TIN GARDNER" on SS Cashy Swamp and ES Roquist Swamp. Wit: JOSEPH MOORE,
ANN MOORE, THOMAS WHIPPLE. *.*.

C 321 THOMAS BLACKMAN & WIFE ANN TO STEPHEN RAGLAND
       Feb. 2, 1730. 10 pds. for 100 A. On NS Morattock River in NW Parish
of Bertie. Part of tract granted RICHARD TURBEVALL by patent dated July 29,
1712 of 510 A. Adj. WILLIAM REAUESESAN. Wit: RICHARD CUERTON, BRYAN RAG-
LAND, ROBERT JONES, jurat. *.*.

C 322 WILLIAM BOON TO NATHAN PLATT
       Nov. 28, 1730. 29 pds. for 100 A. On Ockeneche Swamp. Adj. HENRY
SIMES, ROBERT SIMES. Wit: JOHN PRATT, jurat, JOHN GLOUER, C. EVANS. *.*.

C 323 RICHARD CUERTON & WIFE HANNAH TO STEPHEN RAGLAND of Hanover Co., Va.
       *. 14 pds. for 200 A. On NS Morattock River near Double Bottom
Branch. Adj. RICHARD TURBERVILLE. "...being a parcell which I bought of
THOMAS WHITMELL...." Wit: ROBERT JONES, NATHANIEL MERRITT. *.*.

C 324 ARTHUR WILLIAMS & WIFE MARY TO WILLIAM JONES
       Aug. 10, 1725. 10 pds. for 100 A. On SS Meherin River at Crag
Branch. Purchased of WILLIAM WASHINGTON April 28, 1717. Wit: RICHARD
HORNE, NICHOLAS TINAR. *.*.

C 325 SOLOMON JONES & WIFE ELINOR (ELENOR) TO SAMUEL ELLEBY

April 9, 1730. 50 pds. for 100 A. "...the within mentioned lands
....." Wit: EDWARD HOOD, jurat, JOHN MOHER(?). *.*.

C 325 THOMAS BONNER, cordwinder, to JOHN JENKINS of Nansemond Co., Va.
Aug. 12, 1730. 5 pds. for 100 A. Between THOMAS BIRD, WILLIAM CURLE,
JAMES JENKINS. Wit: JOHN WYNNS, THOMAS BROWN. *.*.

C 326 JOHN EDWARDS, SEN. & WIFE MARY TO JOHN MOORE
*. 25 pds. for 100 A. On ES Turkey Swamp "...on Eastermost side of
JOHN EDWARDS plantation...." Said plantation cont. 200 A. Wit: JAMES
CASTELAW, JONATHAN STANDLEY, HENRY EDWARDS. *.*.

C 327 JOHN EDWARDS & WIFE MARY TO MATTHEW EDWARDS
Feb. 1, 1730. *.*. Power of atty. to ack. sale of 100 A. on Turkey
Swamp to JOHN MOORE. Wit: JAMES CASTELLAW, JONOTHAN STANDLEY, jurat, HENRY
EDMONDS (.). *.*.

C 327 BENJAMIN FOREMAN TO WILLIAM BRYANT
Feb. 1, 1731/32. 26 pds. for 650 A. ON SS Morattock and SS Kehuca
Swamp, and both sides of Marshy Swamp. "...except (150A) that JOHN HALL
now lives...." Wit: RICHARD WILLIAMS, THOMAS BROWN. *.*.

C 328 MATHEW TOBIAS SWANNER TO NICHOLAS TOOPE
July 17, 1730. 25 pds. for 100 A. At Holly Swamp adj. CHRISTOPHER
SEGAR. Wit: JOHN SWENNEY, JOSEPH TOMSON. February Court 1730. THOMAS
HANSFORD, D.C/C.

C 328 JOHN HERRING, JUN. TO RICHARD FRYER
Feb. 7, 1730. "a valuable sum of money" for 160 A. On Rocquist Poc-
oson to Roanoke River. Wit: JOHN HERRING, J. HORO(?). (Also signed
REBECCA HERRING, wife of JOHN).

C 329 LORDS PROPRIETORS TO MAJOR ROBERT WEST
Oct. 19, 1716. Grant. 640 A. "...in Chowan Precinct..." adj. ED-
WARD BRYANT, HENRY BRADLEY. For importation of persons @ 50A/person.
Signed: CHARLES EDEN, esq. "and the rest of our trusty and well beloved
Councillors...." THOMAS KNIGHT, THOMAS POLLOCK, C. GALE, FRANCIS FORSTER,
Recorded in Sec't'y. Office T. KNIGHT Sec't'y. October 20, 1716.

C 330 ROBERT WEST TO SAMUEL ONWELL
Feb. 10, 1730. 50 pds. for "within mentioned patent...." Wit:
ROBERT FORSTER, JAMES MILLIKIN. *.*.

C 330 WILLIAM BRYAN (BRYANT) TO JOHN VEAL of Norfolk Co., Va.
Feb. 9, 1730. 5 pds. for 50 A. By Patent dated Feb. 11, 1725. Wit:
JAMES SUMNER, ROBERT BRASWELL. *.*.

C 331 CHARLES JONES TO CAPT. GEORGE WYNNS
February 1730. 25 pds. for 450 A. On Conaritsa Swamp and East Fork
Cashy Swamp. Adj. ROBERT LANIER. Wit: THOMAS JONES, JOHN WYNNS. February
Court 1730. THOMAS HANSFORD D.C/C.

C 332 PATRICK MAULE TO GEORGE STEVENSON
Jan. 7, 1730. 60 pds. for 240 A. In Ahoskey Woods. Adj. JOHN HAM-
ILTON, OWEN MACDONALD. Wit: WILLIAM GRAY, JAMES TAYLER. *.*.

C 333 STEVEN WILLIAM TO GEORGE NICHOLSON
November 3, 1730. 125 pds. for 550 A. Adj. COTTY CONTHEN(?), GEORGE
SMYTH, JOHN WILLIAMS. Wit: WILLIAM HOLL.(AND)(HALL.), RICHARD WILLIFORD.*.

C 335 EDWARD MOORE TO JOHN HORO
Feb. 9, 1730. 12 pds. for 330 A. On Rocquist Pocoson. Adj. JOHN
HARDY, Esq., MARTEN GARDNER. Wit: THOMAS MEWBORN, JAMES SPAINN. *.*.

C 336 RICHARD MELTON TO RICHARD WILLIAMS
Dec. 30, 1730. 15 pds. for 600 A. On NS Morattock River adj. BENJA-
MIN FOREMAN. Granted to R. MELTON March 9, 1717. Wit: JOHN BROWN, THOMAS
BROWN, GEORGE WILLIAMS. *.*.

C 337 RICHARD MELTON TO BENJAMIN FOREMAN
Dec. 30, 1730. Power of atty. to ack. land on Roanoke River (NS)

cont. 600 A. to RICHARD WILLIAMS. Wit: JOHN BROWN, THOMAS BROWN, GEORGE WILLIAMS. *.*.

C 337 WILLIAM GILBERT TO SAMUEL MATHER of Perquimmons Precinct
     Dec. 1, 1730. 40 pds. for 200 A. On Chincapen Swamp and Flat Swamp. Wit: LAWRANCE MAGUE, JOHN BRYANT. *.*.

C 333 WILLIAM BRYANT TO JOHN VEAL of Norfolk Co., Va.
     Feb. 9, 1730. 8 pds. for 86 A. On NS Morattock River and Bridger's Creek. Granted April 1, 1723. Adj. WILLIAM BRYANT, TIMOTHY CUMINGIM. Wit: JOSEPH SUMNER, ROBERT BRASWELL. *.*.

C 339 JOHN MACKINNE TO JONATHAN WHITE
     Feb. 8, 1730. 15 pds. for 308 A. On SS Morattock River and Elk Marsh. Patent dated Feb. 1, 1725. Wit: JAMES MILLIKIN, jurat, WILLIAM HOGGATT, NATHAN JOYNER. *.*.

C 340 SAMUEL WIGGANS (WIGGENS) & WIFE ELIZABETH TO THOMAS DUFFIELD
     Nov. 12, 1730. 40 pds. for 75 A. On SS Bridger Creek. Adj. CHARLES STEVENS, CLEMENT STRATFORD. Wit: JOHN SHOLAR, JAMES CASTEN. *.*.

C 341 JOHN STEVENS TO NATHAN JOYNER
     Feb. 8, 1730. 15 pds. for 100 A. On SS Morattock River and NS Conaconary Swamp. Wit: JAMES MILLIKIN, jurat, WILLIAM HOGGATT, JOHN MACKINNE.*

C 342 THOMAS ARINGTON & WIFE MARY TO STEVEN RAGLAND of Hanover Co., Va.
     Feb. 3, 1730. *. 160 A. On NS Morattock River Adj. RICHARD TUBERVILLE, JOHN HATHHORN. Wit: RICHARD ALLEN, ROBERT JONES, DANIEL KENDRETT (KENDRILL). *.*.

C 343 RICHARD FRYER TO JOHN HERRING
     Feb. 9, 1730. 50 pds. for 150 A. On WS Cashy River. Adj. THOMAS WHITMELL, _____GUSTON, CULLEN POLLOCK, WILL JONES. Wit: T. HORO, JOHN HERRING. *.*.

C 344 JOHN BRYANT TO SAMUEL ONVINE (ONWINE, ONWELL)
     Feb. 1730. 100 pds. for 160 A. Part of tract which formerly belonged to EDWARD TAYLER. Adj. LAWARANCE MAGUE on Chowan River. Wit: WILLIAM CRANFORD, WILLIAM KEATON. *.*.

C 345 JOHN BRYANT TO CHRISTIAN HEIDLEBURGH
     Power of atty. to ack. sale to SAMUEL ONWINE. Wit: WILLIAM GILBERT, jurat, WILLIAM KEATON. *.*.

C 346 WILLIAM BRYANT & WIFE MARY TO JOHN VEAL of Norfolk Co., Va.
     Feb. 9, 1730. 32 pds. for 320 A. Part of 640 A. granted March 9, 1717. Adj. WILLIAM BRIDGERS. Wit: JAMES SUMNER, ROBERT BRASWELL. *.*.

C 347 LORDS PROPRIETORS TO CAPT. DAVID HENDERSON
     April 1, 1720. Grant. 640 A. On WS Chowan River adj. MAJOR WEST. For importation of person @ 50 A/person. Signed: CHARLES EDEN, Esq. Governor, J. LOVICK, sec't'y., WILLIAM REED, THOMAS POLLOCK, ALFRED JONES. *.*

C 347 CAPT. DAVID HENDERSON TO SAMUEL ONWEN
     May 19, 1725. *. 640 A. "I the subscriber make over all my Right title of within mentioned patent...to SAMUEL ONWEN...." Wit: THOMAS BRADWELL, JOHN GOLSON. *.*.

C 348 LORDS PROPRIETORS TO CAPT. DAVID HENDERSON
     July 20, 1717. Grant. 640 A. In Chowan Precinct. Adj. ROBERT EVANS, MAJ. ROBERT WEST, Widow BARNES(?). For importation of persons @ 50 A/person. Signed: Hon. CHARLES EDEN, Esq. Governor, THOMAS KNIGHT, THOMAS POLLOCK, N. CHEVIN, WILLIAM REED. July 21, 1717. Recorded in Secretary's Office, THOMAS KNIGHT, sec't'y.

C 348 DAVID HENDERSON TO SAMUEL ONWINN
     May 19, 1725. *. 640 A. Above mentioned patent. Wit: THOMAS BRADWELL, JOHN GOLSON. *.*.

C 349 LORDS PROPRIETORS TO MAJOR ROBERT WEST
     July 21, 1717. Grant. 640 A. on WS Chowan River. Adj. Widow BARNES,

EDWARD BRYAN. Signed: Hon. CHARLES EDEN, Esq. Governor, THOMAS KNIGHT, Secretary, N. CHEVIN, THOMAS POLLOCK, FRANCIS FORSTER. *.*.

C 349   MAJOR ROBERT WEST TO DAVID TREESE
        Jan. 3, 1729/30. *. 640 A. Above mentioned patent. Wit: WILLIAM FLEETWOOD. _____. *.*.

C 349   ROBERT HILL TO WILLIAM PARSON
        Aug. 4, 1730. 4 pds. for 640 A. Adj. ABRAHAM MACKELMER on Stonehouse Creek. Wit: JOHN TOMKINS, FRANCIS YOUNG. August Court 1730. THOMAS HANSFORD D.C/C.

C 350   JOHN SKITTLETHARP & WIFE MARY TO JOHN RAY & WIFE MARY
        Oct. 13, 1729. 60 A. For love and affection. On NS Cashy River. Adj. JOHN BIRD, JOHN SKITTLETHORNE. Wit: JOHN BIRD, EDWARD DAVIS. N.C. Court December 1729. C. GALE, C.J. THOMAS HANSFORD D.C/C.

C 351   WILLIAM CRANFORD TO WILLIAM BUSH
        Aug. 11, 1730. 6 pds. for 120 A. On Wiccacon Creek whereon WILLIAM CRANFORD now lives. Adj. THOMAS MACLENDON, DENNIS MACLENDON, dec'd. Formerly surveyed for ABRAHAM BLEWLET. Wit: LAZARUS THOMAS, JOSEPH JOHN ALSTON.

C 352   ROBERT HILL TO JOHN TOMKINS
        March 29, 1730. 15 pds. for 100 A. On Beaverdam Creek commonly called Stonehouse Creek. Adj. THOMAS ELLIS (ELLENBERG), FRANCIS YOUNG. Wit: WILLIAM PERSON, FRANCIS YOUNG, EDWARD YOUNG. *.*.

C 353   MARTEN CROMEN TO THOMAS KERNY (KEARNEY) (CARNEY)
        March 30, 1730. 100 pds. for 229 A. On Casia River Adj. ____ BIRD, LUKE MEAZEL. Patent granted EDWARD STANDING Oct. 19, 1716. Wit: BENJAMIN HILL, THOMAS JONES. N. C. Court April 3, 1730. C. GALE, C.J.

C 354   ABRAHAM MACKELMORE TO WILLIAM PEISON
        Aug. 11, 1730. 2 pds. for 2 A. On Stonehouse Creek. Adj. ROBERT HILL. Wit: ROBERT HILL, FRANCIS YOUNG. August Court 1730. THOMAS HANSFORD D.C/C.

C 355   JOHN LOVICK TO JOSEPH JENOURE
        Dec. 26, 1729. 200 pds. for 890 A. On ES Meherrin Creek and Elm Swamp. Adj. JOHN COTTON, _____MOORE. Wit: ROBERT FORSTER, FRANCIS CLAXTON. N.C. Court May 2, 1730. C. GALE, C.J.

C 355   MARTIN CROMEN TO DARDY (DARBY) DEMPIER (DEMPSIR), cooper
        Aug. 1, 1730. 30 pds. for 388 A. On NS Morattock River. Adj. EDWARD SMITHWICK, TERRENCE BURN. On Charlton's Creek. Wit: SAMUL RATLIF(?), ELIZABETH RATLIF. *.*.

C 357   MARTIN CROMEN TO THOMAS SPEIRS
        Aug. 10, 1730. Power of atty. to ack. sale to DARBY DEMSEE. Wit: ED. KEARNEY, THOMAS KEARNEY, jurat. *.*.

C 357   MARTEN CROMEN TO THOMAS COPELAND
        May 25, 1730. 25 pds. for 250 A. In Tyrell Precinct On NS Flat Swamp. Wit: JAMES JENEURE, ROBERT FORSTER. *.*.

C 358   MICHAEL KING of Kesia in Bertie TO PATRICK CANADY
        May 30, 1730. 60 pds. for 100 A. On Wills Quarter Swamp and Beaverdam Swamp. Wit: MARTIN CROMEN. *.*.

C 359   MICHAEL KING TO JAMES CORIE
        Aug. 8, 1730. Power of atty. to ack. sale on Will's Quarter Swamp to PATRICK CANADY. Wit: THOMAS MICHEAL (MITCHELL?), jurat, RICHARD BIRD.*.

        Note Here:"There are two pages lost out of the Old Book B. And begins again as underneath. I find by the old Alpabet one of the deeds missing is LOVICK to SHELTON."

C 359   JOHN DAVERSON (DAVISON) TO EDWARD BARNES
        (Badly defaced)
        Aug. 11, 1730. *. 464 A. "...said JOHN DAVISON...cont. 464 A. dated

April 1, 1723...." Wit: JAMES HOLLAND, LAWRANCE WOLFERSTON, THOMAS PAGE.*.

C 360 JACOB BRASSWELL & WIFE ELISABETH TO WILLIAM RUFFIN
       Aug. 8, 1727. 11 pds. for 278 A. On SS Morattock River In Uasary
Meadow and Hog Pen Meadow. Adj. JOHN COTTEN, RICHARD BRASWELL. Part of
tract formerly granted JACOB BRASSWELL for 528 A. on April 1, 1723. Wit:
THOMAS HART, JOHN HART. *.*.

C 361 JOHN DEW, SEN. TO JAMES BRYANT, SEN.
       July 25, 1730. 10 pds. for *. On NS Meherrin River on line between
DEW and BRYANT adj. _____BRITT. Wit: ABRAHAM DEW, JOSEPH DEW. *.*.

C 362 JOHN TURBERVILLE & WIFE ELISABETH TO THOMAS HARRINGTON
       Aug. 5, 1730. 20 pds. for 100 A. On NS Morattock River and WS
Turberville (Turbeville) Run. Adj. JOHN COLSON, RALPH MASON and Racoon
Branch. Wit: SETH HATCHER, jurat, JAMES EDMONDS. *.*.

C 362 DANIEL CRAWLEY TO WILLIAM LITTLE
       *. 20 pds. for 200 A. On Occanechy Neck and NES Roanoke River. Part
of a larger tract granted by CRAWLEY to ROBERT LAND (LONG) at mouth of
Quanque Gut. Adj. _____PACE, _____CLARK, GIDEON GIBSON. Wit: ROBERT
FORSTER, J. PRATT. N. C. Court Dec. 12, 1730. C. GALE, C.J.

C 363 EDWARD MOSELEY TO RICHARD EVERARD, Baronet
       (Badly defaced)
       June 12, 1730. *. 1900 A. On NS Morattock River and Irwin's Creek.
Signed: R. EVERARD, C. GALE, J. LOVICK, EDW. MOSELEY, ROBERT WEST, J. PAC-
LIN, T. POLLOCK, C. GALE(?), J. WORLEY. "Rec'd. the Purchase money f__me.
W. LITTLE, R. GALE."

C 363 EDWARD MOSELEY of Chowan TO HON. SIR RICHARD EVERARD, Bar't. Gov. of
       N.C. July 17, 1730. 5 sh. and other considerations. for 1900 A.
On Irvine Creek. Granted to me by patent June 12, 1730. Wit: THOMAS
JONES, jurat, R. FORSTER, JOHN FLACONER. August Court 1730. *.*.

C 363 THOMAS JONES of New Hanover Precinct TO JOHN LOVICK, Esq.
       Sep. 18, 1730. *. 964 A. On Blewwater Branch and Catawiskie Swamp.
Wit: WILLIAM LITTLE, THOMAS POLLOCK, R. FORSTER. N.C. Court Sep. 19,
1730. C. GALE, C.J.

C 364 WILLIAM BOON TO WILLIAM LITTLE
       Nov. 17, 1730. 150 pds. for 550 A. Surveyed to JAMES BOON. On WS
Miery Meadow. 100 A. sold to JOHN BOBBIT; 100 A. sold to HENRY SIMES where
CHAS. EVANS now lives. 150 A. sold by SIMES to WM. LITTLE. Adj. JAMES
SIMES. Wit: R. FORSTER, J. PRATT. N.C. Court 1730. C. GALE, C.J.

C 365 JOHN SANDERS TO WILLIAM LITTLE
       Jan. 20, 1730. 60 pds. for *. On Occaneche Neck "betwixt" WILLIAM
BOON and JAMES GEE. On ES Roanoke River. Surveyed to BARNABE MACKINNE.
Wit: ROBERT FORSTER, J. PRATT, THOMAS BRYANT. N.C. Court Dec. 12, 1731.
C. GALE, C.J.

C 366 "Bertie at a Court held for said Prec't at Court House on Tueasday
10 day Nov'r. Anno Dom. 1730. Present His Majesties Justices. In the
attatchment broght by WILLIAM LITTLE assigner vs JOHN KELLEY for 60 pds.
Sterling the Execution against the goods of the defendent being Returned
mulla Bina(?) the plantiff prayed that appraisers be (appt.) to appraise
land of defendent...pursuant an act of assembly against fugitive...the
following persons (appt'd.) JAMES MILLIKIN, JOHN LAW, JOHN BOBBIT, GEORGE
SMITH, ANDREW IRELAND, PETER JONES, WILLIAM BALDWIN, WILLIAM HODGES or any
six of them...to evaluate land of defendent...Copy RT. FORSTER, clerk."
       "November 20, 1730...lands of JOHN KELLEY...to be the same value in
Satisfaction the Judgement before me....Signed: THOMAS BRYANT
       We...appraisers value the land of JOHN KELLEY...200 acres on Occa-
neche Neck where said KELLEY formerly lived and reversion of 50 acres to
ROGER CASE during life where CASE sometimes lived...Land being part of
patent surveyed to KELLEY...below lands of JOHN COTTON...valued at 23 pds.
sterling...JOHN LANE, ANDREW IRELAND, GEORGE SMITH, WILLIAM BALWIN, PETER
JONES, WILLIAM HODGES." (note: name could be HOLLEY).

       Note: pages 367, 368, 369 blank.

92

"The following Deeds is Transcribed from Book E which said book was began in May 1739..."

C 370 FRANCIS MCCLENDEN & WIFE ELINER & ISAAC HILL TO JOSEPH PERRY of
        Chowan. *. 60 pds. for 150 A. In Chincapin Neck at mouth of Holly
Swamp. Wit: JOHN THOMAS, jurat, JOHN WILLS. *.*.

C 371 GEORGE WALSTON TO JOHN BOWER (BOWEN)
        April 30, 1739. 30 pds. for 284 A. On Deep Run. Adj. WILLIAM ROW-
LAND, PHILLIP WALSTON in Bear Swamp. Wit: RICHARD LEARY, ABRAHAM HERRING,
PHILLIP WALSTON, jurat. May Court 1739. *.

C 372 DAVID JORNIGIND TO JOHN ROBINS
        May 6, 1739. 20 pds. for 100 A. On WS Chowan River. Part of tract
granted RICHARD HOLLAND by patent dated April 1, 1723. Wit: JAMES MANNY,
jurat, WILLIAM ROBINS. May Court 1739. *.

C 374 JOHN DREWRY of Craven County TO JOHN ROBINS
        May 6, 1739. 70 pds. for 100 A. Part of tract granted JOHN DAVISON
by patent April 1, 1723. On Miery Meadow adj. JOHN HOBBS. Wit: JAMES
MANNY, jurat, WILLIAM ROBINS. May Court 1739. *.*.

C 375 EDWARD BYRD & WIFE ANNE TO COLL. ROBERT WEST
        May 7, 1739. 500 pds. for 200 A. On Cashoke Creek at mouth of Miery
Branch and Folly Branch. Wit: ROBERT PATTERSON, JOHN ASHWORTH, PENELOPE
WIN___(?). *.*.

C 375 JOHN WHEELER (WHEATER) TO ROWLAND WILLIAMS
        Dec. 7, 1739. 35 pds. for 90 A. "...with a going Mill...." On Mill
Swamp. Wit: WILLIAM RUSHING, JUN., ROBERT CARSON. May Court 1739. *.

C 377 WILLIAM KENNADY of Tirell Precinct TO JAMES LEGGETT
        Feb. 5, 1735/36. *. 200 A. "...all my right title in all my prop-
erty except a greave and ten foot belonging to it...." In Kesia Neck
formerly called "Terance" adj. JOHN SMITHWICK, JUN., EDWARD SMITHWICK, JUN.
dec'd. Left by E. SMITHWICK. "...The rest of his estate unto his beloved
wife GRACE SMITHWICK during her life...then to her children...said GRACE
making deed of gift to FRANCIS HOBSON...and HOBSON making me a deed before
the plantation was made...in the year 1722...." Wit: WILLIAM GARDNER, JOHN
WALSTON. August Court 1736. JOHN WYNNS C/C.

END OF DEED BOOK C

D 1 JOHN GRUSSETT TO JOHN HOBSON
        Aug. 1, 1733. 59 pds. for *. On NS Roquiss(?) adj. BRANTLY(?).
Part of patent for 200 A. Wit: JOHN EDWARDS, jurat, JOHN _____. August
Court 1733. JOHN WYNNS D C/C. (This deed badly defaced.)

D 2 JOHN HERRING TO THOMAS WHITMELL
        May 14, 1733. 100 pds. for 150 A. On WS Cashy River adj. GARDNER,
JOHN GRAY, JOHNSON. Wit: JOHN GRAY, jurat, ALEX.R. THOMPSON. August Court
1733. JOHN WYNNS D.C/C.

D 4 LORDS PROPRIETORS TO JOHN PACE
        April 1, 1713. Grant. 640 A. On ES Maratock River below Occanee-
chey. Adj. MATTHEW STURDIVENT. Signed: "Hon. THOMAS POLLOCK, Esq. President of the Councell & Commander in Chief and the rest of the Trusty & well
beloved Councellors." THOMAS POLLOCK, THOMAS BOYDE, T. KNIGHT, C. GALE,
T. KNIGHT, Sec'ty. April 9, 1713.

D 4 JOHN PACE TO WILLIAM PACE
        Sep. 14, 1732. *.*. "...out of respect to my brother...and in obe-
dience to my Fathers Last Will and Testament in which he did bequeath the
within lands to my Brother but the writer through Ignorance did omit the
words to him and his heirs...I therefore make over...to him and his heirs
...the within mentioned lands...." Wit: JOHN GRAY, jurat, _____WATFORD.
August Court 1733. JOHN WYNNS D.C/C.

D 5 JOHN TAYLOE (TAYLOR) TO JOHN TYNER
        April 21, 1733. 10 pds. for 100 A. In Maherring Woods adj. Kirby's

Creek, THOMAS MANDEW. Patent dated April 1, 1723. Wit: JOHN TYNER, NICH-
OLAS TYNER, NATHANIEL COOPER. August Court 1733. JOHN WYNNS D.C/C.

D 6   JOSIAS CLAPHAM TO CHRISTOPHER GEWIN, JUN.
       April 7, 1733. 31 pds. for 150 A. On Runaroy Marsh and NS Morratock
River and Flaggy Run. Adj. HENRY ROADS. Wit: JOHN HARRELL, JOHN HARRELL,
JUN, ISAAC HARRELL. August Court 1733. JOHN WYNNS D.C/C.

D 7   JOSIAS CLAPHAM TO CHRITOPHER GEWIN, JUN.
       Aug. 11, 1733. 5 pds. for 20 A. On NE corner adj. ROBERT WEST.
Wit: GEORGE HOUSE, JOHN HARRELL, JUN., jurat. August Court 1733. JOHN
WYNNS D.C/C.

D 8   GEORGE NICHOLSON TO ANTHONY WEBB
       March 6, 1732. 31 pds. for 550 A. At "billey bank" adj. Pitt
Bladdar, GEORGE SMITH, JOHN WILLIAMS. Wit: HENRY WHITHURST, SAMUEL WEBB,
jurat, WILLIS NICHOLAS, JACOB TAYLOR. August Court 1733. JOHN WYNNS D.C/C

D 9   GEORGE NICHOLSON TO ANTHONY WEBB of Virginia
       March 6, 1732. 50 pds. 295 A. Part of two tracts on Wiccacon Creek.
Adj. WILLIAM WILLIFORD, STEPHEN WILLIAMS, CHRISTOPHER HOLLYMAN. Wit: HENRY
WHITHURST, SAMUEL WEBB, jurat, WILLIS NICHOLAS, JACOB TAYLOR. August Court
1733. JOHN WYNNS D.C/C.

D 10   HENRY VIZE TO ROBERT FORSTER
       Aug. 14, 1733. 20 pds. for 300 A. On Horse Swamp adj. LAZARUS THOMAS,
_____EVANS. Wit: JOHN WYNNS, BENJAMIN WYNNS. August Court 1733. *.*.

D 12   ROBERT FORSTER TO JOHN HODGSON
       Aug. 7, 1733. 25 pds. for "within mentioned land." Wit: JOHN WYNNS,
THOMAS JONES. August Court 1733. JOHN WYNNS D.C/C.

D 12   JOHN LOVICK, Executor for THOMAS BETTERLY, TO MILES GALE of Edenton
       Sep. 14, 1733. 386 pds. for 1826 A. "...THOMAS BETTERLY late of
Edenton Dec'd Dyed Seized of Severall Tracts of land...one tract lying in
Bertie Precinct on the north side of Morratock River...containing one thou-
sand four hundred and Twenty acres (adj. HENRY SPELLER)...and one tract
containing four hundred acres...on North side of Morratock River ...on
Chickery Pocoson...." Adj. EDWARD SMITHWICK, COGSWELL & DOMINY, MARTIN
GRIFFIN, JOHN HARLOE. "...Said BETTERLY by Last will & Testament dated
June 4, 1729 did appoint JOHN LOVICK his executor...." MILES GALE was
highest bidder. Bought 1420 A. for 365 pds. and 400 A. for 21 pds. (current Bills of the Province). Wit: WILLIAM LITTLE, PENELOPE LITTLE.
Sep. 14, 1733. WILLIAM LITTLE, Chief Justice. JOHN WYNNS, recorder.

D 13   CHARLES JONES, SEN. TO CHARLES JONES
       Aug. 23, 1733. 260 A. for "natural love and Effection unto my son
..." To him and to his heirs forever "...and wanting heirs to my son LANCE-
LOT JONES and his heirs...." On NS Ahotskey Swamp at Stony Creek Road adj.
CHRISTOPHER HOLLIMAN (HOLLYMAN). Wit: THOMAS BIRD, SEN., jurat, LANCELOT
JONES. November Court 1733. JOHN WYNNS D.C/C.

D 14   JONATHAN STANDLEY of Chowan Precinct TO JOHN COLLINS of Chowan Pre-
       cinct Oct. 27, 1733. 200 pds. for 300 A. On NES Cashy River.
One tract purchased from RICHARD BOON(?) Jan. 17, 1716. One tract for 100
A. purchased of JOHN SHORTT and Elizabeth ROSE by deed dated Feb. 3, 1720.
Both tracts formerly taken up and patented by JOHN HAWKINS. On NS Cashy
at Jack's Creek(?). Wit: JOHN WYNNS, THOMAS CREW. November Court 1733. *.

D 16   EDWARD MOOR TO JONATHAN STANDLEY
       Nov. 13, 1733. 30 pds. for 250 A. On SS Ahotsky Swamp adj. JOHN
DAVIDSON whereon STEPHEN HOWARD did live at Turkey Swamp adj. JOHN MOLTON
and JOHN BARFIELD. Wit: THOMAS CREW, JOHN COLLINS. November Court 1733.*.

D 17   MATTHEW TOBIAS SWANNER TO WILLIAM BUSH, carpenter
       Nov. 20, 1732. 220 pds. for 200 A. Land formerly granted to LEWIS
WILLIAMS by patent dated April 1, 1713. On NS Wiccacon Creek at Holly
Swamp. Adj. NICHOLLAS TOOP(?), CHRISTOPHER SEGOR. Wit: JOHN WYNNS, jurat,
WILLIAM MACKHENRY, MARY WYNNS. November Court 1733. JOHN WYNNS D.C/C.

D 19   JOHN SWENNY TO CAPT. JOHN VANPELT

Sep. 17, 1733. IOO A. "for some money discounted by Capt. JOHN VAN-PELT." On ES Deep Branch. Wit: JOHN WYNNS, jurat, NICHOLAS SESSOMS. November Court 1733. JOHN WYNNS D.C/C.

D 19   JONATHAN TAYLOR & WIFE CATHERINE TO GEORGE POLLOCK, merchant
May 14, 1733. 10 pds. for 640 A. On SS Morratock River "half a mile below Quitsnah." Wit: JOHN WHITE, JAMES BLACK, jurat. November Court 1733.

D 20   WILLIAM LITTLE TO THOMAS BANKS, "taylor"
Oct. 25, 1733. 6 pds. for 640 A. On SWS Chowan River "at a certain place called Little Town"..."and the other Lying in Chinckapin Neck called Plum Tree Neck" cont. 200 A. Bought by WILLIAM LITTLE from JENNETT BANKS "and also all the remaining part of good & chattles before in Deed made over by the said JENNETT BANKS...." Wit: THOMAS JONES, jurat, JOHN BEVARLY. November Court 1733. JOHN WYNNS D.C/C.

D 21   JAMES RUTLAND TO GEORGE STEVENSON (STEPHENSON)
May 8, 1733. 100 pds. for 130 A. At SAndy Run. Part of land formerly granted to ROBERT SHERWOOD for 640 A. dated April 5, 1720. Wit: JOHN HART, ELIZABETH BRADDY(?). November Court 1733. JOHN WYNNS D.C/C.

D 22   JAMES SUMNER of Chowan Precinct & JOHN DREW TO JOHN ELLYSON (ELISON) of Chowan. Sep. 1, 1733. 15 pds. for 200 A. "in a Valley nigh the head of Great Branch" on the land whereon DAVID JARNAGAN now lives called Indian Town Land on Chowan River. Adj. RICHARD HOLLAND. Now in possession of JAMES MANNEY. Wit: SARAH LEE, SARAH DREWRY, FRUZAN(?) LEWIS (her mark). November Court 1733. JOHN WYNNS D.C/C.

D 23   CORNELIUS PIERCE & WIFE MARY TO THOMAS BROWNE
Sep. 10, 1733. 35 pds. for 440 A. On NS Roanoke River (Roanoak). Part of a tract granted to BENJAMIN FOREMAN, SEN. on March 1, 1719. The whole tract being 540 A. This was given by BENJAMIN FOREMAN to CORNELIUS PIERCE on Nov. 10, 1724. Wit: EDWARD BROWNE, RICHARD WILLIAMS, JAMES BROWNE, jurat. November Court 1733. JOHN WYNNS D.C/C.

D 24   WILLIAM WILLIAMS & WIFE DEBORAH TO MATHEW KINCHIN of Isle of Wight Co., Va. Feb. 11, 1734/35. 300 A. for "a valuable sum in hand" On SS Maherring River. Adj. FRANCIS BOYKINS, JAMES TURNER. Part of patent granted to JAMES TURNER by the Hon. CHARLES EDEN by date March 1, 1719. Wit: SAMUEL TAYLOR, jurat, W. KINCHIN, WILLIAM ARRINGTON. February Court 1733. JOHN WYNNS D.C/C.

D 29   SUSANNA CLERK (CLARK) TO JAMES JOYNOR
Feb. 13, 1723/33. 50 A. for "a valuable consideration." At "the Elbow tree of the old County Line" adj. THOMAS BOYKINS on Meherring River. Wit: JOHN JOYNOR, SOLOMON JOYNER, jurat, JOHN LOTH(?), ELIAS BRADDY. February 1733.

D 25   JOSEPH WALL & WIFE MARY TO SAMUEL TAYLOR of Surry Co., Va.
Feb. 11, 1734/35. 100 A. for "a valuable sum." Part of 640 A. granted to JAMES TURNER by CHARLES EDEN on March 1, 1719. "...and made over in open court August 1727 by said JAMES TURNER to JOSEPH WALL...." On SS Maherring River. At present in actual possession of SAMUELL TAYLOR. Adj. JAMES HOWELL, SEN., SAMUEL TAYLOR, EDWARD HOOD, THOMAS HOWELL. At Reedy Branch. Wit: JOHN SIMPSON, MA(?) KINCHEN, SAMUEL HOLLYMAN. February Court 1733. JOHN WYNNS D.C/C.

D 27   CHRISTOPHER GEWIN, JUN. TO ROBERT HODGES
Aug. 30, 1733. 20 pence for 20 A. Adj. ROBERT WEST. Wit: JOHN HARRELL, jurat, JOSEPH HARRELL. February Court 1733. JOHN WYNNS D.C/C.

D 28   CHRISTOPHER GEWIN, JUN. (GUIN) TO ROBERT HODGES
Aug. 30, 1733/34. 32 pds. for 150 A. On NS Morratock River at "Remaroy Marsh(?)" at Flaggy Run. Adj. HENRY ROADES. Wit: JOHN HARRELL, jurat, JOSEPH HARRELL. February Court 1733. JOHN WYNNS D.C/C.

D 30   JOHN WORSLAND & WIFE MARGRETT of Roanoak TO JAMES BARNES (BARNS)
Nov. 4, 1733. 20 pds. for 100 A. In "Roanoke Precinct." Adj. RICHARD BRASSWELL, CHARLES STEVENSON, SAMUEL CANADY. Wit: ELIZABETH CANADY, ARCH(?) THOMPSON, ROBERT RUFFIN, jurat. February Court 1733. *.

D 32   JOHN BRYANT (BRYAN) TO JOHN GLOVER
        Feb. 11, 1733/34. 50 pds. for 100 A. On Chowan River at Cotton
Bottom below the Ferry Point. Part of 640 A. granted to RICHARD BOOTH by
patent and given by his Will to his daughter ELIZABETH DUNN and to me (JOHN
BRYAN) by Deed from ELIZABETH DUNN. Wit: WILLIAM GLOVER, LEWIS BRYAN.
February Court 1733. JOHN WYNNS D.C/C.

D 33   LORDS PROPRIETORS TO CAPT. DAVID HENDERSON
        April 1, 1720. Grant. 640 A. On WS Chowan River adj. MAJOR WEST.
For importation of persons. 50 A/person. Signed: CHARLES EDEN, Esq. Re-
corded in Sec't'y. Office. J. LOVICK, Sec't'y. FRED. JONES, RICH. SANDER-
SON, C. EDEN, THOS. POLLOCK, WM. REED.

D 33   DAVID HENDERSON TO SAMUEL ONWIN
        May 9, 1725. *.*. "all my right Title and Interest of within men-
tioned patent." Wit: THOMAS BRADWELL, JOHN GOLSON. *. ROBERT FORSTER C/C.

D 33   SAMUEL ONWIN TO DAVID ATKINS
        Feb. 12, 1733/34. *.*. "all my right Title to within mentioned
lands." Wit: THOMAS JACKSON, NICHOLAS FAIRLESS. February Court 1733/34.*.

D 33   THOMAS HANSFORD & WIFE BRIDGET TO EDWARD HARE of Chowan Precinct
        Feb. 12, 1733. 30 pds. for 300 A. At Miery Branch. On NS Deep
Creek. Adj. LAZARUS THOMAS and the Main County Road at Holly Branch. Wit:
JOHN BROWN, JOHN THOMAS. February Court 1733. JOHN WYNNS D.C/C.

D 35   THOMAS HOBBEY (HOBBY) of Edgecombe Precinct TO JOHN JENKINS of Edge-
        combe Precinct. Feb. 12, 1733/34. 20 pds. for *. On Yurahaw
Swamp adj. JOHN BLACKMAN, WILLIAM BRASSWELL. Wit: CHARLES HORNE, JOSEPH
SUMNER. February Court 1733/34. JOHN WYNNS D.C/C.

D 36   ROBERT EVANS (EVINS) TO GEORGE DOWNING
        Feb. 10, 1733/34. 50 pds. for 150 A. On SS Cuttawitskey Swamp. Adj.
COLL. MAULE, JAMES WOOD. Wit: NICHOLAS FAIRLESS, JOHN DAWSON. February
Court 1733. JOHN WYNNS D.C/C.

D 37   CHRISTOPHER LAINE (LANE) & WIFE CHRISTAINNA TO ROBERT EVANS (EVINS)
        Jan. 21, 1733/34. "love and Effection...all and singular Our Goods
Chattles personal Estate whatsoever Utensils Household stuff Implements and
all things whatsoever of what nature kind and Property...." Wit: PETER
EVANS, NICHOLAS FAIRLESS, jurat. February Court 1733. JOHN WYNNS D.C/C.

D 38   ANDREW IRELAND TO JOHN HODGSON
        June 1, 1733. 12 pds. for 160 A. On NS Marratock River on Long
Meadow. Part of tract formerly granted to RICHARD MELTON for 640 A. by
patent dated April 1, 1723. Wit: BENJAMIN HILL, jurat, JOHN PATTERSON.
February Court 1733. JOHN WYNNS D.C/C.

D 39   THOMAS BROWN (BROWNE) TO JOSEPH DARDEN (DURDEN)
        Nov. 29, 1716. 50 pds. for 210 A. Part of 540 A. patent. On NS
Maherring River on the "Islands of the River" at Spring Branch. Wit: JOHN
BROWN, _____WILLIAMS, THOMAS JARNAGAN (TARNAGAN). February Court 1733. *.

D 40   WILLIAM WHITEHEAD of Edgecombe Precinct TO JOHN DANIELL (DANIEL) "of
        Government aforesaid". January 2, 1733. 30 pds. for 300 A. On SS
Pottycasey Creek. Part of tract granted WILLIAM WHITEHEAD by patent dated
March 30, 1721. Adj. THOMAS BROWN, FRANCIS PARKER. Wit: FR. PARKER, jurat,
JOHN DICKINSON, PETER DANIELL. February Court 1733. JOHN WYNNS D.C/C.

D 41   JAMES BARNES (BARNS) & WIFE MARTHA TO JONATHAN TARTT
        Feb. 11, 1733/34. 35 pds. for 200 A. On NS Marratock "within the
Ursaray Meadow" in Gum Swamp. adj. GEORGE STEVENS, WILLIAM WILLIAMS, RICH-
ARD BRASSWELL at Hogpen Meadow. Adj. JOHN COTTON (COTTEN), WILLIAM RUFFIN,
JOSEPH WIMBERLEY, GEORGE STEVENS(?). Wit: WILLIAM MOOR, ALEX'R. CAMPBELL,
JAMES MOORE. February Court 1733. JOHN WYNNS D.C/C.

D 43   TIMOTHY RYALL TO NEEDHAM BRYAN (BRYANT)
        Feb. 11, 1733/34. 15 pds. for 200 A. On NS Flaggy Run. Adj. JOHN
HARRELL, JOSEPH MOOR. Wit: JOHN HARRELL, jurat, JOHN HARRELL, JUN., JOHN
BOREFIELD. February Court 1733. JOHN WYNNS D.C/C.

D 44 JOHN WILLSON (WELLSON) & WIFE PRISCILLA TO CAPT. JOHN VANPELT, SEN.
Jan. 17, 1733/34. 200 pds. for 640 A. On WS Chinkapin Creek at
"upper most side of" Miery Branch. Wit: JOHN WYNNS, jurat, FRANCIS BROWNE.
February Court 1733. JOHN WYNNS D.C/C.

D 45 THOMAS JOHNSON TO THOMAS BANKS, "taylor"
Jan. 19, 1733. 20 pds. for 150 A. On WS Chowan River. Adj. THOMAS
BYRD, ABRAHAM BLEWLETT. Now in possession of THOMAS BANKS. At Deep Branch.
Wit: JOHN WYNNS, jurat, WILLIAM WILLIAMSON. February Court 1733. *.

D 46 CHARLES JONES, SEN. TO LANCELOT JONES
Aug. 23, 1733. 200 A. "for natural love and Effection for my son
LANCELOT...for want of (his) heirs...to my son CHARLES JONES and his heirs
...." Adj. JOHN RASBERRY, _____ BUSH. Wit: THOMAS BIRD (BYRD), jurat,
CHARLES JONES, JUN. February Court 1733. JOHN WYNNS D.C/C.

D 47 JOHN GEANY TO THOMAS GEANY
Jan. 19, 1733. 60 pds. for 300 A. On Geany Swamp adj. COLL. BRANCH?
Wit: JOHN DUFFIELD, STEPHEN GEANY. February Court 1733. JOHN WYNNS D.C/C.

D 48 CHARLES JONES TO WILLIAM RUTTER
Nov. 5, 1733. 10 pds. for 100 A. Adj. ARON OLIVER, JOHN RASBERRY.
Wit: CHARLES JONES, JAMES OVERTON. February Court 1733. JOHN WYNNS D.C/C.

D 48 LEWIS BRYAN TO NICHOLAS THOMPSON of Surry Co., Va.
Jan. 8, 1733/34. 100 pds. for 130 A. On NS Sandy Run. Adj. WILLIAM
GRAY, OWEN MACKDANIEL, RICHARD MELTON. Wit: JOHN GRAY, jurat, TO'S(?)
HARDIE. February Court 1733. JOHN WYNNS D.C/C.

D 50 CHRISTOPHER GEWIN (GUIN) TO ABRAHAM HARRELL
Aug. 3, 1733. 32 pds. for 150 A. On NS Marratock River. Adj. JAMES
PARKER, OWEN O DANIELL, WILLIAM EASON. Wit: JOHN HARRELL, jurat, JOHN
HARRELL, JUN. February Court 1733. JOHN WYNNS D.C/C.

D 51 RICHARD HORN (HORNE) of Edgecombe Precinct TO JOHN TAYLOR
March 4, 1734. 40 pds. for 300 A. In Pottycasey Woods adj. THOMAS
HORN. "part of Patent of land dated 1668." Wit: ROBERT LASSITER (LASIS-
TER), JOHN BOHOON, CHARLES CAVENAH. May 6, 1734. JOHN WYNNS D.C/C.

D 52 WILLIAM WARR (WAR) TO SOLOMON FULLER
May 13, 1734. 1600 lbs. of pork. for 100 A. Part of tract patented
by JOSEPH LANE, JUN. Wit: JOHN THOMAS, EZEKIEL FULLER. May Court 1734. *.

D 53 SAMUEL CANADAY of Edgecombe Precinct TO CHARLES STEVENSON
Sep. 5, 1733. 80 pds. for 100 A. On NS Marratock River adj. ARTHUR
WHITEHEAD, RICHARD BRASSWELL. Part of tract formerly granted WILLIAM WHITE-
HEAD for 195 A. dated April 1, 1723. Wit: JOHN HART, BENJAMIN STEVENSON,
MARY FRAIZAR. May Court 1734. JOHN WYNNS D.C/C.

D 54 WILLIAM WILLSON (WILSON) TO THOMAS WILLIAMS
*. 100 pds. for 609 A. On NS Casshy Swamp. Wit: ABRAHAM SHEPHERD,
JOHN SWENNY. May Court 1734. JOHN WYNNS D.C/C.

D 55 CHARLES BARBOR (BARBER) TO THOMAS RYAN
April 27, 1734. 15 pds. for 640 A. On Cuckallmaker's Creek adj.
ISAAC HILL. Wit: JOHN PENNY, CHARLES BARBER. May Court 1734. JOHN WYNNS *.

D 56 SAMUELL HERRING TO JOHN CLEMET (CLEMENT)
May 14, 1734. 42 pds. for 640 A. On ES Cashy River in "Bucklesberry
Parcoson" adj. LAURANCE LARSON. Wit: THOMAS WHITMELL, JUN., OWEN O'DANIELL.
May Court 1734. JOHN WYNNS D.C/C.

D 57 ISAAC WILLIAMS of Chowan TO CHARLES GAVIN
Aug. 29, 1733. 40 "barrills of good merchantable pitch" for 200 A.
Adj. ARON OLIVER. Wit: JOHN PAGETT, SAMUELL MERRITT, WILLIAM RODGERS. May
Court 1734. JOHN WYNNS D.C/C.

D 59 THOMAS RYAN TO JOHN PENNY
April 27, 1734. 15 pds. for 200 A. Part of pattent that CHARLES
BARBOR "taken up on Cuckall Makers Creek." Adj. THOMAS RYAN, RICHARD

WILLIAMS, JOHN WALLIS. Wit: CHARLES BARBOR, THOMAS RYAN. May Court 1734.*.

D 60   JAMES ROBERTS & WIFE CORDELIA TO MARTIN GUARDINER (GARDNER)
       May 11, 1734. 30 pds. for 88 A. On NS Roquess Swamp. Wit: ABRAHAM
SHEPHERD, WILLIAM GARDNER, OWEN O'DANIELL. May Court 1734. *.

D 61   WILLIAM WILLSON of Cashia TO DUKE ROBINSON
       April 13, 1734. "some mony" for 50 A. On SS Cashy Swamp. Wit: JOHN
SWENNY, jurat, JOHN GRANT. May Court 1734. JOHN WYNNS D.C/C.

D 62   OWEN O'DANIEL TO ABRAHAM SHEPHARD (SHEPHERD)
       May 14, 1734. 50 pds. for 400 A. At Great Branch adj. JOHN EDWARDS
at "Miery Branch that runs out of Cashy Swamp." Wit: JAMES ROBERTS, WILLIAM
GARDNER. May Court 1734. JOHN WYNNS D.C/C.

D 63   JOHN GRAY & WIFE ANN TO JOHN HOW
       May 14, 1734. 20 pds. for 300 A. On ES Cashy River at Licking
Branch and Turkey Swamp. Plantation known by the name Turkey Neck. Adj.
THOMAS JONES. Wit: THOMAS KEARNY, JAMES CONNER, jurat. May Court 1734. *.

D 64   WILLIAM GLOVER TO WILLIAM NORWOOD
       Aug. 8, 1733. 50 pds. for 100 A. At the fork of Beaverdam adj.
GLOVER. Wit: MARTIN LYONS, jurat, JOHN DOYLE, NATHANIEL NORWOOD. May
Court 1734. JOHN WYNNS D. C./C.   D 65 Memorandum: "Full and peaceable pos-
session and seizin was this day given and delivered...." November 28, 1733.
Wit: MARTIN LYONS, JOHN DOYLE, NATHANIEL NORWOOD.

D 66   FINCHER (FINCHOR) HAYNE TO ROBERT FORSTER
       Nov. 14, 1730. 400 pds. for 800 A. On Chowan River at Petty Shore.
Adj. SAMUEL WILLIAMS. Plus all cattle, horses, hoggs and one Negroe slave
named Captain. Wit: THOMAS BRYANT, J. PRATT, WILLIAM LITTLE. *. C. GALE,CJ

D 66   ROBERT FORSTER TO FINCHER HAYNE
       May 13, 1734. 400 pds. for "within mentioned lands." Wit: T.
BARKER, THOMAS JONES. May Court 1734. JOHN WYNNS D.C/C.

D 67   RICHARD PACE, JUN. TO JAMES CAIN
       May 13, 1734. 20 pds. for 100 A. On Yawrahaw Swamp. Part of tract
granted BARTHOLEMEW CHAVERS for 300 A. by patent dated March 1, 1713. Wit:
DAVIE HOPPER, SAMUELL COTTEN. May Court 1734. JOHN WYNNS D.C/C.

D 67   JOHN NAIRN TO JAMES BLOUNT (BLUNT)
       May 6, 1734. 75 pds. for 320 A. On SS Marratock River adj. NICHOLAS
CRISP on Rainbow Banks at Connehoe Creek adj. JOHN SPEIR. Wit: WILL. NAIRN,
JOHN ANDERSON, JUN. May Court 1734. JOHN WYNNS D.C/C.

D 69   JAMES BLUNT & WIFE CATHARINE (KATHERINE) TO THOMAS WATSON
       Aug. 28, 1733. 12 pds. for 200 A. to "our well beloved friend."
Adj. Cashy Swamp. Wit: PETER HEASE(?), JOHN WATSON. May Court 1734. *.

D 70   THOMAS SUTTON & WIFE JUDITH TO JOHN LEURTON
May 8, 1734. 72 pds. for 640 A. Land formerly belonged to JOHN PLOWMAN; by
him sold to JAMES TILTON, and by TILTON exchanged for a tract where JOHN
COOK now dwells. On Cypress Meadow adj. DUCKINGFIELD. Wit: RICHARD SPARK-
MAN, PETER BARBERIE. May Court 1734. JOHN WYNNS D.C/C.

D 71   WILLIAM JONES & WIFE MARY of Chowan Precinct TO JAMES CASTELLAW
       April 12, 1721. 23 pds. for 150 A. On SS Cashy River adj. COLL.
POLLOCK, RICHARD FRYER, MARTIN GARDINER. Wit: J. PLOWMAN, MARY WHITE.
Chowan Court April 1721. "JOHN EDWARDS by power of atty. from said CASTEL-
LAW..." ack. sale. THOMAS HENMAN C/C. D 73 "At a Court held for Chowan
Precinct at the Court House in Queen Ann Town the third Tuesday in Aprill
1721 WILLIAM JONES and MARY his wife came into court and ack. the within
deed...." "We the subscribers do assign all our Right Title and Interest
of the within mentioned Deed of Sale unto HENRY GUSTON and JAMES MILLIKIN
..." Aug. 16, 1726. Signed: JAMES CASTELLAW, SARAH CASTELLAW. Wit:
THOMAS SMITH, JAMES BLACK. Oct. 28, 1726. N.C. Court. C. GALE, C.J. ROB-
ERT FORSTER, C/C.
       (CASTELLAW TO GUSTAN & MILLIKIN contained in above transaction.)

D 73   HENRY GUSTON & JAMES MILLIKIN TO JOSHUA WILKINSON

Feb. 10, 1733/34. *.*. "We..,do sign over all our Right Title and Interest of the within mentioned Deed of Sale to JOSHUA WILKINSON...." Wit: JOHN CONNER, JOHN GRAY. May Court 1734. JOHN WYNNS D.C/C.

D 73   THOMAS SUTTON & WIFE JUDITH TO ISAAC GRAGORY, marriner
May 9, 1734. 200 A. for "Love good Will & Effection." Part of a tract "which I elapsed from ELIZABETH JONES...(262 A. dated April 4, 1722) whereof I exchanged with JAMES TILTON and is now in possession of JOHN COOK the said TILTON's wifes Husband and this same two hundred acres I assigned Over to Mary Jones the 7th of Sept'r. 1723 which MARY JONES is now marryed to the said ISAAC GREGORY...said assignment not being so full as...ISAAC GREGORY desires it...." Wit: SUSANAH HENDRICKS, HANNAH HENDRECKS. May Court 1734. JOHN WYNNS D.C/C.

D 75   JAMES KETO (KITO) & WIFE MARTHA TO ISAAC GREGORY
May 11, 1734. (This is an exchange of properties: JAMES KETO makes over to ISAAC GREGORY one tract of 150 A. in exchange for two tracts total- ing 150 A. made over to him by GREGORY.) "...a tract of land made over to me by ISAAC GREGORY in exchange for the same land which is known by the name of Rocky Branch...which was patented in ELIZABETH JONES name Aprill 1, 1714...and elapsed by THOMAS SUTTON April 4, 1722...and by SUTTON made over to MARY JONES Sep. 7, 1723 and by deed of gift to ISAAC GREGORY Hus- band of said MARY 9th May 1734. ...I do acknowledge myself fully satisfied ...and make over to ISAAC GREGORY two tracts joyning together...." GREGORY tract on SS Black Walnut Swamp by name of Rocky Branch cont. 150 A. KETO tracts: On Cashoke Creek in all cont. 150 A. (1) 50 A. made over by Deed of Sale dated 1715 to "MARTHA CLARK my Mother" (2) the other 100 A. "...by JOHN HAWKINS...to my brother by deed of sale to WILLIAM KETO dated April 16, 1715...and by their deaths now become mine...." Wit: THOMAS HAWKINS, jurat, JOHN LEURTON. May Court 1734. JOHN WYNNS D.C/C.

D 76   MARY GREGORY TO THOMAS SUTTON
May 9, 1734. *.*. Power of atty. to ack. sale of 150 A. to JAMES KETER (KETO) also 50 A. to WILLIAM HARDY, JUN. Land on SS Black Walnut Swamp. Wit: ROGER SNELL, RICHARD SPARKMAN, jurat. May Court 1734. *.

D 76   ISAAC GREGORY (GRIGORY), marriner, TO JAMES KETTO (KETER, KETO,
KETTS, KETOE, KETTOE) May 11, 1734. (An exchange: KETO gives tract at mouth of Cashoke cont. 150 A. for 150 A. given by Gregory on Black Walnut Swamp.) 150 A. at mouth of Cashoke below JAMES LOCKHART made over to me by JAMES KETTS (KETER) being the remaining 150 A. and middle part of 262 A. patented by ELIZABETH JONES Aprill 1, 1714 and known by name "Rocky Branch." Bounded by WILLIAM HARDY, JUN., JOHN COOK. Wit: JOHN LUERTON, THOMAS HAWKINS. May Court 1734. JOHN WYNNS D.C/C.

D 78   ISAAC GREGORY (GRIGORY), marriner, & WIFE MARY TO WILLIAM HARDY, JUN.
April 6, 1734. 32 pds. for 50 A. Land that did belong to MARY JONES the said ISAAC GREGORY's wife called Rocky Branch. Adj. Capt. DAVID HENDER- SON at Black Walnut Swamp at mouth of Rocky Branch. Wit: JOHN LUERTON, JAMES KETTER. May Court 1734. JOHN WYNNS D.C/C.

D 79   NICHOLLAS TOOPE (TOOP) TO CHRISTOPHER SEGRO (SEGAR)
Sep. 14, 1733. 50 pds. for 100 A. At Holly Swamp. Wit: THOMAS HANS- FORD, J. HODGSON. May Court 1734. JOHN WYNNS D.C/C.

D 81   CHARLES SOWELL TO JAMES THICKPEN
Feb. 24, 1732/33. 60 pds. for 100 A. "at mouth of a Swamp commonly known by the name Horse Swamp." Adj. RICHARD SOWELL, CHARLES GAVIN. Wit: JOHN AVERRITT, JANE SMITH. May Court 1734. JOHN WYNNS D.C/C.

D 82   JOSEPH PARKER of Chowan Precinct TO JAMES MAGLOHON
May 15, 1734. 40 pds. for 200 A. On Wiccacon Swamp and Wiccacon Creek. Wit: JOHN WHITE, (JUN.?), NICHOLAS FAIRLESS. May Court 1734. *.

D 84   JOHN HOMES, JUN. of Edgecombe Precinct TO JAMES WOOD
May 14, 1734. 100 pds. for 300 A. On WS Conaritsa Swamp. By patent dated Dec. 22, 1724. Wit: JOHN HOMES, JAMES HOLLAND. May Court 1734. *.

D 85   JAMES WOOD TO JAMES HOMES
May 14, 1734. 30 pds. for 140 A. On NS Morattock River called

"Peach Blossom." By patent granted to JOHN STEWARD on March 1, 1721. Adj.
EDWARD HOWARD. Wit: JOHN HOMES, JAMES HOLLAND. May Court 1734. *.

D 86   RICHARD FRYER of Craven Precinct TO SAMUELL HERRING
        May 15, 1734. 160 pds. for 160 A. ON NS Ruquiss Pocoson "at the
Neck where the Great Branch falls into the Pocoson" Part of a tract cont.
260 A. Wit: JOHN HODGSON, THOMAS SUTTON. May Court 1734. JOHN WYNNS DCC

D 87   WILLIAM CURLEIGH (CURLEE) & WIFE MARTHA TO THOMAS HANSFORD
        Feb. 12, 1733. 280 pds. for *. On Ahotskey Ridge. Wit: R. FORSTER,
THOMAS CREW. February Court 1733. "MARTHA...privately examined by PETER
WEST one of the Justices of our said Court Declares that she acknowledges
the same freely...." May Court 1734.

D 89   JOHN GLOVER & WIFE MARY TO JEREMIAH MCGLOHON
        Feb. 10, 1733. 45 pds. for 100 A. At Lower side of an Island at
Loosing Swamp. Wit: JOHN BRYAN, LEWIS BRYAN. February Court 1733. *.
"MARY...privately examined by THOMAS KEARNEY Gent. one of the Justices of
our said Court...acknowledges freely...." May Court 1734.

D 90   WILLIAM VINSON TO BENJAMIN HILL
        March 21, 1733/34. 50 pds. for 100 A. Part of 300 A. granted to
THOMAS VINSON by patent dated March 9, 1717/18. Wit: JOHN EGERTON, THOMAS
VINSON(?). May Court 1734. JOHN WYNNS D.C/C.

D 91   JOSEPH HODGSON (HUDGSON), JUN. of Chowan TO DANIEL FRAZOR
        April 18, 1728. 35 pds. for 100 A. On Cashoke Creek adj. WILLIAM
BURK, CAPT. HENDERSON. Land held by JOHN CROMBIE sold to JACOB HARDY and
by JACOB HARDY ack. to JAMES CASTELLAW and by CASTELLAW assigned to JOSEPH
HUDGSON, JUN. on Oct. 16, 1722. Wit: GEORGE ALLEN, RICHARD SWINSON. N.C.
Court. April 18, 1728. C. GALE, C.J., EDW. MASHBORNE D.C/C.

D 92   DANIEL FRAZOR TO COLL. ROBERT WEST
        May 6, 1734. "...all my Right Title and interest to within mention-
ed lands...in consideration for which WEST has given me in exchange (200 A)
...being part of tract where DANIEL FRAZOR now lives...." Wit: NICHOLAS
FAIRLESS, THOMAS SUTTON, THOMAS ASHLEY, RICHARD SPARKMAN. May Court 1734.*.

D 93   COLL. ROBERT WEST TO DANIELL FRAZOR
        May 6, 1734. (exchange: 100 A. for 200 A.) Land at mouth of Wild
Catt Gutt on Loosing Swamp. Wit: NICHOLAS FAIRLESS, THOMAS ASHLEY, RICHARD
SPERKMAN, THOMAS SUTTON. May Court 1734. JOHN WYNNS D.C/C.

D 94   WILLIAM BROWNE (BROWN) of Edgecombe Precinct TO JAMES WOOD
        April 13, 1734. 25 pds. for *. On SS Morratock River near Beaver-
dam. Adj. DANIEL MCDANIEL. Being land formerly bought of DANIEL MCDANIEL
by Deed dated March 29, 1729. Wit: ROBERT BUTLER, JOHN BALLARD. May Court
1734. JOHN WYNNS D.C/C.

D 95   THOMAS VINSON TO BENJAMIN HILL
        March 21, 1733/34. 50 pds. for 200 A. On Maherring Creek. By
VINSON's patent for 300 A. dated March 9, 1717/18. 100 A. of patent sold
to WILLIAM VINSON. Wit: JOHN EGERTON, WILLIAM VINSON, jurat. May Court
1734. JOHN WYNNS D.C/C.

D 96   ROBERT WARREN TO PELEG ROGERS
        May 17, 1734. 50 pds. for 300 A. On Horse Swamp adj. JACOB LEWIS,
EDWARD HOWARD. Wit: WILLIAM COTTON, WILLIAM ARRINGTON. May Court 1734. *.

D 97   MATHIAS TOBIAS SWANNER (SWANNOR) TO RICHARD WILLIFORD
        May 15, 1734. *. 180 A. Adj. FRANCIS MCCLENDON "...as appears by
the pattent...." Wit: JOHN SWENNY, THOMAS BYRD (?). May Court 1734. *.

D 98   ROBERT LANIER TO RICHARD WILLIFORD
        Feb. 10, 1732/33. 52 pds. for 350 A. On the Beaverdam Swamp that
leads to Loosing Swamp Adj. THOMAS DANIELS. Wit: WILLIAM BUSH, JOHN
SWENNY, jurat. May Court 1734. JOHN WYNNS D.C/C.

D 98   WILLIAM BROWNE & WIFE CHARITY TO WILLIAM AVERITT (EVERITT)
        May 11, 1734. 20 pds. for 320 A. On SS Morratock River at Cabin

Branch and NS Connehoe Creek. Wit: ANTHONY WEBB, JOHN BROWN, JOHN ANDER-
SON. May Court 1734. JOHN WYNNS D.C/C.

D 99   JAMES JENKINS (JINKINS) & WIFE BRIGETT TO HENRY BONNER
        Nov. 9, 1733. 120 pds. for 440 A. On SS Ahotskey Swamp. Adj.
CHARLES JONES. Now in actual possession of BONNER. Wit: THOMAS BONNER,
SIMON HOMES, jurat. May Court 1734. JOHN WYNNS D.C/C.

D 100   JOHN GLOVER & WILLIAM NORWOOD: PARTITION
        Nov. 20, 1733. *. 340 A. "...having taken up a certain tract of land
...and having obtained a pattent for the same under the Hand of GEORGE BUR-
RINGTON, Esq....(dated) 7th day of November one thousand seven hundred and
twenty three...." Adj. WILLIAM GLOVER. All land on SS of dividing line to
belong to JOHN GLOVER: all land on NS dividing line to belong to WILLIAM
NORWOOD. Wit: MARTIN LYONS, jurat, JOHN DOYLE, NATHANIEL NORWOOD. May
Court 1734. JOHN WYNNS D.C/C.

D 102   JOHN LURETON (LUERTON) TO JAMES LOCKHART
        Sep. 4, 1733. 38 pds. 6 sh. for 100 A. On NS Cashoke Creek at mouth
of Reedy Branch. Adj. DANIEL SMITH, MASY(?) JONES, JOHN HAWKINS to "JOHN
LUERTONs Spring Branch." Wit: JOHN CLEMET, THOMAS BEDFORD. N.C. Court
Sep. 4, 1733. WM. LITTLE, C.J. JOHN WYNNS D.C/C.

D 103   WILLIAM DANIEL TO JONATHAN GILBERT, millwright
        Aug. 3, 1734. 745 pds. for 8 tracts of land. (1) On Deep Creek be-
tween "said creek and Wisktfor(?) Branch" adj. Coll. FREDERICK JONES "formerly JOHN BAY's" which land was granted to JAMES RUTLAND by pattent dated
April 1, 1714 and conveyed by RUTLAND to WILLIAM DANIEL. (2) Cont. 640 A.
adj. THOMAS JOHNSON, ROBERT LANIER, MARTHA WILLIAMS (formerly JOHN WILLIAMS)
Said land granted to WILLIAM DANIEL April 1, 1730. (3) 300 A. on Miery
Branch adj. JAMES RUTLAND. Sold to WILLIAM DANIEL by WILLIAM HARDIN JONES
by Deed dated 1728. (4) On SS Deep Creek cont. 100 A. adj. STEPHEN
WILLIAMS, ROBERT ROGERS at May Spring Branch. Land sold to DANIEL by LAZ-
ARUS THOMAS by Deed dated 1730. (5) On Deep Creek cont. 100 A. Part of
tract formerly belonging to Coll. FREDERICK JONES. Sold to DANIEL by WILL-
IAM LITTLE, Esq. by Deed dated Feb. 10, 1725. (6) On Deep Creek cont. 100
A. at Deep Creek Bridge. Sold to DANIEL by JAMES RUTLAND Feb. 9, 1724. (7)
130 A. at Deep Branch on NWS Deep Creek, sold to DANIEL by JAMES PEAK May
11, 1726. Adj. land formerly JOHN FIERYBENT's. (8) 640 A. at Holly Swamp
adj. JAMES' CURLEE at Flatt Swamp. Sold to DANIEL by ROBERT LANIER. Wit:
WILLIAM BADHAM, JOHN HODGSON, jurat. August Court 1734. ROBERT FORSTER C/C

D 107   JOHN BRYAN (BRYANT), merchant, TO JONATHAN MILLER
        June 3, 1734. 25 pds. for 560 A. On WS Cypress Swamp. adj. JOHN
DAVISON at Mulberry Branch and Miery Branch. Said land granted by patent
dated April 1, 1723. Wit: W. BADHAM, jurat, J. MICHENER. August Court
1734. JOHN WYNNS D. C/C.

D 108   THOMAS HARDY TO HENRY KING, planter, & THOMAS ASHBORN, "taylor"
        Feb. 27, 1733/34. 16 pds. for *. On SS Buckesberry "Parcoson."
Formerly belonging to JOHN COOK. At Reedy Branch adj. JOHN HOLLBROOK. Wit:
THOMAS BEDFORD, JOHN WEBB. August Court 1734. JOHN WYNNS D.C/C.

D 109   THOMAS LAMB TO ARTHUR WILLIAMS
        Aug. 6, 1734. 12 pds. for 100 A. On NS Kirby's Creek. Patent
granted to ROBERT SHERROD on March 1, 1719. "...mine by Deed from SHERROD
26th May (1730)...." Wit: WILLIAM HOULT, JOHN ROGERS, JOSHUA LAMB. August
Court 1734. JOHN WYNNS D.C/C.

D 110   JOHN ROGERS TO WILLIAM HOULT (HOLT)
        Aug. 6, 1734. 40 pds. for 118 A. On NS Maherring River adj. WILLIAM
BROWN. Part of patent for 540 A. granted THOMAS BROWN Nov. 29, 1716. By
BROWN and wife CHRISTIAN BROWN made over to ROGERS by Deed November 21,
1718. Wit: THOMAS LAMB, jurat, JOHN ROGERS, JOSHUA LAMB. August Court
1734. JOHN WYNNS D.C/C.

D 111   JOHN EDWARDS & WIFE ELIZABETH TO JOHN ROWLAND
        Aug. 12, 1734. 10 pds. for 200 A. Adj. ABRAHAM SHEPPERD, MARTIN
GARDNER, JOHN EDWARDS, ROBERT HINDS. Wit: WILLIAM GARDINER, RICHARD ROW-
LAND. August Court 1734. JOHN WYNNS D.C/C.

D 113　ISAAC BRAWLER TO CULLIMAR SESSUMS
　　　　Aug. 5, 1734.　60 pds. for 100 A. On WS Eastern Forke of GEORGE
WYNN's Mill Pond.　Wit: JOHN WYNNS, JOSEPH WYNNS, JOHN ASKEW.　August Court
1734.　JOHN WYNNS D.C/C.

D 114　JOHN PATTERSON TO THOMAS VINCENT
　　　　Aug. 7, 1734.　20 pds. for 400 A. On NS Urah Swamp. commonly known
as "Powdering Tubb" at Bear Swamp.　Said land "Elapsed from GABRIEL PARKER
by ROBERT PATTERSON by grant bearing date 30th day 1720 and now in actual
possession of THOMAS VINCENT...."　Wit: JOHN SUTTON, JOHN DICKINSON.　Aug.
Court 1734.　JOHN WYNNS D.C/C.

D 115　RICHARD WORRELL of Isle of Wight Co., Va. TO JOHN BARDEN
　　　　Sep. 29, 1730.　3 pds. 10 sh. for 40 A. On the River Islands at
Cabin Branch.　Wit: ABRAHAM DEW, SAMUEL WAID, jurat.　August Court 1734.
JOHN WYNNS D.C/C.

D 116　JAMES SWAIN TO WILLIAM CHARLTON, JUN.
　　　　April 28, 1729.　7 pds. for 320 A. On SS Smithwick Creek adj. JOHN
SWAIN.　Part of a tract surveyed by JAMES SWAIN.　Wit: WILLIAM CHARLTON,
JOHN DAVIS.　N.C. Court Sep. 13, 1729.　C. GALE, C.J. ROBERT FORSTER C/C.

D 117　WILLIAM CHARLTON TO MATHEW TOBIAS SWANNER
　　　　Aug. 8, 1734.　80 pds. for "within mentioned parcill."　Wit: ALEX-
ANDER CAMPBELL, jurat, JOHN WYNNS.　August Court 1734.　JOHN WYNNS D.C/C.

D 117　OWEN MACK DANIEL TO JOHN BUTLER
　　　　Dec. 15, 1733.　17 pds. 10 sh. for *.　Part of patent formerly
granted MARTIN CROMEN dated May 1, 1668 cont. 320 A. At Flatt Swamp and
Cabin Neck.　Wit: JOHN HARRELL, SARAH HARRELL, August Court 1734.　*.

D 118　JOHN CRICKETT TO JOHN RASBERRY, hatmaker
　　　　Aug. 14, 1734.　30 pds. for 220 A. On Cashy Swamp adj. CHARLES JONES.
"that tract which the said RASBERRY conveyed unto me...in August Court 1730
...."　Wit: JOHN WYNNS, PELEG ROGERS.　August Court 1734.　JOHN WYNNS D.C/C

D 119　GEORGE WYNNS TO JOHN RASBERRY, hatmaker
　　　　Aug. 14, 1734.　45 pds. for 450 A. In Cashy Swamp. adj. ROBERT
LANIER.　Patent "...being due for importation of persons one person for
every fifty acres as appears on Record...."　Wit: JOHN WYNNS, ROBERT FORS-
TER.　August Court 1734.　JOHN WYNNS D.C/C.

D 121　DANIEL O'QUIN TO PATRICK O'QUIN
　　　　Aug. 13, 1734.　60 pds. for 200 A. At Causway(?) Branch on "Cutta-
witskey old Swamp."　Adj. JAMES WOOD, DANIEL O'QUIN and Poplar Swamp.　Wit:
WILLIAM CURLEE, JAMES LASISTER, JOHN SUTTON.　August Court 1734.　*.

D 122　MARTIN CROMEN TO JAMES CASTELLAW
　　　　May 8, 1733.　20 pds. for 200 A. On Cashy River.　By patent granted
NATHAN MOOR and by him sold to CROMEN and recorded in Chowan Precinct.　Wit:
THOMAS KEARNEY, jurat, WILLIAM KENNEDAY, SOLLMON ALSTON.　August Court 1734.

D 123　HUGH HYMAN (HIGHMAN) of Cashy Neck TO WILLIAM ASHBORN
　　　　Nov. 7, 1733.　"one Negro girl" for 225 A. Out of 400 A. patent at
Berry Meadow on Herring Creek.　Wit: WILLIAM LATTIMER, MICHEL KING.　Aug.
Court 1734.　JOHN WYNNS D.C/C.

D 123　WILLIAM EASON & WIFE ANN TO GEORGE HOUSE
　　　　April 4, 1731.　"freely and Volluntarily give and grant" 40 A. of a
"certain piece of Marsh and Meadow ground" on Runaroy Marsh.　Which land
was sold by HENRY WEST and JAMES SMITH to GEORGE HOUSE "...and is found to
be WILLIAM EASON's Pattent bearing date 1723 and in GEORGE HOUSEs sale
bearing date 1730...."　Adj. GEORGE HARRELL, EDWARD HARRELL, JOHN YELVERTON,
JAMES PARKER.　Wit: JOHN HARRELL, JOHN HENNANT, JUN.　August Court 1734.　*.

D 124　JOHN GLOVER & WILLIAM NORWOOD TO WILLIAM GLOVER
　　　　Nov. 28, 1723.　50 pds. for 100 A. On Spring Branch adj. WILLIAM
GLOVER.　Wit: MARTIN LYONS, jurat, JOHN DOYLE, NATHANIEL NORWOOD.　August
Court 1734.　JOHN WYNNS D.C/C.

D 125　THOMAS AVANT (EVENT,AVENT) of Surry Co., Va. TO THOMAS AVANT, JUN.

Nov. 2, 1733. "love goodwill and Effection" for 100 A. "unto my loving son." On NS Morratock River. Part of patent of THOMAS EVENT, SEN. for 640 A. That part from WILLIAM EVANT divided "by a line of markt trees". Wit: JOHN SPANN(SPAIN), MARTIN LYONS, jurat. August Court 1734. *.

D 126 JOHN HODGSON TO WILLIAM RUFFIN
Aug. 15, 1734. 12 pds. for 160 A. On Long Meadow. Part of a tract granted RICHARD MELTON for 640 A. On April 1, 1723. "whereon ANDREW IRE-LAND now dwells." Wit: THOMAS CREW, JOHN WYNNS. August Court 1734. *.

D 126 JAMES SANDERS of Edgecombe Precinct TO PELEG RODGERS (ROGERS)
Aug. 11, 1734. 300 A. "...in Consideration of An Error apparrent Error in a Deed of Sale from me the said SANDERS to ROBERT WARREN dated 13th day of Feby 1728...." A deed for same land to me dated Feb. 7, 1725 from JOHN HOWARD. "...All interest in said land...to PELEG ROGERS...." On Horse Swamp adj. JACOB LEWIS, EDWARD HOWARD, ROBERT LANIER. Wit: JOHN CRICKETT, EDWARD OATLAW (OUTLAW). August Court 1734. JOHN WYNNS D.C/C.

D 128 LORDS PROPRIETORS TO CULLEN POLLOCK
April 18, 1730. Grant. 640 A. On Beaverdam Swamp adj. THOMAS POL-LOCK at mouth of Bull Swamp Branch. For importation of persons: 50 A/person. Signed in Office of Sec't'y. "Sir RICHARD EVERART, Barronet Governor of North Carolina and ye rest of trusty and well beloved Councellors ....": _____WORLEY, ROBERT WEST, RICHARD SANDERSON, EDMOND GALE, THOMAS POL-LOCK. ROBERT FORSTER, deputy Sec't'y.

D 129 CULLEN POLLOCK TO WILLIAM BENTLEY
Sep. 5, 1733. 20 pds. for "within pattent...." "...I shall defend Title from me or my heirs or from my brother THOMAS POLLOCK...reserving to me and my heirs all the Timber...and (right) to Cutt and Carry same except the oak and as much other Timber as he shall have Occassion for any plantation to use...." Also I make over 50 A. lying between this patent and the swamp. Wit: JOHN STANCILL, MARY WEST. N.C. Court August 28, 1734. W. SMITH, C.J. JOHN WYNNS D.C/C.

D 129 WILLIAM BENTLEY of "Terryl Precinct" to JOHN BENTLEY
Aug. 3, 1734. 14 pds. for "All the Timber that is or shall be on the Said land to have free (egress etc.) to Cutt and Carry off the said land...Except the Oak and other Timber he or his heirs shall have occassion for any plantation to use...." Land on Beaverdam Swamp at mouth of Bull Branch. Wit: JAMES LEGETT, JOHN STANSELL. N. C. Court Aug. 28, 1734. W. SMITH, C.J. *.

D 130 JOHN SESSIONS TO JAMES LEGETT
Aug. 1, 1734. *. On Main Swamp of Roquiss. Wit: WILLIAM BENTLEY, WILLIAM PETERS. N.C. Court August 28, 1734. W. SMITH, C.J. JOHN WYNNS *.

D 131 EDMOND SMITHERWICK of "Terrill Precinct: TO JAMES LEGETT
June 29, 1734. 60 pds. for 273 A. In Cashy Neck "joyning to said LEGGETTs dwelling plantation" commonly known as Trowells "containing by the said TROWELLs Deed to me two hundred and seventy three acres." Wit: WIL-LIAM BENTLEY, EDWARD GRIFFIN. N.C. Court Aug. 28, 1734. W. SMITH, C.J. JOHN WYNNS D. Reg. (Deputy Register).

D 132 COLL. JOHN LOVICK TO JOHN SPEIR
Nov. 1, 1735. 30 pds. "silver mony sixty four penny weight to the Pound." for 640 A. In Goose Meadow adj. JAMES TURNER at Gum Swamp, GOV. EDEN's corner. On SS Moratock River "at head of Scotland Neck." By patent granted JOHN LOVICK dated July 20, 1730, and since conveyed to JOHN SPEIR. Wit: ANNO TENOURE(?), DAVID O'SHEAL. N.C. Court Nov. 7, 1732. WM. LITTLE, C.J. JOHN WYNNS D.C/C.

D 133 HENRY OVERSTREET & WILLIAM JONES, JUN. TO HENRY JARNAGAN, SEN.
Nov. 8, 1734. 9 pds. 1 sh. 7 p. for 340 A. On SS Cashy Swamp. adj. GEORGE WILLIAMS, THOMAS MANN. Wit: HENRY JARNAGAN, JUN., JOHN BLACKMAN, JUN. November Court 1734. JOHN WYNNS D.C/C.

D 135 WILLIAM HOLT (HOULT, HOLTE) TO JAMES WILKINS
Nov. 12, 1734. 50 pds. for 118 A. On NS Meherring River adj. WILL-IAM BROWN. Part of patent (+) dated Nov. 29, 1716 for 540 A. Wit: HENRY

GAY, BRYAN MACLAM(?). November Court 1734. JOHN WYNNS D.C/C. (+ patent in name of THOMAS BROWN.)

D 136   WILLIAM JONES TO HENRY OVERSTREET
        Nov. 11, 1734. 3 pds. for 50 A. On NS Marratock River adj. HENRY JARNAGAN on Appletree Swamp adj. THOMAS BARTON. Wit: JOHN BECTON, JOHN BLACKMAN. November Court 1734. JOHN WYNNS D.C/C.

D 137   HENRY JARNAGAN (JERNIGAN) TO HENRY OVERSTREET
        March 7, 1733/34. "nine pounds seven" for 50 A. On NS Marratock River at Appletree Swamp adj. WILLIAM JONES. Wit: NEEDHAM BRYAN, JOHN BLACKMAN, SAMUEL DICKINS. November Court 1734. JOHN WYNNS D.C/C.

D 139   HENRY JARNAGAN (JERNAGAN) of Nansemond Co., Va. TO JAMES TUDAR (TU-
        DOR) Nov. 29, 1732. 10 pds. for 100 A. At Village Swamp. adj. JOHN WILLIAMS. Land formerly granted GEORGE STEVENSON for 640 A. dated August 1728. Wit: NEEDHAM BRYAN, THEOPHILLIS WILLIAMS. November Court 1734. JOHN WYNNS D.C/C.

D 140   WILLIAM EVANS (EVINS) TO JOHN WILLOBY
        Nov. 12, 1734. 37 pds. for 100 A. On SS Horse Swamp. adj. LAZARUS THOMAS, JOHN THOMAS. Wit: WILLIAM RASBURY, FINCHER HAYNE, HENRY MAYNOR. November Court 1734. JOHN WYNNS D.C/C.

D 141   JAMES HOWARD, SARAH CREW & THOMAS CREW TO JOHN JENKINS (JINKINS),
        wheelwright Nov. 1734. 40 pds. for 300 A. "Wee JAMES HOWARD SARAH CREW and THOMAS CREW in Right of his Wife SARAH CREW Exec.rs. of the Last Will and Testament of JAMES HOWARD dec'd late of Bertie Precinct... (sell land as decreed." On NS Cashy by patent dated 1726. commonly known as "Speights Land." Wit: RICHARD ROWLAND, jurat, CATHERINE ROWLAND. November Court 1734. JOHN WYNNS D.C/C.

D 142   WILLIAM MCHENRY (MACKHENRY) TO JEREMIAH MAGLAHON
        Aug. 5, 1734. 50 pds. for 100 A. On Loosing Swamp adj. ROBERT EVANS "along a concluded line between HENRY BRADLEY and Edward Tidmon...." Wit: JOHN THOMAS, JOHN MITCHELL, jurat. November Court 1734. JOHN WYNNS D.C/C.

D 144   WILLIAM LEE, cooper, TO THOMAS LEE, cooper
        Oct. 12, 1734. 150 A. "For Love goodwill and Efeection...unto my son THOMAS LEE...." On SWS Brooks Creek and NS Wiccacon Creek at Ferry Landing "on southern side of Main Road." Wit: JOHN WYNNS, jurat, JOHN KEEFE. November Court 1734. JOHN WYNNS D.C/C.

D 145   JOHN EDWARDS & WIFE ELIZABETH TO JOHN WIMBERLY (WIMBERLEY)
        *. 270 pds. for 600 A. Of this 500 A. out of patent dated July 20, 1717 adj. WILLIAM JONES on SWS Cashy Swamp. 100 A. out of a deed that bears date May 14, 1723 on SWS Cashy Swamp adj. MARTIN GUARDINER "in the meadow." Wit: NEEDHAM BRYAN, ED. WIGGINS, jurat. November Court 1734. *.

D 146   SAMUEL POWERS TO GODFREY LEE
        Feb. 4, 1734. 30 pds. for 480 A. On NS Maherring "...by pattent... as appears in the SecEys Office" commonly called "Mulberry old Field." Wit: J. BONDE, SAM.LL ELLSON. N.C. Court Feb. 6, 1734. W. SMITH, C.J. *.

D 147   SAMUEL POWERS TO THOMAS JARNAGAN
        May 6, 1734. 100 pds. for 480 A. On WS Chowan River adj. GODFREY LEE. By patent dated Nov. 2, 1727. Wit: WILLIAM WHITFIELD, SIMON HOMES, HENRY BONNER. N.C. Court Feb. 18, 1734. W. SMITH, C.J. JOHN WYNNS D.C/C.

D 149   SAMUEL THOMAS & WIFE ELIZABETH TO JOHN BOYD
        Oct. 24, 1734. 60 pds. for 150 A. "where said SAMUEL now lives" On SS Yawrahaw Swamp. Part of tract granted WILLIAM BRASSWELL "Aprill 1, MDCCIVX" (1706). On WS Quankey branch "above the old field." Wit: JOHN DICKINSON, jurat, DANIEL DICKINSON, JOHN CROWELL, ANDREW IRWING. May Court 1735. JOHN WYNNS D.C/C.

D 150   WILLIAM BRASSWELL of Edgecombe Precinct TO "the Reverend JOHN BOYD
        Minister of the Gospell" May 25, 1734. 30 pds. for *. "where JOHN BOYD doth now dwell" on SS Yawrahaw Swamp at mouth of Great Branch adj. ROBERT BRASSWELL on Poplar Branch. Part of tract of 600 A. granted WM.

BRASSWELL April 1, 1714. Wit: ALEXANDER WIGHT, jurat. *. May Court 1735 *.

D 152 HENRY OVERSTREET TO THEOPHILLIS PUGH of Nansemond Co., Va.
        May 10, 1735. 800 pds. for 150 A. plus 50 A. plus chattels. (1) On
Appletree Swamp adj. WILLIAM JONES, HENRY JARNAGAN. (2) 50 A. at head of
Roques (3) 150 A. "whereon ANN OVERSTREET doth now live." The 150 A. pur-
chased of WILLIAM JONES and HENRY JARNAGAN. The 50 A. purchased of ROBERT
RADFORD. In addition 2 Negros named Peter & Jamy; 20 head cattle and hoggs;
100 head of hoggs. Wit: JAMES MILLIKIN, JOSEPH MOOR, JOHN KIRKPATRICK.
May Court 1735. *.

D 154 ABRAHAM MACLIMER TO WILLIAM GILLUM
        May 10, 1735. 5 pds. for 100 A. On NS Morratock River "Down the old
County line." Wit: JOHN DOYLE, JOHN MECHUMP, M. LYONS. May Court 1735. *.

D 155 ABRAHAM MACLIMER (MACKLEMOOR) TO WILLIAM CLANTON
        May 12, 1735. 5 pds. for 100 A. On NS Marratock River at "Pigion
Ruste Creek." Wit: M. LYONS, JOHN DOYLE, JOHN COTTON. May Court 1735. *.

D 156 WILLIAM BATTLE of Nansemond Co., Va. TO JOSEPH WIMBERLY
        February *. *. 160 pds. for 300 A. At a dividing line between JAMES
WILLIAMSON and JONATHAN TAYLOR on Roquess Swamp. Part of patent granted
JAMES WILLIAMSON April 5, 1720 and part of a patent granted JOHN SMITHER-
WICK Aug. 7, 1720. Wit: WILLIAM BUTLER, WILLIAM BATTLE, JUN., JOHN BATTLE,
jurat. May Court 1735. JOHN WYNNS D.C/C.

D 157 ABRAHAM SHEPPERD & WIFE CATHERINE TO JOSEPH WIMBERLY
        May 13, 1735. 50 pds. for 100 A. Adj. EDWARD WINGATE. Wit: JOHN
DAWSON, JOHN RHODES, NEEDHAM BRYAN. May Court 1735. *.

D 159 JOHN HAYS TO HUGH HYMAN (HIGHMAN, HYGHMAN)
        Dec. 14, 1734. 70 pds. for 100 A. On Roquess. Part of patent of
LUKE MEZLE and conveyed by him to GEORGE CLERK, dec'd, and by CLERK's executors to JOHN COLLSON. Wit: JAMES LEGETT, JOSEPH MESSERS(?). May Court
1735. JOHN WYNNS D.C/C.

D 160 WILLIAM EVINS (EVANS) TO PELEG ROGERS
        May 13, 1735. 150 pds. for 300 A. "two percells" (1) in Horse
Swamp adj. JOHN WILLOBY, LAZARUS THOMAS, ROBERT WARREN. (2) adj. ROBERT
FORSTER, JAMES OVERTON, ROBERT WARREN. Wit: JOHN ASKEW, JAMES OVERTON.
May Court 1735. JOHN WYNNS D.C/C.

D 161 FINCHOR HAYNE TO JOHN ASKEW
        Feb. 10, 1734/35. Power of atty. to "...receive...Sums of mony...
due me...to Commence & procecute in my name any actions or Avtions suite or
Suits in Law...perfoem any other Lawfull Act...I might (do) Personally...."
Wit: JOHN WYNNS, jurat, JOHN EARLY, JUN. May Court "MDCCXXXV" (1735) *.

D 162 WILLIAM LEE TO HENRY MAYNOR
        Feb. 4, 1734/35. 30 pds. for 100 A. On Brooks Creek. Wit: JOHN
ASKEW, jurat, CHARLES HARDIE, JOHN WYNNS. May Court 1735. JOHN WYNNS DCC.

D 163 WILLIAM ASKEW, cordwinder, Of Isle of Wight Co., Va. TO JOHN ASKEW
        May 7, 1734. 80 pds. for 175 A. "...to my brother JOHN ASKEW of
Bertie Precinct...." By patent dated Aug. 27, 1714 to RICHARD WILLIAMSON.
Wit: JOHN WYNNS, MARY WYNNS. May Court 1735. JOHN WYNNS D.C/C.

D 164 JOHN LEE TO THOMAS SPITE
        Oct. 19, 1734. 80 pds. for 300 A. On NS Connehoe Creek. Part of
a grant to JOHN LEE dated Sep. 28, 1730(?) adj. WILLIAM AVERIT land which
was "bought out of the same Patent." Wit: JOSEPH MOOR, jurat, JOHN
BALLARD(?), ROBERT BUTLER. May Court 1735. JOHN WYNNS D.C/C.

D 166 ABRAHAM DEW of Edgecombe Precinct to JOHN HOBBS "of said Precinct &
        Province. May 13, 1735. 6 pds. for 150 A. On NS Maherring River
"Joyning to JOHN ROADS Land" at Horse Pasture Creek on "Gardiners path."
Part of a patent granted to DEW. Wit: ANTHONY WEBB. *. May Court 1735. *.

D 167 ANTHONY GANT of Edgecombe Precinct TO ABRAHAM MACLIMER (MACKLEMORE)
        May 8, 1734. 8 pds. for 100 A. On NS Marratock River at "old County

Line" at "Pigion Ruste Creek." Wit: JOHN DOYLE, MARTIN LYONS, jurat. May
Court 1735. JOHN WYNNS D.C/C.

D 168 WILLIAM CAIN TO THOMAS TAYLOR "of Western Branch of Elisabeth River
       Virginia" May 12, 1735. 18 pds. for 290 A. Adj. WILLIAM BENNETT.
Wit: J. EDWARDS, WILLIAM THOMAS. May Court 1735. JOHN WYNNS D.C/C.

D 169 RICHARD WILLIFORD & WIFE ABIGAIL TO WILLIAM WILLIFORD
       March 5, 1734. 50 pds. for 100 A. "formerly purchased of WILLIAM
ASKEY" at Beach Swamp adj. JOHN JONES at Head of Pitt Blade Branch. Wit:
JOHN HOWARD, JOHN GILBERT. May Court 1735. JOHN WYNNS D.C/C.

D 172 JOHN BONDE TO JOSIAH COOPERLY "Late of Baltimore County in the Pro-
       vince of Maryland" May 5, 1735. 25 pds. for 540 A. On NS Meheron
River adj. MARY BRASSWELL, ___FAULK, JOHN CHESHIRE. Patent to SAMUEL
ELSON March 26, 1723. Wit: JAMES CASTELLAW, PETER WEST. May Court 1735.
ROBERT FORSTER C/C.

D 170 JOHN SPEIR TO ROBERT HILLIARD
       May 10, 1735. 80 pds. "silver mony at the weight now current in
Virginia" for 710 A. On SS Cypress Swamp at Dividing Branch at JAMES
DENTON's Headline adj. BENTON and SPEIR. At Kekoekey(?) Swamp on SS Marratock River. Part of 580 A. granted JAMES DENTON April 6, 1722 "whereof is
two hundred and sixty acres of the said Pattent as will more largely appear
by Deed Dated the Seventh day of December (1727)...to SPEIR by JAMES DENTON
...the other (450 A.) by patent dated Aprill 6, 1722...." Altogether 710
A. Wit: JOHN WILKS (?), BENJAMIN JOHNSTON, JAMES MOOR. May Court 1735. *.

D 175 JOSEPH WIMBERLEY TO JAMES BARNS
       May 13, 1735. 45 pds. for 140 A. Adj. RICHARD BRASSWELL "by the
Meadowside." Wit: JOHN DAWSON, WILLIAM WILLSON, WILLIAM KILLINGSWORTH.
May Court 1735. *.

D 176 MARGARET RAILEY & JOHN HUGS (HUSE, HUGES) & WIFE ELIZABETH TO JAMES
       RUTLAND *. 50 pds. for 220 A. On SS Poplar Swamp adj. ABRAHAM
BLULET, ANDREW BARAN. Ours by deed dated Aug. 15, 1720. Wit: WILLIAM
WHITFIELD, GEORGE POWELL, ELIZABETH WHITFIELD. May Court 1735. *.

D 177 JOHN SPANN & WIFE MARY (SPAN) TO DAVID RAZOR
       Jan. 23, 1734. 100 pds. for 300 A. Part of grant to SPAN dated Dec-
ember 12, 1727. in "upper Parish Bertie Precinct" On NS Morattock River at
"Plunketts line and Falling Run." At Green Creek. Wit: RICHARD HEAD,
jurat, WILLIAM ARNOLE, JOHN ARNOLE. May Court 1735. JOHN WYNNS D.C/C.

D 179 JOHN SPANN TO RICHARD HEAD
       Jan. 26, 1734. 100 pds. for 140 A. In "upper Parish Bertie Precinct"
on NS Morattock at Green Creek adj. GEORGE NORWOOD, ROBERT WEB at Pond of
Green Creek. Granted to JOHN SPAN by patent of 440 A. dated Dec. 24, 1729.
Wit: DAVID RAZOR, jurat, WILLIAM ARNOLE. May Court 1735. JOHN WYNNS D.C/C

D 180 ROBERT IVEY of Edgecombe Precinct TO JASPOR STUART (STEWARD, STEW-
       ART) Nov. 7, 1734. 50 pds. for 240 A. in Upper Parish of Bertie
Precinct. On NS Morattock River adj. JOHN GLOVER, THOMAS BRADFORD "JOHN
SPANNs former corner." Granted to JOHN SPANN April 8, 1730. Wit: SILVES-
TER ESTES, WILLIAM GLOVER, jurat, JOHN GLOVER. May Court 1735. *.

D 182 THOMAS JARRILL of Isle of White TO SARAH PARKER of Surry Co.
       Feb. 12, 1734. *. 606 A. to "my well beloved daughter SARAH PARKER
...." On NS Morattock River and ES Occanecha Swamp. Wit: BENJAMIN HILL,
JOHN DEW. May Court 1735. JOHN WYNNS D.C/C.

D 182 JOHN RAY & WIFE MARY TO NATHANIELL HILL
       May 9, 1735. *. *. Power of atty. to ack. plantation to JOHN AIRES.
Wit: NAT'LL. HILL, JOHN BUTLER, jurat. May Court 1735 *.

D 183 JOHN RAY, cordwinder, & WIFE MARY TO JOHN AIRES
       March 7, 1734. 40 pds. for 50 A. On NS Casia River adj. JOHN BIRD,
ROBERT SHARMAN. Wit: ROBERT SHARMAN, ELIZABETH ROZETT. May Court 1735. *.

D 184 THOMAS TURNER of New England TO JAMES BULLOCK

March 25, 1735. *.*. Power of atty. to recover and receive. Wit: JOHN HOW, jurat, THOMAS WHITMELL. May Court 1735. JOHN WYNNS D.C/C.

D 185 OWEN MCDANIELL TO JOHN WARD
Aug. 17, 1734. 17 pds. 10 sh. for 320 A. On NS Flatt Swamp. Part of patent granted MARTIN CROWMAN Oct. 16, 1729. Adj. JOHN BUTLER. Wit: JOHN HARRILL, ISAAC HARRILL. May Court 1735. JOHN WYNNS D.C/C.

D 186 WILLIAM PADGETT TO CHARLES SOWELL
April 9, 1735. 50 pds. for 230 A. On Chowan River adj. CHARLES GAVIN, JOHN AVERETT. At Deep Bottom on Bear Swamp. "being half of Culliver survey." Wit: JOHN AVERAT, JOHN PADGETT. May Court 1735. *.

D 188 GODPHREY LEE TO RICHARD LEE
____ 13, 1734. 15 pds. for 270 A. SS Indian Creek adj. RICHARD HOLLAND. Now in possession of DAVID JARNAKIN. On "Godphreys Great Branch." Wit: HENRY GAY, WILLIAM GAY, JOHN ELLSON, JOHN LEE. May Court 1735. *.

D 189 JOHN CRICKETT TO JOSEPH WILLEY
May 13, 1735. "valuable consideration" for 550 A. On NES Casia Swamp. Adj. THOMAS POLLOCK, WILLIAM WILLSSON. Wit: JOHN RASBURY, RALPH AMBERRY. May Court 1735. JOHN WYNNS D.C/C.

D 190 FRANCIS PARKER "of fishing creek in Edgecombe precinct" TO HENRY EVERARD Feb. 12, 1734. 9 pds. for 640 A. On NS Morattock River adj. JOHN BLUNT, THOMAS BUSBY, RICHARD MELTON. Wit: THOMAS HARRELL, jurat, JOHN BECTON. May Court 1735. JOHN WYNNS D.C/C.

D 191 HENRY AVEREY & WIFE MARY (AVERAD) TO JOSEPH THOMAS
May 12, 1735. 92 pds. 10 sh. for 640 A. On NS Roanoke River adj. JOHN BLUNT, THOMAS BUSBY, RICHARD MELTON. Wit: JOHN HARILL, JOSEPH HARRILL, EDWARD HARRILL. May Court 1735. JOHN WYNNS D.C/C.

D 192 JOHN BRYAN of Craven Precinct TO CHARLES RICKETTS (RICKETS)
May 1, 1735. 30 pds. for 320 A. in St. Johns Neck. On SWS Chowan River adj. FRANCIS BROWN at Cypress Swamp. "at a concluded line between CHARLES RICKETTS & MORDECAY WHITE...." Wit: LEWIS BRYAN, JOHN PADGETT. May Court 1735. JOHN WYNNS D.C/C.

D 193 WILLIAM BRYAN of Pasquotank Precinct TO CHARLES RICKETTS
May 1, 1735. 60 pds. for 430 A. In St. Johns Neck on ES Cypress Swamp adj. WILLIAM WEST "left to me by my fathers will." Wit: LEWIS BRYAN, JOHN PADGETT. May Court 1735. JOHN WYNNS D.C/C.

D 194 CHARLES GAVIN TO ROBERT ROGERS, JUN. of Chowan Precinct
Feb. 18, 1734. 35 "Barrills of Tar" for 85 A. "all but about five or six acres of my land on the Upper side over the creek...." On Woodwards Creek at Long Branch. Wit: WILLIAM SPARKMAN, NICHOLAS FAIRLESS. May Court 1735. JOHN WYNNS D.C/C.

D 196 ABRAHAM ODAM of Chowan Precinct TO WALTER BROWN
May 14, 1735. 10 pds. for 100 A. On SS Cutawitskey Meadow at mouth of Long Branch adj. BRYAN O'QUIN. Wit: JAMES BARNS, JOHN VANN, JUN. May Court 1735. JOHN WYNNS D.C/C.

D 197 JOHN GRADY (GRADDY) & WIFE MARY TO ALEXANDER COTTON
Jan. 22, 1734. 150 pds. for 320 A. Known by name of Deep Creek. Granted to JOHN BAYS on April 19, 1714. At fork of Deep Creek and head of "Wisktfor branch." Wit: JOB RODGERS, JONAS GRIFFIN. May Court 1735. *.

D 198 THOMAS BIRD (BYRD), cooper, TO HONNOUR(?) BAKER, THOMAS BIRD, JUN., HENRY BIRD & EDMOND BIRD Aug. 9, 1735. *. for "...love goodwill and Effection...unto my children..." (1) To my daughter HONOUR BAKER land on SS Ahoskey Swamp cont. 200 A. at Snake Branch. (2) To THOMAS BIRD, JUN. land on WS Loosing Swamp. cont. 640 A. (3) To HENRY BIRD land at fork between Ahoskey Swamp and Loosing Swamp cont. 325 A. (4) To EDMOND BIRD land at Ahotskey Swamp cont. 325 A. between HONOUR, THOMAS and HENRY... "the manor plantation whereon I now live." Wit: JOHN WYNNS, jurat, WILLIAM BAKER. August Court 1735. JOHN WYNNS D.C/C.

D 199 ABRAHAM BRAWLETT TO JOSEPH THOMPSON (THOMSON), JUN., laborer

July 24, 1735. 16 pds. for 120 A. On WS Holly Swamp. Wit: JOSEPH MAYNOR, JOHN WILLOBY. August Court 1735. JOHN WYNNS D.C/C.

D 200 HENRY VIZE, carpenter, to JOHN CLARK
Jan. 10, 1734/35. "for loe I bear" 100 A. On SS Horse Swamp. Wit: CHRIS. HOLLIMAN, ISAAC BRAWLER, FINCHER HAYNES. August Court 1735. *.

D 201 GEORGE WILLIAMS TO JAMES BROWN
Aug. 12, 1735. 40 sh. for 260 A. on fork "betwixt" south and middle branch of Casia "on NS of the Southern branch in THOMAS MANNs Line." By patent granted to GEORGE WILLIAMS. Wit: BENJAMIN WYNNS, RICHARD WILLIAMS. August Court 1735. JOHN WYNNS D.C/C.

D 203 ALEXANDER BEAN of Edgecombe Precinct TO RICHARD PACE
March 7, 1734. 18 pds. for 190 A. Part of patent for 340 A. dated March 1, 1719, The "above one hundred and ninty acres...sold to me by DAVID COMMINGS...." Adj. JOHN GREEN where "JOHN BROWN alias DICTUM forty foot(?)" now dwells. Wit: JOHN PRATT, JAMES MILLIKIN, CHRIS. BANE. August Court 1735. JOHN WYNNS D.C/C.

D 204 PATRICK RYON TO WILLIAM MOOR
March 17, 1734. 20 pds. for 300 A. "...plantation whereon I now live with one half the tract of Land which is mentioned in the Pattant Granted to GEORGE SKIPPER Bearing Date the first Day of Febby 1725...." Wit: BENJAMIN HILL, JAMES IRELAND, WILLIAM HALL. August Court 1735. *.

D 205 RICHARD PACE, JUN. TO RICHARD PACE, SEN.
May 14, 1735. 5 pds. for 40 A. Part of tract granted to JOHN GREEN for 440 A. On March 1, 1719 and sold to me by GREEN. At Little Runn. Wit: JOHN CRICKETT, JAMES CANE, jurat, WILLIAM WILLIFORD. August Court 1735. *.

D 206 EDWARD ANDERSON & THOMAS BRYANT TO WILLIAM BODIE
June 17, 1734. 30 pds. for 440 A. "...between Executor of JOHN AND-ERSON and THOMAS BRYANT Attorney of the said JOHN ANDERSON of the one part ...." On NS Bridgers Creek and NS Morattock River which land belonged to JOHN BLACKMAN and was made over to JOHN ANDERSON. Wit: JOHN DAWSON, WILL-IAM CAIN. August Court 1735. JOHN WYNNS D.C/C.

D 208 JOHN COOK TO WILLIAM WEAVER
Aug. 11, 1735. For "payment received" 100 A. On NS Morattock River at "Benefields Pond" at Canoe Creek. By a patent granted to JOHN COOK in 1725. In Upper Parish of Bertie Precinct. Wit: AARON FUSSELL (FASSELL), RICHARD HEAD. August Court 1735. JOHN WYNNS D.C/C.

D 209 COLLIN (COLTEN) SESSUMS TO JAMES VOLLANTINE
June 30, 1735. 100 pds. for 220 A. Part of a larger patent of JAMES BOON's. Wit: MARY FAIRLESS, NICHOLAS FAIRLESS, jurat. August Court 1735. JOHN WYNNS D.C/C.

D 210 WILLIAM EVANS TO JAMES OVERTON
Aug. 8, 1735. 25 pds. for 110 A. In NW Parish. adj. WILLIAM RUT-TERS, ROBERT WARREN at Horse Penns. Wit: THOMAS WILLOBY, JOSEPH ALBERT. August Court 1735. JOHN WYNNS D.C/C.

D 212 JOHN RASBURY, SEN. TO JAMES ROADS
May 15, 1735. 7 pds. for 250 A. On White Oak Swamp. adj. WILLIAM RUTTER. Wit: JOHN EARLY, jurat, JAMES OVERTON, ANTHONY WEBB. August Court 1735. JOHN WYNNS D.C/C.

D 213 JOSEPH COTTON & BENTON MOOR TO ROBERT FORSTER
*. 200 pds. for 640 A. On SS Meherring Creek on Elm Swamp. "all the land bounded by Meherring Creek and Elm Swamp." By our patent dated Oct. 1, 1726 to JOHN BENTON MOOR and by a deed from WILLIAM HOWELL to JOSEPH COTTON. Wit: WILLIAM WHITFIELD, JOHN BROWN, EDWARD BROWN. August Court 1735. JOHN WYNNS D.C/C.

D 214 WILLIAM DANIEL TO JAMES JENKINS, bricklayer
Aug. 8, 1732. for "a valuable consideration." 50 A. On NS Deep Creek at "Mr. PEEKs corner tree." Wit: THOMAS HANSFORD, jurat, THOMAS JOHNSON. November Court 1735. JOHN WYNNS D.C/C.

108

D 215   DANIEL HENMAR "of Baufort Prect." TO COLL. BENJAMIN HILL
        March 23, 1735(34). 100 pds. for "Three Horses with some Tables
chairs bedd sheeting Platy knives & forks with Several other kinds and
sorts of Goods & Moveables.... one hundred pounds Lawful money of Great
Brittain on the ninth Day of May wch shall happen in the year 1737 for
redemption of the said Bargained Premisses...." Wit: JOHN POWER, jurat.

D 216   "Inventory of Goods sold and Delivered to COLL. BENJAMIN HILL of
        Bertie Precinct the 23rd Day of March 1734/35
one Bed Bolster   sass pan
Two Pillows & one quilt   candle stick
one Pair Sheets   4 dishes
one Brass Kettle   1 Doz'n. Plates
The above reced from Mr. RAINSETT(?) L t him   F(pds) 104:___:___
1 Small Table cost. . . . .   6:___:___
1 sarce Pann . . . .   2:___:___
1 Frying Pan . . . .   2:___:___
1 small Kettle . . . .   8:___:___
3 Matted Chairs . . . .   2:___:___
1 Pair Pott Hooks . . . .   1:___:___
1 Pewter Dish . . . .   1:___:___
1 Bason 1 Tongs . . . .   1:___:___
1 Doz Soop Plates Pewter . . . .   7:___:___
Tea Kettle . . . . 10:___:___
Coffee Pott . . . .   5:___:___
1 Pair Hillards . . . .   1: 10:___
1 Desk Ceadar . . . . 30:___:___
1 Desk Oak . . . . 20:___:___
1 chest Drawers . . . . 20:___:___
2 arm chairs . . . . 14:___:___
6 Plain Chairs . . . . 25: 4:___
1 Bedstead 5 Blanketts 1 Quilt . . . . 50:___:___
1 Large Table . . . . 10:___:___
1 Grid Iron . . . .   1: 10:___
1 Gun 1 Pair Pistols 8 Guinies . . . . 80:___:___
1 Tin Coffee Pott & 1 Pint Pott Lanthern 2 Frik'ds(?) and
  1 Flower box & grater. . . . .   5:___:___
1 Small Looking Glass . . . .   1:___:___
2 Mens Saddles 1 womans . . . . 40:___:___
4 Trunks & chest 1 Box(?).   6:___:___
1 Doz of delf plates Six Basons five cups & Sawcers 1 Quart
  Mug 1 pint 1 Tea Pott . . . . 10:___:___
1 Sett Casters & 3 Tumblers . . . .   6: 4:___
1 Salon 4 Glasses 2 Lyons . . . .   3:___:___
2 Silver Salts 2 Guinnies . . . . 20:___:___
3 Large Silver spoons 5 Tea Spoons a strainer & pair
  Tongs 3 pds. St. . . . . 30:___:___
1 Silver Cup 7 pd Ster'l. . . . . 3: 10:___
3 washing Tubs a pale & 3 bucketts . . . . ___: 10:___
3 Pair Holland Sheets 3 Pair pillow cases . . . . 50:___:___
3 Table Cloaths 10 Napkins . . . . 20:___:___
8 Towells & 3 Ozanbrigs sheets . . . .   5:___:___
2 matmpes(?) . . . . 20:___:___
5 Doz. books Vallue about . . . . 100:___:___
1 Doz. Silver handled knives & 1 Doz Silver handled forks . . 70:___:___
1 Morter . . . .   2:___:___
1 Pair Brass Candlesticks . . . .   2:___:___
1 Mare 12 Horses . . . . 160:___:___
"The above is a Just and true Inventory of the Goods I have sold and Delivered unto COLL. BENJAMIN HILL for the consideration of 100 sterling as (of)
the Bill of Sale...March 23, 1734/35. D. HENMAR. added to the Inventory:
2 Bed Ticks whole pieces
2 Diamond Rings full 1 stone L Diamond
1 Gold Necklaces & Lockett   "
Wit: JOHN POWER, jurat. May Court 1735. JOHN WYNNS D.C/C.

D 218   JOHN BYRD TO ROBERT BELL
        Jan. 28, 1734/35. *.*. Power of atty. to ack. deed of sale for
120 A. dated Jan. 15, 1734 unto ROBERT SHERMAN. Wit: WILLIAM BYRD, JOHN
BELL, ABRAHAM JORDAN. N.C. Court January 29, 1734. W. SMITH, C.J.

D 219 JOHN BYRD & WIFE MARY TO ROBERT SHORMAN (SHERMAN)
          Jan. 15, 1734. 120 pds. for 120 A. Land between THOMAS SUTTON,
JOSEPH SKITTLETHARP, JOHN HAIR. Wit: NATHANIEL HILL, THOMAS SUTTON. N.C.
Court January 29, 1734. W. SMITH, C.J. JOHN WYNNS D.C/C.

D 220 EDWARD OUTLAW TO EDWARD OUTLAW, JUN.
          Oct. 6, 1735. *. 320 A. "...for Love & Effection...unto my son ED-
WARD OUTLAW...." Land in Flatt Swamp. adj. JOHN HOWARD. Wit: WILL SMITH,
RICHARD PHILLIPS. N.C. Court Oct. 9, 1735. W. SMITH, C.J. JOHN WYNNS DCC.

D 220 JONATHAN GILBERT TO RICHARD PHILLIPS
          Sep. 19, 1735. 52 pds. for 200 A. At Deep Creek. "...mine by deed
from WILLIAM DANIEL...." Wit: EDWARD OUTLAW, SARAH WILKERSON, MARY OUTLAW.
N.C. Court Oct. 9, 1735. W. SMITH, C.J. JOHN WYNNS D.C/C.

D 222 RICHARD VICK & WIFE SARAH of Isle of Wight, Va. TO WILLIAM SHUFFELL
          "of county aforesaid". July 20, 1735. 10 pds. 10 sh. for 130 A.
At Pottycasey Creek adj. JOHN TINNEY. Land formerly granted THOMAS KIRBY
by patent "and by him Elapsed and become due to the said RICHARD VICK...."
Patent to VICK dated July 20, 1726. Wit: J. TURNER, JACOB VICK. November
Court 1735. JOHN WYNNS D.C/C.

D 223 JOHN DUFFIELD TO CAPT. THOMAS BRYANT
          Sep. 13, 1735. 5 pds. for 50 A. On NS Bridgers Creek. "...formerly
VOLLANTINE BRASSWELLs & CULLEN POLLOCKs corner...." By grant to VOLLANTINE
BRASSWELL dated 1717, and by BRASSWELL conveyed to JOHN POPE by Deed. By
POPE conveyed to JOHN DUFFIELD. Wit: PETER WEST, EDWARD OUTLAW, JOHN
LEASEY. November Court 1735. JOHN WYNNS D.C/C.

D 224 ELIAS HODGES of Edgecombe Precinct TO JOHN SPEIR "of the said pre-
          cinct" Sep. 29, 1735. 600 pds. for 320 A. At mouth of Kakukey
(Kehucke) Swamp adj. COLL. FREDERICK JONES. On SS of "Roanoke or Morratock
River" at Cowpen Branch. Part of patent to FRED JONES, and since conveyed
by WILLIAM HARDIN JONES to ELIAS HODGES by deed dated Feb. 27, 1730. Wit:
EDMOND WIGGINS, JOHN MOLTON, JUN., BENJAMIN HODGES. November Court 1735. *.

D 225 WILLIAM BARDEN TO ABRAHAM BURTON
          Aug. 12, 1735. 20 pds. for 150 A. Part of patent for 320 A. granted
to SAMUEL PEACOCK on April 7, 1730. Land on SS Maherring River at Crane-
pond Swamp. Wit: JOHN HARRELL, ARTHUR WILLIAMS, THOMAS BRYANT. November
Court 1735. JOHN WYNNS D.C/C.

D 227 WILLIAM BALDWIN of Lains Creek Parish in Surry Co. TO JOHN WEBB
          May 10, 1735. 7 pds. for 150 A. On NS Marratock River. Part of a
patent granted to WILLIAM BALDWIN for 400 A. on Dec. 1, 1727. Land on
Lower side of ...Little Swamp. Adj. ELIZABETH REGAN at Little Cypress
Swamp. Wit: JOSEPH WALL, THOMAS WALL, jurat. November Court 1735. *.

D 228 ARTHUR WILLIAMS TO THOMAS FUTERRILL, JUN.
          Oct. 15, 1735. 10 pds. 10 sh. for 300 A. Land on NS Pottycasey
Creek bounded by Hunting Quarter Swamp. Granted by patent April 6, 1722.
Wit: THOMAS BRYANT, JOHN HARRELL, JOHN HENKINS. November Court 1735. *.

D 229 ANTHONY WILLIAMS TO SIMON HOLMS
          Oct. 3, 1735. 125 pds. for 390 A. On SWS Ahoskey Swamp adj. WILLIAM
CURLEE. Granted April 1, 1723. Wit: JOHN DUFFIELD, WILLIAM WHEELER, ELIZ-
BETH BONNER. November Court 1735. JOHN WYNNS D.C/C.

D 230 PHILLIP PEIRCE TO WILLIAM BARDEN
          May 13, 1735. 5 pds. for 100 A. On SS Marratock River and SS Conn-
hoe Creek at Nairns Branch upon Indian Path. Part of patent granted to
JOHN MACKDONALD for 640 A. dated Oct. 16, 1728. Wit: FRANCIS PARKER, ED-
MUND WIGGINS. November Court 1735. JOHN WYNNS D.C/C.

D 232 ISRAEL JOYNOR & WIFE ELIZABETH TO NATHAN WILLIAMS
          *. 40 pds. for 640 A. A tract granted to JOYNOR on March 1, 1719.
On SS Maherring River at mouth of Cypress Swamp. Wit: CHAPLIN WILLIAMS,
jurat, BENJAMIN WILLIAMS, NATHANIEL JONES. November Court 1735. *.

D 233 THOMAS BONNER TO BENTON MOOR

110

        Oct. 21, 1732. 80 pds. for 350 A. On SWS Ahotskey Swamp. adj.
WILLIAM BYRD. Wit: JOHN DUFFIELD, THOMAS BYRD, SIMON HOLMS. November
Court 1735. JOHN WYNNS D.C/C.

D 234 FRANCIS MACKLENDON (MCCLENDON) TO THOMAS GREEN, blacksmith
        Aug. 14, 1735. 50 pds. for 510 A. On NWS Barbeque Swamp adj. GEORGE
WYNNS, WILLIAM CRANFORD (CRAWFORD) at Briery Branch. Wit: JOHN WYNNS,
jurat, THOMAS LEE, JAMES CASTELLAW. November Court 1735. JOHN WYNNS D.C/C.

D 236 JAMES FARECHILD (FAIRCHILD) TO THOMAS & MARGARETT JOHNSON
        Oct. 25, 1735. 10 pds. for 50 A. Sold to "...THOMAS JOHNSON in be-
half of MARGARETT JOHNSON his wife...." Adj. ROBERT EVANS, ROBERT FORSTER,
WILLIAM BAKER. Wit: JOHN WYNNS, jurat, ROBERT EVINS. November Court 1735.

D 235 JAMES CASTELLAW, Treasurer of Bertie Precinct, TO JAMES HOLLEY
        Oct. 31, 1735. 53 pds. for 117 A. "...According to the Directions
of an Act of Assembly of this Province Entitled an Act for making & Emit-
ting the sum of Forthy Thousand Pounds Publick Bills of Creditt of North
Carolina Do hereby Grant sell (Ensseolss) convey and Confirm unto the said
JAMES HOLLEY.... Land on SS Barbeque Swamp. Land formerly mortgaged by
ANDREW STEVENSON dec'd. late of said precinct...for non payment...land was
sold at Punlick Vendice (vendue)...to JAMES HOLLEY highest bidder...." Wit:
JOHN WYNNS, FRANCIS MACKLENDON. November Court 1735. JOHN WYNNS D.C/C.

D 237 PELEG ROGERS TO WILLIAM EVINS
        Nov. 13, 1735. 100 pds. for 300 A. On Horse Swamp adj. JACOB LEWIS,
EDWARD HOWARD, ROBERT LANIER. Wit: FINCHOR HAYNE, JOHN WYNNS. November
Court 1735. JOHN WYNNS D.C/C.

D 238 CLEM(ENT) STRATFORD of Isle of Wight Co., Va. TO JAMES TURNER
        Aug. 4, 1735. A valluable Sum for 200 A. On SS Pottycase Creek
Swamp. Part of a patent granted GEORGE SKIPPER, JUN. for 640 A. by Hon.
CHARLES EDEN. Wit: LAWRANCE SMITH, NICHOLLAS MONGER, RICHARD HOLLEMAN.
February Court 1735. JOHN WYNNS D.C/C.

D 240 RALF MASON (MASSON) & WIFE HANNAH of Edgecombe Precinct to HENRY
        HORNE Feb. 2, 1735/36. 50 pds. for 100 A. On NS Marattuck River
between WILLIAM REEVES and JOHN GRAY at Spring Branch and Turbevills
Branch.. Being the land that ISAAC PRICE bought of JOSEPH COLSON. and then
ISAAC PRICE dying without children fell to his wife which is now become the
wife of me RALF MASSON.... Wit: JOHN JONES, jurat, FRANCIS JONES, PHILIP
JONES. February Court 1735. JOHN WYNNS D.C/C.

D 241 BARNABE MACKINNE TO PETER JONES
        *. 5 pds. for 100 A. PETER JONES son of PETER JONES...Land on
Occaneechy Swamp. Grant dated April 2, 1730. *.*.

        NOTE HERE: Pages 243-244 are missing. Self contained index Book D
shows that deeds 244 KIRBY TO WARD and 243 MCKINNE TO KINCHIN would appear
here.

D 245 THOMAS KIRBE TO THOMAS WARD
        Note: deed defaced. Previous page missing. Begins:...February 1725
This is probably patent date.
        March 4, 1733/34. *.*. Land on NS Pottecasi Creek at THOMAS DRAKE's
corner. Wit: ARTHUR WILLIAMS, jurat, WILLIAM PERSON (PERSSON), S. PEACOCK.
February Court 1735. JOHN WYNNS D.C/C.

D 246 THOMAS JURNIGAN TO WILLIAM MARTAIN
        *. 50 pds. for 140 A. On SS Meherrin Creek at Elm Swamp. By patent
dated March 9, 1717/18. Wit: JAMES J (or G)____, GEORGE JURNIGAN. February Court 1735. JOHN WYNNS D.C/C. NOTE: Badly defaced deed.

D 247 ROBERT EVANS TO NICHOLAS FAIRLESS
        April 1735. 60 pds. for 640 A. Adj. WILLIAM MAUL on Killam (Swamp)
at TREDDLE KEEFE's corner adj. JAMES BONS (BOON?). Granted to JOHN CHERRY-
HOLME on April 6, 1722. now due ROBERT EVANS by an order of councill. Wit:
JOHN BRASSWELL, CHRISTOPHER ZEHN(?) (XOHN?) (CHERRYHOLME?). February Court
MDCCXXXV. JOHN WYNNS D.C/C.
Note: Defaced deed.

D 249   JOHN DEW, SEN. TO WILLIAM GAY
        Feb. 1, 1735. 10 pds. for 200 A. On Buckharn Swamp adj. WILLIAM
WHITTY.   Wit: JOHN WYNNS, WILLIAM MEARS. February Court 1735. *.

D 250   CHARLES SOWELL TO JAMES THICKPEN
        Feb. 4, 1732/33. 60 pds. for 100 A. At mouth of a Swamp commonly
known by the name Horse Swamp. Adj. RICHARD SOWELL, CHARLES GAVIN. Wit:
JOHN AVERITT, JANE SMITH. May Court 1734. JOHN WYNNS D.C/C.

D 252   JAMES THICKPEN TO ADAM HARRELL (HARRILL)
        April 23, 1735. 70 pds. for *. "my right title and interest to the
within mentioned deed...." Wit: JOHN WYNNS, jurat, WILLIAM PADGETT. February Court 1735. JOHN WYNNS D.C/C.

D 252   JAMES GLISON TO EDEN BAILS
        Sep. 17, 1734. 100 pds. for 125 A. On "Cusshoake Creek" Formerly
belonged to WILLIAM BURT was Excheated by me JAMES GLISON." Wit: WILLIAM
LATTIMER, ANDREW IRELAND, DANIEL GLISSON. February Court 1735. *.

D 253   WILLIAM WILLIAMS TO SAMUEL ALLEN
        Aug. 12, 1735. 9 pds. for 100 A. On SS "Popler Run." By patent to
LEWIS WILLIAMS dated Aug. 17, 1714. "...grandfather to WILLIAM WILLIAMS
...." Wit: BENJAMIN WYNNS, jurat, EVAN RAGLAND. February Court 1735. *.

D 255   JAMES JENKINGS (JENKINS, JENNKINS) TO SIMON HOMES
        Feb. 1733/34. "a sum of money" for 100 A. Money secured by DAVID
WARD. Land on SS Ahoska Swamp at Curlees Branch. Wit: HENRY BONNER, jurat,
JOHN SMITH. February Court 1735. JOHN WYNNS D.C/C.

D 256   WILLIAM BUSH, "carpinter," TO JOHN BUSH
        Jenty (January?) 31, 1735. 220 pds. for 200 A. To my son JOHN BUSH.
Plantation whereon WILLIAM BUSH now dwells on NS Wiccacon Creek at Holly
Swamp adj. CHRISTOPHER SEGAR. "...freee of all Incumberances one mortgage
to DAVID HENDERSON only Except'd..." JOHN WYNNS, jurat, JOHN WILLIAMS,
SARAH ROBERTS. February Court 1735. JOHN WYNNS D.C/C.

D 257   CHARLES GAVIN TO WILLIAM SPARKMAN
        "31st Day of Jenty Anno Domini 1735." 20 pds. for 100 A. At Long
Branch adj. Newbys Mill Pond. Wit: JOHN WYNNS, jurat, OBEDIAH SOWELL,
JOHN WILLIAMS. February Court 1735. JOHN WYNNS D.C/C.

D 259   JAMES HOWARD TO PETER WEST
        Feb. 11, 1735/36. 50 pds. for 300 A. Part of patent granted to
JAMES HOWARD on April 1, 1723. Adj. WILLIAM EVINS, BRIDGETT RASBERRY, ____
WEST, ____ KING. Wit: JOHN WYNNS, BENJAMIN WYNNS, jurat. February Court
1735. JOHN WYNNS D.C/C.

D 260   JOHN AVERRETT TO THOMAS SOWELL
        Feb. 10, 1735/36. 100 pds. for 230 A. Adj. THOMAS WARF at the river
percoson...being half of CHARLES GULEFORD Survey...." Wit: CHARLES SOWELL,
RICHARD SOWELL. February Court 1735. JOHN WYNNS D.C/C.

D 262   JOHN GILBERT & WIFE SARAH TO JOHN HOLLEY
        Feb. 12, 1725/26. * 120 A. "...(for) love Good will & Effection
which we have and do bear unto our son in Law & son JOHN HOLLEY...(two
parcels) joyning together...." On SS Wiccacon Creek adj. JOHN MORRISS,
JOHN VANPELT, "BUSHes land...being the manner plantation and lands adjoyning whereon we lastly Dwelt as by the Deed of Sale from RICHARD MALPASS to
JOHN BUSH...." Wit: JOHN WYNNS, JOSEPH MAYNOR. February Court 1735. *.

D 262   WILLIAM BYRD & WIFE JEAN TO MIKEL KING
        Feb. 10, 1734. 700 pds. for 225 A. On WS Cashoke Creek at Maple
Branch adj. EDWARD BIRD, COLL. ROBERT WEST, GEORGE BELL. Wit: ROBERT
SHARMAN, EDMUND DAVIS. N.C. Court Oct. 30, 1735. W. SMITH, C.J. *.

D 264   MICHAEL KING TO MOSES SPEIGHT of Perquimmons Precinct
        Oct. 30, 1735. 1400 pds. for 200 A. In Cashie Neck adj. EDMUND
SMITHWICK, SAMUEL SMITHWICK at Burnt Branch to Marrattick thorowfair.
Formerly surveyed to EDMUND SMITHWICK and conveyed to MICHAEL KING by deed.
Wit: WILLIAM BYRD, WILLIAM HERRITAGE. N.C. Court Oct. 10, 1735. *. *.

D 266 JOHN BOBBIT TO BARRABY MELTON
       May 1, 1736. 30 pds. for 300 A. On NS Maratuck River adj. HEZEKIAH
MASSIES(?) dec'd. "on side of Oconetchy Swamp" Being part of tract granted
to JOHN BOBBIT by patent for 600 A. dated March 1, 1719. Wit: HENRY HORNE,
jurat, ROBERT MIMS, LIONER MIMS. May Court 1736. JOHN WYNNS D.C/C.

D 268 RICHARD ALLEN TO WILLIAM SHORT
       May 11, 1736. 15 pds. for 140 A. On NWS Ready Run adj. RICHARD TUR-
BEVILE, RALPH MASON. Wit: HENRY HORNE, jurat, JOHN LOW (LAW?). May Court
1736. JOHN WYNNS D.C/C.

D 270 WILLIAM EVANS TO JOHN THOMAS
       May 1, 1736. 35 pds. for 350 A. On ES Mill Creek Swamp. Was granted
by patent dated March 1, 1719 to DAVID HAGANS "was elapsed for want of
seating"; then granted to WILLIAM POPE, and by him deeded to EVANS. Wit:
PHILLIP THOMAS, THOMAS SLOYET(?). May Court 1736. JOHN WYNNS D.C/C.

D 271 SAMUEL ELDRIGE TO BENJAMIN WILLIAMS of Isle of Wight Co., Va.
       *. 10 pds. for 260 A. Part of a 530 A. tract granted to REBECKKA
BRASSWELL on March 1, 1719. Land on SS Meherrin River at "old cuntry line"
adj. Brasswell Branch. Wit: JOHN THOMAS, T. BODDEY, WILLIAM PACE. May
Court 1736. JOHN WYNNS D.C/C.

D 272 CULLEN POLLOCK of Tyrrell Precinct & GEORGE POLLOCK of Bertie Pre-
       cinct TO LAMB HARDY Feb. 7, 1735/36. 40 pds. for 200 A. On
Bryery Branch adj. JOHN LOVICK. GEORGE and CULLEN POLLOCK acting as execu-
tors of estate of THOMAS POLLOCK. Wit: WILLIAM FLEETWOOD, jurat, JOHN
BARNHARD, WILLIAM HARDY, SHOENNE WOLF (WOFF?). May Court 1736. *.

D 274 CULLEN POLLOCK of Tyrrell Precinct & GEORGE POLLOCK of Bertie Pre-
       cinct TO WILLIAM FLEETWOOD Feb. 7, 1735/36. 32 pds. for 100 A.
On Flat Swamp adj. JOHN LOVICK, _____FLEETWOOD. GEORGE and CULLEN POLLOCK
acting as executors of estate THOMAS POLLOCK. Wit: WILLIAM HARDY, LAMB
HARDY, jurat, JOHN BARNHARD. May Court 1736. JOHN WYNNS D.C/C. (also
witnessed by SHOENNE WOLF.)

D 275 THOMAS WATSON TO HENRY JERNIGAN (JARNAGAN)
       * 1735. 12 pds. for 200 A. On SS Chassha Swamp. Wit: HENRY BAKER,
JUN., JACOB JERNIGAN, ANNE JERNIGAN. May Court 1736. JOHN WYNNS D.C/C.

D 276 JOHN HERRING TO ABRAM HERRING
       May 10, 1736. 100 pds. for 380 A. On SS Bear Swamp. Part of patent
granted JOHN HERRING on Aug. 10, 1720. Wit: ROBERT WARRIN, SIMON HERRING.
May Court 1736. JOHN WYNNS D.C/C.

D 278 JOHN GOVER & WIFE MARY TO WILLIAM WELSON (WESON), SEN. of Chowan
       Precinct March 25, 1736. 50 pds. for 155 A. On ES Loosing Swamp.
Wit: WILLIAM PERSEY(?), CONSST. LUTEN, THOMAS WALTON, jurat. May Court
1736. JOHN WYNNS D.C/C.

D 280 JOHN GLOVER & WIFE MARY TO THOMAS WALTON, JUN. of Chowan Precinct
       March 4, 1736. 350 pds. for 228 A. Adj. THOMAS WARR "along the
River side to a small Run below the ferry point known by the name of Cotten
Bottom." Wit: WILLIAM PERSEY, WILLIAM WESON, jurat, CALAB STEPHENS. May
Court 1736. JOHN WYNNS D.C/C.

D 282 BARNABE MACKINNE TO BARTHOLOMEW CHAVERS TO WILLIAM PACE
       "Jen'ry 6, 1735." "a valuable sum of money" for 540 A. "...a sum
of money paid to BATHOLOMEW CHAVERS by WILLIAM PACE...being lost by the
aforesaid CHAVERS for want of (?) as the law doth direct...becomes due to
me BARNABE MACKINNE...by a Relaps patten...dated 30th Day of July 1726...."
Wit: RICHARD PACE, JUN., jurat, CHRISTIAN MACKINNE, JANE MACKINNE. May
Court 1736. JOHN WYNNS D.C/C.

D 283 ABRAHAM BRAWLER TO CHRISTOPHER SEGAR
       May 1736. 4 pds. for 25 A. Adj. Segar, JOSEPH TOMSON, WILLIAM
WARREN. Wit: JOHN WYNNS, jurat, THOMAS CREW. May Court 1736. *.

D 284 JOHN DUFFIELD TO WILLIAM BODDIE
       Feb. 13, 1735/36. 14 pds. for 150 A. "Plantation whereon I now

dwell...part of land I bought of JOHN POPE at Bridgeres (Bridgers) Creek
...." Adj. VOLINTINE BRASSWELL(?)...to the main road...." Wit: JOHN DAW-
SON, jurat, JOHN BODDIE. May Court 1736. JOHN WYNNS D.C/C.

D 285   ROBERT LANIER of "Tarrell Precinct" TO WILLIAM SPIKES of Chowan Pre-
            cinct. May 10, 1736. 15 pds. for 150 A. On "Bever dam swamp at
the Bridge" At Spring Branch. Wit: JOHN THOMAS, jurat, JACOB JERNIGAN,
THOMAS JERNIGAN. May Court 1736. JOHN WYNNS D.C/C.

D 287   JOHN MANN TO THOMAS MANN
            May 12, 1736. "for love and Effection to my Brother...In obediance
to the Last Will & Testament of my dec'd. Father THOMAS MANN where in he
bequeathed to his son (my brother, THOMAS MANN) his plantation on Wiccacon
Creek but the will not being duly witnessed...decends to me...." On SS
Wiccacon Creek adj. TRIDDLE KEEF, WILLIAM DOWNING, JOSEPH WATSFORD, JOHN
WYNNS, "to a line parting my land from JOHN WYNNS" ...Land conveyed him by
ROBERT FORSTER assignee of THOMAS BRAY assignee of SARAH SMITH pet. agst.
my s'd Father in the Court of Chancery.... Wit: JOHN WYNNS, JOHN DAWSON.
May Court 1736. JOHN WYNNS D.C/C.

D 288   JOHN JONES of Edgecombe Precinct to ANTHONY WILLIAMS
            Dec. 27, 1735. 120 pds. for 560 A. On NS Buck Swamp adj. CHARLES
JONES in the Flat Pocoson. Wit: JOHN DUFFIELD, THOMAS DAVIS, CHARLES JOHES
(JONES?). May Court 1735. JOHN WYNNS D.C/C.

D 289   WILLIAM HARRIS & WIFE WINNEFORD TO WILLIAM GRIFFIN
            March 15, 1732. 30 pds. for 320 A. At mouth of Steward's Branch "up
the Lower prong of the branch" on Casiah Swamp. Wit: J. HOW, jurat, HARB-
ERT JURCHARD(?), WILLIAM STANDLEYE. August Court 1733. JOHN WYNNS D.C/C.

D 291   MARY GRIFFIN (GRIFFEN) "relige WILLIAM GRIFFIN" TO THOMAS COWMAN
            April 16, 1736. 25 pds. for 320 A. "exec'r. to the Last will &
testament (of WILLIAM GRIFFIN) in which he did bequeath all his Estate both
real and personal to me...within deed of sale" At Swactes(?) Branch (Stewart's?) adj. RICHARD BRASWELL on Cashay Swamp. Wit: JOHN GRAY, JAMES
BULLAHE, EDWARD MOOR. May Court 1736. "JOHN COOK by virtue of a letter of
attorney duly proved...acknowledged the above assignment...." JOHN WYNNS *.

D 292   JOHN GLISSON & WIFE JANE TO SAMUEL DICKINS
            May 8, 1734. 35 pds. for 135 A. On NS Cashay Swamp. Wit: HENRY
BAKER, jurat, JOHN FRYSSLE(?). May Court 1736. JOHN WYNNS D.C/C.

D 293   MARTAIN LIONS (LIONE, LYONS) TO WILLIAM NORWOOD
            March 26, 1736. 60 pds. for 100 A. In "uppermost parish of bertie
precinct" On NS Morattock River at Falling Run adj. ABRAHAM SKOT and land
formerly belonging to NATHANIEL NORWOOD and MARTAIN LYONS. Part of patent
granted M. LYONS on Dec. 24, 1729. Wit: DAVID RAZOR, JOHN FRY. May Court
1736. JOHN WYNNS D.C/C.

D 295   JOHN PATTERSON TO FRANCIS PARKER
            May 6, 1736. 20 pds. for 120 A. On SS Pottacassie Creek "being ye
lower part of the tract the upper part being now in possession of JOHN &
EDWARD BROWN...." Wit: JOHN BROWN, jurat, MARY BROWN. May Court 1736. *.

D 297   JOHN BEVERLY, SEN. & WIFE MARGARET TO JAMES CASTELAW
            May 16, 1736. 600 pds. for 640 A. On Meherring Creek. By patent to
BEVERLY dated March 1, 1721. Wit: THOMAS BRYANT, jurat, JOHN COX, MARGRETT
BEVERLY. May Court 1736. JOHN WYNNS D.C/C.

D 298   JONATHAN GILBERT of Perquimmons Precinct TO JOB ROGERS
            *. 150 pds. for 200 A. At Deep Creek Bridge "up the main road" adj.
EDWARD HAIR, STEPHEN WILLIAMS, ROBERT ROGERS. First tract cont. 100 A. (2)
also 1/2 water mill and land. Wit: ROBERT GILBERT, JOSEPH GILBERT. May
Court 1736. JOHN WYNNS D.C/C.

D 299   GEORGE PHENNEY & WIFE PENELOPE TO THOMAS JONES of Norfolk Co., Va.
            Oct. 14, 1735. 5000 pds. for 13,947 A. (1) "...that Edenhouse plan-
tation containing by Estimation seven hundred & thirty three acres..." (2)
2000 A. at Salmon Creek called the Back Lands (3) all that piece on the
Blue Water cont. 964 A. (4) all that piece at Mount Royal on NS Morratock

114

River cont.560 A. (5) all that piece in Edgecombe Precinct cont. 4500 A.
called Lovick's Field at the branch of "Tarr River" (6) all that piece at
Fishing Creek cont. 3200 A. (7) all that parcel in Bath County on SS "Nuse
River" cont. 1350 A. called Slate Landing (State?) (8) 640 A. on NS Nuse
River in Bath County at the mouth of Swift Creek. (9) on NS Nuse River
"butted...as by patent...." Wit: THOMAS ASHLEY, jurat, JOHN ASSHLEY. May
Court 1736. JOHN WYNNS D.C/C.

D 301   Dec. 7, 1735. "This may certify that I...Examined Mrs. PENELOPE
PHENNEY wife to GEORGE PHENNEY of Bertie precinct...privately whether
(lands) delivered to THOMAS JONES of Norfolk County...was Volantary and
free consent...without compulsion of her said husband...(she) answered
(that) she signed freely...." PETER WEST.

D 302   THOMAS JONES of Norfolk Co., Va. TO GEORGE PHENNEY
        Dec. 16, 1735.   5600 pds. for (1) Edenhouse plantation cont. 733 A.
(2) 2000 A. on Salmon Creek called "the Backlands" (3) 964 A. on the Blue
Water (4) 560 A. at Mount Royal on NS Moratock River (5) land in Edgecombe
"on the Branch of Tarr River" cont. 4500 A. called "Lovicksfield" (6) land
at Fishing Creek cont. 3200 A. (7) 1350 A. in Bath County on SS Nuse
called "Slate Landing" (8) 640 A. on NS Nuse River in Bath County at mouth
of Swift Creek (9) tract on NS Nuse River cont. 640 A. at mouth of Swift
Creek. (Note: This last appears to be an erroneous repetition of tract #8.)
Wit: ELIZABETH SCOLLEY, JOHN CAKE, GEORGE STRAGHAN. May Court 1736. *.

D 306   CULLEN POLLOCK of Tyrrell Precinct & GEORGE POLLOCK of Bertie Pre-
        cinct TO THOMAS RYAN (RYON) June 20, 1736. 30 pds. for 394 A.
"Executors to the Estate of Mr. Thomas Pollock" Land at "Grills Corner
tree" adj. MR. PHENNEY. Wit: ROBERT WEST, GEORGE HENDERSON, JAMES MCLAUGH-
LIN. N.C. Court July 30, 1736. W. SMITH, C.J. JOHN WYNNS D.C/C.

D 304   JOHN LOVICK TO MILES GALE
        Jan. 19, 1730 ("A° Tertio") 386 pds. for 1820 A. "three several
tracts or plantations of Land lying between Moratock & Cashara River in
prec't. (aforesaid) containing in the whole according to Computation
eighteen hundred and twenty acres late the Estate of THOMAS BETTERLY of
Edenton feltmaker dec'd. in pursuance to the will of s'd. BETTERLY bearing
date the fourth day of June 1729 were Exposed to sell at publick Vandue
(vendue) by JOHN LOVICK Esq...at the Gen'l. court house in Edenton at which
sale or Vandoue MILES GALE of Edenton...appeared to be highest bidder...215
pds. for 300 A., 150 pds. for 1020 A., 21 pds for 400 A. (1) on NS Moratock River cont. 140 A. adj. HENRY SPE___ dec'd., COGSWELL & DOMINY which
cont. 300 A. and 1120 A. as by grant from said BETTERLY to GEORGE BROMLEY
dated June 15, 1726. which may more fully appear by the will of GEORGE
BROMLEY (2) another tract on NS Moratock and SS Conarax Branch(?) at Chick-
errie Pocoson adj. EDWARD SMITHWICK, COGSWELL & DOMINY, MARTIN GRIFFIN,
JOHN HARLOW. Wit: ROBERT FORSTER, THOMAS JONES, FRANCIS CLAXTON. N.C.
Court April 20, 1730. JOHN WYNNS D.C/C.

D 308   JACOBB PARROTT & WIFE MARTHA TO THOMAS RYON
        May 1, 1736. 450 pds. for 200 A. On Chowan Sound adj. land of
GEORGE POLLOCK. Wit: JOHN PADGETT, ROBERT SANDERLIN. August Court 1736.
JOHN WYNNS D.C/C.

D 310   THOMAS RYAN & WIFE MARTHA TO JACOB PARROTT
        Aug. 30, 1735. 200 pds. for 440 A. On Cuckellmaker Swamp adj. ISAAC
HILL, JOHN PENNEY, CHARLES BARKER. Wit: WILLIAM FLEETWOOD, EDWARD RASOR.
August Court 1736. JOHN WYNNS D.C/C.

D 311   MARTIN LYONS TO JOHN ROOK
        Aug. 12, 1736. 6 pds. for 200 A. On NS Bever Pond Creek on the
"County Line." Wit: JOHN WYNNS, PETER WEST. August Court 1736. *.

D 313   WILLIAM BRASSWELL of Edgecombe Precinct TO "REVERAND MR. JOHN BOYD
        Minister of the Gospel" May 25, 1734. 30 pds. for 300 A. On SS
Yawraha Swamp at mouth of Great Branch adj. ROBERT BRASSWELL. Part of
tract cont. 600 A. granted said WILLIAM BRASSWELL on April 1, 1714. Wit:
ELLEX'R. WIGHT, jurat, WILLIAM SHUFFILD, RICHARD TAYLOR. August Court 1736.
JOHN WYNNS D.C/C. "The underwritten was signed (&) sealed in presence of
us the above. ANDREW IRWING, jurat."

D 315 SAMUEL DICKINS TO JOHN SHOLER (SHOALAR)
       Aug. 11, 1736. 10 pds. for 135 A. On NES Cashy Swamp. Wit: SAMUEL
DICKENS, JAMES HOWARD, JAMES PARKER, JOHN BARNES. August Court 1736. *.

D 317 MARTIN LYONS TO JOHN BREWER
       Aug. 12, 1736. 4 pds. for 200 A. At County Line in "Pits Branch" to
Reedy Branch. Wit: THOMAS CREW, JOHN WYNNS. August Court 1736. *.

D 318 ROBERT SHERARD TO ARTHUR SHERARD (SHEROD)
       Aug. 10, 1736. 8 pds. for 160 A. On NS Kerby Creek. Adj. BENJAMIN
FOREMAN on Little Swamp. Part of patent granted ROBERT SHERARD on March 1,
1719. Wit: ARTHUR WILLIAMS TUNER(?), JOHN FARROW. August Court 1736. *.

D 320 JOSEPH BOON (BOONE) TO CAROWLUS ANDERSON
       Aug. 10, 1736. 5 pds. for 50 A. On Mehron River at the Great Gutt.
Being part of a patent formerly granted to WILLIAM BOON for 423 A. dated
Dec. 3, 1720. Wit: JOHN DEW, JOHN WORRELL. August Court 1736. *.

D 321 BENJAMIN JOYNER TO JOHN SMELLY
       Nov. 6, 1734. 8 pds. 10 sh. for 100 A. Part of patent containing
200 A. dated April 1, 1723. On NS Kirbeys Creek adj. ROBERT SMELLY, JOHN
FARROW. Wit: ROBERT SMELLY, WILLIAM SMELLY, GEORGE BUNTEN. August Court
1736. JOHN WYNNS D.C/C.

D 323 PETER HAYS (HAYZE) TO JOHN WATSON
       October *, 1734. 20 pds. for 200 A. On "southermost" branch of
Casey (Cashiah) Swamp. adj. THOMAS MANN. Wit: THOMAS HAYS, THOMAS WATSON.
August Court 1736. JOHN WYNNS D.C/C.

       NOTE HERE: THIS ENDS DEED BOOK D

E 1   JOHN BRYANT (BRYAN) TO FRANCIS BROWN (BROUN)
       Jan. 16, 1726. 16 pds. for 200 A. On St (Sanet) John's Neck on SWS
Chowan River and Cypress Swamp adj. HENRY ROADS. Wit: LAWRENCE MAGUE, SAM-
UEL BOLLIAM. May Court 1727. *.*.

E 2   JOHN BRYAN TO ISAAC HILL
       Power of atty. to ack. above deed. Wit: EDW. MASHBORNE D.C/C.

E 3   FRANCIS BROWN TO JOHN SOWELL, cooper
       Aug. 9, 1736. 50 pds. for 200 A. "within mentioned "Plantation."
Wit: JOHN WYNNS, jurat, JOHN WILLIAMS. August Court 1736. JOHN WYNNS D.CC

E 3   NICHOLLAS SESSUMS TO PETER HAYES (HAZE)
       October *, 1733. 20 pds. for 420 A. On Cashy Swamp on "southermost"
branch." Adj. THOMAS MANN. Wit: THOMAS MANN, JOHN WATSON. August Court
1736. JOHN WYNNS D.C/C.

E 5   JAMES JENKINS, bricklayer, of Edgecombe Precinct to EDWARD HARE of
       Chowan Pre'ct. March 12, 1735/36. 40 pds. for 50 A. On NS Deep
Creek. Adj. "(land) formerly MR. PEEK's.) Wit: JOHN MACKINNE, MARY PARKER,
EPAPHRODITUS MOORE, jurat. August Court 1736. *.

E 6   ROBERT ANDERSON of "Tyrrel" TO JAMES LEGATT
       *. 150 pds. for 150 A. In Kesia Neck. Land called "Frances" adj.
land of JOHN SMITHWICK's called "Moodye"(Moodge). Land formerly belonged
to EDWARD SMITHWICK, JR. Left by last will and testament to his wife,
GRACE. Given by her to her sons FRANCIS HOBSON and JOHN HOBSON. Sold by
the HOBSONs to ROBERT ANDERSON. Wit: GRACE KENNEDY, WILLIAM KENNEDY.
August Court 1736. JOHN WYNNS D.C/C.

       NOTE HERE: Pages 7 & 8 are blank.

E 9   SARAH HOBSON TO FRANCIS HOBSON & MARY HOBSON
       Aug. 10, 1736. *. "...for love good will and affection..." To my
loving son, FRANCIS HOBSON and my daughter MARY HOBSON. (1) To FRANCIS one
Negro boy called Seasor, 1 brass kettle (kittle), 1 case of bottles, 1 sett
of Coopers tools, 1 gun, 3 augurs, 3 chizells, 3 pewter dishes, 2 deap
plates, 3 files. To Mary: One Negro boy called Pomp, 1 feather bed, 3 pewter dishes, 2 pewter plates, 1 tankard, 1 year old heifer. "...to be

116

delivered to them when they become of age..." Wit: WILLIAM KENNEDY, GEORGE
COCKBURN. August Court 1736. JOHN WYNNS D.C/C.

E 9   ABRAHAM JORDAN TO JOHN BYRD
       Sep. 29, 1735. 175 pds. for 340 A. Part of tract containing 640 A.
granted to Capt. ROBERT WEST on Dec. 1, 1712. Conveyed by him to SOLOMON
JORDAN. On NS Cashy River "at the River Pocoson" adj. ROBERT BYRD, WILLIAM
GARDNER. "...it being all the land I now hold...." Between WILLIAM GARD-
NER, JOSEPH SKITTLETHORP, JOHN AIRS. Wit: ROBERT SHARMAN, THOMAS HAWKINS,
JOHN BUTLER. August Court 1736. JOHN WYNNS D.C/C.

E 11   RICHARD BYRD TO EDWARD BYRD
       Feb. 6, 1735. 500 pds. for 200 A. On NS Cashoke Creek at Miery
Branch "it being the branch that parts COLL. ROBERT WEST...." To head of
Folly Branch; to Beaver Dam Swamp. Wit: ROBERT SHERMAN, RICHARD S.(?)
PICKERING, JOHN BYRD. August Court 1736. JOHN WYNNS D.C/C.

E 13   EDWARD BYRD TO MIKEL KING
       May 5, 1736. 200 pds. for 250 A. Part of a tract granted EDWARD
BYRD on Oct. 9, 1716. At fork of Maple Branch adj. JOHN HOLBROOK at Round
Pocoson, also adj. THOMAS MITCHELL. Wit: ROBERT SHARMAN, JOHN BUTLER,
WILLIAM BYRD. August Court 1736. JOHN WYNNS D.C/C.

E 14   THOMAS RYAN & WIFE MARTHA TO JACOB PARROTT
       May 1, 1735. 200 pds. for 200 A. In Ducking Run "joyning on Mr.
DUCKINGFIELDs land", JOHN HARDY, THOMAS ASHLEY, JUN., "to LUCRITE HICK
land" at Troublesome Branch. Wit: EDWARD RAZER, WILLIAM ASHLEY, JOHN PAD-
GETT. August Court 1736. JOHN WYNNS D.C/C.

E 16   CHARLES GAVIN TO WILLIAM ROGERS
       Sep. 20, 1735. "sixty barrills of good and merchantable Pitch" for
500 A. adj. AARON OLIVER. Wit: JOHN PADGETT, NICHOLAS FAIRLESS, jurat.
August Court 1736. JOHN WYNNS D.C/C.

E 17   THOMAS MANDEW TO BENJAMIN BUNN
       Aug. 11, 1735. 100 A. Gift. "...to my grandson, BENJAMIN BUNN...
(land...whereon the said BENJAMIN BUNN's Mother now lives...." On SS
Corory (corary) Swamp. Wit: ISAAC RICKS, H. TUDAR, jurat. August Court
1736. JOHN WYNNS DC/C.

E 19   THOMAS MANDEW TO JAMES TINER
       Aug. 7, 1735. 45 pds. for 620 A. On SS Kerby Creek on Branch
Carony. 620 A. formerly granted to THOMAS MANDEW on April 1, 1723. Wit:
WILLIAM BUNN, jurat, H. TUDAR. August Court 1736. JOHN WYNNS D.C/C.

E 20   DOM REX TO JOHN WYNNS
       April 5, 1741. Grant. 150 A. "GEORGE the second by the Grace of
God of Great Britain, France and Ireland, King, Defender of the Faith...."
Land on ES Chinkapin Creek. Adj. JOHN SMITH at Flat Swamp and Killem Swamp
"...To hold...as of our manner of Greenich in our County of Kent...paying
to us and our heirs and successors forever the yearly rent of four shillings proclamation for every hundred acres...." Land must be cleared and
cultivated at rate of 3 A/100 A. Signed: "GABRIEL JOHNSTON, Esq. our Captain General and Governor in chief at Edenton." By His Ex'c'ly's Command
NATHANIEL RICE, Sec't'y. ROBERT HAMILTON, Dep.

E 22   JOHN WYNNS TO HENRY VANPELT
       May 12, 1741. 50 pds. for 150 A. "...my right title and interest
...to within tract...." Wit: WILLIAM BLY, JOHN KENNEY. May Court 1741.
BENJAMIN HILL C/C. JOHN WYNNS D.C/C.

E 22   WILLIAM BALDWIN TO JOHN WILLIAMS
       Jan. 12, 1735. *. 113 A. In "upper parish Bertie" on NS Meratock
River on WS Little Swamp. Part of tract formerly granted to JOSEPH LANE
for 213 A. on Feb. 1, 1725 and sold to BALDWIN by LANE. Wit: THOMAS PHIL-
LIPS, jurat, SAMUEL DUKE. August Court 1736. JOHN WYNNS D.C/C.

E 23   RICHARD PACE, JUN. TO WILLIAM NICHOLS of Upper Parish Nansemond
       County, Va. July 29, 1736. "ten pds current Spanish money by
weight" for 340 A. Two plantations on NS Maratuck River. Part of 340 A.

granted to DAVID CUMING March 1, 1719 (190 A.). Sold by CUMING to ALEX-
ANDER BANE. The remaining part purchased by WILLIAM PACE: 50 A. of WILLIAM
FROST; the other 100 of DAVID CUMING. Conveyance dated May 16, 1726. Wit:
WILLIAM PACE, MOSES COLEMAN, jurat. August Court 1736. JOHN WYNNS D.C/C.

E 26   THOMAS SMITH TO FRANCIS MYRICK of Isle of Wight County, Va.
        Sep. 22, 1735. "a valuable sum" for 300 A. By patent dated Febru-
ary 1, 1725 on NS Morratock River at mouth of Lizard Creek. Wit: LEWIS
DATRIE, JOSEPH PARKER, jurat, CHARLES TRAVERS, jurat. August Court 1736. *

E 27   THOMAS HARRINGTON TO JAMES PARHAM
        June 24, 1736. 10 sh. for 260 A. (One year lease.) Two tracts on
NS Roanoke River "part of a greater quantity formerly granted to RALPH
MASSON...." (1) Purchased by HARRINGTON of JOHN COLSON (160 A.) adj. RALPH
MASSON, GURBAVILLE (TURBAVILLE), FOSTER MASSON. (2) Purchased by HARRING-
TON of JOHN TURBAVILL. 100 A. on WS Turbavil Run adj. JOHN COLSON on WS
Raccoon Branch at RALPH MASONs Line. Wit: ALEXANDER SOUTHERLAND, WILLIAM
SHORT. August Court 1736. JOHN WYNNS D.C/C.

E 29   THOMAS HARRINGTON TO JAMES PARHAM
        June 25, 1736. 48 pds. for 260 A. On NS Roanoke River. (This is
sale of above described land.) Wit: ALEXANDER SOUTHERLAND, BATT. PATTERSON,
WILLIAM SHORT. August Court 1736. JOHN WYNNS D.C/C.

E 31   JOHN FARROW TO JOHN SMELLY
        Aug. 9, 1736. 3 pds. 7 sh. for 50 A. Part of patent of 200 A.
granted to JOHN FARROW on April 1, 1723. On SS Maherring River and Kirbey
Creek. Wit: ROBERT SMELLE, BENJAMIN JOYNER. August Court 1736. *.

E 32   JOHN BRYANT TO WILLIAM BRYANT
        May 12, 1736. Gift. 100 A. "...tender effection, love and good will
I bear unto my son WILLIAM BRYANT...." Plantation whereon I now dwell...
being land purchased of WILLIAM BOON. "...from after the day of my death
...but in case (he) should die without issue of his body...(to) return to
my son BARNABE BRYANT...." Wit: JOHN DAVIS, JOHN DAVIS, JUN. August Court
1736. JOHN WYNNS D.C/C.

E 33   MICHIAL DORMAN TO GEORGE DOWNING
        Jan. 6, 1735. "a likely Negro man or woman" for 608 A. On SS Ura
Swamp, WS Ura Path. By patent of MICHAEL (MICHIAL) DORMAN. Wit: JAMES
BRYANT, jurat, JOHN SUTTON. November Court 1736. JOHN WYNNS D.C/C.

E 34   FRANCIS PARKER TO HUGH HORTON (HORTEN)
        Nov. 9, 1735. 50 pds. for 140 A. "at a Beech at the confluence (of)
Potecasie Creek and Panther Swamp...." Wit: JOHN HORTEN, WILLIAM MEARS.
November Court 1736. JOHN WYNNS D.C/C.

E 35   WILLIAM CURLEE TO JOHN COTTON (COTTEN)
        Nov. 9, 1736. 50 pds. for 200 A. On NS Ahosskey Marsh adj. JOHN
COLTON at head of Little Branch adj. WILLIAM CURLEE. Part of patent grant-
ed to SARAH SMITH for 640 A. Wit: ALEXANDER CAMPBELL, GEORGE POWELL.
November Court 1736. JOHN WYNNS D.C/C.

E 37   OEN (OWEN) MACKDANIEL (MCDANIEL) TO EDWARD TOOLE
        Aug. 1, 1736. 25 pds. for 200 A. At Jumping Run and Flagg Run adj.
THOMAS BUSBY. Part of a patent formerly granted to JOHN NAIRN dated April
5, 1720. Made over by conveyance to OEN MACKDANIEL in 1725. Wit: JOHN
HARRELL, JOHN HARRELL, JUN., GEORGE HOUSE. November Court 1736. *.

E 39   WILLIAM KINCHEN, SEN. TO GEORGE WILLIAMS
        Nov. 1, 1736. "a valuable sum" for 300 A. "...a valuable sum paid
by GEORGE WILLIAMS to MATTHEW KINCHEN, Dec'd. of Isle of Wight County...
which I acknowledge in behalf of MATTHEW KINCHEN unto GEORGE WILLIAMS...."
Adj. FRANCIS BOYKINS. Part of a patent to JAMES TURNER granted by Hon.
CHARLES EDEN containing 540 A. dated March 1, 1709. Land in Cypress Swamp
on NS Maherring River. Made over May 1733 to WILLIAM WILLIAMS and by WIL-
LIAMS to MATTHEW KINCHEN. Now in actual possession of GEORGE WILLIAMS.
Wit: JOHN EDWARDS, jurat, R. WILLIAMS. November Court 1736. *.

E 41   RICHARD VICK of Virginia TO WILLIAM SHUFFELL

November *, 1736. 50 pds. for 200 A. On Potekesey Creek and SWS
Piney Branch near Pattays Delight and Tinseys(?) Branch. Granted by paten
April 1, 1723. Wit: ALEXANDER CAMPBELL, JOHN RISE (RESE?). November
Court 1736. JOHN WYNNS D.C/C.

E 42   JOHN MOORE TO TITUS MOORE
       March 21, 1735/36. 12 pds. 10 sh. for 100 A. Part of a conveyance
made over by THEOPHILUS WILLIAMS to JOSEPH BALLARD dated March 1, 1727/28.
Wit: THOMAS HARRELL, GEORGE HOUSE, HENRY AVEREY. November Court 1736. *.

E 44   JAMES PARKER, JUN. TO JOHN BARNES (BARNS), "joyner"
       Oct. 8, 1736. 10 pds. for 350 A. Part of a patent to JAMES PARKER,
SEN. on NS Cashy Swamp. Wit: FRANCIS HOBSON, JAMES HATCHESSON. November
Court 1736. JOHN WYNNS D.C/C.

E 45   THOMAS WALTON, JUN. of Chowan Precinct TO THOMAS HANSFORD
       Nov. 8, 1736. 20 sh. for 278 A. One year lease. Land on Chowan
River adj. THOMAS WARR, ROBERT WARREN, WILLIAM BROGDEN. Being land con-
veyed to WALTON by JOHN GLOVER and MARY, his wife. Wit: J. PRATT, JOHN
WYNNS, THOMAS CREW. November Court 1736. JOHN WYNNS D.C/C.

E 46   THOMAS WALTON (WALTEN), JUN. & WIFE SARAH of Chowan Precinct TO
       THOMAS HANSFORD. Nov. 9, 1736. 400 pds. for 278 A. Land prev-
iously leased for one year. On Chowan River adj. THOMAS WARR, WILLIAM BROG-
DEB. "...land lately conveyed to said WALTON by JOHN GLOVER...." Wit: J.
PRATT, JOHN WYNNS, THOMAS CREW. "...SARAH WALTON, privately examined by
JOHN EDWARDS, Gent. one of the Justices of our said Court, declares that
she acknowledges her dowrie thereto freely...." November Court 1736. *.

E 49   JOHN BALLARD of Edgecombe Precinct TO JOHN MOORE
       Feb. 10, 1735. 25 pds. for 200 A. Between Cossey and Maratuck River.
Wit: HENRY AVERE, PETEGROVE SALSBERRY, jurat, THOMAS HARRELL. November
Court 1736. JOHN WYNNS D.C/C.

E 50   JAMES HUTCHESSON TO THOMAS DAUGHTRIE
       Nov. 9, 1736. 15 pds. for 320 A. At head of Catawitskey Swamp. Adj.
____MAUL. Wit: JOHN SUTTON, WILLIAM EDENS. November Court 1736. *.

E 52   JOHN HATCHER of Edgecombe Precinct TO THOMAS WIMBERLY
       Feb. 2, 1736. 40 pds. for 579 A. On SWS Cashy Swamp adj. MARTIN
GARDNER. Part of a patent formerly granted to EDWARD MOOR on July 20, 1717.
Wit: JOHN WIMBERLY, NEEDHAM BRYANT, jurat, PETEGROVE SALSBERRY. November
Court 1736. JOHN WYNNS D.C/C.

E 54   JAMES WOOD & WIFE SARAH TO ABRAHAM CARNAL, SEN. of "upper Nansemond
       parrish in the Colony of Virginia" Nov. 11, 1736. 110 pds. for
840 A. (1) On SS Maratock River in Edgecombe Precinct bought by JAMES WOOD
from JOHN WILLIAMS. Deed dated December 16, 1728. (2) "another percel" of
200 A. in Edgecombe Precinct on SS Morrattock River which JAMES WOOD bought
of WILLIAM BROWN on April 13, 1734. On Beaverdam in the River Pocoson adj.
DANIEL MACKDANIEL. Wit: ROBERT BUTLER, JOHN BATTLE, JOHN BROWN. "...SARAH,
the wife of said JAMES WOOD, being privately examined by THOMAS HANSFORD,
Gent., one of the Justices of the said court, declares that she acknowledges her dowrie thereto, freely, which motion is declared registered...."
November Court 1736 JOHN WYNNS D.C/C.

E 56   ALEXANDER VALINTINE (VALLANTINE), cooper, TO HENRY VALLANTINE
       Aug. 16, 1736. Deed of gift. 220 A. "...to answer the last request
of my now deceased Brother, james vallintine, late of this Precinct, with
consideration of the love I bear unto my Brother, HENRY VALLANTINE...(the)
plantation on which my brother JAMES lived...." Land conveyed to JAMES
VALLINTINE by CULLMER SESSUMS assignee of JAMES BOONE, "patentee." Wit:
JOHN WYNNS, PETER EVANS, BENJAMIN WYNNS. November Court 1736. *.

E 57   WILLIAM PAGETT, JUN. TO MARTIN NOWELL
       June 12, 1736. 30 pds. for 100 A. At head of Mare Branch adj. WIL-
LIAM PAGETT. At "...a line parting the said land and MAULs land." Wit:
JOHN WYNNS D.C/C.

E 59   EDWARD TIDMON (TIDMAN) & WIFE MARGRETT TO DANIEL BROWN

Nov. 4, 1736. 40 pds. for 100 A. On Chinkapin Creek adj. JOHN
YOUNG(?), WILLIAM DOWNING, FRANCIS BROWN. "being plantation lately belong-
ing to RICH'D BROWN, deceased...." Wit: JOHN WYNNS, jurat, JAMES JENKINS,
SARAH WYNNS. November Court 1736. JOHN WYNNS D.C/C.

E 60   ROBERT EVANS, yeoman, TO GODFREY HOOKER & BENJAMIN HOOKER
        Nov. 8, 1736. 12 pds. for 100 A. "...GODFREY HOOKER, late of the
said Precinct, deceased, pursuant to...his last will and Testament...convey
...to BENJAMIN HOOKER, an infant son to the said GODFREY...." Land on WS
Chowan River Pocoson at Fairchild Branch. Wit: JOHN WYNNS, jurat, BENJAMIN
WYNNS, JOSEPH WYNNS. November Court 1736. JOHN WYNNS D.C/C.

E 61   JOHN MORRISS, "tarburner," TO JOHN WYNNS
        Nov. 6, 1736. 150 pds. for 300 A. On SS Wiccacon Creek adj. land
lately Capt. BOON's and now in possession of WYNNS. From Long Branch to
"the main road" to a path that goes to WILLIAM HOOKER's. At Tarr Kiln
Branch and Flatted Gutt "joyning on s'd WYNNS now Dewlling Plantation."
Wit: THOMAS BARKER, jurat, JOHN KEEFE, ELIZABETH BOONS. November Court
1736. JOHN WYNNS D.C/C.

E 62   ROBERT EVANS, yeoman, TO ROBERT FORSTER late of Edenton
        Nov. 9, 1736. 35 pds. for 40 A. Land on WS Chowan River Pocoson
adj. ROBERT FORSTER and Fairchild Branch. Wit: JOHN WYNNS, BENJAMIN WYNNS,
THOMAS BARKER, jurat, JOSEPH WYNNS. November Court 1736. JOHN WYNNS D.C/C

E 63   THOMAS BYRD, cooper, TO BENJAMIN WYNNS
        Nov. 10, 1736. 80 pds. for 300 A. On SWS Chowan River adj. SAMUEL
WILLIAMS. Wit: JAMES BAKER, jurat, HENRY BYRD. November Court 1736. *.

E 64   THOMAS BANKS TO WILLIAM LEWIS, "cordwainer"
        Nov. 10, 1736. Deed of Gift. 200 A. "...unto my son-in-law WILLIAM
LEWIS...." Land in Chinkapen Neck adj. JOHN VANPELT "being my plantation
in Plum Tree Neck formerly conveyed to ABRAHAM BLEWLET from WILLIAM BUSH."
Wit: ISAAC LEWIS, THOMAS LEE, jurat. November Court 1736. *.

E 65   JOHN MCFARLIN & WIFE THOMASIN TO JOHN GRAY
        Sep. 23, 1735. "...for love; respect we bear to our loving friend,
JOHN GRAY, and more especially for his bond for three hundred pounds...for
our maintainance for our natural lives...(the) plantation where we now live
in Chowan Precinct" Also all cattle, hogs, a black horse, 3 beds and furniture, pots, "kittles", axes, hoes "and all & sundry of our movables mentioned and unmentioned...by the delivery of one Turf, and the goods by the
delivery of one chear before the assigning & ensealing hereof...." Wit:
JOSEPH HARDE, GEORGE TURNAGE, jurat. N.C. Court Nov. 1, 1735. W. SMITH,
C.J. JOHN WYNNS D.C/C.

E 66   NICHOLAS BOON TO JOHN BRYANT
        Feb. 10, 1735. 4 pds. for 100 A. On SES Coresey (?) Swamp. Part
of a patent granted to THOMAS BOON for 250 A. dated August 4, 1723. Wit:
EDWARD CHITTY, ELIAS FORT(?), STEPHEN STRICKLAND. February Court 1736. *.

E 68   ROBERT ANDERSON TO JOHN JOHNSON
        Jan. 29, 1736. 70 pds. for 540 A. ("beside the hundred excepted").
"...all that tract of land with the appurtenances thereunto belonging, excepting one hundred acres lying upon WILLIAM SMITH's line...." Adj. JOHN
SESSIENS "up Churyantock"(?). Wit: GEORGE PIERCE, jurat, HELEN OVERSTREET.
February Court 1736. JOHN WYNNS D.C/C.

E 69   WILLIAM CRAWLEY of Virginia TO GEORGE NORWOOD
        Jan. 22, 1736. 20 pds. for 320 A. On NS Morrattock River "the low-
ard Half of a tract of land that way surveyed for the said HENRY JONES; for
which he obtained a patent the 28 day of July 1713, from the counsel bord
in North Carolina...." Wit: DAVID RAZOR (REZOR), JOHN GLOVER, jurat, ANNE
RAZOR. February Court 1736. JOHN WYNNS D.C/C.

E 70   MARTIN LYONS TO WILLIAM NORWOOD
        * 1736. 2 pds. for 40 A. At Bear Branch adj. WILLIAM GLOVER, ABRA-
HAM SCOTT, JOHN GLOVER, WILLIAM NORWOOD. Wit: JAMES PARRISH, NATHAN NOR-
WOOD. February Court 1736. JOHN WYNNS D.C/C.

E 72   THOMAS ALTMAN of "upper Parrish of the Isle of W. County" TO WILLIAM
        CRAFFORD (CRAFFERD) Feb. 1, 1736. 8 pds. for 200 A. On SS Meher-
ring River at Kirbey's Creek on Meadow Branch and Maple Branch. Wit: JAMES
BROWN, JOHN LOHEN. February Court 1736. JOHN WYNNS D.C/C.

E 73   NICHOLAS BOONE (BOON) TO CAROLAS ANDERSON
        Feb. 7, 1736. 6 pds. for 150 A. On SES Corewy(?) Swamp. Part of a
patent granted to THOMAS BOONE for 250 A. on Aug. 4, 1723. Wit: THOMAS
BOON, JOHN DICKENSON, JOHN BRIENT. February Court 1736. JOHN WYNNS D.C/C.

E 74   WILLIAM DOWNING, SEN. of Mount Pleasant in Bertie TO WILLIAM DOWNING,
        JUN. of Boston, New England, marriner. January 1736. 825 A(plus).
(1) 100 A. on WS Chowan River formerly called Woodward's land bounded by
patent formerly granted to JOHN SMITH. Except 100 A. in possession of JO-
SEPH NEWBY. (2) 100 A. on SS Wiccacon Creek adj. JOHN YOUNG, FRANCIS BROWN
at Reedy Branch. (3) 1/2 tract cont. 450 A. Bounded by a deed from WILLIAM
STEPHENS & ELIZABETH STEPHENS to WILLIAM SHARP dated July 7, 1714. (4) A
tract in Chowan Precinct bounded by a patent granted by CHARLES EDEN to
WILLIAM DOWNING dated Dec. 6, 1720. Wit: JOHN WYNNS, jurat, SARAH WYNNS,
EDWARD TIDMAN. N.C. Court February 14, 1736. W. SMITH, C.J. *.

E 76   WILLIAM DOWNING, SEN. of Mt. Pleasant in Bertie TO WILLIAM DOWNING,
        JUN. of Boston, New England, marriner. Jan. 12, 1736. Gift.
"all my right, title, interest, property, claim and demand whatsoever...in
my estate of inheriatnce in Newfoud land at St. John's Harbour...." Wit:
JOHN WYNNS, jurat, SARAH WYNNS, EDWARD TIDMON. February Court 1736. *.

E 77   WILLIAM DOWNING, JUN., marriner, of Boston, New England TO WILLIAM
        DOWNING, SEN. Jan. 12, 1736. "...bound in the sum of one thou-
sand pounds current money of said Province...the condition of the above
obligation is such that WILLIAM DOWNING, JUN....hath received a deed of
gift of four percels of land lying in North Carolina...WILLIAM DOWNING, JUN.
(and heirs) will in all things consent...and abide by...the future disposal
of the said WILLIAM DOWNING, SEN. other lands and estate...." Wit: JOHN
WYNNS, jurat, EDWARD TIDMON, SARAH WYNNS. February Court 1736. *.

E 78   WILLIAM DOWNING, JUN., marriner, of Boston, New England TO WILLIAM
        DOWNING SEN. of Mt. Pleasant, Bertie. Jan. 12, 1736. "...in con-
sideration of Deed of Gift (of land) in Newfoundland at St. John's Harbour
...do pay or cause to be paid...one full half of all the issues, rents and
clear profits of the estate of inheritance which shall acrue...dureing the
natural life of...WILLIAM DOWNING, SEN...also in consideration aforesaid I
bind myself in case a Bill of Exchange, drawn by him the said WM. DOWNING,
SEN. on one JOHN MASTERS of Bristol, for fifty pounds sterling, be not answered nor twenty pounds sterling put thereof, to pay unto the bearer of the
said bill...upon demand, provided no future draught be made thereon...."
Wit: JOHN WYNNS, jurat, SARAH WYNNS, EDWARD TIDMON. February Court 1736.*.

E 79   SOLOMON ALSTEN TO JOHN PERRY of Chowan Precinct
        Dec. 15, 1736. 20 pds. for 260 A. At mouth of Bryant Branch on Bar-
beque Swamp at Chinkapin. Adj. FRANCIS MACLENDON. Wit: RICHARD BOND,
WILLIAM PERRY. February Court 1736. JOHN WYNNS D.C/C.

E 80   THOMAS TULLY (TULLEY) TO DANIEL O'QUIN, SEN. (OCQUIN)
        Dec. 2, 1736. 6 pds. for 167 A. In Northern woods of Morattock
River on SS Pottacasie Creek adj. THOMAS FUTERELL. Which land was purchas-
ed of JOHN GODLEY. Granted to GODLEY by patent bearing date Aug. 2, 1729.
Wit: JOHN SUTTON, jurat, EDWARD HENDERSON. February Court 1736. *.

E 82   ISAAC SANDERS TO JOHN THOMAS
        Dec. 8, 1736. 80 pds. for 100 A. NS Wiccacon Creek at mouth of
Horsehung Branch "to the German's line." Wit: JOHN BROWN, BENJAMIN WYNNS.
February Court 1736. JOHN WYNNS D.C/C.

E 83   BENJAMIN WARREN TO GEORGE WHITE
        Feb. 13, 1727/28. 50 pds. for 150 A. On Obreys Branch adj. HENRY
BRADLEY, JOHN SMITH, ____BARKER. Wit: LEWIS BRYAN, jurat, HENRY BRADLEY.
February Court 1727. EDWARD MASHBORNE D.C/C.

E 85   GEORGE WHITE TO GEORGE SMITH

          Feb. 28, 1735. 80 pds. for 150 A. "within mentioned plantation."
Wit: GEORGE TURNIDGE, JAMES HOLLEY, jurat. February Court 1736. *.

E 85   THOMAS GOFFEE of "Terryll Precinct" TO BENJAMIN WYNNS
          Jan. 18, 1736. 40 pds. for 100 A. On NWS Wiccacon Creek at mouth of
JOSEPH WYNN's Mill Swamp at Turkey Cock Branch. "...one lease for fifteen
years, bearing date Nov 13th Anno Domini 1734 only excepted...." Wit:
JOSEPH WYNNS, jurat, WILLIAM WYNNS. February Court 1736. JOHN WYNNS D.C/C

E 87   JOHN EARLY, SEN. TO JOHN PERRY (PERREY) of Chowan Precinct
          Feb. 8, 1736. 10 pds. for 340 A. On NS Quakison Swamp "according to
courses of the Patent." Wit: JOHN EARLY, JUN., SOLOMON ALSTON, jurat. February Court 1736. JOHN WYNNS D.C/C.

E 88   JOHN JENKINS of Edgecombe Precinct TO SAMUEL ALLEN
          Feb. 7, 1736. 5 pds. for 100 A. Land adj. ANDREW BARON, LEWIS WIL-
LIAMS, JAMES WOOD. Wit: JAMES BARFIELD, jurat, THOMAS THARP. February
Court 1736. JOHN WYNNS D.C/C.

E 89   NICHOLAS TOMPSON & WIFE SARAH of Surry County, Va. TO GREEN HILL
          Nov. 20, 1736. 20 pds. for 330 A. On NS SAndy Run adj. WILLIAM GRAY,
OWEN MCDANIEL, RICHARD MILTON. Wit: JOHN HART, THOMAS HART. February
Court 1736. JOHN WYNNS D.C/C.

E 91   ANNE TUDAR, "widdow", TO THOMAS RAYSON
          Jan. 27, 1736. 5 pds. for 100 A. "...The said land is taken out of
a tract of land that was formerly granted to GEORGE STEPHENSON; six hundred
& forty acres Patent bearing date the eight day of August Anno Domini 1728
...." Adj. JOHN WILLIAMS at Village Swamp. Wit: THEOPHILUS WILLIAMS,
jurat, JOHN HERRARD, HENRY BAKER, JUN. February Court 1736. JOHN WYNNS *.

E 93   EDWARD BRYAN, SEN. of Craven Precinct and County of Bath TO THOMAS
          BYRD, JUN. Dec. 13, 1736. 65 pds. for 317 A. On WS Canaan Swamp
at Great Branch. Between THOMAS BYRD, JUN. and JAMES MAGLOHAN. Wit: HENRY
BYRD, jurat, LUCE BRYAN, LEWIS ____. *. JOHN WYNNS D.C/C.

E 95   JOHN KEEFE TO TREDDLE KEEFE
          Dec. 9, 1736. Trade. 50 A. "...in consideration of a percel of
land on Flat Swamp...conveyed to JAMES AVERETT...." Land now traded on SS
Wiccacon Creek at Keef Swamp adj. JOHN WYNNS, THOMAS WYNNS, TREDDLE KEEFE's
"manner plantation." Wit: JOHN WYNNS, GEORGE SMITH, JOHN WILLIAMS. February Court 1736. JOHN WYNNS D.C/C.

E 96   JOHN BROWNE TO ISAAC SANDERS
          Dec. 8, 1736. 20 pds. for 100 A. "By the Path Side." Wit: JOHN
THOMAS, BENJAMIN WYNNS. February Court 1736. JOHN WYNNS D.C/C.

E 97   JOHN THOMAS TO ISAAC SANDERS
          Dec. 8, 1736. 80 pds. for 200 A. On ES Holly Swamp at Catron Creek
Road. Adj. JOHN BROWN, EDWARD HARE, WILLIAM DOWNING, land formerly WILLIAM
DANIEL's, land formerly JAMES RUTLAND's. Wit: JOHN BROWN, BENJAMIN WYNNS.
February Court 1736. JOHN WYNNS D.C/C.

E 98   ISAAC BRAWLEY TO CULIMER SESSUMS
          Nov. 20, 1736. 80 pds. for 350 A. "...land conveyed to me from
MATTHEW TOBIAS SWANNER & JANE his wife by a Deed; dated the twenty second
day of Aprill Anno Dom. 1730...(excepting ten feet square, including my
Mother's Grave...)...." Wit: JOHN WYNNS, JOSEPH WYNNS, BENJAMIN WYNNS,
jurat, WILLIAM WYNNS. February Court 1736. JOHN WYNNS D.C/C.

E 99   LAURENCE BAKER of Isle of Wight Co., Va. TO WILLIAM CARTER
          Dec. 16, 1735. 3,000 pds. pork for 310 A. "...land whereon said
CARTER dwells...." Patented to BAKER April 1, 1723. Wit: JAMES CARTER,
jurat, RICHARD WIGGINS, THOMAS THACK. February Court 1736. JOHN WYNNS *.

E 101   LUKE MIZLE TO SUSANAH MIZLE, "my daughture"
          Feb. 7, 1737. 50 pds. for 200 A. "...joyning upon the land of
EDWARD COLLINS, JOHN LEGETT and JAMES LEGETT in Kesia Neck...." Wit: JAMES
WARD, JA(MES) PRICE. February Court 1736. JOHN WYNNS D.C/C.

E 102   LUKE MEAZLE TO EDWARD & MARY COLLINS
        Feb. 7, 1737. *. 250 A. "...natural love and effection...unto ED-
WARD COLLINS and MARY his wife...and to heirs of said EDWARD begotten on
the body of the afores'd MARY and (in) default of such issue to the aforesaid EDWARD and his issue...." Land in Kesia Neck adj. JOHN COLESON. Wit:
JAMES WARD, jurat, JAMES PRICE. February Court 1736. JOHN WYNNS D.C/C.

E 103   JAMES WOOD TO WILLIAM PICKET
        Dec. 10, 1735. 10 pds. for 100 A. On Catawitsky Meadow adj. PATRICK
O'QUIN. Wit: JOHN SUTTON, jurat, DANIEL O'QUIN, JUN. February Court 1736.
JOHN WYNNS D.C/C.

E 105   HENRY JERNIGAN (JARNAGAN) of Nansemond Co., Va. TO JOHN BLACKMAN
        Nov. 29, 1735. 10 pds. for 100 A. Part of a tract formerly granted
to GEORGE STEVENSON for 640 A. dated Aug. 8, 1728. Wit: NEEDHAM BRYAN,
THEOPHILUS WILLIAMS, jurat. February Court 1736. JOHN WYNNS D.C/C.

E 107   JOHN EDWARDS, SEN. & WIFE MARY TO JOHN EDWARDS, JUN.
        Oct. 23, 1736. Gift. "...love unto our loving son, JOHN EDWARDS...
our plantation whereon we now live; and one negro fellow Tom and two negro
girls called Dena and Phillis; one feather bed and furniture...in consideration...for JOHN haveing paid or post bond for a debt due from us to
THEOPH'S PUGH, merchant, in Virginia, being eight thousand weight of fresh
pork...(we make over) to our son for his safety all goods and chattles...
lands, negroes, stock of cattle, horses, hoggs and movables of all sorts...
(he) permitting us to live in the house...during our natural lives, and
provide for us food and payment according to his circumstances...." Wit:
THOMAS WHITMELL, GARRARD VANUPSTALL, jurat. February Court 1736. *.

E 108   JOHN EDWARDS, SEN. & WIFE MARY TO JOHN EDWARDS, JUN.
        Oct. 23, 1736. Deed of Gift. "A true and just Inventory of what
(we give) our dutifull son, JOHN EDWARDS....":

one negro man	two iron kittles
two negro girls	one copper d'o.
one feather bed & furniture	four pewter dishes
one chest	four plates
one trunk	eleven pewter basons
one mare	nine head of sheep
all stock of hoggs	all my cattle
two iron potts	300 A. land

Wit: GARRARD VANUPSTALL, jurat, THOMAS WHITMELL. February Court 1736. *.

E 109   HENRY BRADLEY, JUN. of Craven Precinct TO EDWARD WILLIAMS
        Sep. 4, 1736. 100 pds. for 70 A. On Chinkapen Neck at mouth of
Spring Branch. Adj. NICHOLAS SESSUMS "acruing quitrents & the Publick
mortgage only excepted." Wit: JOHN WYNNS, JOSEPH WYNNS, jurat. February
Court 1736. JOHN WYNNS D.C/C.

E 110   SIMON HOMES TO WILLIAM BAKER & JAMES BAKER
        Dec. 10, 1736. 9 pds. for 50 A. "excepting one acre whereon the
mill shall stand on Snake Branch. To William Baker during his natural
life, and afterwards to his son, JAMES BAKER, his heirs and assigns forever. Wit: GEORGE BRAWLER, JOHN WYNNS, jurat. February Court 1736. *.

E 111   WILLIAM WHITEHEAD of Edgecombe Precinct TO ANDREW TAYLOR (TAYLER,
        TAYLOE) Feb. 14, 1735. 6 pds. for 100 A. On WS Marratock River
and Uraha Swamp. Adj. JAMES GRAY, THOMAS TAYLOE. By patent granted to
WILLIAM WHITEHEAD for 490 A. Wit: JOHN EDWARDS, jurat, ELIAS FORT. February Court 1736. JOHN WYNNS D.C/C.

E 113   WILLIAM SMITH TO EDWARD COLLINS
        Jan. 12, 1735. 250 pds. for 185 A. On Rocquiss "on the Indian Line"
Adj. ROBERT ANDERSON, JOHN SESSIONS. Wit: HUGH GRIMES, JOHN WATSEN, JOHN
LEGGETT, jurat. February Court 1736. JOHN WYNNS D.C/C.

E 114   RICHARD BRASSWELL TO JAMES WOOD
        April 8, 1737. 100 pds. for 500 A. On WS Farriss's Branch adj. JON-
ATHAN STANLEY. Wit: JOHN SUTTON, GEORGE DOWNING, jurat, JACOB BRASSWELL.
May Court 1737. JOHN WYNNS D.C/C.

E 115   RICHARD MYRICK & WIFE ELIZABETH TO RICHARD MOOR (MOORE), SEN.

Sep. 18, 1736. 60 pds. for 240 A. On NS Roanoke adj. THOMAS AVANT.
By patent granted Feb. 24, 1729. Wit: RICHARD CUERTON, jurat, WILLIAM
AVENT, THOMAS AVENT, jurat. May Court 1737. JOHN WYNNS D.C/C.

E 117 RICHARD MYRICK & WIFE ELIZABETH TO RICHARD MOORE, SEN.
    Sep. 18, 1735. 60 pds. for 300 A. "...land that I bou't. of JONA-
THAN DAVIS and THOMAS AVENT and was granted by Patent unto CHARLES KIMBLE,
it being the remaining part of KIMBLE's Survey...for (530A.) dated the
first of Aprill 1723...." Adj. JOHN MOOR's land bought of THOMAS AVENT for
230 A. Wit: RICHARD CUERTON, jurat, WILLIAM AVENT, THOMAS AVANT, jurat.
May Court 1737. JOHN WYNNS D.C/C.

E 119 JAMES BALFOUR & WIFE ELIZABETH of Hanover County, Va. TO RICHARD
    MOOR, SEN. Nov. 17, 1736. 20 pds. for 640 A. On NS Moratuck
River adj. THOMAS EVANS on Stoney Creek. Being land that was granted Capt.
JOHN GADDY by patent for 640 A. dated March 1, 1719. Wit: BUCKLEY KIM-
BROUGH, jurat, WILLIAM WESSTON, ELIZABETH KIMBROUGH. May Court 1737. *.

E 121 JOHN ALSTON of Chowan Precinct TO THOMAS PILAND
    Feb. 18, 1736. 40 pds. for 124 A. On SES Ahoskey Swamp by patent
dated April 1, 1723 to GEORGE POWELL. Conveyed by deed to ALSTON August
11, 1726. Wit: HENRY BAKER, JOSEPH VANN, MARY NORRIS. May Court 1737. *.

E 123 SAMUEL POWERS TO GODFREY LEE
    May 9, 1737. 30 pds. for 480 A. Land commonly called "the Mulberry
Old Fields." On NS Chowan River adj. GODFREY LEE, COLL. WILLIAM LITTLE. On
Fort Branch "bounded by the patent." Wit: J. EDWARDS, JOHN DAWSON, jurat,
THOMAS BRYANT. May Court 1737. JOHN WYNNS D.C/C.

E 124 RICHARD BRASSWELL, JUN. of Edgecombe Precinct TO JOHN DAWSON
    June 4, 1736. 10 pds. for 76 A. On Oura(?) Meadows adj. GEORGE
STEPHENSON and "his father's corner tree." Wit: WILLIAM WILLSON, jurat,
EZEKIAL FULLARD. May Court 1737. JOHN WYNNS D.C/C.

E 125 JOHN DEW, JUN. TO JOHN WORRILL
    May 9, 1737. 10 pds. for 250 A. On SS Meheron River and SS Kirby
Creek at Ready Branch. Wit: WILLIAM RICKS, JACOB RICKS, SARAH STONE. May
Court 1737. JOHN WYNNS D.C/C.

E 127 JOHN DEW, SEN. TO HENRY GAY
    Nov. 4, 1736. 7 pds. 10 sh. for 150 A. On WS Chowan River and Bock-
horn Swamp. Part of a tract granted to JOHN DEW by patent. Adj. WILLIAM
GAY, JOHN DEW, ABRAHAM DEW, JOHN CHACHERS. Wit: JOHN DEW, JUN., JOHN
DEBERRY. May Court 1737. JOHN WYNNS D.C/C.

E 129 HENRY VIZE, carpenter, TO WILLIAM MIDDLETON, carpenter
    Dec. 8, 1736. 60 pds. for 150 A. On Horse Swamp adj. JOHN CLARK.
Subject only to quit rents and "one mortgage to the Treasury of Bertie Precinct for thirty pounds (to wit: the payments hereafter growing due only
excepted)...." Wit: ANTHONY WEBB, JAMES OVERTON, NATHANIEL NICHOLAS. May
Court 1737. JOHN WYNNS D.C/C.

E 130 CHARLES JONES, JUN. TO HENRY VIZE
    May 10, 1737. 42 pds. for 260 A. Between LANLOW (LANCELOT) JONES &
CHRISTOPHER HOLLYMAN on "Hodgskey Swamp" at Stoney Creek and Stoney Creek
Road. Wit: FINCHER HAYNES, WILLIAM WARREN, WILLIAM WILLIAMSON, jurat. May
Court 1737. JOHN WYNNS D.C/C.

E 131 GEORGE SMITH & WIFE CHRISTIAN of Chinkapen Creek TO JOHN WYNNS
    Jan. 18, 1736. 140 pds. for 150 A. Land on Chinkapen Creek (Neck)
adj. Wiccacon Creek and "the Main Road near the entrance of the causeway of
Wiccacon Bridge." Adj. DENNIS MCCLENDON, deceased, and JOHN MORRIS. "...
excepting twenty feet square including the Burying Place thereon..." Wit:
EDWARD TIDMON, JOHN HALLUM, ALLEN VOLLANTINE, jurat. May Court 1737. *.

E 133 JOHN WYNNS TO THOMAS JOHNSON
    May 9, 1737. 5 pds. for 20 A. on Wiccacon Creek and ES "of the
Gutt" to Pole Bridge Branch. "...excepting 20 feet square where the Burying Place is...." Wit: JOHN HALLUM, PETER WEST. May Court 1737. *.

E 134 JOHN KEEFE (KEEF) & TREDDLE KEEFE TO JOHN WYNNS

Nov. 18, 1736. 30 pds. for 100 A. On SS Wiccacon Creek being called "the Blind Islands." Adj. WILLIAM DOWNING, THOMAS MANN "at the edge of the Hills next to the said TREDDLE KEEFE's Ferry." Wit: ELIZABETH BOON, WILLIAM STOKES, JOHN HOOKER, JOSEPH WATSFORD, JOHN WILLIAMS. May Court 1737. JOHN WYNNS D.C/C.

E 135 JOHN MALPUSS TO WILLIAM WILLIAMSON
May 2, 1737. 50 pds. for 260 A. In two parcels)1) At the mouth of Chinkapen Branch 100 A. (2) On SWS of mouth of Chinkapen adj. "JAMES BOONs former line (now WILLIAM ROGERS)", "THOMAS ROGER's former line (now the said WILLIAMSONs)." Wit: JOHN WYNNS, WILLIAM HOOKER, jurat, PETER WEST. May Court 1737. JOHN WYNNS D.C/C.

E 137 JOHN RASBERRY TO JOHN THOMAS
*. 50 pds. for 100 A. On Conaritsis Swamp and ES Rattlesnake Branch at Buck Branch. Adj. ROBERT LANIER (LYNEARS). Wit: THOMAS LEE, FRANCIS MCCLENDON. May Court 1737. JOHN WYNNS D.C/C.

E 138 GEORGE DOWNING TO SIMON WEST
May 11, 1737. 50 pds. for 150 A. On SS Catawhitskey Swamp. Adj. COLL. MAUL, JAMES WOOD. Wit: JOHN SUTTON, JOHN DICKENSON, DANIEL DICKENSON. May Court 1737. JOHN WYNNS D.C/C.

E 140 ROBERT FORSTER of Edenton TO JOHN WYNNS
June 4, 1736. Power of atty. "...to execute and perform my office as deputy clerk of the said precinct..." Authorized to pay Mr. JOHN HODG-SON any or all such monies (excepting his own salary and debts owing to MARTIN LYONS and necessary disbursements for "my" plantation). Also power to build or improve plantation and "to dispose of negroes or other appurte-nances...." Wit: JOHN MATHES, JOHN HODGSON. May Court 1737. JOHN WYNNS *.

E 141 THOMAS RYAN & WIFE MARTHA TO PENELOPE PHENEY (PHENNEY), spinster
May 5, 1737. 50 pds. for 200 A. On the Sound adj. Mr. CULLEN POLLOCK. "Received of PENELOPE PHENNEY the sum of fifty pounds current money of Virginia, being the consideration within mentioned...I have pri-vately examined Mrs. MARTHA RYAN...she vollantarly consented to the sign-ing...." May 7, 1737. J. HOLLBROOK. Wit: J. HOLLBROOK, BENJAMIN HILL, THOMAS JONES, JOHN WYNNS DC/C.

E 142 LORDS PROPRIETORS TO WILLIAM ROADS
April 1, 1723. Grant. 640 A. "...according to one great Deed of Grant, bearing date the first day of May anno Domini 1668, given unto our County of Albemarle...doe hereby grant ROADS...a tract of land containing six hundred and forty acres...." On WS Cypress Swamp at COLL. MAUL's corner. For importation of persons: 50A/person. Rent of 1 sh. a year to be paid 29th September. Provided he "plant or cause to be planted within three years" Signed: WM. REED, Esq. President of "councel." Wit: J. LOVICK, FRANCIS FOSTER, M. MOORE, RICHARD SANDERSON. Sec't'y's. Office. J. LOVICK, sec't'y.

E 143 HENRY RODES TO THOMAS FREEMAN
Sep. 22, 1733. *.*. "...my right, title and intrest of within men-tioned Patent...." Wit: JOHN PARKER, THOMAS WALLIS. N.C. Court August 13, 1737. W. SMITH, C.J. JOHN WYNNS D.C/C.

E 144 FRANCIS BENTEN (BENTON) TO JOHN CARRILL
Nov. 13, 1736. 100 pds. for 340 A. On Elm Swamp. "...mine by Patent bearing date November the twelf one thousand seven hundred & twenty three...." Wit: WILLIAM WHITFIELD, ELIZABETH WHITFIELD, jurat, JOBE STAPLES. August Court 1737. JOHN WYNNS D.C/C.

E 145 SAMUEL CHAMBERLIN of Virginia TO JOHN RICHARDS
April 29, 1737. 40 pds. for 470 A. Adj. ARTHUR KAVANAUGH(KANANAUGH) at Falling Run on "HARRINGTON's line" and "MALLORYes line." Wit: JOSHUA STEP(?), jurat, GEORGE SENIOR, THOMAS O'CANING(?), H. HARRIS. August Court 1737. JOHN WYNNS D.C/C.

E 147 HENRY TURNER of Edgecombe Precinct TO THOMAS HART
Aug. 6, 1736. *. for 100 A. "...the residue of a Patent that was granted to HENRY TURNER by the Hon. CHARLES EDEN, Esq....March 1, 1719."

Patent for 167 A. Wit: THOMAS HART, jurat, WILLIAM WALKER. August Court 1737. JOHN WYNNS D.C/C.

E 148   THOMAS FUTERELL, SEN. TO JAMES LASITER
        March 3, 1735. 40 pds. for 185 A. On NWS Yeaurah Swamp "to the middle branch." Wit: JOHN SUTTON, THOMAS FUTERELL. August Court 1737. JOHN WYNNS D.C/C.

E 149   FRANCIS MCCLENDEN TO EDWARD TIDMAN (TIDMON)
        Feb. 8, 1736. 60 pds. for 100 A. On SS Stony Creek at "the corner tree in the Patent line of the whole survey," adj. Stoney Creek Road. Wit: JOHN WYNNS, M. LYONS. February Court 1736. *.

E 151   EDWARD TIDMON TO JOSEPH BURDELL of Chowan Precinct, "tayler"
        July 27, 1737. 60 pds. for "the aforementioned percel of land."
Wit: JOHN WYNNS, jurat, BENJAMIN WYNNS. August Court 1737. JOHN WYNNS *.

E 154   SAMUEL PEACOCK TO JOHN PEACOCK
        May 2, 1736. Deed of Gift. 100 A. "...love, goodwill & affection ...to my loving son, JOHN PEACOCK...." Adj. ABRAHAM BURTON (BURTEN). "...to him and the male heirs of his body lawfully begotten, forever..." Wit: WILLIAM ELDRIDGE, NICHOLAS MUNGER, ARTHUR WILLIAM, JUN. August Court 1737.

E 155   SAMUEL PEACOCK & WIFE MARY TO LAWRENCE SMITH of Virginia
        April 5, 1737. "a valuable sum" for 640 A. On NS Pottekasy Swamp and NS Morrattock River. A patent granted to HENRY COMPTON by Sir RICHARD EVERARD by date Dec. 1, 1727. Wit: SAMUEL TAYLER, FRANCIS DELOATCH, MARY TAYLER. August Court 1737. *.

E 157   WILLIAM PEEKE TO JOHN WILLIAMS, cooper
        April 15, 1737. 20 pds. for 500 A. On WS Holly Branch and Miery Branch adj. MICHAEL HILL, FRANCIS MCCLENDON. Wit: JOHN WYNNS, jurat, SARAH WYNNS, ELIZABETH BOON. August Court 1737. *.

E 158   JOHN HERRING, JUN. & WIFE REBECCA TO JOSEPH HARDEE (HARDY)
        March 17, 1736. 160 pds. for 150 A. On ES Cashy River adj. JOHN HOW, EDWARD MOOR at mouth of Licking Branch "thence along lines of Patent." Wit: THOMAS TURNER, JOHN ROWS, SESSION(?) HERRING, jurat. "I, REBECCA HERRING, wife of JOHN HERRING, JUN. do assign over...all my right of dowrie of the within deed...." Wit: JOHN PRICE, CATRINE HERRING. August Court 1737.

E 160   JOHN COWARD & WIFE ELIZABETH TO JOSEPH WIMBERLY
        March 28, 1737. 50 pds. for 250 A. Adj. WILLIAM CHARLTON. Wit: EDWARD VAN, HENRY VAN, JONATHAN TAYLOR (TAYLER), jurat. August Court 1737.*.

E 161   WILLIAM SPEIGHT of Nansemond Co., Va. TO FRANCIS PARKER
        Aug. 9, 1737. 15 pds. for 150 A. At "Beaver Dam Swamp at the Bridge and running down the Road to the head line." At mouth of Spring Branch. Wit: RICHARD WITHFERD(?), FRANCIS SPEIGHT, JOHN BREWER. August Court 1737.

E 163   HENRY HORNE TO THOMAS HORNE
        July 6, 1737. 20 pds. for 110 A. On upper end of Ahoskey Pocoson adj. JOHN DAVISON. Land bought of HENRY BAKER, and granted to WILLIAM FAULK by patent for 110 A. Feb. 1, 1725. Wit: CHARLES HORNE, MICHAEL HORNE, MOSES HORNE. August Court 1737. *.

E 165   NATHANIEL SANDERS & WIFE MARY TO THOMAS HART
        March 21, 1735. 30 pds. for 200 A. On NS Marotuck River at Miery Marsh. Adj. WILLIAM HILLIARD. Wit: JOHN HART, HOWELL BROWN, jurat. August Court 1737. *.

E 166   JOHN RASBERRY & WIFE BRIDGET TO JONATHAN KITTERLIN of Chowan Precinct. July 26, 1736. 30 pds. for 470 A. On Conritsy Swamp and Buck Branch. Adj. ROBERT LANIER, THOMAS POLLOCK. Wit: JOSEPH BORDILL, JAMES MAGLAHON, JOSEPH ARLINE. August Court 1737. *.

E 168   HENRY BAKER TO PETTIGROVE SALSBERRY
        Aug. 10, 1737. 30 pds. for 640 A. On SS Morattock River. Patent granted to WILLIAM GRAY April 1, 1725 and by GRAY sold to WILLIAM GRIFFIN

by deed dated Feb. 13, 1727, and by GRIFFIN sold to HENRY BAKER by deed
dated Aug. 12, 1728. Wit: JOHN HENARD, HENRY BAKER, JUN. Aug. Court 1737.*.

E 169   JOHN WYNNS TO THOMAS FINCH
        * 11, 1737. 50 pds. for 155 A. Adj. PETER WEST, ROBERT LANIER. Wit:
BENJAMIN HILL, JOHN POWERS. Aug. Court 1735. *.

E 171   JOHN WHITE, SEN., yeoman, TO WILLIAM WESSON of Chowan Precinct
        June 9, 1737. 400 pds. for 320 A. Adj. EDWARD BRYAN, MEDIA WHITE.
Wit: JOHN HOWELL, jurat, JOHN WESTON. Aug. Court 1737. *.

E 172   JACOB RICKS & WIFE ESTHER TO JAMES HUTCHESSON
        Aug. 9, 1737. 60 pds. for 600 A. At mouth of Placket Branch on Anton-
key Marsh. Adj. HARDY COUNSELL, RICHARD WASHINGTON. Wit: WILLIAM RICKS,
JOHN SUTTON. Aug. Court 1737. ESTHER RICKS was privately examined by ROW-
LAND WILLIAMS, GENT., one of the Justices of "our said court". *.

E 174   PETEGROVE (PEDEGEVE) SALSBERRY TO GEORGE SPIVEY of Nansemond Co, Va.
        Nov. 4, 1737. 200 Pds. for 300 A. Adj. WILLIAM HINTON, THEOPHILUS
WILLIAMS, THOMAS BOND. "out of a Patent granted to WILLIAM GRAY" dated Apr.
1, 1725. Wit: EPAP. MOOR, LITTLETON SPIVEY. Nov. Court 1737. *.

E 176   WILLIAM KINCHEN & WIFE MARY TO JOHN DEBERRY
        Nov. 5, 1737. 95 pds. for 627 A. On Meherring River at mouth of
Middle Branch. At "Boon's corner tree". Wit: WILLIAM KINCHEN, JUN., THOMAS
HUMPHREY, jurat. Nov. 1737. *.

E 178   GEORGE STEVENSON TO WILLIAM LIVINGSTON
        Sept. 7, 1730. 120 pds. for 363 A. Adj. WILLIAM GRAY on Sandy Run.
At mouth of Haw Branch adj. ROBERT SHERWOOD. "is part of two tracts of land
the one formerly granted to ROBERT SHERWOOD for (640A.) dated fifth Aprill
one thousand seven hundred and twenty; the other granted to GEORGE STEVEN-
SON for three hundred and thirty four acres dated the first day Febry. one
thousand seven hundred and twenty five..." Wit: W. RUFFEN, jurat, SARAH
RUFFEN, THOMAS WATSON. Nov. Court 1737. "Present his Majesty's Justices".*.

E 179   BENJAMIN FOREMAN of Edgecombe Precinct TO MARMADUKE NORFLEET of
        Perquimmons Precinct   Aug. 7, 1737. 7 pds. for 100 A. On NS Mora-
tuck adj. GEORGE WILLIAMS. Part of a patent for 500 A. formerly granted
March 1, 1721. Wit: JOHN ANDERSON, JOHN HINE(?), JOSEPH WALL, Pat. Car.
N.C. Court 1737. Present his majesty's Justices. *.

E 180   WILLIAM BALDWIN of Surry Co., Va. TO THOMAS HOWELL, JUN.
        May 10, 1737. 20 pds. for 250 A. "...being lower half of a certain
tract first granted to WILLIAM JONES for six hundred and forty acres...
dated (Feb. 26, 1711)...and by him conveyed to said BALDWIN..." On Moratuck River between WILLIAM BALDWIN, JOHN BALDWIN. Wit: JOHN BALDWIN, jurat,
RICHARD MESSEY, SUSANAH MESSEY. N.C. Court Nov. 1737. "Present his Majestys
Justices". *.

E 182   THOMAS BRADFORD & WIFE ELIZABETH & SAMUEL NORWOOD & WIFE MARY TO
        BARRABY MELTON   Sept. 3, 1737. 20 pds. for 150 A. On NS Moratuck
River "beginning at the bent of a Branch, binding on MELTON's own land..."
Part of a tract granted to WILLIAM REEVES for 440 A. dated March 13, 1721.
Wit: JAMES SMITH, JOHN CLARK, JOHN PATTERSON. N.C. Court Nov. 1737. *.

E 184   JOHN JERNAGAN of Nansemond Co, Va. TO THOMAS CARRELL
        Oct. 7, 1733. 60 pds. for 100 A. On SS Loosing Swamp. Wit: THOMAS
JONES, WILLIAM STANDLEY, JACOB JERNIGAN. N.C. Court 1737. *.

E 187   JOHN RASBERRY TO JOHN PORTER, JUN. of Nansemond Co., Va.
        Nov. 8, 1737. 15 pds. for 300 A. On SWS of a branch of Cashie River
adj. JOSEPH HOVER(HOOERD's?). Wit: JOHN RASBERRY, JOHN COLE. N.C. Court
1737. "Present his Majesty's Justices." *.

E 188   ALEXANDER CAMPBELL TO SIMEN (SIMON) WEST
        Dec. 1, 1736. 50 pds. for 150 A. On SS Catawhickey Swamp adj. Coll.
MAUL, JAMES WOOD. Wit: JAMES WOOD, SARAH WOOD. N.C. Court Nov. 1737. *.

E 190   HENRY BAKER of Chowan Precinct TO JOHN CAMPBELL
        Feb. 14, 1737. 40 pds. for 130 A. On WS Chowan River adj. _____

BEVERLY, "line formerly THOMAS JERNIGAN's, line formerly JAMES BOON's now JOSEPH ANDERSON's...". Part of a patent granted to WILLIAM MAUL (MAULE) dated April 1, 1720. Conveyed by MAULE to said BAKER. Wit: BENJAMIN HILL, DAVID MEADE, JOSEPH ANDERSON. Feb. Court 1737. *.

E 191 JAMES BROWN TO EDWARD HARRELL
       Dec. 24, 1737. 12 pds. for 260 A. "in the fork between the South & Middle Branch of the Cashy at the neck where the two branches meet". Adj. THOMAS MANN. By patent formerly granted to GEORGE WILLIAMS. Wit: JOHN HARRELL, FRANCIS PARKER. Feb. Court 1737. *.

E 193 PHILLIP PEARCE of Edgecombe Precinct TO JOHN BALLARD
       Feb. 13, 1737. 10 pds. for 150 A. Part of a tract PEARCE bought of DANIEL MCDANIEL on Conneyhoe Creek. Adj. ARTHUR SHERROD, JOHN FORT. Wit: ROBERT BUTLER, WILLIAM EVERETT. Feb. Court 1737. *.

E 194 PHILLIP PEARCE of Edgecombe Precinct TO ARTHUR SHERROD "of precinct aforesaid". On SS Conneyhoe Creek in Edgecombe Precinct. Part of tract bought of DANIEL MCDANIEL. Adj. WILLIAM BARDEN, JOHN BALLARD and Old Indian Path. Wit: CHARLES HORNE, JOHN BALLARD. Feb. Court 1737. *.

E 195 JAMES SMITH "of Terell Precinct" TO RICHARD ALLEN
       Feb. 14, 1737. 30 pds. for 100 A. On NS Moratuck at Runarry Marsh. Part of a tract made over by JOHN SPEIR to JAMES SMITH on Sept. 10, 1733. Bounded by "a tree called Deer's Eyes". Adj. JOHN YEALVENTON (YELVERTON) at Deep Marsh on the dividing line between GEORGE POLLOCK & JAMES SMITH. Wit: SAMUEL ALLEN, PATRICK OCQUIN. Feb. Court 1737. *.

E 197 THOMAS JONES & WIFE ANNE TO JOHN MOOR (MOORE), blacksmith
       Feb. 13, 1737. 400 pds. for 963 A.(?) Land in Bear Swamp near Kesia River. 423 A. by patent dated March 5, 1721/22. "the other containing five hundred and forty acres contained by patent bearing date the 19th day of January 1715". Wit: JONATHAN STANDLEY, WILLIAM STANDLEY. Feb. Court 1737.*.

E 199 WALTER LASHLEY of Virginia TO PATRICK LASHLEY & WILLIAM LASHLEY
       Aug. 17, 1737. 5 pds. for 640 A. "beginning at a Hoggberry JOHN GILLUM's corner tree" to Dogwood Hill and Pine Hill on the River. Wit: JOHN GILLUM, jurat, JAMES MACLIMER. Feb. Court 1737.*.

E 200 RICHARD PACE TO EDWARD EARP
       Feb. 13, 1737. 15 pds. for 250 A. On NS Mooratock River adj. Coll. POLLOCK, SAMUEL PEET, JOHN GILLUM, "a line of GREEN's & PACE's". Part of a patent granted to RICHARD PACE for 500 A. on July 28, 1720. Wit: THOMAS BRYANT, THOMAS PACE, SAMUEL PEETE. Feb. Court 1737. *.

E 202 RICHARD PACE, JUN. TO ROBERT DUKES
       Feb. 13, 1737. 13 pds. for 200 A. On NS Chowanoke Swamp, NS Moratoke River, NS Yawnehoke Swamp. Part of patent granted to JOHN GREEN on March 1, 1719. Part sold to RALPH MASON and by MASON sold to RICHARD PACE, SEN. Part of patent sold to BARTHOLOMEW CHAVAS and by him sold to BARNABY MACKINNEY, SEN. This part now conveyed was sold by GREEN to RICHARD PACE, JUN. Land adj. RICHARD PACE, SEN., BARNABY MCKINNEY, ROBERT DUKES. Wit: WILLIAM PACE, jurat, GEORGE POWERS. Feb. Court 1737. *.

E 203 JAMES BARNES (BARNS) & WIFE MARTHA TO JOHN MCWILLIAMS (MACWILLIAMS)
       Feb. 14, 1737. 50 pds. for 180 A. Plantation bought of JOSEPH WIMBERLY. 140 A. of the 180 A. "that did and doth still belong to the plantation, the other forty beginneth and is boundeth thus:" Adj. FORT's Meadow, ROBERT RUFFIN, "as will apear by Deed given from WIMBERLY to me". Wit: JOHN DAWSON, WILLIAM KILLINGSWORTH, BENJAMIN STEVENSON. Feb. Court 1737. *.

E 204 WILLIAM PATCHETT (PATCHET) of Craven Precinct TO JOSEPH NEWBY of Perquimmons Precinct. Feb. 4, 1737/38. 100 pds. for 127 A. On WS Chowan River adj. DENNIS MACKLENDLE. Wit: EBENEZER HASON, JONATHAN MILLER. Feb. Court 1737. *.

E 207 JAMES RUTLAND TO WILLIAM EDENS
       Aug. 15, 1737. 15 pds. for 30 A. On NS Moratuck River between Sandy Run and Ahoskey Pocoson. Adj. GEORGE STEVENSON at Licking Branch. Adj. THOMAS WATSON. Part of tract formerly granted to ROBERT SHERWOOD for 640 A. on April 5, 1720 "and is now come due the said RUTLAND". Wit: CHARLES HORNE,

WILLIAM GRADDY. Feb. Court 1737. *.

E 208 JOHN GILLUM of Surry Co, Va. TO HOSEA TAPLEY
       June 13, 1737. 70 pds. for 600 A. On NS Maratock River "in an Is-
land" Adj. WILLIAM WYCH. Granted to HINCHY GILLUM, deceased. Wit: JOHN
GILLUM, JUN., GEORGE JORDAIN, GEORGE JORDAIN, JUN., jurat, ANNE JORDAIN.
Feb. Court 1737. *.

E 210 JOHN HERRING, JUN. & WIFE REBECCA TO JOHN HOW
       April 7, 1737. 100 pds. for 150 A. On NES Cassay River. Part of a
tract patented by THOMAS JONES and purchased by JOHN HERRING, JUN. of JOHN
JONES, son of THOMAS JONES deceased. At a dividing line between HERRING &
HOW. Adj. JOHN EDWARDS at Licking Branch. Wit: JOHN HERRING, CHARLES BAR-
BER, JOHN WALLIS, jurat. Feb. Court 1737. *.

E 212 RICHARD PACE TO SAMUEL PEETE,"phisein"
       Feb. 13, 1737. 25 pds. for 250 A. On NS Maratock River. Adj. Coll.
POLLOCK at Yarahaw Swamp. Wit: THOMAS BRYANT, EDWARD EARP, THOMAS PACE,
jurat. Feb. Court 1737. *.

E 213 COLL. ROBERT WEST TO WILLIAM SHOALER (SHOLER)
       Feb. 15, 1737/38. 20 pds. for 400 A. On WS Cashy Swamp. Wit: JONA-
THAN STANLEY, JOHN SHOLER. Feb. Court 1737.*.

E 215 COLL. ROBERT WEST TO DANIEL HYSMITH
       Feb. 15, 1737/38. *. for 400 A. On WS Cashy Swamp on Bevardam. Wit:
JONATHAN STANLEY, JOHN SHOLAR. Feb. Court 1737. *.

E 216 JOHN WEBB & WIFE ANN TO COLL. ROBERT WEST
       Feb. 7, 1737. 50 pds. for 100 A. On Beverdam Swamp at Poplar Branch
and Miery Branch. Adj. CAPT. DAVID HENDERSON "which was land left by Mr.
THOMAS BALL unto his Daughter, now wife unto JOHN WEBB, and the said WEBB
and his wife do hereby acknowledge...sale". Signed: JOHN WEBB, ANN WEBB,
WILLIAM BALL. Wit: HANNAH DOYLE, JOHN HOLBROOK,JOHN HOLBROOK, JUN. Feb.
Court 1737. *.

E 217 JOHN GRAY TO JOHN SHARER
       Aug. 12, 1737. 60 pds. for 320 A. On NS Yourha Swamp at RODGERSES
Branch. Wit: LAWRENCE DAUTREE(DAUGHTREE), jurat, JOSEPH SHERAR. Feb. Court
1737. *.

E 219 ANTHONY HERRING TO JANE GLISSON
       Dec. 14, 1737. 20 pds. for 213 A. Part of a patent formerly granted
to JOHN WILLIAMS and willed unto· ANTHONY HERRING. Adj. WILLIAM HINTON at
Village Swamp. Wit: JOHN HINNANT, jurat, JOHN HARRELL. Feb. Court 1737.*.

E 221 EDWARD BYRD & WIFE ANN TO RODGER SNELL
       *. 200 pds. for 250 A. Adj. MICHAEL KING, JOHN HOLBROOK,EDWARD BYRD,
JOHN BYRD(BIRD), THOMAS MITCHELL. On ES Round Pocoson. Wit: THOMAS SUTTEN,
WILLIAM BIRD, MICHAEL LEE. Feb. Court 1737.

E 223 JANE GLISSON (GLISSEN) TO JOHN HINNART
       *. 2 pds. for 13 A. Part of patent formerly granted JOHN WILLIAMS,
JUN., and made over to ANTHONY HERRING and thence to JANE GLISSEN. On Village Swamp. Feb. Court 1737. *.

E 225 JONATHAN TAYLER (TAYLOR) TO HENRY BATE
       Feb. 1, 1737. 600 pds. for 300 A. On NS Morattuck River adj. _____
MOSELEY. At Quitzna Swamp. Wit: THOMAS WHITMELL, jurat, WILLIAM PIERCE,
REBECCA PIERCE. Feb. Court 1737. *.

E 226 FRANCIS MCCLENDON (MACK CLENDON) TO RICHARD WILLIFORD
       Oct. 25, 1736. 30 pds. for 100 A. On Beaverdam Swamp at "Ploomtree
Branch". Wit: JOHN THOMAS, THOMAS SUTTON. Feb. Court 1737. *.

E 228 JOHN RICHARDS, carpenter, TO JAMES PARHAM
       March 6, 1737. 10 pds. for 100 A. On NS "Morratuck River alis Roa-
noake". Adj. RALPH MASON, ____ HAWTHORN. It is the remainder of MASON's survey. Wit: P. SMITH, W. SHERT(?), WILLIAM REEEDS(?). May Court 1738. *.

E 229 GEORGE TURNAGE TO JOSEPH OATS of Perquimmons Precinct

Feb. 4, 1737/38. 100 pds. for 130 A. On Chinkapin Creek. Adj. JOHN MACKFARLIN, COLL. MAUL "in a meadow by a branch". Wit: THOMAS HANSFORD, PAUL PEARCEY. May Court 1738. *.

E 231 ISAAC WILLIAM & WIFE MARTHA TO THOMAS BOND
Dec. 8, 1735. " a consideration of a likely negro to my liking and ten pounds Virginia currency by bond" for 100 A. On Village Swamp Adj. JOHN WILLIAMS, THEOPHILUS WILLIAMS, ISAAC WILLIAMS. Wit: THEOPHILUS WILLIAMS, JOHN WILLIAMS, jurat. Mary Court 1738. *.

E 233 HENRY JARNEKEN (JARNEKIN) & WIFE ANN TO THEOPHILUS PUGH of Virginia
*. 22 pds. for 100 A. On NS Roanoake River adj. PUGH and JOSEPH BLACKMAN. Wit: NEEDHAM BRYAN, JOHN ABBETT (ABBOTT?), NEEDHAM BRYAN, JUN., jurat. May Court 1738. *.

E 235 LAURENCE MCGUE TO JOHN HOWELL
May 1, 1738. 50 "barrells of good lawful pitch, and in good bar- rells'. For 200 A. On WS Chowan River adj. EDWARD TAYLER. Wit: JOHN HOWELL, JOSEPH HARDE. May Court 1738. *.

E 236 JOHN MANN (MAN) of Edgecombe Precinct TO JAMES BROWN
May 8, 1738. 30 pds. for 640 A. On SWS Cashy Swamp. Wit: JOHN BATTLE, THOMAS MANN, WILLIAM DRAKE. May Court 1738. *.

E 238 JOHN WHITE TO HENRY VANPELT
March 17, 1736. 145 pds. for 200 A. On Chinkapin Swamp. Adj. "JOHN PETTYFERS former corner tree". Wit: THOMAS HANSFORD, jurat, BRIDGET HANS- FERD(?), ELIZABETH LAND. May Court 1738. *.

E 239 EDWARD TIDMAN(TIDMON) & WIFE MARGRET TO DANIEL BROWN
Nov. 4, 1736. 40 pds. for 100 A. On ES Chinkapen Creek. Adj. JOHN YOUNG, WILLIAM DOWNING, CAPT. FRANCIS BROWN "(it being the plantation late- ly belonging to RICH'D. BROWN, dec'd.)". Wit: JOHN WYNNS, JUN., JAMES JENKINS, SARAH WYNNS. Nov. Court 1736. *.

E 240 DANIEL BROWN(BROWNE) TO FRANCIS BROWN, yeoman
March 11, 1737/38. 56 pds. for "all my right, title, interest, property and demand...in...the above land...". Wit: JOHN WYNNS, Jurat, ISAAC LEWIS. May Court 1738. *.

E 241 ROBERT HILL TO THOMAS DELOOCH
Aug. 30, 1737. 5 sh. for 80 A. On SS Fountain's Creek. By patent dated Feb. 22, 1724. Wit: SAM'LL. TAYLOR (TAYLER), jurat. NAT. (?) COOK. May Court 1738. *.

E 243 ROBERT HILL TO THOMAS JORDAIN "of Branswick County", Va.
Oct. 14, 1737. 5 sh. for 80 A. By patent dated Feb. 22, 1724. Wit: EDWARD FLOOD, SAMUEL TAYLOR, jurat. May Court 1738. *.

E 244 JOHN BRETT (BRET) TO WILLIAM AUSTIN
Feb. 12, 1735. 6 pds. 10 sh. for 100 A. On NS Meherin River "being a tract of land formerly relapst by JOHN COUNCIL". Adj. ALEXANDER SHERRETT (SHERED, SHERARD) at Haw Branch. Wit: JOHN POWER, JOSEPH BRETT, jurat, MARY POWER. May Court 1738.*.

E 246 WILLIAM PAGETT (PAGET) & WIFE JANE of Craven Prec't. TO OBEDIAH
SOWELL. April 22, 1737. 17 pds. for 200 A. On Horse Swamp. Adj. RICHARD SOWELL, JUN., CHARLES SOWELL. Wit: JOHN WYNNS, jurat, WILLIAM PAGETT, CHARLES GAVIN, JOHN PAGETT, WILLIAM PAGETT. May Court 1738. *.

E 247 THOMAS JARNAGAN (JARNIGAN) TO JETHREW BUTLER
Feb. 14, 1737/38. 60 pds. for 213 A. On Roanoake River adj. JOHN ELVERTON, JAMES BLOUNT. Wit: WILLIAM WHITFIELD, MATTHEW WHITFIELD, JOHN JONES, jurat. May Court 1738. *.

E 248 JOSEPH WALL, SEN. & WIFE MARY of Edgecombe Prec't. TO SAMUEL TAYLER
(TAYLOR). Feb. 1, 1737/38. "a valuable sum" for 175 A. Part of a patent for 325 A. On SS Meherin River at Cypress Swamp and Old County Line. Adj. ____DELOOCH, ARTHUR COOK, S. TAYLOR. Wit: THOMAS PHILLIPS, jurat, NICHOLAS MONGER, jurat. May Court 1738. *.

E 250   JOSEPH WALL, SEN. & WIFE MARY of Edgecombe Prec't. TO THOMAS PHILLIPS
         Feb. 1, 1737/38. "a valuable sum" for 150 A. Part of patent to
JOSEPH WALL on SS Meherrin River at Old County Line. Wit: SAM'LL TAYLER,
jurat, NICHOLAS MONGER, jurat. May Court 1738. *.

E 251   JOHN BLACKMAN TO DOCTOR JAMES FLOOD of Edgecombe Prec't.
         March 38 (28?), 1737/38. 188 pds. for 100 A. On Village Swamp. Adj.
"widow CHESSER". Wit: SAMUEL SNOWDEN, WILLIAM KILLINGSWORTH, jurat. May
Court 1738. *.

E 253   ROBERT WARREN & WIFE HANNAH TO JOHN MITCHENER
         *. 300 pds. for 980 A. Two tracts (1) Plantation where JOSEPH WARREN
now lives on Horse Swamp adj. JOHN BARFIELD, THOMAS STURGES. Cont. 340 A.
(2) 640 A. formerly bought of JOHN WILLIAMS adj. LAZARUS THOMAS at White
Oad Swamp. Adj. JOHN EARLY. Formerly granted to ARON OLIVER March 11, 1719/
20. Wit: THOMAS HANSFORD, jurat, BRIDGETT HANSFORD. May Court 1738. *.

E 255   DINAH TAYLER of Virginia TO JOSEPH WATSFORD, SEN.
         July 17, 1737. 100 pds. for 640 A. On the "Long Branch of Killum"
at Small Branch and Poly Branch. Adj. THOMAS MANN, JAMES BOON. Wit: JOHN
JOYCE, ALEXANDER VALLINTINE, Jurat. May Court 1738. *.

E 256   THOMAS KERNEY & WIFE SARAH of Edgecombe Prec't. TO DAVID MEADE,
         merchant, of Nansemond, Va.   March 29, 1738. 5 pds. for 229 A. One
year lease. Land on Keisah River "formerly belonging to MARTIN CROMEY and
whereon said KEARNEY lately dwelt". Adj. ____BIRD, LUKE MEASLE. Also a term
of an additional year if desired. Wit: ROBERT FORSTER, jurat, THOMAS JONES.
Aug. Court 1738. *.

E 258   THOMAS KERNEY & WIFE SARAH of Edgecombe Prec't. TO DAVID MEADE of
         Nansemond, Va.   March 30, 1738. 80 pds. for 229 A. Oand now in
possession of MEADE by virtue of previous lease. On Kesia River. Formerly
belonging to MARTIN KERNEY. Adj. ____BIRD, LUKE MEASSLE. Wit: ROBERT FORS-
TER, jurat, THOMAS JONES. Aug. Court 1738. *.

E 262   JOHN MCCASKEY, "sadler", of Tyrrell Prec't. TO JAMES DONAVAN,
         "marriner".   * 22, 1737. 120 pds. for 22 A. On Kesia River on
River Pocoson. Adj. PETER GRAY, PETER STANSELL, dec'd, ARTHUR DUGGALL,
Dec'd. "excepting twenty feet square round about the grave and place where
ARTHUR DUGALL was buried...the same to remain the property of JOHN MCCASKEY,
his heirs...forever...". Wit: WILLIAM ASHBURN, jurat, JONATHAN REDDINGS,
WILLIAM BALL. Aug. Court 1738. *. Note here: At one place in this deed JOHN
MCCASKEY is called "JOHN DONOVAN".

E 264   THOMAS YATES TO JOHN BAZEMORE
         Jan. 21, 1738. 200 pds. for 317 A. On Loosing (Lossing) Swamp. Wit:
WILLIAM YATES, WILLIAM EVENS, JOHN FRYARS. Aug. Court 1738. *.

E 265   HENRY VALLANTINE (VOLLANTINE) TO ALEXANDER VOLLANTINE
         April 8, 1738. 100 pds. for 220 A. On Killum Swamp at mouth of
Holly Branch adj. "the now dwelling place of ALLEX'R. VOLLANTINE". Wit:
JOHN WYNNS, jurat, SARAH WYNNS, BENJAMIN MAYNER. May Court 1738. *.

E 266   OEN MCDANIEL (MACKDANIEL) TO EDWARD TOOLE
         Nov. 29, 1737. 24 pds. for 200 A. Part of patent granted to JOHN
NAIRN April 5, 1720 and since conveyed to OEN MCDANIEL. At Jumping Run
"nigh Flaggy Run" Adj. THOMAS BUSBY "it being the same land that the former
conveyance from OEN MCDANIEL to EDWARD TOOLE was for, but by a default in
laying of the land, did not lay of the said TOOL's due, and now hath made
an addition to make two hundred acres...". Wit: JOHN YELVERTON, JOHN
HARRELL, jurat. May Court 1738.*.

E 268   JAMES SMITH TO JOHN SMITH
         April 19, 1738. 30 pds. for 150 A. Part of a conveyance from JOHN
SPIER to JAMES SMITH on Sept. 10, 1731. At the head of Deep Marsh, Adj.
JOHN YELVERTON, COLL. THOMAS POLLOCK, GEORGE POLLOCK, JAMES SMITH, RICHARD
ALLEN, JOHN SMITH. Wit: JOHN HARRELL, jurat, JONAS MAUND, SAMUEL FALK.
May Court 1738. *.

E 268   JAMES SMITH TO JOHN SMITH
         April 19, 1738. 30 pds. for 150 A. Part of a conveyance lately made

over by JOHN SPIER to JAMES SMITH dated Sept. 10, 1731. Adj. JOHN YELVERTON, Coll. THOMAS POLLOCK, GEORGE POLLOCK, JAMES SMITH, RICHARD ALLEN, JOHN SMITH at the head of Deep Marsh. Wit: JOHN HARRELL, jurat, JONAS MAUND, SAMUEL FALK. May Court 1738. *.

E 270 JOHN HOLLY (HOLLEY) TO EDWARD TIDMON
       March 17, 1737. 50 pds. for 170 A. On SS Wiccacon Creek in Chinka-
pen Neck. Adj. JOHN MORRIS, JOHN VANPELT, ____ BUSH. "Is the land conveyed
to JOHN HOLLY, Dec'd. by JOHN BUSH & RICHARD MALPASS, dec'd., by their sep-
erate deeds joyning together...". Wit: JOHN WYNNS, PETER WEST, SARAH WYNNS,
THOMAS BYRD, JUN., jurat, ESBELL BYRD. May Court 1738. *.

E 271 WILLIAM PACE TO THOMAS PACE
       May 8, 1738. 15 pds. for 340 A. Part of patent granted BARTHOLEMEW
CHEAVONS "being lost for want of seating became due Major BARNABE MACKINNE
for five hundred and forty acres...". On Yaurwehoh Swamp. Patent date
July 30, 1726. Sold by MCKINNE to PACE. "In JOSEPH LANDS Ianwehoh Swamp(?)".
Adj. Cashy Road, DAVID CUMMINGS. Wit: RICHARD PACE, JUN., RICHARD PACE,
SEN. May Court 1738. *.

E 273 HENRY BAKER of Chowan Precinct TO WILLIAM HORNE
       Jan. 20, 1737/38. 25 pds. for 260 A. On Ahosey Swamp (Ahoskey Marsh)
"at head of Branches". Patented to HENRY BAKER April 6, 1722. Wit: CHARLES
HORNE, Jurat, SOLOMON BARFIELD, jurat, CHRIS'N. CUWELL(?). May Court 1738.*.

E 275 JOHN MISHEW TO WILLIAM FROST
       Feb. 20, 1737. 12 pds. for 100 A. On NS Morratock River. Adj. JOS-
EPH REGAN, DANIEL REGAN. Land granted to WILLIAM BALDWIN Dec. 1, 1727. Wit:
JOSEPH RICHARDSON, jurat, JACOB ELLIS. May Court 1738. *.

E 276 WILLIAM CROSBY (CROSBEY) of Onslow Precinct TO ROBERT FORSTER
       March 10, 1737. 11 pds. for 640 A. On SS Pottecasey "being called
Grub Neck" between Pottecasie and Catowatskey Swamp at Blundering Branch.
Adj. ROBERT PARSON. Wit: JOHN BROWN, JOHN BROWN, JUN., jurat, JOSEPH JONES.
May Court 1738. *.

E 278 MICHAEL KING TO JOHN WALLIS
       April 27, 1738. 400 pds. for 540 A. Part of 640 A. tract granted
KING on Feb. 5, 1725. At WILLS Quarter Swamp adj. PATRICK CANADAY, JONATHAN
STANLEY, SEN. Wit: JOHN WYNNS, jurat, THOMAS RYAN. May Court 1738. *.

E 280 BENJAMIN SHERROD of Chowan Prec't. TO HENRY DAWSON of Isle of Wight
       Co., Va.   Aug. 4, 1738. 30 pds. for 100 A. "Being same purchased
of BENJ'A. FOREMAN" On SS Meherring River on Great Creek. Adj. WILLIAM
SHERROD at the "Main Creek". Wit: CHAPLIN WILLIAMS, JOHN DEBERRY, THOMAS
THORNTON(?). Aug. Court 1738. *.

E 281 JAMES HUTCHESSON TO ISAAC HUNTER
       Aug. 4, 1738. 60 pds. for 320 A. In Ahoskey Woods. Adj. Coll. MAUL.
Part of patent dated Aug. 2, 1730. Wit: JOHN HART, W. RUFFIN. Aug. Court
1738. *.

E 282 TREDDLE KEEFE, yeoman, TO JOHN WYNNS, yeoman
       Aug. 4, 1738. 400 pds. for 840 A. Two tracts: (1) 200 A. on SS
Wiccacon Creek "the ferry plantation" at Keef's Swamp. "Land of JOHN WYNNS
conveyed to him by me and my brother, JOHN KEEFE". Also adj. THOMAS MANN.
(2) On "Flat Swamp joyning KILLUM". Cont. 640 A. Adj. PENELOPE MAUL, ALLEX-
ANDER VALLANTINE, FRANCIS BROWN. "except twenty feet square, including the
Burying Place". Wit: GEORGE BOWLER, JOHN WILLIAMS, BRAY HARGROVE. Aug.
Court 1738. *.

E 284 JOHN MALPUSS TO CALEB STEVENS of Chowan Prec't.
       Oct. 17, 1737. 100 pds. for 200 A. By patent to JOHN ODAM dated
April 19, 1719. Adj. LAZARUS THOMAS. Wit: JOHN BYRD, FRANCIS ELLINOR, jurat,
AZURIAH HUSSER (HUSSEN?). Aug. Court 1738. *.

E 285 THOMAS WALTEN (WALTON), JUN. & WIFE SARAH of Chowan Prec't. TO
       MATTHEW SPIVEY, cooper, of Chowan. Oct. 28, 1737. 20 pds. for 100
A. "of woodland ground" at Robin's Beaverdam at Hoskey Swamp. MATTHEW
SPIVEY is son of ABRAHAM SPIVEY. Wit: JAMES BAKER, WILLIAM POYNTER. Aug.
Court 1738. *.

132

E 287 JAMES CASTELLAW, TRASURER, TO JOHN SAVAGE
     April 16, 1737. 101 pds. for 100 A. On WS Kesai River "including
the house and plantation whereon the late MARTIN CROMEN of this Precinct
lived". Adj. JAMES FROST. "Being mortgaged to the publick by the late MAR-
TIN CROMEN, for the sum of seventy pounds, taken out of the Publick Treasury, as appears by his bond to the late Hon'ble Coll. THOMAS POLLOCK,
bearing date Aprill the 30th 1730, and by him forfeited to the Publick for
the non-payment...and by me sold at the Court House at publick vandue...to
JOHN SAVAGE...". Wit: THOMAS SUTTEN, DANIEL HENDRICKS, HENRY DAY. August
Court 1738. *.

E 288 JOHN ROWS TO THOMAS RYAN
     Aug. 8, 1738. 200 pds. for 170 A. On NS Cashia Swamp. adj. Coll.
ROBERT WEST, THOMAS WEST. Wit: EDWARD RASOR (RASSOR), ROBERT SANDERLIN.
Aug. Court 1738. *.

E 289 WILLIAM CURLEE TO THOMAS BARKER
     Aug. 9, 1738. 25 pds. for 440 A. Part of 640 A. granted to SARAH
SMITH on March 1, 1720. On SS Ahoskey Meadow adj. THOMAS DIAL, JOHN COTTON.
Wit: ROBERT FORSTER, DAVID MEADE, JOHN HAFFORD. Aug. Court 1738. *.

E 291 JACOB JARNAGAN & FEABY JARNAGAN & HENRY OBERRY TO JOHN HARRELL
     March 22, 1737. 11 pds. for 24-A. "a tract of woodland" In Cassey
(Carsey) Swamp adj. EDWARD HARRELL, THOMAS MANN(MAN). Wit: EDWARD HARRELL,
JOHN HARRELL, JUN. Aug. Court 1738. *.

E 292 JOHN BAREFIELD & WIFE ELIZABETH "of the County of Bath in Onslow
Precinct" TO WILLIAM CURLEE "of the same County in Craven Precinct"
*. 1738. Gift. 140 A. "out of the pure love and free good-will that we...
bear unto WILLIAM CURLEE". Land at the head of Ahosky Meadows "being land
that was patented to SARAH SMITH" on March 1, 1721. Wit: JOB BROOKS, JAMES
CURLEE, jurat, WILLIAM KELLEY. Aug. Court 1738. *.

E 293 NICHOLAS FAIRLESS, yeoman, TO TREDDLE KEEFE
     Aug. 7, 1738. 125 pds. for 640 A. In Killum Woods. Land now in
actual possession of the said KEEFE. Adj. PENELOPE MAUL, ALEXANDER VAL-
LANTINE. Wit: J. HOLLBROOK JOHN WYNNS. Aug. Court 1738. *.

E 294 MATTHEW TOBIAS SWANNER of Tyrrell Prec't. TO JOHN WYNNS
     July 31, 1738. 1000 pds. for 870 A. "...three percels of land lying
together". On NS Wiccacon Creek. (1) 420 A. adj. JOHN THOMAS, JOSEPH WYNNS,
CULLMUR SESSUMS, EDWARD HARE, JOHN BROWN, JOHN BUSH. (2) Land on Ahotsky
Ridge of 450 A. bounded by patent to SWANNER dated April 5, 1720. Except
about 100 A. conveyed to WILLIAM MEARS. Wit: GEORGE BAWLER(?), jurat, BRAY
HARGROVE, WILLIAM EVANS, MARY WILLOBE. Aug. Court 1738. *. (Note: Although
the deed says it is a transfer of "three percels", only two are actually
listed.)

E 296 MARTIN GRIFFIN "of Terril Precinct" TO EDWARD FRIZBEY, "haltmaker"
     Aug. 5, 1738. 250 pds. for 230 A. On NS Morattuck River "at fork
of the Southern Branch of Rocquiss". Land whereon THOMAS MERSES formerly
lived. Bounded by patent. Wit: ANTHONY WILLIAM, jurat, JAMES WARD(?WARCE?)
Aug. Court 1738. *.

E 297 WILLIAM EVANS TO EDWARD OUTLAW
     Oct. 9, 1736. 150 pds. for 300 A. On horse Swamp. Adj. JACOB LEWIS,
EDWARD HOWARD, ROBERT LANIER. Mine by deed from PELEG ROGERS dated Nov. 13,
1735. Wit: WILLIAM WHITFIELD, EDWARD ROBERTS, JOSEPH JONES, JUN. Aug. Court
1738. *.

E 299 THOMAS THOMPSON & HUGH SCOTT of Boston TO ANDREW THOMPSON
     *. 1800 pds. for "one full sixth part of the plantation on which the
aford DAVID HENDERSON, and of which the said DAVID was seized of in fee
simple...". 580 A. "...and also one sixth part of all and every part of the
lands & plantation belonging to DAVID HENDERSON, containing three thousand
acres...". Land in Tyrrell Precinct. Also 1/6 negroes of DAVID HENDERSON,
1/6 of all stock, 1/6 of all house hold goods, 1/6 of crop of plantation,
and "all within doors, or without". Wit: GEORGE PATTERSON, JAMES CASTELLAW,
THOMAS RYAN, jurat. *.(Note Here: THOMAS THOMPSON of Bertie; HUGH SCOTT of
Boston.)

E 301   JOHN BONDE TO JAMES CARTER of Virginia
        Aug. 23, 1737. 20 pds. for 520 A. On NS Meheron River. Bounded by a
patent dated March 26, 1723. "Excepting twenty acres of the land which is
to be laid off for the said BONDE...lying on the river, joyning to KERSEY's
Landing, the which land is commonly known by the name KERSEY's Neck...".
Wit: GEORGE WILLIAM jurat, JOHN WILLIAMS. Aug. Court 1738. *.

E 302   THOMAS COULDING, of Nansemond Co., Va. TO JOHN STAFFERD
        Aug. 7, 1738. 200 pds. for 300 A. Part of a 530 A. tract granted to
THOMAS JARNIGAN on March 9, 1717. On Pasture Branch adj. JOHN BEVERLEY,
JOHN HOMES at Elm Swamp, Old Cow Path to Flatt Branch "near Meherrin Creek".
Wit: ROBERT FORSTER, T. BARKER, JAMES MANEY. Aug. Court 1738. *.

E 304   ARTHUR BIGGINS of Virginia TO JOHN HILL
        Aug. 1, 1738. 20 pds. for 320 A. On NS Marrattock River. The upper-
most half of a tract surveyed for JOHN HATHHORN that "BIGGINS bought of
HATHHORN & WILLIAM MAUL, Deputy Surveyor" dated Jan. 24, 1712. Wit: JOHN
HILL, jurat, GEORGE BREWER, NATHANIEL HILL. Aug. Court 1738. *.

E 305   JOSEPH WIMBERLY TO ROBERT HUNTER of Chowan
        Aug. 8, 1738. 72 pds. for 300 A. "at dividing line JAMES WILLIAMSON
& JONATHAN TAYLER next to Rocquis Swamp". Part of a patent granted JAMES
WILLIAMSON on April 5, 1729 and part of a patent to JOHN SMITH dated Aug.
7, 1720. Wit: WILLIAM SPUE, JOHN JORDAN, JOHN SUMNER. Aug. Court 1738.*.

E 308   ROBERT SHERMAN (SHARMAN) & WIFE LUCY TO THOMAS RYAN
        Aug. 5, 1738. 200 pds. for 130 A. Adj. THOMAS SUTTON on SS Cashia
River. Adj. "JOSEPH KITTLETHARPS former line". Wit: JOHN WYNNS, CHARLES
SOWELL. Aug. Court 1738. *.

E 309   WILLIAM BALL TO THOMAS RYAN
        Feb. 7, 1737. 100 pds. for 400 A. On Cashoke Swamp adj. Coll. ROBERT
WEST on Beaverdam, Capt. DAVID HENDERSON, JAMES CARTER, JOHN VANTEEN(?).
Wit: JOSIAH REDDICK,THOMAS TODD, jurat, EDWARD RASER. Aug. Court 1738. *.

E 310   WILLIAM CHARLTEN & WIFE MARY TO WILLIAM JORDAN
        May 6, 1738. 250 pds. for 300 A. On Morrattock River adj. WILLIAM
WARD, JOSEPH JORDAN. Wit: JOSEPH JORDAN, jurat, PHILLIP WARD. Aug. Court
1738. *.

E 312   ELIZABETH MATTHEWS TO JOHN WYNNS
        Nov. 5, 1736. 40 pds. for 200 A. On NS Wiccacon Creek adj. RICHARD
HARRELL, THOMAS JOHNSON, WILLIAM BAKER "as reputed and known bounds to the
creek...except twenty feet square, including my father's and three brothers'
& sisters' graves...and JOSEPH MAYNER AND MARY MAYNOR, my guardians and
mother and father-in-law, doth hereby give, and freely surrender up for
part of the consideration money...". Signed: ELIZABETH MATTHEWS, JOSEPH
MAYNOR, MARY MAYNOR. Wit: JOSEPH WYNNS, jurat, BENJAMIN WYNNS, WILLIAM
WYNNS. Aug. Court 1738. *.

E 313   MICHAEL HANLEY & WIFE SARAH TO JOHN JOHNSON
        Aug. 7, 1738. 15 pds. for 340 A. Part of 640 A. patent to RICHARD
MELTON dated May 17, 1731 on SS Mahering River. Wit: MATTHEW SELLERS, JOHN
BARDIN, jurat, BENJAMIN SELLERS. Aug. Court 1738. *.

E 315   JAMES RUTLAND & WIFE ELIZABETH TO JOHN PERREY
        July 24, 1738. 60 pds. for 220 A. Full contents of Patent granted
OEN MCDANIEL dated March 1, 1719 at Poplar Swamp adj. ABRAHAM BLEWLET. Wit:
ROBERT SHARMAN, GEORGE BAWLER. Aug. Court 1738. *.

E 317   ABRAHAM SHEPPARD & CATERNE(?) TO JOHN WIMBERLY
        *. 50 pds. for 400 A. at fork of Cashy Swamp at Miery Branch. Wit:
JAMES CASTELLAW, EDWARD OUTLAW, MATTHEW WHITFIELD. Aug. Court 1738.*.

E 319   WILLIAM CHARLTEN & WIFE MARY TO JOSEPH JORDAN
        May 6, 1738. 100 pds. for 300 A. "all that tract whereon I now live"
Adj. RICHARD SWAIN at head of Sakeykee(?) Creek at Spring Branch adj. ____
WARD, ____SWAIN. Wit: WILLIAM JORDAN, jurat, PHILLIP WARD. Aug. Court 1738.*.

E 321   THOAMS DAVIS TO WILLIAM CATHCART, merchant
        Aug. 10, 1738. 150 pds. for 400 A. In Ahotskey Swamp adj. JAMES

HOWARD, CHARLES JONES, ROBERT LANIER. Wit: ROBERT FORSTER, T. BARKER. Aug. Court 1738. *.

E 322 OSBURN (OSSBURN) JEFFREYS TO WILLIAM HILLIARD
        Aug. 8, 1738. 30 pds. for 300 A. On NS Morrattuck River at Cow Meadow. Tract formerly granted SIMON JEFFREYS on Aug. 3, 1725. "and by him relapst for want of seating and due to said OSBURN JEFFREYS by an order of council, bearing date the 17th day of March 1728...". Wit: J. BODDIE, BENJAMIN JOHNSTON. Aug. Court 1738. *.

E 323 WILLIAM MEAZELL (MEAZEL) of "Terrell Precinct" TO JOHN SMITHWICK
        *. 250 pds. for 100 A. On NS Moratuck River. Part of a larger tract bought of EDWARD SMITHWICK at Opossum Hill Creek. Wit: CHARLTEN MIZELL, JOHN MIZELL, WILLIAM JORDAN, jurat. Aug. Court 1738. *.

E 325 GEORGE STEVENSON TO PATTRICK ROOCH
        Aug. 1, 1738. 25 pds. for 100 A. At Sandy Run on East Prong of Haw Branch. Part of a tract formerly granted ROBERT SHERROD for 640 A. dated April 5, 1720. Wit: W. RUFFIN, jurat, THOMAS WALTEN, WILLIAM LIVINGSTON. Aug. Court 1738. *.

E 326 WILLIAM DUFFILL & WIFE SARAH TO THOMAS WALTEN
        *. 15 pds. for 150 A. On ES Fourth Branch at Briery Branch adj. "line formerly belonging unto JOHN DAVISEN". Wit: WILLIAM PERREY, jurat, MATTHEW SPIVEY. Aug. Court 1738. *.

E 328 JOHN HERRING & WIFE CATHERINE TO WILLIAM BYRD
        July 22, 1738. 500 pds. for 600 A. Patent by JOHN HERRING Oct. 8, 1717 at WILLS Quarter Swamp. Wit: ARTHUR WILLIAMS, JOHN HERRING, JUN., JAMES CORRIE. Aug. Court 1738. *.

E 329 WILLIAM RUFFIN & WIFE SARAH TO ROBERT RUFFIN
        Nov. 14, 1738. 50 pds. for 278 A. On Horsepen Meadow at Pole Meadow. Adj. RICHARD BRASSWELL, JOHN COLTEN (COTTEN). Wit: JOHN HART, JOEL NEWSOME, NATHANIEL RUFFIN. Nov. Court 1738. *.

E 331 FRANCIS MALLORY of Virginia TO STEPHEN RAGLAND
        *. 100 pds. for 320 A. On NS Morattock River. Being the lower half of a tract granted to JOHN HATHHORN for 640 A. on July 29, 1712. Wit: JOHN HILL, EVAN RAGLAND, THOMAS MATTHEWS, jurat. Aug. Court 1738. *.

E 333 STEPHEN RAGLAND & WIFE MARY TO EVAN RAGLAND
        *. 8 pds. for 200 A. On NS Moratuck River at Double Bottom Branch. Adj. RICHARD TURBERVIL at TURBERVIL's Branch. Land bought of RICHARD CUERTON (?CRERTRIN?). Wit: WILLIAM SHORTER, THOMAS MATTHEWS, jurat. Aug. Court 1738. *.

E 334 JOHN PERREY & WIFE SARAH of Chowan Precinct TO ISAAC HUNTER "of
        county and Precinct aforesaid". June 13, 1737- 55 pds. for 640 A. Being in Rich Square. Land formerly granted to TIMOTHY CUNINGHAM on March 9, 1717 "and became due EDWARD HOWCOTT by Order of Council bearing date the 11th day of Nov. 1724". Patent date July 30, 1724. Wit: HENRY HUNTER, RICHARD BOND, ELISHA HUNTER. Aug. Court 1738. *.

E 337 EDWARD OUTLAW, JUN. TO RICHARD SANDERS
        April 15, 1738. 100 pds. for 300 A. In Horse Swamp adj. JACOB LEWIS, EDWARD HOWARD, ROBERT LANIER. By deed from WILLIAM EVANS dated Oct. 9, 1736. Wit: ALLEX. COTTEN, WILLIAM WHITFIELD, EDWARD OUTLAW, SEN. Aug. Court 1738.*.

E 338 JAMES FROST "alias BURT" TO JOHN SAVAGE
        May 27, 1737. 12 pds. for 100 A. "JAMES FROST alias BURT, son of JOAN BURT". Land on SS Kesey River adj. land formerly CROMED's(?), and land formerly ASHIA SMITH's. Wit: JAMES LEGETT, ALLEX. THOMPSON, JAMES CASTELLAW, jurat. Aug. Court 1738. *.

E 339 JOHN COLLINS, SEN. of Chowan Precinct TO MARTHA BRYANT
        Aug. 8, 1738. Gift. One negro girl named Hannah. "for...love and goodwill and affection...toward my loving daughter, MARTHA BRYANT...her heirs, but for want of any such heir, then I do give the said Negro girl, Hannah, to the next heir in law...". Wit: A. WILLIAMS, HENRY HORNE, HENRY JONES, SEN. Aug. Court 1738. *.

E 340 ROBERT ROGERS of Chowan Precinct TO EDWARD WRIGHT of Nansemond Co,Va.
Nov. 13, 1738. 40 pds. for 630 A. On WS Chowan River at Deep Creek
and at Catherine's Creek. By patent dated Dec. 14, 1725 to LAZARUS THOMAS
and then "by endorsement" dated Nov. 14, 1727 assigned to ROBERT ROGERS.
Wit: JETHRO SUMNER, WILLIAM WRIGHT, jurat, ROBERT ROGERS, JUN. Nov. Court
1738. *.

E 343 JAMES CARTER TO NATHANIEL FIELD of Nansemond Co., Va.
Nov. 18, 1738. 20 pds. for 440 A. On NS Meherrin River "which was
granted SAMEUL ELLSON by WILLIAM REED late Governour of North Carolina as
by one patent bearing date March 26th 1723". Adj. MARY BRASSWELL, ____FAULK,
____CHESHIRE. Wit: BENJAMIN HILL, JAMES WILKINS, Jurat. Nov. Court 1738.*.

E 345 EVAN RAGLAND TO WILLIAM SHORT
Nov. 14, 1738. 30 pds. for 200 A. "a parcel...which I bought of my
father STEPHEN RAGLAND" On NS Moratock River at Double Bottom Branch. Adj.
RICHARD TURBERVIL AND Turbervil Branch. Wit: PHILLIP SMITH, HENRY JONES.
Nov. Court 1738. *.

E 346 STEPHEN GANEY (GAINEY) TO BENJAMIN HILL
Dec. 23, 1737. 153 pds. for 150 A. On SS Meherrin (Meheran) River
at Rattle Snake Valley adj. THOMAS GAINEY. Wit: JOHN BONDE, PAT ROOCH,
SAMUEL MERRIT, jurat. Nov. Court 1738. *.

E 348 JOHN SPIER TO WILLIAM GARROTT
Oct. 13, 1738. 20 pds. for 100 A. At Ahotskey Swamp and Spier
Branch at Piney Branch. Adj. ____MATHEWS, THOMAS DAVIS. Wit: PETER WEST,
jurat, PETER WEST, JUN. Nov. Court 1738. *.

E 349 JOHN BALDWIN of Edgecombe Precinct TO WILLIAM SMITH
Nov. 10, 1738. 6 pds. for 50 A. Adj. HENRY JONES, GEORGE SMITH. Wit:
GEORGE SMITH, JEREMIAH SMITH. Nov. Court 1738. *.

E 350 WILLIAM BALDWIN of Surry Co., Va. TO SAMUEL BUXTON of James City Co.,
Va. May 4, 1738. 22 pds. 10 sh. for 250 A. On NS Moratuck River.
Part of 640 A. survey to WILLIAM JONES dated Feb. 26, 1711/12 and by him
conveyed to JOSEPH LANE, JUN. and from LANE conveyed to WILLIAM HOGGATT and
from HOGGAT to BALDWIN. Adj. THOMAS HARRELL, JUN. at Spring Branch. Wit:
JOHN BALDWIN, jurat, RICHARD MASSEY, SUSANAH MASSEY. Nov. Court 1738. *.

E 352 WILLIAM GARROTT TO MOSE PRICE
Oct. 13, 1738. 10 pds. for 50 A. At Ahoskey Swamp at the mouth of
Piney Branch adj. THOMAS DAVIS. Wit: PETER WEST, jurat, PETER WEST, JUN.
Nov. Court 1738. *.

E 353 NATHANIEL HILL TO DANIEL LEE
Aug. 4, 1738. Settlement of damage suit. "NATHANIEL HILL...by assaul-
ting and beating DANIEL LEE...hath unfortunately deprived him of the use of
his limbs whereby he is unable to do any work for the support of himself
and family and the said DANIEL LEE having brought suit for the recovery of
damages on that account...it was agreed in open court...that for and during
the natural life of him the said DANIEL...to give him...within two months
two cows and calves and two sows and hoggs...and (for 5 sh.)....that plantation containing seventy five acres...during (his) natural life...and the
sum of thirty pounds current bills of the province in each and every year
of the natural life of him...every first day of August...". Wit: J. MONT-
GOMERY, THOMAS JONES. Aug. 4, 1738. W. SMITH, C.J.

E 354 JOHN MANN of Edgecombe Precinct TO MARY SPIKES (SPEIGHT) of Per-
quimmons Precinct. Nov. 11, 1738. 8 pds. for 250 A. At fork of
Killum Swamp and Flatt Swamp adj. FRANCIS BROWN. Part of a grant to THOMAS
MANN for 500 A. dated Nov. 4, 1707. Wit: GEORGE WIMBERLY, FREDERICK JONES,
SAMUEL PARKER. Nov. Court 1738. *.

E 355 LANCELOT JONES TO HENRY VIZE
April 15, 1738. 25 pds. for 50 A. At Ahoske Swamp adj. CHARLES JONES.
Wit: ANTHONY WEBB, Jurat, CHRIS. HOLLIMAN, LANCELOT JONES. Nov. Court 1738.*.

E 357 THOMAS HANSFORD & WIFE BRIDGETT TO JOHN CATHCART of Genoch in North
Britain & WILLIAM CATHCART "of Precinct and Province aforesaid"
March 21, 1737. 500 pds. for 300 A. At Ahotskey Ridge. Granted by patent to

ROBERT LANIER on April 1, 1723. Wit: JOHN BYRD, JOSEPH ANDERSON. Nov. Court 1738. *.

E 308 WILLIAM MEARS & WIFE SARAH TO JOHN CATHCART of Genoch in North Bri-
      tain & WILLIAM CATHCART "Practitiann in Phisic"   Nov. 17, 1738. 135
pds. for 100 A. Wit: ROBERT ROGERS, WILLIAM GARRETT. Nov. Court 1738. *.

E 360 THOMAS YATES TO JOHN GRAVES & WIFE FRANCES
       Dec. 9, 1738. Gift. 150 A. "During the natural Life and after their
Decease to their son JAMES GRAVES and his heirs forever". Adj. ISAAC HILL,
THOMAS POLLOCK. Wit: JOSEPH HARISON, JOHN CRICKET. N.C. Court Nov. 9, 1738.
"Proved before me Let it be Registred". W. SMITH.

E 361 THEOPHILUS WILLIAMS TO JOHN PRATT "attorney at Law"
       Oct. 11, 1738. 45 pds. for 300 A. Part of a tract granted to the
aforesaid THEOPHILUS WILLIAMS by date August 8, 1728. At Falling Run adj.
JOHN WILLIAMS, ____CASTELLAW, WILLIAM GRAY. Wit: HENRY BAKER, JUN., jurat,
NEEDHAM BRYAN. Nov. Court 1738. *.

E 363 WILLIAM MOORE TO BENJAMIN HILL
       Jan. 19, 1737. 25 pds. for 100 A. On NS Meheron Creek. Wit: J. BONDE,
JOHN LAMAN, jurat, JOHN HENDERSON. "Know...that I JUDITH MOORE...have for
five pounds...by Coll. BENJAMIN HILL relinquished all my Right Title and
Interest to within land...". Jan. 19, 1737. Wit: J. BONDE, JOHN LAMAN, JOHN
HENDERSON. Nov. Court 1738. *.

E 364 GEORGE BELL TO THOMAS SUTTAN (SUTTON)
       Nov. 11, 1738. 200 pds. for 640 A. Adj. WILLIAM REDITS, COLL. POLL-
OCK. Wit: ARCHBIL BELL, DEBORY BELL, MARY BELL. Nov. Court 1738. *.

E 366 JOSEPH JONES & WIFE CHARITY TO ROBERT ROGERS
       Nov. 17, 1738. 120 pds. for 250 A. In Ahotskie Woods adj. JOHN JONES,
____EDWARDS, ____HOWARDS. Wit: JOHN SUTTON, THOMAS JACKSON. Nov. Court 1738.*.

E 367 EDWARD HOWCUTT & WIFE ELIZABETH TO JOHN HOWCUTT (HOWCOTT)
       Sept. 26, 1737. Exchange. 40 A. "in consideration of a Piece of land
in Exchange from my brother JOHN HOWCUTT...". Adj. WILLIAM WILLIAMSON. Wit:
JOHN WYNNS, jurat, WILLIAM ROGERS, RICHARD WILLIAMSON. Nov. Court 1738.*.

E 368 WILLIAM WILLIAMSON, Yeoman, & WIFE MARY TO JOHN HOWCUTT
       Sept. 26, 1737. Exchange. 106 A. "...exchange...a certain plantation
where RICHARD MALPASS formerly lived..." At Chinkapin Branch and Mill Creek.
Adj. "RICHARD SOWELLS slash". Wit: JOHN WYNNS, WILLIAM A. ROGERS, RICHARD
WILLIAMS. Nov. Court 1738. *.

E 369 JOHN HOWCOTT (HOWCUTT), yeoman, TO EDWARD HOWCOTT
       Sept. 26, 1737. Exchange. 80 A. "...in Consideration of a plantation
in Exchange from my Brother EDWARD HOWCOTT of Bertie Precinct yeoman..."
Land at Mill Creek adj. JOSEPH NEWBY, Firebent(?) Branch, Capt. DOWNING's
Path to Deep Bottom issuing out of Vixes Branch. Wit: JOHN WYNNS, WILLIAM
ROGERS, RICHARD WILLIAMSON. Nov. Court 1738. *.

E 370 JOHN HOWCOTT (HOWCUTT), yeoman, TO WILLIAM WILLIAMSON
       Sept. 26, 1737. Exchange. 40 A. "...in Consideration of a Piece of
Land in Exchange from WILLIAMSON of Bertie Precinct...". Land on Vixes
Branch at mouth of Sandy Run adj. WILLIAM WILLIAMSON. Wit: JOHN WYNNS,
WILLIAM ROGERS, RICHARD WILLIAMSON. Nov. Court 1738. *.

E 372 WILLIAM RUFFIN & WIFE SARAH TO ETHELRED RUFFIN
       Nov. 14, 1738. 50 pds. for 320 A. At Long Meadow adj. JOHN HART.
Wit: JOHN HART, JOEL NEWSOME, NATHANIEL RUFFIN. Nov. Court 1738. *.

E 373 SAMUEL PRESTON TO RICHARD HINES
       March 4, 1737/38. 20 pds. for 75 A. On Wortom Swamp. Adj. JOSEPH
MENTON(?), RICHARD HINES. Wit: JOHN SHOALAR, RICHARD RONLAND (?RENLAND).
Nov. Court 1738. *.

E 375 JOSEPH NIXON TO JOSEPH HOUGH
       Oct. 21, 1738. 20 pds. for 640 A. On NS Meherrin River adj. WILLIAM
FAULK. Land formerly granted JOHN CHESTER by patent dated March 1, 1719.
Wit: WILLIAM WHITFIELD, JOHN RASBERRY, JAMES MAGLOHON. Nov. Court 1738. *.

E 377 JOHN LUERTON TO EDWARD BYRD
        Oct. 27, 1738. 40 pds. for 220 A. Part of tract "...bound by a tree
in an Island..." at the "main swamp commonly called Cypress Swamp". Wit:
RICHARD LEARY, MARY JONES. Nov. Court 1738. *.

E 378 WILLIAM BENNETT TO WILLIAM BOONE
        May 10, 1738. 5 pds. for 100 A. On SS Yourah Swamp and NS Roanoak
River adj. BENNETT's patent at Kain's Path. Part of patent to WILLIAM BEN-
NETT for 260 A. granted Aug. 4, 1730. Wit: THOMAS BRYANT, WILLIAM TAYLOR.
May Court 1738. *.

E 379 MARY MORSE TO JOHN MORSE
        Feb. 8, 1738. Gift. *. "...love and good will which I bear to the
said JOHN MORSE...His heirs and assigns forever...all that percel of Land
which fell to me by my Brother JOHN M. WILLIAM's Death...". On NS Morattock
River "within Ursura Meadows". Wit: JOHN HART, jurat, NATHANIEL RUFFIN,
SAMUEL RUFFIN. Feb. Court 1738. *.

E 380 JOSEPH WALL, SEN. TO EDWARD HOOD
        Sept. 5, 1738. 10 pds. for 10 A. On SS "of the great Branch called
Hopkins branch". Being part of a tract formerly granted JAMES TURNER "ad-
joining to Land formerly was made over in open court by JOHN SIMPSON to
WILLIAM WALL, Deceased...with Relinquishment of my wifes Dowry...". Wit:
NICHOLAS MONGER, RICHARD WALL, JUN., Jurat. Feb. Court 1738. *.

E 381 JOSEPH WALL, JUN. of Edgecombe Precinct TO EDWARD HOOD
        Feb. 13, 1738. 14 pds. for 180 A. On SS Meherrin River. Land "grant-
ed JOHN SIMPSON by WILLIAM REED, Esq. President of the Providence" dated
Nov. 7, 1723. Adj. JAMES TURNER at TURNER's Branch, HOPKINS HOWELL. Wit:
THOMAS JACKSON, THOMAS RYNA. Feb. Court 1738. *.

E 383 BENJAMIN FOREMAN TO THOMAS ANDREWS (ANDEROS)
        Feb. 3, 1738. 40 pds. for 720 A. Part of two patents: (1) One dated
April 1, 1718. (2) One dated March 1, 1721. Land at low grounds of the
River. adj. RICHARD MELTON, GEORGE WILLIAMS. Part of patent for 500 A. ex-
cepting 100 A. sold to MARMADUKE NORFLEET. Wit: JOHN ANDERSON, SAMUEL GANER
(?), SEN., jurat, SAMUEL GANER, JUN. Feb. Court 1738. *.

E 384 JOHN BELL, merchant, TO ARCHIBALD BELL
        Dec. 29, 1738. 60 pds. for 320 A. On ES Cushie River at Buckles Bary
Pocoson. Adj. LAURANCE SARSUMS. Wit: WILLIAM BYRD, JOHN BUTLER. Feb. Court
1738. *.

E 386 MARY JONES TO THOMAS ASHBURN, "tayler"
        Land "along Morattock Bay taking in Tarrupin Point". Adj. Capt.
DAVID HENDERSON. Wit: THOMAS RYAN, jurat, JOHN LUERTON, RICHARD LEARY. Feb.
Court 1738. *.

E 387 JAMES MCGLOHON TO ELIAS STALLINGS of Chowan Precinct
        Feb. 12, 1738. 20 pds. for 317 A. Sold by WILLIAM CARTER and wife
MARTHA to JAMES MCGLOHON on Feb. 9, 1726. Wit: JOHN WYNNS, SAMUEL ALLEN.
Feb. Court 1738. *.

E 389 PETER JOLLY (JOLLISH) TO JOHN JONES
        Feb. 13, 1738. 100 pds. for 150 A. On WS Chowan River and NWS Deep
Creek adj. JAMES BOON (?), FREDERICK JONES, RICHARD BARFIELD. Wit: THOMAS
WHITMELL, THOMAS CREW, JOHN BELL. Feb. Court 1738. *.

E 390 JONATHAN STANLEY, SEN. TO THOMAS HUDSON
        March 21, 1737/38. 30 pds. for 100 A. On WS Turkey Swamp. adj. STAN-
LEY "at a line of Marked trees made by consent of both parties". Wit: JOHN
BROWN, WILLIAM RONSHAM, WILLIAM MEARS. Feb. Court 1738. *.

E 392 PHILLIP WALSTON TO BENJAMIN LEWIS
        Feb. 14, 1738. 45 pds. for 100 A. On SS Rockquist Swamp. "now in
actual possession of BENJAMIN LEWIS". Adj. _____ASHLEY. Wit: THOMAS WHITMELL,
PHILL WALSTON. Feb. Court 1738. *.

E 394 THOMAS BANKS, taylor, & WIFE JANET (JENNET) TO WILLIAM BARKER
        Feb. 5, 1738. 7 pds. 10 sh. for 200 A. On SWS Chowan River at di-
viding line between BENJAMIN WYNNS "and Lightwood with conveyeances and

138

Egress(?) for fifteen barrels of tar". Wit: JOHN WYNNS, ROBERT HILL, ROBERT MULLIGAN. Feb. Court 1738. *.

E 393   ELIZABETH PARKER, widow, TO MARTHA PARKER
        July 1, 1738. Gift. Household goods. "...love good will and affec-
tion...towards my well beloved Child MARTHA PARKER...one good Bed and furniture and one Large Chest with a Drawer in it and one small red Leather
Guilded trunk and one great Tankard and one Pottle Brass Skillet and two
Large Pewter Dishes Marked Thus AwM and MW and one good Pewter Poringer and
salt seller and one small Bason marked Thus X and Two Large basons marked
Thus X and five pewter plates Marked Thus X and two Cows and Calves and
half their Increase and one Iron Pot holding about five gallons & one Iron
Kittle holding about a gallon & a half and a good Box Iron with a Brass
Knob and Heaters..." To her and her lawful begotten heirs. Wit: JOHN BATTLE,
JOHN BROWN, jurat. Feb. Court 1738. *.

E 395   LITTLETON SPIVEY TO EALEE THOMAS
        Nov. 13, 1738. 30 pds. for 220 A. On NS Morrattock River adj. JAMES
BENTS, THOMAS BUSBYS. To a dividing line between SPIVEY & PAGE. Wit: GEORGE
HOUSE, JAMES CARTER, LUKE THOMAS, jurat. Feb. Court 1738. *.

E 397   JAMES ROADS TO JOHN VICKINS
        Dec. 29, 1738. 30 pds. for 250 A. Adj. WILLIAM RUTONS "to a Tarkiln".
Wit: J. EARLY, JUN., WILLIAM RASBERRY. Feb. Court 1738. *.

E 398   HENRY BONNER TO JAMES WOOD
        Nov. 20, 1738. 200 pds. for 400 A. At Ahotskey Swamp. Adj. CHARLES
JONES. Wit: ABRAHAM O'DHAM, JOHN SUTTON, Jurat. Feb. Court 1738. *.

E 400   WILLIAM CHARLTON of Craven Precinct TO EDWARD FRISBIE
        Feb. 19, 1738. 70 pds. for 100 A. "Patented in the name of JOHN HAR-
LOW and sold by HARLOW to WILLIAM COWARD deceased and sold by JOHN COWARD
to JOSEPH WHITE...". Adj. EDWARD FRISBIE. Wit: FRANCIS PENVIN, JOHN WARBUL-
LAN. N.C. Court March 31, 1739. W. SMITH, C.J.

E 401   JAMES CASTELLAW TO JOHN STAFFORD of Nansemond Co., Va., merchant
        Aug. 4, 1738. 800 pds. for 640 A. On Meherrin Creek. Which land CAS-
TELLAW bought of JOHN BEVERLY and which was granted to BEVERLY by patent
dated March 1, 1720. Wit: ROBERT FORSTER, THOMAS BANKER (?BARKER), THOMAS
JACKSON. Aug. Court 1739. JOHN WYNNS D.C/C.

E 402   JOHN BUSH TO ANDREW THOMPSON, cordwainer, & WALTER ACKMAN (AIKMAN)
        & GEORGE PATTERSON.   *. 138 pds. for 200 A. Land granted to LEWIS
WILLIAMS on April 1, 1713. On NS Wiccacon Creek at Holly Swamp. adj. NICHO-
LAS TOOP, CHRISTOPHER SEGAN. Wit: THOMAS RYAN, JOHN EARLY, CHARITY WILLIAMS.
Feb. Court 1738. *.

E 403   JOHN CARRILL TO SAMUEL SARSUMS
        June 14, 1738. 30 pds. for 100 A. Adj. JONATHAN GILBERT, JOHN CAR-
RELL, ALEXANDER COTTON. Wit: WILLIAM WHITFIELD, ALEXANDER COTTAN, jurat,
ANN COTTAN. Feb. Court 1738. *.

E 405   THOMAS PILAND of Chowan Precinct TO WILLIAM PERRY
        Feb. 1, 1738. 95 pds. for 124 A. On ES Ahotsky Swamp. Granted to
GEORGE POWELL April 1, 1723. "and is now become due to the said PILAND".
Wit: DAVID LEWIS, THOMAS BARNES, JOHN THOMAS, Jurat. Feb. Court 1738. *.

E 407   RICHARD PHILLIPS TO EDWARD OUTLAW
        May 18, 1738. 50 pds. for 100 A. At "Deep Creek Bridge then down
the road to a branch". Wit: JOHN WYNNS, jurat, SARAH WILKINSON, CATHERINE
PENNEY. Feb. Court 1738.

E 408   OSBORNE JEFFRYS TO SAMUEL WILLIAMS
        Feb. 12, 1738. 5 pds. for 90 A. In Ursura Meadows on ES Morattuck
River. Land formerly granted SAMUEL MERRETT "on south easterly side of a
large crooked meadow". Adj. The Neck Land at Cattail Swamp at the "High
Land" at Sherrard's Great Marsh, MERRETTS old south line. Wit: ARTHUR
SHEROD, BENJAMIN STEVENSON, SAMPSON WILLIAMS. Feb. Court 1738. *.

E 410   JAMES WILLIAMSON TO JONATHAN TAYLOR
        July 11, 1738. 100 pds. for 100 A. On ES Quitzna Swamp and NS

Morattuck River adj. HENRY BATES, JOSEPH WIMBERLY. Wit: H. BATE, jurat, MARTHA BATES, JOHN BARTAN. Feb. Court 1738. *.

E 412   JAMES DONAVAN, marriner, TO DAVID MEADE of Nansemond Co, Va.,merchant
        Feb. 14, 1738. 20 pds. for 22 A. On Cashy River Pocoson. Adj. PETER
GRAY, PETER STANCILL, deceased, ARTHUR DUGGELL, deceased. "Land conveyed me
from JOHN MCCASKEY by a Deed dated 22nd April 1737...Except a burying Place
reserved in the said MCCASKEYS Deed". Wit: THOMAS WHITMELL, JOHN HILL. Feb.
Court 1738. *.

E 413   MARY MACKLEMORE (MACKLIMORE) TO ADKINS MACKLIMORE & YOUNG MACKLIMORE
        Feb. 8, 1736/37. Gift. Land and household furniture. "...love...to-
ward my well beloved Children ADKINS MACKLIMORE and YOUNG MACKLIMORE my two
sons..." To ADKINS: one bed and furniture, two pewter dishes, three plates,
one iron pot, one young horse, and nine head of cattle, and the one half of
my stock of hoggs and one survey of land above the Pigeon Roost. To YOUNG:
One negro girl called Febly with all her future increase, one feather bed
and furniture, one Iron pott, three pewter dishes, one bason, three plates,
eight head of cattle, one half my stock of hoggs and one certain survey of
land below WILLIAM GILLAM "and if my mare brings another colt or filly then
the same shall be my son YOUNG's". Wit: CORNELIUS KEITH, JAMES SPAKS(?),
ELIZABETH KEITH. Feb. Court 1738. *.

E 414   JOHN GILLUM of Surry Co., Va. TO EDWARD CLANTON "of the Colony afore-
        said and County of Brunswick"   Nov. 1, 1738. 40 pds. for 290 A. On
NS Morrattuck River between JOHN GILLUM & GEORGE JORDAN at Dogwood Run. Wit:
GEORGE NORWOOD, JOHN NORWOOD. Feb. Court 1738. *.

E 416   JENNETT BANKS TO JOHN WYNNS
        Feb. 5, 1738. Power of atty. "I JENNETT BANKS wife of THOMAS BANKS
do hereby Impower my friend JOHN WYNNS to be my true and Lawful attorney...
to acknowledge...sale...to ROBERT HILL". 395 A. Wit: WILLIAM BARKER (BANKER),
ROBERT MULLIGAN. Feb. Court 1738. *.

E 416   THOMAS BANKS, "taylor", & WIFE JENNETT TO ROBERT HILL
        Feb. 5, 1738. 35 pds. for 395 A. On SWS Chowan River on Chowan Riv-
er Pocoson. Adj. ABRAHAM BLEWLETT, CAPT. BARKER "one acre of land to be
Laid out of the choice of my wife JENNETT BANKS to Include the now Manor
house During Her Life and Lightwood and conveniences and proper Egress for
thirty barrells of tar...". Wit: JOHN WYNNS, WILLIAM BARKER, ROBERT MULLI-
GAN. Feb. Court 1738. *.

E 418   WILLIAM WALSTON TO THOMAS TURNER, trader
        Oct. 31, 1738. 600 pds. for 540 A. On Roquis Creek at "Rasutske path"
"Note also that the aforesaid land was conveyed to me by a Deed of Gift
from my Grandfather WILLIAM WALSTON bearing date the 21st of July 1719...".
Wit: JOHN GRAY, JOSEPH HARDEE, jurat. Feb. Court 1738. *.

E 420   WILLIAM GARRETT & WIFE MARY TO JOHN CATHCART of Genoch in Great
        Britain & WILLIAM CATHCART, "Practitianer of Phisick"   Jan. 16,
1738/39. 40 pds. for 50 A. On Ahosky Swamp adj. MATTHEW's Line. Wit: ROB-
ERT ROGERS, jurat, MARY ROGERS. Feb. Court 1738. "Received of Doc'r WM.
CATHCART the sum of forty pounds...".

E 422   JOHN GRAY TO JOHN CATHCART of Genoch in Great Britain & WILLIAM
        CATHCART, "Practitioner in Phisick"   Feb. 13, 1738/39. 15 pds. for
200 A. On WS Chowan River. Wit: ROBERT ROGERS, THOMAS JONES, EDWARD BUXTON.
Feb. Court 1738. *.

E 423   JOHN BEVERLY & JOHN BERVERLY TO THEOPHILUS PUGH of Nansemond Co, Va.
        Dec. 12, 1738. 500 pds. for 640 A. "between JOHN BEVERLY & ROBERT
BEVERLY his brother sons of JOHN BEVERLY late of Bertie Precinct, deceased
...their Two manor Plantations...late dwelling place of JOHN BEVERLY, SEN.
and JOHN BEVERLY, JUN...which patent was given by the last will and Testament of JOHN BEVERLY...to his sons JOHN BEVERLY and ROBERT BEVERLY...Will
dated Dec. 22, 1737...". Patent date March 20, 1721. Signed: JOHN BEVERLY,
ANNE BEVERLY, ROBERT BEVERLY, ELINOR BEVERLY. "The said THEOPHILUS PUGH put
in the actual possession of the Lands...by the delivery of Turf and Twigg
in the Presence of us...". Wit: THOMAS NEWBY, JOHN WEBB, jurat, RICHARD
TAYLOR, jurat. Feb. Court 1738. *.

E 426   DANIEL HOUGH & WIFE MARGARETT TO THEOPHILUS PUGH of Nansemond Co, Va.
        Dec. 11, 1738.   300 pds. "DANIEL HOUGH and MARGRETT his wife the
late Widow and Relect of JOHN BEVERLY Deceased...by the Last will and testament of JOHN BEVERLY...his aforesaid widow...was left in possession of two
manor plantations whereon JOHN BEVERLY her Husband Deceased and JOHN BEVER-
LY her Eldest son were seated with six hundred and forty acres thereunto
belonging During the Time of Her Natural Life and Whereas JOHN BEVERLY and
ROBERT BEVERLY Her two sons hath...with the consent of MARGRETT their Mother (for 25 pds.)...being left in the hands of THEOPHILUS PUGH Gent. to
and for the Future Benefit and support of DANIEL HOUGH and MARGARETT His
Wife during their natural lives...Reserving...unto DANIEL HOUGH and MAR-
GRETT...benefit of a stand of wheat...egress and regress for all their
stock...to be fed and foddered...also the right to remove...all chattels.."
Wit: THOMAS NEWBY, JOHN WEBB, jurat, RICHARD TAYLOR, jurat. Feb. Court 1738.
*. (Note Here: MARGARET sold her interest for: "the sum of twenty five
pounds current money of Virginia or Two hundred pounds current Province
Bill money of North Carolina".

E 428   JOHN BEVERLY & WIFE ANNE TO THEOPHILUS PUGH of Nansemond Co, Va.
        Dec. 11, 1738.   15 pds. for *. "one percel of wood Land Ground".
Formerly patented by JAMES PARKER Nov. 7, 1723. Parker sold to JOHN BEVERLY
father of said JOHN BEVERLY. Land on NES Cashy Swamp. Adj. THOMAS READS(?),
HENRY ROADS. Wit: THOMAS NEWBY, JOHN WEBB, jurat, RICHARD TAYLOR, jurat.
Feb. Court 1738. *.

E 431   DANIEL HOUGH & WIFE MARGARETT & JOHN BEVERLY & ROBERT BEVERLY TO
        THEOPHILUS PUGH of Nansemond Co, Va.   Dec. 11, 1738. 5000 pds. *.
"...(We find ourselves) justly Indebted unto THEOPHILUS PUGH...or his Cer-
tain Attorney...(in) Quantity of five thousand pounds of current Province
Bill money...the condition is such...(that we convey) two manor plantations
whereon JOHN BEVERLY, SEN. Deceased and JOHN BEVERLY his son were Lately
seated...and also one other Tract...containing five hundred and forty acres
...". Wit: THOMAS NEWBY, JOHN WEBB, jurat, RICHARD TAYLOR, jurat. Feb.
Court 1738. *.

E 433   LORDS PROPRIETORS TO PHILLIP WALSTON
        April 1, 1720. Grant. 600 A. "...according to our Great Deed of
Grant bearing Date the first of May Anno 1668...". Land in Chowan Precinct
on NES Cashia River adj. CHARLES BARBER, on "Isaac Creek"(?), THOMAS JONES,
JONATHAN STANLEY. For importation of persons. Signed CHARLES EDEN, Esq.
Governor. WM. REED, JOHN HARKLEFIELD, THOMAS POLLOCK, RICHARD SANDERSON.
Recorded in Secretary's Office. J. LOVICK, sec't'y.

E 434   PHILLIP WALSTON TO JOSHUA WILKINSON, Taylor
        Feb. 10, 1737/38. 30 pds. for *. "within mentioned Land". Wit:
CHARLES MIZELL, JAMES SWAIN. Feb. Court 1738. *.

F 434   THOMAS JONES & WIFE ELIZABETH of Chowan Precinct TO JOHN CATHCART of
        Genoch in North Britain & WILLIAM CATHCART "Practitioner in Phisick"
July 31, 1738. 400 pds. for 640 A. In NS Antonky Marsh. Adj. JAMES HUTCHE-
SON. Wit: ANNE FORSTER, J. HODGSON. NC. Court Jan. 29, 1738. "...acknow-
ledged before me Mrs. ELIZABETH JONES being privately examined..." W. SMITH
C.J.

E 437   JOHN SPIER of Edgecombe Precinct TO WILLIAM SPIER "of the said
        Precinct".   May 7, 1739. 10 pds. for 200 A. On NS Fishing Creek.
Plantation whereon SPIER now dwells. Adj. WILLIAM SPIER and ELIAS HODGES at
Lodging Branch. Part of a tract patented to JOHN SPIER Feb. 17, 1737 for
450 A. Wit: *.*. May Court 1739. *.

E 438   JOHN SPIER of Edgecombe Precinct TO JOSEPH WALL
        May 7, 1739. 5 pds. for 50 A. On NS Fishing Creek at Short Swamp.
Adj. WILLIAM SPIER. By patent dated Feb. 17, 1737. Wit: *.*. May Court 1739*.

E 439   JOHN SPIER (SPEIR) of Edgecombe Precinct TO ELIAS HODGES "of said
        Precinct".   May 7, 1739. 30 pds. for 200 A. On NS Fishing Creek at
Short Swamp. Between ELIAS HODGES and WILLIAM SPIER. Part of 450 A. patented Feb. 17, 1737. Wit: *.*. May Court 1738. *.

E 441   JAMES WOOD TO WILLIAM DUFFIELD & WIFE SARAH
        May 9, 1739. Gift. 500 A. "...love good will and affection I bear

unto my well beloved Son in Law WILLIAM DUFFILL and SARAH his wife...during
their Natural Lives...". Land at a branch called HARRISS's Branch adj. RICH-
ARD BRASSWELL, JONATHAN STANLEY. Wit: ANDREW IRWING, ROBERT FORSTER, JOHN
SUTTON. May Court 1739. *. (Note: This property lent for life "after their
decease to be Equally Divided between...(their) two eldest Daughters...".)

E 441   GEORGE WYNNS TO JOSEPH WYNNS
        Nov. 10, 1738. Gift. 100 A. "...love...unto my Son JOSEPH WYNNS..."
Land on NS Wiccacon Creek at "mouth of the said JOSEPH WYNNS Hill Swamp".
At Horse Hung Branch. Wit: BENJAMIN WYNNS, CULMUR SESSAMS, jurat. May Court
1739. *.

E 442   JOHN WYNNS, yeoman, TO JOSEPH WYNNS
        Nov. 10, 1738. 40 pds. for 280 A. On NS Wiccacon Creek "at mouth of
Germans will Branch" at Horse Hung Branch. Adj. JOSEPH WYNNS, CULMUR SES-
SUMS, EDWARD HANES, JOHN BROWN, "BUSHES former Land". Wit: BENJAMIN WYNNS,
W. WYNNS. May Court 1739. *.

E 444   JOSEPH WYNNS TO CULMUR SESSUMS, yeoman
        Nov. 11, 1738. 70 pds. for 150 A. On NS Wiccacon Creek at Mill
Swamp at the "Main Road to the Head Line of the Survey of the Germans Land".
Adj. EDWARD HANES, "CULMER SESSUMS other land". Wit: JOHN WYNNS, BENJAMIN
WYNNS. May Court 1739. *.

E 445   JOHN WYNNS, yeoman, TO WILLIAM WYNNS
        May 1, 1739. 300 pds. for 450 A. Land called "Ahotskey Ridge" adj.
____CATHCART, "to land which I purchased from SWANNER". The same land con-
veyed to WYNNS by MATTHEW TOBIAS SWANNER by deed dated July 31, 1738. Wit:
PETER WEST, J. EDWARDS. May Court 1739. *.

E 446   JOHN WYNNS, yeoman, TO JOHN BAKER
        May 7, 1739. 60 pds. for 320 A. On ES Flat Swamp "below BAKERS now
settlement". Adj. ALEXANDER VOLLANTINE, PENELOPE MAUL. Wit: JOSEPH ANDERSON,
BENJAMIN BAKER. May Court 1739. *.

E 447   JOHN HALLUM TO JOHN WYNNS
        May 1, 1739. 25 pds. for 50 A. On NS Wiccacon Creek. Adj. THOMAS
LEE, WILLIAM PEEK, THOMAS LEE. Wit: EBENEZER SLANSON, ISAAC LEWIS, HENRY
MAYNOR, Jurat. May Court 1739. *.

E 448   GEORGE DEMSEY TO SAMUEL JONES
        Dec. 13, 1738. 40 pds. for 388 A. On NS Morattuck River adj. EDWARD
SMITHWICK (SMITHHICK?), TERRENCE BERNS at Charlton Creek and Pely Branch.
Wit: THOMAS RYAN, ROBERT SANDERLIN. May Court 1739. *.

E 450   JAMES BARFIELD TO WILLIAM PERRY
        March 1, 1738. 200 pds. for 100 A. "land formerly belonging to
LEWIS JONES bequeathed and given to him by his Grandfather LEWIS WILLIAMS
deceased...". On NS western fork of Poplar Branch near Cutewitskey Marsh to
"the lower side of an old field lately belonging to LEWIS WILLIAMS deceased
...". Wit: JOHN BATTLE, ELIZABETH BATTLE, SARAH BATTLE. May Court 1739. *.

E 451   JOHN PATCHETT of Craven Precinct TO WILLIAM PERRY
        Feb. 2, 1738. 10 pds. for 100 A. On NS western fork of Poplar Run
(Branch) adj. "tract formerly belonging to LEWIS JONES which he had left
him by his Grandfather LEWIS WILLIAMS Dec'd...". Wit: HENRY BONNER (BANNER),
SOLOMON BARFIELD, jurat. May Court 1739. *.

E 453   JOHN MACKDANIEL TO ANDREW COLLINS
        Dec. 29, 1738. 15 pds. for 95 A. On NS Yourah Swamp adj. JOHN TUL-
LEY. Wit: JOHN SUTTON, jurat, ISAAC PARKER, ANN PARKER. May Court 1739. *.

E 454   EDWARD BROWN of Edgecombe Precinct TO   BROWN
        March 6, 1738. *. Part of a tract which was formerly surveyed for
THOMAS BROWN & ROBERT PATTERSON. "lying in Chowan Precinct; but now Bertie".
On SS Pottacasie Swamp. The upper half of a 300 A. tract. Wit: DAVID PARKER,
BRYANT OQUIN, JOHN DICKINSON. May Court 1739. *.

E 456   HENRY HORNE TO PHILLIP SMITH
        Nov. 20, 1738. 15 pds. for 100 A. Between WILLIAM REEVES & JOHN
GRAY on NS Morattuck River at Spring Branch and Fevbevil's (?Turbevil) Run.

Wit: HENRY JONES, HENRY JONES, PHILLIP JONES. May Court 1739. *.

E 457 PEDEGROVE SALSBERRY & WIFE SARAH TO TITUS MOORE (MOOR)
      May 8, 1739. 80 pds. for 40 A. "at the Head of a Tract of Land
called Snowfield". Adj. WILLIAM TURNER, WILLIAM EASON, HENRY SLUCRITS(?Note
Here: Above this name in different ink at a much later date has been added
the name Averitt). Wit: CHARLES HORNE, THOMAS HARRELL. May Court 1739.*.

E 459 JAMES CAIN of "Edgecomb County" TO EDWARD EARP
      May 1, 1739. 25 pds. for 130 A. Two "percels". (1) 100 A. Land con-
veyed to CAIN by Deed of Sale of RICHARD PACE which PACE bought of BARTHO-
LOMEW CAHVES. (2) 30 A. Part of parcel "Bequeathed to the said JAMES CAIN
by the Last will and Testament of WILLIAM CAIN Dec'd...". Sold to WILLIAM
CAIN by HENRY SIMS. "The both percels of Land are adjoyning". Land on Thomas Branch. Wit: THOMAS BRYANT, BENJAMIN TOOLER, jurat. May Court 1739.*.

E 461 TREDDLE KEEFE, yeoman, TO EBONEZER SLANSON
      May 5, 1739. 40 pds. for 200 A. In Killum Woods "upon the Hew'd
Bridge branch". Wit: JOHN WYNNS, jurat, ISAAC LEWIS, HENRY MAYNOR. May
Court 1739. *.

E 462 THOMAS WILSON & WIFE MARY TO WILLIAM GUNN of Brunswick County, Va.
      March 15, 1738. 20 pds. for 400 A. On NS Roanoke River. By patent
Nov. 15, 1728. Wit: CORNELIUS KEITH, JOHN COOTLE, THOMAS FRASHER, jurat.
May Court 1739. *.

E 464 EDWARD EARP TO BENJAMIN FULLER
      April 25, 1739. 12 pds. 10 sh. for 250 A. "taken out of a patent
granted unto RICHARD PACE for five hundred acres". On NS Moratuck River adj.
JOHN GREEN, DOCTOR SAMUEL PEETE. Wit: SAMUEL PEETE, JOHN SWENNY, EZEKIEL
FULLER. May Court 1739. *.

E 465 ROBERT WEST & WIFE FRANCES TO EDWARD BYRD
      May 7, 1739. 400 pds. for 400 A. On Beaverdam. (1) 220 A. adj. land
formerly THOMAS BALL's, dec'd, DAVID HENDERSON's dec'd, WILLIAM BURT at
Reedy Branch, JOSEPH HUDGSON. (2) 100 A. adj. land formerly bought of JOHN
WEBB at Poplar Branch adj. CAPT. DAVID HENDERSON. (3) 100 A. bought of
DANIEL FRAZER at Cashoak Creek adj. WILLIAM BURT. Wit: ROBERT PATTERSON,
JOHN ASHWORTH, PENELOPE WINANT. May Court 1739. *.

E 467 WILLIAM GRAY of New Hanover Precinct TO PEDEGROVE SALSBURY
      Dec. 8, 1736. 30 pds. for 40 A. Adj. "Snowfields" at Fallen Run.
Adj. WILLIAM GRAY, WILLIAM EASON. Wit: JOHN GRAY, FRANCIS HARRELL, THOMAS
HARRELL, jurat. May Court 1739. *.

E 469 ROBERT WEBB, cordwainer of Surry Co., Va. & WIFE ELIZABETH TO JOHN
      DAY. July 10, 1739. 30 pds. for 159 A. On NS Marratock River adj.
BLANS line, WILLIAM BUGGS on Canoe Creek. By patent for 459 A. dated July
10, 1739. Wit: RICHARD HED, HATHELL NORROD. Aug. Court 1739. *.

E 471 JOHN DAWSON TO COL. ROBERT WEST
      Nov. 30, 1738. 30 pds. for 640 A. On NS Morratock River adj. SAMUEL
MERRET. Land granted to THOMAS SMITH "and by him Elapsed for want of due
seating and planting". Grant for 340 A. Wit: THOMAS WHITMELL, JAMES BEESE-
LEY. Aug. Court 1739. JOHN WYNNS D.C/C. (Note Here: This deed says in one
place 640 A., in another 340 A. The latter is probably correct.)

E 472 HENRY JARNAGAN TO BENJAMIN HILL
      July 27, 1739. 26 pds. 15 sh. for 300 A. On Meherrin(Maherrin)
Creek. "...all that percell of land whereon he the said HENRY now Dwells
and left him by the will of His Father Dec'd as also that Percell of Land
left by his said Father to his Brother lately dec'd and now heir at Law to
his said brother...". Wit: ROBERT FORSTER, THOMAS JONES, JOHN CAMPBELL.
Aug. Court 1739. JOHN WYNNS D.C/C.

E 474 PHILLIP THOMAS TO WILLIAM THOMAS
      June 22, 1739. 40 pds. for 180 A. On Yourahaw Woods and NS Marra-
tock River. "being about half a tract of Land granted to HENRY SIMS by
patent...(March 1, 1719)". Adj. WILLIAM CAIN. Wit: JOHN DAWSON, Jurat, JOHN
BODDIE, THOMAS SMITH. Aug. Court 1739. JOHN WYNNS D.C/C.

E 475   SAMUEL ALLEN TO ROBERT BEVARLEY
        May 9, 1739. 40 pds. for 200 A. At Poplar Branch. adj. ANDREW BAR-
RANS, LEWIS WILLIAMS. Wit: NICHOLAS FAIRLESS, PETER PEIRCEY, WILLIAM WHIT-
FIELD, jurat. August Court 1739. *.

E 477   JAMES CASTELLAW, Treasurer, TO THOMAS ASHLEY, Sen.
        May 12, 1736. 90 pds. for 640 A. On Salmon Creek. "Tracts of Land
belonging to the Late Mr. LAWRENCE SAUNSON (SARSON?) and by him forfeited
to the Public by a Mortgage to the Late Coll. THOS. POLLOCK Treasurer...(by
1729 Act)...and sold by me at the Court house at publick vendue..." By patent to LAWRANCE SARSON dated October 20, 1716. Wit: JAMES LOCKHART, JOHN
DAWSON. Aug. Court 1739. *.

E 478   HOSEA TAPLEY TO GEORGE MORRIS
        Feb. 6, 1738. 10 pds. for 100 A. On NS Morratock River. Part of
tract granted HENCHY (HENCHY) GILLUM for 600 A. Wit: JOHN DAY, jurat, JOHN
MORRIS. Aug. Court 1739. JOHN WYNNS D.C/C.

E 480   WILLIAM PACE & JOHN PACE & ELIZABETH MOOR, "Relict of JOHN PACE late
        of Bertie County Dec'd" TO JOHN CORLEW of Yorkhumton Parish of York
Co, Va. Aug. 13, 1739. 35 pds. 5 sh. for 200 A. On SS Roanoke River. On
SS of a grant to JOHN PACE late of Bertie. Adj. DANIEL CRAWLEY, COLL. WILL-
IAM LITTLE, JOHN LEWS (LAWS?), WILLIAM PACE. This is a one year lease. "to
be fully ended...& paying unto (them)...the rent of one year of Indian Corn
at the feast of St. Michaell the arch angel...". Wit: A. GILES, jurat,
THOMAS VINCE, SARAH MIMS. Aug. Court 1739. JOHN WYNNS D.C/C.

E 482   WILLIAM PACE & JOHN PACE & ELIZABETH MOOR, Relect of JOHN PACE,Dec'd,
        TO JOHN CORLEW of Yorkhampton Parish in York County, Va. Aug. 14,
1739. 25 pds. 5 sh. for 200 A. (Land described above.) Wit: A. GILES, jurat, THOMAS VINCE, SARAH MIMS. Aug. Court 1739. *.

E 485   JOHN MAN of Edgecomb(e) & THOMAS MAN TO MARY SPEIGHT, widow of
        Perquimmons County. Nov. 6, 1739. 75 pds. for 150 A. "...money
paid & already received by my brother THOMAS MAN...land patented to THOMAS
MAN father...and by the last will & Testament...Descended to his sons JOHN
MAN & THOMAS MAN...the will not being duly witnessed the Right of Inheri-
tance fell more particularly to the aforesaid JOHN MAN and in fullfilling
the Desire and will...(JOHN) Hath Given a Deed of Gift to his Brother THOMAS
MAN JUN." Gift dated May 12, 1736 for 490 A. Wit: LEMUEL REDDECK, WILLIAM
TAYLOR, jurat, JAMES BROWN. May Court 1740. *.

E 487   GEORGE SPIVEY of Nancemond Co., Va. TO CALEB SPIVEY
        Aug. 14, 1739. 200 pds. for 300 A. On Village Swamp adj. THEOPHILUS
WILLIAMS, WILLIAM HINTON, THOMAS BONDS. By patent to WILLIAM GRAY dated
April 1, 1725. Wit: JAMES LASITER, WILLIAM RASBERRY, ISAAC SPEIGHT. August
Court 1739. JOHN WYNNS D.C/C.

E 489   JAMES RUSSELL TO JOHN ROGERS
        Aug. 5, 1736. 100 pds. for 100 A. In Kashy Neck on NWS Herring Run
between WILLIAM ASHBORN, WILLIAM KENNEDAYS, JOHN GRIFFIN. Out of patent
dated April 1, 1720 for 420 A. Wit: WILLIAM LATTIMER, JOHN WALBUTTON, jurat.
Aug. Court 1739. *.

E 490   WILLIAM RUSSELL of Tyrrell Precinct TO WILLIAM ASHBORNE (ASHBURN)
        May 30, 1738. 125 pds. for 200 A. In Cashy Neck at Spring Branch.
Wit: JOHN CASKEY, MOSES TOMLINSON, THOMAS WHITMELL, jurat. Aug. Court 1739.*.

E 492   PETER WEST TO CHARLES SKINNER
        Aug. 17, 1739. 10 pds. for 100 A. On SS Cowhaul Pocoson at Little
Cowhaul and Great Cowhaul. "...Memorandum that if at any time I am mind to
Dispose of the said Land if Mr. PETER WEST will give as much as any other
person will he shall have the first refusal if he wont his agreed to sell
the said Land to any other person to my advantage CHARLES SKINNER". Wit: J.
PRATT. Aug. Court 1739. *.

E 493   LANCELOT JONES TO JOHN RASBERRY
        Feb. 17, 1738/39. 30 pds. for 150 A. At Main Swamp adj. CHARLES
JONES, HENRY VIZE. Wit: JOHN VICKENS, WILLIAM RASBERRY. Aug. Court 1739.*.

E 495   ISAAC RICKS TO JACOB RICKS

Oct. 7, 1738. 30 pds. for *. On SS Kirby's Creek at Reedy Branch. Part of patent granted April 6, 1722. Wit: J. DEW, WILLIAM RICKS, JOHN WORRELL. Aug. Court 1739. *.

E 497 EDWARD CHITTY, husbandman, TO ABRAHAM BAGGAT
Aug. 14, 1739. Gift. "...love...unto my well beloved Nephew ABRAHAM BAGGAT...after my Decease and the Decease of SUSANNAH my wife...". Land on NS Maherring River. Wit: ABRAHAM BAGGAT, ROBERT WILLIAMS, MATTHEW STRICK-LAND. Aug. Court 1739. *.

E 498 JAMES BROWN TO JOHN HARRILL (HARRELL)
Feb. 13, 1738/39. 50 pds. for 200 A. On WS Cashy Swamp. Part of a survey granted THOMAS MANN for 640 A. dated Feb. 1, 1725. Wit: HENRY HORNE, EDWARD HARRELL, OWEN RYALLS. Aug. Court 1739. *.

E 500 WILLIAM MIDDLETON TO ANTHONY WEBB
Aug. 16, 1739. 80 pds. for 150 A. On Horse Swamp adj. JOHN CLARK. Land bought by Middleton of HENRY VIZE between JOHN CLARK's "and the land called BARNESE's". Wit: FRANCIS PARKER, HENRY VIZE. Aug. Court 1739. *.

E 501 JOHN TAYLOR TO THOMAS HORN
May 8, 1739. 8 pds. for 300 A. On NWS Pottycasie. Adj. THOMAS HORN "at a mutual Dividing Line between me and the said THOMAS HORN". Wit: JOHN SUTTON, WILLIAM RICKS. Aug. Court 1739. *.

E 503 WILLIAM HOOKS of Edgecomb(e) Co. TO JAMES MANNEY, merchant
April 14, 1739. 12 pds. for 250 A. On NS Indian Creek Swamp on NS Chowan River at Creek Swamp. It being a tract granted to JOHN HOOKS, SEN. by patent dated April 1, 1723. Wit: JAMES BARNES, THOMAS CREW. Aug. Court 1739.*.

E 504 WILLIAM REEVES of Edgecomb(e) Co. TO ROBERT HARRIS
Aug. 8, 1739. 40 pds. for 230 A. On NS Morratock River adj. STEPHEN RAGLAND at fork of TURBEFIELD's Run. Wit: STEPHEN RAGLAND, jurat, JOHN STODGHILL. Aug. Court 1739. *.

E 506 JOHN VANPELT TO JACOB VANPELT
July 30, 1739. 100 pds. for 100 A. In Chinkapen Neck on ES Deep Branch. Wit: DANIEL VANPELT, HENRY VIZE. Aug. Court 1739. *.

E 507 JOSEPH HOUGH TO ELIZABETH CHESHERE (CHESHIRE)
Aug. 15, 1739. 20 pds. for 140 A. (Note Here: Marginal note "..erasures in old book...") Land on NS Maherring River adj. "the King's Land". Wit: WILLIAM MACKY, EDWARD HARBENT. Nov. Court 1739. *.

E 509 LORDS PROPRIETORS TO JOHN BENTLEY
April 6, 1722. Grant. 300 A. In Chowan Precinct at Roquess Swamp adj. Coll. POLLOCK, JAMES WILLIAMSON, JOHN SMITH. "due for the Importation of six persons.." Signed THOMAS POLLOCK. Recorded in Sect'y. Office. J. LOVICK, Sec't'y. JOHN BLOUNT, RICH. SANDERSON, THOMAS POLLOCK, JUN. *.*.

E 509 JOHN BENTLEY TO JEREMIAH BENTLEY
April 12, 1739. Gift. *. "within mentioned patent...unto my well beloved Son JEREMIAH BENTLEY...". Wit: JOHN SMITHWICK, JOHN BENTLEY, JUN. Nov. Court 1739. *.

E 510 JOHN BENTLEY TO JOSIAS GRIFFIN
Nov. 6, 1739. 180 pds. for *. Adj. JOHN HARLO, MARTIN GRIFFIN, HUGH HYMAN, TITUS LEGGET, JAMES LEGGET, ___ POLLOCK. Wit: EDWARD COLLINS, MARY COLLINS. Nov. Court 1739. JOHN WYNNS D.C/C.

E 511 THOMAS HOWELL & WIFE ELIZABETH TO SAMUEL TAYLOR
Aug. 3, 1739. "valuable sum" for 100 A. Part of a patent of 640 A. granted to JAMES TURNER March 1, 1719. Land on SS Meherrin River. Adj. JOSEPH WALL, SAMUEL TAYLOR. Land made over by JAMES TURNER TO THOMAS HARRELL, SEN. on May 1, 1725. Wit: THOMAS PHILLIPS, JONES COOK, ARTHUR COOK, WILLIAM GOODSON, SAMUEL BUXTON. Nov. Court 1739. *.

E 513 THEOPHILUS WILLIAMS & WIFE CHRISTIAN TO THOMAS BARKER
May 17, 1739. 40 pds. for 400 A. Part of a tract granted to JOHN WILLIAMS, JUN. and part of a tract granted THEOPHILUS PUGH containing 400 A. At Village Swamp adj. THOMAS BOND at Falling Run. Wit: PETTYGOVE SALSBERRY,

RICHARD MODLIN (MEDLIN). Nov. Court 1739. JOHN WYNNS, D.C/C.

E 514 WILLIAM WHITEHEAD TO JAMES GUYE
       Oct. 1, 1739. 10 pds. for 100 A. On NS Roanoke River adj. CAPT.
THOMAS BRYANT, WILLIAM CAIN. Part of patent to WILLIAM WHITEHEAD for 490 A.
dated August 10, 1720. Wit: J. EDWARDS, JUN., JOLEN POPE. Nov.Court 1740.*.

E 516 WILLIAM SMELLEY "of county of Brownswick in Virginia" TO JOHN DEBERRY
       Oct. 23, 1739. 18 pds. for 200 A. On SS Maherring River whereon
BENJAMIN JOHNSON now lives. BEing upper half of patent. Part of 300 A.
granted to SMELLEY Feb. 1, 1725. Wit: ARTER STEVENS, ROBERT COB, jurat.
Nov. Court 1739. *.

E 517 JOSEPH BOONE TO HUMPHREY PRYER
       Aug. 31, 1738. "12 barrills of good Stone Pitch" for 210 A. In
Maherring Woods adj. JOSEPH BOON. By patent to BOON. Wit: JOHN DEW, jurat,
BENJAMIN HILL, MATTHEW SELLERS. Nov. Court 1739. *.

E 519 JOHNSAND CORBAT (CORBETT) of Isle of Wight Co, Va. TO JOHN TARNE of
       Surry Co, Va.   Nov. 4, 1739. 6 pds. for 145 A. On SS Indian Creek.
Adj. GODPHREY LEE, EDWARD BARRISS(?). Also adj. land granted JOHN HOOKS,
JUN. by patent dated Nov. 1, 1723. Wit: JAMES MANNEY, THOMAS TARNE. Nov.
Court 1739. *.

E 521 GODFREY LEE & WIFE SARAH TO THOMAS TARNE
       Nov. 12, 1739. 15 pds. for 270 A. On WS Chowan River at Indian Creek
adj. GODFREY LEE & RICHARD LEE. Land granted to EDWARD BARNES "by Relaps
Bearing Date October 1726". Wit: JAMES MANNY, HENRY GRAY, JUN. Nov. Court
1739. *.

E 522 JOSHUA LEE & WIFE MARY TO WILLIAM BATTLE of Chowan County
       Aug. 22, 1739. 40 pds. for 150 A. On NS Indian Creek Swamp "to the
former Virginia Line" at Watering Branch. Adj. THOMAS THORN. Part of patent
granted "JOHN LEE dec'd and Given by the said JOHN LEE in his Last will &
Testament to JOSHUA LEE his son...". Wit: HENRY GRAY, ELISHA WILLIAMS,
jurat, JAMES GRAY. Nov. Court 1739. *.

E 524 ABRAHAM BRAWLER TO ISAAC BRAWLER, yeoman
       Dec. 30, 1738. 30 pds. for 320 A. On WS Holly Swamp adj. JONATHAN
GILBERT at Flat Swamp. Wit: JOSEPH MAYNOR, BENJAMIN WYNNS. Nov. Court 1739.*.

E 525 NICHOLLUS BOONE (BOON) TO ARTHUR STEVENSON
       Oct. 17, 1739. 20 pds. for 125 A. On SS Maherring River adj. CAROLUS
ANDERSON, ELIAS FORD, JOSEPH STRICKLAND, WILLIAM ELDRIDGE, ROBERT COBB,
ARTHUR STEVENSON. By patent dated Dec. 3, 1720. Wit: JOSEPH COBB, JUN.,
ROBERT COBB, ABRAHAM STEVENSON. Nov. Court 1739. JOHN WYNNS D.C/C.

E 527 ISAAC SPEIGHT of Perquimmons Co. TO JOHN MANN of Edgecomb(e) Co.
       Nov. 14, 1739. "I...find myself indebted...in the amount...of five
hundred Pounds Cur't & Lawfull money of the Provence...to which payment...
I do bind myself and my heirs...Dated this XIV day of Nov'r MDCCXXXIX...
The conditions are such that JOHN MANN has sold unto MARY SPEIGHT one hundred and fifty acres being the Remainder of 640 acres of Land contained in
a pattent granted to THOS. MANN father of the s'd. JNO. MANN as may appear
by a Deed of Bargain & Sale bearing the date the sixth day of Nov'r 1739...
but there being a dispute about the Title...and one JOHN WYNN pretends a
title to the said Land...the agreement being that said JOHN MANN was to
sell to the said MARY only his Right to the s'd Land...the condition is
such that (MARY SPEIGHT) never trouble or demand any sum...from the said
JOHN MANN..." Wit: LEMUEL REDDECK, WILLIAM TAYLER. Nov. Court 1739.*.

E 528 JOHN WALLIS (WALLESS) & WIFE SARAH TO DANIEL PERRINE
       July 20, 1739. 50 pds. for 150 A. On SS Wills Quarter Swamp. Wit:
JOSEPH HARDEE, jurat, MARY HARDEE, CHARLES HARDEE. Nov. Court 1739. *.

E 530 JOHN BASS TO GEORGE ANDERSON
       Jan. 13, 1738. 10 pds. for 260 A. On NS Maratoke River at Bear
Swamp adj. ROBERT HOUSE. Part of a patent to JOHN BASS, JUN. for 410 A.
Wit: J. EDWARDS, jurat, THOMAS EDWARDS. Nov. Court 1739. *.

E 532 JOHN JENKINS of Edgecomb(e) Co. TO BENJAMIN JOHNSTON

Nov. 2, 1739. 20 pds. for 600 A. On Yorahoh Swamp adj. JOHN BLACK-MAN, WILLIAM BRASSWELL. Wit: JAMES BARNETT, J. EDWARDS, jurat. Nov. Court 1739. *.

E 533 ROBERT BUTLER of Edgecomb(e) Co. TO WILLIAM TAYLOR (TALER)
July 12, 1739. 30 pds. for 200 A. On SS Merattuck River adj. FRANCIS ROUNTREE, JOHN BALLARD. Wit: NEEDHAM BRYAN, jurat, SUSAN BRYAN, WILLIAM BRYAN. Nov. Court 1739. *.

E 535 SAMUEL GARLAND of Isle of Wight Co, Va. TO PETER GARLAND
Oct. 11, 1739. 4 pds. for 100 A. On NS Maherring River adj. EDWARD BARNES. Part of patent to ROBERT BRASSWELL for 580 A. dated March 1, 1719. Wit: JOHN WATTS, jurat, JOHN DRIVER, GILES DRIVER. Nov. Court 1739. *.

E 537 JOHN SPEIR TO WILLIAM BIRD
Aug. 13, 1739. 70 pds. for 100 A. At Spring Branch adj. JOHN SPEIR. Wit: WILLIAM WHITFIELD, jurat, JOHN GRADDY, LUKE WHITFIELD. Nov. Court 1739.

E 539 NATHANIEL PLATT & WIFE MARTHA TO ROLAND WILLIAMS
April 18, 1739. 37 pds. for 100 A. On Ocheneche Neck at Cypress Branch adj. WILLIAM BROWN, ROBERT SIMS. Wit: ____WATFORD, AUGUSTUS MOORE, jurat, JOHN COTTON. Nov. Court 1739. *.

E 541 ROBERT BEVARLEY & WIFE ELLINOR TO JOHN JONES
Sept. 3, 1739. 320 pds. for 200 A. At fork of Poplar Branch adj. ANDREW BARRON, LEWIS WILLIAMS, JAMES WOOD. "...with corn Tobacco Pease Beans and things thereon now..." Wit: ROBERT ROGERS, jurat, GEORGE DOWNING, HENRY BONNER. Nov. Court 1739. *.

E 543 JOHN MORRISS & WIFE REBECCA of Chinkapen Neck TO THOMAS BANKS,
"tayler". *. 240 pds. for 150 A. On SS Wiccacon Creek in Chinkapin Neck. Conveyed to MORRISS by RICHARD WILLIFORD by deed dated July 10, 1728. At Neetops Marsh adj. EDWARD TIDMON at Deep Branch. Adj. DENNIS MACKLENDON, JOHN WYNNS. Wit: JOHN WYNNS, EDWARD TIDMON, WILLIAM LEWIS. Nov. Court 1739*.

E 544 THOMAS BANKS, "taylor" TO WILLIAM BARTAN of Isle of Wight Co, Va.
Oct. 30, 1739. 22 pds. for 195 A. On SS Chowan River adj. WILLIAM BARKER, ROBERT HILL. Wit: JOHN WYNNS, jurat, JAMES MAGLOHAN, SARAH WYNNS. Nov. Court 1739. JOHN WYNNS D.C/C.

E 545 FRANCIS MCCLENDON of Craven Co., yeoman, TO JOHN MORRISS
Sept. 26, 1739. 75 pds. for 318 A. In Chinkapen Neck of SS Bevardam Swamp at branch of Canaan Swamp adj. RICHARD WILLIFORD. Wit: JOHN WYNNS, jurat, W. WYNNS. Nov. Court 1739. *.

E 547 SAMUEL ALLEN TO RICHARD ALLEN
Nov. 12, 1739. 100 pds. for 100 A. On Marratock River at Runaroy Marsh "at a tree called Deers eye". Adj. ____POLLOCK. Wit: JOHN ABBOTT, JOHN WYNNS. Nov. Court 1739. *.

E 548 BARRABE MELTON TO JOHN LYDE (LIDE) "late of Charles City County in
Virginia". August 2, 1739. 30 pds. for 250 A. On Roanoak River adj. JOHN BUDTON of Virginia, HENRY JONES, ELIZABETH MESSE, "plantation formerly belonging to JOHN LEONARD". Wit: JOHN JONES, THEOPHILUS WILLIAMS, THOMAS COMAN. Nov. Court 1739. *.

E 550 ELIAS FORT TO ABRAHAM STEPHANSON
October 23, 1739. 5 pds. for 150 A. On SS Maherring River adj. WILLIAM BOON, JOHN BRYANT, ____BENNET. "one hundred and fifty acres of woodland ground..." Bought of THOMAS BOON by deed dated November 9, 1728. Part of a patent to WILLIAM BENNET for 600 A. dated April 1, 1723. Wit: ARTHUR WILLIAMS, RICHARD WASHINGTON, JOHN WASHINGTON. Nov. Court 1739. *.

E 551 ELIAS FORT TO ABRAHAM STEPHENSON
November 4, 1739. 40 pds. for 147 A. On SS Maherring River at Is-land Gutt at mouth of Myerrey at Old County Line. Part of a patent to WILLIAM BOON for 423 A. dated December 3, 1720. "...and (100 A) of the said Divident was first transfered by the said BOON to SAM'LL CANEDAY by deed dated July 15th 1721...". Wit: ARTHUR WILLIAMS, RICHARD WASHINGTON, JOHN WASHINGTON. Nov. Court 1739. *.

E 553 NICHOLAS BOON TO ROBERT COBB
       October 17, 1739. 20 pds. for 165 A. On SS Maherring River. Adj.
JOHN DEBARG, WILLIAM ELDRIDGE, ARTHUR STEPHENS, ROBERT COBB, NICHOLAS BOON.
Land purchased of WILLIAM BENNET by deed dated May 14, 1723. Wit: JOSEPH
COBB, JUN., CHARLES ANDERSON, ABRAHAM STEVENSON. Nov. Court 1739. *.

E 555 JOHN WILLIAMS TO THOMAS RICHARDSON
       January 20, 1738/39. 10 pds. for 113 A. At head of Little Swamp on
NS Morattock River adj. BENJAMIN THOMAS. Part of tract granted JOSEPH LANE
bearing date 1668. Purchased by WILLIAM BALDWIN "and Divided by the said
BALDWIN between the said JOHN WILLIAMS and EDWARD GOODSON, JUN...". Wit:
JOHN GILL, jurat, GEORGE SMITH, THOMAS HILL. Nov. Court 1739. *.

E 557 JAMES WILLIAM & WIFE REBECCA TO ROBERT HICKS, "marrinor"
       October 17, 1739. 140 pds. for *. JAMES WILLIAMS "late of Boston in
the county of Suffolk and Province of Massachusetts Bay in New England
Marrinor". Land on NS Roanoke River and ES Jump and Run. adj. "Land formerly belonging to JAMES BLOUNT byt now JEFFREY BUTLER...". Adj. THOMAS PAGE.
Wit: JOHN CLARK, LOTT LEWIS. December 1, 1739. Signed: "Suffolk Boston
Oct'r 17th 1739 HABIJAH SAVAGE (Jus Pec)". W. SMITH C.J. "Recorded in ye
secretarys office NATH RILL sec...Rec'd on the day of the date hereof Mr.
ROBT HICKS the sum of one hundred and forty Pounds in full consideration
and purchase of the afore Devised Premises by me JAMES WILLIAMS...".

E 559 NATHANIEL HILL TO THOMAS RYAN
       July 23, 1739. 1400 pds. for 640 A. On SS Salmon Creek. "I the said
NATHANIEL HILL for myself my sons MICHEAL and NATHANIEL our heirs..." Wit:
JOHN FRYARS, JOHN CANNER, ANN FRYARS. February Court 1739. *.

E 562 HENRY BARNS TO THOMAS HANSFORD
       December 20, 1739. Power of atty. "THOMAS HANSFORD of Bertie County
one of his Majestys Justices for the said county..." Power to ack. sale of
120 A. on WS Chowan River adj. LAURENCE MAJUE, WILLIAM WESTAN. Wit: SAMUEL
BASEMAN (BOZEMAN), jurat, JACOB PRESSAN, SARAH PRESSAN (PRESSON), MILDRED
MCKENZIE. Dec. 20, 1739. KEN MCKENZIE. "The above power of Attorney this
day was ack'd before me one of his Majestys Justices of the peace for this
county of Surry in Virginia". Feb. Court 1739.*.

E 562 THOMAS HANSFORD TO MEDIA WHITE
       February 11, 1739. 80 pds. for 320 A. On WS Chowan River adj.
LAURENCE MACGUE (MAGUE). Land formerly JAMES CURLEE's and now held by
MAGUE. Part of a larger tract for 640 A. granted to THOMAS MANN by date
April 1, 1713. Wit: THOMAS JACKSON, JAMES MANEY. Feb. Court 1739. *.

                          End of Deed Book E

BERTIE COUNTY DEED BOOK F

1739 - 1744

F 1 FRANCIS McCLENDON & WIFE ELINOR & ISAAC HILL TO JOSEPH PERRY of
Chowan Precinct. Jan. 2, 1738. 60 pds. for 150 A. In Chinkapin Neck
at the mouth of the Holley Swamp. At Bare (Bear) Swamp. Wit: JOHN THOMAS,
jurat, JOHN WILLIS. May Court 1739. *.

F 2 GEORGE WATSON & WIFE TO JOHN BOWIN
April 30, 1739. 30 pds. for 184 A. At Deep Run on Bear Swamp adj.
WILLIAM NEWLAND, PHILLIP WALSTON. Wit: RICHARD LEARY, ABRAHAM HERRING,
PHILLIP WALSTON, jurat. May Court 1739. *.

F 4 DAVID JORNEJEND TO JOHN ROBINS
May 6, 1739. 20 pds. for 100 A. On WS Chowan River at Gem Pond. Part
of a tract granted to RICHARD HOLLAND by patent April 1, 1723. Wit: JAMES
MANNEY, jurat, WILLIAM ROBINS. May Court 1739. *.

F 5 JOHN DREWRY (DRURY) of Craven County TO JOHN ROBINS
May 6, 1739. 70 pds. for 100 A. At Miery Meadow adj. JOHN HOBBS.
Part of a tract granted to JOHN DAVERSON by patent dated April 1, 1723. Wit:
JOSEPH MANEY, jurat, WILLIAM ROBINS. May Court 1739. *.

F 6 EDWARD BYRD & WIFE ANN (ANNE) TO COLL. ROBERT WEST
May 7, 1739. 500 pds. for 200 A. on Cashoak Creek at the mouth of
Miery Branch and Folly Branch adj. Coll. Robert West. Wit: ROBERT PATTERSON,
JOHN ASHWORTH, PENELOPE WINANTS. May Court 1739. *.

F 7 JOHN WHEELER TO ROWLAND WILLIAMS
Dec. 7, 1739. 35 pds. for 90 A. on NES Mill Swamp. Wit: WILLIAM
RUSHING, JUN. (RUSHIN), ROBERT CROSON. May Court 1739. *.

F 9 HENRY MAYNOR TO ROBERT MILLIKIN
May 5, 1739. 40 pds. for 200 A. Adj. FINCHOR HAYNS, ROBERT HILL,
THOMAS BANKS, BENJAMIN WYNNS. Wit: JOHN WYNNS, ISAAC LEWIS, EBENEZER
SLANSON. May Court 1739. *.

F 9 JOHN PRATT, WILLIAM CATHCART, EDWARD BUXTON, JOHN HODGSON TO DOM REX
May 8, 1739. "...(the) Obligation is such that JOHN PRATT by his
Excellency GABRIEL JOHNSTON Esq. Governor and Commander in Chief of the
Provence...by his Commission bearing date the 26th day of March 1739 was
Constituted & Appointed Sheriff of the County of Bertie...for two years...
he (JOHN PRATT) shall execute perform and Discharge the Office of sheriff.."
Wit: JOHN WYNNS, R. ROGERS. May Court 1739. *.

F 10 MICHAEL RISHA TO JOHN CRICKETT
Aug. 22, 1736. 120 pds. for 180 A. + 200 A. Two tracts on SS Cypress
Swamp adj. MICHAEL RISHA. Wit: RICHARD MALPASS, MARY MALPASS. N.C. Court
July 28, 1737. W. SMITH, C.J.

F 12 THOMAS ASHLEY, blacksmith, & WIFE ANN TO EDWARD HOWKETT (HOCUTT),SEN.
Aug. 30, 1739. 60 pds. for 340 A. On Rawquiss Swamp. Tract granted
to JAMES CASTELLAW by patent. Adj. PHILLIP WALSTON, JONATHAN STANLY, COLL.
CULLEN POLLOCK. Wit: MICHAEL SLAUGHTER, DAVID AMBROS. N.C. Court Aug. 3,
1739. W. SMITH, C.J.

F 13 ROBERT FORSTER of Edgecombe County TO JOHN EDWARDS
Dec. 1, 1739. 400 pds. for 890 A. At Elm Swamp on Meherrin Creek at
the Round Pocoson. Adj. WILLIAM MOOR. Wit: JAMES CRAVEN, ISAAC(?) ARKAND
(?ARTHAND?). N.C. Court December 18, 1739. W. Smith C.J.

F 14 HENRY ROADS & WIFE MARY of "Onsloe" Precinct on New River TO THOMAS
PARKER of Chowan Precinct. March 9, 1731. 130 pds. for 400 A. Land
on Cypress Swamp at Tumbling Branch adj. JOHN BRYAN. Wit: JOHN PARKER,
JOSEPH PARKER, JAMES PARKER. N.C. Court. March 28, 1740. W.SMITH, C.J.

F 16 JAMES CASTELLAW & WIFE SARAH TO GEORGE STRAUGHAN
July 9, 1739. 230 pds. for 170 A. On Roquis Creek adj. LUKE MEIZLE.
Wit: JAMES WATSON, JAMES THOMSON. Aug. Court 1739. *.

F 17 NATHANIEL HILL TO JAMES CASTELLAW
      Aug. 16, 1739. 400 pds. for 640 A. On NS Cashy River at Poplar Run.
"(I)...do...defend...against the Lawfull Claims of my sons MICHAEL and
NATHANIEL..." Wit: ALLEXANDER COTTON, NEEDHAM BRYAN, J. EDWARDS. August
Court 1739. *.

F 18 JAMES CASTELLAW & WIFE SARAH TO MOSES SPEIGHT
      Dec. 13, 1736. 600 pds. for 400 A. On SS Cashy River adj. MOSES
SPEIGHT, JOHN WARBULTON (WARBUTTON). "the plantation lately belonging to
JOHN HOBSON Dec'd..." On Herring Creek whereon PETER BASBARRIE (?BARNABY?)
SEN. now lives..." By deed of Sale from SAMUEL SMITHWICK of Tyrrell Pre-
cinct to the said CASTELLAW. Wit: THOMAS JACKSON, CHARLES McDONALL, THOMAS
CREW. Aug. Court 1739. *.

F 20 RICHARD ALLEN & WIFE TO SAMUELL ALLEN
      May 27, 1739. 600 pds. for 100 A. On NS Merattock River adj. "Deers
Eyes", JOHN YELVERTON, the dividing line between POLLOCK & ALLEN. Wit:
JACOB ALLEN, RICHARD ALLEN, JONAS STALLINGS, jurat. Aug. Court 1739. *.

F 21 CHARLES McDOWALL, Taylor, & WIFE ELIZABETH of Chowan Precinct TO
      SAMUEL ALLEN. August 4, 1739. 35 pds. for 132 A. On Cashy River at
Thomsons Landing. Wit: JAMES BRADLEY, RICHARD ALLEN, JUN. Aug. Court 1739.*.

F 23 MOSES SPEIGHT TO THOMAS RYAN
      July 23, 1739. 401 pds. & 8 sh. for 200 A. In Cashy Neck at dividing
line between EDMOND SMITHERWICK and SAMUEL SMITHERWICK at head of Burnt
Branch. Which land was conveyed by EDMOND SMITHERWICK to MICHAEL KING and
by the said KING to MOSES SPEIGHT. Wit: JOHN FRYARS, ANDREW THOMSON, jurat,
JOHN CONNER. August Court 1739. *.

F 24 DAVID THOMSON TO ANDREW THOMASON & GEORGE PATTERSON
      Aug. 9, 1739. 1000 pds. for 3580 A. One sixth interest in same. (1)
"one full sixth part of the Plantation on which the aforesaid DAVID HENDER-
SON...was seized..". (2) "One sixth part of all and every part of the lands
and Plantations belonging to DAVID HENDERSON containing three thousand
acres...in Tyrell County..". (3) one sixth part of Negroes. (4) One sixth
part of all stock. (5) one sixth part of all crops. "..to be defended
against me and my heirs...and HUGH SCOTT of Boston..". Wit: THOMAS RYAN,
jurat, JAMES THOMSON, JOHN THOMASON. August Court 1739. *.

F 26 JACOB JARNAGAN TO THOMAS BARKER
      July 19, 1739. 50 pds. for 10 A. Adj. BARKER, THOMAS REASON. Wit:
MATTHEW WHITFIELD, JUN., GEORGE SMITH. *.*.

F 27 MEDIA (MEDEA) WHITE TO JOHN PERRY (PERREY) of Chowan County
      Feb. 13, 1739. 400 pds. for 320 A. On WS Chowan River adj. land for-
merly JAMES CURLEES...now held by LAURENCE MAGUE. Wit: THOMAS HANSFORD,
THOMAS JACKSON. Feb. Court 1739. *.

F 28 DAVID DUN of Craven County TO THOMAS HANSFORD
      June 10, 1740. 20 pds. for 100 A. on Chowan River below Ferry Point.
Adj. ROBERT WARREN. Land known as Cotton Bottom. "...land given ELIZABETH
DUN by her father RICHARD BOOTH dec'd. by Will...". Wit: JOHN HOWELL, SEN.,
JOHN HOWELL, JUN. Aug. Court 1740. *.

F 28 JOHN AIRES TO JOHN BYRD
      Jan. 5, 1739. 90 pds. for 50 A. On NS Cashy River adj. ROBERT BYRD,
THOMAS RYAN, "the Widow STEWARDS...". Wit: NATHANIEL HILL, jurat, JOHN RAY.
Feb. Court 1739. *.

F 29 JOHN BARFIELD (BAREFIELD) TO DAVID WARD
      Oct. 16, 1735. 20 pds. for 125 A. on Wattom at Huckleberry Branch adj.
RICHARD HINES, NATHAN ROWLAND at Cashy Swamp. Wit: WILLIAM WHITFIELD,
EDWARD ROBERTS, JOHN JENKINS. N.C. Court Oct. 16, 1735. W. SMITH, C.J.

F 30 JOHN SUTTON TO ANDREW IRVING
      Oct. 24, 1739. 96 pds. for 100 A. On NS Cuttawitskey Meadow. At div-
iding line between JOHN DICKASON and FRANCIS PRIDGEON. Adj. HUGH MORTON.
Wit: GEORGE DOWNING, JOHN SPEIR, MARY DOWNING, jurat. Feb. Court 1739. *.

F 31   EDWARD OUTLAW & GEORGE OUTLAW of Chowan Precinct TO THEPHILLUS PUGH,
       merchant, of Nansemond, Virginia. "(EDWARD)...eldest son of EDWARD
OUTLAW late of the said County Dec'd. and GEORGE OUTLAW another of the sons
of the said EDWARD OUTLAW Dec'd..." Land on Chowan River adj. PETER EVANS
at the Main Road. Wit: MICHAEL JACKSON, WILLIAM PUGH, RICHARD HARGROUSS.
Feb. Court 1739.. *.

F 31   "...at the same time PATIENCE OUTLAW wife of said EDW'D OUTLAW being
       Privately Examined persuant to an Actt...did freely consent...".

F 33   WILLIAM McCONE TO THOMAS DAVIS
       Feb. 12, 1739. Deed of Gift. 100 A. "...in Consideration of the Love
good Will and Effection...unto my Brother in Law THOMAS DAVIS..." Land on
SS Horse Pasture Creek adj. EDWARD POWERS at Hawtree Branch. Wit: JOHN
WYNNS, JOHN BATTLE. Feb. Court 1739. *.

F 33   JOSEPH NIXON TO JAMES WASHINGTON of Surry County, Virginia.
       May 13, 1740. 35 pds. for 300 A. On SS Meherring River adj. JOHN
NELLSON, HENRY WHEELER "thence along a line of Markt trees that BENJAMIN
FOREMAN formerly made Between MATA SELLERS land and the said NIXONS land..",
OWEN McCRAVEY, land known as BENJAMIN FOREMAN Plantation. Wit: SAMUEL
TAYLOR, THOMAS MURRELL, RICHARD WALL. May Court 1740. *.

F 34   NATHANIEL FIELD & WIFE ELIZABETH TO JOHN BYNAM of Surry County, Va.
       May 8, 1740. 15 pds. for 200 A. On NS Meherron River adj. MARY BRASS-
WELL. Beling the upper part of a patent granted to SAMUELL ELSON dated
March 26, 1723. Wit: JAMES WASHINGTON, RICHARD WASHINGTON, ARTHUR WASHING-
TON. May Court 1740. *.

F 35   ABRAHAM BURTON & WIFE ANNE TO THOMAS MURRELL of Southworke Parish in
       Surry County, (Va.) May 13, 1740. 40 pds. for 150 A. Part of a pa-
tent for 320 A. granted to SAMUEL PEACOCK on April 7, 1730 and sold to
WILLIAM BARDEN and by BARDEN sold to ABRAHAM BURTON by deed dated August
12, 1735. Land on SS Meherrin River at Crane Pond. Wit: JAMES WASHINGTON,
RICHARD WASHINGTON, SAMUEL PEACOCK. May Court 1740. *.

F 36   JOHN BRYANT TO CAROLUS ANDERSON
       Oct. 16, 1739. 5 pds. for 100 A. Part of a tract sold by WILLIAM
BENNETT to THOMAS BOON, JUN. and by BOON transferred to JOHN BRYANT by deed
Nov. 9, 1724. Part of a patent for 600 A. granted to WILLIAM BENNETT dated
1723. Land on SS Meherrin River adj. JOHN NELLSON, WILLIAM BOON. Wit: JOHN
BRIANT, JOHN DEBERRY, SARAH REVETT. May Court 1740. *.

F 38   WILLIAM McCONE (MACONE) TO JOHN MACONE
       Feb. 12, 1739. Deed of Gift. 100 A. "unto my Loving Brother John
MACONE..." On WS Main Road "from MRS. CHESHIRES Ferry to BARKERs Ferry near
Horse Pasture Creek..." Part of 240 A. which "Edward Powers conveyed to our
Father JOHN MACONE..." on Feb. 4, 1732. Wit: JOHN WYNNS, J. DEW. February
Court 1739. *.

F 38   RICHARD WASHINGTON TO JOHN WASHINGTON
       Dec. 24, 1739. 15 pds. for 335 A. On WS Hunting Quarter Swamp. Being
a patent granted RICHARD WASHINGTON Aug. 4, 1723. The manor plantation of
RICHARD WASHINGTON. Wit: ARTHUR WASHINGTON, RICHARD WASHINGTON, MARY WASH-
INGTON, EDWARD HUDGSON. Feb. Court 1739. *.

F 39   JOHN BUTTER (BUTLER) & WIFE ELIZABETH TO WILLIAM BATTLE of Chowan
       County. Feb. 11, 1739. 10 sh. for 2 A. on SS Indian Creek Swamp adj.
BATTLE. Wit: WILLIAM BARNES, jurat, JOHN WYNNS. Feb. Court 1739. *.

F 40   THOMAS RYAN TO NATHANIEL HILL
       July 23, 1739. 245 pds. for 180 A. On NS Cashy Swamp adj. Coll.
ROBERT WEST, THOMAS WEST. Wit: JOHN FRYARS, JOHN CONNER, ANN FRYARS. Feb.
Court 1739. *.

F 42   ABRAHAM HERRON (HERRIN) TO JOHN AIRES
       Nov. 7, 1739. "Six Thousand Weight of Fresh Pork and Twenty days
Work". 380 A. On SS Bear Swamp. Wit: JOHN RAY, JOHN BOWIN. Feb. Court 1739.*.

F 43   SIMON HOMES TO JAMES WOOD

Feb. 13, 1739/40. 25 pds. for 100 A. Part of a tract granted WILLIAM CURLEE in 1720 and granted by deed to SIMON HOMES. On SWS Ahotsky Swamp. Wit: JOHN PORTER, SEN., WILLIAM WHITFIELD, JUN. Feb. Court 1739. *.

F 44 JAMES FARECHILD TO THOMAS JOHNSTON
Nov. 10, 1729. 7 pds. for 150 A. At Haw Branch adj. GODPHREY HOOKER, ROBERT EVANS, MR. POLLOCK, WILLIAM BAKER. Part of 200 A. which FAIRCHILD bought of JOHN MAINER, SEN. Wit: SAMUELL WILLIAMS, ELIZABETH WILLIAMS. November Court 1739. Thomas Crew, D.C/C.

F 45 THOMAS JOHNSON TO SAMUEL GREEN of "Perquimons County"
Feb. 11, 1739. 40 pds. for 150 A. Wit: JOHN WYNNS, JAMES(?) ARTHAND (?). Feb. Court 1739. *.

F 46 RICHARD MARTIN & WIFE ELIZABETH TO THOMAS JACKSON
January 14, 1739. 175 pds. for 140 A. on SS Meherrin Creek at Little Gutt "to the Old Indian (Path) going over the Elm Swamp". Wit: JOB ROGERS, SUSAN LOCKIER. Feb. Court 1739. *.

F 47 ABRAHAM DEW of Edgecombe County TO JOHN HOBS (HOBBS)
Feb. 12, 1739/40. 20 "Barrells of Good Merchantable full Bound Tarr". For 200 A. Part of a patent granted ABRAHAM DEW on NS Meherrin River at Gardners Path at Head of Horse Pasture Creek adj. JOHN ROGERS. Wit: J. DEW, WILLIAM BARDIN, JOHN WILLIAMS, JUN. Feb. Court 1739. *.

F 48 RICHARD LEE TO JOHN BUTLER (BUTTER)
Sept. 29, 1739. 40 pds. for 270 A. on SS Indian Creek adj. RICHARD HOLLAND. Now in possession of DAVID JARNAGAN. Adj. GODFREY LEE at "a Great Branch...commonly called GODFREY LEEs great Branch...". to the main run of Indian Creek. Wit: JAMES MANEY, HENRY GAY. Feb. Court 1739. *

F 49 NICHOLAS TYNER & WIFE ELIZABETH TO WILLIAM TYNER
Feb. 7, 1739. Deed of Gift. 300 A. "for the value and Respect... unto my Son... Excepting my Liberty and Tollaration therein and thereon dureing my natural Life..". Land on SS Maherrin River and SS Little Swamp. Wit: J. DEW, jurat, RICHARD BARLEY. Feb. Court 1739. *.

F 50 NICHOLAS TYNER, SEN. TO NICHOLAS TYNER, JUN.
Feb. 7, 1739. Deed of Gift. 400 A. "...for the value and Respect that I Bear to my son NICHOLAS TYNER, JUN...". Land on SWS Little Swamp adj. JOHN BARNES. Wit: J. DEW, RICHARD BAILEY. Feb. Court 1739. *.

F 51 BARNABY MACKINNE of Edgecombe County TO WILLIAM BAYLE (BAILEY)
Jan. 9, 1739. 6 pds. for 100 A. "..at Mauls upper line known by the name of Swanson Survey" to Deep Valley. Being part of a tract of land granted to said BARNABE MACKINNE by patent bearing date July 30, 1726. Wit: THOMAS CREW, WILLIAM HURST. Feb. Court 1739. *.

E 52 THOMAS WARD TO THOMAS FUTERRILL
March 8, 1739. 10 pds. for 290 A. On NS Pottacasie Creek adj. THOMAS DRAKE. Wit: MATTHEW MASHBORNE, THOMAS FUTERRILL, JUN., JOHN SUTTON. Feb. Court 1739. *.

F 53 RICHARD SOWELL, son of CHARLES SOWELL TO JOHN WELSSON, yeoman
April 14, 1740. 50 pds. for 230 A. "a certain Parcell of Land which my Dec'd. father Devised to me..." At mouth of Bare Swamp adj. WELLSON, OBEDIAH SOWELL. Wit: JOHN WYNNS, DANIEL BROWN, MARTIN NOWELL. May Ct. 1740.*.

F 54 JOHN PATTERSON TO JOHN NIXON
May 10, 1737. 50 pds. for 629 A. On Meherring Creek. Wit: JOHN SUTTON, MARY SUTTON, MARY CARTER. *.

F 55 JOSEPH NIXON TO ANDREW IRELAND
July 6, 1739. *.*. "...all my Right Title and Interest Claim or Demand in and to the within contained deed...". Wit: ARTHUR WILLIAMS, MATTHEW SELLERS, jurat. Feb. Court 1739. *.

F 55 JOSEPH GARLING of "Isle of White County", TO JOHN MELLER
Jan. 10, 1739. 6 pds. for 100 A. On SS "JOHN VEGENs line" adj. JONA-THAN SANDERS. Wit: JAMES MANEY, jurat, PETER GARLING. Feb. Court 1739. *.

F 56 THOMAS TURNER of Isle of Wight County, Va. TO WILLIAM HART
Nov. 12, 1739. "a valuable sum" for 180 A. On SS Maherrin River.
Land granted to THOMAS TURNER by Hon. CHARLES EDEN ESQ. by date March 1,
1719 "now in actual possession of WILLIAM HART". Adj. ISRAEL JOYNER. Wit:
JAMES TURNER, JOSEPH PLATTS, JOHN SIMPSON, FRANCIS BOYKIN. Feb. Court 1739.*.

F 57 JAMES TURNER & WIFE ANN of Isle of Wight Co., Va. TO WILLIAM HART
Nov. 12, 1739. "a valuable sum" for 100 A. Part of a patent of 640 A.
dated March 1, 1719. Land on SS Meherrin River. Now in actual possession of
HART. Wit: JAMES TURNER, Jurat, JO(SEPH) PLATTS, JOHN SIMPSON. February
Court 1739. *.

F 57 JAMES TURNER & WIFE ANN of Isle of Wight County, Va. TO WILLIAM HART
Nov. 12, 1739. "a valuable sum" for 100 A. Part of a patent of 640 A.
dated March 1, 1719. On SS Meherrin River. Now in actual possession of
WILLIAM HART. Wit: JAMES TURNER, Jurat, JOS(EPH) PLATTS, JOHN SIMPSON.
February Court 1739. *.

F 59 JAMES TURNER & WIFE ANN of Isle of Wight County, Va. TO FRANCIS BOYKIN
Feb. 9, 1739. " a valuable sum" for 290 A. On SS Maherring River.
Land granted to SIMON BRYANT by WILLIAM REED, ESQ. President and Commander
in Chief of North Carolina by date Nov. 7, 1723. On Cypress Swamp adj.
HENRY TURNER. Land being in actual possession of FRANCIS BOYKIN. Wit:
WILLIAM HART, jurat, JOHN SIMPSON. Feb. Court 1739. *.

F 60 JAMES BOON of Craven County TO JOHN TAYLOR, SEN.
Jan. 1, 1739. 6 pds. for 100 A. On SS Maherrin River adj. ARTHUR
WILLIAMS on NS Kirbys Creek at Spring Branch. Part of a patent formerly
granted to JOSEPH BOON dated March 1, 1719. Wit: JOHN DEW, jurat, RICHARD
BAILEY, JAMES HOLLAND. Feb. Court 1739. *.

F 61 RICHARD BAILEY TO GEORGE BUNTIN
Feb. 6, 1739. 10 pds. for 200 A. On SS Maherring River at Spring
Branch on Kirbys Creek. Being part of patent formerly granted to JOSEPH
BOON for 480 A. dated March 1, 1719. Wit: JOHN DEW, NICHOLAS TYNER. Feb.
Court 1739. *.

F 62 CHARLES KERBY (KIRBY) TO THOMAS AULTMAN
Feb. 11, 1739. 10 pds. for 200 A. On SS Kirbys Creek. Part of patent
granted CHARLES KIRBY on Dec. 1, 1727. Wit: ARTHUR WILLIAMS, Jurat, JOHN
DEW, ROBERT WILLIAMS. Feb. Court 1739. *.

F 63 JAMES NELSON TO WILLIAM NELSON
Jan. 30, 1739. 20 pds. for 200 A. Land granted to TIMOTHY HIGNS by
patent dated April 1, 1723. On NES Hunting Quarter Swamp. Wit: JOHN DEW,
jurat, ELIZABETH TAYLOR. Feb. Court 1739. *.

F 64 JOHN GRAY & WIFE ANN TO JAMES CARTER
Aug. 10, 1737. 60 pds. for 315 A. On NS Sandy Run. Wit: JAMES
THOMPSON, JOHN FREEMAN, MOORE CARTER. May Court 1740. *.

F 66 PEDEGROVE SALSBERRY TO ISAAC HARRELL
Aug. 11, 1739. 7 pds. for 140 A. On NS Maratuck River adj. "SPIVEYS
Line", WILLIAM TURNER, JOHN MOOR, WILLIAM EASON. Wit: JACOB JERNIGAN, JOHN
MOOR, WILLIAM BRYANT. Mary Court 1740. *.

F 68 DAVID OSHEAL of Nansemond County, Va. TO JOHN WYNNS
Sept. 5, 1739. 20 pds. "within mentioned patent". Wit: MICHAEL
JACKSON, WILLIAM WYNNS, Jurat, J. OSHEAL. May Court 1740. *.

F 67 LORDS PROPRIETORS TO DAVID OSHEAL
Aug. 5, 1729. Grant. 440 A. "...according to Our great Deed of
grant bearing date the first day of May Anno Domini 1668...". Land on WS
Ahotskey Ridge at Timber Branch adj. ROBERT LANIER, EDWARD HOWARD, JOSEPH
JONES, JOHN JONES, JUN. Land formerly granted by patent to JAMES HAMELTON
Aug. 4, 1726 and "lapsed for not seating". Signed: RICH'D. EVERARD, E.
MOSELEY, C. GALE, ROB'T. WEST, J. LOVICK, Sec't'y., JOHN BLOUNT, JOHN PATIN.

F 69 JOHN WYNNS TO JOHN CATHCART "of Genoch in great Britain" & WILLIAM
CATHCART of Bertie County. Feb. 13, 1739. 21 pds. 1 sh. *.*. Wit:
DAVID COLTRANE.*.*.

F 69 BENJAMIN BRITT (BRETT) & WIFE CHARITY TO THOMAS BRITT
      Jan.23 1739. 12 pds. for 100 A. On NS Meherring River "...Out of the
Original patent by the Last Will and Testament of JOHN BRITT Deceased." Wit:
WILLIAM MACKY, NATHAN BRITT, jurat. May Court 1740. *.

F 70 JOSEPH MAYNOR TO CULLMUR SESSUMS, Yeoman
      Feb. 11, 1739. 35 pds. for 100 A. On Beavardam Branch. Wit: JOSEPH
MAYNOR, BENJAMIN WYNNS, Jurat. W. WYNNS. May Court 1740. *.

F 71 ROBERT ROGERS, Ordinary Keeper, & WIFE MARY TO THEOPHILUS PUGH of
      Nansemond County, Va. March 14, 1739. 60 pds. for 250 A. Land for-
merly in Chowan Precinct in Ahotskey Woods. Adj. JA. EVARARD, R'D. HAR-
GRAUSS, WILLIAM PUGH. May Court 1740. *.

F 74 THOMAS BONNER TO JAMES WOOD
      March 20, 1739. 20 pds. for 300 A. On SS Ahoskey Swamp adj. BENTON
MOOR. Wit: ___ROGERS, MARY ROGERS, JOHN WYNNS, jurat. May Court 1740. *.

F 75 ABRAHAM BRAWLER TO CHRISTOPHER SEGAR, blacksmith
      March 14, 1739. 70 pds. for 195 A. On WS Holly Swamp at Northern
Branch of William Creek at mouth of Reedy Branch "at dividing line between
said land and WILLIAM WARRENS Land". Adj. GODWINS Land, ISAAC BRAWLER at
Flatt Swamp. Wit: JOHN WYNNS, jurat, WILLIAM SPARKMAN. May Court 1740. *.

F 76 JOHN SPEIR of Edgecombe County TO JAMES BIRD
      Feb. 18, 1739. 10 pds. for 100 A. On SS Short Swamp. By patent to
JOHN SPEIR dated Feb. 17, 1737. Wit: ROBERT HILLIARD, THOMAS DOWLS, SAMUEL
WIGGINS, JOHN WYNNS, jurat. May Court 1740. *.

F 77 JOHN JENKINS TO PATRICK O QUIN
      July 6, 1739. 20 pds. for 30 A. On SS Catawatskey Meadow at West
Branch. Adj. EDWARD HOWCOTT, PATRICK OQUIN, JOHN JENKINS. Wit: MARY ANDER-
SON, JAMES BAREFIELD, jurat. May Court 1740. *.

F 78 WILLIAM WHITEHEAD of Edgecombe Precinct TO JOHN BODDIE
      May 12, 1740. 20 pds. for 200 A. On NS Swift Creek at mouth of Little
Gutt adj. JOHN SCOTT, JOSEPH NIXON at Meadow Branch. Wit: LEWIS DAVIS,
THOMAS HILL, THOMAS THARP, jurat. May Court 1740. *.

F 79 RICHARD SUMNER TO GEORGE DOWNING
      May 6, 1740. 25 pds. for 200 A. On NS Catawitskey Meadow at GRAY's
Pocoson. Wit: JAMES BRYANT, JOHN OCQUIN, JOHN SUTTON, Jurat. May Court 1740.*.

F 80 JONATHAN TAYLOR TO HENRY BATE, "province Sergeon"
      Sept. 18, 1739. 145 pds. for 100 A. On NS Morattuck River and ES
Quitsnay Swamp. Land the said TAYLOR bought of JAMES WILLIAMSON. Adj. BATES,
WIMBERLY. Wit: HENRY HUNTER, Jurat, GAR'D. VANUPSTALL, WILLIAM PERREY. May
Court 1740. *.

F 82 WILLIAM MOORE TO JAMES PARTRAM
      March 3, 1739. 20 pds. for 300 A. On NS "Morratock River alis Roan-
oak" on Jacks Swamp. Wit: PHIL SMITH, ROBERT HARRIS, Jurat, JOHN RICHARDSON.
May Court 1740. *.

F 83 ISAAC BRAWLER, yeoman, TO CHRISTOPHER SEGAR
      April 14, 1740. 100 pds. for 320 A. On WS Holly Swamp and N branch
of Wiccacon Creek. Adj. JONATHAN GILBERT at Flatt Swamp. Wit: THOMAS DIXON,
jurat, JOHN DEW, MR. SHIVERS(?). May Court 1740. *.

F 84 WILLIAM WATERS TO MARY DEMSEY
      June 4, 1739. 9 pds. for 10 A. On SW branch of Salmon Creek on "Mr.
DUCKINFIELDS Line" and "LUEEYS Oldfield" (?). Wit: THOMAS RYAN, Jurat,
WILLIAM ASHLEY. May Court 1740. *.

F 85 JAMES SKIPPER (SKIPER, SKIPOR) & WIFE MARY TO JOHN HILLIARD
      Dec. 24, 1739. 20 pds. for 195 A. Being part of two patents (1)Dated
February 1, 1725 (2) August 10 17(?). Containing all land of both patents
except 100 A. made over to WILLIAM HALL. Wit: JOHN DAWSON, jurat, WILLIAM
HALL, SOL'N DAWSON. *.*. "...MARY SKIPER do Resign all my Rights of Dower
in said plantation...".

F 86   GEORGE MORRIS TO EDWARD JACKSON of Charles City County, Va.
       Feb. 9, 1739. 17 pds. 10 sh. A tract of land patented by HINCHE
GILLUM and sold to HOSEA TAPLEY cont. 600 A. On NS Meratuck River "on the
side of Creek that makes the Islands". Wit: JOHN BRADLEY, HOSEA TAPLEY,
THOMAS GOOD, AARON FUSSELL, Jurat. May Court 1740. *.

F 88   MOSES PRICE & WIFE ANN TO JOHN CATHCART of Genoch of North Britain &
       WILLIAM CATHCART, "practitioner in Phisick"   Oct. 26, 1739. 50 pds.
for 50 A. At Mouth of Piney Branch on Ahoskey Swamp at MATTHEWS Line. Wit:
ROBERT ROGERS, Jurat, MOOR CARTER. May Court 1740. *.

F 89   JONATHAN GILBERT of Perquimmons Precinct TO JOB ROGERS
       *. 150 pds. for 200 A. At Deep Creek Bridge adj. EDWARD HAIR, STEPHEN
WILLIAMS at May Spring Branch. "..and that the said land and Half the s'd
Mill...". Wit: ROBERT GILBERT, jurat, JOSEPH GILBERT. May Court 1736. *.

F 90   JOB ROGERS TO JONATHAN GILBERT
       Feb. 9, 1739. *.*. "...all my Right Title & Interest in the within
deed of sale...". Wit: THOMAS JACKSON, JOSEPH MAYNOR. May Court 1740. *.

F 91   SAMUEL SIZEMORE of Chowan Precinct TO ISAAC LEWIS
       July * 1720. 40 pds. for *. Land adj. RALPH OUTLAW "a Place settled
and Built upon by one THOMAS RODE on Catewhiske Swamp commonly known &
called by the Name Rodes folly...". Wit: RT. HICKS, BARA___ MACKINNE. "At
Court held for Chowan Precinct at the Court House in Queen Anns Town on
30th day of July 1720..." THOMAS HENMAN C/C.

F 92   ISAAC LEWIS TO WILLIAM MOOR of Ahoskey
       Nov. 3, 1739. 22 pds. *. "within mentioned lands". Wit: THOMAS JONES,
PETER PEIRCY. May Court 1740. *.

F 92   OSBORNE JEFFREYS TO WILLIAM HILLIARD
       May 12, 1740. 20 pds. for 400 A. On NES Moratuck River. Land granted
JEFFREYS by patent March 17, 1728. At Hog Pen Meadow. Wit: ISAAC PARKER,
JOELL NEWGUM, DANIEL DICKINSON. May Court 1740. *.

F 93   JOHN BEVERLY TO ROBERT ROGERS
       May 25, 1740. 240 pds. for 440 A. At Head of Ahorsekin Marsh. Wit:
JAMES ARTHAND, ROBERT HARRIS. May Court 1740. *.

F 94   JOHN PERREY & WIFE SARAH TO THEOPHILUS PUGH of Upper Parish Nansemond
       County, Va., merchant. Feb. 12, 1739. 100 pds. for 250 A. "...being
in Bertie Precinct formerly called Chowan Prec't on Wicacone Pocoson". Land
formerly surveyed for George Gladstain and by him assigned to WILLIAM BROWN
"and the said WILLIAM BROWN dying the...Land Decended to his son BEAL BROWN
and by the said BEAL BROWN...sold...to EDWARD HOWCOTT and by (HOWCOTT) sold
unto JOHN PERRY..." By patent to EDWARD HOWCUTT bearing date the first day
of April in the year 1720. Wit: JOHN WYNNS, THOMAS JACKSON, WILLIAM TWEEDIE.
May Court 1740. *. "...SARAH the wife of the s'd JOHN PERREY being privately
Examined by NEEDHAM BRYANT ESQ. & Declares she Ack'd the same freely..."

F 97   THOMAS BARKER TO JOHN BEVERLY
       May 14, 1740. 5 sh. for 440 A. At head of Ahorseskin Marsh. Land
purchased of WILLIAM CURLEIGH. Wit: J. PRATT, JOHN ABBOT(ABBOTT), Jurat,
JAMES ARTHAND. May Court 1740. *.

F 98   WILLIAM ELDRIDGE TO WILLIAM TALOR
       May 10, 1740. 12 pds. for 170 A. On SS Meherron River at Cabbin
Branch. Adj. HENRY GAY. By patent to ELDRIDGE dated Feb. 1, 1725. Wit: J.
DEW, DANIEL OQUIN, JOHN BRYANT. May Court 1740. *.

F 99   PEDEGROVE SALSBERRY & WIFE SARAH of Society Parish, Bertie Co. TO
       ADAM RABEY. April 19, 1740. 25 pds. for 200 A. On NS Roanoake River
adj. NEEDHAM BRYANT, MATTHEW TURNER, ISAAC HARRELL, CALEPH SPIVEY, THEOPHI-
LUS WILLIAMS. Wit: MOSES ELLIS, GEORGE HOPE, AARON ELLIS. May Court 1740.*.

F 100 CAROLUS ANDERSON TO BENJAMIN COBB
       Oct. 16, 1739. 10 pds. for 150 A. Part of patent granted THOMAS
BOON for 250 A. dated Aug. 4, 1723. On SES Conoroy Swamp. Said land now in
possession of COBB. Wit: JOSEPH COBB, JUN., NICHOLAS BOON, ABRAHAM
STEVENSON. May Court 1740. *.

F 101 RICHARD WILLIAMS TO JEAN (JANE) BROWN
May 10, 1740. 12 pds. for 200 A. JANE BROWN "formerly wife of THOMAS BROWN Dec'd...I do make over to her Lawfull son ARTHUR BROWN...". Part of a tract containing 640 A. which GEORGE WILLIAMS bought of RICHARD MELTON. Adj. BENJAMIN FOREMAN, JEAN BROWN, RICHARD MELTON. Wit: JOHN WYNNS, J. HOLLBROOK. May Court 1740. *.

F 102 THOMAS SPELLER TO ALEXANDER RAY
March 24, 1740. 100 pds. for 300 A. Adj. RICHARD SWAIN, MILES GALES, _____ FRISBIE. Wit: EDWARD COLLINS, WILLIAM WARD. May Court 1740. *.

F 105 JOHN MOOR TO RICHARD MOOR
Feb. 13, 1739. Gift. 200 A. "JOHN MOOR son of RICHARD MOOR Late Dec'd...and RICHARD MOOR son of RICHARD MOOR aforesaid..." Land on NS Morattoak River. Being land late RICHARD MOOR bought of THOMAS AVENT by deed dated July 16, 1716 "...and is Mannor Plantation RICHARD MOOR now lives on ..." Wit: P(?) SMITH, ROBERT HARRIS. Feb. Court 1739. *.

F 105 JOHN WYNNS TO JOHN KEEFE
Feb. 4, 1739. 80 pds. for 150 A. "JOHN WYNNS Attorney of GEORGE SMITH Late of Bertie County..." Land on ES Chinkapen Creek "near the fort Bridge the Plantation whence the said SMITH Lately Removed..." Adj. OBREYs Branch, BENJAMIN BAKER. Wit: JAMES(?) ARTHAND, *. Feb. Court 1739. *.

F 106 HENRY JONES TO PHILLIP JONES
Aug. 20, 1739. Gift. 230 A."...Between HENRY JONES son of HENRY JONES Late Dec'd...and PHILLIP JONES (well beloved Brother)..." Land on NS Moratuck River at mouth of Deep Bottom. Adj. WILLIAM REAVES, BARRABE MELTON "Being land that HENRY JONES Dec'd bought of JOHN LEONARD..." Wit: HENRY HORNE, EVAN RAGLAND, JAMES JONES. Feb. Court 1739. *.

F 107 JAMES TART TO SAMUEL WILLIAMS, SEN.
Feb. 12, 1739. 50 pds. for 99 A. plus 100 A. "...being all the Land sold to me and Contained in Two Deeds one sold to me by CHARLES STEPHENSON bearing Date Nov. the fourteenth day Anno 1727 the other bearing Date the Twelfth day of February 1738 and Purchased from OSBERN JEFFREYS..." Adj. SAMUEL MERRITTS at SES Long Creek Meadow at Cattail Swash adj. RICHARD BRASSWELL. Wit: ROBERT WILKINS, JONATHAN FORT, SAMUEL RUFFIN, Jurat. Feb. Court 1739. *.

F 109 JOHN MOOR TO RICHARD MOOR
Feb. 10, 1739/40. Gift. 120 A. "Between JOHN MOOR son of RICHARD MOOR Late Dec'd...and RICHARD MOOR son of aforesaid RICHARD MOOR..." Adj. RICHARD MOOR's present manor house plantation. Wit: P. SMITH, ROBERT HARRIS. Feb. Court 1739. *.

F 111 JOHN WILLIAMS & WIFE ANN TO THOMAS WHITMELL
Jan. 21, 1739. 40 pds. for 440 A. Adj. THOMAS TURNER on Branch of Rocquiss, JOHN EDWARDS. Wit: SAMUEL HERRING, ARTHUR WILLIAMS, ISAAC WILLIAMS. Feb. Court 1739. *.

F 112 JOHN WALLIS, "weaver", & WIFE SARAH TO THOMAS JENKINS
Sept. 2, 1739. 50 pds. for 200 A. On Wills Quarter Swamp at JOHN WILLIAM's corner. Wit: MARTHA FEWAUSE, ELIZABETH FEWAUSE, JOSEPH HARDEE. Feb. Court 1739. *.

F 114 HENRY JONES TO JAMES JONES
Aug. 20, 1739. Gift. 240 A. "HENRY JONES Son of HENRY JONES late Dec'd...(to my well beloved brother)...JAMES JONES...the Manor Plantation whereon his father Last Lived...Part of Patent to HENRY JONES Dec'd for (640 A.)...bearing date 26th day Feb. 1711/12..." Wit: HENRY HORNE, EVAN RAGLAND, PHILLIP JONES. Feb. Court 1739. *.

F 115 GEORGE DOWNING & WIFE MARY TO FREDERICK JONES
March 5, 1738. Exchange. 608 A. "...in consideration (by) FREDERICK JONES by Sufficient Deed...bearing Equall Date...Land containing five hundred and forty five acres...on South East Side of Catawiskey Swamp... granted JOHN JONES, SEN. Dec'd. and by Last Will and Testament...to FREDERICK JONES..." To FREDERICK JONES 608 A. tract whereon GEORGE DOWNING now dwells being tract granted RICHARD KILLINGSWORTH, dec'd. and by KILLINGSWORTH sold to MICHAEL DORMAN and by DORMAN sold to DOWNING. This tract on

WS Ura Path. KILLINGSWORTH patent date March 1, 1719. Wit: ALLEXANDER CAMPBELL, JAMES BRYANT, jurat. Feb. Court 1739. *.

F 117   JOHN YEALVANTON (YELVERTON) TO OWEN ROYALL
        Oct. 24, 1739. 24 pds. for 213 A. Part of patent formerly granted JAMES BLOUNT. Cont. 213 A. and made over to JOHN YELVERTON. Adj. land formerly THOMAS BUSBY's at Beaver Swash on Morrattock River at dividing line between JOHN YELVERTON and JOHN BLOUNT. Wit: JOHN HARRELL, LITTLETON SPIVEY, JOHN YEALVERTON. Feb. Court 1739. *.

F 119   JOHN GRAY TO PHIL (PHILLIP) SMITH
        May 8, 1739. 53 pds. for 750 A. On NS Moratock River adj. JOHN PACE, RICHARD TUBERVIL, WILLIAM TURBERVIL at Reedy Run Pocoson. Granted by patent to JOHN PACE & RICHARD TURBERVIL dated 1719. Wit: JOSEPH BRYAN, JOHN MACKFARLING. Feb. Court 1739. *.

F 120   BARNABY MACKINNE of Edgecombe County TO THOMAS HOWELL
        Jan. 28, 1739. 12 pds. 10 sh. for 100 A. On NS Moratock River being part of tract of 640 A. granted to JOHN GREEN by patent July 29, 1712 and by GREEN sold to BARTHOLEMEW CHAVOORS and by the said CHAVOORS sold to MACKINNE. Adj. WILLIAM JONES on Yeorah Swamp. Wit: WILLIAM BAYLEY, WILLIAM HURST, jurat. Feb. Court 1739. *.

F 121   JOHN BROWNE TO JOHN BATTLE
        Feb. 2, 1739. 32 pds. for 330 A. Being land granted JOHN BROWNE on Nov. 8, 1721 at mouth of Blundering Branch at Catawatskey Swamp. Wit: ISAAC CARTER, jurat, WILLIAM KNIGHT, MARY BROWN. Feb. Court 1739. *.

F 122   ROBERT ELLIS TO PHILLIP SMITH
        Feb. 9, 1740. 25 pds. for 300 A. Adj. EMANUEL ROGERS, PHILLIP SMITH, "Late JOHN GRAYS land", PHILLIP SMITH, "ROBERT ELLIS Dec'd.". Wit: ROBERT HARRIS, jurat, JOHN WILLEY, JOHN MOOR. Feb. Court 1739. *.

F 124   WILLIAM LATTIMORE & WIFE ELIZABETH TO JOHN BRADLEY
        Dec. 21, 1739. 350 pds. for 250 A. Plantation formerly called PERRYS Plantation "it being in Cashy". "...freely aquited...onley the said JOHN BRADLEY is to pay the one Half of the Quitrents of the bargained Premisses to Our Sovreign Lord the King or his Debts which is behind...". Wit: WILLIAM ASHBORNE, JOHN ROGERS, WILLIAM ROGERS. Feb. Court 1739. *.

F 125   LORDS PROPRIETORS TO WILLIAM GRAY
        Feb. 1, 1725. Grant 350 A. "...according to Our great Deed of grant bearing date the first day of May Anno Domini 1668 Given to Our County of Albemarle..." Land in St. John's Neck at Tubling Branch adj. JOHN BRYANT, SEN. at Teemer (?Fremer?) Branch. Signed: SIR RICHARD EVERARD, Barr't Gov'n, J. LOVICK, C. GALE, T. HARVEY, T. POLLOCK, JOHN BLOUNT, E. MOSELEY. J. LOVICK Sec't'y. Rec. in Sec't'y Office.

F 126   NICHOLAS MEDLIN (MEDLINE) & WIFE ANN TO JAMES STEWART
        Dec. 5, 1739. 160 pds. for 440 A. Part of land contained in 640 A. whereon MEDLIN now lives on NS Moratock River adj. FRANCIS PARKER. "to a branch of the Cashy", THOMAS BUSBY. Wit: WILLIAM LIVINGSTON, jurat, JAMES RUTLAND, WILLIAM EDEN. Feb. Court 1739. *.

F 128   JACOB MAYNOR TO HENRY MAYNOR
        Dec. 1, 1739. 35 pds. for 80 A. At DAWS's Road. Wit: BENJAMIN WYNNS, jurat, G. WINS. Aug. Court 1740. *.

F 129   THOMAS RAYSON TO THOMAS BARKER
        Dec. 24, 1739. 10 pds. for 100 A. Land RAYSON bought of ANN TUDOR adj. BARKER, JOHN WILLIAMS at Village Swamp. Wit: PETTIGROVE SALSBERRY, JOHN PUGH. Aug. Court 1740. *.

F 130   WILLIAM ARRINGTON TO SAMUEL SANDS
        Feb. 9, 1739. 20(pds.) for 160 A. On SS Meherrin River. Granted to JOSEPH WALL "but now come to ...ARRINGTON by Order of Councill...". By date Aug. 10, 1728. Wit: GEORGE WILLIAMS, EDWARD HOOD. Aug. Court 1740. *.

F 131   HENRY VIZE TO JOHN MITCHENER
        Aug. 13, 1740. 150 pds. for 310 A. On ES Stoney Creek Road at CHRISTOPHER HOLLYMAN's corner on Ahoskey Swamp at mouth of Buck Branch adj.

JOHN RASBERRY, CHARLES JONES. Wit: THOMAS DIXON, jurat, JAMES MAGLOHON, DEMSEY WOOD. August Court 1740. *.

F 132 JACOB CARTER TO ISAAC CARTER
       July 24, 1740. Gift. 200 A. "...JACOB CARTER Heir at Law to MOOR
CARTER Dec'd...Love good will and affection unto my well beloved Brother
ISAAC CARTER..." Land on SS Meherin River. "...An Equall Devision of four
Hundred acres granted to my father Dec'd...by patent Feb'y the first 1725.."
Adj. SAMUEL BROWN. Wit: ISAAC CARTER, JOHN SUTTON, jurat, FREDERICK JONES.
Aug. Court 1740. *.

F 133 WILLIAM BRYANT & WIFE of Edgecombe County TO THOMAS UZELL of Nanse-
       mond County, Va. May 20, 1740. 1000 pds. for "a certain planta-
tion" plus 100 A. Land on NS Meherrin River "being plantation whereon JAMES
BRYANT formerly Lived and part of the patent Granted to RICHARD BRASSWELL
and also one hundred Acres of Land bought of JOHN DEW by Deed bearing Date
the 25th day of July 1730..." Wit: JAMES UZZELL, THOMAS WHITFIELD, W.
BAKER. Aug. Court 1740. *.

F 133 EDWARD COLLINS TO JOHN EDWARDS
       August 9, 1740. 400 pds. for 185 A. On WS Rocquiss Swamp adj. ____
SESSIONS, ROBERT ANDERSON. Wit: JAMES MADAIN(?), THOMAS WHITMELL, jurat,
CHARLES HARDEE, DANIEL PAYENS. Aug. Court 1740. *.

F 135 JAMES RUTLAND TO THOMAS BAREFIELD
       Aug. 12, 1740. 24 pds. for 230 A. Adj. "...(land) that was marked
out for ROBERT MACKFRILEY", ROBERT SHERWOOD on Sandy Run. Part of patent
granted to ROBERT SHERWOOD for 640 A. dated April 5, 1720. "now become due
JAMES RUTLAND". Wit: CHARLES HORNE, jurat, JAMES RUTLAND. Aug. Court 1740.*.

F 136 WILLIAM BRYANT of Edgecombe County TO THOMAS UZZELL of Nansemond Co.
       May 20, 1740. 25 pds. for 320 A. Land whereon JAMES BRYAND Dec'd.
formerly lived. Patent granted to RICHARD BRASSWELL for 640 A. dated Nov.
24, 1706. "...which patent being Indorsed to JAMES BRYANT SEN. the fourth
day of March 1708 and Recorded in Chowan County.." adj. JOHN DUKES, "Being
the same (300 A.) of land given JAMES BRYANT by his father JAMES BRYANT
Dec'd and also one hundred acres I bought of JOHN DEW (dated July 25, 1730)
...".+Wit: THOMAS WHITFIELD, W. BAKER. Aug. Court 1740.
+Land adj. JOHN DEW, WILLIAM BRYANT, BRITT's corner.

F 137 JONATHAN SANDERSON TO BARRIT MOUNTGOMERY (MONTGOMERY)
       April 26, 1740. 30 pds. for 100 A. On WS Chowan River and NS Bock-
horne Swamp. Part of tract to ROBERT BRASSWELL by patent dated March 1,
1719. Wit: JAMES MANEY, jurat, THOMAS PRETTER. Aug. Court 1740.*.

F 139 THOMAS LOVICK of Carteret County TO THOMAS ASHLEY
       Aug. 2, 1740. 40 pds. for 150 A. "...THOMAS LOVICK appointed Execu-
tor in Last Will and Testament of LAURENCE LARSON Late of the County of
Bertie...sell(s) unto THOMAS ASHLEY..." Land on Blackwaknut Swamp adj. ____
HARDY. Land granted THOMAS POLLOCK and assigned to LAURENCE LARSON by deed
April 5, 1720. Wit: ROBERT LOVICK, JAMES CARLEE. Aug. Court 1740. *.

F 140 WILLIAM GRAY TO WILLIAM TURNER of Isle of Wight County, Va.
       Aug. 11, 1740. 26 pds. for 420 A. "In woods betwixt Keshy and Mor-
rattock" being part of tract called Snowfield. By patent March 30, 1721.
Adj. NEEDHAM BRYANT at Runaroy Path at Alligator Marsh. Wit: JOHN GRAY,
JAMES WATSON. Aug. Court 1740. *.

F 141 HUGH HORTON of Northwest Parish (Bertie) TO JOHN HART
       Aug. 13, 1740. 100 pds. for 640 A. "...at a Beech in the Confluence
of Potakasey Creek & Panther Swamp..." Wit: ISAAC HUNTER, jurat, JONATHAN
TART, PHILLIP EVENS. August Court 1740. *.

F 142 JONATHAN GILBERT, "Mill Wright", TO THOMAS PENNEY (PENNY)
       Feb. 12, 1739. 5 sh. for 130 A. On SS Chowan River adj. JOHN FERRY-
BENT's line (Fierybent) to Deep Creek. "...(Except a Convenient Road to be
Laid Out by the Partie to the Deed to a Saw or other mill when Erected by
said JONATHAN GILBERT on Deep Creek and also the Liberty to make a conven-
ient Landing on the neat point of Land below where the s'd THOS. PENNY now
Dwells..." Wit: JOB ROGERS, jurat, BRIGETT PHILLIPS. Aug. Court 1740. *.

F 143   JOSEPH OATES TO JOHN GRAY, surveyor
         Sept. 25, 1739. 100 pds. for 130 A. On Chinkapin Creek between JOHN
MACKFARLEN and COLL. MAUL. Wit: JAMES BEESLEY(?), JOHN MACKFARLEN. Aug.
Court 1740. *.

F 144   CHARLES STEVENSON TO SAMUEL COTTON
         Feb. 6, 1739. 20 pds. for 100 A. On NS Moratuck River adj. JOHN
COTTON, RICHARD MILTON at Village Swamp. Wit: JOHN HART, JOHN DAWSON. Aug.
Court 1740. *.

F 145   JAMES RUTLAND, JUN. TO WILLIAM MOOR
         Nov. 19, 1739. 66 pds. for 65 A. On SS Ahotskey Marsh at a branch
commonly called HENARDS Branch adj. BAKER. Part of patent formerly granted
JAMES RUTLAND, JUN. "for seventy acres". Dated April 6, 1724. Wit: CHARLES
HORNE, jurat, ROBERT WHITFIELD. Aug. Court 1740. *.

F 147   SAMUEL BUXTON TO THOMAS PACE
         *. 5 pds. for 50 A. "...a Certain Woodland piece of ground and Tract
of Land Containing Fifty Acres..." Between BUXTON and THOMAS HOWELL. Adj.
PENELOPE MAUL. Wit: WILLIAM PACE, jurat, SAMUELL BUXTON, JUN., BENJAMIN
BUXTON. Aug. Court 1740. *.

F 148   WILLIAM HORNE TO CHARLES HORNE
         Aug. 9, 1740. 15 pds. for 130 A. At head of the branches of Ahosskey
Swamp. Part of a patent granted HENRY BAKER for 260 A. dated April 6, 1722.
Wit: ROBERT WHITFIELD, WILLIAM MOOR, jurat. Aug. Court 1740. *.

F 150   WILLIAM DUFFIELD TO WILLIAM PULLEY
         May 13, 1740. 60 pds. for 75 A. on SS Bridgers Creek adj. CHARLES
STEVENSON, CLAMMON STAFFORD. Part of a tract formerly granted GEORGE
STEVENSON. Wit: JAMES TART, JOHN HART, SIMON WEST. Aug. Court 1740. *.

F 151   ALEXANDER BALLANTINE TO ROBERT SHARMAN (SHERMAN), "Schoolmaster"
         March 26, 1740. 18 pds. 10 sh. for 100 A. At "forke of Poly Branch"
adj. JOSEPH WATFORD, TREDDLE KEEF at Bridge Branch. Wit: JOHN WYNNS, jurat,
THOMAS LEE. Aug. Court 1740. *.

F 152   JACOB VANPELT, yeoman, TO JOHN VANPELT, yeoman
         Sept. 29, 1739. 160 pds. for *. Land in Chinkaoen Neck "...which
the said JOHN VANPELT lately Conveyed me and was conveyed to him by JOHN
SWENNEY..." Wit: JOHN WYNNS, jurat, DANIEL VANPELT, WILLIAM WYNNS, BENJAMIN
WYNNS. Nov. Court 1740. *.

F 153   JOHN PRATT TO ROBERT FORSTER of Edgecome County
         Nov. 3, 1740. 20 pds. for 100 A. On NS Roanoak River "...was for-
merly the Estate of GIDEON GIBSON and by him sold to me..." Wit: WILL.
CATHCART, ALEXANDER M:CULLOCK. N.C. Court Nov. 3, 1740. W. SMITH, C.J.

F 154   THOMAS MILNER, yeoman, of Nansemond County, Va. TO WILLIAM GODWIN
         Oct. 30, 1740. 35 pds. for 227 A. Two tracts: (1)"...Plantation
whereon GODWIN now dwells and whereon EDWARD HOWARD lately Dwelt..." In
fork of Horse Swamp at mouth of Flatt Swamp. (2) "one other parcel of Land
out of the s'd HOWARDS patent Land to be laid in a square and to Include
one hundred and Seventy three acres...". (Tract 1 cont. 227A; tract 2 cont.
173 A.). Wit: SAMUEL WEBB, jurat, MARTHA MILNER. Nov. Court 1740. *.

F 155   JAMES WILLIAMSON & WIFE SARAH TO JAMES HURST
         July 26, 1740. 40 pds. for 100 A. Adj. HENRY BATES, _____WINGATE.
Wit: WILLIAM PERCE, WILLIAM KELLEY. Nov. Court 1740. *.

F 157   ISAAC HILL TO JAMES CONSTANT of Chowan County
         Jan. 28, 1739. 200 pds. for 640 A. on WS Chowan River "...which
land was Surveyed for ISAAC HILL Grandfather to ISAAC HILL...by a draught
of patent bearing Date the twenty fifth day of March (May?) which was in
the year of Our Lord Christ Sixteen Hundred and Ninety nine...(which) Descending to him the said ISAAC HILL from his Grandfather..." Wit: WILLIAM
WESSON, jurat, WILLIAM WESSTON, JUN. Nov. Court 1740. *.

F 159   JOHN & JOSEPH SNOWDEN of Perquimmons Co. TO SAMUEL & EDWIN GODWIN
         of Isle of Wight Co., Va. Nov. 15, 1739. 25 pds. for 515 A. on ES
Flatt & Horse Swamp. Bounded by patent to LAZARUS THOMAS dated March 1,1719

and sold "to our father THOMAS SNOWDEN..." Wit: JOHN WYNNS, jurat, SARAH
WYNNS. Nov. Court 1740. *.

F 160 WILLIAM BAREFIELD (BARFIELD) TO THOMAS COWMAN
        Aug. 11, 1740. "a white horse and one Thousand Pounds of Good mer-
chantable Pork..." This consideration to be paid to brother JAMES BARFIELD.
Land on NS Ahoskey Marsh. Part of patent granted to JOHN COTTON dec'd. adj.
RICHARD BARFIELD, Coll. MAUL, JOHN COTTON. Wit: ARTHUR COTTON, WILLIAM
HOBBY, JOHN OLEPHANT. Nov. Court 1740. *.

F 162 JAMES RUTLAND TO JAMES RUTLAND, JUN.
        Nov. 13, 1740. 100 pds. for 400 A. In two tracts: (1) 160 A. by pa-
tent granted to OWEN McDANIEL March 1, 1719 (2) 240 A. granted to GEORGE
STEVENS July 30, 1726. Wit: JOHN RUTLAND, JEAN LEVERNICK. Nov. Court 1740.*.

F 163 JAMES RUTLAND, JUN. TO JAMES RUTLAND, SEN.
        Nov. 13, 1740. 100 pds. for 286 A. On WS Ahoskey Swamp adj. "JAMES
RUTLAND the Elder", JAMES WOOD, GEORGE SMITH. Land granted JAMES RUTLAND,
JUN. Nov. 17, 1723. Wit: JOHN RUTLAND, JEAN LEVERRICK. Nov. Court 1740.*.

F 164 NATHANIEL HILL TO SAMUEL COOK
        Nov. 11, 1740. 20 pds. for 100 A. On Blackwalnut Swamp adj. LAWRENCE
SARSON, JOHN HARDY. Wit: JOSIAH REDDICK, WILLIAM ASHLEY, RICHARD ASHLEY.
Nov. Court 1740. *.

F 166 ANTHONY WILLIAMS, yeoman, TO JOHN WYNNS
        Dec. 18, 1738. *.*. "...(I) appoint my friend JOHN WYNNS to be my
true and Lawful Attorney...to sell my tract of Land I purchased of JOHN
JONES upon the Northside of Ahoskey Swamp Containing five hundred and Seventy acres..." Wit: GEORGE BOWLER, WILLIAM GAROT, JOHN SPEIR, jurat. November
Court 1740. *.

F 166 JOHN WYNNS TO WILLIS NICHOLAS
        Nov. 12, 1740. 30 pds. *. "...JOHN WYNNS...attorney of ANTHONY
WILLIAMS Late of Bertie County...(sells) Land ANTHONY WILLIAMS purchased of
JOHN JONES son of CHARLES JONES..." On NS Ahotskey Swamp. By patent to
JOHN JONES dated Nov. 11, 1719. Wit: WILLIAM GODWIN, EDMOND GODWIN. Nov.
Court 1740. *.

F 167 WILLIAM & ELIZABETH MOOR TO JAMES MUNFORD of Prince George Co., Va.
        Oct. 29, 1740. 86 pds. for 640 A. On NS Roanoak River "where the
Countery Line crosses the River...". Wit: ROBERT COOK, THOMAS STEVENS,JUN.,
HENRY ROTTENBERRY. Nov. Court 1740. *.

F 169 THOMAS GOODSON & WIFE ELIZABETH of Edgecombe County TO THOMAS RICH-
ARDSON. Feb. 26, 1739. 6 pds. for 100 A. On WHEELER's Mill Swamp.
Part of a patent granted to WILLIAM ARRINGTON dated Aug. 10, 1728. Adj.
JOSEPH RICHARDSON. Wit: SAMUEL BUXTON, Jun., ROBERT DUKES, SAMUEL BUXTON,
jurat. Nov. Court 1740. *.

F 169 MARGRET (MARGARET) BEVERLEY, widow, TO JOHN & ROBERT BEVERLEY
        May 5, 1738. Gift. "...Natural Love and affection...to my Two Sons
JOHN BEVERLEY & ROBERT BEVERLEY...as also is due Regard the Last Will and
Testament of my Late Dec'd Husband JOHN BEVERLEY...and to prevent any Law
Suits or Contentions from a Mis Construction of the said Will and Testament
...all the Estate bequeathed unto me by my said Late Husband..." (1) All
Negroes (2) household goods (3) cattle, sheep, horses and other stock. "The
said Negroes and stock to the use of MARGARET BEVERLEY during her Natural
Life and widowhood...". Wit: DANIEL HOUGH, THOMAS CREW, jurat, GEORGE
OUTLAW. *.*.

F 170 FRANCIS STRINGER of Craven Co., "Practitioner in Phisick & Chyrurgery"
        TO DANIEL HOUGH. Nov. 13, 1740. 500 pds. for stock, negroes,
household furniture. MARGARET BEVERLEY now wife of DANIEL HOUGH, formerly
widow of JOHN BEVERLEY made over to her sons, JOHN & ROBERT BEVERLEY, certain property. The sons sold this property (see F 169) to FRANCIS STRINGER
by instruement of deed dated Oct. 23, 1740. Wit: JOSEPH JONES, H. VERNON.
Nov. Court 1740. *.

F 173 WILLIAM WHITFIELD & WIFE ELIZABETH TO THOMAS WALKER of Norfolk Co.Va.
        Nov. 13, 1740. 65 pds. for 200 A. Commonly called Red Ridge

Plantation. WHITFIELD's by deed dated Oct. 24, 1729. Wit: JOSEPH OATES, WILLIAM WESSTON. Nov. Court 1740. *. "...ELIZABETH WHITFIELD being privately Examined by THOMAS HANSFORD Esq. acknowledges the Same freely..."

F 174 CHARLES SKINNER, "Talor", TO PETER WEST
Aug. 22, 1740. 40 pds. for 100 A. Land Skinner bought of WEST. Wit: WILLIAM PUGH, jurat, PETER WEST, JUN. Nov. Court 1740. *.

F 175 THOMAS HOWELL & WIFE ELIZABETH TO ISAAC EDWARDS of Norfolk Co., Va.
Feb. 9, 1741. 25 pds. for 250 A. "...the Lowest Half of a Certain Tract at first Granted to WILLIAM JONES for six Hundred and forty Acres..." dated Feb. 26, 1711/12. By JONES conveyed to JOSEPH LANE, JUN. and from LANE "to the said BOLDING" and from BOLDING to HOWELL. Land on Moratock River adj. "BOLDING and his son JOHN BOLDING...". Wit: EDWARD HOOD, THOMAS DIXON, WILLIAM WILLIFORD. Feb. Court 1740. "...ELIZABETH HOWELL wife of ...THOAMS HOWELL being privately Examined by one of the Justices of Our s'd Court Declares that she acknowledges freely..." BENJAMIN HILL, C/C.

F 177 JOHN LUERTON TO JOSIAH REDDICK
Sept. 26, 1740. 400 pds. for 200 A. On Salmon Creek at Poplar Run. Wit: RICHARD ASHLEY, JOHN ASHLEY, THOMAS GOODMAN. N.C. Court Sept. 26, 1740. W. SMITH, C.J.

F 176 ELIZABETH KINCHIN of Isle of Wight Co., Va. TO WILLIAM KINCHIN
Nov. 23, 1740. Gift. "...Love and Goodwill I Bear to my son WILLIAM KINCHIN...and Likewise to my Grandson WILLIAM KINCHIN and son to aforesaid WILLIAM KINCHIN being of Edgcomb County...". (1) To my son Two Negroes, Secor & Rose (2) to my Grandson "my goods & chattles now in possession of said WILLIAM Delivered with an inventory signed by my own hand...". Wit: R. WILLIAM, THOMAS GOODWIN, WILLIAM TAYLOR. N.C. Court Feb. 11, 1740.*.

F 178 WILLIAM BAYLE, carpenter, TO WILLIAM HURST of Edgecombe Co.
Oct. 15, 1740. 10 pds. for 100 A. Land on Roanoke adj. COLL. MAUL's upper line, MACKINNE's head line to Deep Bottom. Part of tract sold to BAYLE for 739 A. by COLL. BARNABY MACKINNE dated 1739. Wit: JOHN DAWSON, THOMAS PARKER. N.C. Court Feb. 11, 1740. W. SMITH C.J.

F 179 THOMAS BARFIELD TO JOHN WILKS
Sept. 30, 1740. 9 pds. 10 sh. for 150 A. On head of Cashy on WS of "a Branch that falls into the middle swamp of the Branches of the Casy". Adj. JAMES RUTLAND, HENRY HORNE. Part of patent formerly granted ABELL CURLESS for 640 A. dated August 1, 1726. Wit: CHARLES HORNE, MOSES HORNE. Feb. Court 1740. BENJAMIN HILL C/C.

F 180 THOMAS BARKER & WIFE FERIBE TO JACOB JARNAGAN
Sept. 21, 1739. 50 pds. for 10 A. On SS Moratuck River adj. JOSEPH BLACKMAN "by the Pond side". Wit: MATTHEW WHITFIELD, jurat, PETYGROSS SALSBERRY, JOHN PUGH. Feb. Court 1740. Benjamin Hill C/C.

F 182 JOHN LEE & WIFE MARY of Edgecombe County TO THEOPHILUS PUGH of Nansemond Co, Va. Aug. 21, 1740. 200 pds. for 640 A. On WS Keneetoe Creek. Being tract granted JOHN LEE by patent dated Sept. 28, 1730. Wit: T. BARKER, JOHN PUGH, W. TAYLOR, jurat. Feb. Court 1740. *.

F 183 ARTHUR SHERRARD & WIFE MARY TO ROBERT SHERRARD
* 1740. 20 pds. for 90 A. On Conneyhoe Creek adj. WILLIAM BARDEN on Old Indian Path, JOHN BALLARD. Wit: HENRY SOWERLY, JOHN SHERARD. February Court 1740. *.

F 184 PETER WEST TO THOMAS CLIFFIN (CLIFTING)
Feb. 11, 1740. 9 pds. for 200 A. Adj. JACOB LEWIS on Waiding Branch on Horse Swamp. Wit: PETER WEST. *.*. Feb. Court 1740. *.

F 185 JAMES BRANTLEY & LEWIS BRANTLEY TO WILLIAM RUTLIDGE
June 3, 1740. 10 pds. for 100 A. On NS Morattock River adj. SAMUEL WILLIAMS at Peahill Creek. Wit: JAMES MACKLIMORE, Jurat, ALLEXANDER SOUTHERLAND. Feb. Court 1740. *.

F 186 JAMES RUTLAND, SEN. TO GEORGE BURNETT
Feb. 10, 1742. 14 pds. for 200 A. "...at Head of Branch of Cashy called Wattom...". On NS Cashy Swamp at Flatt Branch. Part of patent to

ROBERT RADFORD for 450 A. dated April 1, 1723. Wit: HENRY HORNE, JONATHAN TART, JOHN WILKES. *.*.

F 188   ANTHONY WEBB TO SAMUEL WEBB
        Jan. 9, 1740.   100 pds. for 275 A. "Half that Tract or parcel of Land GEORGE NICHOLSON bought of STEPHEN WILLIAMS being the East side of Land Including the House & plantation...". Wit: NATHANIEL NICHOLAS, NATHANIEL NICHOLAS (this name twice as witness), WILLIAM WEBB. Feb. Court 1740. *.

F 189   ANTHONY WEBB TO NATHANIEL NICHOLAS
        Jan. 10, 1740.   100 pds. for 275 A. "Half that Tract or parcel of Lands that GEORGE NICHOLSON bought of STEPHEN WILLIAMS being the West side of said tract...". Between NATHANIEL NICHOLAS and SAMUEL WEBB in Northwest Parish. Wit: JESSE WOOD, THOMAS OUTLAW, DEMSE WOOD. Feb. Court 1740. *.

F 190   JAMES CAIN & HARDY CAIN of Edgecombe County TO JOHN BASS
        Dec. 16, 1740.   30 pds. for 150 A. On NS Roanoak in Uraha Woods adj. WILLIAM THOMAS "Lately made for EDWARD ARPE...". Part of patent granted HENRY SIMS for 360 A. dated March 1, 1719. Wit: SAMUEL PEETE (PEEK), JOHN EDWARDS.   Feb. Court 1740. *.

F 191   DANIEL PUGH of Nansemond Co., Va. TO SAMUEL RUFFIN
        Oct. 8, 1740.   40 pds. for 500 A. By deed to DANIEL PUGH 1723. Wit: JAMES EVERARD, GEORGE DOWNING, jurat, JOHN REID. Feb. Court 1740. *.

F 192   THOMAS MILNER of Nansemond Co., Va. TO PAUL PENDER
        July 14, 1740.   9 pds. for 227 A. On Flatt Swamp adj. ROBERT LANIER. Wit: HENRY BLOODWORTH, jurat, JOHN JONES. Feb. Court 1740. *.

F 193   JOSIAH REDDICK TO JOHN COOK
        Feb. 9, 1740.   440 pds. for 200 A. On Salmon Creek. Wit: WILLIAM HARDY, WILLIAM ASHLEY. Feb. Court 1740. BENJAMIN HILL C/C.

F 194   JAMES BRANTLEY & LEWIS BRANTLEY of Isle of Wight Co, Va. TO SAMUEL WILLIAMS.   June 3, 1740.   15 pds. for 150 A. "on Bank of Moratock River" at Peahill. Wit: JAMES MACKLIMORE, jurat, ALEXANDER SOUTHERLAND. Feb. Court 1740. *.

F 195   BENJAMIN SELLERS of Edgecombe County TO BENJAMIN HILL
        SS Meheren River and NS Kirby Creek "one parcel of fifty acres my father MATTHEW SELLERS Bought of BENJAMIN FOREMAN whereon my mother now lives and the other fifty acres which my father bought of JOHN MAHARE and also one hundred & Seventy Acres patented in my Fathers names all the s'd Lands Joining Together..." Wit: JOHN CAMPBELL, jurat, CHRISTOPHER LAHEY, SAMUEL MIRRET. Feb. Court 1740. *.

F 196   WILLIAM BENNETT TO THOMAS SMITH
        Sept. 19, 1739.   7 pds. 10 sh. for 150 A. Granted me by patent Aug. 14, 1730 on Yawrha Swamp. Wit: WILLIAM BODDIE, jurat, JOHN BODDIE, WILLIAM BENNET. Feb. Court 1740. Benjamin Hill, C/C.

F 197   BENJAMIN GRIFFIN of Craven County TO JOSEPH SCOTT
        Aug. 29, 1740. 40 pds. for 400 A. (50A. + 350 A.) "one plantation that WILLIAM GOODMAN Built on & Seated...". Also 350 A. granted WILLIAM GOODMAN Aug. 5, 1727 on Potecasey adj. THOMAS BONNER, THOMAS BROWN, ARON ODOM at Bells Branch. Wit: JAMES DENTON, jurat, PATRICK CAR, LEONARD LANKSTON. Feb. Court 1740. *.

F 199   ROBERT LANIER TO JOHN GILBERT
        July 6, 1740.   22 pds 10 sh. for 367 A. On WS Chowan on Conneritsat. Wit: THOMAS KEARNEY, EDMOND KEARNEY, JOHN HOLLEY, jurat. Feb. Court 1740. *.

F 200   JOHN SCOTT & WIFE MARY TO THOMAS BLOUNT "Late of Edenton, Mercht."
        Feb. 18, 1740.   180 pds. for 271 A. On SWS Cashy Swamp adj. JOHN HARDY. By grant to JOHN GRIFFIN for 591 A. "and was given by WILLIAM GRIFFIN son of s'd JOHN GRIFFIN to his wife MARY GRIFFIN by will..." Except one piece sold by WILLIAM GRIFFIN unto SAMUEL BASS cont. 320 A. Land ajd. BASS and JOHN THOMAS. "Except a mortgage due on it for fifty four pounds Bills.." Wit: SARAH HUNTER, ELIZABETH WHITMELL.   N.C. Court April 19, 1741.W.SMITH C.J.

F 201   WILLIAM DOWNING of Mount Pleasant TO JOHN WYNNS
        March 4, 1739. 1400 pds. for 550 A. At Mount Pleasant on SWS Chowan
River at mouth of Wildcatt Gutt adj. POLLOCK, SHARP at the head of Goose
Creek and Wiccacon Creek. Wit: ROBERT SHERMAN, JOHN HOOKER, jurat, WILLIAM
HOOKER. Feb. Court 1740. BENJAMIN HILL C/C.

F 202   DANIEL REGIN TO ROBERT CLARY
        Aug. 25, 1740. Power of atty. to recover monies owed "...sole power
...concerning all Lands to me belonging in the Government of North Carolina
and Virginia...To Let Lease & act as I myself might...". Particularly on
tract now in possession of JOSEPH BRIDGERS. To sell tract to BRIDGERS.
Wit: GEORGE WILLIAMS, WILLIAM ARRINGTON, EDWARD HOOD, jurat. Feb. Court 1740.*.

F 203   PETER EDMONDSON of Dorchester Co., Maryland TO THOMAS JACKSON
        Sept. 12, 1740. Power of atty. "to collect sums owed...(in) money
Tobacco or any other Merchantable: Sufficient...". Wit: PAUL PHABEN, jurat,
EST. JACKSON. Feb. Court 1740. *.

F 204   JOHN GLOVER & WIFE MARY of Edgecombe County TO JOHN JESTICE
        Oct. 9, 1740. 30 pds. for 210 A. adj. WILLIAM GLOVER. Wit: JAMES
PARRISH, WILLIAM NORWOOD, jurat, WILLIAM GLOVER, JUN. May Court 1741. *.

F 204   ELIZABETH KINCHIN TO WILLIAM KINCHIN, SEN.
        Nov. 22, 1740. Deed of Gift. "An Inventory of all & singular the
Estate Goods & Chattles of ELIZABETH KINCHIN Late of the Isle of Wight
County in Virginia...". 1 Negro man Secor, 1 Negro woman Rose, 29 pds. cash,
4 beds & furniture, 2 potts, 5 dishes 2 doz. plates, chest of drawers, 10
Leather chairs, 1 Large Bible, 3 Brass Candlesticks, 3 punch Bowls, 2 Black
Trunks. Wit: R. WILLIAMS, WILLIAM TAYLOR, THOMAS GODWIN. *.*.

F 205   JAMES BARNES TO ELIAS WILLIS
        April 29, 1740/41. 30 pds. for 100 A. Part of a tract formerly
granted WILLIAM WHITEHEAD April 1, 1720. Adj. RICHARD BRASSWELL. Signed
JAMES BARNES, MATTHEW BARNES. Wit: ROBERT RUFFIN, ISAAC HUNTER, E. BUXTON.
May Court 1741. *.

F 206   PHILLIP OREILLY of Brunswick Co., Va. TO EDWARD HOOD
        Power of Atty. March 19, 1735/36. To sell to THOMAS WILSON of
Brunswick County a tract called Copper Hill on Roanoak River "being the
Tenth part of the s'd Mine and Tennor of Land". Wit: SAMUELL TAYLOR "one of
his majestys Justices for Bertie Precinct", NICHOLAS MONGER. May Court 1741.*.

F 207   BRYAN OCQUIN, JOSEPH JONES & FREDERICK JONES TO JANE CARTER
        *. 34 pds. "...obligation is such (that we)...do Save Harmless and
Endemnified the s'd JANE CARTER from all & every part of the estate of
PATIENCE OCQUIN Granddaughter to MOOR CARTER Dec'd. bill the Next Court to
be held for this County on Timber Branch...". Wit: JOHN SUTTON, JOHN
DICKINSON, KINDRED CARTER, jurat. *.*.

F 207   JOSHUA WILKINSON TO MARY HARY (HARDEE)
        July 21, 1739. 20 pds. for 100 A. On NES Kesiah River adj. JOHN
MOOR, STEWART, BARBER, WILLIAMS. Wit: JOSEPH HARDEE, jurat, MARY HARDEE,
CHARLES HARDEE. May Court 1741. Benjamin Hill C/C.

F 209   JOHN WYNNS TO WILLIAM HOOKER & JOHN HOOKER
        April 17, 1741. 100 pds. for 250 A. The SE or upper Half of a Tract
of Land which was granted to me by patent March 6, 1740. On SW Quoyokoson
Swamp at Mare Branch. "...dureing the Natural Life of the s'd WILLIAM
HOOKER and to the s'd JOHN HOOKER his heirs and assignes forever...". Wit:
PER. EVANS, ROBERT HILL. May Court 1741. *.

F 209   WILLIAM BLY of Chowan County TO JOHN WYNNS.
        May 11, 1741. 40 pds. for 360 A. On SWS Quoyokason Swamp at mouth
of Crooked Branch. Part of a patent granted BLY for 560 A. on March 11, 1740.
Wit: JOAN RADOLPH STAINFIELD, SAMUELL NORTHEY, JOHN CAMPBELL, jurat. May
Court 1741. *.

F 210   ROBERT CLARY TO BENJAMIN FUTERILL
        May 13, 1741. 90 pds. for 168 A. On NS Potteycasey Creek at Hunting
Quarter Swamp. Part of a tract formerly granted RICHARD WASHINGTON for 335
A. August 4, 1723. Wit: THOS. FUTRILL, *. May Court 1741. *.

F 211   ROBERT HINES of Craven County TO GEORGE HOUSE
        March 30, 1741. 96 pds. for 240 A. On Casia Branch adj. ABRAHAM
SHEPPARD at Rocquiss Branch. Wit: ANTHONY HERRING, GEORGE JARNIGAN, WILLIAM
HINES. May Court 1741. Benjamin Hill, C/C.

F 212   JOHN BUTLER TO JAMES MANNEY (MANEY)
        Jan. 3, 1740. 35 pds. for 270 A. On SS Indian Creek adj. RICHARD
HOLLAND. Now in possession of DAVID JONIJEND at "GODFREY LEES great Branch".
Part of a tract granted GODFREY LEE. Wit: DAVID JONIJEND, jurat, ABRAHAM
PAGE. May Court 1741. *.

F 214   JOHN DAY & WIFE JEAN TO EDMUND DAY
        May 9, 1741. 45 pds. for 250 A. Being part of a patent granted
ROBERT WEBB Feb. 1725. In Upper Parish of Bertie on NS Moratuck at "BLANS
line" on Green Creek adj. WILLIAM BRIGGS on Canoe Creek. Wit: JASPER STEW-
ART, jurat, RICHARD CROSS, JOHN SPANN. *. *.

F 215   JOHN PHILLIPS & THOMAS MOY TO JOSEPH ROGERS of Surry Co, Va.
        May 6, 1741. 26 pds. for 400 A. On SS Meheron River adj. ISRAEL
JOYNER "in the Creek Branch". Wit: JAMES WASHINGTON, JOHN NICHOLSON(?),
HENRY SOWERLY. May Court 1741. *.

F 216   BENJAMIN HILL TO WILLIAM WHITFIELD, JUN.
        May 14, 1741. 20 pds. for 300 A. On NS Meheron Creek at Bels Branch.
Wit: JOHN WYNNS, BENJAMIN WYNNS. May Court 1741. BENJAMIN HILL, C/C.

F 217   SIMON WEST TO JAMES WOOD
        Aug. 25, 1740. 50 pds. for 150 A. On SS Catawhisky Swamp. Adj. Coll.
MAUL, JAMES WOOD. Wit: JOHN OLEPHANT, MOSES WOOD, THOMAS COOK. May Court
1741. *.

F 218   JOHN JENKINS TO WILLIAM PERREY
        April 2, 1740. 50 pds. for 200 A. On Poplar Swamp adj. JOHN JONES,
LEWIS JONES, PATRICK OQUIN. Wit: MARY ANDERSON, JAMES BARFIELD, J. EDWARDS,
NOAH PREDHAM, jurat, SARAH PREDHAM. May Court 1741. *.

F 219   HENRY BRANCH TO MEDIA WHITE
        July 23, 1740. 26 pds. for 200 A. In two tracts. (1) at Reedy
Branch adj. JOHN CRICKET (2) a parcel adj. the above land and purchased
from COLL. POLLOCK. Wit: THOMAS HANSFORD, jurat, JOHN FERRIS. May Court
1741. Benjamin Hill C/C.

F 221   JOHN HINTON TO MICAJAH HINTON
        May 11, 1741. 40 pds. for 250 A. On Village Pond at Little Marsh
adj. JAMES BLOUNT's former line. Part of a patent bought by WILLIAM HINTON
of JAMES BLOUNT. Wit: PATRICK CAR, JOHN HINNANT, MOSES BENTON.May Court 1741.

F 222   HENRY SOWERBY TO JOHN NICHOLSON of Surry Co, Va.
        May 11, 1741. Mortgage. 550 A. "...(I) am bound...in the just Sum
of one Hundred Ninety Eight pounds current money of Virginia...do defend (to
him) a certain parcel of land..." On SS Meherrin River. Wit: NATHANIEL
FIELD, JOSEPH JOHN SNIPES. May Court 1741. *.

F 223   HENRY SOWERBY TO JOHN NICHOLSON of Surry Co, Va.
        May 11, 1741. 98 pds. for 550 A. Land on SS Meherrin River adj.
JAMES WASHINGTON. Wit: JAMES WASHINGTON, NATHANIEL FIELD, JOSEPH JOHN
SNIPES. May Court 1741. *.

F 224   WILLIAM REEVES of Edgecombe County TO ROBERT HICKS, "marriner" of
        NW Parish, Bertie.   April 13, 1741. 3 pds. for 30 A. Land in NW
Parish Bertie on NS Roanoak River. "to an Old field formerly JANE JOHNSES
..." Wit: ROBERT HARRIS, JAMES PARHAM, jurat. May Court 1741. *.

F 226   STEPHEN RAGLAND TO ROBERT HICKS
        April 15, 1741. 3 pds. for 40 A. Land in NW Parish at mouth of Dou-
ble Branch at headline between RAGLAND & HICKS ajd. "an Oldfield formerly
JANE JOHNSES..." Wit: ROBERT HARRIS, JAMES PARHAM, jurat. May Court 1741. *.

F 227   JOHN SHERARD (SHERRARD) TO JOHN NICHOLSON
        Feb. 6, 1740. 45 pds. for 100 A. Part of patent to HENRY WHEELER
Feb. 9, 1714. "...(JOHN SHERRARD's) by virtue of a Devie to him made in the

164

Last Will & Testament of his father ROB'T SHERRARD Dec'd..." Wit: JAMES WASHINGTON, THOMAS MURRETT, HENRY SOWERLY, ROBERT THARP. May Court 1741. *.

F 228 JOHN SHERARD TO JOHN NICHOLSON of Surry Co., Va.
Feb. 6, 1740. 220 pds. for 100 A. +100 A. A 220 pd. bond to assure delivery. (1) "one hundred acres of High Land" (2) also 100 A. bought of EMPEROR WHEELER on SS Meherrin River. Wit: JAMES WASHINGTON, HENRY SOWERLY, THOMAS MURRETH, ROBERT THARP. May Court 1741. *.

F 229 JOHN BENTLEY, SEN. TO JOHN MANNING
Sept. 9, 1740. 185 pds. for 225 A. In Coshie Neck at a Gutt coming out of Cypress Creek on NWS adj. JEREMIAH BENTLEY, JAMES BESLY, CHARLES MANNING, JOHN MANNING at Charlton Creek Pocoson. Wit: JEREMIAH BENTLEY, jurat, JOHN BENTLEY, JUN. May Court 1741. *.

F 230 WILLIAM BOONE & WIFE ALEE TO THOMAS UNDERWOOD
*. 9 pds. 10 sh. for 100 A. Part of patent to WILLIAM BOONE on SS Meherrin River dated May 9, 1741. Land now in actual possession of THOMAS UNDERWOOD. Wit: ABRAHAM BAGGETT, NICHOLAS BOONE. May Court 1741. *.

F 233 DANIEL PORINE TO GARRARD VANUPSTALL
May 11, 1741. 100 pds. for 150 A. On ES Wills Quarter Swamp at Broad Branch. Wit: THOMAS WHITMELL, ELIZABETH WHITMELL, SE., ELIZABETH WHITMELL, JUN. May Court 1741. *.

F 231 SAMUEL ONWIN TO JAMES AVERITT
May 7, 1741. 100 pds. for 320 A. "Taken out of a Patent formerly granted to Cap't. DAVID HENDERSON bearing Date the 20th day of July 1717 ...". Adj. Coll. ROBERT WEST (now in possession of THOMAS NEWBOORN). Wit: THOMAS RYAN, JOHN BELL, THOMAS YETS. May Court 1741. *.

F 234 EDWARD BRYAN & WIFE MARTHA TO THOMAS WHITMELL
April 8, 1741. 100 pds. for 275 A. "...one half a patent for 550 A. granted ELIZABETH WEST & MARTHA WEST dated the thirteenth day of Aprill Anno Domini one Thousand Seven (hundred) Twenty four...". Wit: THOMAS BLOUNT, WILLIAM WESTON, SEN., JAMES CASTELLAW. N.C. Court April 8, 1741. W. Smith, C.J.

F 236 CHARLES PATE & WIFE SARAH of Craven County TO ROBERT HOWELL
Oct. 7, 1740. 36 pds. for 260 A. On NS Rocquiss Swamp. Adj. JOHN EDWARDS. Wit: JAMES CASTELLAW, jurat, JAMES BAKER, THOMAS COPLEN. May Court 1741. Benjamin Hill, C/C.

F 238 THOMAS FUTRILL TO BENJAMIN FUTRILL
April 23, 1739. 40 pds. for 150 A. On Hunting Quarter Swamp at Pottecasie Creek. Part of tract formerly granted ARTHUR WILLIAMS for 300 A. dated April 6, 1722. Wit: JOHN HART, JOHN FUTRILL. May Court 1741. *.

F 238 ROBERT CLARY TO JOHN FUTRILL
May 13, 1741. *. 167 A. On NS Pottecasie Creek at Hunting Quarter Swamp. Part of a tract formerly granted RICHARD WASHINGTON for 335 A. dated Aug. 4, 1723. Wit: THOMAS FUTRILL, ROBERT CLARY. May Court 1741. *.

F 239 ARTHUR HARRIS TO HOSEA TAPLEY
Feb. 7, 1739. 200 pds. Two tracts. (1) plantation whereon ARTHUR HARRIS now dwells on NS Morrattock River cont. 320 A. Part of a greater tract adj. JOHN HILL. (2) No description of second tract. "...and said HARRIS is to Build a Barn for the s'd TAPLEY forty foot in Length Twenty foot in Bredth Twelve foot pitched and Two Shedds Ten foot wide the Same Length of the House and to be done well and workmanlike on or by the Last day of July Next..." Wit: THOMAS SMITH, ANNE CREWS, EDWARD CREWS. May Court 1741. Benjamin Hill C/C. "Memorandum...between ARTHUR HARRIS and HOSEA TAPLEY that whereas there is a Dispute Between JOHN HILL and ARTHUR HARRIS concerning the Two Hundred acres of Land within mentioned that if s'd JOHN HILL after a survey has not his Compliment and by that means recover part or all the Two Hundred Acres that the s'd HARRIS is to pay at the Rate of Ten pounds current money of Virginia (per) Hundred...if HILL recover any other way after the survey it is to be wholly at the s'd TAPLEYs Loss.." Wit: THOMAS SMITH, EDWARD CREWS, ANNE CREWS.

F 241 JOHN GILBERT TO JOHN HOLLY

July 7, 1740. 50 pds. for 157 A. On Conaritsay Swamp between GIL-
BERT & HOLLY adj. JOHN THOMAS. Wit: JAMES BAKER, JOHN THOMAS, jurat. May
Court 1741. *.

F 240   WILLIAM WILSON (WILLSON) & WIFE JUDITH TO JAMES WILLSON
        April 10, 1741. Gift. 180 A. "...parental Love & affection that...I
do bear Towards my well beloved son JAMES WILLSON..."Land in Ursara Meadows
"at this Time my Dwelling Plantation..." adj. ARTHUR WHITEHEAD on SS Fish
Meadow, JOHN COTTON. Wit: ISAAC HUNTER, JOHN DAVESON. May Court 1741. *.

F 243   FRANCIS PRIDGEON TO ROBERT LASITER
        Aug. 24, 1740. 15 cows, 1 horse, 1 mare, 1 Rigg & 1 pair Blanketts.
For 90 A. on NS Yarorah Swamp. Wit: JAMES LASITER, jurat, JOHN SUTTON. May
Court 1741. *.

F 244   JOHN JONES of Chowan County TO WILLIAM PERRY (PERREY)
        Feb. 11, 1740. 6 pds. for 100 A. On Poplar Swamp adj. PATRICK OCQUIN.
Wit: WILLIAM PUGH, JACOB CARTER, jurat, JOHN SUTTON. May Court 1741. *.

F 245   NATHANIEL FIELD, shoemaker, TO ROBERT THARP of Surry Co, Va.
        March 6, 1740. 20 pds. for 170 A. On NS Meherrin River adj. BENJAMIN
HILL and land bought of JOSEPH HOUGH. Wit: JOHN NICOLSON, JOHN BYNUM, ELIZ-
ABETH TAID, JAMES WASHINGTON, NATHAN BRITT. May Court 1741. *.

F 246   ARTHUR SMITH, ELIZABETH SMITH & JAMES ALLEN of Surry Co., Va. TO
        CHAPLIN WILLIAMS of Isle of Wight Co., Va. March 21, 1740. 15 pds.
for 210 A. On NS Meherrin River at the County Line. Being a tract formerly
granted Mrs. ELIZABETH ALLEN dated Nov. 19, 1728. Wit: THOMAS WILLIAMS,
JOSHUA DAWSON, FRANCIS GREGORY. May Court 1741. *.

F 247   WILLIAM GUNN TO COLL. BENJAMIN HILL
        Feb. 25, 1740. 240 pds. for 400 A. On NS Roanoak River. By patent
dated Nov. 15, 1728. By deed from THOMAS WILLSON dated March 15, 1738. Wit:
JOHN CAMPBELL, jurat, MARY LAHEY. May Court 1741. *.

F 248   JOHN WIGGINS (WIGENS) & WIFE MARY TO JOHN BARNES (BARNS)
        Feb. 3, 1740. 2 pds. 10 sh. for *. "a small parcel of Land being
Part of a Tract I bought of BARNARD BAUGER containing fifty acres..." On NS
Meherrin on Buckhorn Swamp at a dividing line between WIGGINS and WILLIAM
WHITLEY. Wit: WILLIAM WHITLEE, WILLIAM WIGENS, SAMUEL WARREN. May Court 1741.*.

F 249   PELEG ROGERS of Edgecomb County TO JOHN MITCHENER
        May 19, 1740. 150 pds. for 300 A. In two parcels (1) One the side of
Horse Swamp adj. JOHN WILLOBY, LAZARUS THOMAS, ROBERT WARREN (2) Adj. ROBERT
FORSTER, JAMES OVERTON, ROBERT WARREN. Wit: WILLIAM GODWIN, JUN., THOMAS
DIXON, JOB ROGERS. May Court 1741. *.

F 250   ANDREW THOMPSON TO GEORGE PATTERSON
        May 6, 1740. 300 pds. for 580 A. On Meratock Bay which land THOMP-
SON "bought of Uncles THOMAS THOMPSON & DAVID THOMPSON of the Sheir of
Beirth and THOMAS THOMSON of the Shair of Sterling North Britain.." Wit:
THOMAS RYAN, R. HERTELL, JOHN WYNNS. May Court 1741. BENJAMIN HILL, C/C.
(Note the name spelled both THOMSON and THOMPSON in this deed.)

F 252   ROBERT HARRIS & WIFE LAMENDA TO STEPHEN RAGLAND
        Oct. 16, 1740. 60 pds. for 230 A. "ROBERT MORRIS Late of Hanover
County Virginia now of Bertie County...". Land on Roanoak River adj. RAG-
LAND at TURBEVILL's Run. Wit: P. SMITH, NATHANIEL HILL, JNARM'D (?) BROWN.
May Court 1741. *.

F 253   THOMAS BIRD TO CHARLES JONES, JUN.
        Nov. 6, 1740. 10 pds. for 100 A. On NS Mill Pond at Spring Branch.
Wit: EDMOND BIRD (BYRD), JOHN BRIEER(?). May Court 1741. *.

F 254   JOHN MITCHENER TO STEPHEN SHIVERS
        May 12, 1741. 30 pds. for 50 A. Adj. JOHN RASBERRY at Buck Branch
on NS Horsky Swamp adj. CHARLES JONES on NS Stoney Creek Road adj. LANCILET
JONES. Wit: WILLIAM GODWIN, Jurat, JOHN WILLIBE. May Court 1741. *.

F 255   JOHN WASHINGTON TO ROBERT CLARY
        Oct. 4, 1740. 800 lbs. Pork & 1 Horse Bridle & Saddle & 1 gun for

335 A. On NS Pottacasie Creek at Poplar Branch on WS Hunting Quarter Swamp.
Wit: THOMAS FEWTRELL, BENJAMIN FEWTRELL, jurat, JOHN SUTTON. MAY COURT 1741.*.

F 256 RICHARD BROWN & WIFE ANNE TO JOHN HODGSON of Chowan County
       Feb. 13, 1740. 600 pds. for 320 A. +240 A. "...(RICHARD BROWN) &
ANNE His wife only Daughter of FINCHOR HAYNE late of the County afores'd
Dec'd..." Two tracts. (1) Land on Chowan River adj. SAMUEL WILLIAMS, JOHN
BROWN. (2) Land between JOHN MAYNOR, JACOB LEWIS at head of BROOKES Creek
cont. 240 A. - which two tracts were formerly FINCHOR HAYNE's - and all
other lands of FINCHOR HAYNE on Pettyshore adj. two tracts not here parti-
cularly mentioned. "(Except the Dower of ANNE Late widow of the s'd FINCHER
HAYNE if any she can claim)" Wit: JOHN WYNNS, BENJAMIN HILL. N.C. Court
Feb. 17, 1740. W. SMITH C.J.

F 259 THOMAS WHITMELL & WIFE ELIZABETH TO EDWARD BRYAN
       March 7, 1741. 600 pds. for 1/2 120 A. formerly sold to
THOMAS WEST by LAURENCE SARSON by deed July 4, 1720. Registered in General
Court Register Book November 24, 1720. "ELIZABETH WHITMELL being first pri-
vately Examined..." Wit: THOMAS BLOUNT, WILLIAM WESTON, SEN., JAMES CASTEL-
LAW. N.C. Court April 8, 1741. W. Smith C.J.

F 263 THOMAS SPELLER TO JOSEPH JORDAN
       Feb. 5, 1740. 3 pds. for 2 A. On Sohikey Creek adj. JAMES WARD &
WILLIAM JORDAN. Wit: WILLIAM JORDAN, JAMES WARD, Aug. Court 1741. BENJAMIN
HILL C/C.

F 261 EDWARD BRYAN, "marriner" TO THOMAS SLAUGHTER
       Aug. 11, 1741. *. 313 A. "...EDWARD BRYAN...the only Acting Executor
of the Last will & Testament of LAWRENCE MAYGUE of the county af's'd Planter Dec'd...ordered (this land) sold by his executors...". Part of a 516 A.
tract formerly belonging to THOMAS BRAY of Chowan. By deed from BRAY Nov.
3, 1718. Adj. JOHN HOWELL on Mill Swamp on Chowan River "on which a mill
now stands belonging to JOHN HOWELL...". Wit: WILLIAM WESSTON, JOHN HOOKER,
jurat. Aug. Court 1741. *.

F 264 DANIEL DOMONY (DOMINY) & WIFE ANNE of Easthampton in Co. of Suffolk
       in Province of New York to ANDREW OLIVER & ANDREW MOORE, merchants
March 5, 1741. 65 pds. for 1600 A. On NS Moratoke River adj. Mr. SMITHWICK.
By patent granted to NATHANIEL DOMINY and ROBERT COGWELL "by his Excellency
the most noble HENERY DUKE of BEAUFORT Palatine and the rest of the true and
absolute Lords Proprietors...". Dated Aug. 29, 1713. Recorded in Office
of the Sec't'y. Sept. 9, 1713. Wit: NATHNAIEL TALMAGE, JONATHAN STRATTON.
Suffolk Court March 6, 1741. "Court of Common Pleas". Signed: THOMAS CHAT-
FIELD, Judge. Dec. 28, 1742. W. Smith C.J.

F 265 LEWIS BRYAN of Craven Co. TO EDWARD BRYAN
       Nov. 14, 1740. 457 pds. 10 sh. for 300 A. On WS Chowan adj. EDWARD
BRYAN. Part of tract where JOHN HOWELL now lives & plantation where EDWARD
BRYAN now lives. "Land left the said LEWIS BRYAN by the will of his father
...". Wit: WILLIAM WESTON, jurat, SAMUEL OSTEEN. Aug. Court 1741. *.

F 267 SIMON BRYAN of Pasquotank Co. TO EDWARD BRYAN
       June 15, 1741. 200 pds. for 320 A. On Chinkapen Swamp "being a par-
cel of land given to the said SIMON BRYAN by his father LEWIS BRYANs Last
Will and Testament..". Wit: WILLIAM WESTON, Jurat, BENJAMIN BAILEY, EPHRAIM
WESTON. Aug. Court 1741. *.

F 267 JOHN SMITHWICK TO MARY DUGGAN
       Aug. 7, 1741. Gift. 125 A. "Love good will & affection...unto my
well beloved Daughter MARY DUGGAN wife of WILLIAM DUGGAN...to MARY and her
lawfully begotten heirs forever...to WILLIAM DUGGAN for the Term of Life.."
Land between Moratack River and Charlton's Creek. "...if MARY have no issue
to return to the Lawful heirs of JOHN SMITHWICK...". Wit: *.*. Aug. Court
1741. *.

F 268 WILLIAM SPARKEMAN, yeoman, TO JOHN PURVISS of Nansemond Co., Va.
       July 7, 1741. 220 pds. for 100 A. Land on Mill Neck at Newbys Mill
Pond. Wit: JOHN WYNNS, jurat, JOHN HOOKER. Aug. Court 1741. *.

F 269 WILLIAM WHITLEY TO JOHN BARNS
       *. 3 pds. for a "Small parcel". Part of a survey bought of WILLIAM

WHITLEY on NS Buckhorn Swamp at Old County Line adj. JOHN WIGENS & WILLIAM WHITLEY. Wit: IRELAND WHITLEY, J. WYNNS. Aug. Court 1741. *.

F 270 DOM REX TO JOHN PRATT
        Nov. 20, 1739 Grant. 300 A. Land adj. WILLIAMSON, JOHN SMITH. "yearly rent of four shillings for every hundred acres". Signed: GABRIEL JOHNSTON, ESQ. Our Captain General Governor in Chief at Newbern. Enrolled in the Auditor Generalls office (Nov. 20, 1739). NICH. FOX pro Auditor. Recorded in Sec't'y. Office NICHOLAS FOX Sec't'y. Examined pro Atty Gen'll NICH. FOX.

F 271 JOHN PRATT TO WILLIAM BRYAN
        May 19, 1740. 30 pds. for 300 A. within mentioned patent. Wit: NEEDHAM BRYAN, jurat, GEORGE JERNIGAN. Aug. Court 1741. *.

F 272 WILLIAM ASHBURN TO THOMAS BREWER of Nansemond Co., Va.
        May 18, 1741. 20 pds. for 225 A. On Main Branch of Herring Creek called Perrys Meadow. Bought of HUGH HIGHMAN by deed Nov. 7, 1733. Wit: THOMAS HOLLADAY, jurat, WILLIAM CAMPBELL, HENRY SHIVERS. Aug. Court 1741.*.

F 272 ANDREW IRELAND TO BENJAMIN HILL
        July 23, 1741. 400 pds. for 629 A. "...JOHN PATTERSON by deed poll Bearing Date the Tenth day of May Anno Domini 1737...comfirm unto JOHN NIXON...all his plantation...in Bertie Precinct (as then called) But now Bertie County...JOHN NIXON is now Dec'd Intestate...land came to JOSEPH NIXON Eldest son & Heir at law...indorsed (by JOSEPH NIXON) the sixth day of July Anno 1739 to me...". Land on Meherrin Creek. Wit: JAMES ARTHANS, jurat, WILL CATHCART. Aug. Court 1741. *.

F 274 WILLIAM BUSH, "carpenter" of Craven Co. TO ISAAC HILL
        May 7, 1741. 130 pds. for 276 A. In two parcels. (1) In Chinkapen Neck 156 A. on Long Meadow now in possession of ISAAC HILL. (2) 120 A. adj. "THOS. or DENNIS McCLENDONS Deed...". One mortgage to the Treasury of Bertie Precinct and quitrents due Nov. 20, 1732. Wit: JAMES WILLIAMS, jurat, LEWIS WILLIAMS. Aug. Court 1741. *.

F 275 JOHN SPANN & WIFE MARY TO SILVESTER ESTES
        Aug. 8, 1741. 100 pds. for 160 A. In Upper Parish Bertie on NS Morattock River by patent to SPANN for 160 A. Wit: JASPER STEWART, jurat, DAVID ROZAR, RICHARD CROSS. Aug. Court 1741. *.

F 276 CHARLES STEVENSON TO JOHN JAMESON
        June 5, 1741. 98 pds. 10 sh. for 1280 A. On Roanoak River at mouth of Long Gutt adj. JAMES CASTELLAW. "Mine by patent." Wit: JOHN DAWSON, GEORGE DOWNING, jurat. Aug. Court 1741. *.

F 277 JOHN MOOR & RICHARD MOOR TO WILLIAM ACOCK
        July 5, 1741. 80 pds. for 640 A. On NS Moratuck River adj. THOMAS AVENT on Stoney Creek. Land granted by patent to JOHN GADDIS dated March 5, 1719. Wit: WILLIAM SHORTER, JOHN BROWN, ELIZABETH SHORTER, THOMAS PACE, jurat, THOMAS AVENT. Aug. Court 1741. *.

F 242 JAMES BLOUNT of Craven County TO JETHRO BUTLER
        *. 25 pds. for 220 A. On NS Morattock River "Nigh the River Bank" at dividing line between JETHRO BUTLER & ROBERT HICKS adj. land that BUTLER bought of THOMAS JARNAGAN. Wit: OEN MACKDANIEL, Jurat, GEORGE BELL, JOHN HARRELL. Aug. Court 1741. *.

F 280 WILLIAM PEEKE TO JOHN WYNNS, yeoman
        March 17, 1741. 100 pds. for 150 A. On NS Wiccacon Creek adj. WYNNS, THOMAS LEE, WILLIAM LEE on Dunns Swamp. Wit: BENJAMIN WYNNS, jurat, SARAH WYNNS. Aug. Court 1741. *.

F 281 JOHN WYNNS TO WILLIAM FREEMAN of Chowan Co.
        Aug. 3, 1741. 50 pds. for 300 A. On SWS Quoyokason Swamp at Crooked Branch. Assigned to me by WILLIAM BLY. Wit: THOMAS JACKSON, JAMES DROUGHIM, THOMAS OUTLAW. Nov. Court 1741. *.

F 282 THOMAS MARTIN of Western Branch of Norfolk Co., Va. TO JOSEPH OATES
        Feb. 8, 1739. Exchange. 300 A. (1) JOHN ODAM to MARTIN. Land at Sumerton Chappull in Nansemond Co, Va. "...and also for & by order of JANE

PAGETT One of the Daughters & Heir of JOHN ODAM Dec'd & Late of Bertie Coun-
ty...delivered to JOSEPH OATES...and by order of JANE PAGETT (all their
deeds being lost) all that tract of Land lying at Mount Pleasant or Pitch
Landing & Joyning to WILLIAM PAGETTS Land..." (2) 100 A. by patent date
Feb. 1704 (or 5/6) "That I sold to JOHN ODAM her father in the year (1721)".
Wit: WALTER DROUHAM, JOHN IVES, RICHARD POWELL. NC Court July 29, 1741.
J. Montgomery C.J.

F 283 JONATHAN MILLER & WIFE SUSANNAH TO GEORGE PATTERSON
       Feb. 1, 1741/42. 45 pds. for 150 A. In Buckleberry Pocoson known by
the name Island. Adj. ARCHIBALD BELL, JAMES NEWLAND, JOSEPH REDDILL. Wit:
THOMAS RYAN, LOVICK YOUNG. Feb. Court 1741. Benjamin Hill C/C.

F 284 JAMES CASTELLAW TO GEORGE PATTERSON
       Aug. 31, 1741. 60 pds. for (part of) 580 A. "...DAVID HENDERSON
Dec'd. did by his Last will & Testament in Writing bearing date the thir-
teenth of February 1735 give & bequeath unto his nephew GEORGE HENDERSON &
to the six children which his sister JANET had in Scotland by ANDREW THOMP-
SON...GEORGE HENDERSON one of the legatees is since dead & whereas JOHN
THOMPSON Eldest son and Heir of JOHN THOMPSON of Cambasdrenny in North
Britain Dec'd THOMAS WINGATE of Meclewood and GRIZEL his wife & WALTER AICK-
MAN of Carsebonny and ISOBELL his wife, which the s'd JOHN THOMPSON Dec'd
GRIZEL & ISOBELL were three of the six children of ANDREW THOMPSON Dec'd by
JANET his wife and only sister of the said DAVID HENDERSON...". By Deed Aug.
29, 1740 appt. JAMES CASTELLAW atty. to receive and dispose of their inher-
itance of DAVID HENDERSON. 580 A. their share of Land on Moratuck Bay. Wit:
THOMAS WHITMELL, jurat, HENRY DAY. November Court 1741. BENJAMIN HILL C/C.

F 286 JAMES TINER TO SAMUEL STRICKLAND
       Sept. 15, 1741. 20 pds. for 150 A. On SS Kirbys Creek at Mandew
Branch. Part of patent granted THOMAS MANDEW on April 1, 1723. Wit: J. DEW,
CAROLUS ANDERSON. Nov. Court 1741. *.

F 287 WILLIAM GUNN TO BENJAMIN HILL, merchant
       Feb. 5, 1740. Power of Atty. to collect debts. Wit: JOHN CAMPBELL,
WILLIAM STOKES. Nov. Court 1741. BENJAMIN HILL, C/C.

F 288 JOSEPH PLATTS & WIFE MARY TO HENRY HOWELL
       April 5, 1741. "a valuable sum" for 225 A. On SS Meherrin River adj.
JAMES TURNER, THOMAS PHILLIPS. Part of patent granted THOMAS HOWELL by
WILLIAM REED, ESQ. for 450 A. dated April 5, 1723. Wit: JOHN EXUM, SAMUELL
TAYLOR, HOPKINS HOWELL. Nov. Court 1741. *.

F 289 WILLIAM GUNN & WIFE RUTH TO BENJAMIN HILL
       Feb. 24, 1740. 35 pds. for (Bill of Sale): 4 negros Tom, Benbow,
Dina and her child, 1 molatto Boy named Daniel. Now in possession of GEORGE
GOULD. "(Iwill) warrant & Defend the said Negros & Molatto Boy to the s'd
HILL During the life of my Wife RUTH..." Wit: JOHN CAMPBELL, WILLIAM
STOKES. Nov. Court 1741. *.

F 289 JOHN WALBUTTON TO JOHN JORDAN
       Dec. 12, 1740. 50 pds. for 120 A. On Heron Creek adj. JOHN BRADLEYS,
WILLIAM ASHBURN, JOHN ROGERS, ____ SAVAGE. The remains of a patent of ROB-
ERT WALBUTTON dated April 1, 1720. Wit: WILLIAM ASHBURN, JOHN BRADLEY,
jurat, WILLIAM HARRISON. Nov. Court 1741. *.

F 290 THOMAS TAYOR of Western Branch of Elizabeth River, Va. to JOSEPH
       RICHERSON (RICHARDSON) Oct. 8, 1741. 75 pds. for 290 A. Adj. WILL-
IAM BENNET. Wit: JOHN IVEY, THOMAS TUCKER, JOSEPH GRANT, jurat. Nov. Court
1741. *.

F 292 JOHN PRATT, High Sheriff Exq. of Bertie County TO JOHN HODGSON &
       WILLIAM CATHCART. Nov. 1, 1740. 100 pds. for 300 A. Part of tract
granted THEOPHILUS WILLIAMS by date Aug. 8, 1728 on Falling Run adj. JOHN
WILLIAMS, ____ CASTELLAW, WILLIAM GRAY. Wit: J. MONTGOMERY, BENJAMIN HILL,
jurat. Nov. Court 1741. *.

F 293 ROBERT EDWARDS TO THOMAS WARD
       Aug. 28, 1741. 30 pds. for 100 A. On NS "Panter Swamp" adj. MOAB
WILLIAMS & Cross Branch. Part of patent formerly granted ROBERT EDWARDS
bearing date Feb. 1, 1725. Wit: J. DEW, JOSEPH WARD. Nov. Court 1741. *.

F 293 ROBERT EDWARDS, SEN. TO THOMAS WARD
       Aug. 6, 1741. 20 pds. for 350 A. In Little Creek at asture Branch.
Part of patent formerly granted TIMOTHY HIGNS March 1, 1719. Wit: JOHN DEW,
jurat, JOHN WORRELL. Nov. Court 1741. BENJAMIN HILL C/C.

F 295 WILLIAM GUNN TO BENJAMIN HILL
       Feb. 24, 1740. 35 pds. for (Bill of Sale) "Two Large Glasses with
stones on Writing Desk on Ovil Tale one Round D one Easy Chair one Dozen of
Chairs one pleat Warmer Two Corner Coberts one pair English Quem stones one
p'r Large Iron Doggs four feather Beds & Ordinary Furniture one Chest of
Drawers the Oyster shells & Lime on the Plantation some hides & Two Iron
Potts with Sundry other Household goods..." Wit: JOHN CAMPBELL, MARY CAMP-
BELL. Nov. Court 1741. *.

F 296 WILLIAM WYNNS, yeoman, TO THEOPHILUS PUGH, merchant, of Nansemond
       Co., Va. Aug. 11, 1741. 20 pds. for 450 A. On Ahoskey Ridge adj.
____CATHCART. Wit: THOMAS JACKSON, JAMES MANNEY, JOHN WYNNS. Nov. Court
1741. *.

F 298 JOHN JAMES (JEMMISSON), "Physician" & WIFE ELIZABETH TO THEOPHILUS
       PUGH, Merchant, of Virginia. Aug. 19, 1741. 150 pds. for 1280 A.
On Roanoak River at mouth of a large Gutt adj. JAMES CASTELLAW. "Included
in a Patent of the said Land granted unto CHARLES STEVENSON..." Dated Feb.
14, 1739. Included in a deed from STEVENSON to JAMMESSON. Wit: JAMES EVER-
ARD, CHRISTOPHER GARDNER. Nov. Court 1741. *.

F 301 FREDERICK JONES TO THEOPHILUS PUGH, merchant, of Virginia
       March 13, 1742. 130 pds. for 608 A. In two tracts: (1) On SS Ura
Swamp on WS Ura Path. Land granted RICHARD KILLINGSWORTH by patent March 1,
1719. (2) Adj. first parcel Purchased of GEORGE DOWNING by deed March 5,
1728. cont. 200 A. Wit: NEEDHAM BRYAN, HENRY AVERITT, JAMES EVERARD. N.C.
Court April 4, 1742. J. MONTGOMERY, C.J.

F 302 JOHN GANEY of Craven Co. TO JOHN DEW
       May 25, 1741. 36 pds. for 200 A. Part of patent formerly granted
RICHARD WASHINGTON on Nov. 7, 1723 in Potecasie Woods on Patties Delight
adj. RICHARD VICK. Wit: RICHARD WASHINGTON, THOMAS GARREY, NATHANIEL FIELDS.
Nov. Court 1741. BENJAMIN HILL C/C.

F 303 WILLIAM FAULK of Tyrrell Co. TO BENJAMIN HILL
       Sept. 17, 1741. 500 pds. for 500 A. On NS Meherrin. By patent June
7, 1739 to WILLIAM FAULK. Wit: THOMAS JONES, jurat. JAMES ARTHAND. Nov.
Court 1741. *.

F 304 WILLIAM AUSTON TO THOMAS UZZELL
       Aug. 7, 1741. 25 pds. for 100 A. On NS Meherrin River adj. ALLEXAN-
DER SHERARD on Haw Branch. Wit: JAMES WASHINGTON, jurat, JOHN DEW, JOHN
NICOLSON. Nov. Court 1741. *.

F 305 JOHN WYNNS, yeoman, TO WILLIAM WYNNS, yeoman
       March 23, 1740. 1700 pds. for 550 A. Land on Mount Pleasant on SWS
Chowan River at Wild Cat Gutt at POLLOCKS Line, SHARPS line at Goose Creek
& Wiccacon Creek. "One Lease to WILLIAM DOWNING excepted". Wit: JOHN HOOKER,
FRANCIS BROWN, JUN. Nov. Court 1741. *.

F 306 EDWARD WINGATE of New Hanover Co. TO JONATHAN TAYLOR
       *. 200 pds. for 200 A. Part of a tract WINGATE purchased of Doc'r
JAMES WILLIAMSON on NS Morrattock River adj. EDMOND SMITHWICK, ABRAHAM
SHEPPARD. Wit: H. HUNTER, W. DANIEL, WILLIAM PERRY, jurat. Nov. Court 1741.*.

F 308 JAMES PARKER, SEN., carpenter, TO WILLIAM SHOLAR
       Nov. 9, 1741. "consideration of a mare" for 150 A. Part of a patent
to JAMES PARKER on NS Cashy Swamp. adj. WILLIAM SHOLAR. Wit: RUTH PARKER,
RICHARD ROWLAND. Nov. Court 1741. Benjamin Hill C/C.

F 309 JAMES WILLIAMSON & WIFE SARAH TO WILLIAM PEIRCEY
       July 29, 1740. 100 pds. for 70 A. Adj. HENRY HUNTER, JOHNSONS Branch
"thence along the Bredth of the ridge". Wit: HENRY HUNTER, JOHN GRAY, SARAH
HUNTER, THOMAS TAYLOR, jurat. November Court 1741. *.

F 311 JOHN HOWELL, SEN. TO MATTHEW HOWELL

Oct. 9, 1741. Gift 340 A. "Natural good Will & affection I bear Towards my Son MATTHEW HOWELL..." On WS Chowan River adj. RICHARD BOOTH. Wit:
SARAH HOWELL, ARTHUR HOWELL, JOSEPH HARDEE. Nov. Court 1741. *.

F 311   THOMAS GANEY & WIFE MARTHA TO JOHN GRIFFIN of Surry Co., Va.
Aug. 6, 1741. 150 pds. for 950 A. on SS Meherrin at mouth of Spring
Branch to Rattle Snake Valley adj. THOMAS GANEY. Land granted to his father
WILLIAM GANEY by patent March 27, 1713. Wit: JAMES WASHINGTON, RICHARD
WASHINGTON, THOMAS UZZELL. Nov. Court 1741. "...and at the Same time MARTHA
the Wife of the s'd THOMAS being first Privately Examined by WILLIAM CATH-
CART Esq....acknowledges freely..." *.

F 312   NATHANIEL KEELE TO MATTHEW WHITFIELD of New Hanover Co.
Jan. 19, 1740. Power of atty. to collect debts and manage Plantation
on W Branch of New River formerly belonging to JETHRO MASHBORNE cont. 200
A. Wit: WILLIAM WHITFIELD, jurat, J. ARYARS. Feb. Court 1741. *.

F 313   JOHN GRAY, surveyor, TO JOHN WILSON
Sept. 1, 1740. 100 pds. for 130 A. On ES Chinkapen Swamp adj. Col.
MAUL. Wit: WILLIAM GRAY, JOHN GRAY, JOHN GRAY, JUN. Feb. Court 1741. *.

F 314   JOHN GRAY TO THOMAS PARKER
Feb. 10, 1741/42. 110 pds. for 640 A. On WS Chowan River in St.
Johns Neck adj. JOHN BRYAN on Cypress Swamp at Tumbling Branch and Femur
Branch at Chinkapen Creek. Wit: JOHN FREEMAN, jurat, *.*. Feb. Court 1741.*.

F 316   JOHN MACKFARLING & WIFE THOMASINA TO JOHN GRAY
Sept. 23, 1735. 300 pds. for *. "...Love and Respect...unto our
friend JOHN GRAY and more especially for his Bond for three Hundred Pounds
...Plantation whereon we now live in Chowan Precinct From SAMUEL WOODWARD
to PHILLIP BROWN by deed and by BROWN bequeathed in Last Will & Testament
unto us..." Also all cattle, hogs, a black horse, 3 beds, furniture, pots,
kittles, oxes, hoes "...and all movables mentioned & unmentioned..." JOS.
HARDEE, GEORGE TURNEDGE, jurat. N.C. Court Nov. 1, 1735. S. SMITH C.J.

F 316   JOHN GRAY TO JOHN WILSON Late of Province of New York
Aug. 1, 1740. 100 pds. for *. "within mentioned plantation (& appurtenances)" Wit: WILLIAM GRAY, JOHN GRAY, JUN. Feb. Court 1741. *.

F 317   SAMUELL RUFFIN of Northampton Co. TO ROBERT PEELLE, JUN. of Nansemond Co, Va. *1741/42. 40 pds. for 500 A. On Catowisky Meadow.
Granted by patent Nov. 11, 1719 to ROBERT HICKS "...by him Elapsed for want
and due Seating & planting...came due JAMES WOOD..." WOOD's patent date
April 1, 1723. Wit: ISAAC CARTER, JACOB CARTER. Feb. Court 1741. *.

F 318   JOHN HARRELL TO JAMES HARRELL
Feb. 4, 1741. 10 pds. for 50 A. JAMES HARRELL brother to JOHN
HARRELL. Land "being the Lower end of the Land I bought of JAMES BROWN for
Two Hundred Acres more of less..." Granted by patent to THOMAS MANN for 640
A. Feb. 1, 1725. Wit: CHRISTOPHER HARRELL, HENRY HARRELL. Feb. Court 1741.*.

F 319   THOMAS STEVENSON & WIFE REBECCA TO WILLIAM WEAVER (WEVER)
*. 70 pds. for 300 A. Adj. ALLEXANDER COTTEN, JONATHAN CLIFTS, THO-
MAS JOHNSTON. Wit: THOMAS ARCHER, ELIZABETH STAPLES. Feb. Court 1741. *.

F 320   JAMES RUTLAND TO THOMAS JONES of Pettyshoar
Oct. 12, 1741. 20 pds. for 130 A. Land on Deed Creek adj. JOB ROGERS,
JONATHAN GILBERT, JOHN GILBERT. Wit: R. FORSTER, WILL CATHCART. Feb. Court
1741. *.

F 321   THOMAS JONES of Pettyshoar TO JAMES RUTLAND, JUN.
Oct. 12, 1741. 80 pds. for 300 A. On Woatom. Granted THOMAS JONES
"by the Late Lords proprietors their Governour & Council..." Sept. 22, 1730.
Adj. PETER WEST. Wit: R. FORSTER, WILL CATHCART. Feb. Court 1741. *.

F 322   CHARLES RICKETTS TO THOMAS RYAN (RIAN)
Feb. 9, 1741/42. 100 pds. for 430 A. Patent date March 9, 1717/18
to LEWIS BRYAN. By him sold to s'd RICHETTS. Land in St. John's Neck on ES
Cypress Swamp adj. WILLIAM WEST, JAMES TURNER. Wit: WILLIAM TOOD, jurat,
WILLIAM RICKETS, JOHN RICKETS. Feb. Court 1741. *.

F 324 JOHN BRYAN of Craven Co. TO JOHN GRAY
       Jan. 20, 1739/40. 100 pds. for 640 A. On WS Chowan River in St.
Johns Neck adj. JOHN BRYAN on Cypress Swamp at head of Femur Branch of
Chinkapen Creek. Wit: WILLIAM GRAY, JOHN WILSON, jurat. Feb. Court 1741. *.

F 325 PHILLIP WALSTON, SEN. TO GEORGE, HENRY,PHILLIP, PHILLIP (the son of
       WILLIAM), & AVERILLE WALSTON. March 17, 1740/41. Gift (will) Land
and Negroes. "...Natural Love and Effection that I bear unto my children...
and to my wife.." To my wife AVERILLE 1/2 plantation during her life and
widowhood. To HENRY: 400 A. ajd. JAMES NEWLAND. Also negro boy Quash. Not
to be sold during life of grantor. To PHILLIP a negro Prince and a boy
called Jack...labor of same reserved during life of grantor. To GEORGE 400
A. on Kesia where I now dwell. A negro boy called Sezar. Life right of both
reserved by grantor. To EASTER 200 A. on SWS Bare Swamp and a negro girl
called Vilott. Not to be sold during life of grantor without consent. To
JEAN 200 A. on Bare Swamp and a negro girl Cate also reserved during life
of grantor. To MARY "Negro Jenny after my decease and her increase reserving for myself only the first child". To NANCY, EASTER, JANE, MARY all my
stock of cattle equally except 5 cows and calves, 2 steers (use reserved of
all during life of grantor) also all sheep - reserve 1/2 all wool during
life. To grandson PHILLIP WALSTON, son of WILLIAM and ELIZABETH WALSTON, 1
negro girl Rose. If she should breed each of his brothers and sisters should
have one negro. Wit: JAMES WATSON, THOMAS WHITMELL, THOMAS RYAN. Feb. Court
1741. *.

F 326 WILLIAM WHITFIELD & WIFE RACHEL TO HENRY COPELAND of Nansemond Co, Va.
       Nov. 12, 1741. 25 pds. for 300 A. On NS Meherrin Creek at Bells
Branch adj. ARON ODAM. Wit: JAMES COPELAND, DANIEL ROGERS, WILLIAM WHITFIELD.
Feb. Court 1741. *.

F 328 JOHN GRANT TO THOMAS BASS
       Dec. 24, 1741. 70 pds. for 240 A. Adj. AMON GRANT. Wit: THOMAS WHIT-
MELL, jurat, THOMAS CASTELLAW. Feb. Court 1741. *.

F 329 THOMAS FUTRILL & WIFE ANN TO JOEL NEWSUM
       Jan. 21, 1741. 15 pds. for 100 A. In Northampton Precinct on Yourar
Swamp and Yourhar Road. Part of 640 A. surveyed by WILLIAM BRASSWELL, Dec'd.
Wit: JOHN DICKINSON, jurat. Feb. Court 1741. *.

F 330 THOMAS MANN of Edgecombe TO MARY SPEIGHT, widow
       Feb. 8, 1741. 75 pds. for 490 A. "MARY SPEIGHT widow and Relect of
THOMAS SPEIGHT Late of Perquimmons County..." Land on Wiccacon Creek adj.
JOHN WYNNS, WILLIAM DOWNING, JOSEPH WOTSFORD. Wit: JOHN HOOKER, JOS(EPH)
OATES, THOMAS BANKS. N.C. Court April 2, 1742. J. Montgomery, C.J.

F 332 JOHN MANN of Edgecombe Co. TO MARY SPEIGHT
       April 9, 1742. "a valuable sum" for 150 A. "MARY SPEIGHT Widow and
Relect of THOMAS SPEIGHT Late of Perquimmons..." Land on Wiccacon Creek adj.
JOHN WYNNS "and land lately conveyed to MARY SPEIGHT by THOMAS MANN..."
Land granted to THOMAS MANN Father of s'd JOHN MANN of Dec. 17, 1716. Wit:
WILLIAM WEST, JAMES CANE, JOSEPH PERREY. May Court 1742. Thomas Crew C/C.

F 334 THOMAS RYAN TO EDWARD RASOR
       April 1, 1742. 140 pds. for 350 A. Adj. "Mr. DUCKENFIELDS Line" on
Green Branch at Salmon Creek. Wit: THOMAS JONES, JAMES McMANUS, EDWARD
BRYAN. N.C. Court April 1, 1742. J. MONTGOMERY C.J.

F 335 WILLIAM CATHCART & WIFE PENELOPE TO THOMAS JONES
       Oct. 19, 1742. 2000 pds. for 9470 A. "WM. CATHCART & PENELOPE his
wife Heirs of WILLIAM MAUL Esq. Late of the s'd County..." (1) 640 A. on NS
Morratock River called "Boath" by patent Jan. 23, 1713. (2) 2500 A. on Ahotsky & Catawiskey Swamp called "Summersett" Patent dated November 29, 1716.
(3) Tract of 3000 A. in Chowan on SS Morratock called "Caledonia" by purchase dated Oct. 19, 1722. (4) 170 A. between Catawiskey & Ahotsky by patent dated April 1, 1723. (5) 640 A. on Roonaroy Meadows by patent dated
Feb. 1, 1725. (6) 640 A. by Deed Poll in Chowan Precinct on SWS Chowan
River bought from JAMES BLOUNT's wife CATHERINE by WILLIAM MAUL in 1721.
(7) 640 A. On Roonaroy by patent date Feb. 1, 1725. (8) A patent from LEWIS
BRYAN to PENELOPE for 640 A. on Moratock River dated Aug. 18, 1726. "...on
the whole nine Thousand four hundred and seventy acres..." Wit: BENJAMIN
HILL, THOMAS CREW. N.C. Court Oct. 20, 1742. W. SMITH, C.J. "Mrs. PENELOPE

172

CATHCART was Privately Examined...acknowledge freely..." PETER WEST, Justice.

F 336 THOMAS JONES TO WILLIAM CATHCART
        Oct. 29, 1742. 2000 pds. for 9470 A. (Same tracts as in preceding
deed.) Wit: T. BARKER, ABRAHAM BLACKSHALL, BENJAMIN HILL. N.C. Court Oct.
29, 1742. W. SMITH, C.J.

F 338 JOHN BRADELY of Craven TO GEORGE STRACKEN
        Oct. 12, 1741. 130 pds. for 320 A. At mouth of Reedy Branch adj.
LAURENCE McGUE at Cypress Swamp. Wit: JOHN WHITE, ROBERT CLARK, JOHN GRAY.
March 4, 1741. J. MONTGOMERY C.J.

F 339 ISAAC SANDERS, yeoman, TO GABRIEL MANLEY
        March 27, 1742. 20 pds. for 100 A. *. Wit: FRANCIS BROWN, BENJAMIN
WYNNS. May Court 1742. THOMAS CREW C/C.

F 339 JOHN CRICKETT, "Taylor", TO WILLIAM SPARKMAN
        May 10, 1742. 27 pds. for 180 A. On SS Cypress Swamp "Round about
Pond". Wit: JOHN WYNNS, GEORGE DAUGHAN. May Court 1742. *.

F 340 JOHN JAMESON, "Practitioner in Phisick", & WIFE ELIZABETH TO JAMES
        WILKINS of Northampton Co. May 8, 1742. 48 pds. for 110 A. Land
in Northampton adj. WEST DURDEN [these may be two surnames WEST and DURDEN]
WILLIAM BROWN, JAMES WILKINS. Part of 540 A. grant to THOMAS BROWN by
patent Nov. 29, 1716. On NS Maherine River. Wit: JOHN SUTTON, EDWARD OUTLAW.
May Court 1742. THOMAS CREW C/C.

F 342 WILLIAM WHITFIELD TO THOMAS WALKER
        March 18, 1741/42. 35 pds. for 300 A. At Pottecasie Branch adj.
THOMAS JONES at "THOMASES Path". Plantation whereon JOHN GRADDY formerly
lived "...& the plantation that WILLIAM WHITFIELD JUN. now liveth..." Wit:
EDWARD OUTLAW, PATIENCE OUTLAW, DANIEL SELLEVENT, WILLIAM WHITFIELD, JUN.
May Court 1742. *.

F 342 HENRY MAYNOR, yeoman, TO CHRISTOPHER ROBERTSON
        May 8, 1742. 13 pds. 10 sh. for 175 A. Adj. JOHN HODGSON, ISAAC
LEWIS, ROBERT MILLIKIN. Wit: GEORGE WYNNS, BENJAMIN WYNNS. May Court 1742.*.

F 343 WILLIAM WYNNS, Yeoman, TO BENJAMIN TURNER of Isle of Wight Co, Va.
        May 10, 1742. 30 pds. for 100 A. Near Mount Pleasant adj. WILLIAM
SHARP at Dogwood Branch, ELEAZAR QUINBY. "Excepting always the Guarantee of
a Lease made by JOHN WYNNS to WILLIAM DOWNING and others on the s'd Pocoson
..." Wit: BENJAMIN WYNNS, HENRY MAYNOR. May Court 1742. *.

F 344 SOLOMON JOYNER of Edgecombe Co. & JOHN JOYNER & WIFE ELIZABETH of
        Isle of Wight Co, Va. TO JOSEPH WITHERINGTON of Surry Co, Va.
Feb. 7, 1741. 25 pds. for 256 A. A Patent granted JOHN BROWN for 256 A.
July 28, 1713 on "Bank of the River" adj. JAMES CURLEE, JOHN SMYTH. Wit:
JAMES WASHINGTON, HENRY CRAFFORD, MORNING CRAFFORD, JOHN SHERARD, WILLIAM
PLYANT, JOHN FORT (FOORT). May Court 1742. THOMAS CREW C/C.

F 345 SOLOMON JOYNER of Edgecombe Co. TO JOSEPH WITHERINGTON of Surry Co,
        Va. Feb. 9, 1741. 200 pds. for 256 A. on Chowan River. "...Bound
to him for 200 pds...obligation is such that (we)..shall Refund unto the
s'd JOSEPH WITHERINGTON his heirs the purchase money in the s'd Deed mentioned with reasonable allowance for all improvements that shall thereon be
made..." Wit: JAMES WASHINGTON, WILLIAM PLYANT, JOHN SHERARD, JOHN FOORT.
May Court 1742. Thomas Crew C/C.

F 347 ROBERT FORSTER of Edgecombe Co. TO JACOB SHARP of Surry Co.
        May 10, 1742. 130 pds. for 675 A. In three parcels (1) 140 A. on
upper side of Wiccacon Creek adj. NORVIL. Granted FORSTER by patent Feb.
28, 1739. (2) On WS Chowan River on upper side Wiccacon Creek to Hodge
Creek. Granted FORSTER Feb. 15, 1739 cont. 395 A. (3) 40 A. on WS Chowan
River Pocoson at Fairchild Branch which land was purchased of ROBERT EVANS
by Deed Nov. 9, 1736. Altogether 675 A. Wit: JOHN BROWN, BENJAMIN HILL,
J. HODGSON. May Court 1742. *.

F 348 JOHN WYNNS TO JACOB SHARP of Virginia
        May 13, 1742. 100 pds. for 50 A. On NS Wiccacon Creek adj. lands of
ROBERT FORSTER of Edgecombe, WILLIAM BAKER. "...s'd land late conveyed from

JAMES FAIRCHILD to MARGRETT JOHNSON & by her assigned to me.." Wit: THOMAS
CREW, THOMAS JACKSON. May Court 1742. *.

F 349   WILLIAM WYNNS, Yeoman, TO WILLIAM KIRBY of Isle of Wight, Va.,"Turner"
        May 10, 1742. 30 pds. for 100 A. Near Mount Pleasant adj. WILLIAM
SHARP, BENJAMIN TURNER. "Except always the Guarantee of a Lease to WILLIAM
DOWNING.." Wit: BENJAMIN WYNNS, HENRY MAYNOR. May Court 1742. *.

F 350   JOHN WATSON of Edgecombe TO WILLIAM BOYT
        May 8, 1742. 20 pds. for 200 A. On SWS Cashia Swamp adj. land for-
merly THOMAS MANN's at Winningham Branch. Part of patent granted NICHOLAS
SESSUMS for 420 A. dated Feb. 1, 1725. Wit: RICHARD ROBERTS, JAMES WATTSON.
May Court 1742. THOMAS CREW C/C.

F 351   MARGUERY GILBERT TO WILLIAM WRIGHT, JUN. of Nansemond Co, Va.
        Feb. 15, 1741. 25 pds. for 200 A. "...being part of a Debt due to
the s'd WILLIAM WRIGHT by a Bill for thirty five pounds Current money of
Virginia from JONATHAN GILBERT De'd'd..." Land on Main Road to EDWARD HARE
at Deep Creek. "(MARGUERY) Right & Lawfull authority by the Last Will and
Testament of the s'd JONATHAN GILBERT Dec'd...(to sell)" Wit: ANN COTTEN,
JOHN BRADDY, ANTHONY WEBB. May Court 1742. *.

F 352   THOMAS STEVENSON TO JOHN ARCHER
        March 6, 1742. 40 pds. for 200 A. "on the Hot House in EDWARD CAR-
TERS Line" adj. PETER WEST. Wit: EDWARD MOOR, PETER WEST, JUN. May Court
1742. *.

F 353   THOMAS PARKER, "Turner" TO JOHN FREEMAN
        April 7, 1742. 60 pds. for 290 A. In St. Johns Neck at Cypress
Swamp near Tumbling Branch at Chinkapen Swamp on Femur Branch. Wit: JOHN
WELLS, BENNET BAKER, JOHN SOWELL. May Court 1742. *.

F 354   JAMES FLOOD, "Practitioner of Physick" TO THEOPHILUS PUGH of Nanse-
        mond Co, Va.   Oct. 20, 1741. 460 pds. for 100 A. On Village Swamp
adj. Widow CHESHER. Wit: WILLIAM TAYLOR, JACK JERNIGAN, THOMAS PRICE. May
Court 1742. *.

F 355   GABRIEL JOHNSTON ESQ. & WIFE PENELOPE TO ROBERT WEST
        Aug. 18, 1741. Gift & Exchange. "...Consideration of a marriage al-
ready Had & Solemnized Between the s'd GABRIEL JOHNSTON & PENELOPE his wife
and of the affection PENELOPE has for her husband...all the lands which she
is seized in this Government to be Settled & assured to the s'd GABRIEL
JOHNSTON...do grant bargain and sell to ROBERT WEST all that Plantation
known as Edenhouse...(cont. 900 A.)...and also that tract on Salmon Creek
called the Back Lands containing Two Thousand Acres...and a tract called
Mount Royall...on North Side of Roanoke River containing...five hundred &
Sixty acres...and also all the Island called Lovicks Island...on Roanoke...
(cont. 640 A.)...also a tract called Lovickfield on a Brnach of Tarr River
in Edgecombe County containing four thousand five Hundred acres...also all
the tract...containing Two Several Grants...at mouth of Swift Creek on
Northside of Neuse River in Craven County containing twelve Hundred &
Eighty acres..." Wit: J. MONTGOMERY, EDWARD GRIFFITH. N.C. Court Aug. 18,
1741. JOHN WYNNS. "...PENELOPE privately examined...acknowledges freely..."
J. MONTGOMERY C.J.

F 356   CAPT. JAMES McDOWELL TO JOHN BRADLEY
        May 11, 1743. *.*. "(I)...stand firmly indebted unto JOHN BRADLEY...
in the sum of Four Thousand Pounds...I bind my heirs...(and) do make over
by Deed of Gift...the Plantation whereon I live in Cashoke with all household Furniture...five Negros...to JOHN BRADLEY for the use of MARGRETT my
wife then the obligation to be void and of none Effect & Virtue..." Wit:
CHARLES MITCHELL, JAMES CAMPBELL, HENRY DELON (C/C). Aug. Court 1743.
JOHN WYNNS, Register.

F 357   ROBERT EVANS & WIFE ANN TO JOHN HARRELL
        June 5, 1742. 12 pds. for 265 A. On ES Brookses Creek adj. JOHN
HUTSON, ELIJAH DIXON(?)(DACOS). Wit: BENJAMIN WYNNS, WILLIAM WYNNS. Aug.
Court 1742. HENRY DELON C/C. JOHN WYNNS, Register.

F 358   WILLIAM WILLIAMSON, Yeoman TO ELEAZAR QUIMBEY, carpenter.
        July 9, 1741. 35 pds. for 100 A. Land purchased of JOHN MALPASS at

174

Deep Bottom adj. "Bounds I Gave JOHN HOUCUTT". Adj. Chinkapen Swamp, RICH-
ARD SOWELL, LEONARD GREEN,WILLIAM ROGERS. Wit: JOHN WYNNS, SARAH WYNNS.
May Court 1742. *.*.

F 359   DAVID LEGGETT TO TITUS LEGGETT
        Dec. 9, 1741 60 pds. for 50 A. On SS Rocquis Creek adj. "JOHN STE-
PHENS, alis STRAUHOUS Line to the Landing Branch..." Wit: JOHN SMITHWICK,
JAMES LEGGETT. Aug. Court 1742. HENRY DELON C/C.

F 360   JOHN WILLIAMS, Cooper, TO THOMAS GREEN
        Aug. 7, 1742. 30 pds. for 240 A. Adj. "Formerly JAMES BOONS Corner",
GEORGE WYNNS. Wit: JOHN WILLIAMS, EDWARD WILLIAMS, BENJAMIN WILLIAMS. Aug.
Court 1742. *.

F 361   WILLIAM BUSH, yeoman of Craven Co. TO JOHN PERREY
        May 22, 1742. 40 pds. for 260 A. On WS Barbeque Swamp adj. JOHN
PERREY. Wit: GEORGE WYNNS, BENJAMIN WYNNS. Aug. Court 1742. *.

F 362   JOHN WILLIAMS, cooper, TO MICHAELL WARD
        Aug. 7, 1742. 25 pds. for 100 A. On NS Quiockison Swamp adj. ALLEX-
ANDER CANNADAY. Wit: EDWARD WILLIAMS, BENJAMIN WYNNS. Aug. Court 1742. *.

F 363   THOMAS MACCLENDON of Craven Co. TO WILLIAM LEWIS
        Nov. 13, 1741. 150 pds. for 350 A. In Chinkapen Neck at mouth of
Holly Branch. Wit: WILLIAM WYNNS, THOMAS BANKS. Aug. Court 1742. *.

F 364   JOSEPH NEWBY of Perquimmons TO EPHRAIM HUNTER of Chowan
        Oct. 17, 1741. 150 pds. for 2 tracts and a mill. (1) On ES Mill
Creek at Chowan River adj. DENNIS McCLENDON. Formerly surveyed for WILL
PAGET and by him conveyed to JOSEPH NEWBY cont. 127 A. (2) 100 A. on WS
Mill Creek adj. EDWARD HOWCUTT. Also a mill. (3) Also all patents, grants,
deeds now in possession of JOSEPH NEWBY. Wit: JOHN FREEMAN, PETER BYROM.
Aug. Court 1742. *.

F 366   SAMUELL HERRING of Craven Co. TO NATHAN MIERS
        May 11, 1742. 45 pds. for 300 A. On NS Rocquiss Pussoson at Broad
Branch adj. JAMES WILLIAMS, THOMAS WIMBERLEY. Wit: ANTHONY HERRING, THOMAS
JONES. Aug. Court 1742. *.

F 367   LEWIS BRIANT (BRYAN) of Craven Co. TO ADEM HARRELL (HARRILL)
        March 17, 1742. 150 pds. for 400 A. On WS Chinkapen adj. ALLEXANDER
STEEL, HENRY VANPELT. Land granted WILLIAM CRANFORD by patent March 13,
1741. Wit: JOHN WHITE, JOHN BEASLEY. Aug. Court 1742. *.

F 368   SUSANNAH COLLSON & JOHN COLLSON TO THOMAS BLOUNT & THOMAS WHITMELL
        Dec. 16, 1741. June 19, 1742. 500 pds. for 600 A. "...Executors
of the Last will and Testament of JOHN COLLSON SEN. Dec'd...except for
thirty two pounds quit rents Deducted is paid by THOMAS COLLINS..." Land
on SS Rocquis Creek. Part of tract to LUKE MEAZLE and conveyed to TIMOTHY
TRULOVE and by TRULOVE to GEORGE CLARK GLOVER Dec'd. And by JONATHAN TAYLOR,
legatee, and JAMES WILLIAMSON, administrators, "..by and to this s'd GEORGE
CLARKs will conveyed by deed to JOHN COLLSON SEN. Dec'd...out of this COLL-
SON sold three hundred acres..." Land adj. JOHN STEVENSON, ___HAYS. Wit:
EDWARD COLLINS, MARY COLLINS. Aug. Court 1742. HENRY DELON, C/C.

F 369   JOSEPH WILLIE (WILLEY) TO THOMAS HOLDER
        Nov. 20 1735. 40 pds. for 180 A. On NES Cashie Swamp adj. THOMAS
WILLIAMS. Wit: JOHN THOMAS, JOHN BAZEMORE. Aug. Court 1742. *.

F 371   THOMAS ASHLEY, SEN. TO THOMAS ASHLEY, JUN.
        Aug. 10, 1742. 100 pds. for 120 A. On Cashoke Creek adj. HENRY VAN
LUVEN. Wit: JOHN HILL, WILLIAM ASHLEY. Aug. Court 1742. *.

F 372   JEREMIAH BENTLEY & WIFE JEAN TO ROBERT HUNTER of Chowan Co.
        May 10, 1742. 425 pds. for 300 A. On Rocquiss Swamp adj. Coll.
POLLOCK, JAMES WILLIAMSON, JOHN SMITHWICK.(SMITHWEEK). Wit: H. HUNTER, JOHN
WATSON, MARY WOTSON, ELIZABETH CLARK. Aug. Court 1742. *.

F 373   JOSEPH WILLIE TO WILLIAM VINEER
        Nov. 26, 1735. 40 pds. for 180 A. On NES Cashie Swamp. Wit: JOHN
THOMAS, JOHN BASEMORE. Aug. Court 1742. *.

F 374 THOMAS YATES & WIFE BRIDGETT TO THOMAS JACKSON
        Aug. 11, 1742. 40 pds. for 200 A. CHARLES JONES made a deed of gift
to BRIDGETT RASBERRY April 23, 1725 "the Now wife of THOMAS YATES.." for
200 A. Land on Horse Swamp adj. JAMES HOWARD, PETER WEST at Cow Hall. Wit:
THOMAS DAVIS, SAMUEL ORMES. Aug. Court 1742. *.

F 375 ROGER SNELL, cooper, TO JAMES McDOWALL, merchant
        *. 400 pds. for 200 A. Adj.HENRY KING, COLL. ROBERT WEST, ROBERT
BELL, dec'd., THOMAS MITCHELL, dec'd. Wit: JOHN HILL, ANDREW THOMSON,
WILLIAM BALL. Aug. Court 1742. HENRY DELON C/C.

F 376 THOMAS RYAN TO HENRY COBB
        March 16, 1742. 40 pds. for 400 A. At Cookown Branch, Beavardam,
ARNOLs Branch. "...to the Road that goes to WILLIAM BIRDS on Plowmans Line
..." Wit: WILLIAM LAURENCE, JAMES NEWLAND. Aug. Court 1742. *.

F 377 THOMAS ASHBURN TO JOSEPH DEMSEY
        Aug. 10, 1742. 25 pds. for 78 1/2 A. On SS Bucklesberry Pocoson.
1/2 tract cont. 157 A. formerly belonging to JOHN COOK by patent dated 1721.
Wit: JOSIAH REDDICK, RICHARD ASHLEY, THOMAS RYAN. Aug. Court 1742. *.

F 378 JOHN COLLINS, SEN. & WIFE MARTHA TO THOMAS DAVIS
        Aug. 10, 1742. 70 pds. for 100 A. On NS Kesia River "known by Name
of Roses Old Field". At Issues Creek on Reedy Branch. Wit: THOMAS JACKSON,
ARTHUR WILLIAMS. Aug. Court 1742. *.

F 379 THOMAS SPELLER & WIFE SARAH TO JOSIAH RIDDICK
        March 12, 1741/42. 700 pds. for 800 A. On NS Morrattock at Sakythee
(?) Creek. Part of 1000 A. formerly purchased by HENRY SPELLER from EDWARD
SMITHWICK. Wit: WILLIAM JORDAN, WILLIAM WARD. Aug. Court 1742. *.

F 381 EDWARD COLLINS, yeoman, TO ELIZABETH , EDWARD, ANNE, THOMAS & SARAH
        COLLINS.   Aug. 11, 1742. Deed of Gift. "...good will & Naturall
affection I bear to my children..." (1) To ELIZABETH a negro girl named
Bess and her issue. (2) To EDWARD two boys called Morat and Andy. (3) To
ANNE a girl named Phillis and her issue. (4) To THOMAS a boy called Jupiter.
(5) To SARAH a girl called Judith and her issue. Wit: JOHN HARRELL, JAMES
CASTELLAW, HENRY DAY. Aug. Court 1742. *.

F 381 ISBELL KING widow of Society Parish TO HENRY KING
        Aug. 9, 1742. Deed of Gift. "...for good will & affection...I do
bear to my son HENRY KING of the same Parish & County Miner..." A Negro
girl named Cloe. Wit: ROBERT WEST, STEVENS LEE, ROBERT WEST. Aug. Court 1742.*.

F 382 JAMES WATERS TO ARCHBILL BELL
        *. 120 pds. for 200 A. In Bucklesberry Pocoson. Formerly belonging
to LAWRENCE SARSON. Adj. JOHN REDITT, JOSEPH REDITT. Wit: JAMES CASTELLAW,
MICHAEL KING. Nov. Court 1742. *.

F 382 PETER GRAY TO JOHN EDWARDS
        Aug. 7, 1742. 200 pds. for 480 A. Adj. JOHN EDWARDS dec'd., HARDY's
line, JOHN HOLLBROOK, THOMAS JONES. Wit: JOHN HILL, HENRY DAY. Nov. Court
1742. *.

F 383 JOHN GILBERT & WIFE ELIZABETH TO THOMAS YATES
        Nov. 6, 1742. 50 pds. for 100 A. "...land...given & will'd to me by
JOHN HALE Dec'd..." At White Oak Branch in Middle Swamp. adj. YATES line,
EDWARD TAYLOR, POLLOCK. Wit: JOHN CAKE, ANN CAKE. Nov. Court 1742. *.

F 384 ROBERT EVANS TO PETER EVANS
        June 11, 1742. 85 pds. for 235 A. Two parcels on Petty Shoar (1)
adj. NICHOLLAS FAIRLESS, GODFREY HOOKER cont. 100 A. Part of purchase patent granted to THOMAS POLLOCK January 28, 1705. (2) 135 A. on SE part of
s'd plantation granted ROBERT EVANS Aug. 3, 1723. Wit: BENJAMIN WYNNS, WILL
WYNNS. Feb. Court 1742. *.

F 385 RICHARD ROGERS of Edgecombe TO ELIZABETH ROGERS, widow
        July 3, 1742. 43 pds. for * "...land whereon my brother ROBERT
ROGERS Lived & Died..." In Mill Neck. Wit: JOHN WYNNS, JOSEPH CALES, JOHN
WESTON, WILL'M ROGERS. Nov. Court 1742. *.

F 385 JOHN MOOR, blacksmith, TO JOHN EDWARDS
      Aug. 5, 1742. 100 pds. for 100 A. On Eastermost part of a plantation
formerly belonging to JOHN EDWARDS Dec'd. which cont. 200 A. "...wch was
Equally Divided Betwisch the s'd EDWARDS Dec'd and the s'd MOOR..." Wit:
THOMAS WHITMELL, JOHN HILL. Nov. Court 1742. HENRY DELON C/C.

F 387 JOHN EDWARDS TO CHARLES HARDEE (HADEE)
      Aug 11, 1742. 300 pds. for 480 A. (1) 200 A. adj. JOHN GRAY at
Licking Branch, HENRY EDWARDS at Turkey Swamp. (2) 240 A. adj. JOHN EDWARDS
Dec'd. Wit: THOMAS WHITMELL, JOHN HILL. Nov. Court 1742. *.

F 388 EDWARD OUTLAW TO JOELL SANDERS
      Oct. 8, 1742. 18 pds. for 322 A. *. Wit: THOMAS DIXON, FRANCIS
SANDERS. Feb. Court 1742. *.

F 389 HENRY HUNTER TO ROBERT HUNTER
      Aug. 11, 1742. 80 pds. for 100 A. At dividing line between JAMES
WILLIAMSON & JONATHAN TAYLER on Rocquiss Swamp. Part of a grant to JAMES
WILLIAMSON dated April 5, 1720. Part of grant to JOHN SMITHWICK Aug. 7,
1720. Wit: JOHN HILL, MARTHA HILL, ELIZABETH WHITMELL. Feb. Court 1742. *.

F 390 JOHN MITCHENER, yeoman, TO THOMAS BAKER, yeoman
      Aug. 13, 1742. 15 pds. for 260 A. On Stony Creek Road at CHRISTOPHER
HOLLYMAN's line, adj. STEPHEN SHIVERS. Wit: JOHN WYNNS, JOSEPH BARRADWILL.
Feb. Court 1742. *.

F 390 DANIEL HOUGH TO HENRY WINBORNE & BRYANT HARE of Nansemond Co, Va.
      Dec. 8, 1742. 27 pds. 10 sh. Part of parcel purchased by DANIEL
HOUGH from THOMAS JONES by deed July 13, 1742. Patented by FREDERICK JONES
in 1712. On SS Maherin Creek at Hothouse Branch at Indian Path. Wit: BENJA-
MIN HILL, JOHN WINBORNE, NICHOLAS MONGER. Feb. Court 1742.

F 392 THOMAS BAKER TO CHRISTOPHER HOLLAMAN, SEN.
      Feb. 8, 1742/43. 15 pds. for 260 A. In Hoskey whereon s'd BAKER now
lives. Wit: THOMAS DIXON, WILLIAM WARREN. Feb. Court 1742.

F 392 STAVEN (STEVEN) SHIVERS TO CHARLES JONES
      Sept. 17, 1742. 50 pds. 10 sh. for 50 A. "...Part of patent that
CHARLES JONES JUN'R Tuck up Bearing Date August the first 1725..." On Hoskey
at Buck Branch. Wit: CHRISTOPHER HOLLAMAN, THOMAS DIXON. Feb. Court 1742.*.

F 393 CULLEN POLLOCK of Tyrrell County TO LAMB HARDY
      Jan. 21, 1742/43. 38 pds. for 294 A. "...CULLEN POLLOCK...executor
to estate of m'r THOS POLLOCK..." Land adj. on SS "the Governors line", on
ES THOMAS RYAN, NEHEMIAH WARIN & WILLIAM CAMPBELL. Where JOSEPH DEMPSEY
formerly lived. Wit: NEHEMIAH WARING, WILLIAM CAMPBELL. Feb. Court 1742. *.

F 394 CULLEN POLLOCK of Tyrrell TO WILLIAM CAMPBELL
      Jan. 21, 1743. 42 pds. 18 sh. 8 p. for 250 A. Land on WS Eastermost
Swamp adj. NEHEMIAH WARING. CULLEN POLLOCK acting as executor of estate of
THOMAS POLLOCK. Wit: NEHEMIAH WARING, LAMB HARDY. Feb. Court 1742. *.

F 395 THEOPHILUS WILLIAMS TO JETHRO BUTLER
      Sept. 10, 1742. 25 pds. for 500 A. "...to be laid out according to
the Will of THOMAS BUSBY..." On NES Merattuck River at Beaverdam Branch adj.
ROBERT MELTON. Wit: NEEDHAM BRYAN, JOHN CAMPBELL, STEPHEN BLACKMAN. Feb.
Court 1742. *.

F 396 CHARLES JONES, JUN., YEOMAN, TO BRAY HARGROVE
      May 13, 1742. 60 pds. for 100 A. On NS Mill Pond at Spring Branch.
Wit: JOHN WYNNS, WILLIAM GODWIN. Feb. Court 1742. *.

F 397 JOHN KEEFE TO JAMES WILLIAMS Late of Chinkapen Neck
      June 11, 1742. 110 pds. for 150 A. On ES Chinkapin Swamp. Wit: JOHN
WYNNS, THOMAS LEE. Feb. Court 1742. *.

F 398 PATRICK OCQUIN TO WILLIAM PICKETT
      Aug. 19, 1741. 1000 lbs. pork for 150 A. On War Tom Swamp. Wit:
JOHN SUTTON, WILLIAM PERRY, SAMUEL HOWARD. Feb. Court 1742. HENRY DELON,C/C.

F 399 WILLIAM BOYT of Nansemond Co., Va. TO THOMAS WATSON

July 8, 1742. 20 pds. for 200 A. On Casshy Swamp adj. THOMAS MANN at WININGHAMs Branch. The same that BOYT bought of JOHN WATSON. Part of a patent to NICHOLAS SESSIONS dated Feb. 1, 1725. Wit: HENRY HORNE, JAMES BROWN, ELIZABETH HORNE. Feb. Court 1742. *.

F 400   JOHN HILL TO MEDIA WHITE
        Feb. 8, 1742/43. 65 pds. for 380 A. At Chinkapen Orchard. Wit: JOHN WATSON, ABRAHAM GARDAN. Feb. Court 1742. *.

F 402   RICHARD HODGE of Bluford Co., NC TO GEORGE HOUSE
        Feb. 7, 1742/43. 55 pds. for 150 A. On NS Morattack River at Runerry Marsh on Flagg Run. Adj. ___NAIRON, HENRY ROADES. Wit: JOHN HARRELL, JOSEPH HARRELL. Feb. Court 1742.

F 403   RICHARD HODGE TO GEORGE HOUSE
        Feb. 7, 1742. 15 sh. for 20 A. On NS Morattuck River in NES ROBERT WEST. Wit: JOHN HARRELL, JOSEPH HARRELL, JESSE HARRELL. Feb. Court 1742. *.

F 404   THOMAS BARKER TO JOHN JAMESON
        Aug. 24, 1741. 8 pds. for 600 A. On NS Roanoak River. Land which THOMAS KEARNEY surveyed for THOMAS BARKER. Wit: WILLIAM WHITFIELD, JUN., FARIBE PUGH. Feb. Court 1742. *.

F 405   JOHN HILL TO JOHN OXLY (OXLEY)
        Feb. 9, 1742. 250 pds. for 185 A. At Cuckoldmakers Creek of the great Beavardam. Wit: THOMAS WHITMELL, HENRY DAY. Feb. Court 1742. *.

F 406   BENJAMIN WYNNS, yeoman, TO GEORGE WYNNS
        Feb. 1742. 100 pds. for 100 A. On NS Wiccacon Creek adj. JOSEPH WYNNS, Mill Swamp at Turkey Cock Branch. Wit: JOHN THOMAS, AARON ASKEW. Feb. Court 1742. *.

F 407   JOHN BARFIELD (BEARFIELD) of Onslow Co. TO WILLIAM WILLIFORD
        Oct. 19, 1742. 100 pds. for 100 A. On SS Chowan River at Tuseakey Branch on SS Horse Swamp. Wit: ANTHONY WEBB, EDWARD OUTLAW, ANN RIALL. May Court 1743. *.

F 408   WILLIAM MOOR & EDWARD MOOR TO PETER WEST.
        April 22, 1743. 20 pds. for 150 A. "Land known by name Punkill". Signed: WILLIAM MOOR, EDWARD MOOR, MARY MOOR. Wit: THOMAS WALKER, THOMAS HOLLOWELL. May Court 1743. *.

F 409   JAMES BARFIELD TO JOHN RANDALL of upper Parish Nansemon Co., Va.
        March 9, 1741/42. 12 pds. for 150 A. Adj. BARFIELD, JAMES RUTLAND. Part of a patent to WILLIAM BAKER for 350 A. "Now become Due to this s'd JAMES BARFIELD..." Wit: CHARLES HORNE, WILLIAM MOORE. May Court 1743. *.

F 410   WILLIAM HORNE TO CHARLES HORNE
        May 9, 1743. Gift. 130 A. to well beloved son. Land on Ahoskey Swamp. Being part of land WILLIAM HORNE bought of HENRY BAKER which was granted to BAKER for 260 A. April 6, 1722. Wit: HENRY HORNE, MOSES HORNE, JOHN RANDALL. May Court 1743. *.

F 412   CHARLES HORNE TO MOSES HORNE
        *. 20 pds. for 130 A. In "N Hampton Co". Land bought of WILLIAM HORNE which he bought of HENRY BAKER and is part of BAKER's patent for 260 A. dated April 6, 1722. Wit: HENRY HORNE, JOHN RANDALL, WILLIAM HORNE. May Court 1743. *.

F 413   JOHN RASBERRY TO JOHN VICKARS
        May 10, 1743. 15 pds. for 400 A. At Colt Branch adj. JAMES MAGLAHLANE, JOHN MITCHENER. Being part of 3 patents (1) granted GEORGE SMITH on July 5, 1712. (2) Granted JOHN RASBERRY Nov. 7, 1723. (3) Granted JOHN RASBERRY March 30, 1743. Wit: JAMES THOMSON, THOMAS SUTTON, JOHN MANEING. May Court 1743. *.

F 414   SAMUELL SIZEMORE TO WILLIAM HOOKER, SEN.
        May 9, 1743. 100 pds. for 120 A. "At Main Road at the Head Line" on Sandy Run. Wit: JOHN HOOKER, JAMES HOOKER, WILLIAM FREEMAN. May Court 1743.*.

F 415   THOMAS HOWELL & WIFE GRACE TO WALTER DRAUHAN of Chowan Co.

Nov. 16, 1743 30 pds. for 200 A. On WS Barbeque Swamp "Being Compliment of patent granted THOMAS HOWELL..." By Date June 20, 1741. Wit: JOHN HOWELL, JUN., JOHN HOWELL, JOHN DROUHAN. May Court 1743. *.

417 WILLIAM BLY of Chowan Co. to JOHN PERRY (PERREY)
Nov. 23, 1741. 40 sh. for 200 A. On NES Quoyokason Swamp. Adj. PERRY. Part of patent granted WILLIAM BLY March 10, 1740. Wit: MICHALL WARD, JAMES JONES, NICHOLAS PERREY. May Court 1743. *.

F 418 WILLIAM WYNNS, Yeoman, TO JOHN BARKER of Surry Co., Va.
May 30, 1743. 42 pds. for 150 A. On SWS of Chowan River at Mount Pleasant on Anthony Swamp. Adj. WILLIAM KIRBEY at Goose Creek. Wit: JOHN WYNNS, THOMAS BANKS, WILLUT ROBARS, EBENEZER SLANSON. Aug. Court 1743. *.

F 419 ROBERT SHARMAN & WIFE LUCEY of Northampton Co. TO GEORGE MATHIAS LIVERMAN. Feb. 6, 1741/42. 10 pds. for 100 A. "...in the fork of the Hewed Bridge Branch & the Colley Branch..." adj. JOHN WATFORD, TREDDLE KEEFE, RICHARD HOMES to the east side of Little Branch. Wit: JAMES MANEY, EDWARD BARNES. May Court 1743. Henry DeLon C/C.

F 420 WILLIAM CATHCART & WIFE PENELOPE TO JOHN WYNNS
Sept. 13, 1742. 1100 pds. for 5480 A. "...his wife & Daughter and Sole Heir of WILLIAM MAULE Esq. Late of the s'd County..." Several tracts between Chowan River and Chinkapen Creek. Wit: SARAH HILL, MARY LOVICK. May Court 1743. *.

F 421 JOHN AIRES (ARES) TO ABRAHAM HERRON, JUN.
Dec. 27, 1742. 3000 lbs. fresh pork and 20 days work for 380 A. on SS Bear Swamp. Wit: JOHN SALLIS, ABRAHAM GORDAN. May Court 1743. *.

F 422 WILLIAM PEARES TO THOMAS ODOM
May 7, 1743. 11 pds. for 200 A. On WS Connaritsrat Swamp adj. WILLIAM PEARES. Wit: JAMES HOLLY, JACOB HOLLY, WILLIAM ODOM. May Court 1743.*.

F 423 THOMAS PARKER, "Turner", TO JAMES FREEMAN
April 7, 1742. 33 pds. for 166 A. In St. Johns Neck on Cypress Swamp "near the mouth of Tumbling at Gumbling Branch..." As measured by JOHN WYNNS Deputy Surveyor. Wit: JAMES AVERILL, JOHN SOWELL. May Court 1743. *.

F 424 DANIEL HOUGH TO WILLIAM MOORE
March 17, 1742/43. 3 pds. for 50 A. On Old Indian Path at PETER WEST's corner on WS Hothouse Branch adj. THOMAS JONES. Wit: PETER WEST, JUN., PETER WEST. May Court 1743. *.

F 425 BRAY HARGROVE, yeoman, TO THOMAS BYRD, yeoman
Jan. 21, 1742/43. 100 pds. for 100 A. On NS Mill Pond at Spring Branch. Wit: EDMON(D) HOLEMAN, EDMON(D) BYRD. May Court 1743. *.

F 425 JOHN ASHLEY TO PATIENCE DEMSEY
May 6, 1742. 40 pds. for 50 A. On ES Waters Branch. Wit: JAMES STEWART, THOMAS ASHLEY, ANDREW THOMSON. May Court 1743. *.

F 426 SAMUEL ONWINN TO THOMAS JACKSON
Jan. 10, 1742. 150 pds. for 160 A. On WS Chowan River. Land bought of JOHN BRYANT February 6, 1730. Part of tract formerly belonging to BRYANT. Adj. THOMAS SLAUGHTER on Middle Branch. Wit: W. BAKER, THOMAS YATES, JUN. May Court 1743. *.

F 428 JOHN WYNNS & WIFE SARAH TO THOMAS HANSFORD
May 5, 1743. 200 pds. for 600 A. On Chowan River adj. MAUL's Haven Landing, JOHN DAVERSON, JOHN WILLSON, RICHARD BOOTH. Wit: JOHN LANE, WILL CATHCART. May Court 1743. *. "...SARAH WYNNS...being privately examined... signed freely & without any compulsion..." May 7, 1743. WILL CATHCART.

F 430 JONATHAN STANLEY, JUN., yeoman, TO SOLOMON CHERRY
May 16, 1743. 120 pds. for 320 A. On SS Cashy Swamp. Wit: SAMUEL ORMES, EDWARD BRYAN. May Court 1743. *.

F 430 THOMAS BANKS TO WILLIAM LEWIS, cordwinder
April 30, 1743. Deed of Gift. 150 A. +stock. "...Love good will & Effection...to my son in Law WILLIAM LEWIS...land whereon JOHN KENNEY (my

other son in Law) now dwells in Chinkapen Neck..." On SS Wiccacon Creek.
"...Alson stock of horses cattle sheep & hoggs & house Stuff; furniture &
lumber whatsoever kind is to be found in Amaria..." Wit: JOHN WYNNS, BENJA-
MIN WYNNS. May Court 1743. *.

F 431 JOHN WYNNS ESQ. & WILLIAM BAKER TO ELIZABETH NORVIL (NORVILL), JAMES
       & BENJAMIN NORVIL. April 23, 1743. 250 pds. for 260 A. "... ELIZA-
BETH NORVIL widow and JAMES NORVILL and BENJAMIN NORVILL sons of the s'd
ELIZABETH..." Plantation called "Tarbay" on NS Wiccacon Creek adj. WILLIAM
BAKER, JUN.'s "Lower Landing to the Islands of Tarbay" adj. THOMAS JOHNSON.
For ELIZABETH her lifetime; then the western 160 A. to JAMES & the east 100
A. to BENJAMIN. Wit: WILLIAM HOOKER, JUN., BRAY HARGROVE. May Court 1743.*.

F 432 ELIZABETH & JAMES NORVILL TO JOHN WYNNS
       April 23, 1743. 80 pds. for 30 A. Land on NS Wiccacon Creek cont. 30
A. Wit: WILLIAM HOOKER, JUN., BRAY HARGROVE. May Court 1743. *.

F 433 WILLIAM DOWNING, yeoman, TO EPHRAIM HUNTER, yeoman
       Feb. 5, 1742. 16 pds. for 10 A. On ES Woodwards Creek "including
Part of the said HUNTERs Milldam..." Wit: JOHN WYNNS, ROBERT HOWELL. May
Court 1743. *.

F 434 JOHN WYNNS TO JOHN DAVISON (DAVIRSON)
       Dec. 16, 1742. 132 pds. for 600 A. "...land...including a Place
called MAULs Quarter..." On WS Chowan River. Wit: MARY WOTSFORD, THOMAS
WHITMELL, NEEDHAM BRYAN. Feb. Court 1742. *. Note: a map of described land
is included here.

F 435 JOSHUA WILKINSON, "Taylor" of Tyrrell Co. TO HENRY MARK ANTHONY DELON
       Oct. 7, 1742. 100 pds. for 150 A. On SS Cashia River Pocoson adj.
JOHN GRAY, SEN., THOMAS WHITMELL. Wit: JOHN HILL, SAMUEL WIGGINS. Nov.
Court 1742. *.

F 437 JOSEPH SCITELTHARP & WIFE MARREY TO JAMES MCDOWALL, "mearener"
       *. 100 pds. for 50 A. Adj. JOHN BYRD, ___MORIS. Wit: JOHN RAY,
JAMES MCLAUGHLIN, HENRY KING. Nov. Court 1742. *.

F 438 THOMAS RYAN TO CHARLES JACOCKS
       Nov. 8, 1742. 60 pds. for 200 A. At Haymeadow Branch at the Beavar-
dam. Wit: ARCHBIL BELL, THOMAS SUTTON. Nov. Court 1742. *.

F 439 JOHN PLOWMAN WHITE of Chowan Co. TO THOMAS RYAN
       Jan. 3, 1741/42. 200 pds. for 620 A. Patent date Aug. 30, 1714.
Granted to Captain JOHN PLOWMAN, and left by Will to JOHN PLOWMAN WHITE.
Land called Low Suffolk at Ducken Run. Wit: JAMES MCLAUGHLIN, THOMAS WILL-
IAMSON, GRIFFETH HOWELL. Nov. Court 1742. *.

F 440 GEORGE DEMCEY TO THOMAS RYAN
       Jan. 30, 1741/42. 30 pds. for 10 A. On SWS Salmon Creek. Wit: DAVID
THOMSON, THOMAS MEWBORNE, JOHN HILTON. Nov. Court 1742. *.

F 442 THOMAS RYAN TO WILLIAM FLEETWOOD
       Sept. 9, 1742. 100 pds. for 200 A. On ES Great Beavar Dam adj.
CHARLES JACOCKS in Hay Meadow Branch, "the Govrners Line". Wit: EDWARD
RASOR, LOVICK YOUNG, LAMB HARDY. Nov. Court 1742. *.

F 443 JOHN BYRD TO JAMES MCDOWALL, Merchant
       Nov. 16, 1741. 90 pds. for 50 A. On NS Casia River adj. ROBERT BYRD,
THOMAS RYAN, JOHN MORRIS. Wit: ROBERT WEST, JOHN HILL. Nov. Court 1742. *.

F 444 JAMES AVERITT TO THOMAS RYAN
       Nov. 6, 1742. 100 pds. for 320 A. Patent granted Captain DAVID HEN-
DERSON July 21, 1707. By HENDERSON sold to SAMUEL ONWIN and by ONWIN sold
to AVERITT. Wit: JOHN CRICKETT, EDWARD RASOR(RASSOR). Nov. Court 1742. *.

F 445 JOHN PLOWMAN WHITE of Craven Co., "trader" TO THOMAS RYAN
       Jan. 3, 1741/42. 200 pds. for 640 A. By patent dated Oct. 8, 1717
to Capt. JOHN PLOWMAN and "come to JOHN PLWOMAN WHITE by will..." Including
Beavardam Islands called Norwich. Adj. JOHN HERRING. Wit: JAMES MCLAUGHLIN,
THOMAS WILLIAMSON, GRIFFETH HOWELL. Nov. Court 1742. *.

F 447   THOMAS RYAN TO ANDREW THOMSON, cordwainer
        Nov. 8, 1742. 240 pds. for 620 A. On Low Suffolk Meadow at Ducken
Run. Wit: JOHN COLLINS, JUN., THOMAS DAVIS, JAMES MCLAUGHLIN. NOV. COURT 1742.*.

F 448   SAMUELL JONES TO JAMES LEGETT
        June 2, 1739. 60 pds. for 388 A. "Lately in the Occupation of DARBY
DEMPSIE..." On NS Morrattock River adj. EDWARD SMITHWICK, TERENCE BURNS at
Charlton Creek. Wit: JOSEPH BENTLEY, JOSEPH WIGHT. Feb. Court 1742. *.

F 449   JOHN HILL TO THOMAS RYAN
        Nov. 7, 1742. 60 pds. for 320 A. On WS Chowan River adj. JAMES CON-
STANT, THOMAS YATES at Herring Run. Wit: JAMES CASTELLAW, PHILLIP WALSTON,
WILLIAM BALL. Feb. Court 1742. *.

F 450   MOSES SPEIGHT TO MARY SPEIGHT
        Aug. 19, 1740. Deed of Gift:
Riding horse Spark   5 iron potts
18 head cattle   1 spight
2 feather beds & furniture   6 leather chairs
8 pewter dishes   5 flagg chairs
6 gallon basons   my crops now in the ground
12 pewter plates   "all the rest of my estate"
"...freely & unanimously give and Bequeath unto my Loving Wife MARY
SPEIGHT..." Wit: WILLIAM LATTIMER, ROBERT SMITH, MARY SMITH. Feb. Court
1742. *.

F 450   ALICE THOMAS, widow, TO LUKE THOMAS
        Dec. 29, 1740. Deed of Gift. 220 A. "...to well beloved son LUKE
.." Land adj. JAMES BLUNT, THOMAS BUSBY, ___SPIVIE,___PAGE. Which land
ALICE THOMAS bought of LITTLETON SPIVIE. Wit: WILLIAM CARTER, JAMES THOMAS.
Feb. Court 1742. *.

F 452   CHARLES JONES TO WILLIAM YATES
        July 22, 1742. 70 pds. for 75 A. Adj. MOSES PRICE, WILLIAM RUTTER,
JOHN RASBERRY, CHARLES JONES. Part of tract "granted to my son CHARLES
JONES by Patent bearing Date August the fourth day Anno Dom. 1725..." Wit:
CHRISTOPHER HOLLAMAN, THOMAS DIXON. Feb. Court 1742. *.

F 453   EDWARD MOOR TO JOHN HOW
        Feb. 9, 1730 12 pds. for 339 A. On Rocquis Pocoson adj. JOHN HARDY
ESQ., MARTIN GARDNER. Wit: THOMAS MEWBOORN, JAMES SPEIR. Feb. Court 1730.
RT. FORSTER C/C.

F 454   JOHN HOW TO JOSEPH ALBERT, Labourer
        May 27, 1735. 75 pds. for "My right...to within mentioned land..."
Wit: EDWARD MOOR, JAMES BULLOCK. Feb. Court 1742. HENRY DELON C/C.

F 455   JOHN JOHNSON TO JAMES LEGETT
        March 10, 1739. 50 pds. for 100 A. "Land granted to ROBERT ANDERSON
by Patent bearing Date the 19th day of October 1722..." On NS Chewatock
Swamp adj. MOSES HARE, Indian Line, land formerly WILLIAM KENEDY's. Wit:
WILLIAM KELLEY, JOSEPH WIGHT. Feb. Court 1742. *.

F 455   JOHN HODGSON of Chowan Co. & WILLIAM CATHCART TO THOMAS BARKER
        Dec. 15, 1742. 80 pds. for 300 A. Land sold by THEOPHILUS WILLIAMS
to JOHN PRATT and by PRATT sold to HEDGSON & CATHCART. Wit: JAMES CASTELLAW,
ABRAHAM BLACKALL, ROBERT STEPHENS. Feb. Court 1742. *.

F 456   WILLIAM BLY, yeoman, of Chowan Co. TO MICHAEL WARD, yeoman
        May 9, 1743. 120 pds. for 300 A. On NS Quoyakason Swamp adj. ___
OUTLAW, ___PERREY. Part of patent to BLY dated March 10, 1740. Wit: NICHO-
LAS PERRY, JACOB PERRY, JAMES JONES. May Court 1743. HENRY DELON C/C.

F 457   THOMAS RYAN TO JOHN HORNBECK (HORNBEAK)
        Jan. 27, 1742/43. 100 pds. for 544 A. On ES Middle Swamp at Easter-
most Swamp adj. ___GRILL, "his Excellency", NATHANIEL DUCKENFIELD, EDWARD
RASOR. Wit: ANDREW THOMSON, DAVID ATKINS, NEHEMIAH WARING. May Court 1743.*.

F 459   JOSEPH ALBURSON (ALBERTSON) TO HENRY DELON
        April 13, 1743. 100 pds. for 339 A. On Rocquis Pocoson adj. JOHN
HARDY, MARTIN GARDNER. Wit: HENRY DAY, WILLIAM BLY. May Court 1743. *.

F 460   THOMAS HAWKINS TO GEORGE BELL
        Feb. 1, 1742. 60 pds. for 320 A. In Cypress Swamp "concluding the
lower half of the Island commonly called Fettens Island..." Wit: WILLIAM
BYRD, JEAN BYRD. May Court 1743. *.

F 461   CHARLES JACOCKS TO JAMES LEARY
        April 4, 1743. 30 pds. for 100 A. Called Haymeadow" adj. WILLIAM
FLEETWOOD, THOMAS RYAN. Part of 200 A. bought by JACOCKS from THOMAS RYAN.
Wit: THOMAS RYAN, SAMUEL COOK, MARY COOK. May Court 1743. *.

F 462   THOMAS JOHNSON of Tyrrell Co. TO JAMES LEARY
        Oct. 23, 1742. 80 pds. for 50 A. On NS Cashoke Creek adj. JAMES
LOCKHART, EDEN BAIL. Wit: THOMAS RYAN, RICHARD ASHLEY, WILLIAM WILLSON.
May Court 1743. *.

F 463   CHARLES JACOCKS TO EDWARD BRYAN
        May 10, 1743. 2 pds. 2 sh for 1 A. 3 rod 16 pearches. Part of tract
formerly belonging to JONATHAN JACOCKS at Head of Albemarle Sound near
Blackwalnut Point. adj. EDWARD BRYAN, CHARLES JACOCKS. Wit: SAMUEL ORMES,
SAMUEL DALLING. May Court 1743. *.

F 464   JOHN RASBERRY TO JAMES ROADES of Edgecomb(e) Co.
        May 5, 1743. 60 pds. for 150 A. On White Oak Swamp adj. TARKILN,
WILLIAM RUTTER, Part of a patent dated March 15, 1742. Wit: THOMAS DIXON,
JONATHAN ROBINSON. May Court 1743. *.

F 465   THOMAS RYAN TO DAVID THOMSON, carpenter
        Nov. 29, 1742. 400 pds. for 100 A. On Cashoke Creek Swamp. Adj.
THOMAS ASHBUR, JOHN HOLLBROOK, GEORGE PATERSON, EDWARD BYRD, JAMES CEATON.
Wit: STEPHEN CATTER, JOHN COLLINS, JUN., JONAS CATTELL. May Court 1743. *.

F 466   CHARLES RICHETTS TO GEORGE HUGHS of Chowan Co.
        Dec. 9, 1742. 50 pds. for 700 A. In Cypress Swamp at Miery Branch.
Wit: EPHRAIM WESTON, JOHN MEASELL. May Court 1743. *.

F 467   CULLEN POLLOCK TO NEHEMIAH WARING
        Dec. 25, 1740. 40 pds. for 200 A. CULLEN POLLOCK serving as executor
of the estate of THOMAS POLLOCK. Land on WS Eastermost Swamp adj. WILLIAM
CAMPBELL, _____GRILL. Wit: LAMB HARDY, WILLIAM CAMPBELL. May Court 1743.*.

F 468   WILLIAM DOWNING, yeoman, TO JOHN WYNNS
        Dec. 19, 1742. 100 pds. for 550 A. Land between Wiccacon and Killum
adj. Keef Swamp, WYNNS, THOMAS MANN to Long Branch. "...to Include the
Eastern Half of the Land formerly WILLIAM STEVENS..." Wit: BENJAMIN WYNNS,
AARON ASKEW. Aug. Court 1743. *.

F 469   JOSIAH REDDICK TO JOSEPH JORDAN
        Feb. 24, 1743. 100 pds. for 800 A. At mouth Sohikey Creek adj.GALES.
Wit: WILLIAM JORDAN, MILDRED JORDAN. Aug. Court 1743. JOHN WYNNS D. Reg.

F 470   WILLIAM WYNNS, yeoman, TO ELEAZAR QUINBY, carpenter
        Dec. 18, 1741. 170 pds. for 50 A. On SS Wiccacon Creek near Goose
Creek adj. WILLIAM SHARP, WILLIAM DOWNING, "white oak neck". Wit: JOHN
WYNNS, G. HOOKER, JUN, JAMES HOOKER. May Court 1742. THOMAS CREW C/C. JOHN
WYNNS D.Reg. (copy)

F 471   MARY OWL TO JAMES, ANEILINA, SARAH OWL
        Oct. 1, 1741. Deed of Gift. To children. (1) Negro named Benjamon
to JAMES. If he die without heirs to ANEILINA. (2) To ANEILINA one cow and
one sow. (3) To SARAH one cow and one sow. Wit: THOMAS WILLSON, JOSEPH
THOMAS, ANN THOMAS. Nov. Court 1742. HENRY DELON C/C. Copy JOHN WYNNS D.Reg.

F 472   DANIEL HOUGH TO BENJAMIN HILL
        Dec. 9, 1742. 65 pds. for 200 A. Land whereon HOUGH now dwells
which he bought of THOMAS JONES of Cape Fear on July 30, 1742. Between Blew
Water & Northermost Prong of Hothouse Branch adj. Bevardam Swamp and Potty-
casey Swamp. By patent date 1712. The other portion of 400 A. bought of
JONES sold to BRYANT HAIRE of Virginia. Wit: ED. HACKET, MARY CAMPBELL,
SARAH HILL. Nov. 12, 1743. J. MONTGOMERY, C.J., JOHN WYNNS, D/Reg.

182

F 473   WILLIAM KENNYDY (KENNEDY) TO ROBERT HOWELL
        ___9, 1743. Deed of Gift. 100 A. "...good will.." Land on NS Roquis
Swamp "...being land which JOHN WYNNS surveyed for me the said WILLIAM KEN-
EDY..." Wit: FRANCIS KENNEDY, WILLIAM KENNEDY, JUN. HENRY DELON C/C. Copy
JOHN WYNNS D/Reg.

F 474   THOMAS JONES of New Hanover Co. TO DANIEL HOUGH
        July 30, 1742. 250 pds. for 800 A. Between Blue Water and Northermost
Prong of Hothouse Branch adj. Bevardam Swamp & Pottycasy Swamp and Pottycasy
Creek. Land granted to FREDERICK JONES in 1712. Wit: J. PORTER, A. LIVING-
STON, ___ROSSETT (L. DE ROSETT?), BENJAMIN HILL. N.C. COURT Oct. 28, 1742.
W. SMITH, C.J. Copy JOHN WYNNS D/Reg.

F 475   MARGARETT JONES of Beaufort Co. TO THOMAS RYAN
        *. 2 "likely Young Negros" for 2180 A. MARGARETT JONES a spinster.
"...all her rights to s'd lands formerly Belonging to JOHN HOLBROOK SEN. and
to JOHN HOLBROOK, JUN. & all the goods & Chattles Rights & Credits with all
the Negros & stocks of any kind..." Wit: EDGAR TIPPER, WILLIAM BRIEVLY,
THOMAS WILLIAMSON. Nov. Court 1743. HENRY DELON,C/C, Copy BENJAMIN WYNNS D/R.

F 476   WILLIAM EASON TO THOMAS BARKER
        Jan. 25, 1743. 140 pds. for 440 A. Adj. EDW. HARRELL, THOMAS BARKER,
"land that was given the s'd WILLIAM EASON by his father WILLIAM EASON Deceased in his Last Will & Testament..." Wit: ISAAC EASON, THOMAS PUGH. Feb.
Court 1743. *.*.

F 478   CULLEN POLLOCK of Tyrill Co." TO THOMAS MEWBORN (MEWBOORN)
        Aug. 5, 1743. 36 pds. for 278 A. Acting as executor of the estate of
THOMAS POLLOCK. "...being part of the great Tract of Land that did belong
to my brother THOMAS Dec'd..." On WS Flatt Swamp adj. CAKE. Wit: MOSES(?)
MEWBORN, JAMES GRAVES. Aug. Court 1743. HENRY DELON C/C. BENJ. WYNNS D/Reg.

F 479   CULLEN POLLOCK of Tyrryll Co. TO MOSES MEWBORN (MEWBOORN)
        Aug. 5, 1743. 23 pds. for 126 A. Acting as executor of the estate of
THOMAS POLLOCK. "...Part of great tract that did belong to my brother
THOMAS Dec'd..." On Briery Branch. Wit: JAMES GRAVES, THOMAS MEWBOORN. Aug.
Court 1743. HENRY DELON C/C. Copy JOHN WYNNS D/Reg.

F 480   DOM REX TO JOHN VANPELT
        *. Grant 150 A. "...grant...as of Our Manner of East Greenwich in
Our County of Kent..." Yearly rent of 4 sh/100 A. Land on NS Barbeque Swamp
adj. THOMAS MCCLENDON. Signed: GABRIEL JOHNSTON Capt. General & Gov. in
Chief. At Edenton March 11, 1741. JOHN RICE, Gov. Sec't'y.

Note: a map appears here. "Pursuant to a warrant from his Excely the Gov.
        bearing Date the 20th of Sept 1739...(to lay) for JOHN VANPELT one
hundred & fifty acres...on N side Barbique Swamp...(adj) THOMAS MCCLENDON..
JOHN CONNER Dep. Survey'r."

F 482   JOHN VANPELT (VAN PELT) TO ELIAS STALLINGS, Yeoman
        June 11, 1742. 400 pds. for 150 A. Within mentioned patent. Wit:
DANIEL VANPELT, MARY VANPELT. Aug. Court 1743. *.*.

F 483   CULLEN POLLOCK of Tyrryll TO JOHN GRAVES
        Aug. 5, 1743. 6 pds. 8 sh and "piece of cloath" for 100 A. "...And
seven pounds Eight Shillings it appears to me has been paid to my Brother
THOMAS POLLOCK & a piece of Cloath Weaved for the s'd THOMAS POLLOCKs Negros by JOHN GRAVES...Being part of Great Tract of Land that did belong to
my Brother THOMAS POLLOCK Dec'd..." Wit: JAMES GRAVES, MOSES MEWBOORN. Aug.
Court 1743. HENRY DELON C/C. Copy BENJAMIN WYNNS D/Reg.

F 484   LORDS PROPRIETORS (DOM REX) TO JOHN BENTLY
        Aug. 4, 1723. Grant. 480 A. "...according to Our great Deed of Grant
Bearing Date the first Day of May Anno Dom 1668..." For importation of per-
sons 50 A/person. Land on NS Morrattock River adj. JOHN HARLOW, MARTIN
GRIFFIN, THOMAS POLLOCK. Wit: "WILLIAM REED, President of Our Councill in
Sec't'y Office. J. LOVICK Sec'y. C. GALE, RICH HANDERSON, THOS. POLLOCK In
clerks office May 19, 1739. JNO. WYNNS Clk."

F 485   JAMES BENTLEY TO HUGH HYMEN
        Nov. 17, 1741. 30 pds. for 200 A. "part of within Land Holden by

me..." Wit: THOMAS COLLINS, JOHN MCCASKEY, WILLIAM DUGGAN. Aug. Court 1743.
HENRY DELON C/C. BENJAMIN WYNNS D. Reg.

F 485   THOMAS MEWBOORN, blacksmith, TO THOMAS RYAN
        April 5, 174(3). 360 pds. for 500 A. On WS Eastermost Swamp adj.
CAKE, WILLIAM YEATES, JOHN GULLSON, THOMAS YATES. Wit: JOHN CAKE, JOHN HILL,
ROBERT WEST. Aug. Court 1743. *.*.

F 487   JOHN HILL TO THOMAS RYAN
        Nov. 27, 1742. 500 pds. for 426 1/2 A. On WS Chowan River adj. JOHN
CAKE, JAMES CONSTANT...said land was formerly taken up by ISAAC HILL & then
Left by Will unto JOHN HILL..." Patent bearing Date Anno Dom 1705..." Wit:
JAMES CASTELLAW, PHILLIP WALSTON, WILLIAM BALL. Aug. Court 1743. *.*.

F 488   THOMAS RYAN TO JOHN HOLBROOK (HOOLBROOK)
        May 20, 1743. 640 pds. for 320 A. On WS Chowan River and SS Herring
Runn adj. ISAAC HILL, JUN., THOMAS YATES. Wit: RICHARD ASHLEY, JONAS CAT-
TELL, MARY SUNDERLIN(?). *.*.

F 490   JOHN CAKE TO JOHN HOLBROOK
        Feb. 11, 1743. 60 pds. for 320 A. On WS Squareanea Swamp adj. Coll.
WEST, Coll. POLLOCK,WILLIAM YATES. Land granted to JOHN HOLBROOK, SEN. on
April 1, 1723. Wit: JOSEPH BUTTERTON, THOMAS MEWBOORN, JAMES SOMERELL. Aug.
Court 1743. *.*.

F 491   CULLEN POLLOCK of Terryll Co. TO JAMES GRAVES
        Aug. 5, 1743. 42 pds. for 328 A. Acting as executor of estate of
THOMAS POLLOCK. Land "that Did belong to Dec'd Brother THOMAS POLLOCK..."
On Eastermost Swamp at Briery Branch adj. JOHN CRECKET, THOMAS YATES, JOHN
GRAVES, WILLIAM TOD, Horse Branch. Wit: THOMAS MEWBOORN, MOSES MEWBOORN.
Aug. Court 1743. *.*.

F 492   PETER WEST TO WILLIAM MOOR(E)
        May 1, 1743. Land Division. 300 A. On Hothouse and Pondslash. Land
taken up by PETER WEST - elapsed - then taken up by WILLIAM MOOR. "...it
being unknown to them (WEST & MOORE) which of them hath the best Right to
the s'd Lands...(they) have mutually agreed to Divide the s'd Lands..."
Line to go from THOMAS STEVENSON's corner along the Old Indian Path commonly called Cottons Road. Land to the east of this line to PETER WEST. Land
to the west of this line to WILLIAM MOORE. Wit: J(AMES) OATES, THOMAS
WALKER. Aug. Court 1743. *.*.

F 493   PAUL PENDER, "saddler" TO RICHARD ROBARDS, "cooper"
        March 31, 1743. 14 pds. for 227 A. Land purchased of THOMAS MILNER
on Flatt Swamp adj. EDWARD OUTLAW. Wit: THOMAS DIXON, *. Aug. Court 1743.*.

F 494   CALEB SPIVEY & WIFE ELIZABETH TO THOMAS HARRELL
        June 13, 1743. 40 pds. for 300 A. Adj. WILLIAM HINTON on Village
Swamp, THEOPHILUS WILLIAMS. By patent granted WILLIAM GRAY April 1, 1725.
Wit: NEEDHAM BRYAN, SAMUEL HARRELL, WILLIAM BRYAN. Aug. Court 1743. *.*.

F 495   THOMAS HARRELL TO SAMUELL HARRELL
        June 13, 1743. 20 pds. for 150 A. On ES Village Swamp adj. WILLIAM
HINTON, PETTEGROVE SALSBERRY, THEOPHILUS WILLIAMS, ____BOND. Land granted
WILLIAM GRAY by Patent April 1, 1725. "...& half of a Deed that belongs to
THOS.HARRELL..." Wit: NEEDHAM BRYAN, WILLIAM BRYAN, CALEB SPIVEY. Aug.
Court 1743. *.*.

F 498   NATHAN ROLAND of Edgecombe Co. TO THOMAS PAGE
        Aug. 9, 1743. 7 pds. for 200 A. Adj. ABRAHAM SHEPHERD, MARTIN GARD-
NER, JOHN EDWARDS, ROBERT HINES. Wit: NATHAN ROWLAND, HENRY DELON, SAMUELL
HOWARD. Aug. Court 1743. *.*.

F 499   MARGARET MEDFORD TO ABIGAIL RYALL
        Dec. 6, 1742. 5 pds. for 213 A. "...Being the Land that OWEN RYALL
Bought of JOHN YELVERTON..." Wit: ____BARKER, FARABE BARKER. Aug. Court
1743. *.*.

F 500   JOHN HILL TO ABRAHAM HERRING
        Aug. 10, 1743. 50 pds. for 500 A. On NS Kesia River and NS Buckels-
berry Swamp. Wit: ARTHUR WILLIAMS, JAMES CAMSALEST(?) Aug. Court 1743. *.

184

F 501 SAMUELL HERRING of Craven Co. TO CHARLES KING of Chowan Co.
       Feb. 28, 1742/43. 40 pds. for 100 A. On Roquiss Pocoson at Broad
Branch. Wit: THOMAS JONES, THOMAS WIMBERLY, SAMUEL HERRING, ANTHONY HERRING.
Aug. Court 1743. *.

F 503 MOSES ROUNDTREE TO MOSES HILL
       Sept. 1742. 100 pds. for 160 A. Adj. FRANCIS ROUNTREE on Guys(?)
Hall Swamp. Wit: JESSE ROUNDTREE, FRANCIS ROUNDTREE. Aug. Court 1743. *.

F 504 MOSES ROUNDTREE (ROUNTREE) TO FRANCIS ROUNDTREE
       Aug. 9, 1743. 100 pds. for 320 A. On Guys Hall Swamp adj. JESSE
ROUNDTREE, "along the Old Line". Wit: THOMAS ROUNDTREE, MOSES HILL, JESSE
ROUNDTREE. Aug. Court 1743. *.

F 505 MOSES ROUNDTREE TO JESSE ROUNDTREE
       Sept. 1742. 100 pds. for 160 A. Adj. "the Old Line FRANCIS ROUND-
TREES corner..." Wit: THOMAS ROUNDTREE, Sen., THOMAS ROUNDTREE, MOSES HILL.
Aug. Court 1743. HENRY DELON, C/C.

F 507 JOSEPH OATES of Chowan Co. TO WILLIAM PUGH of Edgecombe Co.
       May 20, "in the seventeenth year of the Reign of Sovreign...George".
60 pds. for 300 A. Adj. EPHRAIM HUNTER &"Cherryholms Old Field". By patent
granted THOMAS MARTIN on February 10, 1704/05. Wit: JOHN MURPHREY, ROBERT
LACITER, FRANCIS GRIFFIN. Aug. Court 1743. *.

F 507 JOHN COLLINS, SEN. TO JETHRO ROUNDTREE
       Feb. 15, 1741/42. 100 pds. for 400 A. On NWS Guy Hall Swamp. Wit:
ROBERT WEST, HENRY DELON. N.C. Court Oct. 28, 1742. W. SMITH, C.J.

F 509 WILLIAM CATHCART TO HUGH HORTON
       Feb. 25, 1742/43. 55 pds. for 50 A. In Ahotskey Swamp adj. MATTHEW's
Line at Ahotskey Run. Wit: THOMAS BONNER, MARY LOVICK. Aug. Court 1743. *.

F 510 JOHN JONES TO JOHN RODOLPH STEINFIELS
       Aug. 2, 1743. 20 pds. for 150 A. On WS Chowan River at Deep Creek
adj. JAMES BOON, FREDERICK JONES, RICHARD BARFIELD. Wit: MATTHRAS JONES,
JAMES COTTON. Aug. Court 1743. *.

F 511 JOHN MITCHINOR of Elesebeth Co., Va., "saddler" TO THOMAS DIXON
       July 2, 1743. 760 pds. for 1280 A. Land purchased of ROBERT WARREN
and PALEG RODGERS. On SS Horse Swamp adj. JOHN WILLOBY, JAMES OVERTON, _____
VICKERS,JOHN EARLEY to Tussockey Branch. Wit: RICHARD ROBERTS, J. EARLEY.
Aug. Court 1743. *.

F 512 WILLIAM SHARP, "joyner" TO JANE QUINBY, "widow"
       Feb. 23, 1732/33. Deed of Gift. Land on SS Wiccacon Creek commonly
called Indian old field. "beginning at my landing..." Wit: JOHN WYNNS, MARY
QUINBY. Aug. Court 1743. *.

F 512 EDWARD HOCOTT of Beaufort Co. TO JOHN EDWARDS of Cashy
       Aug. 11, 1743. 200 pds. for 340 A. On ES Roquiss Swamp adj. PHILLIP
WALSTON, JONATHAN STANLY, CULLEN POLLOCK. Wit: JOHN WYNNS, NOAH PRIDHAM.
Aug. Court 1743. *.

F 513 WILLIAM WYNNS, yeoman, TO WILLIAM ASKEW cordwainer
       Dec. 18, 1741. 200 pds. for 60 A. On SWS Chowan River "whereon
ASKEW now dwells..." At Goose Creek to mouth of Barbeque Branch. Adj. WILL-
IAM SHARP. Wit: JOHN WYNNS, W. HOOKER, JUN., JAMES HOOKER. May Court 1743.*.

F 514 WILLIAM ASKEW TO WILLIAM WYNNS
       May 30, 1743. 200 pds. "...transfer all Lands and appurtenances
conveyed in afore written Deed..." Wit: JOHN ASKEW, HENRY MAYNOR, BENJAMIN
WYNNS. Aug. Court 1743. HENRY DELON C/C.

F 515 DENNIS MCCLENDON, yeoman, of Craven Co. TO RICHARD BROWN
       Feb. 4, 1742/43. 30 pds. for 440 A. On SS Wiccacon Creek in Chinko-
pen Neck adj. JOHN EARLEY, ISAAC HILL, WILLIAM LEWIS, CAPT. VANPELT, THOMAS
BANKS, JOHN WYNNS, RICHARD BROWN. Wit: JOHN THOMAS, BENJAMIN WYNNS. Aug.
Court 1743. *.

F 516 COLL. PETER WEST TO NATHANIELL NICHOLAS

Aug. 12, 1743. 9 pds. for 200 A. At Wading Branch adj. THOMAS CLIF-
TON on Horse Swamp, great Cow Hall, ANTHONY WILLIAMS, JOHN WILLIAMS. Wit:
BNEJAMIN WYNNS, WILLIAM GODWIN. May Court 1744. BENJAMIN WYNNS D/C.

F 517 PETER WEST TO SAMUELL WEBB
       May 3, 1744. 14 pds. for 200 A. On Horse Swamp ajd. RICHARD SANDERS,
THOMAS JACKSON. Land PETER WEST bought of JAMES HOWARD. Wit: ANTHONY WEBB,
WILLISS NICHOLAS, WILLIAM WEBB. May Court 1744. *.

F 518 NEEDHAM BRYAN & WIFE SUSSANAH TO WILLIAM VANN
       May 8, 1744. 17 pds. 10 sh. for 100 A. On NS Flaggey Run adj. JOHN
HARRELL. Wit: JOHN COLLINS, WILLIAM COLLINS. May Court 1744. *.

F 520 NEEDHAM BRYAN & WIFE SUSSANAH of Society Parish TO BARNABY BRYAN(T)
       May 8, 1744. 17 pds. 10 sh. for 100 on NS Flaggy Run ad dividing
line between BARNABY BRYAN & WILLIAM VANN. Wit: JOHN COLLINS, WILLIAM
COLLINS. May Court 1744. *.

F 521 ROBERT GILBERT TO NOAH PRIDHAM
       Dec. 16, 1743. 5 pds. for 380 A. Part of tract of 580 A. purchased
of WILLIAM MOORE on February 10, 1729. Adj. THOMAS ARCHER, JOHN CARTER.
Wit: THOMAS CREW, WILLIAM PERRY, JAMES JONES. May Court 1744. *.

F 522 WILLIAM BARKER, Yeoman, TO THOMAS BASS of Surry Co., Va. cordwainer
       Jan. 14, 1744. 30 pds. for 200 A. On NS Chowan River adj. BENJAMIN
WYNNS. Wit: JOHN WYNNS, THOMAS JOHNSON, THOMAS WASHINGTON. May Court 1744.*.

F 524 WILLIAM RODGERS, cooper, & WIFE ANNE TO WILLIAM LACITER
       Feb. 20, 1743. 50 pds. for 100 A. Land whereon LACITER lives at
mouth of Sandy Run, Chinkopen adj. THOMAS RODGERS. Wit: JOHN WYNNS, ISAAC
HILL, JOSEPH PERRY. May Court 1744. "...ANNE RODGERS being Privately Examined...Declares that she Signed...freely..." J. WYNNS J.P. BENJ. WYNNS D/C.

F 525 ELEAZAR QUINBY & WIFE ANNE TO ISAAC LASITER of Virginia
       Feb. 10, 1743. 20 pds. for 50 A. Adj. WILLIAM SHARP at Goose Creek
on Wiccacon Creek. Wit: JOHN WYNNS, WILLIAM LASSITER. May Court 1744. "...
ANNE LACITER...privately examined...Declares she signed freely..." *.

F 526 JOHN HOCUT, yeoman, TO AARON LASSITER
       Feb. 17, 1743. 120 pds. for 106 A. At mouth of Chinkopen Branch at
Mill Creek adj. RICHARD SOWELL. Wit: JOHN WYNNS, ISAAC HILL, JAMES OATES.
May Court 1744. *.

F 527 ISAAC HILL, yeoman, TO THOMAS ARCHER
       May 1, 1744. "the sum of one whole years work already paid" for 200
A. Land on Holey Branch of Chinkapen Neck. Part of a larger tract granted
to ISAAC HILL adj. JOHN VANPELT. Wit: JOHN WYNNS, JOSEPH WYNNS, ALEXANDER
VOLLANTINE. May Court 1744. *.

F 528 DANIELL HOUGH TO BENJAMIN MILL, merchant
       Aug. 23, 1743. 289 pds. 10 sh. for:

9 cows and 6 calves	1 cross cut saw
4 stears or oxen 6 yrs. old	2 large chests
5 stears or oxen 2 yrs. old	5 axes
3 yearlings	1 broad axe
3 cows	2 tables
4 feather beds & furniture	2 doz. Pewter Plates
4 Iron Pots	5 Pewter dishes
1 Bell Mettle Motor	4 Large Pewter Basons
1 whip saw	1 Negro woman named Bess

Wit: JOHN CAMPBELL of Edenton, Merchant, JOHN RODOLPH STEINFELS of Bertie
Co., "Doct'r". May Court 1744. BENJAMIN WYNNS, D/C.

F 529 JAMES STEWART TO BENJAMIN HILL, merchant
       Feb. 14, 1743. 17 pds. 10 sh. for 440 A. Land whereon STEWART now
lives which was bought of NICHOLAS MEDLIN on NS Morattock River adj. FRAN-
CIS PARKER, THOMAS BUSBY. Wit: JOHN CAMPBELL, MILES GALE, JUN. May Court
1744. *.

F 530 EDWARD FRISBY TO THOMAS BARKER
       March 16, 1744. Power of atty. Wit: THOMAS WHITMELL, ELIZABETH

WHITMELL. May Court 1744. BENAJMIN WYNNS D/C.

F 531 THOMAS RYAN, trader, TO NEHEMIAH WARING
Feb. 9, 1743/44. 1200 pds. (Bond) for 560 A. By virtue of atty. from JOHN GRILL of the Colony of Virginia dated Feb. 16, 1742/43 and proved by oath of NEHEMIAH WARING in May Court 1743. Land on Eastermost Swamp adj. EDWARD RASOR at Salmon Creek adj. THOMAS POLLOCK, JOHN HORNBECK to Middle Swamp. Land by patent to WILLIAM GRILL of Virginia April 1, 1714. Wit: JOHN HORNBECK, JOSPEH ANDREWS, CAESSEED(?) HORNBECK. May Court 1744. *.

F 532 NEHEMIAH WARING TO GEORGE CAPEHART, shoemaker
May 9, 1744. 180 pds. for 210 A. Land on Eastermost Swamp near Salmon Creek. Part of tract formerly belonging to WILLIAM GRILL and now belonging to JOHN CAMPBELL and by CAMPBELL sold to WARING. Adj. THOMAS POLLOCK JOHN CAMPBELL. Wit: JOHN HOLNBECK, WILLIAM YEATES. May Court 1744.*.

F 534 CULLEN POLLOCK of Terry (Tyrell) Co. TO JOHN CAKE
April 12, 1744. 80 pds. for 447 A. Acting as executor to estate of Brother THOMAS POLLOCK. Land at Tods Branch and Flatt Swamp. "...a Tract of land granted to my Father & left to my brother THOMAS POLLOCK Dec'd..." Wit: THOMAS SLATTER, JOHN HOLNBECK. May Court 1744. BENJAMIN WYNNS D/C.

F 535 GEORGE COCKBURN TO DUGOLD (DUGALD)MCKICHAN
April 23, 1744. 320 pds. for 440 A. On NS Roquiss Swamp adj. THOMAS WHITTMELL. Wit: THOMAS WHITMELL, JOHN HILL. May Court 1744. *.

F 536 COURT JUSTICES TO NOAH PRIDHAM
May 10, 1743. "rent hereafter reserved..." 40 year lease for 1 sh./ year rent. Land conveyed to the Justices of the Court by JOHN JONES "whereon the Late court House...now stands..." Signed: J. WYNNS, NEEDHAM BRYAN, JOHN HARRELL. *.*. May Court 1744. *.

F 537 JOHN SPEIR & WIFE JUDITH TO JOHN BAZEMORE
March 6, 1743/44. 25 pds. for 220 A. At mouth of Spring Branch on NS Ahotskey Swamp adj. HUGH HORTON. Wit: WILLIAM WHEELER, HUGH HORTON, ROBERT WILLISS. May Court 1744. *.

F 538 JAMES CASTELLAW TO COURT JUSTICES
May 10, 1744. 5 sh. for 1 A. For public use on NS Cashy River and SS Wills Quarter Swamp. Justices: GEORGE GOULD, WILLIAM CATHCART, THOMAS HANSFORD, GEORGE LOCKHART, THOMAS WHITMELL, JOHN HARRELL, NEEDHAM BRYAN, JOHN WYNNS, JOHN BROWN. Wit: T. BARKER, JOHN HARRELL, THOMAS JONES, R. FORSTER. May Court 1744. BENJAMIN WYNNS D/C.

F 539 MARGERY GILBERT & GIDEON GILBERT TO WILLAIM WRIGHT, JUN. of Nancemond County, Va. Feb. 6, 1743/44. 35 pds. for 300 A. "...Debt due...by a Bill for Thirty five Pounds current money of Virginia from JONATHAN GILBERT Dec'd..." Two parcels. (1) Land at Deep Creek Bridge adj. EDWARD HARE. Cont. 200 A. (2) Land adj. STEPEHN WILLIAMS, ROBERT RODGERS to May Spring Branch cont. 100 A. And also 1/2 Water Mill with 1/2 all Liberties. Land sold by JONATHAN GILBERT to JOB RODGERS and by RODGERS made over again to GILBERT. "by an assignment on the Back of the said Deeds..." Wit: ANTHONY WEBB, WILLIAM RODGERS. Feb. Court 1743. HENRY DELON C/C.

F 541 OWEN MCDANIELL TO SOCIETY PARISH
*. Gift. 1 A. "...for the use of said parish for the placing and building a House thereon for the publick worship of God..." Land at Hins Old Field on WS Jumping Run. Wit: JOHN HARRELL, JOHN WYNNS, NEEDHAM BRYAN. Nov. Court 1743. *.

F 542 JOHN WYNNS TO WILLAIM HOOKER & JOHN HOOKER
April 17, 1741. 100 pds. for 250 A. Upper half of a tract granted March 6, 1740. On WS Quioccasson Swamp adj. Mare Branch "during the natural Life of the s'd WILLIAM HOOKER and the s'd JOHN HOOKER his heirs and assigns forever..." Wit: PETER EVANS, ROBERT HILL. May Court 1741. BENJ. HILL C/C.

F 542 WILLIAM HOOKER & JOHN HOOKER TO JOHN OUTLAW
July 26, 1743. 150 pds. for *. aforementioned lands. Wit: JAMES HOOKER, WILLIAM HOOKER, JUN., BRAY HARGROVE. Nov. Court 1743. *.

F 543 THOMAS DAVIS (DAVICS) TO GARRAD VAN UPSTALL, joyner

Nov. 9, 1743. "goodwill" 100 A. On NS Cashy River adj. WILLIAM COLLINS, known by name of Stoney Landing formerly the property of SAMUELL ALLEN. Wit: NOAH PRIDHAM, HENRY DELON. Nov. Court 1743. HENRY DELON C/C.

F 544   CHRISTIAN REED of Perquimmons Co. TO JOSEPH WYNNS
    July 22, 1743. 70 pds. for 140 A. 1/2 tract cont. 280 A. "who my Father WM. REED Esq. Dec'd Purchased from one RICH'D BARFIELD..." On SS Chowan River and WS Deep Creek. Wit: T. BARKER, JOHN WYNNS. Nov. Court 1743.*.

F 545   SUNDRIES TO WINNEFRED WHITMELL & MARY WHITMELL
    *. Deed of Gift. "... Natural love & affection...to be equally divided when they become of age or at Marriage..." Given by "...wee the subscribers of Edgecombe County & Bertie County..." 2 Negro women and one negro girl named Phillis, Penny, Nancy. Signed: ROBERT HUNTER, ELIZABETH HUNTER, THOMAS WHITMELL, THOMAS BLOUNT, ELIZABETH BLOUNT, JOHN HILL, MARTHA HILL, HE.HUNTERM, SARAH HUNTER. Wit: MOSES HUNTER, JAMES MCKICHAN, THOMAS COLLINS. Nov. Court 1743. HENRY DELON C/C.

F 545   JOHN HILL TO WILLIAM BIRD
    Nov. 9, 1740. 50 pds. for 500 A. On ES Bucklesberry Pocoson adj. NATHANIEL HILL, DAVID HICKS, THOMAS ASHBORN, GEORGE BELL, CHRIS VANLUVEN. Wit: WILLIAM BALL, JOHN BELL. Nov. Court 1743. HENRY DELON C/C.

F 545   JAMES WATERS TO JOHN HILL
    Nov. 9, 1743. 40 pds. for 500 A. On ES Bucklesberry Pocoson adj. NATHANIEL HILL, DAVID HICKS, THOMAS ASHBORN,GEORGE BELL, CHRIS VANLUVEN. Wit: WILLIAM BALL, JOHN BELL. Nov. Court 1743. *.

F 547   JAMES RODES of Edgecombe Co. TO SAMUEL ONWIN
    May 5, 1743. 50 pds. for 150 A. Adj. WILLIAM RUTTER at fork of White Oak Swamp, "to a tarkiln". Part of patent dated March 15, 1742/43. Wit: THOMAS DIXON, JONATHAN ROBINSON. Nov. Court 1743. *.

F 549   THOMAS TURNER & WIFE MARY TO ANDREW THOMPSON
    Nov. 10, 1743. 50 pds. for 200 A. "...a Certain Percell of Land which DAVID HIX died possessed...being a legacy bequeathed by the s'd HICKS to his Daughter MARY HICKS..." Wit: JAMES CASTELLAW, HENRY DELON. Nov. Court 1743. *.

F 549   LUKE MEIZLE (MUZELL), SEN. TO JAMES LEGGETT (LEGET)
    May 5, 1742. 70 pds. for 90 A. In Kesia Neck adj. "MEIZELL Old Line that comes from Morrottock River...", JOHN SMETHWICK, ROBERT ANDERSON, JOHN SESSIONS. Wit: JEREMIAH LEGETT, MERTIN COOK, SARAH LEGETT. Feb. Court 1742.*.

F 550   THEOPHILUS WILLIAMS & WIFE CHRISTIAN TO THEOPHILUS PUGH of Nancemond
    Co., Va.   Sept. 24, 1742. 140 pds. for 240 A. On NS Foaling Run adj. NEEDHAM BRYAN, THOMAS BON, THOMAS BARKER. Part of a patent formerly granted THEOPHILUS WILLIAMS for 640 A. on August 8, 1728. Wit: T. BARKER, WILLIAM TAYLOR, NEEDHAM BRYAN. Nov. Court 1743. *.

F 552   DOM REX TO GEORGE GOULD
    July 26, 1743. Grant. 268 A. On ES Rosuskey (Rususkey) Swamp to the Low Grounds. Signed: GALE, JOHNSTON JNO. RICE pro Sec. February 15, 1743 by EDW GRIFFETH Pro Aud'r.

F 553   PETER GRAY TO ELIZABETH ARMSTRONG
    Jan. 25, 1743/44. Deed of Gift. "...good will & affection I do Bare ...my Estate both Real & Personal...except one cow & calf which after my Decease shall be Delivered to JOHN FRANCIS CULLIFER..." Wit: JAMES LEGGETT, ELISHA WHITFIELD. Feb. Court 1743. *.

F 554   ABRAHAM SHEPHERD TO JONATHAN TART of Northampton Co.
    Jan. 24, 1742. 60 pds. for 335 A. Where Shepherd now dwells on Rocquis Swamp. N.C. Court Nov. 21, 1743. J. MONTGOMERY, C.J.

F 555   EDWARD OUTLAW TO THOMAS HOLLOWELL of Northampton Co.
    Jan. 24, 1742. 254 pds. for 320 A. "...Certain Plantation & Tract of Land that my Father gave me..." On SWS Flatt Swamp. adj.____SANDERS. Wit: WILLIAM GODWIN, JOEL SANDERS. Nov. Court 1743. HENRY DELON C/C.

F 557   THOMAS FINCH & WIFE MARY TO THOMAS WALKER

. 240 pds. for 155 A. Adj. PETER WEST, ____LANIER. Wit: MARG. LACY, THOMAS STEVENSON, ALEX BAYER. Nov. Court 1743..

F 558 WILLIAM MOOR TO THOMAS WALKER
       Dec. 3, 1743. 20 pds. for 50 A. (200A.) On SS Indian Path "purchased out of land DANIEL HOUGHS Deed and out of PETER WESTS patent 150 acres..." Adj. COLL. JONES, PETER WEST, WILLAIM WHITFIELD, Old Tar Kiln. Wit: SIMON HOMES, DANIELL HOUGH. Feb. Court 1743. *.

F 559 SIMON HOMES & WIFE MARY TO THOMAS WALKER
       Dec. 3, 1743. 50 pds. for 340 A. On SWS Ahotskey Swamp adj. WILLIAM CURLEE. Formerly granted by patent April 1, 1723. Wit: WILL MOOR, HENRY BONNER. Feb. Court 1743. *.

F 560 WILLAIM CATHCART TO NOAH PRIDHAM
       Dec. 22, 1743. 170 A. Between Catawhitskey & Ahotskey on Timber Branch adj. JOHN JONES, JOSEPH JONES. Land granted WILLIAM MAUL, Dec'd, on April 1, 1723. *.*. Feb. Court 1743. *.

F 561 JOHN CAMPBELL of Edenton, merchant TO JOSEPH JONES
       Jan. 11, 1743/44. 307 pds. 10 sh. for 234 A. Part of tract known by name Blew Water on SS Cuttawitskey adj. JOSEPH JONES. Wit: MILES GALE, BENJAMIN HILL, WILLIAM HUMFREE. Feb. Court 1743. *.

F 563 THOMAS BIRD, cooper, TO BENJAMIN HOLLYMAN
       May 10, 1743. 80 pds. for 640 A. On WS Chowan River at Loosing Swamp. Wit: CHRISTOPHER HOLLYMAN, HENRY CANADAY. Nov. Court 1743. *.

End of Deed Book F

DEED BOOK G

G 1 EDWARD COLLINS TO HUGH HYMAN, Weaver
      Feb. 26, 1746/47. 20 pds. for 30 A. On Deep Branch. "Land purchased by THOS. COLLINS, Dec'd of the Ex'rs & heirs of JOHN COALSONs Will..." Wit: CHARLES MITCHELL, MARY COLLINS. May Court 1747. BENJAMIN WYNNS, D.C/C.

G 2 THOMAS CASTELLAW & WIFE SARAH TO THOMAS RYAN
      May 4, 1747. 580 pds. for 500 A. On NS Roquiss Swamp commonly known as CASTELLAWS Islands". By deed to me by date Nov. 5, 1744. Wit: THOMAS WHITMELL, RICHARD ASHLEY. May Court 1747. *.

G 3 THOMAS DEANS of Northampton County TO MARY O'QUIN
      May 11, 1747. 2 pds. for 100 A. Land on Wattom Swamp adj. WILLIAM PICKET. Wit: JAMES BOYT, ALEXANDER O'QUIN. May Court 1747.*.

G 5 ISAAC CARTER of Society Parish TO JOSEPH BENTHALL
      May 9, 1747 25 pds. for 200 A. Adj. JOHN BROWN "which was the Line of Doctor SAMUEL BROWN Dec'd..." adj. MOOR CARTER "Just over the N.Hampton County Line...", adj. JACOB CARTER, ISAAC CARTER. Wit: JOHN BROWN, SAMUEL BROWN, ENOCH LEWIS, THOMAS WILLS. *. BENJAMIN WYNNS D.C/C.

G 6 THOMAS BASS, planter TO WILLIAM WILLSON
      Nov. 29, 1746 20 pds. for 240 A. At a branch adj. AMOS GRANT. Wit: THOMAS WHITMELL, JAMES KENEDAY. May Court 1747. BENJAMIN WYNNS D. C/C.

G 7 JOHN THOMAS, cooper, of Tyrell County TO RICHARD BROWN
      Nov. 26, 1745. 20 pds. for 100 A. On NS Wiccacon Creek at the mouth of Horsehung Branch. Wit: BENJAMIN WYNNS, WILLIAM WYNNS. May Court 1747.*.

G 9 JAMES DAVIS alias BOON TO RICHARD BROWN
      May 9, 1747. 32 pds. 10 sh. for 150 A. On SS Wiccacon Creek in Chinopen Neck adj. RICHARD BROWN, WILLIAM LEWIS. Wit: PEGGY WYNNS, BENJAMIN WYNNS. May Court 1747. *.

G 10 JAMES CASTELLAW, Treasurer of Bertie County TO JAMES MCDOWALL,
      merchant. Sept. 27, 1726. 150 pds. for *. Land mortgaged by JOHN HOLBROOK, SEN. Wit: JAMES THOMPSON, JOHN POWER. Apr. 6, 1747. E. HALL, C.J.

G 11   JAMES GRAVES TO ANN REESE, daughter of DAVID REESE, Spinster
       April 20, 1747. 36 pds. for 228 A. Part of a larger tract belonging
to THOMAS POLLOCK Dec'd. on Eastermost Swamp at Horse Branch. Adj. WILLIAM
TODD, THOMAS YEATS, JOHN CRICKET at Briery Branch adj. JOHN RODGERS. Wit:
WILLIAM CAMPBELL, JOHN PUSSELL(?), DAVID ROSE. May Court 1747. *.

G 12   THEOPHILUS PUGH of Nancemond County, Va. TO WILLIAM TAYLOR of Edge-
       combe County.   Oct. 2, "MDCCXL". 170 pds. for *. Land THEOPHILUS
PUGH purchased of WILLIAM CATHCART "the XV day of Jany MDCCXL". Wit: ROBERT
WOOBANK(?), NICHOLAS MASSENBURG, JOHN IVY, BED. DAVENPORT. N.C. Court Sept.
22, 1747. _ HALL, C.J.

G 14   ABRAHAM SMITH & WILLIAM WILLIAMSON TO ANDREW CULLIFER
       March 12, 1746/47. 37 pds. for 25 A. At Sandey Run a branch of Mount
Pleasant Mill Swamp at Indian Path. Adj. POLLOCKS Line. Wit: WILLIAM HOOKER,
JUN., EPHRAIM HUNTER. May Court 1747. BENJAMIN WYNNS, D.C/C.

G 15   RICHARD BROWN TO JAMES DAVIS alias BOON
       July 14, 1746. 30 pds. for 100 A. On NS Wiccacon Creek adj. JOSEPH
WYNNS. Wit: PEGGY WYNNS, BENJAMIN WYNNS. May Court 1747. *.

G 16   HENRY DAY, carpenter TO JAMES MCDOWALL, trader
       Jan. 17, 1745. 500 pds. for * "...all my hogs, cattle, horses, work-
ing Tools & all my Personal Estate..." Wit: JOHN SALLIS, ISABELLA FRAZER.
May Court 1747. *.

G 16   JOHN HOLLEY TO JONATHAN KITRELL
       *. 30 pds. for 167 A. On ES Connaritsit Swamp between JOHN GILBERT
and JONATHAN KITRELL adj. JOHN THOMAS. Wit: JOHN THOMAS, PATIENCE THOMAS.
May Court 1747. *.

G 18   JOSEPH SCOTT TO WILLIAM KNIGHT
       Feb. 10, 1746. 4 pds. for 400 A. (1) one tract "that WILLIAM GOODIN
Built on and Settled" 50 A. (2) 350 A. by patent to WILLIAM GOODMAN dated
Feb. 10, 1746/47. In Pottycasy at THOMAS BONNERS corner adj. THOMAS BROWN,
AARON ODOM Wit: JOHN HARRELL, WILLIAM CORNER. May Court 1747. *.

G 19   WILLIAM KNIGHT TO WILLIAM CONNER.
       Feb. 10, 1746/47. 5 pds. 12 sh. for 125 A. By patent granted WILLIAM
KNIGHT Feb. 10, 1746/47 on Pottcasey Creek adj. LEONARD LANGSTON, HENRY
COUPLAND. Wit: JOHN BROWN, ISAAC CARTER. May Court 1747. *.

G 21   JOHN GRANT TO JOHN BARNS
       March 10, 1746/47. 20 pds. for 200 A. On fork of Buck Swamp. Part of
a patent to THOMAS WHITMELL. Wit: JONATHAN STANDLEY, JUN., JOHN BARNS, JUN.
May Court 1747. *.

G 22   GEORGE GOULD TO THOMAS SLATTER
       July 28, 1746. 100 pds. for 400 A. On Cuccold Makers Swamp adj. JOHN
OXLEY. WILLAIM PRICE, MALACHI WESTON. May Court 1747. *.

G 23   GEORGE GOULD TO THOMAS SLATTER
       July 28, 1746. 100 pds. for 640 A. On WS Cucoldmakers Swamp at JOHN
PERRYS corner adj. GEORGE GOULD. Wit: WILLIAM PRICE, MALACHI WESSTON. May
Court 1747. *.

G 24   HENRY SUMERELL & WIFE SARAH TO THOMAS RYAN
       Feb. 20, 1746. 10 pds. for 240 A. (1) On SS Salmon Creek "formerly
taken up by WILLIAM WATERS..." (2) 100 A. that THOMAS RYAN gave to "our
brother JAMES WATERS Dec'd..." (3) 100 A. on Wills Quarter Swamp. Wit:
HENRY COBB, ARTHUR HOWARD, JOHN OAKS. May Court 1747. *.

G 25   JOSEPH WIMBERLY & WIFE JUDAH TO JOHN SMITH
       September 10, 1746. 50 pds. for 250 A. Land between Roanoke River and
Roquist Swamp at head of Connohax adj. WILLIAM CHARLTON, EDWARD FRISBY.
Wit: NEEDHAM BRYAN, MICAJAH HINTON. May Court 1747. *.

G 27   THOMAS SLATTEN, merchant TO GEORGE GOULD
       July 28, 1746. *.for 316 A. "...in consideration of one thousand &
Forty acres of Land Lying in Cuckoldmakers Swamp...and Two hundred Pounds
Current money of the Province..." Adj. JOHN HOWELLS mill Swamp and the

Chowan River. Wit: WILLIAM RICE, MALACHI WESSTON. May Court 1747. *.

G 28 THOMAS SLATTER TO GEORGE GOULD
      May 13, 1747. 200 pds. for 1040 A. Two tracts: (1) 400 A. on Cuckold-
makers Swamp adj. JOHN OXLEY. (2) 640 A. on Cuckoldmakers adj. JOHN PERRY,
GEORGE GOULD. Wit: JOHN LOVICK, JAMES MCDOWALL, JAMES CASTELLAW. May Court
1747. *.

G 30 EDMOND SMITHWICK & WIFE HANNAH TO JOSEPH JORDAIN
      Jan. 10, 1746. 75 pds. for 297 A. In Sohika Neck. As per patent to
EDMOND SMITHWICK(SMETHWICK) cont. 297 A. By SMITHWICK sold to WILLIAM
LATTIMER & NATHAN MOOR. Wit: MILDRED JORDAN, JOSIAH HART, WILLAIM JORDAN.
May Court 1747. *.

G 31 THOMAS ASHLEY the Elder TO SAMUEL COOK
      May 13, 1747. 4 pds. for 50 A. At Blackwalnut Swamp adj. THOMAS RYAN.
Wit: H. HUNTER, RICHARD ASHLEY. May Court 1747. *.

G 33 WILLIAM PEEK of New Hanover Co. TO ALEXANDER MCCULLOCK
      Aug. 11, 1746. 25 pds. for 300 A. Near Roanoke River at Flaggy Run
"which my Father JAMES PEEK Bought of HENRY AMERSON as by Deed will Appear
Dated the 14th Day Feb'y & Duly Prov'd at August Court 1727..." Wit: BENJA-
MIN HILL, WILLIAM HANSFORD. July 6, 1747. N.C. Court. E. HALL C.J.

G 34 WILLIAM PUGH of Edgecombe Co. TO ISAAC HUNTER of Chowan Co.
      May 9, 1746. 37 pds. 10 sh. for 300 A. Land at Pitch Landing being
held by Patent Granted to THOMAS MERTIN. Adj. EPHRAIM HUNTER, WILLIAM DOWN-
ING, "...on the River Bank..." Wit: ELIZABETH SUMNER, JOSEPH SUMNER, JOHN
SUMNER. N.C. Court June 23, 1747. E. HALL, C.J.

G 35 EPAPHRODITUS MOOR TO BRYAN DAUGHTRY (DAUGHTREE) of Nancemond Co. Va.
      Aug. 11, 1747. 6 pds. 10 sh. for 340 A. By patent granted to MOOR
April 20, 1745 on NS POWELS Pocoson at Buck Branch. Wit: JOHN MOOR, RACHEL
MOOR. Aug. Court 1747. *.

G 37 WILLIAM STANCELL & WIFE AFRICA TO SUSANNAH THOMPSON & HER HEIRS
      Nov. 16, 1745. for "a valluable consideration in hand" 520 A. On Kesia
River "in a square piece" Adj. JOHN SAVAGE, WILLIAM STANCELL. Wit: DAVID
HENDRICKS, ABRAHAM HENDRICKS. Aug. Court 1747. *.

G 38 JOHN HALLUM TO LEWIS WILLIAMS, yeoman
      March 4, 1746. in "consideration of one horse" 359 A. On ES Loosing
Swamp adj. ROBERT EVANS in Peggys Neck, ALEXANDER KENEDAY. Wit: ISAAC HILL,
MARY WILLIAMS. Aug. Court 1747. *.

G 39 JOSEPH JONES TO SARAH HUMFREE
      Aug. 10, 1747. 34 A. "..for Love Good will & affection..to my well be-
loved Daughter.." On Kings Road..."to her and her heirs forever...only
should WILLIAM HUMFREE be Left a Widower he shall & may Quietly & peacably
(occupy) as his own During his Natural Life..." Wit: NATHAN HORTON, ISAAC
CARTER. Aug. Court 1747. *.

G 40 GEORGE WALSTON of Beaufort Co. TO PHILLIP WALSTON, SEN.
      July 24, 1747. 200 pds. for 400 A. At the fork of Bear Swamp on WAL-
STONS Creek. Wit: SARAH WALSTON, JOHN MAY, JOHN HARDY. Aug. Court 1747. *.

G 41 PETTYGROVE SALSBERRY TO NICHOLAS SKINNER
      *. 40 pds. for 300 A. On SS Cashy Swamp "in the fork above JOHN WIM-
BERLY". Wit: THOMAS WHITMELL, SAMUEL ANDREWS. Aug. Court 1747. *.

G 43 JOHN MIZELL TO JOHN SOWELL
      July 26, 1747. 8 pds. for 10 A. *. Wit: JOSEPH EVANS, JEREMIAH
MALPASS. Aug. Court 1747. BENJAMIN WYNNS D.C/C.

G 44 BENJAMIN HILL, merchant, TO WILLIAM YATES, SEN.
      Aug. 6, 1747. 125 pds. for 800 A. (This whole tract seems to contain
400 A., although wording is not clear.) (1) Land DANIEL HUGH bought of
THOMAS JONES of Cape Fear bearing date July 30, 1742. Between Blue Water of
Northermost Prong of Hothouse Branch between Beaverdam Swamp, Pottycasy
Swamp and Pottycasey Creek. Part of a tract granted FREDERICK JONES ESQ.
dated 1712. (2) Other 400 A. from THOMAS JONES Gent. to DANIEL HOUGH sold

to HENRY WINBOURN & BRYANT____. Wit: ALEXANDER MCCULLOK, LUKE LANGSTON. Aug. Court 1747. BENJAMIN WYNNS D.C/C.

G 45 WILLIAM KNIGHT TO ISRAEL JOHNSON, joyner
Aug. 7, 1747. 5 pds. for 100 A. Adj. LEONARD LANGSTON, JAMES DENTON at Bells Branch. Wit: LUKE LANGSTON, WILLIAM YATES. Aug. Court 1747. *.

G 47 RICHARD SWAIN TO GEORGE CLEMONS
Aug. 10, 1747. 15 pds. for 172 A. On S. Branch of Rocquis. Wit: THOMAS SPELLER, WILLIAM SWAIN. Aug. Court 1747. *.

G 48 WILLIAM STANCELL & WIFE AFRICA TO JOSEPH JORDAN
July 5, 1747. 62 pds. 10 sh. for 245 A. On Cashy River at Sohikey Neck. Adj. ____ SAVAGE, JOHN HARRESS, JOHN GORFFITH(?). Wit: ISAIAH JOHNSON, DAVID BROADWELL, JAMES CANADAY. Aug. Court 1747. *. "AFRICA...privately examined by JAMES CASTELLAW ESQ. one of his Majesty Justices of the Peace."

G 50 WILLIAM TURNER & WIFE PATIENCE TO MATTHEW TURNER
Aug. 10, 1747. 13 pds. for 210 A. Part of a tract of land called "Snowfields" granted to WILLIAM GRAY by patent bearing date March 13, 1721. Adj. NEEDHAM BRYAN near Roonoroy Path. Wit: NEEDHAM BRYAN, HENRY AVERET, BARNABY BRYAN. Aug. Court 1747. *.

G 51 WILLIAM CATHCART of Northampton Co. TO JOHN CAMPBELL
Aug. 12, 1747. 20 pds. for 200 A. On WS Chowan River. Wit: T. BARKER, J. SALLIS. Aug. Court 1747. *.

G 53 ANIAH GOFFE Late of Johnston Co., spinster TO GEORGE WYNNS, Yeoman
July 9, 1747._ pd. 10 sh. for 100 A. On NS Wiccacon Creek at Mill Swamp and Turkey Cock Branch. Adj. JOSEPH WYNNS. Wit: GEORGE WYNNS, BENJAMIN WYNNS. Aug. Court 1747. *.

G 54 THOMAS FINCH, Labourer TO RICHARD BROWN
Jan 6, 1746/47. 32 pds. for 272 A. On NES Quoyockason Swamp at Stoney Creek Road adj. JOHN EARLY "originall Pantantee". Wit: BENJAMIN WYNNS, PEGGY WYNNS. Aug. Court 1747. *.

G 55 WILLIAM WYNNS, merchant TO WILLIAM BROWN
Feb. 18, 1746/47. 30 pds. 5 sh. for 240 A. On Brooks Creek "being had to a Deed from JOHN HODGSON to JAMES ROOKINGS..." Wit: P. EVANS, BENJAMIN WYNNS. Aug. Court 1747. *.

G 56 HENRY VAN LUVEN TO THOMAS ASHLEY
July 20, 1747. 10 pds. for 82 A. On WS Cashoke Swamp adj. THOMAS ASHBORNS Corner "to the mouth of a great branch opposite to the old Plantation...to line of VANLUVEN & WEST..." Wit: THOMAS RYAN, ANDREW THOMPSON, ANDREW MOORE. Aug. Court 1747. *.

G 57 THOMAS WHITMELL, Sheriff of the County TO ARCHIBALD BELL
March 21, 1746. 506 Province Bills for 480 A. "...by Virtue of an Execution to me Directed from the Genrall Court against the Lands of LAWRENCE SARSON Dec'd Late of this Province in the said County have Sold at Publick Vendue to ARCHIBALD BELL...under the Seal of ENOCH HALL Chief Justice...Dated at Edenton the 6th Day of November Anno Dom 1746..." Two plantations adj. ARCHIBALD BELL, JAMES MCDOWALS, WILLIAM REDDITS, THOMAS WILLIAMSON, GEORGE HENDERSON Dec'd, JAMES NEELAND, ROBERT LAURENCE, JOSEPH REDDITS. "...232 pds. as well to satisfy THOMAS AMORY of a certain Debt in Genrall Court holden for our said Province at the Court House in Edenton on the last Tuesday in March 1744..." Land in hands of THOMAS LOVICK, executor for LAWRENCE SARSON. Wit: WILL CATHCART, JOHN POWER. Aug. Court 1747.*.

G 58 JAMES PARKER TO DEMSEY GRANT
Aug. 4, 1747. 5 pds. for 100 A. Land formerly granted by Patent to JOHN GRAY on Broad Branch adj. WILLIAM KING. Wit: WILLIAM KING, JONATHAN KITTRELL. Aug. Court 1747. *.

G 60 JOSEPH ANDERSON & WIFE ANN OF Chowan County TO JOHN HULL & ANN HULL
July 9, 1747. "in consideration of the natural love and affection" 1000 A. ANN HULL, one of the daughters of GEORGE MARTIN..."JOSEPH ANDERSON & his wife ANN Sole executors of GEORGE MARTIN Esq, Dec'd her former husband...GEO. MARTIN in his Lifetime (to wit) the Sixth Day of October in the

192

year of our Lord one thousand Seven Hundred & thirty four by his Last Will
& Testament Gave and bequeathed unto his wife all his Real Estate During
the term of Her Natural Life and did Impower her to Dispose of same by Last
Will & Testament...amongst his children..." Land purchased of STEPHEN HOW-
ARD and wife SARAH by Deed dated March 5, 1722/23. Also 900 A. of patent to
JAMES BOON dated Nov. 5, 1716 and by Boon sold to GEORGE MARTIN March 7,
1722/23. Same lands confirmed by PATRICK MAUL and THOMAS JONES to GEORGE
MARTIN by indentures dated Sept. 16, 1730. Wit: ABRAHAM BLACKALL, JAMES
CAMPBELL. July 30, 1747. N.C. Court. ENOCH HALL, C.J.

G 61   JOHN HULL & ANNA HIS WIFE TO JAMES COUPLAND
       July 31, 1747. 100 pds. for 1000 A. On SS Chowan River. Land formerly
RICHARD BARFECTOS(?) now JAMES MCDOWALLS. Adj. land formerly JOHN GRAYS now
belonging to Doctor CATHCART. Adj. BOONS patent. 900 A. Part of a patent to
JAMES BOON and by BOON sold to GEORGE MARTIN of Maryland by deed dated
March 7, 1722/23. 100 A. granted to STEPHEN HOWARD & SARAH HOWARD and sold
to GEORGE MARTIN March 6, 1722/23. Said lands conveyed to JOHN HULL & ANNA
by JOSEPH & ANN ANDERSON, executors of the estate of GEORGE MARTIN. Wit:
LUKE SUMNER, LEMUEL REDDICK, JAMES MANEY. N.C. Court July 31, 1747. *.

G 64   LUKE WHITE, yeoman TO JOHN DAVESON, yeoman
       March 26, 1747. 10 pds. for 100 A. On WS Chowan River at MAULS Creek
adj. THOMAS HANSFORD. Wit: PHILLIP MAGUIRE, MICHAEL BERRY, JOHN DAVESON.
N.C. Court Aug. 27, 1747. E. HALL, C.J.

G 65   JOHN FREEMAN of Chowan County TO SAMUEL FREEMAN
       June 12, 1747. 640 A. "inconsideration of Naturall Love and Affec-
tion...more especially out of the full Complying & Fullfilling of the Last
Will & Testament of my Father WILLIAM FREEMAN Late of Chowan County...
which was proved in due form of Law before WM. SMITH ESQ. & Chief Judge of
the Province aforesaid...He did Bequeath to my two Brothers AARON & SAMUEL
FREEMAN & AARON now being Dec'd before he was of Lawfull age & Dieing Intestate his Inheritance descending to me the Eldest Brother..." Land a
patent to HENRY ROADS April 1, 1723. By him sold to WILLIAM FREEMAN Sept.
22, 1733. Wit: THOMAS WALTON, THOMAS ROUNTREE, JUN, THOMAS ROUNTREE, SEN.
N.C. Court July 31, 1747. E. HALL, C.J.

G 67   WILLIAM WYNNS, merchant TO JOHN VANPELT, yeoman
       March 2, 1746. 80 pds. for 353 A. On WS Chincopen Swamp. WILLIAM
WYNNS acting as attorney for THOMAS MCCLENDON of Craven County. Wit: HENRY
VIZE, WILLIAM SHARP, DNAIEL VANPELT. Nov. Court 1747. BENJAMIN WYNNS D.C/C.

G 68   JOHN JONES, sawyer TO JOHN HOWELL, yeoman
       Nov. 9, 1747. 80 pds. for 150 A. On NS Chinkopen Swamp adj. JOHN WIL-
SON, THOMAS HANSFORD "formerly a corner for BOOTH", to Long Branch. Wit:
JAMES WATSON, JAMES LESSLIE(?) Nov. Court 1747. *.

G 69   JAMES MCDOWALL, merchant TO JOSEPH HARDY, planter
       Nov. 10, 1747. 48 pds. 12 sh. 6 p. for 400 A. On NS Cashy River and
NS Buckelsberry Swamp adj. ROBERT LAURENCE. Wit: JOHN CRICKET, EDWARD RASOR
(RASSOR). Nov. Court 1747. *.

G 71   JOSEPH JONES TO NATHAN HORTON
       *. 20 pds. for 350 A. Part of a tract of JAMES HOWARD on NWS Ahotskey
Swamp adj. EDWARD HOWARD. Wit: WILLIAM HUMFREE, WILLIAM HORTON, ISAAC
CARTER. Nov. Court 1747. *.

G 72   JOHN CAMPBELL of Edenton, Merchant TO JOSEPH JONES
       Sept. 19, 1747. 105 pds. for 730 A. Part of a tract commonly called
Bluewater adj. JOSEPH JONES on SS Catawitskey. Part of 964 A. Wit: BENJA-
MIN HILL, WILLIAM HUMFREE, JOHN RIEUSSET(?). Nov. Court 1747. *.

G 73   RICHARD BROWN, yeoman TO THOMAS FINCH, labourer
       Jan. 5, 1746/47. 50 pds. for 50 A. In Chinkopen Neck. Adj. THOMAS
FINCH, JOHN EARLY. Wit: BENJAMIN WYNNS, PEGGY WYNNS. Nov. Court 1747. *.

G 74   RICHARD BROWN TO FRANCIS BROWN, JUN.
       Nov. 10, 1747. 35 pds. for 100 A. In Chinkopen Neck on SS Wiccacon
Creek to "line lately THOMAS FINCHS", WILLIAM PERRY. Wit: DANIEL VANPELT,
BENJAMIN WYNNS. Nov. Court 1747. *.

G 76   THOMAS FINCH, labourer TO JOSEPH BARRADAIL, taylor
       Oct. 11, 1747.   25 pds. for 496 A. In Chinkopen Neck. Wit: LEWIS
WILLIAMS, BENJAMIN WYNNS. Nov. Court 1747. BENJAMIN WYNNS D.C/C.

G 77   JOSEPH BARRADAIL, taylor TO RICHARD BROWN, yeoman
       Oct. 3, 1747. 30 pds. for 496 A. Land I bought of THOMAS FINCH in
Chinkopen Neck. Part of two tracts "Reference being had to two Severall
Deeds from the said RICHARD BROWN to THOMAS FINCH..." Wit: WILLIAM PERRY,
BENJAMIN WYNNS. Nov. Court 1747. *.

G 78   JOHN BELL TO JOSEPH THOMAS
       Feb. 27, 1746.   50 pds. for 178 A. on NS Cashy Swamp adj. MAJOR WEST.
Wit: THOMAS CASTELLAW, THOMAS SIMONS, PETER DAY. Nov. Court 1747. *.

G 80   MICHAEL HILL TO THOMAS RYAN
       Nov. 10, 1747.   500 pds. for 640 A. On SS Salmon Creek. Wit: JOHN
HARDY, ARTHUR WILLIAMS, NATHANIEL HILL. Nov. Court 1747. *.

G 82   JOHN WYNNS, yeoman TO BENJAMIN BAKER, yeoman
       Oct. 10, 1747.   6 pds. 10 sh. for 162 A. "Between Killum & the Long
Branch" Adj. THOMAS MANN "down the said Manns old Line Now SPEIGHTS", JOHN
WOTSFORD, ALEXANDER VOLLANTINE. Wit: LIDIA PALMER, BENJAMIN NORVILL. Nov.
Court 1747. *.

G 83   THOMAS MORRISS, yeoman TO ANN LOVEWELL, spinster
       July 24, 1747.   5 pds. for 100 A. On a "Branch of Mount Pleasant Mill
Swamp the branch called Chinkopen..." Adj. LASSITER, O'LIVER. Wit: WILLIAM
HOOKER, JUN., STEPHEN HOOKER. Nov. Court 1747. *.

G 84   RICHARD ODAM & SUSANNAH WIDOW OF JACOB ODAM TO JAMES MCDOWALL, merchant
       Oct. 7, 1747.   25 pds. for 100 A. On Connaritsit Swamp adj. NATHANIEL
WILLIAMS, JAMES ROW, "...it being the Land left me by my Father JACOB ODAM
..." Wit: THOMAS ASHLEY, RICHARD ASHLEY, JOHN HENDRICKS. Nov. Court 1747.*.

G 86   MILES GALE of Edenton, mariner TO MILES GALE, JUN. of Edenton
       April 10, 1747.   1420 A. + 400 A. "...given me by my son MILES GALE
.." Land on NS Morattock River adj. HENRY SPELLER now dec'd, COGSWELL &
DOMINI lands. (2) On NS Morattock & SES Conaray(?) on Chickery Pocoson. Adj.
EDWARD SMITHWICK, COGSWELL & DOMINI, MERTIN GRIFFIN, JOHN HARLOE to Conaray
Branch. Wit: JOHN CAMPBELL, JOHN RICE. N.C. Court April 20, 1747. E.HALL C.J.

G 87   LEWIS SOWELL, Yeoman of Johnston County TO JAMES BURRUSS
       March 23, 1746/47.   70 pds. for 200 A. "near the River Pocoson" at
Horse Swamp adj. OBADIAH SOWELL. Wit: WILLIAM HOOKER, JUN., JAMES (B)LUNT
(?). Feb. Court 1747. *.

G 88   JOHN WESTON TO WILLIAM SLOPER, carpenter
       Feb. 9, 1747/48.   100 pds. for 230 A. On Bear Swamp adj. THOMAS SOWELL,
Dec'd, JACOB KEEL, OBADIAH SOWELL. Wit: WILLIAM HOOKER, JUN., JOSEPH PERRY,
WILLIAM WESTON, JUN. Feb. Court 1747. *.

G 89   JOSEPH WATSFORD (WOTSFORD) TO JOHN WYNNS, yeoman
       Aug. 27, 1747.   60 pds. for 320 A. "..land commonly called GEORGES"
on SS Long Branch near the old Cart Way through the said branch. Adj. JOHN
WOTSFORD, ALEXANDER VOLLANTINE, BENJAMIN BAKER. "...Land being Specially
bequeathed to me by the Last Will of my Dec'd father JOSEPH WOTSFORD..."
Wit: WILLIAM WYNNS, JOSEPH PERRY, JOHN WOTSFORD. Feb. Court 1747. *.

G 90   JOHN MOOR, blacksmith TO EPHRAIM WESTON
       Feb. 9, 1747.   5 sh. for 150 A. On Cashy River at Bear Island. Adj.
WILLIAM COLLINS. Wit: THOMAS CASTELLAW, HENRY WALSTON. Feb. Court 1747. *.

G 92   ABEL DEELE TO PETER WEST
       Nov. 21, 1747.   30 pds. for 150 A. On Blue Water adj. PETER WEST, JUN.
Wit: SARAH WEST, DANIEL RODGERS. Feb. Court 1747. *.

G 92   RICHARD BLIZARD TO TIMOTHY VANPELT
       Aug. 7, 1747.   123 pds. for 200 A. On NS Wills Quarter Swamp adj.
JAMES CURRIE on Pell Mell Pocoson. Wit: ABRAHAM JORDAN, JAMES CASTELLAW,
WILLIAM JENKINS. Feb. Court 1747. *.

G 94   ARCHIBALD BELL TO JOHN REDDITT
        Feb. 8, 1747/48.   253 pds. for 280 A. In Buckelsberry Pocoson being
part of 480 A. belonging to the Late LAURENCE SARSON Dec'd including a
plantation whereon JOHN REDDITT now lives adj. WILLIAM REDDITT, THOMAS
WILLIAMSON "...which land was sold by THOMAS WHITMEL Esq. high Sheriff...
under seal of ENOCH HALL, Esq. Chief Justice (Nov. 6, 1746)...and bought by
the subscriber for Five hundred & Six Pounds..." Wit: THOMAS RYAN, THOMAS
WHITMELL, ARTHUR WILLIAMS. Feb. Court 1747. BENJAMIN WYNNS, D.C/C.

G 95   THOMAS BARKER TO JOHN HARRELL
        Nov. 14, 1747.   160 pds. for 640 A. In Roonaroy Meadows adj. THOMAS
and GEORGE POLLOCK's corner, WILLIAM EASON. Land granted to WILLIAM MAUL by
patent dated Feb. 1, 1725. Commonly called Broad Neck Survey. Wit: WILLIAM
NOBLES, MARY PUGH. Feb. Court 1747. *.

G 96   NATHAN ROWLAND of Edgecombe Co. TO DANIEL MURPHEY (MURPHREY)
        Aug. 13, 1747.   30 pds. for 390 A. On ES Cashy Swamp adj. ROADES
Plantation on Wattom Swamp "where is a Beverdam". Wit: JOSEPH MINTON, JOHN
JENKINS. Feb. Court 1747. *.

G 98   DANIEL MURPHREY TO RICHARD HARRELL, SEN. of Nancemond Co, Va.
        Nov. 16, 1747.   30 pds. for 190 A. On Cashy Swamp adj. "ROADS Planta-
tion" at Wattom Swamp. Wit: JOHN HARRELL, FRANCIS HARRELL. Feb. Court 1747.*.

G 100 RICHARD HINES TO WILLIAM SNOWDEN
        May 14, 1747.   10 pds. for 175 A. at Fork of Cashy River and Wattom
Swamp. adj. ROBERT CARTER, DANIEL MURPHREY. Wit: JOSEPH MENTON, RICHARD
ROWLAND. Feb. Court 1747. *.

G 101 WILLIAM WADE TO MOSES WOOD
        Oct. 12, 1747.   10 pds. for 240 A. On SS Sequea Swamp adj. GEORGE
JARNAGAN. Wit: JOSEPH BARRADAIL, THOMAS BAKER, JAMES WOOD. Feb. Court 1747.*.

G 102 HUMPHREY LAURENCE TO GEORGE LAURENCE
        Jan. 9, 1747.   7 pds. 10 sh. for 120 A. "...A Certain Piece of Land
which was Willed to me by my father ROBERT LAURENCE..." On SS Bear Swamp
"...being part of the Land my Father ROBERT LAURENCE Lived on when he died
..."   Wit: WILLIAM LAURENCE, ALEXANDER HAW, JOHN SALLIS. Feb. Court 1747.*.

G 103 MICHAEL HILL TO JAMES CASTELLAW
        Jan. 22, 1748.   500 pds. for 640 A. On NS Cashy River on Eastermost
Branch. Wit: JOHN MOORE, THOMAS CASTELLAW, HENRY WALSTON. Feb.Court 1747.*.

G 104 THOMAS YATES TO JOSEPH JACOCKS
        Feb. 1, 1747.   60 pds. for 100 A. In Middle Swamp at mouth of White
Oak Branch. Adj. THOMAS YATES, EDWARD TAYLER, POLLOCKS corner. Wit: EDWARD
BRYAN, WILLIAM STOKES, JAMES JONES. Feb. Court 1747. *.

G 106 WILLIAM DUFFELL, husbandman TO JUDITH DUFFELL
        .. "...in consideration of Love good Will & affection which I have
* Do bear towards my Loving Daughter JUDITH DUFFELL..." 6 cows, 3 calves,
2 yearlings, 1 feather bed & rugg, 2 blankets, 4 sheets"...& the Pewter
which did belong to her Grandmother & one chest..." Wit: JONATHAN STANDLEY
JUN., CHARLES KING. Feb. Court 1747. *.

G 106 THOMAS WHITMELL, ESQ., JOHN GRAY, GENT. OF BERTIE & THOMAS BLOUNT
        ESQ. of Edgecombe Co. TO DOM REX.   May 15, 1745.   500 pds. for *.
Performance bond for THOMAS WHITMELL. "...to our Said Lord the King his
heirs & Successors..." THOMAS WHITMELL was appointed Sheriff of Bertie
County by commission of GABRIEL JOHNSTON, Governor. Wit: H. HUNTER, BENJA-
MIN WYNNS, J. WYNNS, JOHN BROWN. May Court 1745. *.

G 107 JOHN BROWN, THOMAS BROWN, BENJAMIN WYNNS TO DOM REX
        May 13, 1747.   500 pds. Bond for JOHN BROWN to serve as Sheriff of
Bertie County. Appointed by GABRIEL JOHNSTON. Wit: JOHN WESTON, WILLIAM
WESTON, JUN. May Court 1747. *.

G 108 MOSES SPEIGHT TO MARY SPEIGHT
        Oct. 29, 1740. *Power of Attorney. "...in Consideration of the Love
& affection...(I do have) for my beloved wife MARY SPEIGHT...Power of attorney...Ratifying & by these presents allowing whatsoever MARY SPEIGHT

shall in my name do..." Wit: THOMAS RYAN, JAMES MCADAMS. N.C. Court. Oct. 29, 1741. J. MONTGOMERY, C.J.

G 109 ISABELL KING, widow TO KING CHILDREN
        Sept. 23, 1742. "...(for) Love...I bear to my children MICHAEL, HENRY, JOHN, CATHRINA, ISABELL, PENELOPE, MARY KING...these following Negroes & their increase...Viz. Tower, Hill, Harry, Hannah, Bess, Maria, Armstead...and all other moveable estate..." Wit: ARCHBILL BELL, CHARLES MITCHELL, PETER WYNANT. N.C. Court Oct. 20, 1742. W. SMITH, C.J.

G 110 CULLEN POLLOCK of Tyrrel (Tyrryl) County TO FRANCIS RASOR(RASSOR)
        March 6, 1742. 40 pds. for 200 A. On WS Eastermost Swamp of Salmon Creek on SS of Cross Branch. "By my authority by my Executorship of the Will of Mr. THOMAS POLLOCK Late Dec'd..." Wit: SAMUEL HARDY, LOVICK YOUNG. Aug. Court 1742. HENRY DELON C/C.

G 111 JOHN GRILLS of King William Co. Va. TO THOMAS RYAN
        Feb. 16, 1742/43. Power of attorney. "...in respect to makeing Sale of Certain tract of Land Lying on Salmon Creek..." Signed: "JOHN GRILLS the Son of WILLIAM GRILLS..." Wit: NEHEMIAH WARING, CASPER HORNBECK, JOSEPH STARLING. May Court 1743. HENRY DELON C/C.

G 112 THOMAS MCCLENDON of Craven County TO WILLIAM WYNNS.
        Nov. 16, 1741. Power of Attorney. "...power..to sell..recover...and receive...in my name..." Wit: JOHN ASKEW, BENJAMIN WYNNS, THOMAS MCCLENDON. Aug. Court 1742. *.

G 112 EDWARD WINGATE, SEN. of Lockwoods Folly TO JOHN WINGATE of Lockwoods
        Folly. Jan. 3, 1742/43. Power of Attorney. "...to sell & Dispose of a certain tract of Land lying & being on Roanoke River containing 328 acres ..." Adj. COGSWELL & DOMONICKS Line at JAMES WILLIAMSONS. Wit: WILLIAM FORBES, NEIL MCNEIL, EDWARD WINGATE, JUN. Nov. Court 1743. *.

G 114 DOM REX TO JOHN WYNNS
        April 20, 1745. Grant. 400 A. Land at head of Wild Catt Branch adj. WILLIAM WESTON. Signed: GABRIEL JOHNSTON our Captain General & Governour in Chief at New Bern in this 20th Day of Aprill in the eighteenth year of our Reign Anno Dom 1745..." RT. FORSTER, Dep. Sec. In Auditor Generals Office 20th April 1745. ALEXANDER MCCULLOCK, Dep. Aud.

G 115 JOHN WYNNS TO GEORGE JARNAGAN
        May 13, 1747 9 pds. for 400 A. Within mentioned patent. Wit: THOMAS HANSFORD, JOHN BROWN, THOMAS WHITMELL. May Court 1747. BENJAMIN WYNNS, D.C/C.

G 116 THOMAS JONES of New Hanover Province TO THOMAS WALKER
        Oct. 21, 1746. 75 pds. for 250 (2500?) A. Between JOHN COTTEN, JAMES COTTEN, DANIEL HOUGH. Wit: SAMUEL SWANN, GEORGE NICHOLAS, JOSEPH BLAKE. *. E. HALL, C.J.

G 117 JOHN LEWIS of Isle of Wight Co, Va. TO BENJAMIN HILL
        Nov. 3, 1740. 12 pds. for 400 A. "...Land whereon my Father THOMAS LEWIS formerly lived...which the said THOMAS bought of DANIEL MCDANIEL as by said patent bearing date ninth day of March 1717..." At Bever Dam Swamp on Spring Branch. Adj. THOMAS VENSON, JOHN CROSBEY. Wit: ALEXANDER MCCULLOCK, WILLIAM MANNSELL (MAUNSELL), SARAH MCCULLOCK. N.C. Court. July 27, 1748.*.

G 119 THOMAS PARKER, wheelwright TO JOHN FREEMAN, wheelwright
        Feb. 24, 1747/48. 25 pds. for 150 A. On NS Barbaque Swamp adj. THOMAS MCCLENSONS former line. Also a Grist Water Mill on Barbeque Swamp. Also an acre on SS Barbeque Swamp "which said mill THOS. PARKER & JOHN FREEMAN bought of ELIAS STALLINS..." Wit: BENJAMIN WYNNS, RICHARD BROWN. May Court 1748. JOHN LOVICK C/C.

G 120 MICHAEL HILL TO JOHN HILL
        May 5, 1748. 60 pds. for 460 A. On WS Casia River. Wit: ROBERT HUNTER, MOSES HUNTER, RICHARD MANING. May Court 1748. JOHN LOVICK C/C.

G 122 MICHAEL HILL TO JOHN HILL
        May 5, 1748. 60 pds. for 424 A. On ED Rocquis Swamp adj. JOHN HARDY at BOWERS (BREWERS) Quarter. Wit: ROBERT HUNTER, MOSES HUNTER, RICHARD MANING. May Court 1748. *.

196

G 123 WILLIAM LEWIS, yeoman TO WILLIAM PERRY, yeoman
       Sept. 16, 1747. 50 pds. for 150 A. On Chinkopin Neck and SS Wiccacon
Creek. Cont. 150 A. near Netops Marsh adj. THOMAS FINCH. Wit; JOSEPH BARRA-
DAILE, JOHN REED, BENJAMIN WYNNS D.C/C.

G 125 THOMAS RYAN TO WILLIAM CAMPBELL
       Feb. 19, 1747/48. 20 pds. for 200 A. On Eastermost Swamp adj. WILL-
IAM CAMPBELL, ___GRILL, JOHN NICHOLL. Wit: ANDREW THOMSON, THOMAS ASHBORN,
DAVID RYAN. May Court 1748. JOHN LOVICK C/C.

G 126 THOMAS RYAN TO JOHN SALLIS
       May 11, 1748. 50 pds. for 400 A. Land where PHILLIP WALSTON formerly
lived adj. GEORGE WATSON (WALSTON?) at WALSTON Creek adj. JOHN BOWIN, JAMES
NEWLAND. Wit: JOHN BROWN, PHILLIP WALSTON, SEN. May Court 1748. *.

G 128 JOHN PUGH TO THOMAS BARKER
       April 4, 1748. 85 pds. for 320 A. + 300 A. "Land whereon FRANCIS
PUGH late Father of the said JOHN PUGH did live and is the land that WILL-
IAM EASON did grant to FARLOW (TARLOW) OQUIN by deed of gift July 12, 1722
..." 300 A. granted to TARLOW OQUIN Aug. 4, 1723. Wit: GEORGE LOCKHART,
THOMAS WIGGINS. April Court 1748. JOHN LOVICK C/C.

G 129 WILLIAM BUSH of Johnston Co., yeoman TO BENJAMIN WYNNS
       July 18, 1747. 50 pds. for 700 A. "...WILLIAM BUSH heir at Law to
JOHN BUSH late of Bertie Deceased..." In Chinkapin Neck on Wiccacon Creek
adj. JOHN REED, WILLIAM PERRY, WILLIAM LEWIS, JOHN VANPELT. "whereon my
Father & Grand Father lived and Died..." Wit: JOHN WYNNS, ISAAC BUSH,
FRANCIS MCCLENDON. *.

G 131 RALPH OUTLAW TO THOMAS EASON of Chowan Co.
       Dec. 2, 1747. 20 pds. for 300 A. On SS Ahoskey Swamp adj. CHARLES
JONES. Wit: WILLIAM HUMFREE, WILLIAM OUTLAW. *. *.

G 132 JOHN CAKE TO ELIZABETH SUMEREL
       May 8, 1748. 28 pds. for 147 A. "...paid by my Daughter ELIZABETH
SUMEREL..." Land on Flatt Swamp adj. THOMAS NEWBOURN at Dogwood Branch.
Wit: ANTHONY FILGO, THOMAS NEWBOORN. May Court 1748. *.

G 133 JOHN THOMAS TO JOHN SALLIS
       May 3, 1748. 12 pds. 10 sh. for 100 A. At Buck Branch adj. CALEB
SPIVAY. Wit: JESSE WOOD, CHRISTOPHER HOLLYMAN. May Court 1748. *.

G 135 GEORGE CLEMONTS (CLEMONS) TO HENRY KING
       Oct. 27, 1746. 60 pds. for 100 A. "I...am obliged to HENRY KING of
Chowan County...in Seventy pounds Virginia money...I bind myself (and heirs)
this 27th day of Oct. Anno Dom 1746...whereas...hathe bargained and sold...
one hundred acres of land lying on Rocquis Pocoson...which GEORGE CLEMONS
formerly purchased of JOHN HERRING JUN..." Adj. CHARLES KING as by patent
to JOHN HERRING. Wit: MICHAEL KING, CHARLES KING, THOMAS RETTER. May Court
1748. *.

G 136 GABRIEL JOHNSTON CERTIFICATES OF FREEDOM
       "These are to certify all whom it may concern that Molley a Negro
wench who has lived with me for Sever'l years by past is now Discharged
from my Service and I do hereby Discharge her. GAB. JOHNSTON Edenhouse
July 17, 1747.
These may certify to all concerned that the bearer of this Ceasar a negro
fellow is a freeman and is now Discharged from my Service. GAB. JOHNSTON
Edenhouse July 20, 1747.
The above Certificates was proved in open Court in due form of Law & on
mocon ordered to be recorded. JNO. LOVICK C/C.

G 136 THOMAS WILLIAMSON TO SAMUEL ORMES
       May 30, 1747. 8 pds. for 214 A. On SS Bucklesbury Pocoson Adj.
LAURENCE SARSON, ___ROSE, PHILLIP WALSTON, JOHN HOLBROOK. As by patent
dated April 1, 1723. Wit: WILLIAM STOKES, JOHN COBERT. N.C. Court June 3,
1747. E. HALL, C.J. J. LOVICK C/C.

G 138 JOHN HILL TO JOHN JONES
       July 22, 1746. 20 pds. for 200 A. "...being the residue of a patent
bearing date Nov. 7, 1723..." Adj. EDWARD TAYLOR, COLL. POLLOCK, MEDIA WHITE.

Wit: WILLIAM PEARCE, REBECCA PEARCE. Aug. Court 1748. JOHN LOVICK C/C.

G 140   JAMES CASTELLAW, ESQ. TO WILLIAM CASTELLAW
        Aug. 10, 1746. 10 sh. for 640 A. On NS Cashy River at Poplar (Pap-
lar) Runn. Wit: NEEDHAM BRYAN, GEORGE PATTERSON. Aug. Court 1748. *.

G 141   WILLIAM CRISP & FRANCES CRISP* TO SAMUEL SINGLETON
        Aug. 9, 1746. 30 pds. for 200 A. On NS Rocquis Islands at the edge
of Rocquis Pocoson. Adj. FRANCIS HOBSON to Chiske Swamp, ROBERT HOWELL.
Wit: ROBERT HOWELL, FRANCIS HOBSON. Aug. Court 1746. *. (*There is no mention that FRANCES CRISP is wife of WILLIAM CRISP. The general rule is to
say "...wife of...")

G 143   WILLIAM BLITH TO MICHAEL WARD
        Oct. 28, 1747. 23 pds. for 200 A. On SW side Quonckson Swamp adj.
JOHN BUSH at ES Cablan Branch adj. WILLIAM FREEMAN. "...part of a patent to
him the Said WILLIAM BLITH for Five hundred and Sixty Acres of Land March
the Eleventh day in the year 1740..." Wit: ROBERT DROUGHAN, MICHAEL WARD,
JUN., ROGER BADGETT. Aug. Court 1746. *.

G 144   CHARLES MITCHELL TO COLL. ROBERT WEST
        Aug. 10, 1748. 48 pds. for 280 A. Adj. EDWARD BIRD "...on South
side of the Main road near Kings plantation..." On ES Spring Branch adj.
ROGER SNELL. By patent dated April 10, 1730. Wit: JAMES CASTELLAW, JOHN
LOVICK. Aug. Court 1748. JOHN LOVICK C/C.

G 146   PHILLIP WALSTON, SEN. TO JAMES TRADER
        Nov. 28, 1747. 50 pds. for 400 A. on Walston Creek at Beaver Dam
(actually spelled Damn) Swamp. Whereon said WALSTON now lives adj. HENRY
WALSTON. Wit: JOHN BARNES, JUN., JOHN BARNES. WILLIAM KING. Aug. Court 1748.

G 148   FRANCES RASOR (RASSOR) TO ELIZABETH HARDAY (HARDY)
        Feb. 11, 1748. Gift. 200 A. "...natural love & affection I bear to
my loving and Dutiful Daughter ELIZABETH HARDAY..." Land on WS Eastermost
Swamp or branch of Salmon Creek adj. CAMPBELLS line, POLLOCKS line, COOPERS
branch. Wit: WILLIAM HARDY, WILLIAM KEELER. Aug. Court 1748. *.

G 149   ABRAHAM ODAM TO JAMES ROE, shoemaker
        Feb. 10, 1748. 7 pds. for 100 A. On ES Connoritsat Swamp adj. RICH-
ARD ODAM, JOHN GILBERT. Wit: RICHARD HOLLY, THOMAS ODAM. Aug. Court 1748.*.

G 150   JOHN BAKER, turner TO GEORGE HUGHS, cooper
        April 8, 1748. 125 pds. for 267 A. On ES Barbeque Swamp. "...Accor-
ding to the patent granted to me for the same land dated Sept. 25, 1741..."
Wit: JOHN WYNNS, JAMES JONES. Aug. Court 1748. *.

G 151   JOHN BAKER TO ELIZABETH & SOLOMON NORVILL
        April 16, 1748. 30 pds. for 125 A. On Flatt Swamp adj. ALEXANDER
VOLLANTINE, JOHN WYNN. Wit: JOHN WYNNS, BENJAMIN NORVILL, THOMAS JOHNSTON,
JAMES NORVIL. Aug. Court 1748. *.

G 152   JOHN BAKER, yeoman TO WILLIAM HOOKER, JUN.
        July 2, 1748. 15 pds. for 10 A. Adj. WILLIAM HOOKER, ____NORVILL.
Wit: BENJAMIN NORVILL, SOLOMON NORVILL, JAMES NORVILL. Aug. Court 1748.*.

G 153   JACOB HOLLY of New Hanover Co. TO BENJAMIN CLEMONS of Johnston Co.
        Nov. 30, 1747. 15 pds. for 200 A. Part of a greater tract granted
to THOMAS WHITMELL at the mouth of Mirey Branch adj. ____GRAY on Buck Swamp.
Wit: GEORGE PARKER, WILLIAM EMERSON, PALY PARKER. Aug. Court 1748. *.

G 154   WILLIAM CHARLTON of Craven Co. TO THOMAS NORCOM of Perquimmons Co.
        June 1, 1748. 200 pds. for 300 A. "Land that my father WILLIAM CHARL-
TON made a purchase of from the Indians and is on the North part of my pa-
tent & Includes an Island commonly called the Indian Island..." Wit: LUKE
MIZELL, ELIZABETH MIZELL. Aug. Court 1748. *.

G 155   JOHN GILBERT TO ALEXANDER OLIVER
        Aug. 27, 1747. 11 pds. for 100 A. On Coneratsrat Swamp adj. JOHN
GILBERT, JOHN HOLLY. Wit: WILLIAM WILLIAMSON, WILLIAM BEAGELEN, JOHN SHOLAR.
Aug. Court 1748. JOHN LOVICK, C/C.

G 157   DAVID ATKINS TO BENJAMIN STONE
        *. "valuable consideration" for 320 A. On ES plantation of DAVID
ATKINS adj. MAJOR WEST. Wit: JOHN CAKE, MARY CAKE. Aug. Court 1748. *.

G 158   LORDS PROPRIETORS TO WILLIAM MAULE *
        Feb. 1, 1725. Grant. 640 A. Land on SS Chinkapin Swamp at mouth of
Cypress Swamp adj. HENRY ROADS at Barbeque (Swamp). "...being due from the
Importation of one person for every Fifty acres..." Signed: RICHARD EVERARD,
W. MOSELEY, JOHN BLOUNT, C. GALE, THOMAS POLLOCK, THOMAS HARVEY. Rec. in
Sec'ty Office J. LOVICK Sec'ty. "Enrolled in the Auditor Genrals office
April 1, 1744. ROBERT HAMILTON D. Aud." (*Marginal note beside this deed
says CATHCART TO DAVIESON & WYNNS)

G 159   WILLIAM CATHCART of Northampton Co. TO JOHN DAVERSON & JOHN WYNNS
        Aug. 24, 1748, 5 pds. for "within mentioned patent". Wit: THOMAS
JONES, DAVID THOMPSON. Feb. Court 1748. JOHN LOVICK C/C.

G 159   WILLIAM LEE, JUN. TO THOMAS LEE
        Jan. 7, 1748/49. 20 pds. for 150 A. At Ferry Landing on NS Wiccacon
Creek up the main road adj. HENRY MAYNOR to "the first great Branch of
Brooks Creek". Wit: WILLIAM WYNNS, BENJAMIN WYNNS. Feb. Court 1748. *.

G 161   JAMES CASTELLAW, Public Treasurer of Bertie County TO JOHN SALLIS
        Nov. 13, 1748. 88 pds. 10 sh. for 300 A. Land bounded by a deed
from PELEG ROGERS to WILLIAM EVANS "which said Land was mortgaged by the
said WILLIAM EVANS to me the said Treasurer...became Fortified...and by me
sold at publick Vendue..." Wit: THOMAS WHITMELL, CHRISTIAN PRATT. Feb.
Court 1748. *.

G 162   JAMES CASTELLAW, ESQ. & WILLIAM CASTELLAW, Yeoman TO JOHN SALLIS
        Dec. 24, 1748. *houses. "Those houses that lyes near the Court house
at Cashy commonly known by the name of SYNNOTTS & TOMLINSONS houses...Re-
serving only the use of Two of the houses that Belonged to SYNNOTT for our
own use, not in any wise to Settle person or persons in them unless it be
any workmen that Shall or may be Imployed to work on the Mile...(for 7
years) with power to raise any Stock of Hoggs Cattle Horses or sheep...
(Lease to be renewable). Wit: JOHN CASTELLAW, SARAH SANDERS. Feb. Court 1748.

G 164   BENJAMIN LEWIS of Tyrrell TO PHILIP WALSTON
        Jan. 16, 1748. 20 pds. for 100 A. On ES Roquis Swamp adj. BROGDONS
Line. Wit: SAMUEL SINGLETON, NATHANAEL KNOT. Feb. Court 1748. *.

G 165   WILLIAM YEATS TO JOSEPH JONES
        Aug. 5, 1748. Gift. 1 A. "...(for) good will which I have and do
bear towards my Neighbor(bour) JOSEPH JONES..." Land on NS Blew Water. Wit:
WILLIAM HUMPE. JOHN BRICKELL, CADER SOWELL. Feb. Court 1748. *.

G 166   JOHN PARCEL TO THOMAS RYAN
        *. 100 pds. for 219 A. By deed from Coll. CULLEN POLLOCK to JOHN
ROGERS on WS Eastermost Swamp at Cross Branch. Wit: JOHN NICHOLLS, JOHN
NICHOLLS, JUN., WILLIAM CAMPBELL. Feb. Court 1748. *.

G 167   SAMUEL ORMES TO THOMAS YATES, SEN.
        Sept. 19, 1748. 20 pds. for 514 A. On SS Bucklesbury Pocoson adj.
LAURENCE SARSON, ___ROSE, PHILLIP WALSTON, JOHN HERRING, ___HOLLBROOK. By
patent dated April 1, 1723. Wit: JOSEPH BUTTERTON, JOHN LOVICK. Feb. Court
1748. JOHN LOVICK C/C.

G 168   JOHN JENKINS (JINKINS), canter TO EZAH JOHNSON
        Dec. 17, 1748. 60 pds. for 200 A. On SS Wills Quarter Swamp adj.
JOHN WILLIAMS. Wit: ABRAHAM JORDAN, DAVID BROADWELL. Feb. Court 1748. *.

G 170   WILLIAM JOHNSON of Surry Co., Va. TO FRANCES RASOR
        May 31, 1748. Power of atty. to sell land. 100 A. "...to my well be-
loved friend & Sister..." Land on NES Salmon Creek between CULLEN POLLOCK's
land formerly CARY GODBEY's. That land whereon EDWARD RASOR now dwells & is
held by patent taken out by SUSANNAH JOHNSON. Wit: NATHANIEL JOHNSON,
HANNAH JOHNSON. Feb. Court *. JOHN LOVICK C/C.

G 171   FRANCES RASOR TO EDWARD RASOR
        *. 10 pds. for 100 A. "...By virtue of power of attorney given and

granted unto me by WILLIAM JOHNSON of Surry County..." Land on ES Salmon Creek adj. CULLEN POLLOCK. Land formerly belonging to CARY GODLEY, that tract where EDWARD RASOR now dwells. By patent to SUSANNAH JOHNSON dated April 1712. Wit: WILLIAM FLEETWOOD, LAMB HARDY, WILLIAM HARDY. Feb. Court 1748. *.

G 172 JOHN ELKS TO JACOB LASKER
    May 3, 1748. 10 pds. for 250 A. On SS Flatt Swamp adj. ABSOLOM HOLLAWAY, JOLL SANDERS. Wit: JOHN HARRELL, JOSIAH HARRELL. Feb. Court 1748.*.

G 173 JONATHAN STANDLY, SEN. TO GEORGE STANDLY
    Dec. 13, 1748. 40 pds. for 300 A. "...GEORGE STANDLY the son of JONATHAN STANDLY..." Land granted to JOHN MOLTON by patent March 9, 1717/18. On SS Horskie Swamp. "...only one hundred Excepted called by the Name of Jurnagins thicket..." Wit: JOHN _____, ANTHONY WEBB. Feb. Court 1748. *.

G 175 TIMOTHY VANPELT, carpenter TO THOMAS RYAN
    Feb. 2, 1747/48. 336 pds. for 300 A. and personal property. (1) 200 A. on NS Pellmell Pocoson by patent Feb. 14, 1739. (2) 100 A. On Great Beaver Dam dated Feb. 7, 1746. "...Likewise all my Hoggs mark'd with a Swallow (for?) in the Left Ear and Two under keels in the right Ear..." Wit: THOMAS TURNER, DAVID RYAN, EDWARD HOWARD. Feb. Court 1748. *.

G 177 WILLIAM ASHBURN, taylor TO THOMAS ASHBURN
    Feb. 26, 1747. 200 pds. for 200 A. + Negroes. Land at Cashia adj. RICHARD BRADLY, THOMAS ROGERS. "...also Nan and her son George and a Negro woman named Hannah & her Daughter named Patt..." Wit: WILLIAM TAYLOR, JAMES TART. Feb. Court 1748. *.

G 178 ELIZABETH BAKER, widow TO BENJAMIN BAKER, yeoman
    Oct. 12, 1747. "Stock, household stuff, goods, chattels and other personal estate...(for) Sundry Causes...easpecially for the consideration of the Boarding & Entertainment I have had and Expect to have from my son BENJAMIN BAKER..." Wit: JOHN WYNNS, SARAH WYNNS. Feb. Court 1748. *.

G 179 WILLIAM OUTLAW TO HARMON HOLLIMAN
    July 20, 1748. 15 pds. for 180 A. On ES Harts Delight Pocoson to Beaverdam Pocoson at Spring Branch adj. RICHARD WILLIFORD. Wit: WILLIAM HOSEA, ANN OUTLAW. Feb. Court *. JOHN LOVICK C/C.

G 180 LUKE MIZELL TO RICHARD & SUSANNA TOMLINSON
    Nov. 8, 1748. Gift. 110 A. "...in consideration of the Natural love and affection that I have and do bear unto RICHARD TOMLINSON and SUSANNA his wife...my Son and Daughter...and heirs begotten of the body of said SUSANNAH..." Land adj. JAMES LEGGITT, HUMPHREY BATE. Wit: LUKE MIZELL, JUN., JOHN WILLIAMS. May Court 1749. *.

G 181 WILLIAM HOOKER, Yeoman TO JAMES & STEVAN HOOKER
    April 6, 1749. Gift. 160 A. "...In consideration of Love goodwill and affection unto my Beloved Sons JAMES & STEVAN HOOKER..." Land on SS Wiccacon Creek adj. Coll. POLLOCK, School House Branch, JOHN WYNNS Mill Pond, "the line of my Fathers Patent...", WILLIAM HOOKER, JUN, Sandy Run, _____ OLIVER. Wit: JOHN WYNNS, JOHN BROWN. Jan Court 1749. *.

G 183 GEORGE LOCKHART, JAMES FLOOD, THOMAS RYAN, bondsmen
    May 8, 1749. 500 pds. Bond for GEORGE LOCKHART to be Sheriff of Bertie. Appt. by GABRIEL JOHNSTON, ESQ. for two years. Wit: JOHN HILL, JOHN LOVICK, JOHN SALLIS. *.*.

G 184 THOMAS RYAN TO PETER CHRISTIAN SHROCK, cordwainer
    April 8, 1749. 55 pds. for 70 A. On WS Eastermost Swamp adj. JOHN CAMPBELL, MICHAEL CAPEHART, PETER SHROCK, WILLIAM CAMPBELL. Wit: EDWARD RASOR, JOHN NICHOLLS, THOMAS ASHBURN. May Court 1749. JOHN LOVICK C/C.

G 185 RICHARD BRADLY TO THOMAS ROGERS, JUN.
    Jan. 4, 1747/48. 55 pds. for *. "my Dwelling Plantation in Kesia Neck" on SS Meadows adj. JOSEPH JORDAN, THOMAS ROGERS. Wit: WILLIAM LATTIMER, JOHN ROGERS, ROBERT ROGERS. May Court 1749. JOHN LOVICK C/C.

G 186 THOMAS HANSFORD TO ISAAC HUNTER of Chowan County
    Aug. 9, 1748. 50 pds. for 312 A. On Chowan River adj. WILLIAM

DOWNING, JOHN CHERRYHORN, "NUBYS Corner". Land now in the possession of EPHRAIM HUNTER. By patent to THOMAS HANSFORD dated "Edenton March 11 Anno Dom one Thousand Seven Hundred Forty...being the same land which was former- ly granted to THOMAS MARTIN by Patent (Feb. 28, 1704/05)" Wit: JENKINS HANSFORD, JAMES LESLIE, JOSEPH PERRY. May Court 1749. *.

G 187   THOMAS RYAN TO JOHN NICHOLLS, bricklayer
        Aug. 8, 1748. 800 pds. for 394 A. At Middle Swamp adj. WILLIAM GRILL, Mr. JOHNSTON. Wit: DAVID RYAN, WILLIAM GOODWIN EDWARD HOWARD. May Court 1749.*.

G 189   BEJAMIN WYNNS TO AARON ASKEW, yeoman
        Aug. 8, 1748. 12 pds. 10 sh. Land in Chinopen Neck adj. JOHN VANPELT, Polecat Branch. Wit: JOHN EARLY, THOMAS LEE. May Court 1749. *.

G 190   GEORGE GOULD TO JONATHAN MILLER
        Aug. 4, 1748. 50 pds. for 370 A. On Morulle Branch adj. JOHN PERRY. By grant to GOULD April 20, 1745. Wit: JOHN FIELD, WILLIAM GRAY. *.*.

G 191   BENJAMIN CLEMMONS (CLIMMONS) of Johnston Co. TO JOSHUA SPIVEY of Nansemond Co.   Nov. 15, 1748. 12 pds. for 200 A. "...it being a piece of Land which I purchased of JACOB HALLE..." At mouth of Myre Branch at Buck Swamp adj. JAMES PARKER. Wit: HENRY ROADS, WILLIAM KING, CHARLES KING. May Court 1749. *.

G 191   CHRISTOPHER HOLLIMON TO SAMUEL HOLLIMAN (HOLLIMON)
        May 6, 1749. 40 pds. for 200 A. "...by my Son SAMUEL HOLLIMON..." On SS Horskey Swamp adj. FRANCIS THOMAS(?), WILLIAM WEBB. Wit: WILLIAM WEBB, HENRY REED. *.*.

G 193   MOSES BAKER, Yeoman TO BENJAMIN HOLLIMAN
        Jan. 31, 1748. 30 pds. for 150 A. On ES Chinkapin Creek adj. JOHN SMITH at Flatt Swamp & Killum. Wit: JOHN WYNNS, JOHN SMITH, W. EVENS. May Court 1749. *.

G 194   BENJAMIN WYNNS TO JOSEPH HALL, yeoman
        Aug. 6, 1748. 25 pds. for 200 A. At Chinkapin Neck on Wiccacon Creek adj. AARON ASKEW, GEORGE MATHIAS LEVERMAN at Polecat Branch. "...Quitrents Since 25th day of March 1741 also accruing only Excepted..." Wit: JOHN EARLY, THOMAS LEE. May Court 1749. *.

G 195   THOMAS RYAN TO WILLIAM WILLSON
        Aug. 16, 1748. 120 pds. for 160 A. On NS Cashia Swamp at Poplar Branch. Wit: JOHN NICHOLLS, THOMAS HOULDER, JAMES JOLLY. May Court 1749.*.

G 196   JOHN FREEMAN TO THOMAS FREEMAN
        Aug. 4, 1748. 50 pds. for 150 A. + one water Grist Mill. On NS Bar- beque Swamp adj. THOMAS MACCLENDON, ____ GREEN. "...as by plann thereof Dated 10th day of August 1745..." Wit: PEGGY WYNNS, BENJAMIN ____. May Court 1749. *.

G 197   PETER WEST TO ELIZABETH COTTON & CHILDREN ABNER, CYRUS COTTON
        Nov. 15, 1748. Gift. Negroes. "...for Love that I do bear unto my Daughter ELIZABETH COTTON (I) do freely give unto her children to ABNER & CYRUS COTTON and to all the rest of the children of my s'd Daughter...one Negro woman Named Hannah & one Negro girl Named Butt and one Negro Boy named David & one Negro Girl Named Moll Daughter of the s'd Hannah...to my grandchildren (when they) shall be of the age of twenty one years..." *.*. May Court 1749. *.

G 198   JOHN CRICKET, taylor & Wife MARY TO FRANCIS PENRICE, carpenter of Chowan Co. Nov. 9, 1748. 50 pds. for 95 A. On Flatt Swamp of Cashy River adj. Coll. POLLOCK. Wit: WALTER DRAUGHAN, WILLIAM WOODE, JAMES WORDEN, JOHN CRICKET, JUN. Aug. Court 1749. JOHN LOVICK C/C.

G 199   WILLIAM FLEETWOOD & EDWARD RASOR TO WILLIAM ANDERSON, joyner
        Aug. 8, 1748. 18 pds. for 100 A. On NES Salmon Creek between CULLEN POLLOCK "which was formerly CARY GODBY's and That Tract of Land whereon EDWARD RASOR now dwells...Land held by patent obtained by SUSANNA JOHNSON bearing date the ___Day of April 1712..." Wit: JOHN NICHOLLS, HUMPHREY NI- CHOLLS, ANNA NICHOLLS. Aug. Court 1749. *.

G 200 GARRAD VANUPSTALL TO JOHN SALLIS
        March 8, 1748. 20 pds. for 100 A. On NS Cashy River "which will
appear from a Deed from THOMAS DAVIS to me the said UPSTALL..." Wit: THOMAS
WHITMELL, MARY PACE. Aug. Court 1749. JOHN LOVICK C/C.

G 202 MEDIA WHITE & WIFE ELIZABETH TO EDWARD RICE late of Perquimmons Co.
        May 15, 1749. 8 pds. 15 sh. for 380 A. On Chinkopin Orchard to Gum
Pocoson. Wit: THOMAS SLATTER, GEORGE CROMELL(?). Aug. Court 1750. *.

G 203 GEORGE STRAUGHAN TO WILLIAM BOYCE
        Aug. 9, 1749. 120 pds. for 220 A. On WS Cypress Swamp adj. LAURENCE
MAGEW. Wit: EDWARD COLLINS, WILLIAM EVERIT, WILLIAM SPARKMAN. Aug. Court
1749. *.

G 204 WILLIAM KNIGHT TO WILLIAM BARTER
        Aug. 5, 1749. 5 pds. for 140 A. On NS Poticasy Creek adj. LEONARD
LANSTON, ISRAEL JOHNSON, Bells Branch, HENRY COPLIN, ____BAKERS line. Wit:
JOHN BROWN, JOHN BENTON. Aug. Court 1749. *.

G 206 THOMAS RYAN TO DAVID BROADWELL, carpenter
        Feb. 13, 1749. 106 pds. for 200 A. Adj. JAMES CURRY on Pell Mell
Pocoson. Wit: JAMES CANADAY, DAVID RYAN. Aug. Court 1749. *.

G 207 BARNABY HELY DUNSTAN TO JENKINS HANSFORD
        Nov. 2, 1748. 60 pds. for 640 A. On SS Chinpapin Swamp adj. HERDINE
(?) VANPELT Dec'd. Formerly the Land of JOHN WHITE on PAUL BANCHES Land.
Adj. WILLIAM BADHAM ESQ., Dec'd. Wit: THOMAS HANSFORD, HENRY HANSFORD, WILL-
IAM HANSFORD. Aug. Court 1749. *.

G 209 JAMES LEGGITT TO JOHN ALLEN
        Aug. 8, 1749. 100 pds. for 150 A. On Roquist Swamp. Wit: THOMAS
WHITMELL, SAMUEL SINGLETON(?), WILLIAM LATTIMER, JOSEPH JORDAN. Aug. Court
1749. *.

G 210 JOHN JAMESON & WIFE ELIZABETH TO DAVID MEADE
        Aug. 8, 1749. 150 pds. for 640 A. (600 A. stated also). On NS Roanoke
River adj. CHARLES STEVENS at Village Swamp, JAMES CASTELLAW, ____WILLIAMS,
COLL. JONES. WIT: THOMAS BARKER, JAMES MATTHEWS. Aug. Court *. *.

G 212 WILLIAM KING TO CHARLES KING
        May 31, 1748. Gift. 4 A. "...love good will and affection...toward
my Loving Brother CHARLES KING...(4 A.)...being part of a tract of one
hundred acres which I now dwell..." Adj. CHARLES KING. Wit: CHARLES KING,
SEN., ELIZABETH KING. Aug. Court *. *.

G 212 JOSHUA WILKINSON TO JAMES BULLOCK
        Aug. 1, 1749. 32 pds. for 200 A. At head of Isaac Creek commonly
known as Walstons or Hokeirs Creek. Adj. JOHN WILLIAMS, JOHN MOOR. Wit:
WALTER SESSUMS, JOHN COOK. Aug. Court 1749. *.

G 214 JOHN CRICKET TO JONATHAN STANDLY
        Nov. 19, 1748. 2 pds. for 50 A. On NS Cashy near Lumber Bridge to
an Island. Wit: DAVID STANDLY, EDMOND STANDLY. Aug. Court 1749. *.

G 215 JAMES CURRIE (CURRY) TO THOMAS WHITMELL, merchant
        Aug. 8, 1749. 10 pds. for 50 A. Adj. WHITMELL, "formerly RICHARD
FRYARS Corner tree...Land said WHITMELL bought of JOHN WILLIAMS..." Wit:
WILLIAM WILLIAMS, JOHN BENTON. Aug. Court 1749. JOHN LOVICK C/C.

G 216 EDWARD WRIGHT of Nansemond Co., Va. to BENJAMIN WYNNS
        Jan. 1, 1745. 80 pds. for 630 A. On WS Chowan River. Land that was
sold to EDWARD WRIGHT by ROBERT ROGERS by deed Nov. 13, 1738. Wit: WILLIAM
WRIGHT, JUN., NATHANIEL WRIGHT, JOHN ASKEW. Nov. Court 1749. *.

G 217 RICHARD BROWN, yeoman TO ISAAC HILL, cooper
        June 2, 1749. 3 pds. for 46 A. In Chinkopin Neck adj. THOMAS ARCHER.
Wit: LEWIS WILLIAMS, WILLIAM BROWN. Nov. Court *. JOHN LOVICK C/C.

G 218 JOSHUA STEVANS TO WILLIAM TYNER
        Mar. 10, 1748. 200 pds. for 190 A. On NS Chinkapin Swamp adj. RICHARD
HOMES. Wit: JOHN FREEMAN, JOHN DAVISON, JOHN DAVISON,SEN. Nov. Court 1749. *.

G 220 ABRAHAM HERRING TO ARNOLD HOPKINS
        Jan. 9, 1748/49. 20 pds. for 380 A. On SS Bear Swamp. Wit: JOHN
REDDITT, THOMAS LAWRENCE. November Court 1749. JOHN LOVICK C/C.

G 221 CHARLES HARDY TO JOSEPH WYMBERLY, merchant
        Nov. 15, 1749. 20 pds. for 339 A. On Roquiss Pocoson adj. JOHN
HARDY, MARTIN GARDNER. Wit: JOHN WYNNS, BENJAMIN WYNNS. November Court.*.

G 223 THOMAS WALKER TO PETER WEST
        Oct. 9, 1744. 1 pd. for 100 A. Adj. JACOB LASKER, ___WALKER. Wit:
SARAH WEST, JACOB LASKER, BRYAN HARE. November Court *. JOHN LOVICK C/C.

G 224 JOHN EDWARDS TO JOHN BROGDEN, JUN.
        Nov. 15, 1749. 30 pds. for 340 A. On ES Roquist Swamp adj. PHILLIP
WALSTON, JONATHAN STANDLY, COLL. CULLEN POLLOCK. Wit: JOSEPH WYMBERLY,
SAMUEL MOORE. November Court *. JOHN LOVICK C/C.

G 226 THOMAS FREEMAN TO JAMES HOLLY
        Nov. 15, 1749. 14 pds. for 209 A. On WS Barbeque Swamp. Part of a
patent formerly belonging to JOHN HOWELL, SEN. Wit: JOHN DAVISON, JUN.,
PETER EVANS. November Court *. JOHN LOVICK C/C.

G 227 ARTHUR WILLIAMS TO EDWARD VAN
        *. 20 pds. for 212 A. On ES Roquiss Pocoson. A survey granted to
JOHN WILLIAMS Aug. 8, 1720. Wit: WILLIAM KING, JOSHUA LANG. November
Court *. JOHN LOVICK C/C.

G 228 THOMAS HOLDER TO JOHN SPRING
        Nov. 15, 1749. 1 pd. 10 sh. for 100 A. On NS Cashy Swamp at Water-
ing Hole Branch adj. WILLIAM LEVINER. Wit: EDWARD RASOR, CHARLES MITCHEL.
November Court *. JOHN LOVICK C/C.

G 229 WILLIAM WRIGHT of Nansemond Co., Va. TO BENJAMIN WYNNS
        January *, 1745. 50 pds. for 100 A. On Deep Creek adj. STEPHEN
WILLIAMS, ROBERT ROGERS. Near May Pring Branch. Land purchased of MARGERY
and GIDDEON GILBERT Feb. 6, 1743. Wit: EDWARD WRIGHT, JOHN ASKERS. November Court *. JOHN LOVICK C/C.

G 231 SOLOMON HOMES of Johnston Co. TO DAVID MEADE, merchant, of Nansemond
        Co., Va. Sep. 25, 1749. 60 pds. for 140 A. On NS Roanoke River
at Peach Pocoson adj. EDWARD HOWARD. Part of a tract granted JOHN STEW-
ART(?) March 1, 1721. Wit: WILLIAM WILLIAMS, LAURENCE TOOLE, GURRALDUS(?)
O BRYAN. November Court *. JOHN LOVICK C/C.

G 232 THOMAS FREEMAN TO JOHN REED (READ)
        Oct. 8, 1749. 50 pds. for 151 A. "...One messuage or Tract of Land
with a grinding mill upon it & all that belongs to the s'd mill..." On
Barbeque Swamp adj. THOMAS MCCLINDON, ___GREEN at Chinkapin Fork. Wit:
JOHN SMITH, WILLIAM COLTHRED(?) November Court *. JOHN LOVICK C/C.

G 233 LUKE MIZELL TO MARTHA MIZELL
        Nov. 13, 1749. Gift. 100 A. "...unto my well beloved Daughter..."
Land adj. RICHARD TOMLINSON, JAMES LEGGITT, ___COLLINS. Wit: LUKE MIZELL,
JUN., RICHARD TOMLINSON. November Court *. JOHN LOVICK C/C.

G 235 ANTHONY WILLIAMS of New Hanover Co. TO JOHN WYNNS
        Dec. 29, 1747. Power of atty. 1170 A. Power to "sign deed to JOHN
BAKER son & Legatie of HENRY BAKER Dec'd... Land granted to my Grandfather
LEWIS WILLIAMS...." On Ahotskey Swamp. Wit: JOHN BAKER, ABSOLOM WESTON,
WILLIAM BOONE. November Court 1749. JOHN LOVICK C/C.

G 235 ANTHONY WILLIAMS of New Hanover Co. TO JOHN BAKER, joyner
        *. 10 pds. for 100 A. "...ANTHONY WILLIAMS Heir at Law to LEWIS
WILLIAMS the Elder Late of that part of Chowan now called Bertie County
Dec'd..." Land between Catherine Creek and Deep Creek adj. CAPT. BENJAMIN
WYNNS, EDWARD HARE "the heir or Legatee of WILLIAM GARRAT Dec'd..." Land
to include a place called Hickry Neck patented to LEWIS WILLIAMS April 1,
1713. Signed: JOHN WILLIAMS atty. for ANTHONY WILLIAMS. Wit: PEGGY WYNNS,
BENJAMIN WYNNS. November Court 1749. JOHN LOVICK C/C.

G 237 JONATHAN MELTON of Onslow Co. TO JOHN HARRILL, JUN.

Sep. 27, 1749. 6 pds. for 640 A. Land on NS Roanoke River "...but was formerly called Chowan precinct being Pattant formerly grated to RICHARD MELTON bearing Date 6th day of April 1722...." Adj. GEORGE WILLIAMS, BENJAMIN FOREMAN. Wit: JOHN COOPER, WILLIAM BARBER, WILLIAM TISER. November Court 1749. JOHN LOVICK C/C.

G 238 LUKE MIZELL TO ELIZABETH MIZELL
Nov. 13, 1749. Gift. 100 A. "...To my well beloved Daughter ELIZABETH MIZELL...." Adj. ____COLLINS, MARTHA MIZELL. Wit: LUKE MIZELL, JUN., RICHARD TOMLINSON. November Court 1749. JOHN LOVICK C/C.

G 239 JOHN DAVISON & JOHN WYNNS TO JOHN SMITH of Chinkapin in Bertie
Sep. 1, 1749. 6 pds. 10 sh. for 100 A. Land on SS Chinkapin Swamp at Myery Branch. Wit: ANN REASONS, J. WYNNS. November Court 1719. JOHN LOVICK C/C.

G 240 WILLIAM BUSH TO MICHAEL WARD, JUN.
Oct. 20, 1749. 7 pds. for 210 A. "...WILLIAM BUSH heir at Law to JOHN BUSH late of Bertie Deaseased...." Land on WS Quoyokason Run. By patent to the late JOHN BUSH dated March 9, 1717/18.. "Quitrent preceeding the 29th day of Sep'r 1747 & Since only Excepted...." Wit: J. WYNNS, WILLIAM HOOKER, ANN REASONS. November Court 1749. JOHN LOVICK C/C.

G 241 ISAAC HILL TO DEMSEY WOOD
July 19, 1749. 10 pds. for 50 A. On SS Stoney Creek at Horsepen Branch to Halfmoon Branch. Wit: JOSEPH BARRADIAL, JESSE WOOD. November Court 1749. JOHN LOVICK C/C.

G 242 JOHN BAKER, yeoman TO BENJAMIN WYNNS, carpenter
July 4, 1748. 34 pds. for 100 A. Between Deep Creek & Catron Creek "commonly known as Hickory Neck..." Adj. BENJAMIN WYNNS, EDWARD HARE to Wolfpit Branch. Wit: WILLIAM BROWN, W. SMITH, JOHN ASKEW. November Court 1749. JOHN LOVICK C/C.

G 244 MICHAEL HILL TO SAMUEL COOK
Oct. 19, 1749. 64 pds. for 200 A. In Blackwalnut Swamp adj. ____ HOLBROOK, ____ HILL, THOMAS RYAN, "LAWRENCE SARSONS Dec'd..." Wit: ARTHUR WILLIAMS, JOHN BYRD. November Court 1749. JOHN LOVICK C/C.

G 245 WILLIAM WYNNS, merchant TO JOHN BARTON
July 20, 1749. 50 pds. for 300 A. On SWS Chowan River adj. SAMUEL WILLIAMS, WILLIAM WYNNS at Deep Branch. Wit: JOHN BAKER, CULM. SESSIONS, JAS. HOOKER, GEO. WYNNS, JUN. November Court 1749. JOHN LOVICK C/C.

G 247 WILLIAM WYNNS, merchant TO JOSEPH WYNNS, millwright
Feb. 9, 1748/49. 125 pds. for 130 A. On SWS Chowan River commonly called Mount Pleasant at Wilt Catt Gutt adj. ____POLLOCK, ____SHARP, THOMAS HINES, JOHN BARKER at Anthony Branch on Wiccacon Creek. Wit: JOHN JIMSON, GEO. WYNNS, JUN. November Court 1749. JOHN LOVICK C/C.

G 248 ROBERT ROGERS of Chowan Precinct TO EDWARD WRIGHT of Nansemond Co..
Va. Nov. 13, 1738. 20 pds. for 630 A. At Deep Creek adj. Catherine Creek. By patent dated Sep. 7, 1725 to LAZARUS THOMAS and by sale to ROGERS from THOMAS. Wit: JETHRO SUMNER, WILLIAM WRIGHT, JUN., ROBERT ROGERS, JUN. November Court 1738. JOHN WYNNS C/C.

G 252 EDWARD WRIGHT of Nansemond Co., Va. TO BENJAMIN WYNNS
July 27, 1749. 5 sh. for 630 A. "...Within mentioned deed..." Wit: JOHN BUXTON, JOHN ASKEW. November Court 1749. JOHN LOVICK C/C.

G 252 OWEN DANIEL of Edgecombe Precinct in County of Bath TO RICHARD ROWLAND. Oct. 23, 1734. A Young Horse. For 137 A. "...In consideration of a young Horse...." Land on ES Wattom Swamp at Posom Branch adj. COLL. WEST. Wit: JOHN SHOLAR, WILLIAM GARDNER, MARTIN GARDNER. *.*.

G 253 RICHARD ROWLAND TO JOHN SHOLAR
Feb. 2, 1748/49. *.*. "...my whole wright Title & interest of this within mentioned Deed..." Wit: WILLIAM SHOLAR, W. PICKET. November Court 1749. JOHN LOVICK C/C.

204

G 254   INVENTORY OF GEORGE COULD, ESQ.
     Nov. 14, 1749. "GEO. GOULD late deceased & taken into the possesion
of BENJAMIN HILL & THOMAS BARKER appointed administrators of the Goods and
Chattels...in consequence of the Said GEORGE GOULD..."

1 clock
1 Looking Glass
1 Smaller D'o
8 small pictures in frames
1 desk
1 Tea Chest
2 China Punch Bowls
2 muggs
1 Coffee Mill
2 pair Window curtains
6 Tea Spoons
3 Large Silver Spoons
1 Bed Counter Pan & Pillows
1 Bible
The Religion of Nature Delinated
1 tea board
1 case with bottles
3 pair of shoes
2 Vinigar Cruits
peper box & Equipage
4 small China bowls
5 cups
4 chairs
2 Decanters
17 p's glass
1 flask
5 hides
10 table cloaths
6 towels
10 shirts
2 waist coats
6 caps Linnen
1 Do Veloet(velvet?)
1 pair Steelgards
3 Loves Sugar
6 Candle moulds
8 Dalph plates
2 black Jacks
1 pewter Tankards
1 case of knives & forks
3 brass Candlesticks
1 Spire morter
1 Tea kettle
1 Coffee port
2 chockolat Mills
12 prints in frames
3 pair Stockings
1 fluke Hoe
1 Shear of cotter
4 Brick Moulds
1 branding Iron
1 Garden Rake
2 wedges
2 hand saws
1 spade
2 grubing(?) hoes
1 Grind Stone
The Office of a Justice
   of Peace DON FRANCISCO
   DEQUEVADO
Calves Letters 3 vol.
The whole duty of a
   communicant
1 old Bible

2 tin Collenders & 2 covers
3 Iron pots
1 skillet
1 pot Rack
2 pair hand Irons
1 Gun
1 Pair Boots
1 Search & cover to it
27 Pewter Plates
5 dishes D'o
2 Basons D'o
2 pillow cases
15 sheets
3 old wast coate(s)
2 Flannel
2 Coates
1 pair Cloath Brickers
1 Great Coate
1 Bed tick & Bolster
2 Feather Beds
2 bolsters
3 pillows
1 counterpane
5 Blankets
1 Large hair trunk
1 small D'o
1 red Leather D'o
2 chests
1 Great Wheel
1 box Iron
9 casks
1 Stone Jugg
29 bottles
27 head neat cattle
6 calves
6 horses
1 Mare & Colt
12 sheep
8 Negroes (young & old)
"one D'o said to be sold
   to Mr. WHEATLY..."
2 Sermon Books in Mr
   LOVICKs hands
1 Book at Mr. CRICKETs
1 desk
2 coates
4 wast coates
3 pair Brickes
1 shirt
10 wine glasses
35 head of hogs
   (young & old)
1 silver watch
2 Basons
1 pair silver knee
   buckles
1 bridle & saddle
1 port mantell
1 frock wast coat
   & Briches
1 Sword & Belt
1 Wigg
1 pair chext Trouzers

1 pair of Books at
   Gov'nors
1 pair of money scales
1 fork
1 ink pot
2 horn combs
2 cannesters (Some Tea
   in one)
a few medicines
2 papers spices
1 prayer book
1 Tea cup
5 Nutmegs
A Small parcell of
   Coffee
1 pin cushion
1 bible Mr. LOVICK has
Paradice Lost
Death of Steaven by
   Mr. Watts
miscellanions collections
1 Vol Shakespears
   Plays
one D'o Gaurdian
1 Vol Bens Works
14 cups
12 Sauces
2 China Dishes
3 pair stockings
1 Bobb Wigg
1 Major Wigg
2 pair stockings
13 stocks
2 shirts
1 handkerchief
1 cup
1 Neck cloath
2 spits
1 chain
1 cheese Toaster
1 Grid Iron
5 weeding hoes
6 axes
3 hilling hoes
1 old Tennant Saw
2 handkerchiefs
3 Cravats
2 shirts
2 caps
1 pair Shoe Buckles
1 pair pumps
1 pair Silk Garters
1 Hatt
Virginia Money in a
   Silk purse
   (31 pds, 19 sh 2d)
New Bills
   (50 pds, 8 sh 8d)
Old Bills
   (1 pd, 10 sh)
Encharidon

"...(being) Goods & money belonging to the Estate of GEORGE GOULD Esq late
of North Carolina Deaseased...(taken) in Consequence of Letters of Adminis-

tration granted to them by His Excellency GABRIEL JOHNSTON Esq...." Signed: ELIZABETH GOULD. Wit: THOMAS HANSFORD, JOSEPH BUTTERTON.

G 255 WILLIAM JOHNSON of Surry Co., Va. TO EDWARD RASOR
July 19, 1749. 26 pds. for 740 A. Land on Eastermost Swamp, Salmon Creek adj. CULLEN POLLOCK, SEN., JOHN CAMPBELL. By a patent obtained by WILLIAM GRILLS Dec'd. "...Including the Plantation where the s'd EDWARD RASOR now Dwells, as also that where WILLIAM ANDERSON now Dwells...." Wit: THOMAS RYAN, THOMAS(?) CASTELLAW, WILLIAM RICE. November Court 1749. *.

G 256 MICHAEL & ISBELL KING, mother of MICHAEL TO SIMON BRYAN
Jan. 2, 1749. 66 pds. for 250 A. Land on Maple Branch adj. EDWARD BYRD, ROBERT WEST, THOMAS MITCHEL, ____IDOOLBROOK at Round Pocoson. Wit: EDWARD BRYAN, ROBERT WEST, HUMPHREY LAURENCE. February Court 1749. *.

G 258 WILLIAM ANDREWS TO THOMAS ANDREWS
Feb. 14, 1749. 20 pds. for 100 A. Land by patent dated April 1, 1718 at Mill Branch adj. THOMAS WILLIAMS. Wit: WILLIAM SISE, MATTHEW SEAY, MARTHA ANDREWS. February Court 1749. *.

G 259 THOMAS JACOCKS TO CHARLES JACOCKS
June 29, 1749. Gift. Negro. "...I do freely give to my Nephew... son of CHARLES JACOCKS my Brother a Negro Girl named Aimy She being about Eight years Old...." Wit: SIMON BRYAN, ROBERT WEST, EDWARD BRYAN. *.*.

G 260 MICHAEL WARD TO RODGER BADGETT
Dec. 27, 1749. 28 pds. for 100 A. On SS Quiockson Swamp at Cabin Branch and Crooked Branch. Wit: JOHN DROUGHAN, ROBERT DROUGHAN, JOHN OUT-LAW. February Court 1749. *.

G 261 BARTHOLOMEW FIGURES of Northampton Co. TO JOSEPH WETHERINGTON
Jan. 9, 1749/50. 15 pds. for 50 A. On NS Wiccacon Creek on ES of a Gutt. Wit: RICHARD FIGURES, BARTHOLOMEW FIGURES, JOSEPH FIGURES, WILLIAM FIGURES. February Court 1749. *.

G 262 EDWARD HOCUTT TO BENJAMIN HOOKER
June 3, 1748. 20 pds. for 50 A. On a branch of Mount Pleasant Mill Creek adj. WILLIAM HOOKER, ____ BENNITTS. At Sandy Run. Wit: WILLIAM HOOKER, JUN., STEPHEN HOOKER (HACKER), JAMES BENNITT. February Court 1749.

G 262 MICHAEL HILL TO JAMES MCDOWALL
May 28, 1749. 10 pds. for 100 A. Land on Bucklesbury Swamp adj. JOHN WILLIAMS, ABRAHAM HERRING "Containing one Hundred Ackers Sqwair from the s'd WILLIAMS line...." Wit: JOHN SALLIS, ARNAL HOPKINS. Feb. Court 1749. *.

G 264 ELEXANDER KANADAY TO ROGER BADGETT
Oct. 24, 1749. 60 "Barrells of Tarr" for 150 A. On NS Cabin Branch adj. EDWARD OUTLER, WILLIAM FREEMAN. Wit: WILLIAM HOSEA, ELEXANDER KANA-DAY, WILLIAM WILLAFORD. February Court 1749. *.

G 265 THOMAS ANDREWS TO WILLIAM ANDREWS
Feb. 14, 1749. 20 pds. for 100 A. "...Where THOMAS ANDREWS now liveth being part of one patent bearing Date the first day of March Anno 1721...." At Panter Gut adj. NORFLEETs line on Roanoke River. Wit: WILL-IAM TISE, MATTHEW SEAY, MARTHA ANDREWS. February Court 1749. *.

G 266 FRANCES OLIVER TO JOHN OLIVER
August 1, 1749. Bargain. Negroe plus land. "...FRANCES OLIVER widow and Relict of ANDREWS OLIVER late of Bertie County...." One negro man named Beckwith and a certain parcel of land. "...JOHN OLIVER doth bar-gain covenant and agree with the s'd FRANCES OLIVER to pay all Funeral Charges all Just and Lawfull Debts which was due and owing from the s'd Deceased ANDREW OLIVER's Estate...and to pay and Deliver to s'd FRANCES OLIVER fifteen Barr'l's of Good merchantable corn in the year one Thousand and Seven hundred and Fifty...." Wit: JOSEPH JORDAN, RICHARD TOMLINSON. February Court 1749. *.

G 267 REBECCA PINNER....An Affadidavit
"Bertie County. This day came before me REBECCAH PINNER & made oath

that She Saw her Father JOHN RASBERRY deceased give and Deliver unto JOHN RASBERRY the Son of the s'd Deceased a Certain Negro fellow Called Tom but not that he Should be possessed with him till after the death of the s'd Deceased & his wife. Given under my hand this 6th day of January 1749/40. J. EARLY, J.P." Wit: WILLIAM HOSEA, WILLIAM RASBERRY. *.*.

G 267   THOMAS JOHNSON TO JOSIAH JOHNSON
        Gift. "To my Loving son...my Goods and Chattels Implym's household Stuff Ready money and all other things to me belonging...To be delivered to the s'd JOSIAH JOHNSON (when he) Shall arrive at the age of Eighteen Years ...." Wit: PETER EVANS, JOSEPH HARRELL. February Court 1749. *.

G 268   GEORGE SMITH of New Hannovah TO JOHN HURST of North Hampton
        Jan. 22, 1749/50. 80 pds. for 400 A. On Kesia River at Roquest Swamp. Wit: WILLIAM STOKES, WILLIAM BARBER, PHILLIP WALSTON, DANIEL PEGRAM. February Court 1749. JOHN LOVICK C/C.

G 269   WILLIAM HOOKER, JUN. TO WILLIAM WITHERINGTON
        Feb. 27, 1749/50. 16 pds. for 50 A. On NS Wiccacon Creek Adj. ____ SHARP, ____ BAKER, ____ FIGURES. Wit: BURILL BELL, RICHARD FIGURES, JOSEPH WITHERINGTON. February Court 1749. *.

G 270   WILLIAM SHARP TO PETER EVANS, carpenter
        *. 34 pds. *. Land formerly called Brambles Old Field on Wiccacon Creek at Broad Neck Branch adj. COLL. GEORGE POLLOCK at head of Spring Branch. Wit: WILLIAM HOOKER, JUN., JEAN(?) HOOKER, WILLIAM SHARP. February Court 1749. SAMUEL ORMES C/C.

G 271   JOHN BAZEMORE TO FRANCIS THOMAS
        *. 10 pds. for 50 A. Part of a tract JOHN BAZEMORE bought of HENRY VIZE on NS Hoskey Swamp. Adj. CHRISTOPHER HOLLYMAN, JUN. Wit: WILLIAM HOSEA, JOSEPH HALL. February Court 1749. JOHN LOVICK C/C.

G 272   JOSEPH BLACKMAN of Johnston Co. TO THOMAS BARKER of Edgecombe Co.
        Jan. 13, 1749. 75 pds. for 150 A. On NS Morrattock River adj. JOHN WILLIAMS at Grays Marsh. Adj. THEOPHILUS WILLIAMS. Tract of land formerly granted by patent to GEORGE STEVENSON. Wit: JOHN BROWN, THOMAS PUGH. May Court 1750. JOHN LOVICK C/C.

G 273   JOHN JONES & WIFE JUDITH TO THOMAS WALKER
        May 3, 1750. One Negro Woman for 600 A. "...woman named Moll & her child named Carles...(land) Near Bertie Old Court House...One acre Excepted for the Old Court House which has bin Transferred by the above said JONES ...." By patent dated Dec. 3, 1728. Wit: JOHN BRICKELL, BRYAN HARE, JOHN BROWN. May Court 1750. JOHN LOVICK C/C.

G 275   JOHN LOVICK of Craven Co. TO GABRIEL JOHNSTON
        April 19, 1750. 500 pds. for 2000 A. Land known by the name of Horse Meadow. Adj. HENRY KING at Briery Branch and Flatt Swamp on Great Beaver Dam and ES Vicars Branch. Wit: GEORGE NICHOLAS, SAMUEL ORMES, Edenhouse April 19, 1750. JAMES HASELL, C.J.

G 277   PAUL PENDER TO GILSTRAP WILLIAMS
        April 4, 1750. 24 pds. for 320 A. Land adj. CHARLES ROYALSES. Wit: J. EARLY, JAMES EARLY. May Court 1750. John Lovick c/c.

G 278   JAMES RUTLAND of North Hampton Co. TO JOHN WEST
        Sep. 9, 1749. 9 pds for 100 A. "Night Watom Meadows" at Snuffmill Branch. Part of patent formerly granted THOMAS GENT for 300 A. Dated Sep. 22, 1730. Wit: CHARLES HORNE, MICHAEL HORNE. May Court 1750. *.

G 280   THOMAS SUTTON, JUN. TO JAMES LOCKHART
        April 28, 1750. 50 pds. for 180 A. "...Whereas MARY JONES of the County...mentioned by her Last Will & Testament...bequeathed unto me...her Nephew...that Plantation on which she lived...." Land on Cashoke adj. the Deceased CAPT. HENDERSON. Wit: GEORGE LOCKHART, JOHN BURN, GRISALL BURN. May Court 1750. JOHN LOVICK C/C.

G 281   JOHN REED, miller TO WILLIAM WYNNS
        April 8, 1750. 110 pds for 4 Negro Slaves. "...Slaves...one Negro man named Ceasar, one Negro woman Hannah, one Negro Girl Phebe, one Negro

Boy called Ceasar..." Wit: DANIEL VANPELT, JOSEPH PERRY, RICHARD BROWN.
May Court 1750. JOHN LOVICK C/C.

G 282 MICHAEL HILL TO ROBERT HUNTER
       May 9, 1750. 60 pds. for 205 A. On Fork of Cashy at Wills Quarter
adj. COLL. ROBERT WEST. Wit: JOHN HILL, HUMPHREY BATE. May Court 1750. *.

G 282 JOHN HOWELL TO JOHN BROWN, JOHN WYNNS, THOMAS WHITMELL, Vestrymen
       March 1, 1749. 5 sh. for 1 A. "Vestrymen & Trustees appointed to
build & Errect a Chappell in Society Parrish...Land near the Main Road...
(adj.) the plantation whereon I now live and whereon St. John's Chappell is
to be errected & Built...for use and Benefit and Service of Some Parishion-
ers of Society Parish...and all other Christian Disposed persons for the
use of a church...." Wit: JOHN RIEUSSET, JOHN CAMPBELL. May Court 1750. *.

G 284 WILLIAM STANSSELL & WIFE AFRICA of Johnston Co. TO JOSEPH JORDAN
       May 5, 1750. 15 pds. for 50 A. "...where JOHN HARRIS JUN now liveth
..." A tract commonly called "JNO HARRISS Land." Wit: JOHN HARRISON, JOHN
STANSELL, JUN., REBECCA STANCELL. May Court 1750. JOHN LOVICK C/C.

G 286 HARMON HOLLOMON TO RICHARD WILLIFORD
       *. 14 pds. for 150 A. "...A certain Devident or half Tract of Land
..." On ES Hearts Delight Pocoson at Spring Branch at Beaverdam Pocoson.
Land purchased from WILLIAM OUTLAW which OUTLAW purchased of ROBERT EVANS.
Wit: WILLIAM WILLIFORD, JOHN WYNNS, MOSES WOOD. May Court 1750. JOHN
LOVICK C/C.

G 287 DEMSY WOOD TO JOSEPH (JESSE) WOOD
       Aug. 28, 1749. 7 sh. 6 p. for 100 A. "...of my Brother JOSEPH WOOD
...(bought) of ISAAC HILL...." Land on WS Halfmoon Branch. Wit: WILLIAM
HOSEA, WILLIAM RASBURY. May Court 1750. JOHN LOVICK C/C.

G 288 JOEL SANDERS TO PAUL PENDER
       Oct. 28, 1749. 21 pds. for 320 A. Adj. CHARLES ROYAL, Wit: JAMES
EARLY, JOHN EARLY. May Court 1750. JOHN LOVICK C/C.

G 289 ROBERT WEST TO MICHAEL HILL
       May 9, 1750. 60 pds. for 205 A. At fork of Cashy and Wills Quarter
Swamp in Cashy Swamp. Adj. ROBERT WEST. Wit: JOHN HILL, HUMPHREY BATE.
May Court 1750. JOHN LOVICK C/C.

G 290 THOMAS YEATS TO ANTHONY FILGO
       April 7, 1750. 150 pds. for 340 A. By patent dated April 8, 1745.
Adj. JOHN OXLEY, GEORGE GOULD. Wit: JOHN CAKE, JUN., WILLIAM CAKE. May
Court 1750. JOHN LOVICK C/C.

G 292 GEORGE CAPEHART, shoemaker TO MICHAEL CAPEHART
       Aug. 9, 1750. 6 pds. for 90 A. On NES Eastermost Swamp of Salmon
Creek adj. JOHN CAMPBELL. Wit: EDWARD RASOR, GEORGE CAPEHART, JUN., WILL-
IAM KEETOR. August Court 1750. EDWARD RASOR C/C.

G 293 HENRY VANLUVAN TO HENRY KING
       Aug. 11, 1750. 25 pds for 440 A. Adj. WILLIAM JONES. Out of a pat-
ent of 640 A. Wit: W. DIFES, WILLIAM BELL, JOSEPH HARDY. August Court
1750. EDWARD RASOR. (EDWARD RASOR is listed as Court Recorder.)

G 294 ABSOLOM HOLLOWELL of Surry Co., Va. TO PAUL PENDER
       June 7, 1750. 5 pds. for 320 A. "...Land which fell to me by my
Brother THOMAS HOLLOWELL Deas'd...." On SWS Flat Swamp adj. GILSTRAP WIL-
LIAMS. Wit: WILLIAM GODWIN, GILSTRAP WILLIAMS. August Court 1750. EDWARD
RASOR C/R.

G 295 JOHN PUGH TO JAMES COPELAND of Nansemond Co., Va.
       Aug. 14, 1750. 16 pds. 10 sh for 100 A. "...JOHN PUGH Son of FRAN-
CIS PUGH...." Land on ES Elm Swamp adj. JAMES COPELAND "and formerly known
by JAMES BOONs Corner Tree....", land formerly JOHN BEVERLYs. Wit: THOMAS
JACKSON, JOHN BRICKELL, HENRY HUNTER. August Court 1750. EDWARD RASOR C/R

G 297 JOHN OLIVER & WIFE SARAH of Society Parish TO JOHN SMITH
       March 12, 1749/50. 34 pds. for 200 A. Land in Society Parish adj.

JOHN HUDGSON at Conakogs(?) Run. Part of a tract formerly granted ROBERT COGSWELL and NATHNIEL DOMINY on Aug. 29., 1713. Wit: JOHN HILL, MARTHA HILL. August Court 1750. "...SARAH the wife of JOHN OLIVER was privately Examined by JNO BROWN Esq. one of his Majesty's Justices of the peace for s'd County, sho declared She acknowledged the Same freely willingly and without compultion...." EDWARD RASOR C/R.

G 301 WILLIAM SPEIGHT TO JOHN WATSON
    March 12, 1749/50. 30 pds for 240 A. On Roquiss Swamp by patent Feb. 23, 1727. Wit: HENRY HUNTER, MARY EVERET. August Court 1750. EDWARD RASOR C/R.

G 298 JOSEPH WATSFORD TO JOHN WYNNS, yeoman
    May 10, 1749. 5 pds for 106 A. "Two Percells of Land Joyning to- gether on the North West Side of Longbranch of Killum bequeathed to me by my Deaseased Father JOSEPH WOTSFORD...." Adj. JOHN WOTSFORD, "s'd WYNNS." Wit: ANN REASONS, JOHN SUEISS, THOMAS MORRISS, JOHN WOTSFORD. August Court 1750. EDWARD RASOR C/C.

G 299 JOHN SUTTON TO JAMES LOCKHART of Scotch Hall
    May 17, 1750. 15 pds for 100 A. "...JOHN SUTTON of the province a'f's'd son of THOMAS SUTTON SEN...Whereas MARY JONES my Aunt by her Last Will & Testam't...bequeathed to me JOHN SUTTON...part of that Plantation on which She lived...." In Cashoke. Adj. Hendersons Corner on Moratock Bay at Spring Branch. Wit: GEORGE LOCKHART, NATHANIEL SYLVESTER(?), ELIZABETH LOCKHART. August Court 1750. EDWARD RASOR C/C.

G 302 STEPHEN BROWN TO JOHN SPEIR
    Dec. 11, 1749. 17 pds. for 100 A. "...within the Prongs of Killum" Adj. JOHN WYNNS, JAMES BROWN, FRANCIS BROWN. August Court 1750. *.

G 302 JOHN WYNNS, yeoman TO JAMES BURRASS
    May 5, 1750 (also listed Jan. 1, 1744). 15 pds. for 200 A. Land on SS Flatt Swamp of Killum and ES of the Old Road at Old Bridge. Adj. ‾‾ WHITE. Wit: THOMAS HANSFORD, WILLIAM HANSFORD. August Court 1750. *.

G 303 JOHN JONES[+]TO JOHN HOWELL, yeoman
    Aug. 10, 1750. 50 pds for 150 A. On NS Chinkapin Swamp adj. JOHN WILSON, adj. land "formerly the property of PHILLIP BROWN." Wit: JOHN CAMPBELL, JOHN RICUSSET(?) August Court 1750. (+JOHN JONES listed as a "sawyer.")

G 304 MICHAEL HILL TO THOMAS RYAN
    February * 1749/50. 55 pds for 980 A. (1) 540 A. on NS Buckels Berry Swamp adj. ROBERT LAWRENCE, WILLIAM RIDDITT Deacesed, JOHN WILLIAMS, MR. DUCKENFIELD, JOSEPH HARDY. (2) 440 A. On ES Buckels berry Pocoson adj. JOHN MICHEL, DAVID HICK, THOMAS RYAN, SAMUEL COOK. "Lands was Granted Mr. JOHN HARDY Deaceased and was by Virtue of his Will given to the s'd MICHEL ..." Wit: RICHARD TOMLINSON, DAVID RYAN, JOHN BOWING. August Court 1750.

G 305 JOHN GILBERT TO ISAAC STALLONS (STALIONS)
    March 13, 1749. 25 pds. for 100 A. On ES Coneritsrat Swamp adj. JOHN GILBERT, WILLIAM WILLIAMSON. Wit: JOHN SHOLAR, JOHN WYNNS, RICHARD WILLIFORD. August Court 1750. EDWARD RASOR C/R.

G 306 JOHN CRICKET, taylor to WILLIAM SPARKMAN
    Jan. 3, 1748. 120 pds. for 200 A. adj. MICHAEL RISHA in Lorrill Pocoson. Wit: JOHN NICHOLLS, JUN., JAMES PURSSELL, ROBERT DRAUGHAN. August Court 1750. EDWARD RASOR C/R.

G 307 FRANCES HOBSON of Tyrrell Co. TO ROBERT HOWELL
    July 18, 1750. 20 pds for 100 A. On NS Roquiss Islands. Part of patent of 220 A. Wit: SAMUEL SINGLETON, HANNAH SINGLETON. August Court 1750. EDWARD RASOR C/R.

G 308 JACOB LASHER & WIFE MARY TO EDWARD SCULL OF Nansemond Co., Va.
    Oct. 21, 1749. 12 pds for 250 A. On Flatt Swamp. Wit: PAUL PENDER, SOLOMON PENDER. August Court 1750. EDWARD RASOR C/C.

G 310 JACOB LASHER TO ALEXANDER COTTON

Sep. 9, 1749. 4 pds. 16 sh. for 40 A. "Butted and bounded on the main Road that Leads to THOS. JACKSONs Ferry & the Run of the Elm Swamp..." Wit: SOLOMON PENDER, EDWARD SCULL. August Court 1750. EDWARD RASOR C/C.

G 311   JAMES SEIX TO JOHN DALY
Sep. *, 1750. 15 pds. for stock and corn. "twelve cows & five calves one steer one Bull 3 heifers marked with a Slit in the right ear and a half moon under the left one Black Work horse one bay work Horse and one Young sorrell Stallion three sows twelve shoats four Hoggs marked with same as above and all the Crop of Corn now standing...." Wit: WILLIAM HANSFORD, JOHN WILSON. November Court 1750. SAMUEL ORMES C/C.

G 311   JAMES SEIX & WIFE ANNE TO JOHN DALY
Sep. 25, 1750. 20 pds. for 200 A. "JAMES SEIX of Bertie County Planter and Anne his Wife Daughter and Devisee of HENDRICK VANPELT late of Society Parish.... (land) Devised by HENDRICK VANPELT...to the above said ANNE...." By will dated Sep. 27, 1749. Wit: THOMAS HANSFORD, JOHN WILSON. November Court 1750. SAMUEL ORMES C/C.

G 312   PETER CHRISTIAN SHROCK TO GEORGE CAPEHART
*. 40 pds. for 60 A. On Eastermost Branch of Salmon Creek. Part of a tract formerly granted to WILLIAM GRILLS by patent dated April 1, 1714. Wit: JOHN NICHOLS, JUN., JOHN CRICKET, JUN. November Court 1750. *.

G 313   ISAAC HUNTER, SEN. of Chowan Co. TO ELISHA HUNTER
*. 30 pds. for 140 A. On SS Chowan River known as Pitch Landing adj. EPHRAIM HUNTER, ____ CHERRYHORN, ISAAC HUNTER. Being part of a patent granted THOMAS MARTIN cont. 300 A. and part of a patent to THOMAS HANSFORD cont. 312 A. Wit: JOHN GORDAN, JACOB HUNTER, JESSE HUNTER. November Court 1750. SAMUEL ORMES C/C.

G 315   JAMES WILLIAMSON TO THOMAS WHITMELL, merchant
Oct. 12, 1750. 15 pds. for 500 A. "...being part within the Indian Line..." On Quitsney Swamp adj. DR. BATES, HENRY HUNTER, WILLIAM PIERCE on Rocquis, JOHN JOHNSON at Chucalack Swamp. Wit: ROBERT HUNTER, H. HUNTER, JOHN WATSON. November Court 1750. SAMUEL ORMES C/C.

G 316   EDWARD ROBERTS & WIFE MARY TO MERTIN WHEELER
Oct. 4, 1750. Gift. 250 A. "...in consideration to our well beloved Son in Law MERTIN WHEELER..." Land on SWS Ahotskey Swamp at "end of the great Island...." Adj. "Homes's old Line" at Cabbin Branch. By patent dated 1668. Wit: WILLIAM BIRD, PETER BYROM, CHARLES ROBERTS. November Court 1750. SAMUEL ORMES C/C.

G 317   RALPH OUTLAW TO JAMES HINTON
Oct. 24, 1750. 80 pds. for 500 A. On SS Ahorskey Swamp "between OUTLAW & BONNER" adj. ____ KING, ____ EASON. Wit: WILLIAM HUMFRES, THOMAS OUTLAW. November Court 1750. SAMUEL ORMES C/C.

G 317   WILLIAM HART of Northhampton & DAUGHTERS...An agreement
Aug. 16, 1749. "I...WILLIAM HART...together with my Daughters MARTHA & SARAH had in Wedlock with ELISA HOWELL Daughter of JOHN HOWELL (both Deceased) hereby declare...with other children...and heirs of JOHN HOWELL SENIOR late of Bertie Deceased...agree as follows...JOHN HOWELL dying without Will it was agreed that all his Personall & perishable Estate should be equally Divided & proportioned in seven equal Shares for JOHN HOWELL one, for ROBERT HOWELL one, for THOMAS HOWELL one, for WILLIAM HOWELL one, for ARTHUR HOWELL one (all these Sons of the Deceased & for the Daughters of ELISIA my late wife one share, and for WILLIAM THOMPSON son DAVID THOMPSON & SARAH HOWELL Deceased one Share in the Right of his Said Mother Deceased....I do hereby acknowledge to have received my Part & allotment consisting of two Negroes..." Wit: WILLIAM HART, SIMON SIMPSON, JAMES MCLAHAN. August Court 1750. SAMUEL ORMES C/C.

G 318   ROGER SNELL & WIFE ANN TO PETER WYNANTS(WINANTS), marriner
Jan. 20, 1749. 50 pds. for 250 A. Adj. MICHAEL (MYKELL) KING, JOHN HOLBROOK, EDWARD BYRD, THOMAS MITCHELL at Round Pocoson. Wit: ROBERT WEST, ROBERT WEST, JUN., MICHALL KING. August Court 1750. SAMUEL ORMES C/C.

G 320   ANDREW THOMPSON TO WILLIAM HOOTTEN

June 11, 1750. 30 pds. for 620 A. Land commonly known as Plowmans on low Sullolk meadows at Ducking Run. By patent to CAPT. JOHN PLOWMAN dated Aug. 28, 1714. Wit: EDWARD RASOR, WILLIAM HARDY, JAMES LARY. Aug. Court 1750. SAMUEL ORMES C/C.

G 321 PATRICK OQUIN & WIFE MARTHA TO OODAM (AADAM) RABY of Nansemond Co., Va. May 28, 1750. 67 pds. 10 sh. for 230 A. On Casway Branch at Catawhitskey Old Road adj. JAMES WOODS. On NW Fork Poplar Swamp "betwixt JOHN HARE & PATRCIK OQUIN." Wit: JOHN BROWN, SAMUEL BROWN, JOHN BENTON, ISAAC CARTER, JOHN HARE. August Court 1750. SAMUEL ORMES C/C.

G 322 WILLIAM HARDY, cooper TO LAMB HARDY
Aug. 1, 1750. Gift. 270 A. "...in consideration of Natural good will Love & Affection which I have or bear...to my Son..." Land on SS Salmon Creek adj. THOMAS RYAN. Wit: WILLIAM HARDY, JUN., EDWARD RASOR. August Court 1750. SAMUEL ORMES C/C.

G 323 JOHN STANSELL of Tyrell Co. TO JAMES LEGETT
June 23, 1750. 30 pds. for 100 A. Land in Kesia Neck "formerly be-longing to PETER HANSELL Deseased" Adj. PETER GRAY. Wit: ELISHA WHITFIELD, JER.(?) LEGETT. August Court 1750. SAMUEL ORMES C/C.

G 324 WILLIAM BARBER TO JOHN BARBER
Dec. 16, 1745. 1 sh. for *. "...my right title and Interest to any Land I have in Bertie..." Wit: JAMES CASTELLAW, MIKEL LEE. August Court 1750. SAMUEL ORMES C/C.

G 325 JOHN THOMSON (THOMPSON) TO GEORGE LOCKHART
Jan. 8, 1739/40. 333 pds. 6 sh. 8 p. for 1/2 estate of DAVID HENDER-SON. "...JOHN TOMSON...Son to JOHN THOMSON farmer(?) in Cambusdenny in North Brittain...whereas DAVID HENDERSON deceased did by His Last Will & Testament...(dated Feb. 13, 1735) bequeathed to His Nephew GEORGE HENDERSON & to the Six children which his Sister JENNET HENDERSON had in Scotland by ANDREW THOMPSON all his Estate both real and person to be equally divided ...whereas GEORGE HENDERSON one of the Legatees is since Dead...JOHN THOMP-SON is duly constituted lawfull attorney to (sell) all (DAVID HENDERSON's) lands Tenaments Negroes & all effects & Estate whatsoever...." Legatees represented by JOHN THOMPSON are: (1) JOHN, son of ANDREW and JENNET HENDER-SON THOMPSON. (2) THOMAS WINGATE of Micklewood in North Brittain & GRIZAL his wife, daughter of ANDREW & JENNET THOMPSON. (3) WALTER AIKMAN in Kerse-bonny in Scotland & ISABELL his wife, daughter of ANDREW & JENNET THOMPSON. Wit: JAMES LOCKHART, THOMAS ASHLEY, JOHN COOK. N.C. Court Jan. 11, 1739. W. SMITH C.J.

G 328 JAMES CASTELAW TO THOMAS RYAN
Nov. 9, 1747. (Surety until Dec. 24, 1749.) 375 pds. for Surety Bond. "...THOMAS RYAN (as) attorney for JOHN THOMPSON, GRIZEL THOMSON ISABEL THOMSON with the consent of THOMAS WINGATE and WALTER AIKMAN Hus-bands to the said GRIZEL and ISABELL THOMSON (dated Aug. 29, 1740)...sold one Moiety or half the Personal and real Estate of the late CAPT. DAVID HENDERSON of this County Deceased consisting of Land Negroes cattle and Debts..." Wit: DAVID FOEFE(?), JOSEPH HARDY. Feb. 6, 1750. JAMES HASELL*.

G 328 LUKE MIZELL TO EDWARD COLLINS, yeoman
Feb. 12, 1750. 200 pds. for 200 A. Adj. _____LEGET, RICHARD TOMLIN-SON, _____ STRAUGHAN. Wit: RICHARD TOMLINSON, LUKE MIZELL, JUN. February Court 1750. SAMUEL ORMES C/C.

G 329 JOHN PUGH TO THOMAS PUGH
Jan. 5, 1750. 20 pds for 157 A. THOMAS PUGH brother of JOHN PUGH. Land formerly owned by JONATHAN CLIFF (De'c'd) and by him sold to JAMES PECK and by PECK sold to "...my late Father FRANCIS PUGH..." Wit: SAMUEL WIGGINS, LEWIS HODGSON. February Court 1750. SAMUEL ORMES C/C.

G 331 BARNIBY BRYAN TO NEEDHAM BRYAN
Jan. 27, 1749. Mortgage. 100 A. Land at Flag Run adj. WILLIAM VAN. "...that if the above named BARNYBY BRYAN...do pay unto NEEDHAM BRYAN His Heirs or Assigns the Sum of Twenty one pound one Shilling and eight Pence Silver money...by the Twenty day of January next come two Year than this above written deed...shall be Null and void..." Wit: EDWARD VAN,

JAMES GLISSON. February Court 1750. SAMUEL ORMES C/C.

G 332 HENRY COUPLAND, SEN. of Nansemond Co., Va. TO HENRY COUPLAND, JUN.
       *. Deed of Gift. 300 A. "...Naturall love and affection that I
have and do bare unto my Son HENRY COUPLAND...(300 A.) except the use and
Benefitt of about Seventy five acres out of the afores'd Tract during my
naturall Life..." Land on NS Meherrin Creek at Bells Branch adj. ARON
ODEUMS, CHARLES JENKINS. Land purchased of WILLIAM WHITFIELD by deed November 12, 1741. Wit: CHARLES JENKINS, WILLIAM KNIGHT, WINBORNE JENKINS.
February Court 1750. SAMUEL ORMES C/C.

G 333 GEORGE CAPEHART, shoemaker TO GEORGE CAPEHART, JUN.
       Dec. 5, 1750. Deed of Gift. for 50 A. "...Naturall affection for
my Son GEORGE CAPEHART...fifty acres whereon I now dwell...NB Note that my
aforementioned Son GEORGE CAPEHART is not to be possessed with aforementioned Plantation till after my Decease..." Land on WS Eastermost Swamp of
Salmon Creek adj. GEORGE CAPEHART, JUN. (land bought of PETER SHROCK),
MICHAEL CAPEHART. Wit: EDWARD RASOR, MICHAEL CAPEHART, PETER SHROCK. February Court 1750. SAMUEL ORMES C/C.

G 334 WILLIAM HARDY TO EDWARD RASOR
       Jan. *, 1751. 15 pds. for 50 A. On SS Blackwalnut Swamp adj. land
formerly Capt. DAVID HENDERSON's at Rocky Branch, Land formerly JOHN
JONES's, dec'd. Wit: JOHN BOWIN, JUN., ELIZEBETH RATLIFF, WILLIAM KEETOR.
February Court 1750. SAMUEL ORMES C/C.

G 335 EDWARD RASOR TO WILLIAM HARDY
       Jan. 2, 1750/51. 30 pds. for 300 A. On WS Middle Swamp of Salmon
Creek adj. Green Branch, ____ DUCKENFIELD. Wit: JOHN BROWN, JUN., ELIZE-
BETH RATLIFF, WILLIAM KEETOR. February Court 1750. SAMUEL ORMES C/C.

G 335 EDWARD RASOR TO WILLIAM HARDY
       Jan. 2, 1750/51. 30 pds. for 300 A. In Middle Swamp of Salmon Creek
at Green Branch commonly called Derby's Island. Adj. MR. DUCKENFIELD. By
Deed of sale to EDWARD RASOR from THOMAS RYAN dated April 1, 1742. Wit:
JOHN BOWIN, JUN., ELIZEBETH RATLIFF, WILLIAM KEETOR. February Court 1750.

G 337 EDWARD ROBERT & WIFE MARY of Society Parish to DAVID HORTON
       Oct. 2, 1750. 11 pds. for 400 A. On SS Ahotsky Swamp. By patent
bearing date April 10, 1745. Adj. MERTIN WHEELER at Turkey Swamp. Wit:
JOHN BRICKELL, NATHAN HORTON, MARTIN WHEELER. February Court 1750. *.

G 338 SAMUEL PAGE TO EDWARD HARRELL
       Oct. 6, 1750. 37 pds. for 330 A. Land in Cashey Swamp adj. JAMES
BLUNT, SAMUELL PAGE, EDWARD HARRELL. Land formerly granted HENRY RODES in
1723. Wit: THOMAS PAGE, JOHN HARRELL. February Court 1750. *.

G 339 ARNOLL HOPKINS TO JOHN HOPKINS
       Oct. 6, 1750. 5 pds. for 100 Adj. WILLIAM REDDITS, JOSEPH REDDITT.
Wit: ROBERT LAWRANCE, WILLIAM HOPKINS. February Court 1750. *.

G 340 ROBERT HICKS of Northampton Co. TO JOSEPH WIMBURLY
       Oct. 4, 1750. 30 pds. for 600 A. ON WS Kesia River at Blackmans
Landing adj. Capt. WILLIAM GRIGARREY, ____ WOLSTON. By patent to THOMAS
POLLOCK "& by him an assignment on back of Said Pattent conveyed to GEORGE
HENDERSON to HEW SCOTT of Boston in new England & by a deed...from HEW
SCOTT to ROBERT HICKS...." Wit: WILLIAM HENRY, WILLIAM PTOSON.+ February
Court 1750. SAMUEL ORMES C/C. [+POTSON(?)]

G 341 JOHN PAGE TO DAVID MEADES of Nancemond Co., Va.
       Jan. 15, 1750/51. 13 pds. 10 sh. for 200 A. Adj. ABRAHAM SHEPARD,
MARTIN GARDNER, JOHN EDWARD, ROBERT HINES. Wit: LAURANCE TOOLE, THOMAS
CRAFTS. February Court 1750. SAMUEL ORMES C/C.

G 342 JOHN HURST (HUSK) TO WILLIAM BARBER
       Feb. 12, 1751. 40 pds. for 100 A. *. Wit: WILLIAM HICKS, CHARLES
BARBER. February Court 1750. SAMUEL ORMES C/C.

G 343 JAMES RUTLAND of Northampton Co. TO ARTHUR COTTEN
       July 19, 1750. 12 pds. for 100 A. ON Wattom Swamp adj. PETER WEST.

212

Part of patent of 300 A. to THOMAS JONES dated Sep. 22, 1730. Wit: CHARLES
HORNE, BENJAMIN WYNNS. February Court 1750. SAMUEL ORMES C/C.

G 344 THOMAS JACOCKS TO JAMES COOPER
        Jan. 5, 1751. "in consideration of a Note of Hand for thirty five
Barrels of merchantable full bound Tar..." Land adj. THOMAS YATES, EDWARD
TAYLOR, ____ POLLOCK in Middle Swamp. Wit: SIMON BRYAN, ELISABETH JACOCKS.
February Court 1750. SAMUEL ORMES C/C.

G 345 WILLIAM BROWN, miller TO WILLIAM MIDDLETON
        Nov. 12, 1750. 5 pds. for 50 A. "...being the Plantation whereon my
Father JOHN Lived and Died..." Adj. EDWARD HARE, ISAAC SAUNDERS, GABRIEL
MANLEY. Wit: PETER EVANS, BENJAMIN WYNNS. February Court 1750. *.

G 347 JOSEPH WYNNS, yeoman TO GABRIEL MANLEY
        Feb. 23, 1747/48. 20 pds. for 140 A. Adj. CULMUR SESSUMS. Wit:
WILLIAM BROWN, BENJAMIN WYNNS. February Court 1750. SAMUEL ORMES C/C.

G 348 BENJAMIN WYNNS TO MARY VERLIN, Spinster & Son WILLIAM FAIRLESS of
        Petty Shore. May 1, 1750. 40 pds. for 200 A. WILLIAM FAIRLESS
(FARLESS) son of NICHOLAS FARLESS. Land on SWS Chowan River "...it being
the Plantation of Her late Husband NICHOLAS FARLESS Deceased..." Land mortgaged by NICHOLAS FARLESS and sold at public vendue to BENJAMIN WYNNS. Wit:
PETER EVANS, WILLIAM BROWN. February Court 1750. SAMUEL ORMES C/C.

G 349 WILLIAM HOSEA TO THOMAS YATES (YAITS)
        Feb. 4, 1750. 25 pds. for *. Land bought of NATTANIL NICKLESS on
SS White Oak Run adj. JAMES MACGLAWTRONS at Coult Branch. Adj. THOMAS
DIXON, ____ WESTON. Wit: ISAAC HENDRICKSON, WILLIAM RASBERRY, WILL WEBB.
May Court 1751. SAMUEL ORMES C/C.

G 350 THOMAS RYAN TO JAMES LEARY, SEN.
        May 18, 1751. 37 pds. for 200 A. Land purchased of PLOWMAN WHITE
adj. ____ DUCKENFIELD, WILLIAM HUTTON(?), ____ JOHNSTON, WILLIAM FLEETWOOD.
Wit: DARBY LEARY, ELIZABETH RYAN. May Court 1751. SAMUEL ORMES C/C.

G 351 JAMES LEARY (LARY) TO DARBY LEARY
        May 13, 1751. 12 pds. for 100 pds. Land adj. ____ DUCKENFIELD at
Hay Meadow Branch, ____ FLEETWOOD, Governor's Line. Wit: THOMAS RYAN,
DAVID ALLEN, ELIZABETH RYAN. May Court 1751. SAMUEL ORMES C/C.

G 352 WILLIAM HUTTON (HOOTEN) TO JAMES LEARY
        March 16, 1751. 80 pds. for 134 A. At Ducking Run. Wit: DARBY
LEARY, JAMES LEARY. May Court 1751. SAMUEL ORMES C/C.

G 353 MICHAEL HORNE TO NICHOLAS BAGGETT of Northampton Co.
        Dec. 3, 1750. 25 pds. for 300 A. On Wattom Swamp adj. WILLIAM WHIT-
FIELD. By patent to THOMAS WILSON and by him to PETER WEST by date April 7,
1730. Wit: CHARLES HORNE, JOHN WEST. May Court 1751. SAMUEL ORMES C/C.

G 354 EDWARD CARTER & WIFE MARGARET TO MARGARET NICKEN, wife of JAMES
        NICKEN. May 10, 1750. 1 sh. (Deed of Gift.) for 200 A. "...of one
part and MARGARET NICKEN (our well Beloved Daughter) wife of JAMES NICKEN
and the Heirs of her Body lawfully begotten..." Land in Society Parish on
ES Pottecasie Creek adj. JAMES COTTON, ALEXANDER COTTEN. Wit: JA. LOOCKER-
MAN, JOHN BRICKELL. May Court 1751. SAMUEL ORMES C/C.

G 355 EDWARD CARTER & WIFE MARGARET TO MARY BEST, wife of HENRY BEST
        May 10, 1750. Gift. 200 A. "...(Carters) late of Society Parish...
our well beloved daughter and the Heirs of her Body lawfully begotten...."
Land on ES Pottecasie Creek. Wit: JA. LOOCKERMAN, JOHN BRICKELL. May Court
1751. SAMUEL ORMES C/C.

G 356 MARY HOWCUTT TO JOHN WYNNS, yeoman
        Sep. 18, 1749. 100 pds. for 150 A. "MARY HOWCUTT Relict of JOHN
HOWCUTT and Heir at Law to WILLIAM DOWNING JUN late of Boston in New England...that half Tract of Lightwood Land which CAPT. WILLIAM DOWNING...sold
to his Son WILLIAM..." On Wiccacon Creek adj. JOHN WYNNS. Wit: WILLIAM
HANSFORD, THOMAS HANSFORD, ELEAZ(?) QUINBY. *. SAMUEL ORMES C/C.

G 357 LAMB HARDY TO GOVERNOR GABRIEL JOHNSTON

        May 1, 1751. 20 pds. for 270 A. ON Salmon Creek adj. THOMAS RYAN
"as by Deed of Gift bearing date the first day of August in the Year 1750
from my Father WILLIAM HARDY..." Wit: SAMUEL ORMES, WILLIAM HARDY. May
Court 1751. SAMUEL ORMES C/C.

G 358 GABRIEL JOHNSTON, GOVERNOR TO LAMB HARDY
        May 24, 1751. 20 pds. for 300 A. Adj. GABRIEL JOHNSTON, LAMB HARDY,
JOHN NICHOLS on Middle Swamp of Salmon Creek. Wit: SAMUEL ORMES, WILLIAM
HARDY. May Court 1751. SAMUEL ORMES C/C.

G 360 ANN STEINFELS (STANFIELD), widow TO JOHN CAMPBELL of Edenton
        June 29, 1745. 20 pds. for 150 A. "...ANN STEINFELS Widow Executrix
of the last Will & Testament of JOHN RODOLPH STEINFELS...& sole Heir to his
Estate..." Land on Chowan River on NWS Deep Creek adj. JAMES BOON, FREDER-
ICK JONES, RICHARD BARFIELD. Wit: BENJAMIN HILL, WILLIAM WYNNS, JOHN VER-
LIN. May Court 1751. N.C. Court June 29, 1745. JAMES HASELL, C.J. SAMUEL
ORMES C/C.

G 361 JOHN CAMPBELL TO BENJAMIN HILL
        May 13, 1751. 20 pds. for 150 A. Land on WS Chowan River and NS
Deep Creek adj. JAMES BOON, FREDERICK JONES, RICHARD BARFIELD. Known by
name of Cotton Patch. Wit: THOMAS JONES, JAMES JONES. May Court 1751. *.

G 362 JOHN PERRY, yeoman, & WIFE SARAH TO JOHN PENNEY, yeoman
        Sep. *, 1750. 20 pds. for 200 A. Part of a tract "on the Creek in
JOHN PENNYs Line." Wit: THOMAS WATERS, NICHOLAS PERRY. May Court 1751. *.

G 363 JOHN PERRY TO MARTHEW SPIVY
        May 11, 1751. 7 pds. 10 sh. for 200 A. On NES Quoyokasan Swamp adj.
JOHN PERRY. Being part of a patent granted to WILLIAM BLY dated March 10,
1740 and sold to JOHN PERRY. Wit: WILLIAM RICE, JAMES JONES. May Court
1751. SAMUEL ORMES C/C.

G 364 JONATHAN STANDLY, SEN. of Johnston Co. TO NATHANIEL NICKLESS
        Feb. 28, 1750. 53 pds. for 300 A. ON SS Ahoskey Swamp at Turkey
Swamp adj. THOMAS HUDSON, GEORGE STANDLY "being the plantation whereon I
lately lived...." Wit: GEORGE STANDLY, WILLIAM LEWIS. May Court 1751. *.

G 365 JOHN WYNNS TO JOHN BERRY
        Feb. 22, 1750. 11 pds. for 200 A. On SS Flatt Swamp of Killum.
"Quit Rents since the 15th day of Dec. 1742 accruing only excepted ..."
Wit: ANN REASONS, JOHN CAMPBELL, EZEKIAL SLAWSON. May Court 1751. *.

G 365 DAVID HARRELL TO JESSE HARRELL, ELIAS(?) HARRELL, JOSEPH HARRELL
        *. 1 pd. 10 sh. for 70 A.(?) (200 A.?) "...containing by Estimation
Seventy Acres each being in part of a graint formerly grainted unto the
s'd. DAVID HARRELL bearing daite one Thousand seven hundred and forty nine
...." Wit: JOHN HARRELL, RICHARD WILLEFORD. May Court 1751. *.

G 366 JOHN HARRELL, SEN. TO DAVID, ELIAS, JOSIAH, EZEKIAL HARRELL
        May 13, 1751. Deed of Gift. 640 A. "...for the Love and good will
I have unto my fore Sons...to them and to the lawful heires lawfully Begotten of there Bodye or Bodyes and I lend unto all these my Sons Wifes above
named...the use of what Land I gave her Husband...during there Naturall
Life or Widowhood and after he or there deceas or Marriaidge for want of
such Heires as above mentioned that part of the Land to be sould to them
...of my Sons that is then living or there Lawful Heirs...if any one or
more of my Sons...is willing to sell to any one or more of there Brothers..
his Record in Court will be deamed Soficiant...observing the Rights and
Prividledges above mentioned to myself and there Mother...." Wit:

G 366 JOHN HARRELL, SEN. TO DAVID, ELIAS, JOSIAH, EZEKIAL HARRELL +
        (+ The above seems to be a part of this deed; above is not complete.)
        May 13, 1751. Deed of Gift. 640 A. Land on Runnerry Narshes. "...
For the Love and good will I have unto my fore Sons David Harrell & ELIAS
HARRELL and JOSIAH AND EZEKIAL HARRELL...to them and to the lawful heirs
lawfully Begotten of there Bodye or Bodyes and I lend unto all these my
Sons wifes that is now my Sons Wifes above named...the use of what Land I
gave her Husband...fureing there Naturall Life or Widowhood and after he or
there deceas or Marriadge for want of such Heires as above mentioned that

part of the Land should be sould to them...of my Sons that is then Living
or there Lawfull Heires...if any one or more of my Sons...is willing to
sell there part...and will sell to any one or more of there brothers...his
Record in Court will be deamed Soficiant...observing the Rights and Privi-
dleges above mentioned to myself and there Mother...I likewise give and
grant unto my Son ISRAEL HARDY HARRELL the Plantation whereon I now live
and Dwell...after my Decease and the Decease of His Mother (120 A.)...I
likewise give unto...EZEKIAL and ISRAEL HARDY HARRELL one hundred acres of
Land neigh the Head of Jumping Run fifty acres apeace after our Decease to
them and there heires for Ever...." *.*. May Court 1751. SAMUEL ORMES C/C.

G 368   JENNET BANKS TO WILLIAM LITTLE
        Nov. 12, 1730. 200 pds. for 400A + 200 A + 640 A + cattle + Hogs +
Beds + furniture "...JENNET BANKS Exect & Legatary General to the last
Will & Testament of ABRAHAM BLEWLETT her former Husband Deceas'd now wife
of THOMAS BANKS of Edenton...and is now under coverture with THOMAS BANKS
...(who) by a special Instrument in Writing...dated 17th day of Nov. 1725
hath agreed (for)...JENNET to sell...." (1) 400 Land on SS Catawitsky Swamp
--Also land Grant to BLEWLETT (2) 200 A in Chinkapin Neck in a place called
Plumtree Neck by sole from WILLIAM BLYTH deceased to BLEWLETT (3) Plantation on SS Chowan River cont. 640 A "where the s'd JENNETT now lives..." by
grant to BLEWLETT (4) Also 30 head cattle, 12 head hogs, one bed and furniture, 1 mare & colt. Wit: J. PRATT, JAMES MILLIKIN. May Court 1751.
"This Deed was Exhibited into Court and the similitude of the Hand Writing
of JOHN PRAT one of the Evedinces thereto proved by the oath of THOMAS
BANKS and the similitude of the Hand Writing of JOHN PRATT and JAMES MILLI-
KIN proved by the Oath of THOMAS JONES..." SAMUEL ORMES C/C.

G 369   JOHN BRICKELL & WIFE MARTHA, late of Society Parish TO RUBIN POWELL
        of Norfolk Co., Va. Aug. 12, 1751. 25 pds. (Va.) for 200 A. Land
on ES Pottecasie Creek adj. ____WEST at the Old Indian Path, BRYAN HARE,
HENRY WINBOURN, JOHN BUCHELL. Wit: HENRY WINBOURNE, SAMUEL ORMES. August
Court 1751. Rec. SAMUEL ORMES C/C.

G 370   JOHN CARTER & WIFE ANN, Late of Society Parish TO JOHN COUPLAND, son
        of HENRY of Nansemond Co., Va. Feb. 25, 1750. 45 pds. (Va.) for
350 A. Land on ES Potacosie Creek and NS Hothouse Branch at Petatoe Marsh
and ES "of an Island" By deed of sale from THOMAS WALKER Feb. 11, 1746.
Wit: JOHN BRICKELL, EDWARD MOORE. August Court 1751. *.

G 371   JOHN LEWIS, carpenter, TO JACOB LEWIS
        Sep. 27, 1750. 10 pds. for 96 A. NS Wiccacon Creek. Wit: JOHN
HARRELL, JOSEPH HARRELL. August Court 1751. *.

G 372   CALET STEPHENS of Mill Neck TO WILLIAM STEPHENS
        Dec. 17, 1750. Deed of Gift for 200 A. "...unto my Grandson WILLIAM
STEPHENS after my Decease...." Land adj. RICHARD SOWELL. Wit: WILLIAM
TYNER, WILLIAM COLTHRED. August Court 1751. SAMUEL ORMES C/C.

G 373   JOHN BENTLY TO JESSE BENTLY
        August 10, 1751. 50 pds. for 125 A Land in Cut Cypress Creek at
Gum Branch at Charltons Creek. Wit: JOHN SMETHWICK, HANNAH SMETHWICK,
JAMES BEASLEY. August Court 1751. SAMUEL ORMES C/C.

G 374   FRANCES ROUNTREE (ROUNTRY) TO ISAAC HILL
        March 22, 1750/51. 10 pds. (Va.) for 320 A 1/2 of patent granted to
MOSES ROUNTRY for 640 A on Branch of JOYES (GOYES) HALL and Bacon Hill.
Wit: JOSEPH WIMBERLY, ELIZABETH COWARD. August Court 1751. *.

G 376   PETER HAYES TO JOHN HAYES
        Feb. 16, 1750/51. Deed of Gift for 150 A "in consideration of Love
good will and affection which I have...toward my loving Son, JOHN HAYES..."
Land on SS Cashey Swamp. Wit: CHARLES HORNE. August Court 1751. *.

G 376   WILLIAM RUTLAND of Northhampton Co. TO JOHN WEST
        Jan. 9, 1750/51. 8 pds. (Va.) 100 A. Adj. WILLIAM WHITFIELD, HENRY
BAKER. Part of a patent formerly granted to JAMES RUTLAND for 225 A. Wit:
CHARLES HORNE, JAMES POWELL. August Court 1751. SAMUEL ORMES C/C.

G 377   GEORGE STEVENSON Of Edgecomb Co. TO NEEDHAM BRYAN

July 28, 1751. 15 pds. for 120 A. SS Flage Run Adj. WILLIAM BRYAN
(BRAIN), JOHN HARAL. "Part of a bottom which was granted to GEORGE STEVEN-
SON" by date Feb. 1, 1725. Wit: JOHN SMITH, HENRY HORN, EDWARD PERRITT.
August Court 1751. SAMUEL ORMES C/C.

G 378 WILLIAM BYRD TO WILLIAM FLEETWOOD
       Aug. 12, 1751. 20 pds. (Ster. GB) for 500 A Land on ES Buklersburry
Pocoson adj. THOMAS RYAN, ANDREW THOMSON, THOMAS ASHBURN, GEORGE BELL. At
Horsepen Branch. Wit: JOHN HILL, ARCH. BELL, GEORGE BELL. August Court
1751. SAMUEL ORMES C/C.

G 379 RICHARD SOWELL, yeoman TO JAMES+JORDAN, "cuper" (+JEAMS?)
       July 6, 1751. 10 pds. (Va.) for 80 A land in White Oak Swamp at Mill
Branch adj. OBADIAH SOWELL, _____ KEEL, _____ MORISES. Wit: ELEAZ. QUINBY,
AARON OLIVER, WILLIAM BENNETT. August Court 1751. SAMUEL ORMES C/C.

G 380 AARON OLIVER & WIFE ANN TO WILLIAM LASETOR
       Jan. 5, 1750/51. 25 pds. (Va.) for 400 A. on Long Branch on Horse
Swamp to Woodards Creek near the Mill Path. Wit: SIMON DANIEL, ELEAZ.
QUINBY. August Court 1751. SAMUEL ORMES C/C.

G 382 JOHN WILLIAMS TO JOHN MOON
       20 pds. (G.B.) for 840 A Land on SS Sypress Swamp. Land granted to
JOHN WILLIAMS March 21, 1721. Wit: ROBERT HUNTER, JOHN FIELD, JOSEPH BAR-
RADALE. August Court 1751. SAMUEL ORMES C/C.

G 383 JAMES WILLIAMSON TO HENRY HUNTER
       Oct. 12, 1750. 40 pds. (Va.) for 200 A. Adj. DR. BATES "within the
Indian Line Adj. WILLIAM PIERCE, HENRY HUNTER. Wit: THOMAS WHITMELL, ROB-
ERT HUNTER, JOHN WATSON. August Court 1751. *.

G 384 LENARD GREEN of Edgecombe Co. TO THOMAS MORRISS
       Oct. 17, 1750. 6 pds. (Va.) for 140 A. Adj. ELEAZ. QUINBY, RICHARD
SOWELL. Wit: WILLIAM WYNNS, PETER EVANS, JAMES JONES. August Court 1751.*.

G 385 FRANCIS BROWN, yeoman TO WILLIAM BOON
       Aug. 20, 1750. 35 pds. (Va.) for 200 A. ES Chincapin Creek adj. BEN-
JAMIN BROWN to Wiccacon Creek "excepting one hundred acres of Land more or
less to JOHN WYNNS within the said Dementions..." Wit: WILLIAM WYNNS,
PETER EVANS, ISAAC PERRY. August Court 1751. *.

G 386 ISAAC PIERCE & WIFE ABILINA TO PAUL PENDER
       May 28, 1751. 10 pds. for 100 A. "Abilina...one of the Devisees
named in the last will and testament of JONATHAN GILBERT late of the County
aforesaid deceased father of the said ABILINA..." Land at Deep Creek
Bridge adj. _____ FIERYBENT. Land conveyed by JAMES RUTLAND to WILLIAM DAN-
IEL and by DANIEL to JONATHAN GILBERT where on JONATHAN GILBERT lately
lived. Wit: ALEX. COTTEN, EDWARD ROBERTS, JOHN BAKER. "ABILINA PIERCE,
wife of ISAAC PIERCE named in the annexed Deed appeared before me BENJAMIN
WYNNS one of his Majesty's Justices of the peace...and declared she signed
fully and willingly...." August Court 1751. SAMUEL ORMES C/C.

G 387 RICHARD BROWN TO THOMAS SISON (SISSON)
       June 22, 1751. 45 pds. for 100 A. IN Chinkepen Neck adj. ISAAC HILL
Wit: PEGGY WYNNS, BENJAMIN WYNNS. August Court 1751. *.

G 388 JAMES GRAVES of Tyrell Co. TO WILLIAM TODD(?) (TODDE)
       March 12, 1751. 5 pds. for 100 A. "three yards swuare only accepted
...." adj. THOMAS YATES. Wit: LAMB HARDY, WILLIAM HARDY. August Court
1751. SAMUELORMES C/C.

G 389 ARON OLIVER, yeoman, TO ABRAHAM SMITH
       July 31, 1750. 44 pds. for 100 A. On branches of Sandy Run adj.
THOMAS ROGERS, _____ BENIT. Wit: WM. WYNNS, JAMES BENNIT. August Court 1751.

G 389 ARON OLIVER, yeoman, TO JAMES BENIT, cooper
       July 31, 1750. *. *. Land near Sandy Run adj. JOHN ROGERS, _____
HOOKER. Wit: WM. WYNNS, ABRAHAM SMITH. Augsut Court 1751. *.

G 390 WILLIAM BARKER of Johnston Co. TO THOMAS DUKE

Oct. 29, 1750. 30 pds. for 200 A. SWS Chowan River in Chowan River Pocoson "WILLIAM WYNNS my attorney...." Wit: WILLIAM BARTON, JOHN BARTON, ISAAC PIERCE. Augsut Court 1751. *.

G 391 JOHN SALLIS TO THOMAS RYAN
       Aug. 15, 1751. 20 pds. for 100 A. At Bucks Branch adj. CALIB SPYVEY. Wit: HENRY HUNTER, THOMAS CASTELLOW. August Court 1751. *.

G 392 ROBERT EVANS, yeoman, TO GODFREY HOOKER
       Nov. 8, 1736. 12 pds. for 100 A. "GODFREY HOOKER late of the said Precinct deceased pursuant to the said GODFREY in his last Will and Testament...did set over to BENJAMIN HOOKER as Infant Son to said GODFREY...land" On WS Chowan River Pocoson at Fairchild Branch. Wit: JOSEPH WYNNS, BENJ. WYNNS, JOHN WYNNS. Nov. Court 1736. JOHN WYNNS C/C.

G 392 BENJAMIN HOOKER TO PETER EVANS
       Oct. 27, 1750. *.*. All my Right, title & interest aforesaid land. Wit: JOHN WYNNS, JOHN STINSON. August Court 1751. SAMUEL ORMES C/C.

G 393 DOM REX TO BENJAMIN HELLYMAN
       April 20, "in the Eighteenth Year of our Reign" Grant 253 A on Connaritsat Pocoson. "To SEat and Cultivate according to the proportion of three acres for every Hundred...." Wit: ROBERT FORSTER. New Bern in Auditor General's Office ALEX MCCULLOK Dep. Aud. ROBERT FORSTER D/C.

G 394 BENJAMIN HOLLYMAN TO JOHN WYNNS
       Feb. 9, 1750 10 pds. *. "...BENJAMIN HOLLYMAN the within Patentee..." Wit: ANNE REASONS, JAME BOONE WYNNS. Nov. Court 1751. SAMUEL ORMES C/C.

G 395 THOMAS JOHNSON of Onslow Co. TO THOMAS ARCHER
       July 6, 1750. *. 340 A. adj. ____ JOHNSON, THOMAS STEPHENSON. Wit: MARTTHEW (MATHER) WHITFIELD, WILLIAM COLLER, FRANCIS SANDERS. Nov. 15, 1750. JAMES HASELL.

G 396 WILLIAM WEBB TO HENRY REED
       Aug. 26, 1751. 35 pds. for 200 A. On SS Deep Creek adj. EDWARD HARE. Wit: JOHN REED, ELIZABETH REED. November Court 1751. *.

G 397 WILLIAM COK of Granvill Co. TO JAMES DOUGLASS
       May 17, 1751. 20 pds. for 370 A. "(land) bequeathed and given to him by his Grandfather JOHN BEVERLY Deceased..." On SS Ahotskey Swamp. Wit: NICHOLAS PERRY, ABSALOM SPEIR, MORNING PERRY. November Court 1751. *.

G 398 BENJAMIN HOLOMAN, yeoman, TO EDMON HOLOMAN, yeoman
       Jan. 29, 1744/45 30 pds. for 320 A WS Luesin Swampe. Wit: THOMAS BYRD, JONATHAN THOMAS. November Court 1751. SAMUEL ORMES C/C.

G 399 JOHN SMITH, yeoman, TO BENNETT BAKER, miller
       May 22, 1751. 30 pds. for 200 A. ES Chinkapin Swamp adj. "Land of JAMES HOLLEY bequeathed to JANE his wife by the last Will and Testament of our Father JOHN SMITH Deceased..." adj. JAMES WILLIAMS. Wit: JOHN WYNNS, JOHN FREEMAN, THOMAS PARKER. November Court 1751. SAMUEL ORMES C/C.

G 400 JOHN SALLIS TO WILLIAM LAWRANCE
       Aug. 7, 1751. 16 pds. for 400 A. Adj. GEORGE WALSTON, ARNOLD HOPKINS at Bear Swamp. Wit: JOHN REDDIT, ANN REDDIT. Nov. Court 1751. *.

G 401 CHRISTOPHER HOLLOWMAN, SEN. TO HARMON HOLLOWMAN (HOLLOWMON) (HALLIMON) Aug. 17, 1751. 20 pds. for 200 A. "...my son HARMON HOLLOWMAN...being part of a Tract or Parsell of Land he the said CHRISTOPHER HOLLOWMAN bought of JOHN EARLY on Horskey Swamp. Wit: WILLIAM WEBB, DEMCE WOOD, MARY WOOD. Nov. Court 1751. SAMUEL ORMES C/C.

G 402 WILLIAM BOON TO JOHN REED
       Oct. 21, 1751. 22 pds. for 200 A. ON ES Chincopin Creek at Deep Branch on Wicocorn Creek. "...Excepting one hundred acres of Land more or less to JOHN WYNNS within the said Dementions...." Wit: ROBERT HARDY, WM. LOWTHER (SOWTHER?). November Court 1751. SAMUEL ORMES C/C.

G 403 HENRY AVRIT (EVERIT) (AVRITT) TO CHARLES HARDEE

        * 2 pds. for 503 A On Cashy adj. JOHN GRIFFIN, JOHN PARIS, ____HOB-
SON. Wit: RICHARD TOMLINSON, BARN. BRAIN. November Court 1751. *.

G 404   JOHN BROGDON, JUN. TO PETERSON BROGDON
        Nov. 11, 1751. 30 pds. for 170 A. Adj. PHILIP WALSTON on ES Rocquis
Swamp adj. JONATHAN STANDLEY, CULLIN POLLOCK. Wit: H. HUNTER, SARAH HUNTER,
MARY BROGDEN. Nov. Court 1751. SAMUEL ORMES C/C.

G 406   JOHN COTTON of Northampton County TO BENJAMIN COTTON
        Nov. 6, 1751. Goft for 230 A "in consideration of naturall love,
good will and affection...toward my well beloved Brother BENJAMIN COTTON of
the County & Province afo..." Land at head of "blew Water Swamp" adj. PETER
WEST, COLL. JONES. Land formerly granted by Patent to ANNE JONES by date
April 6, 1722 "and became due to my father, JOHN COTTON, by a marriage to
said ANNE JONES and is now fell due to me by the Death of the said JOHN
COTTON my father...." Wit: CHARLES HORNE, ARTHUR COTTON. Nov. Court 1751.

G 407   ALEXANDER BALLANDINE ("ALIAS VOLLANTINE) cooper TO EDWARD VANN for
        BENJAMIN BAKER. Aug. 24, 1751. 4 pds. 10 sh. for 140 A. "land
whereon said VANN lately dwelt" on SS Killum adj. JOHN WYNNS, JOHN BAKER,
ALEXANDER BALLANDINE. Wit: ARTHUR WILLIAMS, TREDLE KEEPE. Nov. Court 1751.

G 408   JOHN SPEIR, Tyrell County, merchant TO JOHN MACKENZIE, minester of
        Suffolk Parish, Nansemond Co., Virginia. *. 10 pds. for 305 A."...
in the Island of Coronine alias Cororine..." adj. SAMUEL SMITHWICK grant
(dated July 26, 1743) "at the three creeks above Conetrol(?) Old field..."
(1) 100 A. Capt. JOHN SPEIR on Roanoke River at Deep water Pond. (2) 160 A
granted by Hon. JOHN EARL OF GRANVILLE to CAPT. JOHN SPEIR dated Sep. 20,
22nd yr of LORD GEORGE (3) 40 A granted CAPT. NICHOLAS CRISP by date March
26, 1727. Wit: THOMAS WHITMELL, THOMAS SPELLER, W. GRAY. Nov. Court 1751.

G 410   THOMAS JONES of News of Craven County TO HENRY AVARA
        Aug. 27, 1746 "for in consideration of paying of all charges that
shall accrue" 503 A Land by patent April 2, 1726 Land on Cashy adj. JOHN
GRIFFIN, JOHN PAICE, ____HOBSON, HENRY AVARA. Wit: JOHN POYTHRESS(?),
RICHARD NUSUM, WM. CHURCHWELL. Nov. Court 1751. SAMUEL ORMES C/C.

G 411   WILLIAM MIDDLETON, yeoman, TO ISAAC SANDERS
        Oct. 22, 1751. 4 pds. 8 p. for 50 A. Adj. ISAAC SANDERS, GABRIEL
MANLEY "...on the main Roads at the CRoss Roads" on Catron Creek at Holly
Swamp. Wit: WILLIAM GODWIN, RICHARD BROWN, JAMES OVERTON. Nov. Court 1751.

G 412   THOMAS BONNER, SEN. Of Bartie Co. TO JONATHAN THOMAS
        Nov. 8, 1751. 20 pds. for 456 A adj. WILLIAM CARLEE. Wit: THOMAS
BYRD, EDMON HOLLOMAN. Nov. Court 1751. SAMUEL ORMES C/C.

G 413   JOHN REED TO THOMAS GREEN
        April 11, 1751. 40 pds. for 150 A. "...One messuage or tract of Land
with a Grist Mill thereon..." On WS Barbeque Swamp adj. THOMAS MCLENDAL.
Wit: HENRY REED, THOMAS GREEN, JOHN SMITH. Nov. Court 1751. SAMUEL ORMES*.

G 414   HENRY BIRD TO SOLOMON HOLOMON
        Aug. 17, 1751. 14 pds. for 225 A. "...a parsel of Land which I the
sd. HENRY BIRD had left to me by my FAther's last Will & Testament THOMAS
BIRD..." On Half Moon Branch adj. EDMON BIRD, BENJAMIN HOLOMON at Lossing
Swamp at Ahorskee Swamp. Wit: DEMCE WOOD, WILL WEBB, MARY WOOD. February
Court 1752. SAMUEL ORMES C/C.

G 415   DANIEL HIGHSMITH (HYSMITH) TO JOHN DEMERT
        Sep. 30, 1751. 60 pds. for 400 A. On WS Cashy Swamp commonly called
Watton Swamp at Beaver Dam. Wit: THOMAS CREW, NATHAN MYERS. Feb. Court
1752. SAMUEL ORMES C/C.

G 416   THOMAS JONES of Petty Shore TO EDWARD SCULL
        Oct. 1, 1751. 30 pds. for 160 A. At Deep Creek adj. "the late JOB
RODGERS now WILLIAM REEDs line..." on lower side of M in Road, ISAAC
SANDERS, "late JOHN GILBERT, now JOHN CAMPBELLs... Being the parcell
THOMAS JONES purchased from the late JAMES RUTLAND...." Wit: WM. WYNNS,
ISAAC PIERCE. Feb. Court 1752. SAMUEL ORMES C/C.

G 417   JETHRO ROUNDTREE TO MICHAEL COLLINS

June 28, 1751/52. 35 pds. for 400 A. SS Guys Hall Swamp. Wit: JOHN SPRINGE, DEMSEY COLLINS. Feb. Court 1752. SAMUEL ORMES C/C.

G 419 CULLEN POLLOCK TO JOSEPH BARRADAIL
* 1752. 21 pds. 10 sh. for 200 A. On WS Canaan Swamp and NS Sequear Swamp. By Patent formerly granted to THOMAS POLLOCK. Wit: MICHAEL COLLINS, WILLIAM WESTON, WILLIAM GRAY. Feb. Court 1752. SAMUEL ORMES C/C.

G 420 GARRAT VAN UPSTALL, carpenter TO ARTHUR WILLIAMS, cooper
Dec. 20, 1751. 120 pds. for 150 A. Land on SS Wills Quarter Swamp at BRoad Branch. Wit: THOMAS DAVIS, ANN DAVIS. Feb. Court 1752. *.

G 422 JAMES DUGLAS (DOUGLAS) TO BENJAMIN PERRY of Perquimmons Co.
Nov. 29, 1751. 44 pds for 370 A. Land on SS Ahorskey Swamp adj. PETER PARKER By patent to LEONARD LANGSTON bearing date April 6, 1722. Wit CADAR POWELL, GEORGE POWELL, WILLIAM PERRY. Feb. Court 1752. *.

G 423 NEEDHAM BYRAN(BRYAN?) of Johnston Co. TO ARON ELLICE
Jan. 7, 1751. 20 pds. for 100 A. adj. ROBERT HODGES "including the maner Plantation that the said ARON ELLICE now liveth..." On Roquist Creek and "acrose the neck of the Rocquist." Wit: JOHN HARRELL, JOSIAH HARRELL. February Court 1752. SAMUEL ORMES C/C.

G 425 JOHN CRICKET, JUN. TO JAMES THOMAS
Nov. 15, 1751. 25 pds. for 270 A on NS Cashy Swamp "at a large Iz-land" Adj. ____ PRICHARD. Wit: JOHN BARNS, JUN., JOSEPH WIGHT. Feb. Court 1752. SAMUEL ORMES C/C.

G 426 JOHN BARNS TO JOHN CRICKEY
Nov. 15, 1751. 25 pds. for 200 A. On NS Buck Swamp "at RODSes corner tree." Wit: JOHN BARNS, JUN., JAMES THOMAS. February Court 1752. *.

G 427 THOMAS RYAN TO THOMAS HOULDER
Feb. 8, 1752 "in consideration of Sixty Barels Pitch" for 200 A. on NS Cashie Swamp. "...EARL of GRANVILES arrages & quite Rents only excepted ..." Wit: THOMAS WHITMILL, WILLIAM MACKEY, JOHN HARDISON. Feb. Court 1752.

G 428 ALEXANDER MCCULLOK (MCCULLOH) TO THOMAS PUGH
Feb. 9, 1750. 35 pds. for 300 A Near the Roanoke River at Flaggy Run. Adj. land purchased by MCCULLOCK of WILLIAM PEEK which is called "the Emperors." Wit: JAMES CASTER (CARTER), RICHARD OLIVER, BENJAMIN WYNNS. Feb. Court 1752. *.

G 429 THOMAS EASON TO BENTON MOOR
Feb. 10, 1752. 21 pds. 16 sh. for 300 A. ON SS Ahotskie Swamp. Wit: JACOB LASHER(?), JOHN BRICKELL. Feb. Court 1752. *.

G 431 MERTIN (MARTIN) WHEELER of Granville Co. TO MOSES BONNER
Oct. 1, 1751. 30 pds. for 150 A. ON SWS Ahotskie Swamp "at the upper end of the great Island..." Adj. "HOLM's old Line." Wit: JOHN BRICKELL, WILLIAM HUMFREE, THOMAS BONNER, JUN. Feb. Court 1752. *.

G 432 MARY HOCUTT, widow, TO EDWARD HOCUTT
Aug. 20, 1751. 40 pds. for 100 A. On Chowan River Woodardses Creek "otherwise called Mill Creek" to Fierybents Branch. Wit: WILLIAM HOOKER, JUN., WILLIAM BEACHAM, JEAN HOOKER, THOMAS MORRIS. Feb. Court 1752. *.

G 433 NATHANIEL WILLIAMS TO DANIEL MURPHREE
Oct. 17, 1750. 22 pds. for 100 A Land on ES Conoritsrat Swamp at Horsepen Branch to a branch "known as Pauls Branch." Wit: JOHN SHOLAR, WILLIAM SHOLAR, Feb. Court 1752. SAMUEL ORMES C/C.

G 434 ISACK STALLINGS TO JAMES JENKINS (JENKINES)
Aug. 20, 1750. 25 pds. for 360 A. On Cashy Swamp "now called Conna-ritsrat Swamp." A patent granted to ROBERT LANIER May 1, 1668. (Note: This is probably charter date to Lords Proprietors rather than actual patent date to ROBERT LANIER.) Wit: DANIEL MURPHREE, JOHN JENKINS. Feb. Court 1752. SAMUEL ORMES C/C.

G 434 MARY HOWCOTT TO WILLIAM BEACHAM (BEACHUM)

July 30, 1751. 30 pds. for 100 A. Part of patent granted to WILLIAM
DOWING for 540 A. Land adj. EDWARD HOWCUTT, Fierybent Branch, JAMES HINTON.
Wit: THOMAS ACON, ED HOCUTT, WILLIAM HOOKER, JUN., THOMAS MORRIS. Feb.
Court 1752. SAMUEL ORMES C/C.

G 436 EDWARD HOCUTT, yeoman TO JAMES HINTON, JUN.
       *. 80 pds. for 160 A. Land on WS EPHRAM HUNTERs Mill Pond at Vixes
Branch. Adj. JOSEPH WYNNS on Wild Cat Gut. "...except the quitrents that
is due from the 5th day of March Anno Dom. 1748/49..." Wit: WILLIAM HOOKER,
JUN., THOMAS MORRIS, WILLIAM BEACHAM. Feb. Court 1752. *.

G 437 AARON LASETOR (LASSETOR) TO WILLIAM LASETOR
       Jan. 5, 1751. 26 pds. 10 sh. for 100 A. Land at mouth of Chinkapin
Branch at Mill Creek adj. RICHARD SOWELL. Wit: JAMES HINTON, THOMAS MORRIS,
ROBERT HILL. Feb. Court 1752. SAMUEL ORMES C/C.

G 439 EPHRAM HUNTER TO WILLIAM LASETOR, carpenter
       Dec. 16, 1751. 4 pds. 10 sh. for 140 A. "...whc. now remeains mine
that I purchased of WILLIAM ROGERS...." At "Golden Pleain Survay." Adj.
THOMAS MORRIS, EDWARD HOWCUTT, JOHN WYNNS, AARON PLOWER(?). Wit: ELEAZ.
QUINBY, THOMAS MOSES (MORE). Feb. Court 1752. *.

G 440 PETER EVANS, carpenter TO JAMES BAKER
       March 25, 1751. 40 pds. for 100 A. SS Wiccacon Creek at Spring
Branch adj. COLL. POLLOCK, ____ SHARP. Wit: WILLIAM WYNNS, JOSEPH WITHER-
INGTON. Feb. Court 1752. SAMUEL ORMES C/C.

G 441 HENRY DELON of Pasquotank County TO JAMES HAMILTON & WALTER EDGE,
       merchants of Hull in England. Oct. 9, 1750. 790 pds. for 150 A +
1 lot + 2 ships + negro + stock (1) Land on Cashy River which DELON Purchased of JOSHUA WILKINSON. (2) Lot # 7 "...in a place called Nixonton on
Little River in Pasquotank County...known as Water Lott...." (3) A 30 ton
Schooner called "Charming Nancy"...now on a voyage to Antigua..." A Brig-
antine called "Kingston" of 100 tons. (4) A negro woman called Hester (5)
"All my stock of cattle and horses now on my property....Providing that if
HENRY DELON...pay on or upon August next ensuing...(790 pds.)...with five
percent interest (by November 21 next)...then these shall be void." Wit:
JOHN CAMPBELL, THOMAS PIERCE, ROBERT COOK. N.C. Court April 17, 1752.
JAMES HASELL, C.J.

G 443 WILLIAM LITTLE of Edgecomb County TO JOHN BENTON, JUN. of Chowan Co.
       April 30, 1752. 45 pds. for 400 A. On Poplar Swamp Adj. "Lines for-
merly ABRAHAM BLULETs..." at Timber Branch. To Cattawasea(?) Swamp. Land
granted WILLIAM LITTLE, father of WILLIAM LITTLE, JUN. Wit: BENJAMIN WYNNS,
JOHN BRICKELL. May Court 1752. SAMUEL ORMES C/C.

G 445 WILLIAM REDDIT Of Duplin County, blacksmith, TO JOHN REDDITT
       March 3, 1752. 10 pds. for 200 A. ON SS Buckelsbery Swamp adj. ABRA-
HAM HERRING. Wit: ROBERT LAWRENCE, JOHN HOPKINS. May Court 1752. *.

G 446 BENJAMIN WYNNS FOR THOMAS LEE TO BYRANT HARE
       March 6, 1752. 20 pds. for 150 A. "...BENJAMIN WYNNS Executor of the
last Will and Testament of THOMAS LEE late of Bertie County deceased...."
Land between BRooks Creek and "the Main Road that leads to Wiccacon Ferry
...." Wit: JOHN BRICKELL, HENRY WINBOURNE, LUKE RAWLS. May Court 1752. *.

G 448 SMITHWICK WORBORTON (WARBUTTON) TO ABRAHAM BARBEREE (BARBREE)
       Dec. 2, 1751. "a valuable sum in Land" for 125 A Land on Kisia Neck
on NS Maratack River. Being part of a larger tract at SMITHWICK's Branch.
Adj. ____ WEST, TITUS LEGET. Wit: WILLIAM HENRY, JOHN WARBURTON, THOMAS
SAVAGE. May Court 1752. *.

G 449 WILLIAM WARD AND WIFE ANN of Tyrell Co. TO JOHN MACKENZIE, minister,
       of Suffolk Parish, Nansemond Co., Va. March 9, 1752. 80 pds.
for 300 A. ON NS Morattock River adj. LUKE MIZEL. "This day Personally
appeared before me ANN WARD...declared her consent to the said...that she
did sign the said Deed of her own free will without any fear complusion or
perswasion..." May 12, 1752. JOHN BROWN, his Majesty's Justice. Wit:
THOMAS WHITMELL, BENJAMIN WYNNS, W. GRAY. May Court 1752. *.

G 451 JENKINS HANSFORD, merchant TO JONAS TAYLOR, THOMAS SCOTT, WILLIAM
       SCOTT ALL OF NORFOLK CO, VA., ship carpenters.   Dec. 24, 1751.   322
pds. 4 sh. 9 p. Bond for Bond exchange + land sale. 640 A. "...whereas
JONAS TAYLOR, THOMAS SCOTT, WILLIAM SCOTT become jointly & severally bound
to Mess. JOHN BOYD & WILLIAM AITCHISON of...Norfolk...Merchs...(by) bond
(dated 23 day this instant of 322 pds. 4 sh. 9 p.)...with Interest thereon
...(we) give JENKINS HANSFORD & WILLIAM HANSFORD..." Note: This is an exchange of bonds. The HANSFORD Brothers are indebted to the three ships carpenters. They pledge payment in goods to BOYD & AITCHISON to discharge the
bonds. Goods to be delivered by JAMES KANNAN to be deducted from the amount
owed by HANSFORD & HANSFORD. JENKINS HANSFORD further transfers to TAYLOR,
SCOTT & SCOTT land purchased of BARNABY DUNSTAN on Chinquepen Swamp on WS
Chowan River cont. 640 A.   Transfers to be void if bond paid by HANSFORD
by June 3, 1753. Wit: JOHN SCOTT, WILLIAM HANSFORD, PETER PORTLAK(PORTLAKE),
RICHARD GARRETT. NC Court April 11, 1752. JAMES HASELL C.J.

G 453 THOMAS HANSFORD TO JONAS TAYLOR, THOMAS SCOTT, WILLIAM SCOTT OF
       Norfolk Co, Va. Dec. 24, 1751. "for bond secured" for 600 A. + 6
slaves JENKINS HANSFORD & WILLIAM HANSFORD sons of THOMAS HANSFORD. Land
"whereon said THOMAS HANSFORD now liveth". Called Malls Haven on WS Chowan
River. Six slaves named York, Hampton, Eleazer, Phillis, Caesar, Poll with
their future increase. Note: This is a mortgage by THOMAS HANSFORD to se-
cure the debt incurred by his sons, JENKINS & WILLIAM. Transfer to be null
and void if debt is paid by June 23, 1753. Wit: JOHN SCOTT, WILLIAM HANS-
FORD, PETER PORTLAK, RICHARD GARRETT. N.C. Court April 14, 1752. *.

G 456 JOSEPH WYMBERLY, merchant TO FRANCIS CORBIN of Edenton
       Oct. 4, 1753. 5 sh. Lease of 1230 A. (1) 600 A. which JOSEPH WYMBER-
LY purchased of ROBERT HIX Oct. 4, 1750. (2) 100 A. purchased of ABRAHAM
SHEPARD May 13, 1735. (3) 200 A. purchased of JONATHAN TAYLOR on May 25,
1744. (4) 330 A. purchased of JOHN WINGATE on Dec. 3, 1743. "...Unto the
said FRANCIS CORBIN...from the third Day of October Instant for and during
and untill the term of one whole Year...and paying unto the said JOSEPH
WIMBERLY...the Rent of one Pepper Corn only at the Feast of St. Michael the
Archangel next insuing...". Wit: T. BARKER, JAMES CAMPBELL. N.C. Court Oct.
12, 1752. *.

G 457 JOSEPH WIMBERLY TO FRANCIS CORBIN
       Oct. 5, 1752. 129 Pd. 1 sh. 4 p. for 1230 A. (1) 600 A. purchased
of ROBERT HIX on Oct. 4, 1750. (2) 100 A. purchased of ABRAHAM SHEPARD May
13, 1735. (3) 200 A. purchased of JONATHAN TAYLOR May 25, 1744. (4) 330 A.
purchased of JOHN WINGATE Dec. 3, 1743. The money to be paid "the first day
of March next ensuing...with lawfull Interest...at six per centum per annum
...". Wit: T. BARKER, JAMES CAMPBELL. N.C. Court Oct. 12, 1752. JAMES
HASELL, C.J. "Received of FRANCIS CORBIN...being the consideration within
mentioned the fifth day of October 1752. JOS. WIMBERLY."

G 460 JOHN HUSK TO HOZIKIAH (HEZEKIAH) HERRENDEN
       Feb. 14, 1751/52. 17 pds. 10 sh. for 150 A. At Roquiss Bridge by
"Keishey Road" adj. WILLIAM BARBER. Wit: EDWARD COLLINS, JOHN WARBUTTON,
JONATHAN RIDING, SAMUEL ORMES. N.C. Court Oct. 18, *. *.

G 461 DAVID MEADE of Nansemond Co, Va. TO BENJAMIN HILL
       Jan. 13, 1752. 100 pds. for 229 A. On Kesia River formerly belong-
ing to THOMAS KEARNEY and by him sold to MEADE March 30, 1738. Adj. LUKE
MEASLES on the River Pocoson. Wit: JOHN DRIVER, JOHN CAMPBELL, FRANCIS
SHEETS (STREETS). N.C. Court Oct. 16, 1752. *.

G 462 JOHN JEMISON & wife ELIZABETH, Practioner of Phisick, TO WILLIAM
       WILLIAMS of Edgecomb Co. Sept. 24, 1752. 300 pds. for 400 A. Land
adj. THEOPHILUS PUGH on Apple Tree Swamp at Falling Run. Wit: JOHN DAWSON,
DANIEL DAUGHTIE (DAUGHTRIE?), JOSEPH MUMFORD. N.C. Court Sept. 24, 1752.*.

G 465 SAMUEL WILLIAMS of Edgecomb Co. TO THOMAS JONES, attorney at law.
       April 26, 1750. 50 pds. for 150 A. Adj. WILLIAM WYNNS, WILLIAM
BROWN, "a percel of Intailed Land now in possession of THOMAS JONES", The
Chowan River at a place commonly called Petty Shoar. Wit: ALEXANDER MCCULL-
OCK, SAMUEL WILLIAMS, JUN. N.C. Court April 26, 1753. *.

G 466 SAMUEL WILLIAMS of Edgecomb TO THOMAS JONES
       Oct. 24, 1752. 49 pds. for 150 A. "...Whereas by an act of assembly

...ratifyed at Newbern the 14th day of April in the year of our Lord 1749. Instituted an act for Docking Intails of small Estates...that it shall and May be Lawfull for any Person Seized...of Land...not Exceeding the value of Fifty Pounds Sterling money and not being...contiguous to other Intailed Lands...Sue out a Writ from the Secretary's Office...Comanding him to Enquire...the vallue of Such Lands...then a Deed of Bargain and Sale reciting the Title and such...acknowledged...before the Chief Justice ...to Pass in Fee Simple such lands...Reversion (or) Recovery shall be barred in the same manner...to the Laws of England." SAMUEL WILLIAMS by last Will and testament of WILLIAM WILLIAMS dated Dec. 9, 1704(?) is seized of 150 A. and has "Sued out Writ" as directed. JOHN HILL, Sheriff of Bertie and other jurors said the land was of value of 49 pds. of Great Britain and declared clear title. Land on Petty Shore on SS Chowan River adj. JOHN BARTON, WILLIAM BROWN, THOMAS JONES. Wit: ALEXANDER MCCULLOCK, SAMUEL WILLIAMS, JUN. N.C. Court April 26, 1753. JAMES HASELL, C.J.

G 469 ROBERT WEST, SEN. TO THOMAS WEST
       July 8, 1752. Deed of Gift for 200 A. "...in consideration of Love, Goodwill and affection...toward my Loving Sun THOMAS WEST...". Land held by deed from CHARLES MITCHELL to Coll. ROBERT WEST, SEN. Wit: FRANCES POLLOCK, ELIZABETH JONES, EVAN JONES. N.C. Court April 11, 1753. *.

G 470 COLL. ROBERT WEST TO THOMAS WEST of Tyrryl Co.
       July 7, 1752. 100 pds. for 530 A. Land on NS Morattock River adj. ELIZABETH GRIFFIN at Spring Branch at Cushoke Creek. Land granted ROBERT WEST in 1712. Wit: FRANCES POLLOCK, ELIZABETH JONES, EVAN JONES. N.C. Court April 11, 1753. *.

G 472 WILLIAM BEVERLY of Craven Co. TO ARTHUR COTTEN of Northampton Co.
       Nov. 20, 1752. 60 pds. for 300 A. Land on NS Ahotskey Swamp "being a Certain Piece of Land that was given him...by Will by his said Grandfather JOHN BEVERLY, sen...as per patent it being half of the patent formerly granted to MR. JOHN BEVERLY..." Wit: WILLIAM RUTLAND, EDWARD RUTLAND, JOHN COTTEN. N.C. Court April 20, 1753. *.

G 473 ROBERT ROGERS of Chowan Co. TO RICHARD TOMLINSON, Blacksmith
       Oct. 20, 1752. 20 pds. for 200 A. Land on Cashy Neck "whereon the said TOMLINSON now Lives". On Morattock River Pocoson adj.____ASHBORN,____ BRADLEY at Brick House Swamp. Wit: JONATHAN STANDLY, JOHN ROGERS, DAVID STANDLY. N.C. Court April 11, 1753. *.

G 474 THOMAS PUGH TO JOSEPH HARRELL
       April 3, 1753. 55 pds. for 300 A. Land at Flaggy Run adj. JETHRO BUTLER, JOHN HARRELL. Wit: JOHN HARRELL, ABRAHAM HARRELL, MARY HARRELL. May Court 1753. BENJAMIN WYNNS C/C.

G 476 PAUL PENDER TO ALEXANDER COTTEN
       ** 1753. 10 pds. for 100 A. Land at Deep Creek adj. "FIERYBENTS former Line." Wit: BRYAN HARE, ALEXANDER COTTEN, JUN. May Court 1753. *.

G 477 PAUL PENDER TO JOHN WILLOBY
       Feb. 28, 1752. 50 pds. for 75 A. Money paid by "JOHN WILLOBY deceased" and land transferred to his son, JOHN WILLOBY. Land on SS Horse Swamp adj. JOHN WILLOBY, SEN., ROBERT FORSTER, JEREMIAH BARNS. Wit: WILLIAM GODWIN, GILSTRAP WILLIAMS. May Court 1753. BENJAMIN WYNNS C/C.

G 478 JOHN SALLIS of Granville Co. TO JOHN BRICKELL
       May 29, 1752. 15 pds. for 300 A. By Deed from PELEG ROGERS to WILLIAM EVANS "which said Land was mortgaged...to JAMES CASTELLOW GENT., Treasurer...forfeited and sold to JOHN SALLIS..." Wit: JOHN BROWN, REUBEN POWELL, JEREMIAH CREECH. May Court 1753. *.

G 480 JACOB HUMFREYS of Onslow Co. & Wife MARTHA TO JOHN BROWN of Northampton Co. Aug. 22, 1752. *for 320 A. Part of a tract surveyed for THOMAS BROWN and ROBERT PATTISON on Pottacasey Swamp. Wit: MATTHEW MASHBORN, CHARLES COX, ROBERT HUTCHINSON, MOSES MCDANIEL. May Court 1753. *.

G 481 HENRY REED TO EDWARD SCULL (SKULL)
       Oct. 30, 1752. 37 pds. for 200 A. On eastermost side of Deep Creek near Chowan River. At SS Deep Creek Bridge adj. EDWARD HARE. Wit: JOHN BRICKELL, JOHN GILBERT (GILLOT). May Court 1753. *.

G 482 BRYAN HARE TO DAVID SINCLARE (SINCLAR)
     March 30, 1753. 40 pds. for 150 A. Land Between Brooks Creek and
the road to Wiccacon Ferry at Ferry Landing. Wit: BENJAMIN HILL, JOHN BRICK-
ELL. May Court 1753. *.

G 483 NATHANIEL MINGE (MING) of Chowan Co. TO CHRISTIAN PRATT of Orange Co.
     June 25, 1752. 2 pds. for 120 A. Land in Casis Neck adj. LUKE MIZEL,
PHILLIP WARD. By patent dated Feb. 21, 1729 to NATHANIAL MING. Wit: THOMAS
WHITMELL. *. N.C. Court April 23, 1753. JAMES HASELL, C.J.

G 484 MARY HOCOT, widow TO WILLIAM HOOKER, JUN.
     Nov. 1, 1752. 50 pds. for 150 A. Land on WS Chowan River below
Mount Pleasant Plantation adj. EDWARD HOCOT, WILLIAM BEACHUN, JAMES HINTON
at Wild Catt Gutt, JOSEPH WYNNS. Wit: ELEAZER QUINBY, JOHN FANNIN, SARAH
FANNIN, ELIZABETH HOCOTT. May Court 1753. BENJAMIN WYNNS C /C.

G 486 ELIZABETH GOULD, widow TO JOHN BUTTERTON
     Nov. 21, 1752. 50 pds. for 316 A. "ELIZABETH GOULD Widow and Relict
of GEORGE GOULD ESQ." Land at JOHN HOWELS Mill Swamp on Chowan River. "...
Excepted Out of the same half an acre of Land on which a Mill now stands...
belonging to JOHN HOWELL...". Wit: JOHN CAMPBELL, JOHN WILSON. May Court
1753. *.

G 487 WILLIAM SOANE TO JOHN CAMPBELL, merchant
     Sept. 28, 1752. 27 pds. 10 sh. for 272 A. "...WILLIAM SOANE Heir at
Law to his Late Father JOHN SOANE...Deceased Intestate...only Son to the
said JOHN by HANNAH his wife...". Land part of 640 A. formerly granted
RICHARD BOOTH. On WS Chowan River "...Below the ferry Point so called for-
merly whereon CAMPBELL now lives. Adj. JOHN HOWELL. "Excepting ten feet
Square to THOMAS SUTTON for Burying Ground." Wit: JOHN HARDISON, EDWARD
RASOR, JOHN DAILY. May Court 1753. BENJAMIN WYNNS C/C.

G 489 WILLIAM SOANE of Tyrill Co. TO JOHN CAMPBELL, merchant
     Sept 28, 1752. Bond to assure true title for 270 A. "I...Heir at
Law to JOHN SOANES Late of Bertie County Deceased...am firmly bound...in
the amount of Fifty Pounds Sterling Lawfull money of England...". This bond
to be forfeited if land title is not clear. Wit: JOHN HARDISON, EDWARD
RASOR. May Court 1753. *.

G 490 WILLIAM BUSH TO HARDY BUSH
     May 8, 1730. Deed of Gift for 200 A. "...To my Loving Kinsman HARDY
BUSH Orphan Son of JOHN BUSH...Lately Deceased...". Land in Chinkopen Neck
at the mouth of Polecatt Branch at the Gnawing Pond. Adj. THOMAS MCCLENDON.
On Wiccacon Creek. Wit: WILLIAM CRANFORD, JOHN WYNNS. May Court 1730.
THOMAS HANSFORD D.C/C.

G 491 HARDY BUSH TO BENJAMIN WYNNS, yeoman
     July 18, 1752. 12 pds. "...my Right Title and Claim to within men-
tioned Lands...". Wit: THOMAS CASTELLOW, MARY CASTELLOW. May Court 1753.*.

G 492 JOSEPH PERRY TO JESSE WOOD
     July 3, 1752. 25 pds. for 60 A. At Miery Branch and Deertree Branch
adj. "s'd PERRY". Wit: BENJAMIN WYNNS, WILLIAM WYNNS, JAMES WOOD. May Court
1753. BENJAMIN WYNNS C/C.

G 493 MICHAEL KING TO NATHAN MIERS
     Jan. 18, 1753. 28 pds. for 72 A. Land on Broad Branch adj. JOHN
WILLIAMS, JUN., SAMUEL HERRING. Wit: WILLIAM KING, HENRY ROADS, CHARLES
KING. May Court 1753. *.

G 495 JOHN WELLS TO RICHARD FREEMAN of Chowan Co.
     Dec. 26, 1752. 29 pds. for 225 A. Between WALTER DRAUGHAN, JONATHAN
MILLER & JAMES HOLLEY on Barbeque Swamp. Wit: JOHN FREEMAN, THOMAS MORRIS,
JAMES FREEMAN. May Court 1753. *.

G 496 ROBERT WARRIN of Duplin County TO THOMAS PARKER
     Aug. 7, 1752. 40 sh. for 213 A. Land between JOHN DAVIS & HENRY
ROADS. Wit: JOHN FREEMAN, RICHARD RANOR, LAZARUS GARRET. May Court 1753.*.

G 497 GEORGE WYNNS TO WILLIAM ASKEW
     Nov. 6, 1752. 20 pds. for 100 A. Adj. WILLIAM WRIGHT on Deep Branch.

Wit: WILLIAM WYNNS, BENJAMIN WYNNS. May Court 1753. *.

G 499   HENRY KING of Duplin County TO DAVID BRYAN
        May 18, 1752.   30 pds. for 225 A. WS Cashoke Creek adj. EDWARD BIRD,
COLL. ROBERT WEST, GEORGE BELL. Wit: ROBERT WEST, ROBERT WEST, JUN., TAMER
WEST. May Court 1753. *.

G 500   MARY VARLEN, Spinster & WILLIAM FAIRLESS (FAIRLES) TO BLAKE BAKER
        May 2, 1753.   5 sh. Lease for one year for 200 A. SWS Chowan River
at Petty Shore. By deed from BENJAMIN WYNNS dated May 1, 1750 for 40 pds.
"unto MARY VARLEN During her Natural Life and after her Decease to ...WIL-
LIAM FAIRLESS." Wit: JOHN HARRELL, JOHN BAKER, NATHANIEL HARGROVE. May
Court 1753. BENJAMIN WYNNS C/C.

G 501   MARY VERLEN, Spinster, & WILLIAM FAIRLESS TO BLAKE BAKER
        May 3, 1753.   80 pds. for 200 A. Land on SWS Chowan River at Petty
Shore, which land was bought of WILLIAM WYNNS May 7, 1750. Wit: JOHN HAR-
RELL, JOHN BAKER, NATHANIEL HARGROVE. May Court 1753. *.

G 505   JOSEPH WETHERINGTON (WELLINGTON) TO GEORGE WYNNS
        Feb. 6, 1753.   40 pds. for 256 A. SWS Chowan River "Plantation...
whereon WILLIAM WETHERINGTON Lately Lived..." Land adj. JAMES CURLEE, JOHN
SMITH. Wit: WILLIAM WYNNS, BENJMAIN WYNNS. May Court 1753. *.

G 506   RICHARD ROBERTS, cooper, TO JAMES DAVIS
        Nov. 30, 1752.   14 pds. for 200 A. On SWS Flatt Swamp "being the
Land and Plantation which I purchased from PAUL PENDER" adj. EDWARD OUTLAW.
Wit: RICHARD ROBERTS, NICHOLAS ASKEW, BENJAMIN WYNNS. May Court 1753. *.

G 507   GEORGE WYNNS TO WILLIAM WRIGHT, School Master
        June 5, 1752.   20 pds. for 250 A. Land called Red Banks adj. GEORGE
WYNNS on Andersons Neck "called forked branch". At Deep Branch. Wit: WILL-
IAM WYNNS, BENJAMIN WYNNS, WILLIAM WITHERINGTON. May Court 1753. *.

G 509   WILLIAM LEE, Husbandman, TO JOSHUA, FRANCIS & ANN LEE
        Jan. 25, 1752.   5 sh. Deed of Gift for Land and personal property.
"for...Five shillings...and also for the Love good Will and affection...
toward my two sons JOSHUA LEE & FRANCIS LEE and my Daughter ANN LEE...All
my Lands and Tenements Goods and Chattles..." (1) To JOSHUA: "That part of
my land whereon he now lives as already known to be mutually agreed upon.."
(2) To FRANCIS: "the Plantation on which I now live...except the part already Laid off to JOSHUA...". (3) A feather bed to each son, and a feather
bed to ANN. The rest of my estate to be equally divided among my three
children. "Not Intended to be the property of my Sons and Daughter until
after the Death of myself and my wife MARTHA LEE...If either of my Sons
shall Die without issue...the Survivor of them shall...be Invested with the
land before mentioned." Wit: WILLIAM LEE, CHRISTOPHER HOLLOMAN, PEGGY
WYNNS, BENJAMIN WYNNS. May Court 1753. BENJAMIN WYNNS C/C.

G 510   JOHN JOHNSON & MARY JOHNSON TO THOMAS WHITMELL
        May 9, 1753.   200 pds. for 200 A. Land granted JOHN SMITHWICK Aug.
7, 1720. At fork of Roquis Swamp. Called "Battesburg" at a Beach called
Chuattat(?) adj. WHITMELL near Quitsney adj. HENRY HUNTER. Wit: JOHN BRICK-
ELL, BLAKE BAKER, JOHN HARRELL, JUN. May Court 1753. *.

G 512   MICHAEL SANDERS TOOL TO EDWARD TOOL
        Jan. 20, 1753.   47 pds. for 200 A. Adj. NEEDHAM BRYAN, MATTHEW
TURNER, ISAAC HARRELL, CALEB SPIVEY, THEOPHILUS WILLIAMS. Wit: JOHN HARRELL,
JESSE HARRELL, ISRAEL HARRELL, HARDY HARRELL. May Court 1753. *.

G 513   JOHN SMITH, merchant TO BARNABY HELY DUNSTAN, joyner
        May 9, 1753.   40 pds. for 100 A. At a branch issuing out of Cashie
River adj. ROBERT BIRD at the River Pocoson. Wit: JOSEPH JORDAN, ANDREW
BURN, THOMAS SPELLER. May Court 1753. *.

G 515   SAMUEL ONWIN TO WILLIAM CAKE
        May 11, 1753.   5 pds. for 100 A. Land bought of JAMES ROADS adj.
WILLIAM RUTTOR(?) on White Oak Swamp at a Tarkiln. Wit: JAMES YATES, MOSES
MEWBERN, JOHN CAKE, JUN. May Court 1753. *.

G 516 WILLIAM HALY, shipwright TO JOHN CAMPBELL, merchant
       ** 100 pds. for "A Certain Frame of Timber and Vessell" Ship "Now on
the Stocks the Keel in Length Sixty feet and Designed to be compleated and
Built in Bredth Twenty three feet Beam, Depth Eight feet and Height from
upper Deck to the Beams five feet Together with all Iron, Iron Work, Timber,
Planks, Beam, Knees of all kinds and Trunnells a full and Sufficient Quantity to frame, Build, Compleat and Launch when compleated and finished...as
well as my Right...procured of Mr. THOMAS RYAN a certain Tract and percel
of Ground for a Ship Yard Laying on Salmon Creek...and Previledge...to cut
Down Timber necessary for Building Compleating Launching of the said Frame
and Vessell until she is compleat..." My tools and premises procured from
MATTHEW THOMAS, THOMAS RYAN by credit given to JOHN CAMPBELL. "Received...
(money above) also Seven Pounds Like money being for a Beat and Tackel
sold...(to) me" Land "whereon RYAN now dwelleth containing one acre". Wit:
THOMAS RYAN, DAVID RYAN. May Court 1753. *.

G 518 THCMAS & FRANCIS PUGH TO JOHN BROWN
       May 9, 1753. 20 pds. for 157 A. Wit: ALEXANDER COTTEN, JOHN BRICK-
ELL. May Court 1753. BENJAMIN WYNNS C/C.

G 519 WILLIAM GRAY TO JACOB BLOUNT & WIFE BARBARA
       May 5, 1753. 50 pds. for 400 A. On Broadbranch adj. THOMAS TURNER
at ThoroughFare Branch. Wit: THOMAS TURNER, THOMAS WHITMELL, ROBERT HOWELL.
May 10, 1753. *.

G 521 JACOB BLOUNT & wife BARBARA TO WILLIAM GRAY
       May 10, 1753. 50 pds. for 600 A. At Broadbranch adj. WILLIAM GRAY,
THOMAS TURNER "Land given of JOHN GRAY by Will to his Daughter the above
s'd BARBARA...". "...the feme being first privately Examined by ROBERT
HARDY Esquire one of His Majesties Justices of the Peace...". ** May Court
1753. *.

G 522 WILLIAM BIRD of Duplin County TO JOSEPH KNOTT
       Jan. 13, 1753. 500 pds. for 600 A. "...a tract of Land taken up by
JOHN HERRING patent bearing Date the Eight Day of October 17?7...". On
Wills Quarter Swamp Adj. CHARLES BARBER, ROBERT TURNER. Wit: ABRAHAM JORDAN,
NATHANIEL KNOTT, JOSEPH HARDY. May Court 1753. *.

G 524 THOMAS CASTELLOW of Duplin Co. TO JOHN WESTON
       May 22, 1753. 80 pds. for 360 A. Land adj. JOHN PLOWMAN, ___ BARBER
on the River Pocoson. Wit: JOHN HILL, DAVID JERNIGAN. Aug. Court 1753.
SAMUEL ORMES C/C.

G 527 JOSEPH DEMSEY (DEMCEY) TO ROBERT WEST
       May 11, 1752. 60 pds. for 78 1/2 A. Land on SS Buckelsberry Pocoson.
Being Half of a certain tract formerly belonging to Mr. JOHN COOK by patent
1721. The "Eastermost half" of this tract. Wit: WILLIAM BALL, THOMAS OLIVER,
L. LOCKHART. Aug. Court 1753. *.

G 528 JAMES MCGLOHON, son of JERIMAH TO JAMES MCGLOHON, son of JAMES
       May 20, 1753. 3 pds. for 140 A. "JEREMIAH MCGLOHON Son of JERIMIAH
MACGLOHON deceased of Bertie County...to JAMES MCGLOHON son of JAMES MCGLO-
HON..." Land on Wiccacon Creek. Wit: JOSEPH PERRY, THOMAS YATES. Aug. Court
1753. *.

G 529 SAMUEL SINGLETON TO WILLIAM TYLER of "Chowan Court"
       Oct. *, 1752. 35 pds. for 200 A. NS Pocoson adj. ROBERT HOWEL at
Chiske. Wit: JOSEPH ALPHIN, ISIAIAH POWELLS. Aug. Court 1753. *.

G 530 SAMUEL SINGLETON TO PETER BRINKLEY of Chowan County
       Oct. 4, 1752. 30 pds. for 190 A. On NS Rocquiss Swamp adj. JOSEPH
KNOT, FRANCIS HOBSON, THOMAS RYAN. Wit: JOSEPH ALPHIN, ISAIAH POWELL. Aug.
Court 1753. SAMUEL ORMES C/C.

G 531 JOHN HINTON TO JOHNAS HINTON
       Aug. 14, 1753. Deed of Gift for 190 A. "...JOHN HINTON eldest Law-
ful Son of the Deasied WILLIAM HINTON...and JOHNAN (JONAS?) HINTON his
brother...part of a Tract formerly belonging to WILLIAM HINTON...". Land at
_leg Swamp adj. JOHN HINTON, THOMAS BARKER. Wit: WILLIAM WILLIAMS, WILLIAM
JENKISON. Aug. Court 1753. *.

G 533 EPHRAM JOHNS of Bewford County to JACOB JERNEGAN
       * 25 pds. for 90 A. On NS Roanoke River adj. THOMAS BUNTON. Wit:
EDWARD MORE, WILLIAM JUNKISON. Aug. Court 1753. *.

G 534 WILLIAM HOOKES, SEN. TO NATHAN HOOKER
       * Deed of Gift for 100 A. + 10 1/2 A. "...Love good Will and Effec-
tion which I have...Unto my Son NATHAN HOOKER" Two tracts (1) 100 A. on
Flatty Gutt at mouth of Deep Branch to Tarr Kiln Branch adj. COLL. POLLOCK.
(2) 10 1/2 A. at Chappel Spring Branch on Flatty Gutt. Wit: JAMES HOOKER,
ST. HOOKER, BURRILL BELL, JOHN HOOKER. Aug. Court 1753. *.

G 535 DAVID BALLENTINE TO ALEXANDER BALLENTINE
       Feb. 8, 1750/51. Deed of Gift for 220 A. "...(for) the great affec-
tion I have and do bear to my well beloved Brother ALEXANDER BALLENTINE as
well as to fullfill the design on my honoured Father..." Land on Killum
Swamp at mouth of Holley Branch adj. "late dwelling Plantation of ALEXANDER
BALLENTINE (deceased)...". Wit: MALACHI WESTON, ROBERT DROUGHAN. Aug. Court
1753. *.

G 536 DAVID BALLENTINE TO JAMES BALLENTINE
       Feb. 8, 1750/51. Deed of Gift for 100 A. "affection...to my Brother
JAMES BALLENTINE as well as to fullfill the design of my Honoured Father.."
Land on Killum Swamp adj. GEORGE VALLENTINE. Wit: MALACHI WESTON, ROBERT
DROUGHAN. Aug. Court 1753. *.

G 537 DOM REX TO THOMAS ODAM
       April 20, 1745. Grant for 200 A. SS Hearts Delight Pocoson adj.
RICHARD WILLIFRED. Signed: GABRIEL JOHNSTON ESQUIRE Our Captain General and
Governor in Chief at New Bern. April 20, 1745. ROBERT FORSTER, Deputy Sec-
retary. "Enrolled in the Auditor Generals Office 20th April 1745. ALEX.
MCCULLOCH Dep. Aud.

G 538 THOMAS ODAM TO THOMAS OUTLAW
       ** 1752. 12 pds. "within mentioned land". Wit: WILLIAM OUTLAW,
CHARYT COCK. Aug. Court 1753. SAMUEL ORMES C/C.

G 539 JACOB LEWIS TO BENJAMIN WYNNS
       April 22, 1752. 20 pds. for 96 A. NS Wiccacon Creek at the Creek
Pocoson at the Landing. Wit: FRANCIS THOMAS, HARMON HOLLAMAN. Aug. Court
1753. *.

G 540 JOHN CHAMBERS TO WILLIAM NOWLING
       Oct. 10, 1752. 80 pds. for 220 A. At Thoroughfare Pocoson at Little
Meadow Branch. Wit: FRANCIS WALL, JOHN NOWLING. N.C. Court April 11, 1753.
JAMES HASSELL C.J.

G 542 LORDS PROPRIETORS TO ROBERT WEST
       Aug. 10, 1720. Grant for 640 A. On Cassye River "In Chewan Precinct"
adj. "Major WESTS old corner", LAURENCE GARSON. For importation one person
every fifty acres. CHARLES EDEN ESQ. Govr. & the Rest of Our Trusty Councillors, Signed JOHN LOVICH, Sec'y. RICHARD SANDERSON, FRANCIS FOSTER(?),
THOMAS POLLOCK, WILLIAM REED.

G 542 ROBERT WEST, SEN. TO ROBERT WEST, JUN.
       July 8, 1752. Deed of Gift "...unto my loving son ROBERT WEST, JUN
..." Within patent. Wit: EVAN JONES, THOMAS WEST, ELIZABETH JONES, FRANCES
POLLOCK. Aug. Court 1753. SAMUEL ORMES, C/C.

G 543 LORDS PROPRIETORS TO ROBERT WEST
       Dec. 1, 1712. Grant 410 A. "His Excellcy The Most Noble HENRY Duke
of Beaufort Pallatine and the rest of...our Lords Proprietors..." Land at
fork of Kesiah River. Due for importation of persons/every 50 A. Hon'ble
THOMAS POLLOCK Esq. President of the Councell & the rest of our Trusty
Councellors. Recorded in Sec't'y's Office Oct. 9, 1712. T. KNIGHT, Sec'y.
W. REED, THOS. POLLOCK THOS. BOYD, C. GALE, T. KNIGHT.

G 544 ROBERT WEST, SEN. TO ROBERT WEST JUN.
       July 8, 1752. Deed of Gift. All "Right Title and Interest to with-
in mentioned patent". Wit: EVAN JONES, THOMAS WEST, ELIZABETH JONES,
FRANCES POLLOCK. Aug. Court 1753. *.

G 544 JAMES BAKER, yeoman TO SAMUEL HOLLAMAN
     Jan. 12, 1753. 35 pds. for 300 A. Land on SS Ahotokey Swamp. Wit:
PEGGY WYNNS, BENJAMIN WYNNS. Aug. Court 1753. SAMUEL ORMES C/C.

G 546 BLAKE BAKER TO CADAR POWELL
     May 26, 1753. 62 pds. 5 sh. for 640 A. Land "...on the Line that
divides Bertie and Northampton Counties". On Refreshing Meadow in Horskey
Marsh at head of Wiccacon Creek. Adj. RICHARD BARFIELD. Land formerly granted HENRY BAKER by Order of Councill April 1, 1723. Wit: CHARLES HORNE,
WILLIAM RUTLAND. Aug. Court 1753. *.

G 547 JOHN BARTON TO THOMAS JONES
     Feb. 1, 1753. 60 pds. for 300 A. SS Chowan Adj. THOMAS JONES on the
river bank. At mouth of Deep Creek. Wit: WILLIAM WYNNS, ____BARTON. Aug.
Court 1753. *.

G 548 RICHARD HARRELL (HERRELL) TO SAMUEL ANDREWS
     June 5, 1753. 18 pds. * "...being part of a Patent bearing Date
March 1, 1721..." In the Low Grounds of the River adj. MARMEDUKE NORFLEET
at Upper Black Pond. Wit: JOHN HARRELL, THOMAS HAYS. Aug. Court 1753. *.

G 550 ROBERT BIRD TO RICHARD DUNSTAN, joyner
     Feb. 3, 1753. 25 pds. for 200 A. On NS Casy Adj. BARNABY DUNSTAN.
Wit: BARNABY HALY DUNSTAN, JOHN WARD. Aug. Court 1753. *.

G 551 WILLIAM WEBB & WIFE SUSANNAH TO JOHN SUMNER (SUMNAR) of Chowan Co.
     Nov. 2, 1752. 90 pds. for 320 A. Land was sold by GEORGE NICHOLSON
to ANTHONY WEBB and by ANTHONY WEBB bequeathed to his Son WILLIAM WEBB.
Land adj. WILLIAM WILLIFORD. Wit: MOSES SUMNER, WILLIAM SUMNER, SAMUEL
SUMNER. Aug. Court 1753. *.

G 553 WILLIAM WEBB TO JOHN SUMNER of Chowan Co.
     Oct. 28, 1752. 10 pds. for 150 A. Land on NS Wiccacon Creek at
Horse Swamp "below the Hows". Adj. JOHN CLARK. Being the plantation the
HENRY VIZE sold to WILLIAM MIDILTON and s'd MIDILTON sold to ANTHONY WEBB
and by him given to WILLIAM WEBB. Wit: MOSES SUMNER, WILLIAM SKINNER,
SAMUEL SKINNER. Aug. Court 1753. *.

G 555 JAMES HOWARD TO JOSEPH HOWARD
     June 15, 1753. 5 pds. for 200 A. Granted to JAMES HOWARD, SEN. De-
ceased April 1, 1723. On NS Ahotsky Swamp adj. EDWARD HOWARD, JOSEPH HOW-
ARD. Wit: WILLIAM HUMFREE, JOHN HARE, SOLOMON HOWARD. Aug. Court 1753. *.

G 556 JAMES HOWARD TO SAMUEL HOWARD
     May 9, 1752. 16 pds. for 220 A. SWS Conneritsrat Swamp. Patent
granted JAMES HOWARD "deceast". Wit: WILLIAM SHOLER, JOHN SHOLAR. Aug.
Court 1753. *.

G 554 BENNETT BAKER, yeoman TO JAMES WILLIAMS
     Dec. 11, 1752. 15 pds. for 200 A. ES Chinkapin Swamp adj. "JAMES
HOLLY which was bequeathed to JANE his wife by last will of Our Father JOHN
SMITH deceased..." Adj. JAMES WILLIAMS. Wit: JOHN FREEMAN, DAVID BALLENTINE,
WILLIAM COLTHRED. Aug. Court 1753. *.

G 555 HENERY RHODES TO JOHN RHODES
     March 21, 1753. 7 pds. 7 sh. for 200 A. NS Roquis Pocoson on mouth
of Will Hoges Branch. Adj. ____WIMBLEY, NATHAN MIERSES. Wit: WILLIAM KING,
THOMAS ROADES, EDWARD GILLMAN, JUN. Aug. Court 1753. *.

G 557 JOHN SALLIS TO THOMAS RYAN
     May 28, 1752. 20 pds. (Ster. G.B.) for 100 A. On NS Cashy River
adj. WILLIAM COLLINS, Doc't. JAMES FLOOD. By a deed passed from THOMAS
DAVIS to GARRARD VANUPSTALL "and on record in Bertie County". Wit: DAVID
RYAN, ELIZABETH RYAN. Aug. Court 1753. *.

G 559 JOHN NICHOLES TO THOMAS RYAN
     Feb. 5, 1753. 200 pds. for 390 A. Adj. Mrs. JOHNSTON at Middle
Swamp. Wit: ELIZABETH CAMPBELL, HUMPHERY NICHOLLS, WM. NUGENT. Aug. Court
1753. *.

G 560 PATRICK KANADAY, carpanter TO DAVID KANADAY
       June 13, 1752. 10 pds. for 100 A. At Poplar Branch at Wills Quarter
Swamp at Beaverdam adj. MR. KING. Wit: ELIZABETH BUTLER, ART. WILLIAMS,
ABRAHAM JORDAIN. Aug. Court 1753. *.

G 561 WILLIAM WITHERINGTON, yeoman TO JOSEPH WITHERINGTON
       Feb. 6, *. 20 pds. for 50 A. On NS Wiccacon Creek adj. ___SHARP, ___
BAKER, ___FIGURES. Wit: WILLIAM WYNNS, BENJAMIN WYNNS. Aug. Court 1753. *.

G 561 WILLIAM WYNNS, ESQ., attorney for JOHN SPEIR & EZEKIEL SLAWSON TO
       WILLIAM WITHERINGTON. Feb. 6, 1753. 20 pds. for 240 A. + 100 A.
Power of Atty. May 7, 1751. (1) Land in Killum Woods whereon EBENEZER
SLANSON (SLAUSON) lived cont. 240 A. (2) Land where JOHN SPEIR lately lived
cont. 100 A. Wit: BENJAMIN WYNNS, WILLIAM SISSON, GEORGE WYNNS. Aug. Court
1753. *.

G 563 ELEXANDER (ALEXANDER) KENADAY TO MICHELL WARD, JUN.
       Nov. 20, 1750. 17 pds. 10 sh. for 200 A. Land adj. RODGER BADGETT.
Part of patent granted ELEXANDER KANADAY for 640 A. April 6, 1745. Wit:
JOHN SMITH, THOMAS WARD, JAMES DROUGHON. Aug. Court 1753. *.

G 564 WILLIAM PERRY TO MICHAEL WARD, JUN.,yeoman
       March 16, 1750/51. 20 pds. + 100 Barrels of merchantable Tarr" for
300 A. Land on Chinkopen Neck adj. Holey Branch to PELT's Path, ARON
ASCKEW, BENJAMIN WYNNS. Wit: STEPEHN HOOKER, JAMES MCCLOHON, JOHN SMITH.
Aug. Court 1753. SAMUEL ORMES C/C.

                        End of Deed Book G

                        _____

                           DEED BOOK H

H 1 WILLIAM KEETOR, cooper, TO EDWARD RAZOR
     Nov. 12, 1753. 15 pds. for 200 A. WILLIAM KEETOR, son and heir to
JAMES KEETOR, deceased "...one certain messuage Track or Parcell of Land
containing fifty acres...on South side Black Walnut Swamp...upper part of
tract of land that did belong to MARY JONES, whom ISAAC GREGORY married &
by the s'd GREGORY (was)...sold to above JAMES KEETOR..." Wit: MARY DILLON,
H. NICHOLS, WILLIAM HARDY. Nov. Court 1753. SAMUEL ORMES C/C.

H 2 JOHN WESTON & WIFE MARTHA TO GEORGE JERNIGAN
     Sept. 10, 1753. 30 pds. for 200 A. On ES Loosing Swamp "...MARTHA
WESTON, wife of JOHN WESTON...came before me and being privately examined
declared that she signed the above deed of her own free will...without compulsion..." ROBERT HARDY. Nov. 13, 1753. Wit: JOHN SOWELL, BENJAMIN
WYNNS. Nov. Court 1753. *.

H 3 WILLIAM WARD of Tyrrell County TO PHILLIP WARD
     May 7, 1753. 20 pds. for 640 A. Land on NS Moratuck River adj.
CLARK'S corner, GEORGE CLARK, "to a Green on CHARLTON's line", WILLIAM
CHARLTON. On SW branch of Roquist. Wit: WILLIAM HOOKS, THOMAS HOOKS, JAMES
WARD. Nov. Court 1753. *.

H 4 THOMAS WALKER TO WILLIAM WEAVER
     Aug. 27, 1753. 23 pds. for 100 A. Land adj. JOHN CARTERS Mill "that
the said WALKER sold to JOHN CARTER...to a deep bottom near a place called
Morning(?) Glorys whole..." On Pottacasy Branch. Wit: GILLSTRAP WILLIAMS,
ROSANNA WILLIAMS, ELIZABETH PENDER. Nov. Court 1753. *.

H 5 WILLIAM NOWLING TO JOHN WARBURTON
     Aug. 28, 1753. 26 pds. 10 sh. for 112 3/4 A. In Cashie Neck adj.
THOMAS SAVAGE, WILLIAM SMITHWICK, Herron (Heoren?) Creek. Wit: RICHARD
BRADLEY, THOMAS SAVAGE. Nov. Court 1753. *.

H 6 WILLIAM NOWLING TO THOMAS SAVAGE
     Aug. 28, 1753. 26 pds. 10 sh. for 107 A. Land in Cashy Neck on the
Thoroughfare Pocoson at Little Meadow Branch. Wit: RICHARD BRADLEY, JOHN

WARBURTON. Nov. Court 1753. *.

H 7   MARMADUKE ROBERSON of Tyrrell TO LAZARUS SUMERELL
      Oct. 22, 1753. 10 pds. for 50 A. On WS Cashie Swamp. Being part of a
patent formerly granted to WILLIAM WILSON adj. land LAZARUS SUMMERELL
bought of WILLIAM WILSON. Wit: THOMAS RHODES, JOSEPH JOLLY (?), ANN ANBORN
(?) (Note: Erasure in deed here.) Nov. Court 1753. SAMUEL ORMES C/C.

H 8   WILLIAM WILSON TO LAZARUS SUMMERRELL
      Sept. 19, 1753. 10 pds. for 50 A. Part of a patent granted to WIL-
LIAM WILSON "...and includes plantation whereon THOMAS BASS now lives..."
On SS Cashie Swamp adj. THOMAS BASS, MARMADUKE ROBERSON(?). Wit: THOMAS
WHITMELL, ELISABETH WHITMELL, MARTHA WHITMELL. Nov. Court 1753. *.

NOTE: The following several deeds from pages 9 through 36 in Book H relate
to sales at Public auction of land formerly belonging to THEOPHILUS PUGH,
merchant of Bertie. At the time of his death PUGH was indebted to ROBERT
CLARY of London, merchant, in the amount of 9061 pds. 12 sh. 5 p. JAMES
POWER was appointed administrator of the estate of PUGH. At the death of
POWER, before the settlement of PUGH's estate, BENJAMIN HILL was appointed
administrator of PUGH's estate. Suit was brought against PUGH's estate by
ROBERT JONES for recovery of debt. While suit was in progress ROBERT CLARY
died and AMY CLARY, HENRY STEVENS & EDWARD WOODCOCK were appointed administrators of CLARY's estate. At New Bern in March 1753 the case was heard
before Chief Justice JAMES HASSELL. The Sheriff was ordered to seize and
sell the lands to settle the remaining small portion of the debt to the
CLARY estate. The several laws governing this sale were cited in each deed.

H 9   JOHN HILL, Sheriff of Bertie TO ROBERT PEEL of Northampton County
      Aug. 14, 1753. 20 pds. for * A. Land adj. JOHN JONES, EDWARD HOWARD
on ES Ahoskey Swamp. Being the same land THEOPHILUS PUGH bought of ROBERT
ROGERS on March 14, 1739. Wit: WILLIAM MOORE, DAVID DICKINSON, AARON MOORE.
Nov. Court 1753. SAMUEL ORMES C/C.

H 11 JOHN HILL, Sheriff of Bertie TO AARON MOOR
      Aug. 14, 1753. 56 pds. for 250 A. Being the land that THEOPHILUS
PUGH purchased of JOHN PERRY. Wit: ROBERT PEEL, DAVID DICKINSON, WILLIAM
MOORE. Nov. Court 1753. *.

H 13 JOHN HILL, Sheriff of Bertie TO DAVID DICKINSON (DICKENSON)
      Aug. 14, 1753. 50 pds. 5 sh. for Land adj. CATHCART. Being the same
tract that THEOPHILUS PUGH purchased of WILLIAM WYNNS. Wit: WILLIAM MOOR,
ROBERT PEEL, AARON MOORE. Nov. Court 1753. *.

H 16 JOHN HILL, Sheriff of Bertie TO THOMAS BARKER
      Aug. 14, 1753. 117 pds. for 240 A. Land which was conveyed by THEO-
PHILUS WILLIAMS to THEOPHILUS PUGH on Sept. 24, 1742. Adj. NEEDHAM BRYAN,
THOMAS BOND, THOMAS BARKER. Wit: WILLIAM MOORE, ROBERT PEELE, DAVID DICK-
INSON. Nov. Court 1753. *.

H 19 JOHN HILL, Sheriff of Bertie TO THOMAS BARKER
      Aug. 14, 1753. 55 pds. for 100 A. Land on NS Roanoke River adj.
PUGH, JOSEPH BLACKMAN, JOHN BLACKMAN. Being that land conveyed by HENRY
JERNIGAN to THEOPHILUS PUGH. Wit: WILLAIM MOORE, ROBERT PEELE, DAVID
DICKINSON. Nov. Court 1753. *.

H 22 JOHN HILL, Sheriff of Bertie TO THOMAS BARKER
      Aug. 14, 1753. 57 pds. 2 sh. for 100 A. Same land which was bought
by THEOPHILUS PUGH from JAMES FLOOD by deed dated Oct. 20, 1751. Land on
Village Swamp adj. Widow CHESHIRE. Wit: WILLIAM MOORE, ROBERT PEELE. Nov.
Court 1753. *.

H 25 JOHN HILL, Sheriff of Bertie TO THOMAS BARKER
      Aug. 14, 1753. 53 pds. for 180 A. Land sold to JOHN JAMESON and by
JAMESON sold to THEOPHILUS PUGH Aug. 19, 1741. On Roanoke River adj. JAMES
CASTELLAW. Wit: WILLIAM MOORE, ROBERT PEELE, DAVILL(?) DICKINSON. Nov.
Court 1753. *.

H 28 JOHN HILL, Sheriff of Bertie, TO THOMAS BARKER
      Aug. 14, 1753. 18 pds. 10 sh. for 200 A. Two tracts sold by HENRY
OVERSTREET to THEOPHILUS PUGH, deceased, May 10, 1735. (1) Cont. 150 A. on

Apple Tree Swamp adj. WILLIAM JONES, HENRY JERNIGAN. (2) Cont. 50 A. on "Roquess" which was purchased by OVERSTREET from ROBERT RADFORD. Tract #1 was "...where ANN OVERSTREET did live..." Wit: WILLIAM MOORE, ROBERT PEELE, DAVID DICKENSON. Nov. Court 1753. *.

H 31 JOHN HILL TO ALEXANDER COTTEN
      Aug. 14, 1753. 80 pds. 15 sh. for 250 A. Land sold by HILL, Sheriff of Bertie, pursuant to sale of THEOPHILUS PUGH's land. This land bought by PUGH of EDWARD OUTLAW Feb. 15, 1739. Wit: WILLIAM MOORE, ROBERT PEELE. Nov. Court 1753. SAMUEL ORMES C/C.

H 34 JOHN HILL, Sheriff of Bertie, TO SAMUEL WIGGINS
      Aug. 14, 1753. 16 pds. for 540 A. Land sold by JOHN BEVERLY to THEO-PHILUS PUGH on Dec. 11, 1738. On Cashy Swamp at THOMAS ROADS corner adj. HENRY ROADS. Wit: WILLIAM MOORE, ROBERT PEELE, DAVID DICKENSON. Nov. Court 1753. SAMUEL ORMES C/C.

H 37 THOMAS ASHLEY, JUN. TO HUMPHREY LAWRENCE, goldsmith
      Nov. 2, 1753. Deed of Gift. 82 A. "...for love...we bear unto our well beloved Daughter ANN intermarried with the s'd HUMPHREY..."Land on WS Cashoke Swamp. Adj. THOMAS ASHBOURNE, to the Great Branch "opposite the Old Plantation", THOMAS ASHLEY, HENRY VANLUVEN, ROBERT WEST, JUN. The same land wiich was bought of HENRY VANLUVEN July 20, 1747. Wit: SAMUEL ORMES, JANE(?) ORMES. Nov. Court 1753. *.

H 38 GEORGE WYNNS TO BENJAMIN WYNNS
      Sept. 22, 1753. 200 pds.(?) for 270 A. Land on NS Wiccacon Creek adj. JOSEPH WYNNS, CULMER SESSUMS, BENJAMIN WYNNS, JOHN BAKER, JAMES ASKINS (ASKEW?), NICHOLAS ASKINS(?), WILLIAM ASKEW, WILLIAM WRIGHT. Part of land left me by last will & testament of my father, GEORGE WYNNS. Wit: WILLIAM WRIGHT, WILLIAM WYNNS, MARY ASKEW. *. *.

H 39 JOHN SHOLAR TO BENJAMIN CARTER
      Oct. 26, 1753. 10 pds. for 170 A. Land on SES Possum Branch. Part of a parcel lately surveyed by Capt. BENJAMIN WEST. Wit: JOHN BARNS, WILLIAM EDWARDS. Nov. Court 1753. *.

H 39 JOHN GLASS of Northampton County TO SAMUEL ANDREWS
      Nov. 13, 1753. 30 pds. for 120 A. "not far from Roanoke River" Adj. THOMAS WILLIAMS, RICHARD WILLIAMS. *.*. SAMUEL ORMES C/C.

H 40 JOHN HOWELL TO JOHN PERRY, "cooper"
      Oct. 11, 1753. 10 pds. 10 sh. for 100 A. On ES Chinkapin Swamp. Wit: JAMES BUTTERTON, JAMES GLAUGHORN. Nov. Court 1753. *.

H 41 JOHN BAKER, yeoman, TO WILLIAM WITHERINGTON
      Nov. 9, 1753. 25 pds. for 200 A. adj. ROBERT EVANS, WILLIAM BAKER. Wit: RICHARD FIGURES, NICHOLAS ASKEW. Nov. Court 1753. *.

H 42 THOMAS PAGE TO WILLIAM POYTHRISS
      *. 10 pds. for 100 A. adj. GRIMSTUK's(?) line on Jumping Run. Adj. JOHN HARRELL "...out of a deed of grant to THOMAS PAGE..." Wit: MICAJAH HINTON, NEEDHAM BRYAN. Nov. Court 1753. *.

H 44 NATHAN MIERS TO HENRY KING of Chowan County, cooper
      Nov. 1, 1753. "An agreement made and concluded this day...the same parties having met at the Place: to wit: at a Poplar on the Broad Branch... (do agree) that the line (concluded today) here-in-after will be the line.. Notwithstanding any error in any writing heretofore made or any dispute which has heretofore arisen..." Wit: WILLIAM KING, WILLIAM EDWARDS, NATHAN MIERS, BENJAMIN WYNNS. Nov. Court 1753. *.

H 45 JOSEPH WIMBERLY, merchant, TO ARCHIBALD WHITE & JAMES SCOTT of
      Norfolk County, Va. June 20, 1753. 64 pds. for (1) five slaves: three men, a boy, a girl. (2) 30 head cattle. (3) 2 horses branded SOL on one and Y on the other (4) 5 feather beds and furniture (5) 1 desk. Wit: GEORGE COLLINS, DANIEL WHITE, HEZEKIAH MCCLOUD (MCCLINT?)*. JAMES HASSELL, C.J.

H 46 JOSEPH WIMBERLY TO ARCHIBALD WHITE & JAMES SCOTT of "the Borough of
      Norfolk". June 20, 1753. 5 sh. for 640 A. (lease) "Land in the

Precinct of Barti on Moratuck River..." A square mile. Tract granted to THOMAS TAYLOR and by TAYLOR sold to JOSEPH WIMBERLY. Wit: GEORGE COLLINS, JOHN CHESHIRE(?), HEZEKIAH MCCLOUD. March 20, 1754. JAMES HASSELL, C.J.

H 47   JOSEPH WIMBERLY TO ARCHIBALD WHITE & JAMES SCOTT "of the Borough of
       Norfolk".   June 21, 1753.   75 pds. for 640 A. Land already possessed
by virtue of lease. A square mile on Moratuck River. Land originally granted to THOMAS TAYLOR and by TAYLOR sold to WIMBERLY. Wit: GEORGE COLLINS,
JOHN CHESHIRE, HEZEKIAH MCCLOUD(?).*.

H 49   JOSEPH WIMBERLY TO ARCHIBALD WHITE & JAMES SCOTT of Norfolk
       June 20, *. 5 sh. for lease. Two tracts: (1) 289 A. as by patent to
EDWARD MORE and consigned by him to CHARLES HARDY. (2) 150 A. Part of a
larger patent granted to JOSHUA WILKINSON "...and conveyed to me by JAMES
BULLOCK..." Adj. JOHN WILLIAMS. Wit: GEORGE COLLINS, JOHN CHESHIRE, HEZE-
KIAH MCCLOUD(?), DAN'L(?) WHITE. N.C. Court March 20, 1754. *.

H 50   JOSEPH WIMBERLY, merchant, TO ARCHIBALD WHITE & JAMES SCOTT of Norfolk
       June 21, 1753. 50 pds. for *. Land now in their possession by above
lease "...by a Bargain of Sale...for one whole year..." Land granted to
EDWARD MORE and conveyed to CHARLES HARDY and thence to JOSEPH WIMBERLY.
Wit: GEORGE COLLINS, JOHN CHESHIRE, HEZEKIAH MCCLOUD. *.*.

H 51   JOSEPH WIMBERLY, merchant, TO ARCHIBALD WHITE & JAMES SCOTT of Norfolk
       June 20, 1753. 5 sh. for 2 A. On ES Quitsney Swamp. A square one
acre to the side. Wit: GEORGE COLLINS, JOHN CHESHIRE, HEZEKIAH MCCLOUD,
DAVID WHITE. *. JAMES HASELL C.J.

H 52   JOSEPH WIMBERLY, merchant, TO ARCHIBALD WHITE & ISAAC SCOTT of Norfolk
       June 21, 1753. 75 pds. for 2 A. on Quitsny Swamp "together with a
water Mill thereon" Wit: GEORGE COLLINS, JOHN CHESHIRE, HEZEKIAH MCCLOUD,
DAVID WHITE. *.*.   JOSIAH SMITH Esq. Mayor of the Borough of Norfolk
certifies that GEORGE COLLINS, JOHN CHESHIRE, HEZEKIAH MCCLOUD & DANIEL
WHITE appeared to attest to deeds.

H 54   GEORGE JARNAGEN & WIFE HANAH (HANNAH) TO WILLIAM KAIL
       Oct. 13, 1753. 37 pds. for 200 A. At a prong of Wild Catt adj. PAT-
TON line. Wit: JOHN LEWIS, WILLIAM WOOD, WILLIAM COLTHRED(?). May Court
1754.   SAMUEL ORMES C/C.

H 55   RICHARD HARRELL TO JOHN RUTLAND of Northampton County
       Nov. 30, 1753. 4 pds. for 100 A. Being a part of a patent which was
formerly granted to SAMUEL ANDUSS(?) for 160 A. Wit: CHARLES HORNE. May
Court 1754. SAMUEL ORMES C/C.

H 56   ROBERT ROGERS & MARY ROGERS TO RICHARD TOMLINSON
       Dec. 3, 1753. 10 pds. for 50 A. On NS Moratuck River adj. RICHARD
TOMLINSON, WILLIAM ASHBURN "...excepting a burying place of thirty foot for
me and my Ears for ever..." Wit: THOMAS DAVID, DANIEL SALENCEN(?). May
Court 1754. *.

H 57   JOHN WARBURTON TO RICHARD BRADLEY
       Nov. 8, 1753. 12 pds. 10 sh. for 50 A. On Kessie River adj. land
formerly Mr. SMITHWICK's. Wit: TITUS LEGETT, JOHN GIBB. May Court 1754. *.

H 57   JOHN BENTON TO JOHN HARE, yeoman
       Aug. 18, 1753. 22 pds. 10 sh. for 200 A. On Cattawuska Swamp adj.
ABRAHAM BLEWLIT. Wit: JOHN BROWN, ISAAC CARTER, JOSEPH HOWARD, JUN. May
Court 1754. *.

H 58   JAMES HOWARD TO SOLOMON HOWARD
       May 14, 1754. Deed of Gift. *.*. "...for brotherly esteem and good
will toward my brother Solomon Howard...together bound with my Father's
last Will and Testament..." Land on Ahoskey Marsh adj. AARON MOORE at Black
Walnut Branch "according to the bounds of the patent". Wit: JOHN SHOLAR,
WILLIAM SHOLAR. May Court 1754. *.

H 58   CHARLES HARDY TO EDWARD GILMAN
       Nov. 15, 1753. 25 sh. for 150 A. Adj. FRANCIS HOBSON, JOSEPH WHEMAN
(?). Wit: JOHN CRICKET, JUN., THOMAS ROADS. May Court 1754. *.

H 59   WILLIAM WILLSON TO WILLIAM BRYAN
     May * 1754. 20 pds. for 240 A. Adj. AMOS GRANT. *.*. May Court 1754.
SAMUEL ORMES C/C.

H 60   LEONARD LANGSTON TO WILLIAM LANGSTON, FRANCIS LANGSTON, THOMAS &
     RACHEL WILL, LUKE LANGSTON.   Feb. 6, 1754. Deed of Gift. (1) To
LEONARD "...for affection which I bear toward my well beloved son WILLIAM
LANGSTON...the plantation whereon I now live...(and) also a negro boy
called Coffee and the still which is now on said plantation as also four
cows and calves..." (2) "...to my son FRANCIS LANGSTON in the County of
Johnson...a tract of land in the said county whereon he now lives...above
the Fork of Marry(?) Branch..." (3) "...to my son-in-law THOMAS WILLS and
my daughter RACHEL WILLS one hundred acres of land...in Johnson County on
the Wattry(?) Branch...and after their deaths to the lawful heirs of my
daughter RACHEL..." (4) "...to my grandson LUKE LANGSTON son of LEONARD
LANGSTON my negro girl called Lucy..." (5) "...and to my grandson LUKE
LANGSTON I freely give my negro girl called Charity..." (6)"...and to my
well beloved son FRANCIS LANGSTON my Negro woman called Judith..." Wit:
JAMES DEUSON(?) (DAWSON?), JOHN BROWN. May Court 1754. *.

H 61   THOMAS SISSON (SISIN, SISSOM) TO RICHARD BROWN
     April 22, 1754. 44 pds. for 100 A. Land on Chinkapin Neck adj. RICH-
ARD BROWN, ISAAC HILL. Wit: BENJ. WYNNS, WM. WYNNS. May Court 1754. *.

H 62   WILLIAM WESTON & WIFE SARAH of Chowan County TO JOHN SOWELL
     Sept. 10, 1753. 60 pds. for 230 A. Land on ES Loosing Swamp adj.___
WATFORD "...to the Commons..." Wit: JOHN WESTON, BENJAMIN WYNNS. May
Court 1754. *.

H 64   GEORGE BELL TO SMITHEY (SMITHIG?) WARBURTON
     * 18, 1754. 30 pds. for 320 A. Land on Buckelsbury Pocosin. Being
the east half of a 640 A. tract whereon GEORGE BELL did formerly live.
"...mine by right of absolute inheritance..." Wit: WILLIAM BALL, PETE
WYNANTS, WILLIAM HUBBARD. May Court 1754. SAMUEL ORMES C/C.

H 65   JAMES HOWARD TO EDWARD HOWARD
     May 14, 1754. Deed of gift. *. "...for the brotherly esteem...I bear
together bound with my fathers last will and testament...unto my brother
EDWARD HOWARD...Land in the woods betwixt Hoskey and Catawitzky Swamp..."
Adj. JOSEPH JONES, "EDWARD HOWARD deceased line". Wit: JOHN SHOLER, WILL-
IAM SHOLER. May Court 1754. *.

H 65   BURWELL BELL & WIFE SARAH TO RICHARD RAYNER
     June 20, 1753. 20 pds. for 200 A. Land on ES Chinkapin Swamp adj.
WILLIAM TYNER, JOHN FREEMAN. Wit: GEORGE BARLOW, JOSEPH BOONS,____ WYNNS.
May Court 1754. *.

H 67   BURWELL BELL & WIFE SARAH TO JOSEPH EVANS
     Nov. 12, 1753. 70 pds. for 100 A. Land on Long Branch adj. BENJAMIN
BAKER. Wit: GEORGE BARLOW(?), JAMES BOON, ____ WYNNS. (Note: This name may
be JAMES BOONS WYNNS.) May Court 1754. *.

H 68   BURWELL BELL & WIFE SARAH TO SOLOMON HILL
     Feb. 16, 1754. 30(?) pds. for 275 A. Land known as the More Branch
Land(?). Adj. JAMES FLETCHER, PHILIP MEGUIRE(MCQUIN?), JACOB KEEL, DEMSEY
HOWELL, WILLIAM WILLIAMSON. Wit: JAMES BOON WYNNS, GEORGE BARLOW. May Court
1754. *.

H 69   BURELL BELL & WIFE SARAH TO DEMSEY HOWELL
     April 9, 1754. 15 pds. for 25 A. Land on More Branch adj. JACOB KAIL
(?KEEL), BURRELL BELL. Part of a tract known as More Branch Land. Wit:
JAMES BOONS WYNNS, GEORGE BARLOW. May Court 1754. *.

H 70   BURRELL BELL & WIFE SARAH TO JAMES WILLIAMS
     Feb. 8, 1754. 12(?) pds. for 110 A. Land on NS Chinkapin Swamp adj.
BELL & WILLIAMS. Wit: GEORGE BARLOW, JAMES BOONS WYNNS. May Court 1754.*.

H 71   JAMES WOOD TO "eldest daughters of WILLIAM DUFFIELD and SARAH his
     Wife". May 13, 1754. Deed of Gift. *. "JAMES WOOD late of Bertie
County Dec'd did by deed of Gift bearing date the 9th day of May Anno Doni
1739...grant to WILLIAM DUFFIELD & SARAH his wife during the natural lives

...containing 500 acres...after the decease (of JAMES WOOD) the said land to be equally divided between WILLIAM DUFFIELD & his eldest Daughters... (therefore) I JAMES WOOD, eldest son and heir of the s'd JAMES WOOD...do hereby release...also (by) brotherly affection I bear to my sister SARAH... the tract of land of my father's deed of gift..." Wit: DANIEL ROGERS, JOHN HARE. May Court 1754. *.

H 71   RICHARD TOMLINSON & WIFE SUSANNAH TO THOMAS HOWARD
       Nov. 12, 1753. 19 pds. for 110 A. Land in Kesia Neck adj. JAMES LEG-
GET. Wit: MARK GIBSON, LUKE MIZELL, MARTHA MIZELL. May Court 1754. *.

H 73   JOSEPH WATFORD & WIFE ELIZABETH TO GEORGE JERNAGAN
       Sept. 24, 1753. 42 pds. for 360 A. Land on Quarter (?) Branch of
Cannon Woods to Loosing Swamp. Wit: THOMAS WOOD(WARD), JAMES WOOD. May
Court 1754. SAMUEL ORMES C/C.

H 74   JOSEPH HARRELL TO JOHN HARRELL
       Feb. 23, 1754. Deed of Gift. 20 A. "...to my brother...a tract of
land purchased by my Father JOSEPH HARRELL from THOMAS PUGH and commonly
called by the name of Sympsons Old Field...to him during his natural life..
and to his heirs...and for want of such heirs...to me and my heirs after my
Brothers Decease..." Land on Flagg Run adj. JOHN WAREN(?), JAMES PARKER,
JOHN NAREN(?). Wit: JOHN HARRELL, GEORGE HOWSE, EZEKIEL HARRELL. May Court
1754. *.

H 75   ELIZABETH SPELLER TO MICHAEL LEE
       May 15, 1754. 5 pds. for 100 A. On ES Bucklesbery Pocoson adj. the
line of WILLIAM RIDDIT(?) deceased, LAWRENCE SARSON. Wit: JAMES BOON, ED-
WARD GILMAN(?), JUN. May Court 1754. *.

H 75   JOSEPH BARRADAILL TO JAMES WOOD
       May 13, 1754. 22 pds. for 100 A. On SS Stony Creek at Stony Creek
Road to Horse Pen Branch. Wit: ISAAC HILL, CHARLES ROBERTS. May Court 1754.*.

H 76   JOSEPH BARRADAILL TO DEMSEY WOOD
       May 13, 1754. 10 pds. for 75 A. On SS Stoney Creek at Half Moon
Branch. Wit: ISAAC HILL, JAMES(?) DRAGHAN. May Court 1754. *.

H 77   FRANCIS MCCLENDON of Johnston County TO JOSEPH BARRADAILL, "taler"
       & JESSE WOOD.   Dec. 12, 1753. 20 pds. for 150 A. Land at Deer Tree
Branch at Stoney Creek and Horse Pen Branch. Wit: ISAAC HILL, JOHN RAS-
(BERRY?). May Court 1754. *.

H 77   ARNOLD HOPKINS TO JOHN LAURENCE
       Feb. 12, 1754. 20 pds. for *. "...a parcel contained in the patent
granted PHILIP WALSTON late of Granville Co. dec'd and by him sold to JAMES
MCDOWELL..." On SS Beaverdam Swamp adj. MICHAEL HILL. Wit: JOHN REDDITT,
JOHN HOPKINS, WILLIAM BAKER. May Court 1754. *.

H 77   CALEB SPIVEY of "Bluford County" TO GEORGE SPIVEY
       Feb. 16, 1754. 5 pds. for 12 A. At String(?) Branch on Jones Line adj.
JONATHAN SPRING. By patent dated 1725. Wit: NEEDHAM BRYAN, WILLIAM BRYAN,
ABRAHAM(?) WIMB(?). May Court 1754. *.

H 80   THOMAS PAGE TO ARON ELIS
       Sept. 8, 1753. 10 sh. for 200 A. "...out of a deed for 526 Acres
that was granted to THOMAS PAGE...(1753)..." Wit: WILLIAM POYTHRISS(?),
MICAJAH HINTON, JOHN ABINGTON. May Court 1754. *.

H 81   CALEB SPIVEY & WIFE MARY TO JONOTHAN SPIVEY
       *. 5 pds. for 128 A. on Cashy Swamp at R____(?) Branch. By patent
dated June 1, 1725. Wit: NEEDHAM BRYAN, WILLIAM BRYAN, ABRAHAM WIMBERLY.
May Court 1754. *.

H 82   WILLIAM HOLLAND TO THEOPHILUS HOLLAND
       Nov. 12, 1753. Deed of Gift. 125 A. "...to my well beloved son THEO-
PHILUS HOLLAND...to him and his heirs...after my & my Wife's decease..."
Land on NS Cashy Swamp near Wattom Pocoson adj. Widow BURNATI (BURNATT),
NICHOLAS BAGGET "...land I bought of JAMES & WILLIAM RUTLAND..." Wit:
CHARLES HORNE, THOMAS BITTEL. May Court 1734. (Note: This date is copied
exactly. Evidence that the deeds were copied many years after original

execution.) SAMUEL ORMES C/C.

H 8? WILLIAM HOLLAND TO SNELL HOLLAND
    *. Deed of Gift. 125 A. "...to my well beloved son SNELL HOLLAND to him and his heirs forever after my & my wife's decease..." Land on NS Cashy Swamp near Wattom Meadow adj. Widow BURINATT, NICHOLAS BAGGETT "it being the plantation whereon I now live & part of the land I bought of JAMES & WILLIAM RUTLAND..." Wit: CHARLES HORNER(HORNES?), THOMAS BITTEL. May Court 1754. SAMUEL ORMES C/C.

H 84 JOHN WESTON, MALACHI WESTON, KATHERINE WESTON TO JOHN HOWELL
    Feb. 11, 1754. 60 pds. for 200 A. Land on Chowan River "the plantation whereon KATHERINE WESTON now lives..." Adj. JOHN HOWELL, THOMAS WESTON, JOHN PERRY at Deep Bottom. Wit: JOSEPH BUTTERTON, EPHRAIM WESTON. May Court 1754. *.

H 85 RICHARD GARRETT of Chowan County TO HARDY HUNTER
    March 5, 1753. 24 pds. for 320 A. "...being one half a patent for six hundred & forty acres of land granted to HENRY BONNER...(by patent Aug. 6, 1719) and was given by said BONNER to his son HENRY who sold...unto RICHARD GARRETT..." Land on Chinquipin Swamp. Wit: JAMES SUMNER, NICHOLAS HUNTER, HEANCE HOFLER. May Court 1754. *.

H 86 JENKINS HANSFORD & BRIDGET HANSFORD TO WILLIAM SCOTT of Colony of Virginia. "release equity of redemption" for 100 pds. (85 pds. to JENKINS HANSFORD. 15 pds. to BRIDGET HANSFORD) for 100 A. Land on Chowan River known as "Malls Haven whereon THOMAS HANSFORD did live" Now conveyed by JENKINS HANSFORD, son and heir of THOMAS HANSFORD. Indenture made by THOMAS HANSFORD Dec. 4, 1751 for 325 pds. 4 sh. 9 p. did pledge forfeit if note was not paid by June 23, 1753. Land to go to WILLIAM SCOTT, JONAS TAYLOR, and THOMAS SCOTT. By separate indenture THOMAS SCOTT & JONAS TAYLOR made over their claim to WILLIAM SCOTT. Wit: CHARLES READ, WILLIAM FLEETWOOD, CHARLES ELIOTT. May Court 1754. SAMUEL ORMES C/C.

H 88 JOHN BYRD of Duplin Precinct TO PETER YATES "of ye Precinct above said". Feb. 11, 1754. 45 pds. for 340 A. Part of a tract cont. 640 A. patented to Capt. ROBART WEST Dec. 1, 1721. Sold by WEST unto SOLOMON JORDAN. On NS Cashie River adj. ROBERT BYRD, WILLIAM GARDNIER. Wit: WILLIAM JOHN REDDITT(?), JOHN YATES. May Court 1754. *.

H 88 ARTHUR BELL & WIFE SARAH, WILLIAM WIGGINS & WIFE PRICILLA of Edgecombe County TO JOHN RHODES. *. 10 pds. for 250 A. Part of a patent granted to ROBERT MACKRASY April 1, 1725 on Sandyrun Swamp. Wit: THOMAS BROWN, EZEKIEL WIMBERLEY, ARTHUR BROWN. May Court 1754. *.

H 90 THOMAS WALKER TO JAMES OVERTON
    July 9, 1752. 80 pds. for 240 A. Land in Flatt Swamp adj. PETER WEST. Being part of a patent granted THOMAS WALKER April 20, 1754. Wit: JOHN BRICKELL, MARTHA BRICKELL. May Court 1754. *.

H 91 WILLIAM ANDREWS TO JAMES LEARY
    May 15, 1754. 14 pds. for 532 A. Land adj. JOHN HARRELL, RICHARD WILLIAMS, JAMES THOMAS. By deed of grant to WILLIAM ANDREWS dated March 25, 1749. *.*. May Court 1754. *.

H 92 BRIDGETT FOLKES TO JOHN RAINER
    Nov. 12, 1753. 7 pds. for 150 A. Part of a tract bought of JOHN PERRY containing 300 A. on Barbeque Swamp. Wit: JAMES DROUGHHAN, JOHN DROUGHAN, JAMES HOLEY. May Court 1754. *.

H 93 JOHN HILL, Sheriff of Bertie TO GEORGE HOUSE
    Aug. 14, 1753. 11 pds. for 400 A. Sale of lands of THEOPHILUS PUGH (see note on page 228). Land formerly belonging to OWEN MCDANIEL and sold to PUGH April 11, 1735. Adj. JOHN BUTLER. Wit: SAMUEL ORMES, ROBERT JONES, JUN. *. SAMUEL ORMES, C/C.

H 95 JOHN HILL, Sheriff of Bertie, TO WILLIAM MOOR of Nansemond Co, Va.
    Aug. 14, 1753. 62 pds. for 640 A. Sale of lands of THEOPHILUS PUGH. Land formerly belonging to JOHN BEVERLY & ROBERT BEVERLY and sold to PUGH Dec. 11, 1738. Wit: ROBERT PEELE, DAVID DICKINSON, AARON MOORE. May Court 1754. SAMUEL ORMES C/C.

H 97   BENJAMIN COTTEN TO HENRY WINBORNE
         Jan. 20, 1754.   55 pds. for 250 A. Land at head of Blew-Water Swamp
adj. PETER WEST, COL. JONES. By patent April 6, 1722. Wit: JOHN BRICKELL,
BRYAN HARE, JOHN WALKER. May Court 1754. *.

H 98   JESSE WOOD TO WILLIAM SISSON (SESSON)
         Feb. 25, 1754.   30 pds. for 250 A. In two tracts: (1) "being part of
JESSE WOOD's new Patent land containing by estimation two hundred Acres..."
(2) 50 A. adj. first parcel. Being part of JOSEPH PERRY's old patent land
at the mouth of Miry Branch on Bear Swamp. Wit: JOSEPH BARRADAIL, JOSEPH
PERRY. May Court 1754. SAMUEL ORMES C/C.

H 99   ROBERT BELL & GEORGE BELL of Duplin County TO DAVID BRYAN
         Feb. 16, 1754. 16 pds. for 50 A. "on the Folley Line". Given by deed
of gift from WILLIAM BIRD to GEORGE BELL in 1732. Wit: ROBERT WEST, PETER
WINANTS, WILLIAM COTTEN (HOOTEN?). May Court 1754. *.

H 99   THOMAS ASHLEY, SEN., blacksmith, TO RICHARD LAKEY, carpenter
         May 15, 1753. *. 100 A. On NS Blackwalnut Swamp. Adj. land of THOMAS
RYAN, SAMUEL COOKE "which s'd Tract of Parcell with 50 Acres which I sold
to the s'd SAMUEL COOK in all one hundred & 50 acres was conveyed to me
from JOHN LOVICK Executor of the last will & Testament of LAURENCE SARSONS
Deceased as by deed bearing date(Aug. 2, 1740)..." Wit: AARON BOULTON,
DO(?) RYAN.   May Court 1754. *.

H 100   JOHN SMITH TO MARTHA RYAN
          Oct. 14, 1753.   200 pds. for *. "JOHN SMITH, executor to JAMES Mc-
DOWELL, deceased. MARTHA RYAN, executrix of THOMAS RYAN, deceased. Right of
JOHN SMITH in & to the lands of JOHN HOLBROOK...said lands being formerly
purchased by JAMES MCDOWELL of THOMAS READING..." Wit: THOMAS WHITMELL,
JOHN HILL.   May Court 1754. *.

H 101   JOHN SMITH of Chowan County TO THOMAS SUTTON
          Aug. 16, 1754.   100 pds. for 480 A. Power of atty. "...I JOHN SMITH
Executor of the last will and testament of JAMES MCDOWELL deceased...do
impower THOMAS WHITMELL, JOHN HILL...merchants...to sell...all Lands belonging to me as executor..." Signed at Edenton February 18, 1754. Wit:
WILLIAM JACKSON, JACOB MORRELL.   Recorded by JAMES HASELL, Chief Justice of
Bertie County.   SAMUEL ORMES C/C.   THOMAS WHITMELL & JOHN HILL in the
name of JOHN SMITH convey to THOMAS SUTTON 480 A. On Walston Creek in the
Beaverdam Swamp"...on the other side it being the plantation whereon the
s'd JAMES MCDOWELL lately lived and bounded on the upper side of lands
whereon HENRY WALSTON formerly lived..." Wit: SAMUEL ORMES, EDWARD RASOR.
Aug. Court 1754. *.

H 102   ANN HODGES, widow, TO ELIAS HODGES
          Dec. 6, 1751.   Deed of Gift.   A negro boy named Joe "...for natural
love and affection I bear to my son, ELIAS HODGES..." Wit: AARON ELLIS,
THOMAS CREW. Aug. Court 1754. *.

H 103   JOHN CAIN (CANE) & WIFE SARAH of Edgecombe County TO ELIAS HOGGES
          Dec. 22, 1753.   75 pds. for 380 A. At a branch of Roquis adj. SAMUEL
CARRIN (CERRIN) at Flagg Branch. Wit: WILLIAM TAYLER, AARON ELLIS, CHARITY
CARRELL. Aug. Court 1754. *.

H 104   EPHRAIM WESTON, yeoman, TO RALPH OUTLAW
          Aug. 13, 1754.   30 pds. for 120 A. adj. JOSEPH WATFORD at Wild Catt
Branch. Wit: JOHN WESTON, WILLIAM FRAZER, THOMAS JONES. Aug. Court 1754.*.

H 105   THOMAS WHITMELL (WHITMEL) & WIFE ELIZABETH TO JOHN JOHNSON
          Aug. 13, 1754.   80 pds. for 440 A. Being land granted to MARTIN
GARDNER by patent July 31, 1716 and sold by s'd GARDNER to JOHN WILLIAMS
and by WILLIAMS sold to THOMAS WHITMELL. Adj. WILLIAM WALSTON on Rocquiss.
Wit: THOMAS ROADES, JOSEPH THOMAS, DAVID STANLEY. ELIZABETH WHITMELL was
privately examined by JOHN BAKER.

H 106   JOSEPH REDDITT of Dupelan (Duplin) County TO JOHN HOPKINS
          Aug. 1, 1754.   4 pds. for 5 A. adj. JOHN HERRING in Bucklesbury
Swamp. Wit: ARNAL HOPKINS, WILLIAM BAKER, WILLIAM HOPKINS. Aug. Court
1754. SAMUEL ORMES C/C.

H 107   WILLIAM DUFIEL (DUFFIEL) & WIFE SARAH & TITUS EDWARDS TO SOLOMON
        CHERRY.   June 6, 1754. 2 pds. for 4 A. Land on SS Cashiah Swamp
adj. s'd CHERRY at Caleen Branch. Wit: JOHNATHAN STANDLEY, THOMAS WILSON.
Aug. Court 1754. SAMUEL ORMES C/C.

H 108   DAVID RYAN TO JOSEPH HARDY
        June 21, 1754. 20 pds. *. "DAVID RYAN...Heir & Ex tor to the last
will & testament of THOMAS RYAN of the county aforesaid deceased...in consideration of twenty Pounds...to the said THOMAS RYAN...and in further consideration of the sum of five shillings...to DAVID RYAN...execute sale to
JOSEPH HARDY..." Land in Bucklesbury Swamp adj. MR. DUCKENFIELD's line.
Wit: JOHN HILL, EDWARD RASOR, JOHN NICHOLLS. Aug. Court 1754. *.

H 109   CORNELIUS CAMPBELL & WIFE ELIZABETH TO WILLIAM KEETOR
        Aug. 12, 1754. 14 pds. for 100 A. on WS Middle Swamp adj. WILLIAM
HARDY. Wit: WILLIAM HARDY, JOHN BOWIN. Aug. Court 1754. *.

H 110   DAVID MEADE of Nansemond Co., Va. TO WILLIAM GRIST of Beaufort Co.
        June 27, 1754. 45 pds. for 22 A. Land bought of JAMES DONAVAN by
deed Feb. 14, 1738. Wit: JOHN DRIVER, WALTER GIBSON, RICHARD GRIST. Aug.
Court 1754. *.

H 111   JOHN EARLY TO DAVID RYAN, heir of THOMAS RYAN, Deceased.
        .. 1754. *. for 350 A. "...in consideration of the full & clear
discharge from and against a bond...from JOHN EARLY unto THOMAS RYAN...a
deed for land between JAMES WILKON's line and the Holley Swamp...At Horse
Swamp" Adj. ISAAC LEWIS, JAMES WILLIAMSON, LAZARUS THOMAS, WILLIAM WARREN
to the Wiccacon Swamp. Wit: JOHN CRICKET, THOMAS KINSEY, JOHN NICHOLS, JUN.
Aug. Court 1754. *.

H 112   THOMAS WILLIAMS TO WILLIAM HOLLOWELL of Perquimmons Co.
        *. 28 pds. for 200 A. Land adj. WILLIAM ANDREWS, THOMAS ANDREWS at
the Mill Branch. Wit: JOHN HARRELL, GEORGE HARRELL, JOHN SKINNER. Aug.
Court 1754. *.

H 113   NICHOLAS SKINNER TO HENRY KING, son of CHARLES KING of Chowan Co.
        June 8, 1754. 27 pds. 10 sh. for 300 A. On Cashie Swamp "in Fork
above JOHN WIMBERLEY's". Wit: CHARLES KING, JUN., WILLIAM KING, EZEKIEL
WIMBERLEY. Aug. Court 1754. *.

H 114   JACOB JERNIGAN TO JESSE JERNIGHAN (JERNIGAN)
        Jan. 19, 1754. 50 pds. for 90 A. Part of a deed to WILLIAM JONES by
HENRY OVERSTREET. Wit: NEEDHAM BRYAN, WILLIAM BRYAN, LINERD HULL. Aug.
Court 1754. *.

H 115   JESSE JARNIGAN (JERNIGAN) TO JACOB JARNIGAN
        Jan. 19, 1754. 50 pds. for 80 A. "Being a piece of land given to
JESSE JERNIGAN (JARNIGHAM) by Will from HENRY JARNIGHAM his father". Adj.
JACOB JERNIGAN, HENRY JARNIGHAM on Appeltree Swamp. Wit: NEEDHAM BRYAN,
LINARD HULL, SARAH BRYAN. Aug. Court 1754. *.

H 116   PAUL PENDER TO JOHN SEGAR
        July 31, 1754. 320 A. On SWS Flat Swamp adj. GILLSTRAP WILLIAMS.
Wit: J. EARLY, GILLSTRAP WILLIAMS. Aug. Court 1754. *.

H 117   MOSES WOOD TO JAMES MITCHELL
        April 8, 1751. "one Pistol and iffty five barrels of full bound
Tarr" for 240 A. Land on SS Segina Swamp. Wit: THOMAS BAKER, JOHN BAZEMORE,
WILLIAM COLTRED(?). Aug. Court 1754. *.

H 118   BRYAN DAUGHTRY of Northampton Co. TO CADAR POWELL
        *. 16 pds. for 240 A. On NS Powell Pocoson at Buck Branch. Being
part of a patent formerly granted to EPHRODITUS MOORE for 340 A. on April
20, 1745. Wit: VALENTINE FLOYD, JOHN SCREWS. Aug. Court 1754. *.

H 119   FRANCIS HOBSON TO DENISE GLISSON of Terrell Co.
        *. 120 pds. for 140 A. On Roquiss Islands "being the upper part of
a tract containing two hundred and eighty acres..." Adj. HOBSON & GLISSON.
Wit: EDWARD GILLMAN, RICHARD ASHLEY. Aug. Court 1754. *.

H 120   JAMES MCDOWAL TO THOMAS OLIVER, marriner

April 20, 1747. 50 pds. for 150 A. Land by name of Ratcliff Plantation on Poplar Run adj. EPHRAIM LOVERTON. Wit: DAN'L. GRANDIN, JOHN CAMP-
BELL, THOMAS LUCAS. April 4, 1847+. E.J. HALL, C.J. JAMES CRAVEN. +(Note:
The actual date given was 1847. Further evidence of the late copying of
this book.)

H 121 ANTHONEY HERRING of Johnson Co. TO JOSEPH MOORE, JUN. of Edgecombe
Co. Nov. 6, 1754. 18 pds. for 270 A. On Rocquiss Swamp adj. THEO-
PHILUS WILLIAMS. Wit: BRIDGET HERING, SARAH HERING. Nov. Court 1754. SAMUEL
ORMES C/C.

H 122 PETERSON BROGDEN (BROGDON) & WIFE MARY TO BENJAMIN SKILES
*. 38 pds. for 170 A. Adj. PHILIP WALSTON on ES Rocquiss Swamp,
JONATHAN STANDLEY, CULLEN POLLOCK, JOHN BROGDON, JUN., PETERSON BROGDON.
Wit: JOHN ALLEN SEN., JOHN BROGDON, JUN., JOHN ALLEN, JUN. Nov. Court 1754.*.

H 123 GEORGE WYNNS TO BLAKE BAKER
Nov. 2, 1754. 65 pds. for 256 A. On SWS Chowan River adj. JAMES
CURLEE(CURLU), JOHN SMITH. Land granted JOHN BROWN July 1713 "and conveyed
by several conveyeances to sundry persons down to JOSEPH WILLINGTON by deed
...(Feb. 16, 1753) to GEORGE WYNNS..." Wit: WM. WYNNS, WILLIAM THOMAS,
WILLIAM WITHERINGTON. Nov. Court 1754. *.

H 125 THOMAS WILLIAMS TO NICHOLAS SKINNER
Nov. 11, 1754. 28 pds. for 200 A. Part of two parcels formerly
granted to BENJAMIN FOREMAN. (1) By date April 1, 1718. (2) By date 1721.
At Mountain Branch adj. JOHN HARRELL. Wit: JOHN HARRELL, JUN., WILLIAM
ANDREWS, GEORGE HARRELL. Nov. Court 1754. *.

H 126 REUBEN POWELL TO BRIAN HARE, son of EDWARD HARE
Aug. 2, 1754. 9 pds. 10 sh. for 45 A. adj. "...The late WILLIAM
WHITFIELDS now JOHN BRICKELLS line..." To the Indian Path adj. ___ WINBORN,
BRIAN HARE. Wit: JOHN BRICKELL, JAMES REID. Nov. Court 1754. *.

H 127 EDWARD ROBERTS, cooper, & WIFE MARY TO CHARLES ROBERTS
Sept. 23, 1754. 1 sh. Deed of Gift. "...For love goodwill and affection...that we bear to CHARLES ROBERTS..." Land on SS Hotskie Swamp at
Cabin Branch. "...s'd EDWARD is to have his lifetime in the s'd plantation
and one half the use of the apple orchard...and should CHARLES ROBERTS die
without issue the land is to be redeemed to EDWARD ROBERTS..." Land obtained by deed of sale from JOHN HOLMES to EDWARD ROBERTS Feb. 25, 1731/32.
Wit: JOHN BAKER, JOHN BRICKELL. Nov. Court 1754. *.

H 128 EDWARD FRISBEE TO JOSEPH WIMBERLY & WILLIAM PEARCE
July 30, 1744. *. 330 + 400 A. Three tracts of which two are on NS
Morattuck at Rocquiss containing 300 A. one is on SS Nuce River at Scotland
Neck containing 400 A. Wit: THOMAS WHITMELL, H. HUNTER (?). May Court 1754.

H 129 JOSEPH WIMBERLY (WIMBERLEY) & WILLIAM PEIRCE (PEIRCE) TO RICHARD
JOHNSON. Nov. 14, 1754. 60 pds. for 330 A. On NS Morattock on Rocquist Branch "formerly belonging to THOMAS MESSERS(?) and WILLIAM CHARLTON
& conveyed to EDWARD FRISBEE & from FRISBIE to JOSEPH WIMBERLY & WILLIAM
PIERCE..." Wit: ISAAC WIMBERLY, DIANNA SANDERS. Nov. Court 1754. *.

H 130 PAUL PENDER TO THOMAS SPARKMAN of Chowan County
Oct. 18, 1754. 26 pds. + 4 pds. "in credit paid in goods at Virginia
store" For 350 A. On Wiccacon Creek at Horse Swamp adj. ISAAC LEWIS, LAZA-
RUS THOMAS, WILLIAM WARREN. Part of a patent granted to JOHN EARLY, JUN.
March 1, 1721. JOHN (?) BRICKELL, JAMES COFFIELD. Nov. Court 1754. *.

H 132 DANIEL HENDRICKS TO SARAH PRICE
July 16, 1754. 12 pds. 10 sh. *. On Heron Run. Wit: JABESH HEN-
DRICKS, JERMS(?) LINNEARD. Nov. Court 1754. *.

H 133 ISAAC COOK TO SOLOMON TREVITT of Boston in New England, marriner
Jan. 10, 1755. 6 pds. 11 sh. for 100 A. On Blackwalnut Swamp adj.
"...land belonging to the late Mrs. FRANCIS JOHNSON now Mrs. FRANCIS RUTH-
ERFURD...", DAVID COOK "which s'd one hundred acres was bequeathed to ISAAC
COOK by the last will & testament of JOHN COOK Deceased to the said ISAAC's
Father". In addition the consideration of 9 pds. 8 sh. 9 p. will be paid
"on January next ensuing at the house where ISAAC COOK now lives being on

the land of DAVID COOK on Salmon Creek..." Wit: SAMUEL ORMES, JANE ORMES, JR.(?). Feb. Court 1755. SAMUEL ORMES C/C.

H 135   ROBERT PEELE TO BENJAMIN COTTEN
        *. 38 pds. for 250 A. Adj. JOHN JONES, EDWARD HOWARD on Ahoskey Swamp. "It being the same tract I bought at public auction as part of the estate of THEOPHILUS PUGH which s'd PUGH bought of ROBERT ROGERS in March 1739 and deeded to me JOHN HILL, Sheriff (August 14, 1753)..." Wit: HENRY WINBORNE, HENRY BRYAN. Feb. Court 1755. *.

H 136   GEORGE STRACHAN of Cushie Neck TO TITUS LEGGETT (LEGIT)
        Feb. 7, 1755. 25 pds. for 80 A. "On a branch in CASTOLAWS Land". Wit: THOMAS HOWARD, KITRIN HOWARD. Feb. Court 1755. *.

H 137   JESSE WOOD TO MOSES THOMPSON
        Nov. 8, 1754. 20 pds. for 300 A. Part of a patent granted to JESSE WOOD June 11, 1753. Adj. JAMES WOOD, OUTLAW's line, WILLIAM PERRY on Half Moon Branch. Wit: GEORGE BARLOW, THOMAS SISSON. Feb. Court 1755. *.

H 138   WILLIAM WYNNS TO JOHN MITCHELL
        Feb. 20, 1754. 20 sh. for 250 A. Adj. CANADAY's Corner, WARRIN's Corner, WESSON's(?) Corner, MITCHELL's Corner. Wit: GEORGE BARLOW, JAMES BOON. Feb. Court 1755. *.

H 137   JOHN CAMPBELL, Merchant, TO PAUL PINDAR
        *. 25 pds. for 270 A. On Deep Creek adj. JOHN BASS, THOMAS JOHNSTON. Wit: HENRY HILL, JOHN DUNLAP. Feb. Court 1755. *.

H 141   ISAAC HILL TO MOSES HILL
        Feb. 26, 1754. 6 pds. for 320 A. "On the main road through Bacon Hill and Branches of Guy's Hall..." Part of a patent to MOSES ROUNTREE for 640 A. Wit: JOSEPH BARRADAILL, THOMAS BAKER. Feb. Court 1755. *.

H 141   THOMAS BONNER TO JAMES BYRUM
        Sept. 12, 1754. 40 sh. for 100 A. On Kisshy Road. Wit: MOSES BONNER, ARTHUR MOOR. Feb. Court 1755. *.

H 142   RICHARD JOHNSON & WIFE ALICE TO JOHN KITTRILL, JUN.
        Feb. 12, 1755. 65 pds. for 100 A. + 230 A. Two tracts. (1) Cont. by patent 230 A. "it being land MARTIN GRIFFIN sold to EDWARD FRISBIE & from FRISBIE to JOSEPH WIMBERLEY & WILLIAM PIERCE and by WIMBERLEY & PIERCE to s'd JOHNSON..." (2) 100 A. being part of a patent to JOHN HARLOWE and sold by HARLOWE to WILLIAM COWARD and by COWARD's son and heir to JOSEPH WHITE and by the s'd WHITE to WILLIAM CHARLTON and by CHARLTON to RICHARD JOHNSON. Wit: THOMAS WHITMELL, ELIZABETH WHITMELL, MOSES HUNTER. Feb. Court 1755. *.

H 143   MILES GALE & WIFE MARTHA of Chowan TO RICHARD BROWNRIGG (BROWNRIG), merchant.   Sept. 6, 1754. 150 pds. for *. "by bargain & sale to him therof made for one year by Indenture bearing date the day next before the day of the date of these presents..." (1) 1420 A. adj.HENRY SPELLAR (now deceased), COGSWELL & DOMINI at Chickery Pocoson adj. EDWARD SMITHWICK, EDWARD SMITH, MARTIN GRIFFIN, JOHN HARLOE. These parcels sold by JOHN LO-VICK, executor of the last will and testament of THOMAS BETTERLEY, to MILES GALE late of Edenton, Father of the said MILES GALE, party of the first part. LOVICK deed dated Sept. 14, 1733. MARTHA GALE privately examined before the Chief Justice of the Province and relinquished her dower without compulsion. JAMES HASSELL, C.J. Wit: MARTIN GALE, BARKER SWANN, JUN. Feb. Court 1755. SAMUEL ORMES C/C.

H 146   SAMUEL FREEMAN, carpenter, TO PETER EVANS, carpenter
        March 7, 1752. 25 pds. for 640 A. On Cypress Swamp adj. COLL. WILLIAM MAULE. Wit: RICHARD BROWN, JOHN SMITH. Feb. Court 1755. *.

H 147   ALEXANDER KENNEDY (KENNADAY, KINAD) SEN. TO JAMES WARD
        Oct. 30, 1752. 10 sh. for 200 A. on SS Quayakason(?) Swamp at Cashi(?) Road to Cabin Branch. Part of a patent to ALEX KENNEDAY for 640 A. dated 1745. Wit: THOMAS WARD, MICHALL WINGATE, JAMES DROUGHAN. Feb. Court 1755. *.

H 150   THOMAS HOWARD TO RICHARD TOMLINSON

Aug. 16, 1754. 15 pds. for 110 A. In Kesia Neck adj. JAMES LEGETT & EDWARD COLLINS. Wit: JAMES LEGETT, JAMES LEGETT, JUN. Feb. Court 1755. *.

H 150   DAVID RYAN TO PAUL PENDER
        * 1754. 12 pds. for 150 A. On Horse Swamp adj. ISAAC LEWIS "otherwise called JAS WILCOSONS Corner Tree", LAZARUS THOMAS former line. Wit: JOHN CRICKETT, JOHN NICHOLLS, JUN. Feb. Court 1755. *.

H 151   AARON MOOR TO JOHN MINSHAW (MINSHEW) of Chowan County
        March 1, 1755. 30 pds. for 300 A. In Cashy Swamp by patent to JOHN RASBERRY Feb. 4, 1725. Adj. JOSEPH HOWARD, ____ PARKER. Wit: MARTE BRICKELL, JOHN BRICKELL. April Court 1755. BENJAMIN WYNNS C/C.

H 152   HENRY WINBORNE, cooper, & WIFE SARAH TO JOHN BRICKELL
        Oct. 15, 1754. 80 pds. for 200 A. On SS Meherrin Creek on Hothouse Branch at the Indian Path. Land bought by WINBORNE of DANIEL HOUGH "Dec. V, MDCCXLII" Confirmed by a Partition deed of s'd HENRY & BRIAN (STARE?HARE?) bearing date "the Vth day of October MDCCLIV". Wit: BRYAN HARE, REUBEN POWELL, BENJAMIN COTTEN (COTTON). April Court 1755. BENJAMIN WYNNS C/C.

H 154   DAVID SINCLAIR of Pasquotank Co., merchant, TO JAMES STOCKDALE of Great Brittain, merchant.   Aug. 5, 1754. 40 pds. for 150 A. Same land which DAVID SINCLAIR has lately purchased of BRYAN HARE.   Mortgaged for debt of 40 pds. to be paid by "Sept. 10 next ensuing". Wit: JAMES SALISBURY, JOHN SPARKLENG. April 12, 1755. "Received 5th Aug. from JOHN STOCKDALE the sum of 40 pounds currant money above mentioned by me." DAVID SINCLAIR.   JAMES HASSELL, C.J.

H 156   WILLIAM DUFFIELD (DIFFILL) & WIFE SARAH TO TITUS EDWARDS
        Oct. 21, 1754. 8 pds. *. "...half the tract or parcell of land whereon I now dwell...is to include the palntation whereon the DUFFILL & his wife now lives for & during the life of the said WM. DUFFILL & the life of SARAH his wife..." Wit: JOHN SPRING, JOHN HOLDER. April Court 1755. *.

H 157   HENRY WINBORNE of Society Parish & BRIAN HARE, coopers: Land Division.
        Oct. 5, 1754. 400 A. "...did buy in concert (Dec. 8, 1742) of DANIEL HOUGH late of said county a tract of land...by free consent of each other have divided the above mentioned four hundred acres..." Land on SS Maharrin Creek at Hothouse Creek by the side of Indian Path. Wit: JOHN BRICKELL, REUBEN POWELL, BENJAMIN COTTON. April Court 1755. *.

H 157   THOMAS ARCHER TO HANCOCK ARCHER, son of THOMAS ARCHER
        March 29, 1755. 5 sh. for 340 A. Adj. THOMAS JOHNSON, THOMAS STEPHENSON. Wit: THOMAS WARD, BENJAMIN WYNNS. April Court 1755. *.

H 159   JONATHAN THOMAS TO ABRAHAM BLITCHENDEN (BLICHENDEN) of Perquimmons Co.
        Nov. 4, 1754. 24 pds. for 456 A. "the full demintion of the Patton ..." Adj. WILLIAM CURLEE, THOMAS BONER. Wit: THOMAS BYRD, JOSHUA DEAL. April Court 1755. BENJAMIN WYNNS C/C.

H 161   TITUS LEGIT of Cashie TO GEORGE SUTTON
        Nov. 14, 1754. 35 pds. for 100 A. "land which formerly did belong to JOHN WARBURTON..." On SS Cashie River adj. ____SPIKES. Wit: JOHN SMITH, JOHN WARBURTON. April Court 1755. *.

H 162   ELIAS PRICE & WIFE MARY of Upper Parish, Nansemond Co., Va. TO ROBERT HOWELL.   Aug. 7, 1754. 40 sh. for 160 A. On Roquiss Swamp adj. ROBERT HOWELL, FRANCIS HOBSON. Wit: RICHARD TAYLOE, JOSEPH HORTON, DANIL (?) HORTON. April Court 1755. BENJAMIN WYNNS C/C.

H 163   EDWARD HOWCUT (HOWCOT) TO GEORGE BARLOW, merchant
        Nov. 7, 1754. 100 pds. for 100 A. "...being part of the Estate of WILLIAM DOWNING, JUN., late of Boston in New England & sold to EDWARD HOWCUTT father of the afs'd ED. by MARY HOWCUTT relict of JOHN HOWCUTT and heir at law to above WILLIAM DOWNING..." On Mill Creek adj. WILLIAM BUCHAN, WILLIAM HOOKER to Cowan River. Wit: JOSEPH SORRELL, AARON OLIVER, MOSES OLIVER.   April Court 1755. *.

H 164   MICHAEL HILL TO JOSEPH WILLIAMSON
        April 15, 1755. 40 pds. for 200 A. On NS Cashy River at mouth of

Tarkil Branch to Walston's Creek. Wit: JOHN OLIVER, LUKE MIZELL, JUN.
April Court 1755. *.

H 165   WILLIAM BENTLEY TO JOHN WOOD(WARD)
        April 18, 1755. 15 pds. for 100 A. On NS Sypros Krick adj. ANN BEN-
LEY "so that the hundred acres is to be square when laid off by a sirvaor."
Wit: RICHARD TOMLINSON, THOMAS PRICE. April Court 1755. *.

H 166   CHARLES JACOCKS TO JAMES LEARY
        April 4, 1743. 30 pds. for 100 A. At Hay Meadow adj. WILLIAM FLEET-
WOOD, HOWARD RYAN. Part of 200 A. bought by JACOCKS of THOMAS RYAN. Wit:
THOMAS RYAN, SAMUEL COOK. May Court 1743. HENRY DELON C/C.

H 167   JAMES LARY TO EDWARD RASOR
        March 20, 1754. 10 pds. for 100 A. "within mentioned tract". Wit:
H. NICHOLLS, MARY LUTEN. April Court 1755. BENJAMIN WYNNS C/C.

H 168   WILLIAM ROBERSON of Northampton TO WILLIS COLLINS
        Oct. 20, 1754. 10 pds. for 200 A. "Being part in Northampton & part
in Bertie Counties". On Sandy Run adj. ___ HAM, JOHN RUTLAND, WILLIAM RUT-
LAND. Part of a tract granted WILLIAM ROBERSON by deed of grant 22nd day
of June 1749. Wit: CHARLES HORNE, WILLIAM HORNE. April Court 1755. *.

H 169   THOMAS CASTELLAW of Duplin Co. TO THOMAS ROADES
        Feb. 17, 1755. 32 pds. for 185 A. + 140 A. Two tracts on NS Roc-
quis Swamp on a place called Rocquis Islands. (1) A grant to WILLIAM SMITH
April 1, 1723 adj. JAMES CASTELLAW. (2) Adj. first tract being part of a
patent formerly granted JOHN WILLIAMS, JUN. "So as to leave out the other
part of the tract". Wit: THOMAS WHITMELL, MOSES HUNTER, ARTHUR WILLIAMS.
April Court 1755. *.

H 171   JETHRO BUTLER "of Barti County" TO GEORGE HOUSE, SEN.
        April 22, 1755. 4 pds. 6 sh. for 5 A. On Flagg Run adj. JOHN WARRON
(?), GEORGE HOUSE's Old Field. Wit: JOHN CARRELL, THOMAS PUGH, GEORGE
HARRELL. April Court 1755. BENJAMIN WYNNS C/C.

H 172   THOMAS YEATES TO JAMES EARLY
        June 1, 1754. 17 pds. for 200 A. On White Oak Swamp adj. JAMES
MCGLOHON, THOMAS DIXON. Wit: WILLIAM HOSEA, J. EARLY, BENJAMIN WYNNS.
April Court 1755. *.

H 174   JOHN HERRELL (HARRELL), JUN. TO SAMUEL ANDREWS
        Feb. 7, 1754. 2 pds. 13 sh. 9 p. for 200 A. "By deed of Grant from
my Lord Carteret bearing date ye seventh Feb. 1754..." Adj. JOHN ROADES,
JAMES BROWN, NICHOLAS SKINNER, JOHN RUTLAND. Wit: JASPER CHARLTON, JOHN
HARRELL. July Court 1755. BENJAMIN WYNNS C/C.

H 175   JOSEPH HALL TO BENJAMIN WYNNS
        Dec. 7, 1754. 40 pds. for 200 A. In Chinkapen Neck on SS Wiccacon
Creek. Land that was conveyed by BENJAMIN WYNNS to JOSEPH HALL in 1746.
Wit: WILLIAM WYNNS, THOMAS SESSONS. July Court 1755. *.

H 175A MICHAEL HILL TO NATHANIEL HILL, JUN.
        June 2, 1755. 100 pds. for 300 A. Adj. MARTIN GRIFFIN at Spring
Branch on Cashie River. Wit: JOHN HILL, JOHN WEBB, MARTHA HILL. July Court
1755. *.

H 177   PETER EVANS, carpenter, To WILLIAM FARELESS (FAIRLESS), planter
        July 10, 1755. 28 pds. for 120 A. On SS Chowan River "known by name
of BENJAMIN HOOKERS" on Fairchild Branch at Poly Bridge. Wit: JOHN RAY,
MATTHEW HAIRGROVE. July Court 1755. *.

H 178   BENJAMIN HOOKER, yeoman TO WILLIAM HOOKER, planter
        May 19, 1755. 5 pds. for 50 A. On Sandy Run, a branch of Mount
Pleasant Mill Creek adj. WILLIAM HOOKER, BENET (formerly OLIVERS), THOMAS
ROGERS. Wit: JOSHUA BURROS, ANN HARRELL. July Court 1755. *.

H 179   RICHARD HARRELL TO JAMES BROWN
        May 3, 1755. 15 pds. for 110 A. Part of a patent March 1, 1721.
"in the low ground of the river" adj. HARRELL, MARMADUKE NORFLEET to Creek

Pond at Black Pond on Thorney Branch at RATLANDS line (RARTLANDS). Wit:
JOHN HARRELL, JUN., ARTHUR BROWN, JAMES BROWN, JUN. July Court 1755. *.

H 180 JOHN YEALVERTON of Edgecombe Co. to JOHN HARRELL
 March 10, 1755. 5 pds. 5 sh. for 50 A. Adj. ____PARKER, ABRAHAM
HARRELL, GEORGE HOUSE, ____BAKER. Wit: WILLIAM JARNIGAN, AACH(?) HARDY
HARRELL, SAMUEL PITTMAN. July Court 1755. BENJAMIN WYNNS C/C.

H 182 DAVID COOK TO ISAAC COOK
 June 1, 1755. 12 pds. for 50 A. On WS Salmon Creek adj. THOMAS OLI-
VER, NAT. DUCKINFIELD. Wit: CARN'S. CAMPBELL, DAVID RYAN. July Court 1755.*.

H 183 RICHARD LAKEY, joyner, & WIFE MARY TO AARON BUTLER (BOLTON),
 shipwright. July 23, 1755. 37 pds. for 380 A. Land adj. MARY
JONES, THOMAS WEST. "...Land defended to JOHN HOLLBROOK, SEN. & heir of the
said pantantee and from him (he dying intestate and without any children)
to MARGARET JONES as heiress...and by the said MARGARET JONES was conveyed
to THOMAS RYAN by Deed bearing date 29th day of Sept. 1743...and by the
last will & testament of s'd. THOMAS RYAN given before mentioned MARY LAKEY
by the name of MARY RYAN..." On WS Salmon Creek adj. THOMAS OLIVER, NAT.
DUCKINFIELD. July Court 1755. *.

H 184 BENJMAIN WARREN SEN. of Loosing Swamp TO PATIENCE WARREN
 April 17, 1755. 20 pds. for 300 A. On WS Cabin Branch adj. ____
CANADY. Wit: WILLIAM WARREN, SUSANNAH WOOD. July Court 1755. *.

H 187 RICHARD DUNSTAN, joyner, TO BARNABY HELY DUNSTAN, joyner
 Feb. 20, 1755. 40 pds. for 200 A. On NS Cashie River adj. DUNSTAN.
Wit: GEORGE SUTTON, JOSHUA SUTTON. July Court 1755. BENJAMIN WYNNS C/C.

H 188 ISAAC LASSITER, yeoman, TO WILLIAM WITHERINGTON, planter
 June 10, 1755. 25 pds. for 50 A. One certain Island on Wiccacon
Creek adj. WILLIAM SHARP, WILLIAM DOWNING. Wit: WILL. HOOKER, JUN., ELEAZ.
QUINBY, ANN QUINBY. July Court 1755. *.

H 189 RICHARD HINES of Johnson Co., planter, TO JOHN CAMPBELL, blacksmith
 March 15, 1755. 27 pds. for 200 A. On Cashie Swamp adj. RICHARD
HARRELL on Poplar Branch. Wit: JOHN SHOLAR, JOSEPH WINSTON(?). July Court
1755. BENJAMIN WYNNS C/C.

H 190 JOHN MANING, husbandman, TO DINAH HYMAN
 July 19, 1755. Deed of Gift. 60 A. "...love goodwill and affection
for my loving daughter DINAH HYMAN, wife of JOHN HYMAN..." Land on NS Long
Pond and Great Swamp. Wit: JOHN BURNAM, BENJAMIN MANING. July Court 1755.*.

H 191 JOHN MANNING, husbandman, TO BENJAMIN MANNING
 July 15, 1755. Deed of Gift. 200 A. "...love goodwill and affection which I bear to my loving son BENJAMIN MANNING...the plantation whereon I now live...and the plantation whereon my son GEORGE MANNING did live..
all my moveable estate goods and chattles at the decease of me and my wife
MARY MANNING..." Wit: JOHN HYMAN, JOHN BURNAM. July Court 1755. *.

H 192 WILLIAM WITHERINGTON TO JOHN WATSFORD, yeoman
 Aug. 27, 1754. 14 pds. for 100 A. Land where JOHN SPEIR lately
lived. By deed of JOHN SPEIR. Wit: SARY EVANS, JEANIT HOOKER. July Court
1755. BENJAMIN WYNNS C/C.

H 193 GEORGE JORNAKEN, planter, TO RALPH OUTLAW, planter
 July 31, 1755. 3 pds. for 20 A. On SS Wild Catt Branch adj. KAIL's
Line, RALPH OUTLAW's corn field. Wit: WILLIAM WOOD, WILLIAM COLTHRED, EDW.
BRISCO. July Court 1755. *.

H 194 JOHN CAMPBELL, blacksmith, & WIFE MARY TO JONATHAN STANDLEY
 July 9, 1755. 31 pds. for 200 A. On NS Kesia Swamp at Poplar Branch.
Wit: JOS. MINTON, JNO. SHOLAR. July Court 1755. *.

H 195 PETER YEATES TO WILLIAM COLBURN
 March 7, 1754. 16 pds. for 320 A. "...it being one full half of a
tract granted Capt. DAVID HENDERSON (July 20, 1717)...and assigned to SAM-
UEL ONWIN (Sept. 6, 1723)...and by deed to me..." Wit: JOHN YEATES, EDWARD
E. DANIEL. July Court 1755. *.

H 196   SAMUEL ONWIN TO PETER YEATES
        March 15, 1755. 40 pds. for 320 A. "...it being one full half of a
tract...granted Capt. DAVID HENDERSON bearing date (July 20, 1717)...and by
said HENDERSON assigned to me (Sept. 6, 1723)..." Wit: JAMES CANNADAY, JOHN
YEATES, EDWARD EVAN DANIEL. July Court 1755. *.

H 197   JOHN MANNING, husbandman, TO ELIZABETH BURNAM
        July 19, 1755. Deed of Gift. 65 A. "...love and affection which I
have...toward my loving daughter ELIZABETH BURNAM, wife of JOHN BURNAM...
the plantation where she now lives..." On BURNAM's Branch at CHARLOTON's
Creek. Wit: JOHN HYMAN, BENJAMIN MANNING. July Court 1755. *.

H 197   EDWARD COLLINS of Society Parish TO CAPT. BENJAMIN WYNNS & CAPT.
        JOHN HILL, churchwardens for said Parish.   Sept. 5, 1754. 10 sh.
for 1 A. In Sohikey Neck in Society Parish on Burche's Spring "on the upper
or south side of the house in which said BURCH lately lived" at Kings' Road.
"For use in building a chapel". Wit: THOMAS SPEIGHT, WILLIAM GRAY, ELISHA
WHITFIELD. July Court 1755. BENJAMIN WYNNS C/C.

H 198   WILLIAM COWARD & WIFE ANN TO JOHN SMITH
        Feb. 26, 1755. 6 pds. for 50 A. Between Ronoak River and Rocky
Quest Swamp adj. SMITH, HUSTON, POLIX(?). Wit: THOMAS HYMAN, MARY HYMAN.
July Court 1755. *.

H 200   JOHN EARLY, Justice, TO ISAAC HILL, planter
        July 22, 1755. 60 pds. for 200 A. Adj. WILLIAM HOOKER. ____ WYNNS,
THOMAS SESSONS on Wiccacon Creek. Wit: JOHN HILL, JONATHAN STANDLEY, ISAAC
CARTER. July Court 1755. *.

H 201   JOHN HILL, High Sheriff of Bertie, TO WILLIAM COLETHRED
        Nov. 25, 1754. 9 pds. 10 sh. for 200 A. In pursuant to action
brought against WILLIAM WYNNS, Esq., administrator of the estate of "NICHO-
LAS WARD (TURNER) late of said province deceased...BLAKE BAKER, Attorney
for WILLIAM WYNNS..." Debt. of 5 pds. 7 sh. 4 p. Land granted NICHOLAS
WARD (TURNER) by WILLIAM BLYTH Oct. 28, 1747. Adj. ____ BUSH on Cablan
Branch on Quayocoson Swamp adj. WILLIAM FREEMAN. Part of a patent granted
WILLIAM BLYTH for 560 A. on March 11, 1740. Wit: JOHN CAMPBELL, HENN BATE,
ROBERT WEST. Oct. Court 1755. *.

H 203   THOMAS JORDAN SPEIGHT TO JOSEPH JORDAN
        Dec. 7, 1754. 100 pds. for 300 A. In Sohikey Neck adj. Keshia River,
DAVID RYAN at mouth of Herrin Creek, MARY SPEIGHT (land bought of JOHN WAR-
BURTON), JOHN WARBURTON, TITUS LEGITT. Wit: JOHN BELOTE, ISAAC JORDAN,
WILLIAM JORDAN. Oct. Court 1755. *.

H 205   WILLIAM BAKER yeoman, TO JOSEPH WITHERINGTON
        Oct. 21, 1755. 7 pds. 11 sh. 9 p. for 100 A. On Wiccacon Creek adj.
ROBERT EVANS, WILLIAM WITHERINGTON, JOHN BAKER. Wit: JOHN HARRELL, WILLIAM
WITHERINGTON, JOSEPH HARRELL. Oct. Court 1755. *.

H 206   JAMES WOOD & PHILLIP WARD of Terril Co. TO WILLIAM HOOKS
        *. 40 pds. for 320 A. In Kishey Neck adj. ____ CHARLTON, ____CLARK.
Wit: THOMAS HOOKS, MARY WARD. Oct. Court 1755. *.

H 207   WILLIAM WITHERINGTON, Yeoman, TO JOHN BAKER
        *. 25 pds. for 50 A. On Wiccacon Creek at Goose Creek adj. WILLIAM
SHARP. Wit: JOHN HARRELL, JOSEPH WITHERINGTON, JOSEPH HARRELL. Wit: JOHN
HARRELL, JOSEPH WITHERINGTON, JOSEPH HARRELL. Oct. Court 1755. *.

H 208   WILLIAM SMITH, JUN. of Edgecomb Co. TO FREDERICK HOMES
        Aug. 11, 1754. 16 pds. for 100 A. On Ronoak adj. Beaverdam Branch,
RICHARD WILLIAMS. "...(this) tract was will'd to said WM. SMITH JUN. by
THOMAS BUSBEE in his last will and Testament..." Wit: BARNABAS BRYAN, JOHN
FRANCIS SIVEY(?), JAMES BOON, JUDITH THOMAS. Oct. Court 1755. *.

H 210   JOHN DAVISON, Planter, TO JOHN DAVISON, cooper
        April 28, 1755. Deed of Gift. 300 A. "...for good-will & affection
I bear unto my only son JOHN DAVISON JUN..." Land on WS Chowan River. Part
of tract purchased of JOHN WYNNS ESQ. in 1740 cont. 640 A. Wit: JOHN DAVI-
SON, JOSEPH BUTTERTON. Oct. Court 1755. BENJAMIN WYNNS C/C.

H 211   AARON ASKEW, Planter, TO BENJAMIN WYNNS
         July 19, 1755. 20 pds. for 100 A. On Chinkapin Neck. Land formerly
conveyed by said WYNNS to said ASKEW in "174_". Wit: GEORGE WYNNS, RICHARD
BROWN. Oct. Court 1755. BENJAMIN WYNNS C/C.

H 212   GABRIEL MANLY, SEN. & SON ABEL MANLEY TO JAMES DAVIS
         *. 150 A. for 150 A. "bargained and swapped". Land adj. CULMER SES-
SUMS. Wit: ISAAC BRAWLER, MEREY(?) WILLEBEE. Oct. Court 1755. *.

H 213   ALEXANDER SPOTSWOOD COTTON TO SOLOMON PENDER, Joyner
         Feb. 4, 1750/1. 16 pds. for 100 A. On ES Main Road leading to JACK-
SON's Ferry adj. JACOB LASHER, "Cotton's old plantation line". Wit: JOHN
BAKER, JAMES COTTON. Oct. Court 1755. *.

H 214   JAMES HURST of Duplin Co. TO JAMES PEARCE
         Aug. 11, 1755. 10 pds. for 100 A. adj. HENRY BATES, _____ WINGATE.
Wit: H. HUNTER, SARAH HUNTER, HENRY HUNTER. Oct. Court 1755. *.

H 216   WILLIAM YEATES, planter, TO EDWARD VAN DANIEL
         Oct. 8, 1755. 20 pds. for 590 A. Adj. JAMES GRAVES on Gunn(?)(Ginn?)
Branch, THOMAS POLLOCK, JOHN CRICKET, THOMAS RYAN on Eastermost Swamp, JOHN
HOWEL. As per patent dated May 1, 1668. Wit: JOHN YEATES, JOSEPH REDDITT.
May Court 1755. *.

H 217   MOSES THOMPSON, taylor, TO WILLIAM OUTLAW
         July 28, 1755. 30 pds. for 300 A. Part of a patent granted JESSE
WOOD June 11, 1753. Adj. JAMES WOOD, OUTLAW's line, WILLIAM PERRY, at Halfmoon Branch. Wit: SARAH WARREN,ANN OUTLAW, WILLIAM COLTHRED. Oct. Court
1755. BENJAMIN WYNNS C/C.

H 218   WILLIAM YEATES, planter, TO JOHN YEATES
         July 22, 1755 (Oct. 29, 1755). 20 pds. for 214 A. Land on SS Buckles-
bury Pocoson adj. LAURANCE SARSON, _____ROSE, PHILLIP WALSTON, JOHN HERRING,
_____ HOLBROOK. By patent dated Aug. 1, 1723. Wit: JOSEPH REDDITT, EDWARD
VAN DANIEL. Oct. Court 1755. *.

H 219   EDWARD COOPER of Tyrrell, TO WILLIAM YEATS (YEATES), JUN.
         Oct. 27, 1755. 30 pds. for 150 A. Adj. Col. ROBERT WEST at Crofut(?)
Branch on Flagy Branch. Wit: PETER YEATS, EDWARD GRIFFIN. Oct. Court 1755.*.

H 221   JOHN WILLEY of Nansemond Co., Va., shoemaker, TO WILLIAM LANIER
         *. "valuable consideration" for 183 A. Land in Cashy Swamp adj.
THOMAS POLLOCK, deceased. Wit: JOHN BAZEMORE, HENRY BONNER, THOMAS HOLDER.
Oct. Court 1755. *.

H 222   NATHANIEL NICKLESS (NICHOLAS) TO WILLIAM WHARTON
         Aug. 1, 1754. 3 pds. 15 sh. for 320 A. Land on Hart's Delight Poco-
son. Wit: MOSES BONNER, DAVIDE HORTON. Oct. Court 1755. *.

H 223   WILLIAM WITHERINGTON (WEATHERINGTON) TO JAMES ALSTON of Chowan Co.
         *. 7 pds. for 240 A. On Killem woods where EBENEAZER SLAWSON lived.
Wit: JOHN HARRELL, JOSEPH HARRELL, JOSEPH WITHERINGTON. Oct. Court 1755.*.

H 224   JESSE ROUNTREE TO HENRY VALENTINE, Planter
         March 7, 1755. 5 pds. for 160 A. Adj. MOSES HILL. Wit: MOSES HILL,
FRANCIS ROUNTREE, JAMES REID. Oct. Court 1755. *.

H 225   WALTER DROUGHAN TO JOHN DROUGHAN
         Oct. 20, 1755. 10 pds. for 320 A. On Barbury Swamp. Being part of a
tract granted WALTER DROUGHAN for 640 A. in 1739(?). Adj. JONATHAN MILLER,
RICHARD FREEMAN (formerly THOMAS MCCLANDON's) on Miria Branch. Wit: JAMES
COTTON, JOSEPH THOMAS, THOMAS BOSWELL. Oct. Court 1755. *.

H 226   WALTER DROUGHAN TO RICHARD SAKES
         Oct. 24, 1755. 3 pds. for 320 A. On ES Mirea Branch adj. GEORGE
HUGHES, CHARLES RICKETS, JONATHAN MILLER. Being part of a patent granted
WALTER DROUGHAN for 640 A. on Feb. 15, 1739. Wit: JAMES COTTEN, SOLOMON
PENDER, JOSEPH THOMAS. Oct. Court 1755. *.

H 228   JONATHAN KITTRELL TO WILLIAM PIERCE
         Sept. 1, 1755. 27 pds. 15 sh. for 167 A. On ES Connaritsrat Swamp

between JOHN GILBERT (GILBART) and JONATHAN KITTRELL formerly between JOHN HOLLY & JOHN THOMAS. Wit: DANIEL MURPHREE, JAMES DODY. Oct. Court 1755. *.

H 230 ELISHA HUNTER of Chowan Co. TO ROBERT SUMNER of Nansemond Co, Va.
  Aug. 8, 1754. 70 pds. for 140 A. At Pitch Landing on Chowan River at Deep Bottom. Part of a patent granted THOMAS MARTAIN Feb. 28, 1704/05 and by MARTIN sold to JOSEPH OATES Feb. 8, 1739, and by OATES sold to WILLIAM PUGH May 20, 1743, and by PUGH sold to ISAAC HUNTER May 9, 1746, and by HUNTER confirmed to said ELISHA HUNTER. Wit: JOHN BENTON, DAVID SUMNER, JOHN KITTRELL, DEMSEY SUMNER, JOHN FREEMAN, WILLIAM FREEMAN, RICHARD FREEMAN. N.C. Court Oct. 21, 1755. JAMES HASSELL, C.J.

H 232 JOHN KITTRELL of Chowan Co. TO JONATHAN KITTRELL
  Oct. 3, 1755. 5 sh. for 250 A. At Buck Swamp on Poplar Branch adj. WILLIAM KING, AMOS GRANT. Wit: JACOB ADOM, SAMUEL KITTRELL, JACOB ROGERS. Jan. Court 1756. *.

H 233 JAMES BULLOCK TO JOHN WESTON
  *. 25 pds. for 200 A. On NS Cashie River adj. JOHN WILLIAMS, JOHN MOOR at Isaac Creek to Wolf Pitt Branch adj. JOHN WILLIAMS. Wit: JOSEPH WIMBERLY, ISAAC WIMBERLY. Jan Court 1756. *.

H 235 GIDEON GILBERT, wheelright, TO JAMES OVERTON
  Nov. 17, 1755. 5 pds. for 100 A. On NS Flat Swamp. Wit: PAUL PENDER, ABSOLOM SPEIRS. Jan. Court 1756. *.

H 236 BENJAMIN PERRY of Perquimmons Co. TO JOHN TYLER
  March 3, 1755. 5 pds. for 150 A. Adj. PETER PARKER on "the main road". Wit: JOEL HOLLOWELL, NICHOLAS STALLINGS, KIDAR POWELL. Jan. Court 1756. BENJAMIN WINNS C/C.

H 237 WILLIAM LEE TO JOHN VANPELT
  Nov. 7, 1755. 80 pds. for 150 A. On SS Brooks Creek "by estrement of writing bearing date 8th of Aug 1732..." On "the main road to the landing..." Wit: BENJAMIN NORVIL, JOSEPH WETHERINGTON, JAMES SEHNSEN. Jan. Court 1756. *.

H 238 WILLIAM BENTLEY TO JAMES SMITHWICK GARDNER
  Nov. 13, 1755. 45 pds. for 100 A. On NS Cutchypress Creek adj. JOHN WOOD(WARD). Wit: JOHN WARD, EDM. SON(sic), EDMUND SMITHWICK, EDW. SMITHWICK. Jan. Court 1756. *.

H 240 JOHN PAGE TO THOMAS PAGE
  Feb. 11, 1754. 15 pds. for 100 A. On Jumping Run. Wit: FRA'S SEARFON, EDWARD HAWKINS. Jan. Court 1756. *.

H 242 JOHN RODGERS TO JAMES LEGGIT, SEN.
  Jan. 27, 1756. 13 pds. for 100 A. In Kashia Neck adj. JOHN WALLNTEN, JOHN GRIFFIN, WILLIAM KENNEDAY, HUGH HYMAN(?). Wit: WILLIAM YOYL(?), JER. LEGGETT. Jan. Court 1756. *.

H 242 MATTHEW SPIVEY TO WILLIAM WOOD
  March 15, 1753. 20 pds. for 200 A. On ES Quicason Swamp adj. JOHN PERRY, WILLIAM BLINE(?). Wit: THOMAS BAKER, JOSEPH BARRADAIL. Oct. Court 1755. BENJAMIN WYNNS C/C. "Memorandum that I WM. WOOD...do this day assign the above and within deed to JOHN WARD...13th day of Dec 1753..." Wit: WILLIAM WYNNS, JOSEPH WATSFORD. Jan Court 1756. *.

H 244 THOMAS OLIVER, marriner, TO CORNELIUS CAMPBELL, marriner
  Jan. 14, 1756. 64 pds. for 150 A. On Salmon Creek "known by name Ratlefts Plantation" on Poplar Run. Wit: JOHN NICHOLL, THOMAS REEVES, JOHN VANDYKE. Jan. Court 1756. *.

H 245 MOSES HARE & WIFE MARY of Chowan Co. TO JONATHAN STANDLEY
  Dec. 5, 1755. 70 pds. for 240 A. On SS Rocquist Swamp at Chonyatock Swamp. Wit: JONATHAN STANDLEY, JUN., SOLOMON KING, CHARLES KING. Jan. Court 1756. *.

H 246 WILLIAM CAMPBELL & WIFE JUDAH TO SAMUEL WILLIAMS
  Jan. 19, 1756. 40 pds. for 468 A. On "eastermost branch of Salmon Creek" adj. CORNELIUS CAMPBELL, LAND HARDY. Wit: WILLIAM HARDY, son of LAMB,

244

DAVID GASKINS. January Court 1756. BENJAMIN WYNNS C/C.

H 248   WILLIAM BENTLEY TO JERRY BENTLEY
        Nov. 10, 1755. Deed of Gift. For 125 A. "...natural love and affec-
tion...unto my well beloved cousin JERRY BENTLEY son of ANN BENTLEY...in
case he should die without issue then to his sisters..." Land on Gum Branch
at CHARLOTON's Creek. Wit: RICHARD TOMLINSON, MARY JOYNS. Jan. Court 1756.*.

H 249   LUKE MIZELL & LUKE MIZELL, JUN. TO CHARLES BURCH & WIFE ELIZABETH
        *. 30 pds. for 100 A. In Keshy Neck on ES Possum Hill Creek adj.
JOHN SMITHWICK, JAMES LEGGITT. Wit: RICHARD TOMLINSON, JOSEPH WILLIAMSON.
Jan. Court 1756. *.

H 251   RICHARD BROWN TO JOHN KAILE
        Dec. 12, 1751. 150 pds. for 272 A. On NE of Quoyccason Swamp at
Stoney Creek Road adj. JOHN EARLY. Wit: HENRY REED, GEORGE REVIT. Jan.
Court *. BENJAMIN WYNNS C/C.

H 251   CHARLES HARDY TO ROBERT HARDY
        Dec. 27, 1755. 7 pds. 10 sh. for 253 A. Adj. FRANCIS HOBSON, EDWARD
GILMAN, THOMAS JONES, JOSEPH THOMAS. Wit: JOHN WATSON, JOHN ALLEN. Jan.
Court 1756. *.

H 253   JOSEPH REDDITT TO CAPT. THOMAS WEST
        Feb. 19, 1755. 6 pds. 8 sh. for 170 A. In Bucklesbury Pocoson adj.
ARCHIBALD BELL. By patent dated Aug. 1, 1726 to WILLIAM REDDITT. Wit:
WILLIAM BALL, JOHN REDDITT. Jan. Court 1756. *.

H 254   MARTIN GARDNER & WIFE ANAH TO WILLIAM PEARCE (PIERCE)
        Jan. 26, 1756. 15 pds. for 50 A. Adj. HENRY KING on Roquiss Swamp,
JAMES WILLIAMS. Part of patent granted MARTIN GARDNER in 1745. Wit: NEEDHAM
BRYAN, JOHN SHOALAR. Jan. Court 1756. *.

H 255   MICHAEL WARD, JUN. & WIFE FRNC(?) TO WILLIAM WOOD, yeoman
        March 1, 1750. 50 pds. for 210 A. On Quayoccason Swamp. Wit: JOSEPH
PERRY, WILLIAM PERRY, JOHN SMITH. Jan. Court 1756. *.

H 257   MOSES PRICE TO RICHARD BROWN
        May 31, 1742. Exchange. 150 A. "...secured...to...said MOSES his
heirs...at New River by RICHARD BROWN and his wife now release and do sell
by way of swap..." Land on WS White Oak Swamp adj. JACOB LEWIS, CHARLES
JONES, JUN. Wit: JOHN SIVENNEY HENEGAN(?), MARY PRICE. Jan. Court 1756. *.

H 258   THOMAS WALKER & WIFE SUSANNAH of Society Parish to JOHN BRICKELL
        Jan. 14, 1756. 115 pds. for 475 A. Land in Society Parish which
THOMAS WALKER bought in two parcels (1) 275 A. of Whitfield and known by
name of Red Ridge adj. PETER WEST. (2) 200 A. bought of WILLIAM MOORE now
of Granville County commonly called Pond Slash adj. Col.(?) JONES, PETER
WEST, WHITFIELD, Tar Kiln Branch at Indian Path "is contiguous to above
mentioned acres". Wit: MATTH. BRICKELL, *. Jan. Court 1756. *.

H 260   JOHN BRICKELL & MARTHA, his wife, of Society Parish TO MATTHIAS
        BRICKELL. Jan. 18, 1756. 150 pds. for 275 A. Adj. PETER WEST.
Wit: REUBEN POWELL, ABSOLOM CREECH. Jan. Court 1756. *.

H 261   WILLIAM BAKER & WIFE MARTHA TO JESSE BAKER
        *. Deed of Gift. "for love and good will...towards my loving son
JESSE BAKER...I reserve...the said plantation...and chattels in my person
during my own life and the life of my loving wife MARGARET BAKER..." Wit:
THOMAS EVANS, SOLOMON NORVILLE, JOHN HARRELL. April Court 1756. *.

H 262   WILLIAM ROBERSON of Edgecombe Co. TO WILLIAM HOMES
        Feb. 17, 1754. 13 pds. for 200 A. Adj. CHARLES HORN, JOHN WILKS.
Being part of a tract granted June 23, 1749. Wit: CHARLES HORNE, BARNABY
BRYAN. *. BENJAMIN WYNNS C/C.

H 263   JOHN WARBURTON TO BARNABY HELY DUNSTAN, joyner
        *. 35 pds. for 70 A. Between Cashia River and Roanoke River adj.
THOMAS SAVAGE, JOHN DALY. Wit: JOHN WARD, JOHN HYMAN. April Court 1756.*.

H 264   JOHN PERRY, JUN. TO RICHARD LAKEY

April 27, 1756. 80 pds. for 320 A. On West Shore of Chowan River. Adj. land formerly belonging to LAWRENCE MACGUE now belonging to JOSEPH BUTTERTON at Beaverdam Swamp. Being land MEDIA WHITE sold to said PERRY Feb. 13, 1739. Wit: THOMAS WHITMELL, JAMES JONES, EPHRAIM WESTON. April Court 1756. BENJAMIN WYNNS C/C.

H 266 RICHARD LAKEY TO JOHN PERRY, JUN.
       April 27, 1756. 80 pds. for 100 A. + 50 A. Three parcels. (1) On NS Blackwalnut Swamp adj. DAVID RYAN, SAMUEL COOK. Formerly purchased of THOMAS ASHLEY, SEN. (2) 50 A. which THOMAS ASHLEY sold to SAMUEL COOK. (3) 150 A. in all conveyed to THOMAS ASHLEY, SEN. by JOHN LOVICK, executor of last will and testament of LAWRENCE SARSON by deed Aug. 2, 1740 and by ASHLEY conveyed to LAKEY May 16, 1753. Wit: THOMAS WHITMELL, JAMES JONES, EPHRAIM WESTON. April Court 1756. *.

H 267 ALEXANDER KENNEDAY of Albemarle Co. & WIFE ABIGAIL TO BENJAMIN ATWELL
       March 1, 1756. Dower Gift. 90 A. "...ALEXANDER KENNEDAY for in consideration of marrying his daughter doth hereby adknowledge to him...forever..." Place called Cabin Hill adj. WILLIAM WOODS, THOMAS WARD on Cashie Road. Wit: JOHN SAWKILL, EDMUND GLOHON, THOMAS OUTLAW. April Court 1756.*.

H 268 JOHN STALLINGS of Granville Co. & ELIAS STALLINGS, JUN. TO WILLIAM
       BLITCHENDEN.   March 13, 1756. 50 pds. for 416 A. On Spring Branch adj. MARY PARKER, ____ WYNNS. Wit: PEGGY WYNNS, BENJAMIN WYNNS. April Court 1756. BENJAMIN WYNNS C/C.

H 270 FRANCIS HOBSON & WIFE ANN TO JOHN BAZEMORE
       April 27, 1756. 40 pds. for 650 A. By patent Feb. 1, 1725. On Cheskee Swamp. Wit: THOMAS WHITMELL, CHARLES KING, JONATHAN KITRELL. April Court 1756. *.

H 271 BURRELL BELL & WIFE SARAH TO WILLIAM HARE (HAIR)
       March 8, 1756. 20 pds. for 182 A. On Mare Branch at dividing line between HARE and E. SLAUGHSON at Flatt Swamp. Wit: WILLIAM HOOKER, JUN., WILLIAM WILLIAMSON. April Court 1756. *.

H 272 WILLIAM BARBER & WIFE ALLESS TO JOHN HURST, taylor
       Jan. 8, 1756. 30 pds. for 100 A. Near Cashy River adj. land of GEORGE SMITH, dec'd. Wit: JOSEPH HARDY, JOHN ALLEN. April Court 1756. *.

H 273 BARNABY HELY DUNSTAN & WIFE ELIZABETH TO WILLIAM BONNER of Chowan
       Co., joiner.   March 1, 1756. 110 pds. for 300 A. On NES Cashie River at Jacket Branch on line between DUNSTAN and PETER YEATES adj. ____ RYAN to Scittlethorp Branch. Including 110 A. which BARNABY H. DUNSTAN bought of JOHN SMITH May 9, 1753. Also including 100 A. which RICHARD DUNSTAN bought of ROBERT BIRD Feb. 3, 1753 and sold to B.H. DUNSTAN and wife. Wit: EDW. RASOR, TOM SUTTON, GEORGE SUTTON. April Court 1756. *.

H 275 JONATHAN STANDLEY TO JOHN WATSON
       *. 1756. 3 pds. 8 sh. for 12 A. Adj. line formerly ____ HARE's to Whittleberry Branch & Whittleberry Branch (Pond). Wit: JAMES BENTLEY, WILLIAM LIVINGSTON. April Court 1756. *.

H 276 WILLIAM WRIGHT of Perquimmons Co., Schoolmaster, TO BENJAMIN WYNNS
       Feb. 15, 1755. 20 pds. for 250 A. On Wiccacon Creek. Land which WILLIAM WRIGHT bought of GEORGE WYNNS June 5, 1752. Adj. WILLIAM ASKEW. Wit: CULLIN SESOMS, JENNIT SESSUMS. April Court 1756. *.

H 278 JAMES LEGITT TO JOHN LEGETT
       April 28, 1756. Deed of Gift. 600 A. "...for love, good-will and affection...to my beloved grandson JOHN LEGETT son of JAMES LEGETT...reserving only the use thereof to myself and my wife, my son JAMES and his wife during our natural lives..." Land in Cashy Neck at Charlton's Creek adj. HENRY BATES at Simmon's Pond, ____RYAND, ____ GRIFFITH, ____ JORDAN. Wit: JOSEPH JORDAN, JOHN WATSON. April Court 1756. *.

H 279 SAMUEL ORMES TO WILLIAM BALL
       April 3, 1756. 20 pds. *. Land in Gum Swamp adj. THOMAS ASHBURN, NATHANIEL DUCKENFIELD (de'c'd), JOSEPH HARDY. Wit: CHAS. ELIOTT, L. LOCKHART. April Court 1756. *.

H 280   CHARLES BURCH & WIFE ELIZABETH TO LUKE MEZELL, JUN.
        Jan. 27, 1756. 30 pds. for 100 A. Land in Cashie Neck adj. MIZELLE,
EDWARD COLLINS, RICHARD TOMLINSON. Wit: RICHARD TOMLINSON, CHRISTOPHER
BURCH. April Court 1756. BENJAMIN WYNNS C/C.

H 281   THOMAS ROADES & WIFE ELIZABETH TO DAVID STANDLEY
        April 28, 1756. 16 pds. for 175 A. On NS Roquist Swamp at Roquiss
Islands by patent granted WILLIAM SMITH dated April 1, 1723 adj. JAMES CAS-
TELLOW. Wit: JONOTHAN STANDLY, MARY NICHOLAS. April Court 1756. *.

H 283   RICHARD BRADLY TO JOHN DALY of Tyrill, merchant
        Feb. 17, 1756. 90 pds. for 210 A. Plantation formerly called BERRY's
Plantation in Cashie Neck. Wit: CHARLES HARDISON, JOHN OLIVER. April Court
1756. *.

H 284   THOMAS CLIFTON TO ISAAC SANDERS of Chowan Co.
        April 27, 1756. 18 pds. 1 sh. for 200 A. On Chinkopen Ridge adj.
SAMUEL WEBB, JACOB LEWIS (formerly JAMES HOWARD's) at Wading Branch adj.
JOHN JONES (formerly), STEPHEN WILLIAMS (formerly). Wit: MATTH. BRICKELL,
WM. WILLIAMS. April Court 1756. *.

H 285   DENNIS GIBSSON of Tyrrell TO ROBERT HOWELL
        April 3, 1756. 15 pds. for 140 A. On Roquist Islands "...upper part
of a tract containing (280 A.) ..." Wit: FRANCIS HOBSON, ISAAC GLISSON.
April Court 1756. *.

H 286   WILLIAM WILLIAMS TO JOHN HARRELL
        Feb. 15, 1756. *. 60 A. On NS Roanoke River. Part of a patent grant-
ed to BENJAMIN FOREMAN at Mill Branch adj. JOHN HARRELL, JUN. Wit: WILLIAM
ANDREWS, NICHOLAS SKINNER, JOHN HIGGS. April Court 1756. *.

H 288   JOHN PENNY, yeoman, TO LODGE SIMPSON
        March 24, 1756. 22 pds. 10 sh. for 200 A. Adj. JOHN PENNY. Wit:
RICHARD LAKEY, GEORGE MEWBORNE, ANTHO. FILGO. April Court 1756. *.

H 288   JAMES PARKER, SEN. & WIFE SARAH TO JOSEPH PARKER
        April 5, 1756. 10 pds. for 100 A. "...by my son JOSEPH PARKER..."
Land on NS Roquist. Wit: JONATHAN STANDLY, WILLIAM KING. April Court 1756.*.

H 290   THOMAS WILLIAMS TO MARMADULE NORFLEET (NORFLITT) of Perquimmons Co.
        Feb. 10, 1756. 120 pds. for 385 A. On NS Roanoke River at MARMADULE
NORFLITS Mill adj. GEORGE WILLIAMS, JOHN HARRELL at NORFLITT's Road at
Connaquina Swamp, NICHOLAS SKINNER, "MARY WILLIAMS corner Grand Daughter to
GEORGE WILLIAMS Dec'd", THOMAS WILLIAMS. Part of three tracts (1) Granted
GEORGE WILLIAMS March 1, 1721 (2) Granted BENJAMIN FOREMAN March 1721 (3)
Granted GEORGE WILLIAMS April 6, 1722. Wit: WILLIAM ROBINSON, ARTHUR BELL,
WILLIAM DAVIS. April Court 1756. *.

H 291   WILLIAM ROBBISON of Northampton Co. TO MARMADULE NORFLITT (NORFLEET)
        of Perquimmons Co.   April 24, 1756. 5 pds. for 200 A. On NS Roa-
noke River adj. CHARLES HORNE, WILLIAM CARTER at CARTER's Branch. Part of
640 A. tract by grant June 22, 1749. Wit: THOMAS WILLIAMS, GEORGE HARRELL,
JONATHAN ROBERSON. April Court 1756. *.

H 293   SAMUEL WIGGINS & WIFE ELIZABETH TO THOMAS MIERS
        April 8, 1756. 30 pds. for 540 A. On NS Cashy adj. THOMAS RHOADES,
HENRY ROADES. "...The Feme being first privately examined by HENRY HUNTER
one of His Majesty's Justices of the Peace..." Wit: JOHN HINTON, JONAS
HINTON, JACOB BUTLER. April Court 1756. *.

H 295   NEHEMIAH SCOTT of Duplin Co. TO THOMAS BARKER (BAKER) of Chowan Co.
        April 8, 1756. 80 pds. for 125 A. + 13 A. (1) Adj. JAMES BLOUNT,
JOHN HINNART, SAMUEL SMITH, "JOHN WILLIAMS the younger" at Indian Village
Meadow (2) 13 A. in Village Swamp. Wit: THOMAS PUGH, JOSEPH SCOTT. April
Court 1756. *.

H 296   CORNELIUS CAMPBELL & WIFE ELIZABETH TO JOHN CRICKETT
        Nov. 15, 1755. 200 pds. for 390 A. (1) On NS Middle Swamp adj.
WILLIAM GRILL, MRS. JOHNSTON (2) 100 A. adj. first tract adj. land formerly
belonging to THOMAS WHITMELL, EDWARD BRYAN. Wit: D. RYAN, JOHN BRETT, JOHN
ANDYCKE. April Court 1756.

H 298   JOSEPH PARKER TO ROBERT HOWELL
        April 5, 1756. 10 pds. for 100 A. on NS Roquist Swamp. Wit: JONA-
THAN STANDLEY, WILLIAM KING. April Court 1756. BENJAMIN WYNNS C/C.

H 299   PETER HAYS & WIFE BETHER (BUTRICE?) TO THOMAS HAYS
        Dec. 8, 1755. 10 pds. for 100 A. On SS Cashy Swamp. By deed dated
1755. Wit: WILLIAM POYTHRESS, GEORGE VANN, JOHN BRYAN. April Court 1756.*.

H 300   ROBERT CARY of London, merchant, ANN CARY, Relict of ROBERT CARY,
HENRY STEVENS of London, EDWARD WOODCOCK TO THOMAS BARKER. Nov. 2, 1754.
5 sh. One year lease. 240 A. + 1280 A. + 150 A. + 50 A. + 100 A.   ROBERT
CARY, son and heir of ROBERT CARY merchant of London. ANNEY CARY, executrix
of ROBERT CARY. HENRY STEVENS of Doctors Commons, London. EDWARD WOODCOCK
of Lincolns Inn in the county of Middlesex, executors of the last will of
ROBERT CARY. And JOHN MOREY of London Merchant (1) Land sold by THEOPHI-
LUS WILLIAMS to THEOPHILUS PUGH by deed Sept. 24, 1742 on NS Foaling Run
adj. NEEDHAM BRYAN, THOMAS BOND, THOMAS BARKER cont. 240 A. (2) Land con-
veyed by HENRY JARNIGAN to THEOPHILUS PUGH dated April 20, 1738 adj. PUGH,
JOSEPH BLACKMAN, JOHN BLACKMAN cont. 100 A. (3) Tract sold by JOHN JAMESON
to THEOPHILUS PUGH by deed Aug. 19, 1741 on Roanoke River adj. JAMES CAS-
TELLAW cont. 1280 A. (4) two tracts sold by HENRY OVERSTREET to THEOPHILUS
PUGH by deed May 10, 1735 (a) 150 A. on Apple Tree Swamp adj. WILLIAM JONES,
HENRY JERNIGAN (b) cont. 50 A. on Roquis. The 150 A. where ANN OVERSTREET
did live and which HENRY OVERSTREET purchased of WILLIAM JONES & HENRY JAR-
NIGAN and the said 50 A. which HENRY OVERSTREET purchased of ROBERT RADFORD
(5) Tract conveyed by JAMES FLOOD to THEOPHILUS PUGH Oct. 20, 1741 on Vil-
lage Swamp adj. Widow CHESHIRE cont. 100 A. Signed ROBERT JONES, JUN. by
Power of Att'y. Wit: WM. WILLIE, GEORGE PURDIE. N.C. Court March 22, 1755.
JAMES HASELL, C.J.

H 304   ROBERT CARY, ANNEY CARY, HENRY STEVENS, EDWARD WOODCOCK TO THOMAS
        BARKER of Chowan Co.   Nov. 3, 1754. 300 pds. Lands in actualy pos-
session of THOMAS BARKER by virtue of a bargain of lease. Seven tracts
(listed above). Power at atty. from ROBERT CARY to ROBERT JONES, JUN. Wit:
W. WILLIE, GEORGE PURDIE. N.C. Court March 22, 1755. JAMES HASSELL, C.J.

H 307   ROBERT HICKS & WIFE SARAH of Granville Co., merchant TO DAVID MEADE
        of Nansemond Co., Va., merchant.   Dec. 29, 1755. 161 pds. 5 sh.
for 534 A. Land on NS Roanoke River adj. land formerly JAMES BLOUNT's now
JETHRO BUTLER's, THOMAS PAGE on Jumping Run. Tract of land patented Nov.
16, 1723 to JOHN WILLIAMS "who dying intestate it descended to his son
JAMES WILLIAMS who conveyed it to said ROBERT HICKS (Oct. 16, 1739)...ex-
cept four acres now in Possession of JETHRO BUTLER on which he has a corn
field that was formerly JAMES BLOUNT's..." Wit: ____BARKER, JOHN GILCHRIST,
DARWIN ELWICK. May 5, 1756. PETER HENLEY, C.J.

H 309   BURRILL BELL & WIFE SARAH TO DANIEL VANPELT
        Feb. 18, 1756. 20 pds. for 157 A. Adj. JAMES JONES & THOMAS SISSONS,
PETER EVANS, JOHN DAVIDSON, JOHN SMITH on Chinkopen Swamp. Wit: JOHN VAN
PELT, MARY ANN WYNNS. July Court 1756. BENJ. WYNNS C/C.

H 311   RODGER BADGETT TO WILLIAM PERRY
        July 27, 1754. 35 pds. for 250 A. On Quiocison Swamp at Cabbin
Branch adj. EDWARD OUTLAW, WILLIAM FREEMAN. Wit: JOHN FRYARS, JAMES PERRY,
NICHOLAS HUNTER. July Court 1756. *.

H 312   FRANCIS CORBIN of Chowan Co. TO JOSEPH WIMBERLY (WIMBERLEY)
        June 5, 1756. 5 sh. for 600 A. On WS Keisa River near BLACKMON's
Landing adj. CAPT. WM. GREGORY, ____WOLSTON "being one of the tracts of
land mortgaged by said FRANCIS CORBIN by a deed of release dated (Oct. 5,
1752). Wit: ____BARKER, JOHN HARE. July Court 1756. *.

H 314   JOSEPH WIMBERLY TO THOMAS HARE
        June 5, 1756. 100 pds. for 600 A. On Cashy River near BLACKMAN's
Landing adj. CAPT. WILLIAM GREGORY. Wit: ____BARKER, JOHN HARE. July Court
1756. *.

H 315   GIDIAN (GIDEON) GILBERT of Duplin Co. TO EDWARD SKULL
        Nov. 7, 1755. 10 pds. for 50 A. On WS Deep Creek adj. ABIGAL GIL-
BERT at Miery Branch. Wit: RICHARD JONES, BENJAMIN COTTEN. July Court 1756.

H 316   WILLIAM HOOKER, JUN. TO HANCE HOSLER of Chowan Co., bricklayer
        July 6, 1755. 52 pds. for 150 A. Land bought of MARY HOCOTT adj.
HOCOTT, BEACHMANS HERITONS(?), JOSEPH WYNNS. "(defend)...from the lawful
claim of the Widow DOWNING Daughter in Law to CAPT. WILLIAM DOWNING of
Mount Pleasant...(and lawful heirs)". Wit: CHAS. CAMPBELL, HENRY HILL, THO-
MAS GARRETT. July Court 1756. BENJAMIN WYNNS, C/C.

H 317   JOHN PENNY TO JOHN MEWBOORNE
        July 27, 1756. 16 pds. for 100 A. Land assigned to PENNY by THOMAS
RYAN, deceased. On ES Cucoldmakers Swamp adj. GEORGE MEWBORNE (MEWBOORNE).
Wit: LODGE SIMPSON, GEORGE MEWBOORNE. July Court 1756. *.

H 318   WILLIAM ANDERSON, carpenter, & WIFE MARY TO REUBEN FIELDS
        Aug. 13, 1755. 44 pds. for *. Land bought of WILLIAM FLEETWOOD and
EDWARD RASOR by deed Aug. 8, 1748 on ES Salmon Creek adj. CULLEN POLLOCK
(land formerly belonging to CARY GOODBY), EDWARD RASOR. "(Land and)...also
all that crop of corn that is now Growing on the said land & one half of
the Petatoes..." Wit: JOHN CRICKETT, JOHN NICHOLLS, JUN. July Court 1756.*.

H 319   GABRIEL MANLY (MANLEY), cooper, TO BENJAMIN WYNNS
        Sept. 7, 1754. 30 pds. for 200 A. "...land whereon I now live..."
Wit: JOSEPH PERRY, JOHN BARKER. July Court 1756. *.

H 321   PETER EVANS, carpenter, TO SIMON VANPELT
        May 12, 1756. 25 pds. for 640 A. On WS Cypress Swamp adj. Col. WM.
MAUL. Wit: WILLIAM WYNNS, BENJAMIN WYNNS. July Court 1756. *.

H 322   MARY CRICKETT TO CRICKETT CHILDREN
        July 27, 1756. Deed of Gift. "...to my well beloved children THOMAS
CRICKETT, CHARLES CRICKETT and SARAH CRICKETT..." To THOMAS & CHARLES 10
pds. Sterling and a good feather bed and furniture to each. (2) To SARAH
one feather bed and furniture and a negro girl named Cloe. To be delivered
to them when they are of age. Wit: H. NICHOLLS, WM. RICE. July Court 1756.*.

H 325   WILLIAM BAKER TO MOSES WOOD, cooper
        July 9, 1756. 11 pds. for 200 A. On SS Bear Swamp Creek "...being
all the land except one hundred acres bequesthed in the will of JAMES NEW-
LAND to ARNOLD HOPKINS of a patent for 300 acres obtained by JAMES NEWLAND
(April 1, 1727)...and left to the said WILLIAM BAKER..." Wit: ED. RASOR,
HENRY FLEETWOOD. July Court 1756. BENJ. WYNNS C/C.

H 324   ALEXANDER KENNEDAY & WIFE ABIGAIL TO RALPH OUTLAW
        Feb. 28, 1756. 47 pds. 3 sh. 1 p. *. In Quoyccason Swamp. Wit:
WILLIAM FRAZER, JOHN SANKILL (LANKILL?). July Court 1756. *.

H 326   WILLIAM LEVINOR & WIFE MARTHA TO THOMAS WILSON
        April 26, 1756. "seventy five pounds of old Tenner" for 183 A. On
NS Cashy Swamp. Wit: JONATHAN STANDLEY, JONATHAN STANDLEY, JUN. July Court
1756. *.

H 327   HENRY VOLLANTINE TO DANIEL FRAZER
        July 21, 1756. 10 pds. for 160 A. Adj. MOSES HILL. Wit: WILLIAM
THORNTON, CHRISTIAN ROUNDTREE, LESTISHER THORNTON. July Court 1756. *.

H 328   JAMES BENNETT (BENNITT) TO ROBERT SUMNER
        July 24, 1756. 15 pds. for 100 A. On SS Sandy Run adj. WILLIAM
HOOKER, JUN., ABRAHAM SMITH, WILLIAM HOOKER, SEN. Wit: HANSE HOSLER, MOSES
OLIVER, ROBERT SUMNER. July Court 1756. *.

H 330   WILLIAM COLLINS, sadler, TO JESSE COLLINS
        June 29, 1752. 5 pds. for 350 A. On NS Pelmell known by name of
Marbin Hills. Wit: MICHAEL COLLINS, HANCE HOFLER. July Court 1756. *.

H 331   ARCHIBALD (ARCHBILL) BELL TO ROBERT WEST
        March 10, 1756. 16 lbs. pork (prock?) for 320 A. In Bucklesberry
Pocoson adj. LAURENCE SARSON. "signed and sealed in Duplin County". Wit:
WILLIAM BYRD, JOHN BELL, GEORGE BELL. July Court 1756. *.

H 332   ARCHBELL BELL of Duplin Co., TO ROBERT WEST
        July 27, 1756. 75 pds. for 200 A. In Bucklesbery Pocoson adj. JOHN
REDDY, ARCHBELL BELL, LAURENCE SARSONS. Wit: WM. MACKEY, L. WEST. July

Court 1756. BENJ. WYNNS C/C.

H 333   WILLIAM HOOKS TO THOMAS HOOKS
     July 20, 1756. Deed of Gift. 320 A. "...to my loving son THOMAS
HOOKS..." Land in Cashia Neck at CHARLTON's Line, CLARK's Line, PHILLIP
WARD. Wit: JOSEPH WILLIAMSON, THOMAS HOWARD. July Court 1756. *.

H 335   RICHARD BRADLY TO JOHN GIBBS
     Jan. 27, 1756. 12 pds. 10 sh. for 50 A. On SS Cashie River adj. Mr.
SMITHWICK at Herrin Creek. Wit: JOHN WARBURTON, JOSHUA SMITH. July Court
1756. *.

H 335   WILLIAM BROWN TO BENJAMIN BROWN
     Aug. 20, 1755. 25 pds. for 150 A. On Chinkopen Creek "known by name
of Killum old field" at Flatt Swamp. Wit: JOHN FREEMAN, BENJAMIN BAKER, JUN.
July Court 1756. *.

H 336   MARGARET DUKINFIELD TO SAMUEL ORMES
     April 6, 1756. Agreement. "MARGARET DUKINFIELD widow & relect of
NATH'L DUKINFIELD Late of London...SAMUEL ORMES Steward of the s'd NATH.
DUKINFIELD's estate in North Carolina...by agreement August 1, 1740...ORMES
did post bond in amt. 1000 pds. for faithful performance...NATHANIEL DUKIN-
FIELD during his lifetime was satisfied with accounts. Since his death
MARGARET DUKINFIELD is satisfied...This agreement is such that neither MAR-
GARET DUKINFIELD nor other heirs will molest SAMUEL ORMES or bring suit
against SAMUEL ORMES for his handling of the (N.C.) estate of NATH'L DUKIN-
FIELD..." Wit: CHAS. ELIOTT, ELIZ. CAMPBELL. July Court 1756. *.

H 338   JOHN CAMPBELL, Merchant, TO OLIAS (OPIAS?) BEAMAN
     July 29, 1756. 16 pds. for 100 A. On WS Road that leads to Mt. Sion
Store adj. _____ COUPLAND, _____ JACKSON, _____ HARTLEY, _____ NICHOLSON. Wit:
JOS. HARDY, ED. RASOR. July Court 1756. *.

H 340   BARNABY BRYANT & WIFE ELIZABETH of Society Parish TO EDWARD BOYD
     March 29, 1756. 18 pds. for 200 A. Land by patent Dec. 13, 1755.
Adj. _____ HILL, JAMES BROWN, EDWARD HAWKINS. Wit: FRAS. SEARSON, WILLIAM
HOMES. July Court 1756. *.

H 342   BENJAMIN BROWN TO PETER EVANS
     Sept. 10, 1755. 70 pds. for 150 A. "known to be the manner Planta-
tion whereon my deceased Father FRANCIS BROWN lived...and left to me..." By
patent June 1707. On ES Chinkopen Creek at mouth of Great Branch at Miery
Branch. Wit: BURRILL BELL, LEWIS WILLIAMS. July Court 1756. *.

H 343   JAMES DAVIS, yeoman, TO JOSEPH THOMAS
     May 9, 1756. 15 pds. for 200 A. On SWS Flat Swamp being plantation
purchased of RICHARD ROBERTS adj. EDWARD OUTLAW. Wit: MICHAEL COLLINS,
ABSOLOM COLLINS. July Court 1756. *.

H 345   JAMES DAVIS TO JOSEPH THOMAS, yeoman
     May 9, 1756. 15 pds. for 140 A. "on main road, near the end of a
casway..." Adj. CULMER SESSUMS, GABRIEL MANLY. Wit: MICH'L. COLLINS, JESSE
COLLINS, ABSOLOM COLLINS. July Court 1756. *.

H 346   HON. JOHN CARTERET, EARL OF GRANVILLE TO JOHN HARRELL
     March 25, 1749. 3 sh. for 200 A. In Society Parish on NS Roanoke
River adj. RICHARD WILLIAMS at Bushy Gutt, JETHRO BUTLER. Provided land be
seated, a good house be built and land stocked with cattle at rate of five
head/hundred acres. (Money rate: 3 sh Sterling = 4 sh Proclamation).
Signed: EDWARD MOSELEY, by commission. Wit: JOHN WYNNS, BENJ. WYNNS. July
Court 1756. *.

H 350   REUBEN POWELL & WIFE MARY TO JOHN BRICKELL
     Oct. 25, 1756. 50 pds. for 150 A. Adj. PETER WEST at Indian Path,
BRYANT HARE, HENRY WINBOURNE, JOHN BRICKELL, "WHITFIELDS now BRICKELLS".
Excepting 45 A. sold by POWELL to BRYAN HARE, son of EDWARD. Wit: MATTHIAS
BRICKELL. *. Oct. Court 1757. *.

H 351   WILLIAM PERRY TO WILLIAM FREEMAN of Chowan Co.
     Aug. 3, 1756. 35 pds. for 250 A. On Quoyocoason Swamp at Cabbin
Branch adj. EDWARD OUTLAW. Wit: RICHARD FREEMAN, JOSHU FREEMAN, JNO.FREEMAN.

Oct. Court 1756. BENJ. WYNNS C/C.

H 353   WILLIAM RASBERRY TO JOSEPH BARRADAIL
        Oct. 26, 1756.   25 pds. for 340 A. "WILLIAM PERRY...Heir-at-Law to
JOHN RASBERRY Late of Bertie County..." Adj. JOSEPH BARRADAIL, EDWARD HOMES
at Signea Swamp, _____ POLLOCK's line to Canaan Swamp, THOMAS BARKER. Part
of a Patent to JOHN RASBERRY Nov. 16, 1743. Wit: DEMSEY WOOD, WILLIAM HOSEA.
Oct. Court 1756. *.

H 354   BURRELL BELL & WIFE SARAH TO JAMES BOONE WYNNS
        Oct. 26, 1756.   200 pds. for 7713 A.   (1) 5480 A. between Chowan
River and Chinkopen Creek "being a tract granted Col. WILLIAM MAULE which
said land descended to PENELOPE CATHCART wife of Doct'r WM. CATHCART who
was daughter and sole heiress to the s'd Coll. WM. MAULE...and by Do. WILL-
IAM CATHCART and PENELOPE his wife conveyed to JOHN WYNNS..." (Sept. 20,
1742.)   JOHN WYNNS by last will and testament gave to his wife, SARAH, now
wife of said BURRELL BELL. (2) 380 A. conveyed to JOHN WYNNS by JAMES CASTEL-
LAW, the Public Treasurer at sale March 9, 1745. And to SARAH WYNNS by
will. (3) 640 A. conveyed to JOHN WYNNS by TREDDLE KEELE (KEEFE) Aug. 4,
1738 and by WYNNS devised to his wife. (4) 253 A. Patented to BENJAMIN HOL-
LOMAN April 20, 1745 and assigned Feb. 9, 1750 to JOHN WYNNS. (5) 320 A.
patent to Coll. WILLIAM MAULE for 640 A. Feb. 1, 1725 and endorsed by WILL-
IAM CATHCART & wife PENELOPE MAULE CATHCART Aug. 24, 1748 to JOHN DEVEREAUX
and JOHN WYNNS. Wit: JOSEPH PERRY, BENJ. BROWN. Oct. Court 1756. *.

H 358   JAMES BOON WYNNS TO BURRELL BELL
        Oct. 26, 1756.   200 pds. for 7713 A. (tract described above). Wit:
JOS. PERRY, BENJ. BROWN. Oct. Court 1756. *.

H 361   PETER BRINKLEY, SEN. of Perquimmons Co. TO MICHAEL GRITFIN
        Sept. 8, 1756.   20 pds. for 190 A. On NS Roquist Swamp adj. JOSEPH
KNOTT, FRANCIS HOBSON, THOMAS RYAN. Land was granted to JOHN HOBSON by
patent April 1, 1723 and by HOBSON sold to SAMUEL SINGLETON and by SINGLE-
TON sold to PETER BRINKLEY Oct. 4, 1752. Wit: SAMUEL SUMNER, JAMES SPEED(?),
JOHN BRINKLEY. Oct. Court 1756. *.

H 363   JOSEPH HARDY TO WILLIAM KNOTT
        Aug. 25, 1756.   20 pds. for 150 A. In Bucklesbury Pocoson "below
COBBS old field" adj. JOSEPH HARDY, WILLIAM KNOTT, THOMAS ASHBURN at Flaggy
Branch. Wit: WILLIAM BALL, THOMAS WEBB. Oct. Court 1756. *.

H 365   SMETHWICK WARBURTON TO WILLIAM WOOTEN, taylor
        March 29, 1756.   5 pds. for 100 A. In Bucklesbury. Wit: WILLIAM
FLEETWOOD, ROBERT THOMPSON. Oct. Court 1756. *.

H 366   WILLIAM HOMES (HOLMES) & WIFE ANN, late of Bertie, TO JOHN BRICKELL
        Oct. 25, 1756.   10 pds. for 200 A. Adj. CHARLES HORN on WS CARTER's
Branch, JOHN WILKES. Wit: WM. ANDREWS, JOHN GILLECOT. Oct. Court 1756.*.

H 367   SAMUEL ANDREWS & WIFE MARY, late of Bertie, TO REUBEN POWELL
        Oct. 14, 1756.   20 pds. for 200 A. Adj. JOHN RODES (RHODES), JAMES
BROWN, NICHOLAS SKINNER, JOHN RYTLAND, THOMAS BARFIELD. Wit: JNO. BRICKELL,
JAS. CATFIELD (COFFIELD?). Oct. Court 1756. *.

H 369   GEORGE JARNIGAN TO WILLIAM MITCHELL
        Oct. 26, 1756.   25 pds. for 400 A. on SS Sequar Swamp adj. JAMES
MITCHELL, WILLIAM MITCHELL. Wit: WM. WESTON, JAMES MITCHELL. Oct. Court
1756. *.

H 369   JAMES EARLY TO JOHN EARLY
        April 6, 1756.   20 pds. for 200 A. Adj. JAMES MCGLOHON at Colt
Branch, THOMAS DIXON. Wit: RICHARD WILLIFORD, JUN., RICHARD WILLIFORD. Oct.
Court 1756. *.

H 371   MICHAEL WARD, SEN. & WIFE ANN TO RICHARD WARD, yeoman
        Sept. 4, 1756.   Deed of Gift. 300 A. "...for and in consideration
of taken care of both of them as long as they both shall live..." On NS
Quoyoccason Swamp adj. _____ KAIL, _____ WELLS. Being part of a patent to BLY
dated March 10, 1740. Wit: JOHN KAIL, MARTHA SPIVEY, WILLIAM COLTHRED. Oct.
Court 1756. *.

H 372   JOHN BRICKELL, Sheriff of Bertie Co., TO THOMAS WHITMELL
        Jan. 26, 1757. 2 pds. 5 sh. for 100 A. Ordered to sell lands of
JAMES MCDOWALL, held by JOHN SMITH Late of Edgecombe, executor of last will
and testament of JAMES MCDOWALL. By order of a judgement at New Berne to
JAMES HOGAN and wife RUTH in the amount of 33 pds. 6 sh. 9 p. against THO-
MAS NORFLEET, dec'd. Due to the obligations of NORFLEET and MCDOWALL in
their life times. THOMAS WHITMELL appeared at sale and bought within land.
In Bucklesberry Swamp adj. JOHN WILLIAMS, ABRAHAM HERRING. Parcel sold by
MICHAEL HILL to JAMES MCDOWALL by deed May 28, 1748. Wit: BENJ. WYNNS,
BURRELL BELL.   Jan. Court 1757. BENJ. WYNNS C/C.

H 374   JOHN BRICKELL, Sheriff of Bertie Co., TO JOHN HILL
        May 10, 1755. 11 pds. Sale of lands of JAMES MCDOWELL (MCDOWALL).
See above transaction. Land sold by CHARLES HARDY to JAMES MCDOWELL on
Feb. 18, 1745. Adj. JOHN GRAY at Licking Branch, HENRY EDMOND at Turkey
Swamp cont. 240 A. Also 240 A. adj. JOHN EDWARDS, dec'd. Wit: BENJ. WYNNS,
BURRILL BELL, J. EDWARDS.   Jan. court 1757. *.

H 376   ABRAHAM SMITH, yeoman, TO WILLIAM HOOKER, JUN.
        Nov. 25, 1756. 5 pds. for 100 A. On Sandy Run adj. ____ ROYSTER,
AARON OLIVER, THOMAS ROGERS. Wit: JAMES HOOKER, STEPHEN HOOKER, NICHOLAS
ASKEW.   Jan. Court 1757. *.

H 378   EDWARD BRYAN TO ADAM HARRELL
        Jan. 24, 1757. 18 pds. for 320 A. In Chinkopen Swamp adj. ____ GIL-
BIRD, JOHN HOWELL. "A tract of land given to SIMON BRYAN by his Father
LEWIS BRYAN's will and sold to EDWARD BRYAN...by deed (Jan. 15, 1741)..."
Wit: JAMES JONES, WILLIAM COLTHRED, JOHN HURST.   Jan. Court 1757. *.

H 379   JOHN WESTERN TO THOMAS SLATTER
        Jan. 25, 1757. 20 pds. for 200 A. On NS Cashy adj. JOHN WILLIAMS,
JOHN MOOR at Isaac's Creek. Wit: BENJ. WYNNS, DAVID RICE. Jan. Court 1757.

H 380   GEORGE HARRELL TO JOHN HARRELL
        Oct. 15, 1756. 20 pds. for 100 A. On NS Roanoke River. Part of a
grant to JOHN HARRELL, JUN. March 25, 1749 adj. WILLIAM ANDREWS. Wit: JESSE
HARRELL, HARDY HARRELL. Jan. Court 1757. *.

H 381   CHARLES ROBERTS & WIFE RACHEL TO HENRY BYRAM
        Oct. 30, 1756. 10 pds. for 100 A. Adj. DAVID HORTON, MOSES BONNER.
Wit: ANN BURD (BIRD?), RACHEL BRICKELL. Jan. Court 1757. *.

H 383   THOMAS BONNER TO CHRISTOPHER HOLLAMAN
        Jan. 26, 1757. 13 pds. for 100 A. On SS Ahotsdy Swamp at Hogpen
Branch "was left me by the last will and testament of my Father, THOMAS
BONNER late of Bertie County, dec'd..." Wit: BENJAMIN WYNNS, SAMUEL JOHN-
STON, JUN.   Jan. Court 1757. *.

H 384   MICHAEL (MICHALL) COLLINS TO BENJAMIN PERRY
        .. 1756. 14 pds. for 200 A. On Guys Hall Swamp. Wit: JNO. CRICK-
ETT, JAS. HEDGEPETH. Jan. Court 1757. *.

H 385   WILLIAM POYTHRESS & WIFE SARAH TO MATTHEW TURNER
        *. 21 pds. 10 sh. for 100 A. Adj. GRISSTOCK, JOHN HARRELL. Out of
a grant to THOMAS PAGE dated 1753. Wit: HENRY AVERET, GEORGE HOUSE. Jan.
Court 1757. *.

H 387   JOHN HILL TO THOMAS BOSWELL
        Jan. 27, 1757. 11 pds. for 200 A. + 240 A. (1) Adj. JOHN GRAY on
Licking Branch, HENRY ESMOND at Turkey Swamp. (2) 240 A. adj. JOHN EDWARDS
(dec'd). Wit: B. BAKER, BENJ. WYNNS. Jan. Court 1757. *.

H 388   THOMAS WHITMELL TO ARNOLD HOPKINS
        Jan. 7, 1757. 8 pds. for 100 A. In Bucklesbery Swamp adj. JOHN
WILLIAMS. Wit: THOMAS PUGH, WILLIAM KING, CHAS. KING. Jan. Court 1757.*.

H 390   WILLIAM SISSON TO JOSEPH PERRY
        Aug. 24, 1756. 45 pds. for 200 A. + 50 A. (1) Being a part of
JESSE WOOD's patent. (2) 50 A. "being part of JOS. PERRY's old patent" on
Miery Branch at Deer Tree Branch. Wit: JESSEY WOOD, JAMES BROWN. Jan. Court
1757. *.

H 391 JAMES BROWN TO WILLIAM BROWN
        Nov. 16, 1754. 20 pds. for 222 A. "formerly the property of the
deced FRANCIS BROWN" On WS Cypress Swamp. Wit: PETER EVAN, BENJ. BROWN.
Jan. Court 1757. BENJ. WYNNS C/C.

H 392 JOHN BROWN TO BENJAMIN BROWN
        Jan. 13, 1757. 20 pds. for 222 A. "part of a tract formerly the
property of the deceased FRANCIS BROWN". On WS Cypress Swamp "below the
bridge" at Mulberry Branch. Wit: EDMD. HODGSON, FRANCIS BROWN. Jan. Court
1757. BENJ. WYNNS. C/C.

H 393 BENJAMIN BROWN TO LEWIS WILLIAMS
        Dec. 18, 1756. 30 pds. for 250 A. At a Holly on Flatt Swamp at
Killum Swamp. Wit: JOHN SAWKILL, ISAAC HILL, FARABA HILL. Jan. Court 1757.*.

H 394 JOHN WILLIAMS, yeoman, TO BENJAMIN BROWN
        Dec. 18, 1756. 11 pds. for 150 A. In Chinkopen Neck at Black Haw
Branch adj. JOHN EARLY, ISAAC HILL, JOHN WILLIAMS to Rattlesnake Branch.
Wit: JOHN SAWKILL, ISAAC HILL, FARABEE HILL. Jan. Court 1757.*.

H 395 JOHN GLASS & WIFE ELIZABETH of Northampton Co. TO JAMES SEAY
        Jan. 20, 1757. 30 pds. for 120 A. "not far from Roanoke River" Adj.
THOMAS WILLIAMS, RICHARD WILLIAMS. Wit: JOHN RUFFIN,DRED. RUFFIN. Jan.
Court 1757. *.

H 397 EARL OF GRANVILLE TO EDWARD HARRELL
        March 5, 1749. 3 sh. for 190 A. On NES Cashy Swamp adj. GEORGE
BURNETTE (BURNET) "...cultivate at rate of 3 acres for every 100 Acres...
within 21 yrs clear and cultivate the premises after the rate of 21 acres
for every hundred acres...erect a good dwelling house...stock cattle thereon at rate of five head for every hundred acres..." Signed E. MOSELEY.
Wit: JNO. WYNNS, BENJ. WYNNS. Jan. Court 1757. *.

H 401 FRANCIS BROWN TO GEORGE RIBBITT
        Feb. 24, 1757. 33 pds. for 100 A. In Chinkopen Neck on SS Wiccacon
Creek at main road adj. THOS. FINCH (lately), WILLIAM PERRY. Wit: BENJ.
WYNNS, WM. WYNNS, JNO. VANPELT. April Court 1757. *.

H 402 THOMAS MORRIS, slay-maker, TO WILLIAM LASSITER
        Feb. 26, 1757. 32 pds. for 260 A. Land bought of LEONARD GREEN adj.
LASSITER, E. QUINBY on White Oak Swamp, AARON OLIVER on Chinkopen. Wit:
WILLIAM HOOKER. *. BENJ. WYNNS C.C.

H 403 ISRAEL JOHNSON, joyner, TO LEONARD LANGSTON
        Nov. 9, 1756. 10 pds. for 100 A. Adj. JAMES DENTON at Bell's Branch.
Wit: LUKE LANGSTON, ROBERT YEATES, JAMES DENTON. April Court 1757. *.

H 404 ROBERT WEST & THOMAS WEST TO JOHN WEBB
        Oct. 18, 1755. 50 pds. for 330 A. At fork of Cashoke Creek formerly
patented by WILLIAM WEST and at his death descended to ROBERT & THOMAS WEST.
"Patenant by ROBERT WEST in the year one thousand and 744". Wit: ROBERT
WEST, ROGER SNELL, JAMES MCDANIEL. April Court 1757. *.

H 405 STEPHEN WILLIAMS & WIFE ESTHER of Duplin Co. TO JOHN CARTER
        April 23, 1757. 85 pds. for 230 A. "...whereas ANTHONY WILLIAMS
grandfather of the sd. STEPHEN...was in his lifetime possessed of a tract..
containing (560 A.)...by his will...did devise unto his son ANTHONY Father
of said STEPHEN (230 A.)...after death of said ANTHONY, father of said
STEPHEN, the s'd STEPHEN did possess..." Patented April 1, 1714 on Bucky
Swamp. Land at Jackson's Ferry upon Chowan River at Ahotskie Swamp on
Bonner's Bridge. Wit: THOS. WALKER, JOHN BRICKELL, WILLIS NICHOLAS. April
Court 1757. *.

H 408 MICAL BRYAN (BROWN) & WIFE OLIVE (OLLIFF) TO AARON ELLISS
        April 26, 1757. 11 pds. for 100 A. ADj. ROBERT HODGES on "Little
Roquist". Wit: JAMES ABINGTON, ELIAS HODGES. April Court 1757.

H 409 EDWARD BOYD & WIFE ABIGAIL of Society Parish TO SAMUEL JOBE
        Dec. 16, 1756. 16 pds. for 200 A. Land granted to BARNABY BRYANT
Dec. 13, 1755. Wit: WILLIAM POYTHRESS, JAMES ABINGTON. April Court 1757.*.

H 411   JOHN ROBERTSON, SEN. of Chowan Co. TO JOHN ROBERTSON, JUN.
April 22, 1757. Deed of Gift. Chattels.

1 negro man	6 puter basons
2 negro boys	2 soup dishes
3 feather beds & furn.	2 smaller plates
20 head cattle cross left ear	3 plates
nick & square on right ear	2 porringers
3 young cows swallow fork left ear	2 tankards
iron pots	2 punch bowls
skillets	1 linen wheele
feather beds & furn.	1 stone mug
4 sea chests	2 delf punch bowls
1 handmill	2 brass candlesticks
1 gun	pr. small steeyards
2 doz. porringers	2 tables
1 brass candlestick	1 earthen jar
3 mean sifters	2 hominy sifters
2 narrow axes	3 hand saws
2 weeding hoes	1 plough
1 linen wheele	3 narrow axes
1 cotton card	1 cowbell
frying pan	2 ___(?) knives
pr. fire tongs	chizell
1 augue	pr. cart wheels
1 tea pot	4 saddles
2 knives	1 horse

"six books in whose custody they be found"
"sundry house hold goods, being the goods the said JOHN was invested with a
title too by virtue of his marriage to ELIZABETH JONES...(stock mark) given
by THOMAS JONES dec'd..." Wit: JOHN FREEMAN, WILLIAM TYNOR. April Court
1757. BENJ. WYNNS C/C.

H 412   DAVID RYAN TO RICHARD (DICK) LAKEY
Aug. 21, 1756. 12 pds. *. "all interest...I now have in the lands
of JNO HOLLBROOK, dec'd. as was left to the said RICHARD LAKEY's wife by
THOMAS RYAN, dece'd...and also all the right...that the s'd DAVID RYAN hath
to the said lands...purchased by MARITA RYAN of JOHN SMITH executor of
JAMES MCDOWWALL deceast..." Wit: JOHN BESWICK, ANN READ, DANIEL BOWEN.
April Court 1757. *.

H 413   JOHN BRICKELL, sheriff of Bertie, TO BLAKE BAKER
July 28, 1756. 8 pds. for 100 A. Pursuant to a judgement in amount
of 5 pds. 8 sh. 3 p. by RICHARD HOMES vs. WILLIAM HOOKER, JUN. adm. of
EDWARD HOCOTT late of Bertie. Land belonging to EDW. HOCOTT sold by She-
riff to BLAKE BAKER as highest bidder. Near Mount Pleasant on Chowan River.
Wit: BENJAMIN WYNNS, MATT. BRICKELL. April Court 1757. *.

H 415   SAMUEL HOLLAMON TO MOSES SUMNER
Jan. 26, 1757. 11 pds. for 20 A. On NS Ahotsky Swamp. Wit: WM. RAS-
BERRY, JOHN RASBERRY. April Court 1757. *.

H 417   JOHN DEMENT TO WILLIAM EDWARDS
July 26, 1756. *. 200 A. On NES Cashy Swamp adj. BENJ. CARTER. Wit:
JOHN SHOLAR, SOLOMON BARNS. April Court 1757. *.

H 417   EDWARD ROBERTS, Granville Co., TO CHARLES ROBERTS
July 26, 1756. Deed of Gift. *. "unto my well beloved son CHARLES
ROBERTS of Bertie County..." Land adj. WILLIAM BIRD, DAVID HORTON, MOSES
BONNER. Wit: MATTHIAS BRICKELL. *. April Court 1757. *.

H 418   RICHARD LAKEY & WIFE MARY TO JOHN PERRY, JUN.
April 16, 1757. 39 pds. for 320 A. "...land formerly belonging to
THOMAS RYAN dec'd, and by him willed unto his daughter MARY..." On WS Cho-
wan River at Herring Run adj. THOMAS YATES dec'd., ISAAC HILL, JUN. "which
is now in possession of Mrs. ELIZABETH GOULD..." Wit: JOSEPH BUTTERTON,
THOMAS PERRY, HENRY SPELLER. April Court 1757. *.

H 420   EDWARD COLLINS TO EDWARD COLLINS, JUN.
March 2, 1757. 100 pds. for 200 A. Adj. JAMES LEGGITT, RICHARD
TOMLINSON, ___ STRAUGHAN. Wit: JOSEPH WILLIAMSON, THOS. COLLINS. April
Court 1757. *.

H 420   WILLIAM BLITCHENDEN TO EDMUND BIRDE
        Nov. 20, 1756. 20 pds. *. On SS Spring Branch adj. MARY PARKER, ___
WYNNS "together with a pair of millstones now on the said land with all the
iron works belonging to the said mill with priviledge of timber from the
land...and other requirements for a mill on the branch..." Wit: THOMAS CREW.
*. April Court 1757. BENJ. WYNNS C/C.

H 421   WILLIAM SCOTT, shipwright, TO EDWARD COCKRAN
        March 28, 1757. 90 pds. for 600 A. On Chowan River sold by JOHN
WYNNS to THOMAS HANSFORD on May 5, 1743 and sold to WM. SCOTT by BRIDGET
HANSFORD, widow and exec. & JENKINS HANSFORD (Dec. 24, 1751). Adj. Mauls
Haven Landing, JOHN DAVISON, JOHN WILSON, RICHARD BOOTH. Wit: JOHN CAMPBELL,
ALEX FORD. April Court 1757. *.

H 424   HARMON HOLLAMON TO SAMUEL HOLLAMON
        Jan. 25, 1757. 50 pds. for 200 A. Being part of a tract bought of
JOHN EARLY on NS Ahotskey Swamp. Wit: MOSES SUMNER, JOSHUA DEAL. April
Court 1757. *.

H 425   WILLIAM ASHBURN, joyner, & THOMAS ASHBURN, taylor, TO JOHN DALY of
        Tyrrell Co. Feb. 30, 1757. 70 pds. for 200 A. In Cashia Neck adj.
plantation called BERRY's Plantation at Spring Branch. Wit: EDW'D RASOR,
MARY SUTTON, WILLIAM TODD. April Court 1757.*.

H 426   JAMES BOON WYNNS TO JOHN WATSFORD
        April 26, 1757. 10 pds. for 111 A. On NS Long Branch on the main
road. Being land whereon WILLIAM EVANS lately lived. Wit: CULLEN POLLOCK,
BENJAMIN WYNNS. April Court 1757. *.

H 428   JOSEPH THOMAS (THOMPSON) TO JOHN PERSEY (PERRY), cooper
        Dec. 29, 1756. 55 pds. for 320 A. On SS Cashia Swamp. Wit: JOHN
FRYARS, EDWARD HENRY. April Court 1757. *.

H 429   BURRELL BELL TO BENJAMIN WYNNS & NICHOLAS PERRY
        July 18, 1753. Marriage Contract SARAH WYNNS - BURRELL BELL. June
8, 1753. BURRELL BELL & SARAH WYNNS, late relect of JOHN WYNNS agreed to be
married. SARAH WYNNS was possessed of "considerable property and personal
estate consisting of negroes money and other chattels" wished to make pro-
vision for her five children. Five negroes and 25 pds. settled on BENJ.
WYNNS and NICHOLAS PERRY provided SARAH WYNNS have use of them during her
natural life. Should BURRELL BELL survive SARAH; "then in trust for MARY
ANN WYNNS, JOHN AUGUSTUS WYNNS, WINNIFRED CAROLINE WYNNS, WILLIAM WATKINS
WYNNS, SARAH AMELIA WYNNS children of SARAH WYNNS or such of them as shall
be living at that time to be equally divided among them..." Wit: WILLIAM
WYNNS. *. April Court 1757. BENJ. WYNNS C/C.

H 431   JOHN EDWARDS of Northampton Co. TO WILLIAM JENKINS
        April 16, 1756. 40 pds. for 890 A. Adj. WILLIAM MOOR at Maherrin
Creek, JOHN COTTEN. Wit: WILLIAM WINBURNE, CULLEN EDWARDS. N.C. Court May
11, 1756. PETER HENLY, C.J.

H 432   EARL OF GRANVILLE TO GEORGE HOUSE
        June 11, 1753. Grant. 500 A. Adj. NEEDHAM BRYAN, WIDOW BRYAN, ___
WIMBERLEY at Miery Branch. Signed JAMES JONES, FRANCIS CORBIN. Wit: BENJA-
MIN WYNNS, JAMES CAMPBELL. April Court 1757. BENJ. WYNNS C/C.

H 436   SAMUEL ORMES, merchant, TO JOHN HILL & DAVID BRYAN
        July 28, 1757. Power of Atty. To collect debts due me "and more
especially to sell a tract of land a certain Island in Morratock River in
Tyrril County" Cont. 25 A. granted Nov. 21, 1744. Wit: B. BAKER, BENJ.
WYNNS. July Court 1757. *.

H 436   JOHN WILLIAMS TO EZEKIEL WILLIAMS
        Feb. 26, 1757. Deed of Gift. 640 A. To my grandson EZEKIEL WILL-
IAMS. Land adj. PHILLIP WALSTON, CHARLES BARBER, JONATHAN STANDLEY.
Granted by patent Nov. 11, 1719. "also after my decease the bed and furni-
ture whereon I now lie my chest and my trunk and a case of bottles...the
land and the stock thereon to be possessed immediately..." Wit: THOMAS
WHITMELL, PRISCILLA VANPELT, NATHANIEL COOPER. July Court 1757.*.

H 437   MICHAEL WARD, JUN. TO RICHARD WARD

Feb. 7, 1757. 30 pds. for 200 A. Being part of a patent to ALEXAN-
DER KENNEDAY April 6, 1745. The plantation whereon THOMAS WARD now resides
adj. WILLIAM COLTHRED, WILLIAM FREEMAN at Cabbin Branch, PATIENCE WARREN
at Quayoccason Road, WILLIAM WOOD. Wit: GEO. BARLOW, JAMES BOON. July Court
1757. BENJ. WYNNS C/C.

H 438 WILLIAM SLOPER TO THOMAS WHITMELL
April 7, 1748 Deed of Gift. 230 A. "...out of affection I owe to
my loving friend THOMAS WHITMELL..." Land in Mill Neck bought of JOHN WES-
TON. Wit: JOHN GRAY, THOMAS WORSLEY. July Court 1757.

H 439 ELIZABETH HARDY TO BENJAMIN HARDY
July 26, 1757. Deed of Gift. 200 A. "...love...for my dutiful son
BENJAMIN HARDY..." Land on WS of Eastermost branch of Salmon Creek adj.
SAMUEL WILLIAMS, CULLEN POLLOCK at Cross Branch. Wit: WILLIAM HARDY (son of
LAMB), H'Y(?) FLEETWOOD. July Court 1757. *.

H 440 EDWARD VANN & WIFE MARY TO JOHN LAKEY
July 23, 1757. 13 pds. 15 sh. for 200 A. On NWS Eastermost Swamp
adj. JOHN HOWELL, WILLIAM COLEMAN, THOMAS JACKSON, ALEXANDER FORD, JAMES
GRAVES. Wit: JAS. BUTTERTON, HARDY HUNTER. July Court 1757. *.

H 441 WILLIAM BENTLEY TO LUKE WARD
July 26, 1757. 10 pds. 10 sh. for 50 A. Islands of Roanoke adj.
JOHN WARD, JOHN SMITHWICK, _____ BENTLEY. Wit: GEORGE SUTTON, JNO. WARD.
July Court 1757. *.

H 442 MICHAEL WARD TO JAMES WARD (son of MICHAEL)
July 9, 1757. 30 pds. for 100 A. On NS Quayoccason Swamp adj. RALPH
OUTLAW. Wit: GEO. BARLOW, THOMAS WARD, July Court 1757. *.

H 443 CORNELIUS CAMPBELL & WIFE ELIZABETH TO ROBERT DUDLEY
June 10, 1757. 16 pds. for 320 A. Land formerly belonging to JAMES
AVERY "the other half of the tract now in the possession of WILLIAM COLEMAN"
adj. WILLIAM RICE, WILLIAM YEATES. Wit: WILLIAM RICE, MARY LAKEY. July
Court 1757. *.

H 445 JOSEPH RIDING TO WILLIAM COWARD
Dec. 23, 1756. 30 pds. for 100 A. Part of a tract adj. ARTHUR DU-
GALL at Hines Branch. Wit: JOSEPH RIDING, GEORGE SUTTON, JOHN JOHNSTON, WM.
JOHNSTON. July Court 1757. *.

H 446 JOHN WEST & MARY WEST TO MOSES MOORE of Northampton Co.
April 2, 1757. 25 pds. for 100 A. + 100 A. On Wattom Meadow and SS
Smitfruill (Suntfruill?) Branch. (1) Part of a tract formerly granted
THOMAS JONES Sept. 22, 1730 adj. WILLIAM WHITFIELD's old line, HENRY BAKER's
old line. (2) Part of a tract granted JAMES RUTLAND for 225 A. Wit:
CHARLES HORNE, ABSOLOM RAULS, DEMSEY HOLLAND. July Court 1757. *.

H 447 JOHN SOWELL, laborer, TO JAMES WARD
July 16, 1757. 50 pds. for 230 A. JOHN SOWELL "heir at law to JOHN
SOWELL dec'd". Land on ES Loosing Swamp. Wit: JOHN ROOS, BENJ. STREATER,
BENJ. WYNNS. July Court 1757. *.

H 449 RUTH MOORE, ROBERT ROGERS & WIFE MARY of Beaufort Co. TO WALTER
SESSIONS (SISSONS) of Beaufort Co. July 27, 1757. 5 pds. for 100
A. "...RUTH and MARY being daughters of the late EDWARD MOORE of Bertie
County dec'd..." Land on WS Cashiah adj. JOHN HARDY, JAMES CURRY, _____
WHITMELL. Wit: THOS. WHITMELL, JOHN ALLEN, WM. LAURENCE. July Court 1757.

H 450 RUTH MOORE, ROBERT ROGERS & WIFE MARY of Beaufort Co. TO JOHN ALLENS
JUN. July 27, 1757. 20 pds. for 320 A. "...RUTH & MARY being
daughters of the late EDWARD MOORE of Bertie County dec'd...Land on NES
Roquiss Swamp adj. GEORGE COCKBURN at Flatt Pocoson. Part of a patent to
WILLIAM SMITH dated 1721 and purchased of RICHARD ABBE by EDWARD MOORE
Sept. 12, 1724. Wit: JOS. WIMBERLY, JONATHAN STANDLEY. July Court 1757.
"...the Feme being first privately examined by JOSEPH JORDAN ESQ. one of
his Majesties Justices of the Peace for the said county..." JOHN SMITH. *.

H 452 JOHN BAKER, THOMAS PUGH, JAMES JONES TO SOVREIGN LORD GEORGE
July 11, MDCCVII. Performance Bond. In Amount of 1,000 pds. The

condition of the obligation is such that JOHN BAKER is constituted sheriff
of the County of Bertie, and will faithfully perform his duties. Wit: JOHN
HILL, J. PEARSON. July Court 1757. BENJ. WYNNS C/C.

H 453   JOHN BAKER, JOSEPH JORDAN, HENRY HUNTER TO ARTHUR DOBBS, Gov.
        July XXVII, 1757. JOHN BAKER appt. sheriff by commission from the
Governor. Wit: JOHN HILL, BENJ. WYNNS. July Court 1757. *.

H 453   HENRY GLISSON & WIFE CHARITY of Northampton Co. TO ADAM RABY
        Jan. 24, 1757. 4 pds. 6 sh. 10 pds. for 15 A. At Northeast Branch
adj. JOHN HARE. Part of land devised to CHARITY GLISSON by the last will &
testament of her brother PATRICK OQUIN. Wit: ARTHUR COTTEN, NICHOLAS PERRY,
JOHN HARE. Oct. Court 1757. CHARITY GLISSON privately examined by JOHN DUKE
and SAMUEL COTTEN of Northampton Co., two justices. Oct. 4, 1757. *.

H 456   BENJAMIN WYNNS, Clericus Curii, TO JOHN DUKE & SAMUEL COTTEN, Justi-
        ces of Northampton Co. Oct. 24, 1757. Directive. To examine
CHARITY GLISSON re conveyance to ADAM RABY to determine that she made conveyance of own free will. *.*.*.

H 457   STEPHEN HOOKER of Tyrell Co., weaver, TO JAMES HOOKER
        Sept. 6, 1757. 80 pds. for 160 A. + 140 A. (1) On SS Wiccacon Creek
"...given and expressed in a joint deed of gift by WILLIAM HOOKER now deceased..." adj. COL. POLLOCK "to the school house branch", JOHN WYNNS Mill
Pond. (2) Also "my right title...to two other parcels (given in like manner
aforesaid)". Cont. 140 A. adj. POLLOCK, School House Branch, WILLIAM HOOKER
to Sandy Run. ____OLIVER "to the three mile post on the main road". Wit:
ARTHUR YOUNG, ELIZABETH HOCUTT, WILL HOOKER. Oct. Court 1757. *.

H 458   BENJAMIN NORVILLE, cooper, TO WILLIAM BROWN
        Oct. 9, 1756. "sundry good causes" for 260 A. Adj. JESSE BAKER's
lower landing, Tarbay Island, JOSEPH WITHERINGTON. Also 12 head cattle with
cross in left ear and a clit and half moon in right ear. BENJAMIN NORVILLE
is now being sued for debt by GEORGE BARLOW and STEPHEN FOLGER for damages
on detaining his servant. WILLIAM BROWN secured from both these actions.
Wit: JNO. HARRELL, STEPHEN LEE, WILLIAM LEE. Oct. Court 1757. *.

H 460   BENJAMIN NORVILLE & WIFE MARGARET TO JOHN VANPELT
        Nov. *.*. 22 pds. for 150 A. On NS Wiccacon Creek adj. WILLIAM BAKER
(BACOR). Wit: JOHN FLEMMING, THOMAS WILLIAMS. Oct. Court 1757. *.

H 461   BENJAMIN NORVILLE, cooper, TO WILLIAM BROWN (BROWNE)
        Oct. 10, 1757. 25 pds. for 150 A. adj. JOHN VANPELT at Wiccacon
Creek, JOHN BAKER late dec'd. Wit: JNO. HARRELL, JOSEPH HARRELL. Oct. Court
1757. *.

H 462   THOMAS HARRELL, SEN. (ADAM HARRELL, SEN.) TO ADAM HARRELL, JUN., yeoman
        Aug. 18, 1757. 20 pds. for *. On WS Chinkopen adj. ____ PATIFORD,
___ CAMPBELL. Wit: THOMAS HARRELL, WILLIAM HARRELL, WILLIAM COLTHRED. Oct.
Court 1757. BENJ. WYNNS C/C.

H 463   THOMAS ASHBURNE TO JOHN NICHOLLS, bricklayer
        Oct. 26, 1757. 12 pds. for 100 A. At Troublesome Bridge along Ca-
shoke Road. Being part of land bought of ANDREW THOMPSON. Wit: ED. RASOR,
THOMAS SLATTER. Oct. Court 1757. *.

H 464   ADAM HARRELL, SEN., yeoman, TO THOMAS HARRELL
        Aug. 18, 1757. 20 pds. for 200 A. Adj. ___HANSFORD, ___ LASSITER,
___ PELT. Wit: ADAM HARRELL, JUN., WILLIAM HARRELL, WILLIAM COLTHRED. Oct.
Court 1757. *.

H 465   EDWARD SKULL, carpenter, TO JOSEPH JACKSON
        Sept. 10, 1757. 80 pds. for 250 A. "JOSEPH JACKSON, Factor for TIMO-
THY NICHOLSON, THOMAS HARTLEY, merchants in company of White Haven...Great
Britain." Land on both sides of Deep Creek adj. EDW. HARE (now JOHN HARE)
at Miery Branch. And a water grist mill. Wit: BENJ. WYNNS, EDMOND BEEMAN.
Oct. Court 1757.

                        END OF DEED BOOK H

Index prepared by
Miss Karon Mac Smith, Nixon, Texas

Best, Henry 212
  Mary 212
Beswick, John 253
Betterly, Thomas 21, 41, 72, 93(3),
  114(3), 237
Betty 17, 49, 67
Beum, Thomas 69
Beverly, Anne 139, 140
  Elinor 139, 146
  Henry 80
  John 4, 9, 17, 19, 24, 25,
    46(2), 50, 62, 67(3), 73,
    75, 80, 85, 94, 133, 138(2),
    139(6), 140(10), 154(2),
    159(4), 207, 216, 229, 233
  John Jr. 25, 73, 139
  John Sr. 48, 73, 113(2), 139,
    140, 221(2)
  Margaret/Margrett 17, 25,
    113(2), 140, 159(3)
  Robert 139(3), 140(2), 143,
    146, 159(3), 233
  William 221
  127
Biggins, Arthur 133(2)
Bill see Bell
Binum see Bynum
Bird, Ann/Anne 30, 92, 128,
  148, 251
  Barnabee 30
  Edmond 106, 165, 178,
    217, 254
  Edward 3, 54, 111, 116(3),
    128(2), 137, 142, 148, 181,
    197, 205, 209, 223
  Esbell 131
  Henry 106(3), 119, 121,
    217(2)
  Honnour 106
  James 153
  Jean 111, 181
  John 3(2), 8(3), 54, 82(4),
    90(2), 92, 105, 108, 109,
    116(2), 128, 131, 136, 149,
    179(2)
  Mary 54(2), 82, 109, 203, 233
  Rebeckah 54
  Richard 90, 116
  Robert 5494), 116, 149, 179,
    223, 226, 233, 245
  Thomas 2, 4(2), 11, 20(6),
    52(2), 56, 85, 88, 96(2),
    99, 106, 110, 119, 165, 178,
    188, 216, 217(2), 238
  Thomas Jr. 106(3), 116, 121(2),
    131
  Thomas Sr. 93
  William 108, 110, 111(2),
    116, 128, 134, 137, 146,
    175, 181, 187, 209, 215,
    224, 234, 248, 253
Bird, ___ 26, 90, 130(2)
Bittel, Thomas 232, 233
Black, James 3, 41, 94, 97
Blackall, Abraham 172, 180, 192
Blackman see Blackmon
Blackmon, Ann 87
  Elizabeth 7(3)

Blackmon, John 3(2), 4(2), 7(3),
  65, 71, 95, 103(2), 107, 122
  John Jr. 102
  Joseph 78, 129
  Stephen 176
  Thomas 87
Blackmon, ___ 211, 247(2)
Black Haw Branch 252
Black Pond 240
Blackshall see Blackall
Black Walnut Branch 230
Black Walnut Point 181
Black Walnut Swamp 32(2), 83, 84,
  98(4), 157, 159, 190, 203, 211,
  227, 234, 236, 245
Blackwell, Anne 82
  George 31, 82
Bladoe Branch 33
Blake, Joseph 72, 195
  Thomas 2
Blan, ___ 142, 163
Blewlett, Abraham 2, 4. 19, 20,
  24, 25, 90, 95, 105, 119, 133,
  139, 214(4), 219, 230
  Jennet 19, 214
Blewlett, ___ 19, 26
Blichenden see Blitchenden
Bline, William 243
Blind Islands 124
Blitchenden, Abraham 238
  William 245, 254
Blizard, Richard 193
Bloodworth, Henry 161
Blount, Barbara 224(2)
  Catherine/Katherine 1, 3, 18,
    19(2), 97, 171
  Elizabeth 11, 57, 187
  Jacob 224(2)
  James 1, 3, 4, 11(4), 18, 19,
    24, 57, 97(2), 129, 147, 156,
    163(2), 167, 171, 180, 193,
    211, 246, 247(2)
  John 11, 12, 26, 32, 57, 71,
    73(2), 86, 87, 106(2), 144,
    152, 156(2), 198
  Thomas 161, 164, 166, 174, 187,
    194
Blue Water 21, 113, 114, 181, 182,
  188, 190, 192, 193, 198
Blue Water Branch 91
Blue Water Swamp 217, 234
Bluford County 177
Blulet see Blewlett
Blundering Branch 131, 156
Blunt see Blount
Bly, William 114, 162(2), 167,
  178(2), 180(3), 213
Bly, ___ 250
Blyth, William 214, 241(2)
Boath 171
Bobbit(t), John 25(2), 76, 81,
  91(2), 112(2)
  Sarah 25
Boddie, J. 133
  John 113, 142, 153, 161
  T. 112
  William 107, 112, 161
Boddy/Bodie see Boddie

Duffield,
  William cont. 194, 231(2), 232,
    235, 238(23)
Dugall, Arthur 11, 12(4), 15(2),
  21, 130(2), 139, 255
  Sarah 12
Duggan, John 19, 68
  Mary 166(4)
  William 166(2), 183
Duglass see Douglass
Duke(s), Benjamin 85
  John 157, 256(2)
  Robert 129, 159
  Samuel 116
  Thomas 215
Dunlap, John 237
Dunmade, Steven 86
Dunn, David 149
  Elizabeth 95(2), 149
  Francis 28
Dunn,   167
Dunn see also Dew
Dunston, Barnaby 220, 226
  Barnaby Hely 201, 223, 226,
    240, 244, 245(4)
  Elizabeth 245
  Martha 72
  Richard 226, 240(2), 245
Dunston see Dunstan
Duplin County 219, 222, 223,
  224(2), 234(2), 239, 242, 246,
  247, 248(2)
Duplin Precinct 233
Durden see Darden
Durding, Mary 9
Dyall, Thomas 3, 26(2), 27, 30,
  83, 132
Earley see Early
Early, Beershabe 39
  Elmer 85
  J. 184, 206(2), 235, 239
  J. Jr. 138
  James 206, 207, 239, 250
  John 2, 37, 49, 63, 68, 72,
    130, 138, 184(2), 191, 192,
    200(2), 207, 216, 235(2),
    241, 244, 250, 252, 254
  John Jr. 22, 37, 39(2), 104,
    121, 236
  John Sr. 22, 37, 39, 63, 121
Earp, Edward 127, 128, 142(2), 161
Eason, Ann 101
  Isaac 182
  Thomas 196, 218
  William 8(2), 15, 21(2), 26,
    34(2), 41, 58(2), 59, 75(5),
    82, 96, 101(2), 142(2), 152,
    182(3), 196
East Hampton 166
East Greenwich, Kent 166
Eden, C. 59, 82, 95
  Chas. 54
  Charles 8, 19, 31, 38, 44,
    78, 88, 89(2), 90, 94(2),
    110, 117, 120, 124, 140, 152,
    225
  Gov. 80, 102
  Phillip 18, 27, 39
Eden House Plantation 113, 114, 173,
  196(2), 206

Edens, William 118, 127, 156
Edenton 19(2), 24, 41, 50(2), 58,
  65, 76(2), 93(2), 114(2), 116,
  119, 124, 161, 182, 188, 191, 192,
  193(2), 200, 214, 220, 234, 237
Edge, Walter 219
Edgecombe 171, 173
Edgecombe County 144(2), 145(2),
  146, 148, 151(2), 153, 156, 157(2),
  158, 159, 160, 161(2), 162, 163,
  171, 172(4), 173, 181, 184, 187,
  189, 190, 194(2), 206, 214, 215,
  219, 220(3), 233, 234, 236, 240,
  241, 244, 251
Edgecombe Precinct 95(3), 96(2), 98,
  99, 102, 103, 104(3), 105, 106,
  107, 1o9(2), 110, 112, 114(3),
  115, 188(4), 121, 122, 123, 124,
  126, 127(3), 129(2), 130(4),
  135(2), 137, 140, 141, 142, 143,
  153, 203
Edmund(s), Henry 75, 88, 251
  James 91
Edmondson, Peter 162
Edwards, Cullen 254
  Elizabeth 12(2), 15, 49, 81, 100,
    103
  Henry 88, 176
  Isaac 160
  J. 51, 83, 105, 123, 141, 145(2),
    146, 149, 163, 251
  John 15, 21, 24, 41, 62, 71(2),
    75, 78, 79, 92, 97(2), 100(2),
    103, 117, 118, 122, 128, 148,
    155, 157, 161, 164, 175(2),
    176(5), 183, 184, 202, 211,
    251(2), 254
  John Jr. 5(4), 12(2), 13(3), 24,
    49, 60, 79, 122(5)
  John Sr. 60, 88(3), 122(2)
  Martha 5
  Mary 88(2), 122(2)
  Matthew 5(3), 88
  Robert 6, 32(2), 49, 168(2)
  Robert Sr. 169
  Thomas 145
  Titus 235, 238
  William 229(2), 253
Edwards,   136
Egerton, John 2
Eldredge see Eldridge
Eldridge, Samuel 112
  William 14, 15(3), 30, 44, 125,
    145, 147, 154(2)
Elabe/Eleby see Ellerby
Elbow Tree 94
Eleazer 220
Eliott see Eliott
Elison, John 94
Elizabeth Co., Va. 184
Elizabeth River, Va. 105
Elk Marsh 28, 43, 89
Elk Marsh Swamp 81
Elks, John 199
Ellerby, John 87(2)
  Samuel 67
  Thomas 24, 79
Ellice see Ellis
Ellinor, Francis 131

274

Elliott, Charles 233
  Chas. 245, 249
Ellis, Aaron 154, 218(2), 232,
  234(2), 252
  Jacob 131
  Moses 154
  Robert 156(2)
  Thomas 90
Elison/Ellyson see Elison
Elm Swamp 4, 19, 25, 50, 70,
  80, 90, 107(2), 110, 124, 133,
  148, 151, 207, 209
Elson, John 106
  Peace 56
  Sam'll 103
  Samuel 2, 18, 27, 29, 50, 56,
    105, 135, 150
Elverton, John 57, 58, 129
Elwick, Darwin 247
Emerson, Henry 45, 48
  Mary 45
  William 197
Emperors 218
Enbanck see Eubanck
Esmond, Henry 251
Estes, Sylvester 105, 167
Essex Co., Va. 62
Eubanck, George 21, 30, 60, 61(2),
  62(2)
Evans, Evan(s), Ann 21, 29, 37, 39,
  173
  C. 62, 69, 76, 87
  Charles 76
  Chas. 91
  John 60, 75
  Joseph 190, 231
  P. 191
  Per. 162
  Peter 11, 17, 29(2), 74, 95,
    118, 150, 175, 186, 202,
    206(2), 212(2), 215(2), 216,
    219, 237, 239, 247, 248,
    249, 252
  Phillip 157
  Robert 2, 7(2), 26(3), 29,
    37(2), 39, 46, 52, 63, 72,
    76(2), 89, 95(2), 103, 110(4),
    119(2), 151, 172, 173, 175(2),
    190, 207, 216, 241
  Robert Sr. 157
  Sary 240
  T. 76
  Thomas 123, 244
  W. 200
  William 44, 58, 74, 75, 78, 103,
    104, 107, 110, 111, 112(2),
    130, 132(2), 134, 198(2), 221,
    254
Evans, Evan(s),   93
Evant/Event see Avant
Evens/Evins see Evans
Everard, Henry 106
  James 57, 74, 76, 85, 153,
    161, 169(2)
  R. 91
  Sir Richard 31, 38, 40, 44, 55,
    61, 86, 87, 91(2), 102, 125,
    152, 156, 198

Everat see Everett
Everet(t), John 85
  Mary 208
  William 69, 127, 201
Everet(t) see also Averett/Averey
Everit see Everett
Exum, John 168
Fairchild, James 2, 73(2), 84, 110,
  151(2), 173
  Nicholas 66, 119(2), 172, 216,
    239
Falconer, John 91
Falk see Faulke
Falling Run 30, 44, 50, 56, 60, 105,
  113, 124, 136, 142, 144, 168, 220
Fanney/Fanning see Fannin
Fannin, John 25, 80, 222
  Sarah 222
Farechild see Fairchild
Farless see Fairless
Farris's Branch 122
Farror/Farrour see Farrow
Farrow, John 44, 54, 115(2), 117(2)
Fassell see Fussill
Faulke, Jonathan 77
  Samuel 130, 131
  William 39, 51(2), 56, 58, 80,
    125, 135, 169(2)
Faulke,   105, 135
Febly 139
Fellham, James 32
Femur Branch 156, 170, 171, 173
Ferrebent, Christopher 2
  John 17, 29, 100, 157
Ferrebent,   16, 17, 19, 67, 136,
  215, 219, 221
Ferris, John 153
Ferry Landing 103, 198, 222
Ferry Plantation 131
Ferry Point 95, 149, 222
Fettens Island 181
Fewause, Elizabeth 155
  Martha 155
Fewtrell/Fewtrill see Futrell
Field(s), Elizabeth 150
  James 6
  John 200, 215
  Nathaniel 135, 150, 163(2), 165,
    169
  Reuben 248
Fierybent/Firybent see Ferrebent
Figures, Bartholomew 205(2)
  Joseph 205
  Richard 205, 206, 229
  William 205
Figures,   206, 227
Filgo, Anthony 196, 207, 246
Finch, Mary 187
  Thomas 126, 187(2), 191, 192(2),
    193(2), 196
  Thos. 252
Fish Meadow 16, 165
Fishing Creek 50, 55(2), 56, 79,
  106, 114(2), 140(3)
Flaconer see Falconer
Flag Branch 29, 234, 242, 250
Flag Run 69, 75, 79, 117, 177, 210,
  215, 232, 239
Flaggy Run 8, 19, 29(2), 45, 58(2),

Flaggy Run - cont.
59(2), 65, 78, 92, 94, 95, 130,
185(2), 190, 218, 221
Flat Branch 133, 160, 199
Flat Pocoson 75, 113, 255
Flat Swamp 18, 26, 31, 68, 75,
80(2), 86, 89(2), 90(2), 100,
101, 106, 109, 112, 116, 131(3),
135, 141, 145(2), 153(2), 158(2),
161, 182, 183, 186, 187, 196,
197, 200, 206, 207, 208(2),
213, 223, 233, 235, 243, 245,
249(2), 252
Flatty Gut 37, 66, 119, 225(2)
Fleetwood, Henry 248
Hy 255
William 78, 90, 112(2), 114,
179, 181, 199, 200, 212,
215, 233, 239, 248, 250
Fleetwood,   112, 212
Flemming, John 256
Fletcher, James 231
Flewallen, Richard 16(2)
Flint Pocoson 30
Flood, Edward 129
James 130, 173, 199, 226, 228,
247
Floyd, Valentine 235
Foaling Run 187, 247
Foefe, David 210
Folger, Stephen 256
Fok/Folk see Faulke
Folkes, Bridgett 233
Folley Line 234
Folly Branch 92, 116, 148
Foltera Fort 16
Fon, Wm. 30
Foort see Fort
Forbes, William 195
Ford, Alex 254
Alexander 255
Elias 145
Ford,   73, 123
Ford see also Fort
Foreman, Benj'a 131
Benjamin 4, 14(5), 30, 57, 60,
80, 88(3), 115, 126, 137, 150,
155, 161, 203, 236, 246(2)
Benjamin Sr. 94(2)
Verilah/Verrily 4, 57(2)
Fork Branch 46
Fork Field 64
Forster, Ann 140
Fran 33(2), 44, 54
R. 6, 9(3), 31(2), 55, 84,
91(4), 99, 170(2), 180, 186,
Rob. 9
Robert 1(8), 2, 3, 5, 11, 13(2),
19, 20(4), 21, 23, 24, 27(4),
28, 29(3), 31(2), 34, 38,
40(2), 41(3), 43(9), 44(5), 47,
48(2), 49, 50(2), 51(4), 53,
55(3), 57, 61, 64(3), 65,
66(4), 67(7), 68(7), 69(3),
73, 76, 77(4), 78, 79(2), 81,
82(2), 83(2), 84, 86(3),
87(2), 88, 90(2), 93(2), 94,
97(3), 100, 101(2), 102, 104,

Forster,
Robert cont. 105, 107, 110, 113,
114, 119(2), 124, 130(2), 131,
132, 133, 134, 138, 141, 142,
148, 158, 165, 172(4), 216(2),
221, 225
Robt. 10, 12(2), 31
Rt. 34, 195
William 86
Forster see also Foster
Fort, Alec 81
Elias 9(2), 10, 52, 56, 84, 119.
122, 146(2)
Elias Sr. 63
George 75
John 10, 81(2), 127, 172(2)
Jonathan 155
Mary 81(2)
William 81
Fort,   127
Fort see also Ford
Foster, Fran. 31(2), 40, 61, 63, 64
Francis 38, 82, 88, 90, 124, 225
Foster see also Forster
Fountain,   129
Fourth Branch 134
Fowler, Margarett 31
Fox, Nich. 167(2)
Foxhall, Thomas 18
Foyle, Anne 73
James 63(3), 64, 73
Francis 115
Francis, Mr. 62
Frank 44
Frasher/Fraser/Frazor see Frazier
Frazier, Andrew 55
Daniel 55, 99(4), 142, 248
Isabella 189
Mary 96
Thomas 142
William 234, 248
Freeman, Aaron 192(2)
James 178, 222
Jno. 249
John 152, 170, 173, 174, 192,
195(2), 200, 201, 216, 222(2),
226, 231, 249, 253
Joshua 249
Richard 222, 242, 243, 249
Samuel 192(2), 237
Thomas 124, 202(2)
William 167, 177, 192(2), 197,
205, 241, 243, 247, 249, 255
Frisbie, Edward 132, 138(2), 185,
189, 236(3), 237(2)
Frisbie,   155
Frisby/Frizby see Frisbie
Frost, James 42, 132, 134(2)
William 30, 45(2), 51, 84, 117,
131
Frowell, Joseph 41
Tibitha 41
Fry, John 113
Fryar(s), Ann 147, 150
John 130, 147, 149, 150, 247, 254
Richard 41, 50, 75, 79, 88, 89,
97, 98, 201
Fryer see Fryar
Fryssle, John 113

Gray,
William 60(2), 61, 62, 63, 64, 65,
67(3), 70(4), 73, 76, 88, 96,
121, 125(2), 126(2), 136, 142(2),
143, 156, 157, 168, 170(2), 171,
183(2), 191, 200, 218, 224(3),
241
Gray, __ 71, 76, 78, 153, 197, 206
Grayhall Swamp 33
Great Beaver Dam 179, 199, 206
Great Branch 38, 39, 44, 70, 94, 97,
98, 103, 114, 121, 151, 229, 249
Great Britain 29, 238
Great Creek 131
Great Cypress Swamp 80
Great Ditch 37, 57
Great Gut 52, 115
Great Marsh 24, 64, 70(2), 73
Great Meadow 62
Great Quank Creek 86
Great Swamp 72, 240
Green, Ammy/Elimy 30
Edw. 57
Elizabeth 5, 6(4), 10, 16(2),
18
John 30(2), 34, 44, 54(3), 64,
66(3), 71, 74, 76, 79, 81,
107(3), 127(2), 142, 156(2)
Leonard 174, 215, 252
Robert 44, 69(4)
Samuel 151
Thomas 110, 174, 217(2)
William 24, 31, 44, 53, 54,
66(2), 68
Green, __ 105(3), 127, 163, 171,
200, 202, 211(2)
Green Pond Meadow 50
Gregary/Grigory see Gregory
Gregory, Francis 165
Isaac 98(13), 227(2),
Mary 98(3)
William 211, 247(2)
Griffes, Andrew 16
Griffen see Griffin
Griffet/Griffeth see Griffith
Griffin, Benjamin 54, 161
Edw. 59
Edward 102, 242
Elizabeth 9, 221
Francis 184
John 9(2), 10(2), 59, 62(2),
72, 143, 161(2), 169, 217(2),
243
Jonas 106
Josia 144
Joyce 10
Martin/Mertin 9, 19, 74, 93, 132,
144, 182, 193, 237(2), 239
Mary 113, 161
Michael 250
W. 56
William 10(2), 49, 50(2), 56,
62(2), 76, 112, 113(2), 125,
126, 161(2)
Griffith, Edw. 187
Edward 173
Elizabeth 9
John 8, 191
Griffith, __ 245

Grigarry see Gregory
Grill(s), William 1(2), 186(3),
200, 205, 209, 246
Grill(s), __ 114, 180, 181, 196
Grimes, Hugh 222
Sarah 86(2)
William 13
Grimstuck, __ 229
Grisstock, __ 251
Grist, Richard 235
William 235
Groom, John 70
Grub Neck 131
Grumsell, Mary 57
Grussett, John 92
Guardiner see Gardener
Guin see Gewin
Guise Hall Swamp 78, 184(3), 218,
237, 251
Guleford, Charles 111
Gullson, John 183
Gum Branch 11, 214, 244
Gum Pocoson 201
Gum Swamp 65, 79, 95, 102, 245
Gumbling Branch 178
Gunn, Ruth 168(2)
William 142, 165, 168(2), 169
Gunn see also Ginn
Gupson see Gibson
Guston, Alexander 62
Henry 41, 50, 60, 62(2), 65, 66,
72, 75, 76, 81, 97(3)
Guston, __ 66, 89, 242
Guye, James 145
Hacker see Hooker
Hacket, Ed. 181
Hade see Hardy
Hafford, John 132
Hagan(s), Daniel 44, 112
Hainsworth, Rich. 60
Hair(e) see Hare
Hale, John 58(2), 175
Half Moon Branch 203, 207, 217,
232, 237, 242
Hall, E. 188, 190(2), 192(2), 193,
194, 195, 196
E. J. 236
Enoch 191, 192
John 1, 14, 88
Joseph 200, 206, 239(2)
William 69, 75, 88, 107, 153(2)
Hall, __ 189
Halle, Jacob 200
Hallum, John 123(2), 141, 190
Haly, William 224
Ham, __ 239
Hamilton, James 152, 219
John 5, 14, 23, 60, 88
R. 22
Robert 22(3), 116, 198
Hammond, Clement 72, 74, 75
Hampton 220
Handerson see Henderson
Hanes see Hayne(s)
Hanley, Hannah 134(2)
Michael 133
Sarah 133
Hannah 195, 199, 200(2), 206

Holmes,
John 4, 6, 9, 24, 25, 46, 47, 98, 133
John Jr. 98
Mary 188
Richard 178, 253
Simon 100, 103, 109, 110, 111, 122, 150, 151, 188(2)
Soloman 202
Thomas 27(2)
William 244, 249, 250
Holmes, ___ 209, 218
Holnbeck see Hornbeck
Holt(e), William 100(2), 102
Homes see Holmes
Hood, Edward 88, 94, 137(2), 156, 160, 162(2)
Hood, ___ 81
Hooker, Benjamin 19(2), 205, 216(2), 239(2)
Elizabeth 37
G. Jr. 181
Godfrey 10, 37, 57, 66, 119(3), 151, 175, 216(4)
James 177, 181, 184, 186, 199(2) 251, 256
Jas. 203
Jean 206, 218
Jeanet 240
John 124, 162(3), 166(2), 169, 171, 177, 186(3), 225
Nathan 225
St. 225
Stephen 227, 251, 256
Will 256
Will. Jr. 240
William 1, 2, 37, 66, 119, 124, 162(3), 179(2), 186(3), 197, 199, 203, 205, 241, 252, 256(2)
William, Jr. 189, 193(3), 197, 199, 205, 206(2), 218, 219(2), 222 238, 239(2), 245, 248, 251, 253
William Sr. 2, 177, 225, 248
Wm. 24
Hooker, ___ 215
Hookes see Hooks
Hooks, John 51, 62
John Jr. 32(3), 61, 145
John Sr. 61, 144
Martha 32
Thomas 227, 241, 249(2)
William 144, 227, 241, 249
Hoolbrook see Holbrook
Hootten see Hutton
Hope, George 154
Hopkins, Arnal/Arnold 202, 205, 211, 216, 232, 234, 246, 251
John 211, 219, 232, 234
William 210, 234
Hopkins, ___ 137
Hopper, David/Davie 60(2), 71, 75, 81(7), 82, 97
Hord, T. 89
Hornbeak see Hornbeck
Hornbeck, Caesseed [sic] 186
John 180, 186(4)
Horn(e), Charles 95, 125, 127(2), 131, 141, 157, 158(2), 160,

Horn(e)
Charles cont. 177(3), 206, 212(2), 214(2), 217, 226, 230, 232, 239, 244(2), 246, 250, 255
Elizabeth 177
H. 67(3)
Henry 67, 68, 80, 110, 112(2), 125, 134, 141, 144, 155(2), 160, 161, 177(3), 215
Jacob 4
Michael 67(2), 68, 125, 206, 212
Moses 125, 160, 177(2)
Richard 9, 15, 23, 70, 71, 87, 96, 144(3)
Sarah 15
Thomas 23, 96, 125
Thos. 32
William 80, 131, 158, 177(4), 239
Horner, Charles 233
Horo, J. 88
John 88
Horron see Herrin
Horse Branch 189
Horse Creek Swamp 3, 7
Horse Hung Branch 51, 120, 141(2), 188
Horse Pasture Creek 25, 29, 43, 60, 83, 104, 150(2), 151
Horse Pen Branch 203, 215, 218, 232(3)
Horse Pen Meadow 134, 206
Horse Pens 107
Horse Spring Branch 82
Horse Swamp 11(2), 17(2), 18, 20, 21, 40, 46, 55, 72, 74, 75(3), 77(3), 82, 85, 93, 98,, 99, 102, 103, 104, 107, 110, 111, 123, 129, 130, 132, 134, 144, 158(2), 160, 165, 175, 177, 184, 185(2), 193, 215, 221, 226, 235, 236, 237
Horsely, Richard 40(2)
Rd. 32
Horsing Branch 1
Horten see Horton
Horton, David 211, 238, 251, 253
Hugh 117, 157, 184, 186(2)
John 117
Joseph 26(3), 238, 242
Nathan 190, 192, 211
William 11(2), 192
Hosea, William 199, 205, 206(2), 207, 212, 239, 250
Hoskins, Thomas 19(2)
Hosler, Hance 248(3)
Hothouse Branch 9, 173, 176, 178, 181, 182, 183, 190, 214, 238
Hothouse Creek 238
Hough, Daniel 140(5), 159(3), 176(2), 188(2), 190(2), 195, 238(2)
Joseph 136, 144, 165
Margaret 140(6)
Houlder see Holder
Hoult see Holt
House, George 79, 93, 101(3), 117, 118, 138, 163, 177(2), 232, 233, 240, 251, 254
George Jr. 239(2)
Robert 18(2), 31, 145

Hyman, Dinah 240(2)
  Hugh 101, 104, 144, 167, 182,
    188, 243
  John 240(2), 241, 244
  Mary 241
  Thomas 241
Hymen see Hyman
Hysmith see Highsmith
Idolbrook 205
Indian Creek 4, 52, 64, 73, 106,
  145(2), 151(2), 163
Indian Creek Swamp 32, 144, 145,
  150
Indian Island 197
Indian Line 122, 180, 209, 215
Indian Old Field 184
Indian Path 85, 109, 176, 188,
  189, 236, 238, 244, 249
Indian Springs 9
Indian Swamp 14
Indian Town 67
Indian Town Land 94
Indian Village Meadow 72, 256
Indian Village Pond 72
Irby, Henry 21, 30
Ireland, Andrew 46, 49, 52, 53,
  54, 62, 70, 91(2), 95, 102,
  111, 151, 167
  James 33, 107
Irving, Andrew 103, 114, 141, 149
Irving, __ 91
Irwin, Henry 55
Irwing see Irving
Irwin's Island 31
Isaac Creek 140, 201, 243, 251
Island Creek 6(2)
Island Gut 146
Islands of Roanoke 255
Islands of Rocquist 79
Island Swamp 6
Isle of Wight Co., Va. 1, 4, 5, 6(2),
  8, 10(3), 18, 21, 23, 24, 28, 29,
  30, 31, 32, 37, 40, 43, 44(3), 56,
  61, 64(3), 65(2), 67(2), 70(3),
  71, 72, 73, 74(4), 77, 78, 94,
  101, 104, 105, 109(2), 110, 112,
  116, 117, 121, 131, 145, 146(2),
  151, 152(2), 157, 158, 160, 161,
  162, 165, 172(2), 173, 195
Ismay, Thomas 62
Issues Creek 175
Ives, John 168
Ivey, John 168, 185
  Thomas 67
  Robert 73, 105
Ivy see Ivey
Jack 171
Jacket Branch 245
Jack's Creek 93
Jack's Swamp 153
Jackson, Edward 154
  Est. 162
  John 43, 48(2)
  Joseph 256(2)
  Mary 32
  Michael 150, 152
  Rich. 60
  Richard 28(2), 29, 30(2), 32(2),

Jackson,
  Richard cont. 37, 58, 87
  Sarah 28
  Thomas 95, 136, 137, 138, 147,
    149(2), 151, 154(2), 162, 167,
    169, 173, 175(2), 178, 185,
    207, 209, 255
  William 234
Jackson, __ 242, 249, 252
Jacocks, Charles 179(2), 181(4),
  205(2), 239(2)
  Elizabeth 212
  Jonathan 181
  Joseph 194
  Thomas 205, 212
James see Jameson
James City Co., Va. 10, 60(2), 69,
  135
Jameson, John 167, 169(2), 172,
  177, 201, 220, 228(2), 247
  Elizabeth 169, 172, 201, 220
Jammesson see Jameson
Jamy 104
Jansey, Andros 48
Jarnagan see Jernigan
Jarrell, Thomas 23, 64(3), 65(2),
  70(6), 105
  Thomas Sr. 33
Jeffreys, Elizabeth 51, 76
  Osburn(e) 134, 138, 154(2), 155
  Simmon/Simon 2, 9, 13, 18(2), 34,
    43, 47, 49, 51, 56, 60, 70, 81,
    134
Jemmisson see Jameson
Jeneur, James 87, 90
  Joseph 90
Jenkings/Jennkins see Jenkins
Jenkins, Bridget 100
  Charles 211
  James 40, 43, 45(2), 73, 79,
    80, 88(2), 100, 107, 111, 115,
    129, 218
  John 95, 103, 121, 145, 149,
    153(2), 163, 194, 198, 218
  Lewis 62
  Thomas 2(2), 3, 4, 9(2), 16,
    19, 23(2), 27, 48, 52, 53,
    54, 58, 59, 69, 80(2), 83, 155
  Thos. 83
  William 193, 254
  Winborne 210
Jenkins, __ 80
Jenkison, William 224
Jenny 171
Jernigan, Ann/Anne 112, 129
  David 92, 94, 106, 151, 224
  Feaby 132
  George 110, 163, 167, 194, 195,
    227, 230, 232, 240, 250
  Hannah 230
  Henry 103(3), 104(2), 112, 133,
    139, 142(2), 228, 229, 235,
    247(3)
  Henry Jr. 102
  Henry Sr. 102
  Jack 173
  Jacob 112, 113, 126, 132, 149,
    152, 160, 225, 235(3)

Quincy Gut 43
Quitsnah 94, 223
Quitsnah Swamp 128, 138, 153, 209
  230(2)
Rabey, Adam 154, 210, 256(2)
Raby see Rabey
Rachel, John 74
Raccoon Branch 91, 117
Radford, Robert 17, 24, 38, 51,
  56, 104, 164, 229, 247
  Robt. 56
  Susanna 17, 24
Ragland, Bryan 87
  Evan 111, 134(2), 135, 155(2)
  Mary 134
  Stephen/Steven 87(2), 89,
    134(2), 135, 144(2), 163(2),
    165(2)
Railey, Margaret 105
Rainbow Banks 97
Rainer, John 233
Raising, Widow 33
Randall, John 177(3)
Ranor, Richard 222
Rapier, __ 28
Ramsey, John 20
Ras__, John 232
Rasbary/Rasbeary/Rasbury see
  Rasberry
Rasberry, Bridget 20(3), 28, 84,
  111, 125, 175
  Edward 200
  John 11, 20(&), 28, 49, 70,
    82, 84(2), 101(3), 106,
    124, 125, 126(2), 136, 143,
    157, 165, 177(2), 180, 181,
    206(2), 238, 250(2), 253
  John Sr. 107
  William 103, 138, 143(2), 206,
    207, 212, 250
  Wm. 253
Rasor, Anne 119
  Christian 1
  David 105(2), 113, 119, 167
  Ed. 248, 249, 256
  Edw. 245
  Edward 1, 114, 116, 132, 133,
    171, 179(2), 180, 186, 192,
    198(2), 199(2), 200, 202, 205(2),
    207(6), 208(8), 209, 210(2),
    211(5), 222(2), 227, 234, 235,
    239, 248(2)
  Edw'd 254
  Frances 1(4), 197, 198(2)
  Francis 195
  Mart. Fred. 42(2), 84
  Martin Fred. 72, 83
  Martin Frederick 1(2)
  M. F. 1(2)
Rassor see Rasor
Ratcliff, Elizabeth 90, 211(3)
  Samuel 67, 90
Ratcliff Plantation 236, 243
Ratclif see Ratcliff
Ratland/Rartland see Rutland
Rattlesnake Branch 124, 252
Rattlesnake Valley 135, 170
Rauls see Rawls
Rawlison, George 85
Rawls, Absolum 255

Rawls, Luke 219
Ray, Alexander 42, 67(2), 155
  John 82, 90, 105(2), 149, 150,
    179, 239
  Mary 90, 105(2)
Rayford, Martha 5, 10
  Math. 37
  Matthew 52(2)
  Phillip 3, 5, 10, 31, 81, 86(2)
Rayner, Richard 231
Rayson(s), Matthew 82(2), 83
  Thomas 121, 156(2)
Razor/Resor see Rasor
Read see Reed
Reading, Thomas 234
Reads see Rhodes
Reason(s), Ann 203(2), 208, 213,
  216
  Thomas 149
Reauesesan [sic] , William 87
Reaves see Reeves
Reddick, Josiah 133, 159, 160, 161,
  175(2), 181
  Lemuel 143, 145, 192
Reddill, Joseph 168
Reddings see Ridings
Reddish, E. 84
  Edward 84
Redditt(s), Ann 216
  John 175, 194(2), 202, 216, 232,
    244
  Joseph 175, 211, 234, 242(2),
    244
  William 136, 191(2). 194, 211,
    219, 244
  William John 233
Red Banks 223
Reddy, John 248
Red Ridge 9, 65, 77, 244
Red Ridge Plantation 160
Reed, Ann 253
  Charles 233
  Christian 187
  Elizabeth 216
  Henry 200, 216, 217, 221, 244
  John 196(2), 202, 206, 216(2),
    217, 219
  Mary 50
  William 7(2), 13, 16, 17(3), 38,
    48, 50, 55, 61, 73, 82, 89(2),
    124, 135, 137, 168, 182, 187,
    217, 225
  W. 225
  Wm. 31, 33(2), 44, 54, 63, 64,
    78, 95, 128, 140
Reed, __ 9
Reedy Branch 6(2), 7, 11, 14, 23, 27,
  29, 34, 40, 52, 58(2), 75(2), 82,
  85, 94, 100(2), 115, 120, 123,
  142, 144, 153, 163, 172, 175
Reedy Pocoson 51, 81
Reedy Run 29, 112
Reedy Run Pocoson 156
Reedy Swamp 37
Reek, James 7
Reese, Ann 189
  David 189
Reeves, Thomas 243
  William 9, 45, 68, 110, 125,
    144(2), 155, 163

Stewart,
  Sarah 10, 32, 39
  Widow 149
Stewart, __ 66, 112, 162
Stinson, John 216
Stockdale, James 238
  John 238
Stodghill, John 44
Stodgill see Stodghill
Stokes, Jones 69
  Silvanna 72
  William 124, 168(2), 194, 196,
  206
Stone, Benjamin 198
  John 8
  Sarah 123
Stonehane, Thomas 1
Stonehouse Creek 23, 24, 74,
  90(3)
Stonehouse Marsh 77
Stoney Creek 123(2), 125, 167,
  203, 232(3)
Stoney Creek Road 93, 123, 125,
  156, 165, 176, 191, 232, 244
Stoner Landing 187
Strachan see Stracken
Stracken, George 172, 237
Stradford/Stratford see Stanford
Straghan see Straughan
Stratton, Jonathan 166
Straughan, George 114, 148, 201
Straughan, __ 210, 253
Steater see Streeter
Streeter, Benj. 255
  Thomas 48
Street(s), Francis 220
  Thomas 48
Strickland, John 73
  Jos. 73
  Joseph 145
  Martha 23, 37
  Matthew 144
  Samuel 168
  Stephen 119
  William 23, 28, 31, 32, 37, 57
  William Sr. 45
  Wm. 73
Stricklin/Strickling see Strickland
Streite Marsh 43
String Meadow 7, 52
Stringer, Francis 59(2)
Sturdevent, Matthew 92
Sturges see Sturgis
Sturgis, Thomas 40, 82, 130
Sueiss, John 208
Suffolk, Mass. 147(2)
Suffolk Co., N.Y. 166
Suffolk Court 166
Suffolk Meadows 210
Suffolk Parish, Nansemond 217,
  219
Sugg, Anderson 78
Sumerel see Sumerill
Sumerill, Elizabeth 196(2)
  Henry 189
  Lazarus 228(3)
  Sarah 189
Sumerton Chapel, Nansemond 167
Summerset 171

Sumner(s), David 243
  Demsey 243
  Elizabeth 190
  Francis 74
  James 9, 22, 88, 89, 94, 233
  Jethro 135, 203
  John 133, 190, 226(2)
  Joseph 89, 95, 190
  Luke 192
  Mary 46
  Moses 226(2), 253, 254
  Richard 19, 43, 46, 54, 65, 153
  Robert 243, 248(2)
  Samuel 226, 250
  William 226
Sunderlin see Sanderlin
Surginer, John 44, 58, 64(3), 71,
  79
  Robert 64
  William 64, 80
Surginer see also Serginer
Surry Co., Va. 16(5), 17, 18(3),
  28, 34, 44, 45(3), 46(2), 68,
  69(3), 70(3), 71, 72(2), 80,
  84, 94, 96, 101, 105, 121, 126,
  128, 135, 139, 142, 145, 147,
  150(2), 163(3), 164, 165(2),
  170, 172(3), 178, 185, 198, 199,
  205, 207
Sutton, Cost 66
  Elizabeth 32, 83(2), 84
  George 238, 240, 245, 255(2)
  John 2(3), 3(4), 4(4), 5, 7,
  8(3), 9(4), 11(2), 12(2),
  16(2), 17(2), 18(2), 19(2),
  21(2), 23(2), 24(2), 25(3),
  26, 27(4), 38(2), 43, 46, 47,
  48(2), 51(2), 56(4), 57, 59,
  65(2), 68, 69(2), 75, 79,
  101(2), 117, 118, 120, 122(2)
  124, 125, 126, 136, 138,
  141(2), 144, 149, 151(2), 153,
  157, 162, 165(2), 166, 172,
  176, 208(2)
  John Jr. 27
  John Sr. 208
  Joshua 240
  Judith 97, 98
  Mary 3, 27, 28(4), 32, 37(2),
  38, 51, 254
  Nathaniel 54
  Thomas 32(2), 83(3), 97, 98(4),
  99(3), 109(2), 128(2), 132,
  133, 136, 177, 179, 222,
  234(2)
  Thomas Jr. 206
  Thos. 32
  Tom 245
Swain, Anna 42(3)
  James 13(3), 66(2), 67, 101(2),
  140
  John 30, 66
  Richard 19, 41, 42(3), 55, 67,
  133, 135, 155, 191
  William 191
Swain, __ 133
Swainner/Swaner/Swanor see
  Swanner
Swan Pond 53
Swann, Barker Jr. 237

318

Willoby,
John Sr. 221
Mary 132
Merey 242
Thomas 107
Wills, John 92
John Jr. 26(2), 44
Rachel 231
Thomas 188, 231
William 49(2)
Will's Quarter Swamp 3, 82(2), 90(2),
131, 134, 145, 155, 164, 186,
189, 193, 198, 207(2), 218,
224, 227
Willson, John 96, 151(2), 178
Priscilla 96
Richard 49
Thomas 181
William 16, 96, 97, 105, 106,
123, 181, 188, 200
Willson see also Wilson
Wilson, James 39, 70, 165(2)
John 70, 71, 170, 171, 192,
209(2), 222, 254
Judith 165
Mary 142
Rebecca 15, 30
Richard 49
Stewart William 2
Thomas 9(2), 17, 142, 162, 165,
212, 235, 248
William 10, 13, 14(2), 15(2),
17, 30(2), 50, 68, 76, 165,
228(3), 231
Wilson see also Willson
Wim__, Abraham 232
Wimberly, Abraham 232
Ezekiel 233, 235
George 135
Isaac 236, 243
John 103, 105, 118, 190, 235
Jos. 220, 255
Joseph 95, 104(2), 125, 127(2),
133(2), 139, 189, 202(2), 211,
214, 220(4), 229(2), 230(8),
236(3), 237(2), 243, 247(2)
Wimburly see Wimberly
Winant(s), Penelope 142, 148
Pete 231
Peter 195, 209, 234
Winant(s) see also Wynant
Winborne, Henry 176, 191, 214(2),
219, 234, 237, 238(4), 249
John 176
Sarah 238
William 254
Winborne, __ 236
Winbourne see Winborne
Windgate 35
Wingate, Edward 12, 48, 50, 73,
104, 169(2)
Edward Jr. 195
Edward Sr. 195
Grizel 168(2), 210
John 195, 220(2)
Michall sic 237
Thomas 168, 210(2)
Winn, Geo. 51
George 1(2), 10, 12, 13, 17,

Winn,
George - cont. 51(3), 59(2), 78,
88, 101
John 19, 20(2), 23(2), 24, 25,
27(3), 30, 34, 57, 59(2),
76(2), 80(3), 81, 86(2), 88(2)
Penelope 92
Rose 25
Winn, __ 242
Winn see also Wynns
Winningham's Branch 173, 177
Winston, Joseph 240
Wise, Henry 75
Wistfor Branch 100, 106
Witherington, Joseph 172(3), 206,
219, 227,, 241(3), 242, 256
William 206, 223, 227, 239, 236
240(2), 241(3), 242
Withford, Richard 125
Woff see Wolf
Wolf, Shoenne 112(2)
Wolferston, Lawrance 91
Wolf Pit Branch 203, 243
Wolston, __ 211, 247
Woobank, Robert 189
Woodall, Jonathan 11
Woodford, Joseph 70
Wood(s), Benjamin 13(2), 19
Dense/Demsey 157, 161, 203, 207,
216, 217, 232, 250
Edward 79
Edward Jr. 16, 79
Edward Sr. 46
Francis 50
James 8(2), 9(2), 18, 19(3),
21(7), 22(6), 26, 28(3), 32,
38, 39, 56, 65(3), 74, 95,
98(2), 99, 100, 118(4), 121,
122(2), 124, 126(2), 138, 140,
146, 150, 153, 159, 163(2),
170(2), 194, 210, 231(2),
232(5), 237, 241, 242
Jesse 161, 196, 203, 207, 234(2),
237, 242, 251(2)
John 13(3), 51, 59, 72, 239
Jos. 251
Joseph 58, 207(2)
Mary 216, 217
Moses 163, 207, 235, 248
Robert 8
Sarah 19, 118(2), 126
Susannah 240
William 230, 240, 243, 244,
245, 255
Wm. 243
Wood(s) see also Ward
Woodward, Samuel 19, 40, 41, 170
Thomas 232
Woodward, __ 70, 106, 120, 179,
215, 218
Wooten, Thomas 85
William 250
Worborton see Warburton
Worden, James 200
Worley, J. 31, 55, 91
Worley, __ 49, 102
Worrell see Worrill
Worrill, John 115, 123, 144, 169
Richard 101
William 23